# Learning
# Microsoft® Office 97

## PROFESSIONAL VERSION
### ■ WORD ■ EXCEL ■ POWERPOINT ■ ACCESS

**Iris Blanc**
**Cathy Vento**

*To Our Families*
Alan, Pamela, and Jaime–*I.B.*
Jim, Chris, Dirk, Jimmy, Mindi, and Anthony–*C.V.*

| **Managing Editor** | **English Editors** | **Technical Editors** | **Design and Layout** |
|---|---|---|---|
| Jennifer Frew | Aegina Berg | Katherine Bernthal | Maria Kardasheva |
| New York, NY | New York, NY | Westmont, IL | New York, NY |
| **Contributing Author** | Monique Peterson | Carol Havlicek | Udora Phillips |
| Kathy Berkemeyer | New York, NY | Long Beach, NY | New York, NY |
| Westmont, IL | | | |
| | | Cathy Vesecky, | Paul Wray |
| | | Westmont, IL | New York, NY |

# CONTENTS

# Contents

# INTRODUCTION

## About Microsoft® Office 97 Professional

Microsoft ® Office 97 Professional includes Word, Excel, Access, PowerPoint®, Outlook™, Bookshelf Basics, and several other programs, such as Microsoft Internet Explorer. Each of the applications and utilities included in the package can be used separately or they can be used together to produce professional looking documents.

✓ *If you are using the standard Microsoft Office 97 suite package, Access and some bonus applications will not be included. Bonus applications are not covered in this book.*

The following software applications will be covered in Learning Microsoft Office 97:

■ **Word 97**, a word processing program, used for creating and editing documents.

■ **Excel 97**, a spreadsheet program, used for analyses and graphing of numerical data.

■ **Access 97**, a database program, used for organizing and sorting information.

■ **PowerPoint 97**, a presentation graphics program, used for creating visual presentations.

The information created in one application can be shared with other applications. For instance, a spreadsheet created in Excel, or a database created in Access, can easily be incorporated into a memo or letter that is created in Word. Data created in Word, Excel, or Access can be incorporated into PowerPoint. Such integration will be demonstrated in the Integration section of this text.

## About this Book

Learning Microsoft Office 97 will teach you to use and integrate the four mentioned applications in the Microsoft Office Professional 97 suite package on an IBM PC or compatible computer.

Each lesson in this book explains concepts, provides numerous exercises to apply those concepts, and illustrates the necessary keystrokes or mouse actions required to complete the exercises. Lesson summary exercises are provided at the end of each lesson to challenge and reinforce the concepts learned.

After completing the exercises in this book, you will be able to use the basic features of each application in Office 97 with ease.

## How to Use this Book

Each exercise contains four parts:

- **NOTES**     explain the concept and application being introduced.

- **EXERCISE DIRECTIONS**     explain how to complete the exercise.

- **EXERCISES**     allow you to apply the new concept.

- **KEYSTROKES**     outline the keystroke shortcuts and mouse actions required for completing an exercise.

✓ *Keystrokes and mouse actions are only provided when a new concept is being introduced. Therefore, if you forget the keystroke or mouse action required to perform a task, you can use the either the Help feature (explained in the Basics section) or the index of this book to find the procedure.*

Before you begin working on the exercises in any Office 97 application, you should read the first introductory section entitled Basics. This section will explain the screens, the Help feature, working in Windows, toolbars, menus, and other necessary preliminary information.

## Data and Solution Files

The data files are provided on the accompanying CD-ROM. Please read the installation directions on page viii to learn how to access these files. Solutions disks may be purchased separately from DDC Publishing. You may use the data files to complete an exercise without typing lengthy text or data. However, exercise directions are provided for both data disk and non-data disk users. Exercise directions will include a keyboard icon ⌨ to direct non-data disk users to open documents created in a previous exercise and a diskette icon 🖫 to direct data disk users to open the document available on the CD. For example, a typical direction might read: Open ⌨**TRY**, or open 🖫**03TRY**.

The Solution disk may be used for you to compare your work with the final version or solution on disk. Each solution filename begins with the letter "S" and is followed by the exercise number and descriptive filename. For example, **S03TRY** would contain the final solution to the exercise directions in exercise three.

A directory of data disk and solutions disk filenames are provided in the Log of Exercises section of this book.

✓ *Saving files to a network will automatically truncate all filenames to a maximum of eight characters. Therefore, though Windows 95 allows for longer filenames, a maximum of only eight characters can be saved to a network drive.*

## The Teacher's Manual

While this book can be used as a self-paced learning book, a comprehensive Teacher's Manual is also available. The Teacher's Manual contains the following:

- Lesson objectives
- Exercise objectives
- Related vocabulary
- Points to emphasize
- Exercise settings
- A Log of Exercises, which lists filenames in exercise number order
- A Directory of Documents, which lists filenames alphabetically along with the corresponding exercise numbers.
- Solution illustrations

# The enclosed CD-ROM includes . . .

## A Companion Internet Simulation

The CD-ROM that accompanies this book contains a simulation of Internet sites to be used in the Integration lesson. This means that you can complete the exercises without an Internet connection, avoiding modems, connection time and fees, wandering to unrelated sites, and long waits for Web sites to load. It's like being live on the Internet with none of the inconvenience.

For example, in Exercise 10, you will do a multi-level search on a site that gives information on Brazil. Launch the simulation following the detailed directions and follow the prompts at the bottom of your screen to find the information that you need. You will then copy the results of your search into a Word document and use the information in a PowerPoint presentation. Even if you have never been on the Internet before, you will be able to do the exercises. The results are that you learn how to integrate the power of Office 97 with the power of the Internet. (*See installation instructions at the right.*)

## Multimedia Internet Browser Tutorial

For the new user of the Internet, the CD-ROM includes basic computer based training on how to navigate the Internet using a browser. A browser is a program that helps manage the process of locating information on the Word Wide Web. The tutorial introduces the concepts and then shows you how to apply them. (*See installation instructions at the right.*)

## Demo of DDC's Office 97 Multimedia Tutorial

In this excerpt of DDC's Office 97 CBT (Computer Based Training), you will receive a sample of step-by-step directions, illustrations, simulations of desired keystroke or mouse actions, and application problems. (*See installation procedures on the following page.*)

## Installation Instructions

A separate installation is required for each program. At the designated prompt, indicate which program you wish to install. When installation of one program is complete, you may begin again from step one (above, right) to install another.

### System Requirements

| Software | Windows 95 or Windows NT 3.51 (or higher) |
|---|---|
| Hardware | 80486DX or higher, 16 MB RAM, 256 Color Monitor, and CD-ROM Drive- |
| Disk Space | 40 MB available hard disk space |

**To install the programs, place the CD in your CD-ROM drive and follow the listed steps below:**

1. **To install from Windows 95:**
   Click Start on the desktop and click Run.
   **OR**
   **To install from Windows NT:**
   Go to Program Manager in Main, click File,
2. In the Run window, begin a program installation by typing one of the following:
   - *CD-ROM drive letter:*\OFF97INT\SETUP to install the Internet Simulation.
   - *CD-ROM drive letter:*\OFFICE97\SETUP to install the Office 97 CBT.
   - *CD-ROM drive letter:*\NETSIM\SETUP to install the Browser tutorial.
3. Click NEXT at the Setup Wizard screen.
4. At the following screen, click NEXT to create a DDCPUB directory for storing program files. Then click YES to confirm the directory choice.
5. At the following screen, allow the default folder to be named **DDC Publishing**, and click NEXT.
6. At the next screen, choose one of the following options based on your individual system needs:
   *NOTE: A **Typical** installation is standard for most individual installation.*
   - **TYPICAL:** installs a minimum number of files to the hard drive with the majority of files remaining on the CD-ROM.
     ***NOTE: With this installation, the CD must remain in the CD-ROM drive when running the program.***
   - **CUSTOM:** installs only those files that you choose to the hard drive. This is generally only recommended for advanced users of Innovus Multimedia software.

- **Server:** installs the programs on a network server.
7. Click NEXT to begin copying the necessary files to your system.
8. Click OK at the Set Up status Window and then click YES to restart Windows.

To launch a program, click the Start button on the Windows 95 desktop, select Programs, DDC Publishing, and then select one of the following:

- **OFF97INT (to start the Internet Simulation)**
- **DEMO97 (to start the Office97 CBT)**
- **NETCBT (to start the Browser tutorial)**

## Data Files

Since this book is designed to teach you how to use the features of Microsoft Office 97, not how to type, you can use the data files to avoid typing long documents that are used in many of the exercises.

A disk icon 💾 preceding a filename means that there is a data file for the exercise. Follow the exercise directions to open the data file and complete the exercise as indicated.

✓ *Saving files to a network will automatically truncate all filenames to a maximum of eight characters. Therefore, though Windows 95 allows for longer filenames, a maximum of only eight characters can be saved to a network drive.*

**To copy data files on to a hard drive**:
- Open Windows 95 Explorer (Right-click on **Start** button and click **Explore**).

- Be sure that the CD is in your CD-ROM drive. Select the CD-ROM drive letter from the All Folders pane of the Explorer window.

- Click to Select the **DDCdata** folder in the Contents of (CD-ROM Drive letter) pane of the Explorer window.

- Drag the folder onto the letter of your hard drive (usually **C:**) in the All Folders pane of the Explorer Window.

## Advanced Exercises

In addition to the eight comprehensive lessons included in the Word 97 section of this book, two additional lessons, *Merge* and *Columns and Tables; Calculate and Sort*, are provided on the accompanying CD-ROM. Though the procedures in these two lessons cover some advanced techniques, it is recommended that do these exercises.

To access the lessons, follow the installation directions below. You can then print and duplicate the exercises you wish to use.

### To install the Advanced Lessons:

The advanced lessons are stored on the CD-ROM in Adobe's portable display format (PDF). These .PDF files can be viewed and printed through Acrobat Reader. Acrobat Reader is included on the CD; install it on your computer if you do not already have Acrobat Reader. To do so:

1. Locate the Acrobat Reader folder on the CD.
2. Double-click the Setup icon.
3. Respond to the prompts to install Acrobat Reader 3.0.

After installing Acrobat Reader, you may either:

- Leave the advanced lesson files on the CD and open, view and print them from the CD.

- Copy some or all of them to your hard drive using Windows Explorer.

The advanced lesson files are located in the ADVANCED folder on the CD and are named as follows:

MERGE lesson
    merge01.pdf
    merge02.pdf
    merge03.pdf

COLUMNS AND TABLES lesson
    cols01.pdf
    cols02.pdf
    cols03.pdf
    cols04.pdf
    cols05.pdf
    cols06.pdf
    cols06.pdf
    cols07.pdf
    cols08.pdf

The .PDF file ADVCONT.PDF contains a table of contents summarizing the topics covered in the advanced lessons.

# LOG OF EXERCISES

**Word**

| Lesson | Exercise | Filename | Data file | Solution File | Page |
|--------|----------|----------|-----------|---------------|------|
| 1 | 1 | TRY | | S01TRY | 22 |
| | 2 | TRYAGAIN | | S02TRYAGAIN | 27 |
| | 3 | LETTER | | S03LETTE | 30 |
| | 4 | BLOCK | | S04BLOCK | 34 |
| | 5 | PERSONAL | | S05PERSONAL | 38 |
| | 6 | OPEN | | S06OPEN | 39 |
| 2 | 7 | TRY | 07TRY | S07TRY | 42 |
| | 8 | TRYAGAIN | 08TRYAGAIN | S08 TRYIT | 45 |
| | 9 | DIVE | 09DIVE | S09DIVE | 48 |
| | 10 | LETTER | 10LETTER | S10LETTER | 53 |
| | 11 | BLOCK | 11BLOCK | S11BLOCK S11BLOCA | 55 |
| | 12 | PERSONAL, TRYIT, OPEN | 12PERSON 12TRYIT 12OPEN | S12OPEN | 58 |
| | 13 | REGRET | 13REGRET | S13REGRET | 60 |
| | 14 | COMPANY | | S14COMPANY | 63 |
| 3 | 15 | ESTATE | 15ESTATE | S15ESTATE | 66 |
| | 16 | GLOBAL | 16GLOBAL | S16GLOBAL | 70 |
| | 17 | CAFE | 17CAFE | S17CAFE | 74 |
| | 18 | DESIGN | 18DESIGN | S18DESIGN | 77 |
| | 19 | COLOR | 19COLOR | S19COLOR | 80 |
| 4 | 20 | DIVE | 20DIVE | S20DIVE | 84 |
| | 21 | CONNECT | | S21CONNE | 88 |
| | 22 | TIPS | 22TIPS | S22TIPS | 91 |
| | 23 | CONNECT | 23CONNECT | S23CONNECT | 93 |
| | 24 | TIPS | 24TIPS | S24TIPS | 96 |
| | 25 | DIVE | 25DIVE | S25DIVE | 98 |
| 5 | 26 | SOD | 26SOD | S26SOD | 100 |
| | 27 | CONNECT | 27CONNECT | S27CONNECT | 104 |
| | 28 | CARS | | S28CARS | 108 |
| | 29 | GREEN | | S29GREEN | 111 |
| | 30 | BRANCH | 30BRANCH | S30BRANCH | 113 |
| 6 | 31 | SEMINAR | 31SEMINAR | S31SEMINAR | 116 |
| | 32 | PREVIEW | 32PREVIEW | S32PREVIEW | 121 |
| | 33 | VOYAGE | 33VOYAGE | S33VOYAGE | 126 |
| | 34 | USA | 34USA | S34USA | 130 |
| | 35 | PREVIEW USA | 35PREVIEW 35USA | S35PREVIEW S35USA | 133 |
| | 36 | BRAZIL | 36BRAZIL | S36BRAZIL | 138 |
| 7 | 37 | HOTELS GLOBAL DIVE | 37HOTELS 37GLOBAL 37DIVE | S37HOTEL | 141 |
| | 38 | HOMES, ESTATE | 38HOMES, 38ESTATE | S38HOMES | 144 |
| | 39 | WILL | 39WILL | S39WILL | 147 |
| | 40 | MACRO | | | |
| | 41 | SETTLE | | S41SETTLE | 152 |
| | 42 | WORKOUT | | S42WORKOUT | 154 |

**Access**

| Lesson | Exercise | Filename | Data file | Solution File | Page |
|---|---|---|---|---|---|
| 1 | 1 | COMPANY | | S01COMPA | 301 |
| | 2 | COMPANY | 02COMPAN | S02COMPA | 303 |
| | 3 | HUGCLUB | | S03HUGCL | 305 |
| | 4 | COMPANY | 04COMPAN | S04COMPA | 308 |
| | 5 | CLUBS | | S05CLUBS | 311 |
| | 6 | COMPANY | 06COMPAN | S06COMPA | 313 |
| 2 | 7 | CLUBS | 07CLUBS | S07CLUBS | 314 |
| | 8 | COMPANY | 08COMPAN | S08COMPA | 317 |
| | 9 | HUGCLUB | 09HUGCLB | S09MEMFO | 320 |
| | 10 | CLUBS | 10CLUBS | S10CLUBS | 323 |
| | 11 | COMPANY | 11COMPAN | S11COMPA | 326 |
| | 12 | COMPANY | 12COMPAN | S12HARDF | 327 |
| 3 | 13 | HUGCLUB | 13HUGCLB | S13HUGCL | 330 |
| | 14 | COMPANY | 14COMPAN | S14COMPA | 333 |
| | 15 | HUGCLUB | 15HUGCLB | S15HUGCL | 335 |
| | 16 | CLUBS | 16CLUBS | S16CLUBS | 338 |
| | 17 | JANESHOP JANE | 17JANE | S17JANESH S17JANE | 339 |
| 4 | 18 | HUGCLUB | 18HUGCLB | S18HUGCL | 343 |
| | 19 | COMPANY | 19COMPAN | S19COMPA | 346 |
| | 20 | COMPANY | 20COMPAN | S20COMPA | 348 |
| | 21 | COMPANY | 21COMPAN | S21COMPA | 350 |
| | 22 | COMPANY | 22COMPAN | S22COMPA | 351 |
| | 23 | COMPANY | 23COMPAN | S23COMPA | 354 |
| | 24 | COMPANY | 24COMPAN | S24COMPA | 357 |
| 5 | 25 | JANESHOP | 25JANSHP | S25JANSH | 359 |
| | 26 | COMPANY | 26COMPAN | S26COMPA | 362 |
| | 27 | COMPANY | 27COMPAN | S27COMPA | 364 |
| | 28 | ADDRBOOK | | S28ADDRB | 366 |
| | 29 | COLLEGE | | S29COLLE | 367 |

## PowerPoint

| Lesson | Exercise | Filename | Data file | Solution File | Page |
|---|---|---|---|---|---|
| 1 | 1 | KIT<br>FLAGSHIP | | S01KIT<br>S01FLAGSHIP | 377 |
| | 2 | FLAGSHIP<br>KIT | 02FLAGSHIP<br>02KIT | S02FLAGSHIP<br>S02KIT | 382 |
| | 3 | FLAGSHIP<br>KIT | 03FLAGSHIP<br>03KIT | S03FLAGSHIP<br>S03KIT | 385 |
| | 4 | KIT | 04KIT | S04KIT | 389 |
| | 5 | FOOD | | S05FOOD | 393 |
| | 6 | BRAZIL | | S06BRAZIL | 395 |
| 2 | 7 | KIT | 07KIT | S07KIT | 399 |
| | 8 | BRAZIL | 08BRAZIL | S08BRAZIL | 403 |
| | 9 | FLAGSHIP | 09FLAGSHIP | S09FLAGSHIP | 408 |
| | 10 | FOOD | 10FOOD | S10FOOD | 414 |
| | 11 | FLAGSHIP | 11FLAGSHIP | S11FLAGSHIP | 418 |
| | 12 | KIT | 12KIT | S12KIT | 421 |
| | 13 | INVEST | | S13INVEST | 423 |
| 3 | 14 | BRAZIL | 14BRAZIL | S14BRAZIL | 428 |
| | 15 | FOOD | 15FOOD | S15FOOD | 434 |
| | 16 | FLAGSHIP | 16FLAGSHIP | S16FLAGSHIP | 437 |
| | 17 | FOOD | 17FOOD | S17FOOD | 440 |
| | 18 | INVEST | 18INVEST | S18INVEST | 444 |

## Integration

| Exercise | Filename | Data file | Solution File | Page |
|---|---|---|---|---|
| 1 | WAGON<br>PAYMENT<br>PRICE<br>INVENTORY<br>BLOCK | 01WAGON.XLS<br>01PAYMEN.XLS<br>01PRICE.XLS<br>01INVEN.XLS<br>01BLOCK.DOC | | 450 |
| 2 | SKI CURRENCY | 02SKI.DOC<br>02CURRENCY.XLS | S02SKICUR.DOC | 455 |
| 3 | INVEST STOCK | 03INVEST.DOC<br>03STOCK.XLS | S03INVSTK.DOC<br>S03STOCK.XLS | 459 |
| 4 | SKI, CURRENCY | 04SKICUR.DOC<br>04CURREN.XLS | S04SKICU.DOC<br>S04CURRE.XLS | 464 |
| 5 | JANESHOP<br>STOCKEX | 05JANSHOP.MDB | S05STOCK.XLS | 468 |
| 6 | NYMEET<br>HUGCLUB | 06NYMEET.DOC<br>06HUGCLU.MDB | S06NYHUG.DOC | 472 |
| 7 | SKIOUT | 07SKIOUT.DOC<br>07CURREN.XLS | S07SKIOUT.PPT | 476 |
| 8 | TICKLE<br>TOYS | 08TICKLE.DOC<br>08TOYS.XLS | S08TICKLE.DOC | 479 |
| 9 | MEMO<br>FRANCE | 09MEMO.DOC<br>09FRANCE.PPT<br>09APPROV.DOC | S09FRANC.PPT<br>S09APPRO.DOC | 483 |
| 10 | SHOW<br>BRAZIL<br>REPLY<br>INFLATION<br>INVITE<br>COLLEGE | 10SHOW.DOC<br>10BRAZIL.PPT<br>10REPLY.DOC<br>10INFLAT.XLS<br>10INVITE.DOC<br>10COLLEGE.MDB | S10SHOW.DOC<br>S10REPLY.DOC<br>S10BRAZI.PPT<br>S10INVIT.DOC<br>S10BRAZI.DOC | 487 |

# DIRECTORY OF DOCUMENTS

## Word

| Filename | Exercise |
|---|---|
| ANNOUNCE | 45 |
| BLOCK | 4, 11 |
| BRANCH | 30 |
| BRAZIL | 36 |
| CABLE | 48 |
| CAFE | 17 |
| CARS | 28 |
| COASTAL | 43 |
| COLOR | 19 |
| COMPANY | 14 |
| CONNECT | 21, 23, 27 |
| DESIGN | 18 |
| DIVE | 9, 20, 25, 37 |
| ESTATE | 15, 38 |
| FAX | 46 |
| GLOBAL | 16, 37 |
| GREEN | 29 |
| HOMES | 38 |
| HOTELS | 37 |
| JOURNEY | 44 |
| LETTER | 3, 10 |
| MACRO | 40 |
| OPEN | 6, 12 |
| PERSONAL | 5, 12 |
| PREVIEW | 32, 35 |
| REGRET | 13 |
| REGRETS | 47 |
| SEMINAR | 31 |
| SETTLE | 41 |
| SOD | 26 |
| TIPS | 22, 24 |
| TRY | 1, 7 |
| TRYAGAIN | 2, 8 |
| TRYIT | 12 |
| USA | 34, 35 |
| VOYAGE | 33 |
| WILL | 39 |
| WORKOUT | 42 |

## Excel

| Filename | Exercise |
|---|---|
| ACCREC | 30, 33 |
| COMM | 25 |
| DREAM | 32 |
| EXPENSE | 14 |
| INCOME | 15, 18, 19, 23 |
| INVENTORY | 4 |
| MKTG | 16, 27 |
| MKTGSUM | 28 |
| PAY | 3, 7, 12, 17, 20 |
| PAYMENT | 31, 32 |
| PAYTEMP | 26 |
| PRICE | 5, 6 , 10 |
| RATE | 34 |
| REPORT | 11, 13, 21, 22 |
| SABRINA | 24 |
| SALARY | 29 |
| SALES | 2, 8 |
| SPORTS | 35, 36, 37 |
| TOYS | 39 |
| WAGON | 9, 38 |

## Access

| Filename | Exercise |
|---|---|
| ADDRBOOK | 28 |
| CLUBS | 5, 7, 10, 16 |
| COLLEGE | 29 |
| COMPANY | 1, 2, 4, 6, 8, 11, 12, 14, 19, 20, 21, 22, 23, 24, 26, 27 |
| HUGCLUB | 3, 9, 13, 15, 18 |
| JANE | 17 |
| JANESHOP | 17, 25 |

## PowerPoint

| Filename | Exercise |
|---|---|
| BRAZIL | 6, 8, 14 |
| FLAGSHIP | 1 |
| FLAGSHIP | 2, 3, 9, 11, 16 |
| FOOD | 5, 10, 15, 17 |
| INVEST | 13, 18 |
| KIT | 1, 2, 3, 4, 7, 12 |

## Integration

| Filename | Exercise |
|---|---|
| BLOCK | 1 |
| BRAZIL | 10 |
| COLLEGE | 10 |
| CURRENCY | 4 |
| FRANCE | 9 |
| HUGCLUB | 6 |
| INFLATION | 10 |
| INVENTORY | 1 |
| INVEST STOCK | 3 |
| INVITE | 10 |
| JANESHOP | 5 |
| MEMO | 9 |
| NYMEET | 6 |
| PAYMENT | 1 |
| PRICE | 1 |
| REPLY | 10 |
| SHOW | 10 |
| SKI | 4 |
| SKI CURRENCY | 2 |
| SKIOUT | 7 |
| STOCKEX | 5 |
| TICKLE | 8 |
| TOYS | 8 |
| WAGON | 1 |

# Microsoft Office 97 Basics

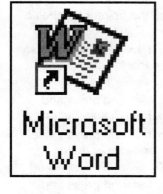

Microsoft Word

Microsoft Excel

Microsoft Access

Microsoft PowerPoint

# Exercise 1

## ■ About Microsoft® Office 97 for Windows® 95 ■ Using The Mouse
## ■ Microsoft Office Shortcut Bar ■ Starting Microsoft Office 97

## NOTES

### About Microsoft® Office 97

■ Microsoft® Office 97 Professional for Windows® 95 provides a full range of powerful programs that may be used independently or in an integrated fashion to efficiently complete all your office applications. Microsoft® Office includes Microsoft Access® (database program), Microsoft Binder® (project organization program), Microsoft Excel® (spreadsheet program), Microsoft Outlook® (information management program), Microsoft PowerPoint® (presentation program), Microsoft Word (word processing program) and Microsoft Bookshelf Basics (reference tools).

■ This text will include instruction on all programs except Microsoft Outlook, Microsoft Bookshelf Basics, and Binder.

### Using the Mouse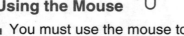

■ You must use the mouse to access many features in Microsoft Office. Therefore, you must become familiar with its operation.

■ When the mouse is moved on the tabletop, a corresponding movement of the mouse pointer occurs on the screen. The mouse pointer changes shape depending on the program in use, the object it is pointing to, and the action it will be performing. The mouse pointer will not move if the mouse is lifted up and placed back on the tabletop.

■ Specific mouse shapes will be discussed within each application as they are activated.

■ All references to the use of mouse buttons in this book refer to the *left* mouse button unless otherwise directed.

■ The mouse terminology and corresponding actions described below will be used throughout the book:

| | |
|---|---|
| **Point to** | Move the mouse (on the tabletop) so the pointer touches a specific item. |
| **Click** | Point to an item and quickly press and release the *left* mouse button. |
| **Right-click** | Point to an item and press and release the *right* mouse button. |
| **Double-click** | Point to an item and press the left mouse button twice in rapid succession. |
| **Drag** | Point to an item and press and hold down the left mouse button while moving the mouse. |
| **Slide** | Move the mouse on the tabletop so that a menu is highlighted. |

✓Note: *You must be using an IntelliMouse to use the following mouse actions.*

| | |
|---|---|
| **Scroll** | Rotate the center wheel of an IntelliMouse forward or backward to move through a document. |
| **Pan** | Press the center wheel of an IntelliMouse and drag the pointer above or below where you first click. The farther you drag from the point of the first click, the faster the document will move. |

| | |
|---|---|
| **AutoScroll** | Click the center wheel of an IntelliMouse to automatically scroll down in a document. Scroll up by moving the pointer above the point of the first click. |
| **Zoom** | Hold down the Ctrl key while you rotate the center wheel of an IntelliMouse to zoom in or out by 10% increments. |

## The Microsoft Office Shortcut Bar

■ After the software is installed, the Microsoft Office Shortcut bar appears on your window display. The Shortcut bar displays buttons (symbols) that represent features found in Microsoft Office. This Shortcut bar is displayed at all times so that you can access Office features from within Windows or from any Office application.

■ The Shortcut bar contains buttons for Getting Results Book, New Office Document, Open a File, Internet Explorer, Bookshelf Basics, New Note, New Message, New Journal Entry, Microsoft Outlook, New Appointment, New Task, and New Contact. The Shortcut bar buttons will be introduced and discussed when they are necessary for an exercise.

### *Shortcut Bar*

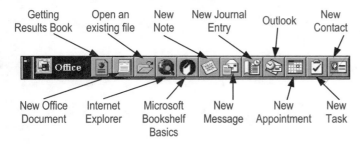

✓Note: *Your Shortcut bar may be different, depending on the office components that are installed on your system.*

■ When you point to a Shortcut bar button, a **ToolTip** displays with an explanation of that button's function.

■ Shortcut bar buttons may be added or deleted to display those features you commonly use.

✓Note: *If the Shortcut bar does not appear after installation, click Start, Program, Start Up. Then, select Microsoft Office Shortcut bar.*

## Starting Microsoft® Office 97

■ There are two ways to start Microsoft Office 97. You can click the New Office Document button on the Shortcut bar, or you can click the Start button on the Windows® 95 Taskbar. The Taskbar appears on your window display when you install Windows 95. It is used to start applications as well as to switch between applications.

Windows 95 taskbar

## Using the Shortcut Bar

■ Once the New Office Document button is selected, a new screen appears displaying tabs that represent various applications. The General tab contains icons that represent new files for Word, Excel, PowerPoint, Access, and Binder. For example, to open the Word program *and* begin a new document, you would click Blank Document, which appears below the Word symbol and then click OK.

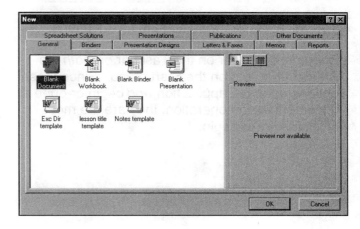

## Using the Start Button on the Windows Taskbar

■ After you click the Start button on the Windows Taskbar, a menu appears. Slide the mouse to highlight Programs. Once Programs is highlighted, a second menu appears listing those programs installed in your computer. Slide the mouse to highlight the desired application, and click to select it.

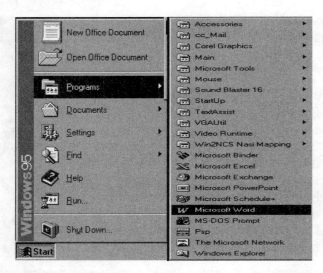

■ You will note, too, that the same two options, New Office Document and Open Office Document, appear on the Taskbar on *both* the Shortcut bar and on the Start menu. Since these options open the application *and* begin or open a document in one operation, they are the most efficient way to begin.

■ If you select New Office Document from the Start menu, the same New screen dialog box with tab selections displays as illustrated on the previous page.

## Closing Programs Using the Mouse

■ To quickly exit a program using the mouse, click the Program Close button (the X in the upper-right corner of the screen). In the illustration below, you will note two Close buttons. The top Close button closes the program; the bottom Close button closes the document window. Other methods of closing programs will be detailed in Exercise 2.

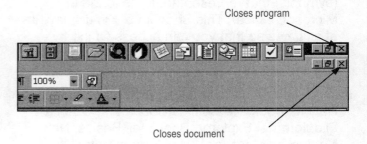

Closes program

Closes document

# EXERCISE DIRECTIONS:

1. Roll the mouse up, down, left, and right on the tabletop or the mousepad.

2. Place the mouse pointer on each button on the Shortcut Bar and note the ToolTips notation for each button.

3. Click the New Office Document button.

   ✓ *The New screen (dialog box) with Blank Document highlighted appears.*

4. Click OK to open a new document in Word.

5. Click the bottom Close button to exit the new Word document.

6. Click the top Close button to exit the Word program.

7. Click Start on the Windows Taskbar.

8. Slide the mouse to highlight Programs, then highlight and click Microsoft Word.

9. Click the top Close button to exit the Word program.

10. Click Start on the Windows Taskbar.

11. Click New Office Document.

    ✓ *The New screen (dialog box) with Blank Document highlighted appears.*

12. Click each tab to view the options and return to the General tab.

13. Double-click Blank Workbook to open a new workbook in Excel.

14. Click on the bottom Close button to exit the new workbook.

15. Click on the top Close button to exit Excel.

# KEYSTROKES

**START OFFICE**

1. Click **Start** on Taskbar........... `Ctrl` + `Esc`
2. Click **Programs** ............................. `P`

3. Select program:

   **Microsoft Access**

   **Microsoft Excel**

   **Microsoft PowerPoint**

   **Microsoft Word**

4. Press **Enter** .................................... `↵`

**CLOSE THE PROGRAM**

Click Program Close `⊠` button.

## Exercise 2

- **Office Windows** ■ **Menus, Toolbars, and Commands**
- **Select Menu Items** ■ **Dialog Box Options**
- **Shortcut Menus**

# NOTES

## Office Windows

■ When you access each Office application, you will see its opening screen. The common parts of all the Office application windows will be illustrated and discussed using the Word screen. The specific screen parts for each Office program will be detailed in the appropriate section of this book.

■ Clicking the **Program Control** button [W], located to the left of the Program Window Title bar, accesses a drop-down menu from which you can choose commands to control the program window.

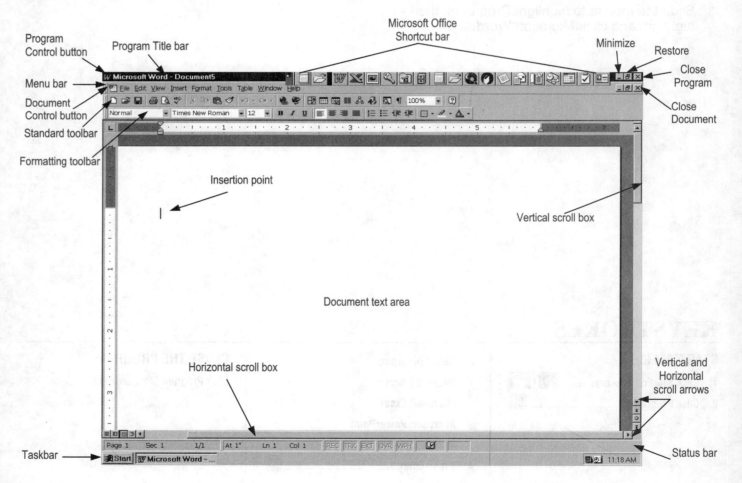

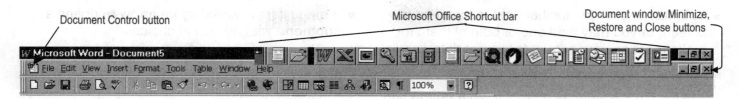

Document Control button
Microsoft Office Shortcut bar
Document window Minimize, Restore and Close buttons

- The **Microsoft Office Shortcut bar** displays buttons that represent features found in Microsoft Office.

- The **Program Window Title bar**, located at the top of the application window, displays the program name (Microsoft Word, Excel, etc.) and may also display the name of an opened file if the document window is maximized.

- The **program window Minimize**, **Restore**, and **Close buttons** are located on the right side of the program title bar. Clicking the Minimize button ▬ shrinks the window into the Microsoft Word button on the Taskbar. Clicking the Restore button 🗗 causes the button to change to a Maximize button 🗖. Clicking the Close button ✕ closes the program.

- The **Menu bar**, located below the title bar, displays menu names from which drop-down menus may be accessed. When you click on a menu, a drop-down menu appears.

- Clicking the **Document Control button** 🔳, located to the left of the Menu bar, accesses a drop-down menu from which you can choose commands to control the document window.

- The **document window Minimize**, **Restore**, and **Close buttons** are located on the right of the menu bar. When the document window is maximized, clicking the Minimize button ▬ shrinks the window to an icon which displays at the bottom of the screen. Clicking the Restore button 🗗 creates a document window (below the toolbars) including a document title bar. The Document Title bar then contains the Document Control button and the Minimize, Maximize, and Close buttons which also appear on the Menu bar. Clicking the Maximize button on the document title bar returns the window to the size of the opening screen. Clicking the Close button closes the document.

- The **toolbars**, located below the menu bar, contain buttons, each of which has a small picture or icon displayed on it, that can be used to select commands quickly.

- Pointing to and resting the pointer on a toolbar button displays a **ToolTip**, which names the button.

- The **Status bar**, located at the bottom of the window, displays information about the current mode or operation.

- The **Horizontal** and **Vertical scroll bars** are used to move the screen view horizontally or vertically. Drag the **Scroll box** on the vertical scroll bar up or down to move more quickly toward the beginning or end of the document.

- The **document text area** is the blank workspace for typing text.

## Menus, Toolbars, and Commands

- The Menu bar and toolbars may be used to access commands. Each application opens with two toolbars. The **Standard toolbar**, located below the main menu bar, contains buttons that accomplish many common tasks easily, like saving and printing a file.

*Word Standard Toolbar*

*Excel Standard Toolbar*

- The **Formatting toolbar**, located below the Standard toolbar, contains buttons that easily change the appearance of data. While each application contains both toolbars and many of the same buttons, the toolbars also contain buttons unique to each program.

*Word Formatting Toolbar*

*Excel Formatting Toolbar*

- You may display the toolbars at the top of your screen, or you may hide one or both of them to make room on your screen for text or data.

- **To select a command from a toolbar:**
  - Use the mouse to point to a toolbar button and click once.

- **To access Menu bar items:**
  - Use the mouse to point to a menu item on the menu bar and click once, or
  - Press Alt + *underlined letter* in the menu name.

- **To select a command from a drop-down menu:**
  - Use the mouse to point to the command on the drop-down menu and click once, or
  - Press the underlined letter in the command name, or
  - Use the up or down arrow key to highlight the command, then press Enter.

- Some menu options are dimmed, while others appear black. Dimmed options are not available for selection at this time, while black options are.

  ✓ Note the drop-down menu that appears when View is selected in Word.

  ✓ Note the drop-down menu that appears when Insert is selected in Excel.

- A check mark next to a drop-down menu item means the option is currently selected.

- A menu item followed by an arrow ▶ opens a **submenu** with additional choices.

- A menu item followed by an **ellipsis** (...) indicates that a dialog box (which requires you to provide additional information to complete a task) is forthcoming.

  ✓ Note: *Icons that appear next to menu items are available on the Standard or Formatting toolbars.*

- Note the Page Setup dialog box below, which appears after you select Page Setup from the File menu, and the Font dialog box, which appears after you select Font from the Format menu.

*Page Setup Dialog Box*

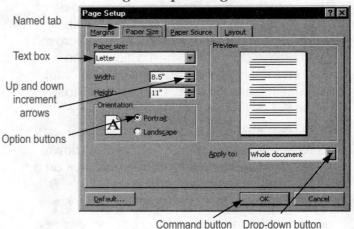

*Font Dialog Box*

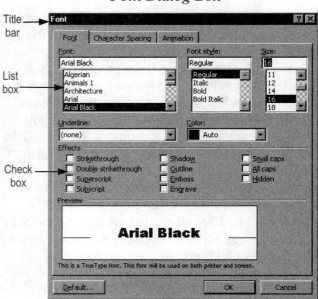

## Dialog Box Options

- A **dialog box** contains different ways to ask you for information. A description of dialog box parts appears below:

  - The **Title bar** identifies the title of the dialog box.

  - A **text box** is a location where you type information.

  - **Command buttons** carry out actions described on the button. When command names have an ellipsis following them, they will access another dialog box.

  - A **drop-down list** is marked with a down arrow. Clicking the drop-down list box accesses a short list of options.

  - An **increment box** provides a space for typing a value. An up or down arrow (usually to the right of the box) gives you a way to select a value with the mouse.

  - A **named tab** is used to display options related to the tab's name in the same dialog box.

  - **Option buttons** are small circular buttons marking options in a set. You may choose only one option from the set. A selected option button contains a dark circle.

  - A **check box** is a small square box where an option may be selected or deselected. A "✔" in the box indicates the option is selected. If several check boxes are offered, you may select more than one.

  - A **list box** displays a list of items from which selections can be made. A list box may have a scroll bar that can be used to show hidden items in the list.

  - A **scroll bar** is a horizontal or vertical bar providing scroll arrows and a scroll box that can be dragged up or down to move more quickly through the file.

    ✓Note:   Note the labeled parts in the dialog boxes.

## Shortcut Menus

- Shortcut menus appear when the *right* mouse button is pressed. The menu items that appear vary depending on the task being performed and the position of the mouse pointer on the screen.

## Mouse and Keystroke Procedures

- Procedures for completing a task will be illustrated throughout this book as shown below. Mouse actions are illustrated on the left, while keystroke procedures are illustrated to the right and keyboard shortcut keys are illustrated below the heading. Use whichever method you find most convenient.

*In this exercise, you will become familiar with the toolbars, Ruler, and drop-down menus.*

# EXERCISE DIRECTIONS

1. Start the Word program.
2. Select View from the Menu bar.
3. Deselect Ruler.
   - ✓ *Note the change in the screen.*
4. Select View; select Toolbars.
5. Deselect Standard.
   - ✓ *Note the change in the screen.*
6. Select View and reselect Ruler to return the ruler to the screen.
7. Select View; select Toolbars. Reselect Standard to return toolbar to the screen.
8. Use the View menu to make the following changes:
   - Deselect Ruler.
   - Select Full Screen.
9. Restore the screen to the default view by clicking Close Full Screen.

10. Click the document minimize button ▬ on the menu bar.
    - ✓ *Note that your document window is reduced to an icon.*
11. Click the document maximize button ▢ to return the window to the previous screen.
12. Select Page Setup from the File menu.
13. Select the Paper Size tab.
14. Click the Paper Size drop-down list arrow and select Legal 8½ x 14 in.
15. Return the paper size to the Letter 8 ½ x 11 in default setting.
16. Click on each tab to note the available options; click Cancel to return to document.
17. Position the mouse pointer anywhere in the document text area and click the right mouse button.
    - ✓ *Note the shortcut menu that appears.*
18. Click the program Close button to close Word.

# KEYSTROKES

## HIDE/DISPLAY TOOLBARS

1. Click **View** .............................. Alt + V
2. Click **Toolbars** .......................... T
3. Select desired toolbar.
4. Repeat steps 1-3 for each additional toolbar you want to appear.

### To customize toolbar(s):

1. Click **View** .............................. Alt + V
2. Click **Toolbars** .......................... T
3. Click **Customize** ........................ C
4. Click **Options** tab .................. Alt + O
5. Select desired toolbar or menu display options.
6. Select **Close** .............................. Enter

## HIDE/DISPLAY RULERS (WORD)

1. Click **View** .............................. Alt + V
2. Click **Ruler** .............................. R

# Exercise 3

■ **Using the Keyboard** ■ **The Zoom Option**
■ **Help Features** ■ **Office Assistant**

## NOTES

### Using the Keyboard

■ Computers contain specialized keys:

- **Function keys** (F1 through F12) perform special functions.

- **Modifier keys** (Shift, Alt, Ctrl) (there are two of each on most keyboards) are used in conjunction with other keys to select certain commands or perform actions. To use a modifier key with another key, you must hold down the modifier key while tapping the other key.

- **Numeric keys**, found on keyboards with a number pad, allow you to enter numbers quickly. When the Num Lock light is ON, the number keys on the pad are operational, as is the decimal point. When the Num Lock light is OFF, the insertion point control keys (Home, PgUp, End, PgDn) are active. The numbers on the top row of the keyboard are always active.

- **Escape key** (Esc) is used to cancel some actions, commands, menus, or an entry.

- **Enter keys** (there are two on most keyboards) are used to complete an entry of data in some applications.

- **Directional arrow keys** are used to move the active screen insertion point.

### The Zoom Option

■ The <u>V</u>iew menu contains a <u>Z</u>oom option that allows you to set the magnification of the data on the screen. When <u>Z</u>oom is selected, the following dialog box appears:

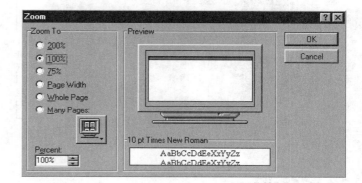

■ By clicking an option button, you can display the text at **200%**, **100%**, **75%**, etc. However, the zoom control box, 75% ▾, located on the Standard toolbar, lets you easily set text magnification without opening the menu or dialog box.

✓ Note: If you are using the IntelliMouse, you can hold down the Ctrl button and roll the wheel on the IntelliMouse to adjust the view by 10% increments (from 10-500%).

✓ Note: To work through the exercises in this text, the Standard and Formatting toolbars as well as the Ruler must be displayed on your screen. If these items are not displayed, follow the keystrokes on page 15.

## Help Features

■ Help is available from a variety of sources in Office. Below is an illustration of the help features available on the Word Help menu. Help menus in Excel, Access, and PowerPoint offer similar options.

   ✓ *Note: The Word Help menu offers assistance for WordPerfect users. On the Excel Help menu, you will find help for Lotus 1-2-3 users.*

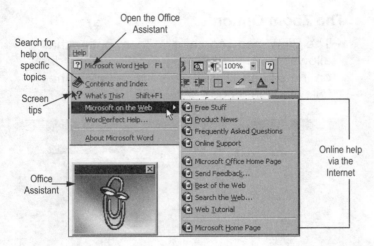

## Office Assistant

■ By default, the Office Assistant appears on screen when you open any of the Office applications. The Office Assistant will answer questions, offer suggestions, and provide help unique to the Office program you are using.

■ When you click on the Assistant, type your question and click Search. The suggested procedures display.

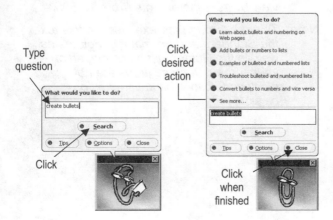

■ The Office Assistant can provide help even when you do not ask for it. For example, if you start typing a letter, the Assistant will open and offer help. You can then access a variety of wizards that can walk you through the procedure, or click Cancel and return to your document.

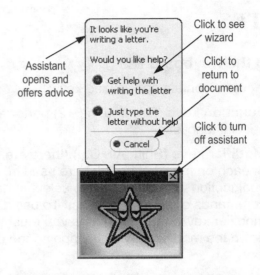

■ The Office Assistant also offers tips about features and keyboard shortcuts. A tip is available when a light bulb appears in the Assistant window. Click the Assistant to view the tip.

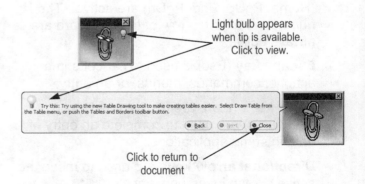

## Office Assistant Options

- You can control the way the Office Assistant appears on screen as well as the kind of information that it presents. You can also turn the Assistant off. If you turn the Assistant off, you can easily turn it on again by clicking the Assistant button 🔲 on the Standard toolbar.

- To change the Assistant options:
  - Click the Office Assistant (if it is on screen) or click the Office Assistant button on the toolbar and click Options. Click the Options tab and select the desired options.

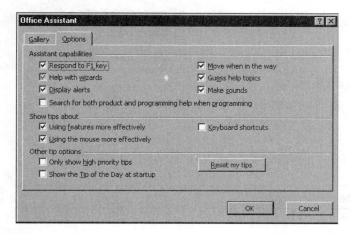

## Select a Different Office Assistant

- The Gallery tab in the Office Assistant dialog box offers several different Assistant characters. Click the Gallery tab on the Office Assistant dialog box and click Next to view the different Assistants.

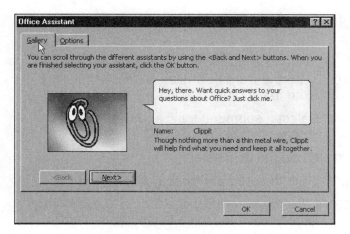

## Contents, Index, and Find

- If you select Contents and Index on the Help menu, you will be able to use the Contents, Index and/or the Find options to look for help.

## Contents

- The **Contents** tab displays a page listing the help contents by topic in the current program. Double-clicking on a topic presents a list of subtopics and/or display screens. Note the Word contents page and an example of a display screen illustrated below.

*Word Contents Page*

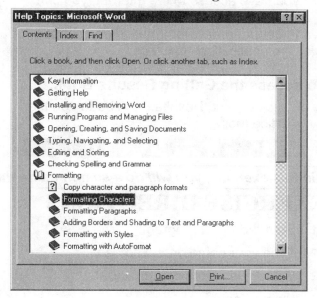

## Index

- The **Index** tab allows you to enter the first few letters of your topic; the index feature then brings you to the index entry. Double-click the entry or select the entry and click Display. The help screen related to your topic is then displayed.

## Find

- The **Find** tab accesses the Help database feature. It allows you to search the Help database for the occurrence of any word or phrase in a help topic. The Index and Find features are similar; however, Find offers more options to search for a topic.

## Screen Tips

■ You can find out information about screen elements by selecting the What's This? feature on the Help menu, then pointing to the element you want information about, and clicking the mouse.

Or you may click the question mark in a dialog box, and click on the option.

## Getting Results Book

✓ Note: The Getting Results book is available only if you installed Microsoft Office from a CD-ROM.

■ If you have access to the Internet, you can connect to Microsoft on the World Wide Web and get up-to-date information and support for all the applications in Office.

## To access the Getting Results Book:

• Click Getting Results Book button on the Office toolbar.

**OR**

• Open the Help menu, select Microsoft on the Web, and select the option you want to connect to. You can move around from option to option once you are connected to the Internet.

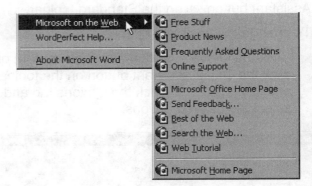

## Exit Help

■ Click Cancel or Close or press Escape exit.

---

*In this exercise, you will do a search using the office Assistant.*

# EXERCISE DIRECTIONS

1. Start the Word program.

2. Type your name on the screen.

3. Select View from the menu bar.

4. Select Zoom.

5. Select the 200% magnification option.

6. Click OK.
   ✓ *Note the change.*

7. Repeat steps 3-6 using the 75% option.

8. Using the Zoom Control box on the Standard toolbar, set the magnification to 150%.

9. Return to 100% magnification using any desired method.

10. Click the Office Assistant button on the Standard toolbar or click on the Office Assistant image.

    • Type Zoom in the question text box and click Search.

    • Read the Search results.

    • Click Tips. Read the tip displayed.

    • Click Close.

11. Start the Excel program.

12. Press F1 to access Help.

13. Type the following question and click Search: How do I hide a toolbar?

14. Double-click one of the topics.

15. Press the Esc key.

16. Select Contents and Index from the Help menu.

17. Click the Index tab.

18. Type the word Formulas, then click Display. Note the submenu topics.

19. Select a submenu topic and view the help screen.

20. Close the help screen.

21. Click the program close button to exit Excel.

22. Click the program close button to exit Word. When prompted to save the file, select No.

# KEYSTROKES

## ZOOM

### To specify a custom zoom:

1. Click on Zoom Control box on the Standard toolbar.

2. Type (10-500) zoom percentage.........................*number*

3. Press **Enter** .................................. `Enter`

### To select a zoom:

1. Click drop-down arrow in `▼` Zoom Control box on Standard toolbar.

2. Select zoom percentages.

### To change zoom with IntelliMouse:

Hold down the Ctrl key and roll the wheel to change zoom option by 10% increments.

## START OFFICE ASSISTANT

*By default, the Office Assistant will appear when you open any Office application. If the Assistant is not on screen, use these steps to activate the Assistant.*

Click Office Assistant button `🔲` on Standard toolbar.

**OR**

Press **F1** .................................. `F1`

*If the Contents, Index, and Find window opens instead of the Office Assistant, the F1 key option has been disabled in the Office Assistant Options dialog box. See below on how to change this option.*

## CLOSE OFFICE ASSISTANT

Click Close button on Office Assistant.

## USE OFFICE ASSISTANT

1. Click Office Assistant......................... `F1`

2. Type question in Assistant text box.

3. Click **Search**........................... `Alt`+`S`

4. Select from list of procedures to view more information.

5. Press **Escape** .............................. `Esc` to close Help window.

## CHANGE OFFICE ASSISTANT OPTIONS

1. Click Office Assistant ...................... `F1`

2. Click **Options** ......................... `Alt`+`O`

3. Click **Options** tab ................... `Alt`+`O`

4. Select desired options.

5. Click **OK**................................. `Enter`

## USE CONTENTS AND INDEX

1. Click **Help** .............................. `Alt`+`H`

2. Click **Contents and Index**................ `C`

### Contents

a. Double-click a book or topic.

b. Double-click a submenu item or a display item.

### Index

a. Type first letters of topic word in step 1 text box.

b. Double-click topic in Step 2 box.

   **OR**

a. Select topic.

b. Click **Display**....................... `Alt`+`D`

### Find

a. Type and enter a search word or phrase in Step 1 text box.

b. Select matching words in Step 2, if presented.

c. Double-click topic in Step 3 box.

   **OR**

a. Select topic.

b. Click **Display**.............................. `D`

## ACCESS SCREEN TIPS

### To View Tips in Dialog Boxes:

Click question mark `?` in dialog box.

**OR**

Point to option and press.......... `Shift`+`F1`

### To View Tip For Region of Screen, Menu, or Toolbar Button:

1. Point to element on screen.

2. Press **Shift+F1** ..................... `Shift`+`F1`

3. Click mouse to view information about desired on screen element.

4. Press Escape................................. `Esc` to close Help.

## EXIT HELP OR HELP SCREENS

Click **Cancel** ....................................... `Esc`

**OR**

Click **Close** button .............................. `✖`

*Next Chapter*

# Microsoft Word 97

**Lesson 1:** Create and Print Documents

**Lesson 2:** Open and Edit Documents

**Lesson 3:** Text Alignments and Enhancements

**Lesson 4:** Format and Edit Documents

**Lesson 5:** Additional Formatting and Editing

**Lesson 6:** Work with Multiple-Page Documents

**Lesson 7:** Work with Multiple Documents; Macros

**Lesson 8:** Clip Art and Templates; Envelopes and Labels

## Lesson 1: Create and Print Documents

- **Start Word** ■ **The Word Window** ■ **Default Settings**
- **If You Make an Error** ■ **Create a New Document**
- **Save a New Document** ■ **Close a Document**

## NOTES:

### Start Word

- Word may be started using any one of the following procedures (*See Office Basics, Lesson 1, page 3.*):

  - *Using the Windows 95 Taskbar.* Click *Start*, highlight *Programs*, highlight and select *Microsoft Word*.

  - *Using the Windows 95 Taskbar.* Click *Start*, highlight and select *New Office Document*, select *Blank Document, OK.*

  - *Using the Shortcut bar: Click Start a New Document, select Blank Document, OK.*

### The Word Window

- Shown below is the Microsoft Word default window. It appears when the program is first started.

- The numbered key on the following pages explains each window area specific to Word.

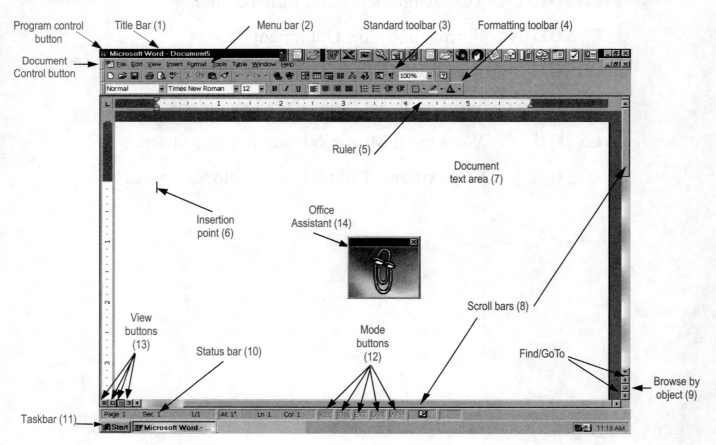

## Title Bar (1)

■ Displays the program and document name.

## Menu Bar (2)

■ Displays items that you can select when executing commands. When an item is selected using either the keyboard or the mouse, a group of subitems appears in a drop-down submenu.

## Standard Toolbar (3)

■ Contains a collection of buttons (pictures) that enable you to accomplish many common word processing tasks easily, like saving and printing a file.

■ When you point to a button on the toolbar, a ToolTip displays.

## Formatting Toolbar (4)

■ Contains a collection of buttons that let you easily change the appearance of your document.

## Ruler (5)

■ Measures the horizontal distance from the left margin of a page. You will learn to use this Ruler and other ruler settings to change tabs, indents, and margins.

## Insertion Point (6)

■ The **Insertion Point** is the blinking vertical line that appears in the upper left-hand corner when Word 97 is started. It indicates where the next character to be keyed will appear and blinks *between* characters, rather than below them.

■ The insertion point does not always appear on the document screen. It may be made visible by clicking the left mouse button at the desired location or by tapping any one of the arrow keys.

## Document Text Area (7)

■ The **document text area** is the blank space for typing text. This area can be maximized by hiding toolbars.

## Scroll Bars (8)

■ **Scroll bars** are used to move the screen view horizontally or vertically. The **scroll box** on the vertical scroll bar can be dragged up or down to move the screen view quickly toward the beginning or end of the document. The scroll box on the horizontal scroll bar can be dragged left or right to move the screen quickly left or right.

## Browse by Object (9)

■ The **Browse by Object** button is used to search a document for a field, endnote, footnote, graphic, comment, section, page, bookmark, table, comment, etc. Click browse by object on scroll bar, select desired item and then click Next/Previous button on scroll bar to move to next/previous item of same type.

## Status Bar (10)

■ Appears at the bottom of the screen. It displays:

| | |
|---|---|
| **Page 1** | The page number. |
| **Sec 1** | The section. |
| **1/1** | The current page and total number of pages in the document (1/1 meaning page one of a one-page document). |
| **At 1"** | The measurement in inches from the top edge of the page to the current location of the insertion point. |
| **Ln 1** | The line number at which the insertion point is currently located. |
| **Col 1** | The distance of the insertion point from the left margin in number of characters. |

## Taskbar (11)

■ The **Taskbar** is used to start applications and switch between applications.

## Mode Buttons (12)

■ Mode buttons are located near the center of the Status bar and may be activated by double-clicking on them. They place Word in various **modes**. (*Modes will be explained in related exercises.*)

## View Buttons (13)

- Word provides various ways to view documents on the screen. The **View buttons** allow you to quickly switch between views. You may also change document views by selecting a particular view from the <u>V</u>iew menu.

  - **Normal view** is the default. It is used for most typing, editing, and formatting.

  - **Page Layout view** is used to see a document just as it will look when printed. This view allows you to see headers and footers, footnotes and endnotes, columns, etc.

  - **Online Layout view** makes it easier to read documents on screen. Text will appear larger and will fit the window, rather than appearing the way it will print. The Document Map pane automatically displays when you switch to Online view.

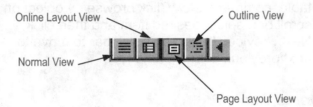

  - **Outline view** allows you to collapse a document to see only the main headings or expand it to see the entire document.

## Office Assistant (14)

- The Assistant (see page 12) can answer questions and offer suggestions about completing a task.

## Default Settings

- The following are Word's default settings for margins, tabs, line spacing, font, font size, and text alignment:

| | |
|---|---|
| Margins: | 1.25" on the left and right |
| | 1" on the top and bottom |

✓ *Note: Word assumes you are working on a standard 8.5" x 11 page. The At indicator in the Status bar shows the insertion point as measured in inches from the top of the page.*

| | |
|---|---|
| Tabs: | every .5 inches across the page. |
| Line spacing: | Single |
| Font: | Times New Roman |
| Font size: | 12 point |
| Text alignment: | Left |

## If You Make an Error...

- The following keys will get you out of trouble or offer help:

  - **Backspace** — Will erase characters to the immediate left of the insertion point.

  - **Escape** — (or clicking a **Cancel** button) will back you out of most commands without executing them.

  - **F1** — Will access Help from the Office Assistant.

*Standard Toolbar*

*Formatting Toolbar*

## Create a New Document

- When you start Word, a blank screen appears, ready for you to begin keyboarding text. Word assigns "Document1" in the title bar as the document name (until you provide a name).

- As you type, the **Col** (Column) **indicator** in the Status bar changes. As text advances to another line, the **Ln** (Line) **indicator** also changes. If you move the insertion point, the **Col** and **Ln** indicators display the new location of the insertion point.

- The **At indicator** displays the vertical position of the insertion point as measured in inches from the top edge of the page.

- As text is typed, the insertion point automatically advances to the next line. This is called **word wrap** or **wraparound**. It is only necessary to use the Enter key at the end of a short line or to begin a new paragraph.

## Save a Document

- Documents must be given a name for identification. A **filename** may contain a maximum of 255 characters, can include spaces, and is automatically assigned the file extension **.doc**. If you choose not to assign a filename, Word assigns a filename for you. It uses the first phrase of text up to a punctuation mark, new line or character, or paragraph mark, then adds .doc as the filename extension. Filenames and extensions are separated by a period.

    *EXAMPLE*:

    **filename.extension**

- Filenames are displayed in the case in which you type them. If you type a filename in uppercase, it will appear in uppercase. You cannot, however, save one filename in uppercase and save another using the same name in lowercase.

- When saving a file, you must indicate the location where you wish to save it. Documents may be saved on a removable disk or on an internal hard drive. If you save a file to a removable disk, you must indicate that you are saving to the A or B drive. The hard drive is usually designated as the C drive.

- If you save to the hard drive, Word provides folders that you may use to save your work.

Or, you may create your own folders in which to save your work. You will learn to create folders (or directories) in a later exercise. You should use a floppy disk to save the exercises in this book.

- When saving a file for the first time, select **Save** from the **File** menu or click the Save button on the Standard toolbar. The following Save As dialog box appears:

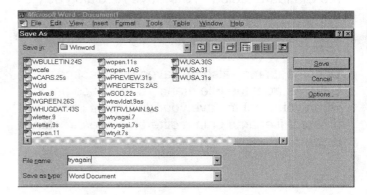

- Note the Save in drop-down list box. Word displays the current location, or folder, where you can save your file. The large area below the Save in box displays the contents of current folder.

- If you wish to save your file to a removable disk, click the list arrow next to the Save in box and double-click 3½" Floppy (A:).

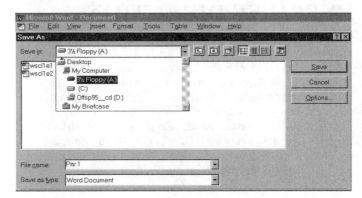

- Once this location is specified, the large area below the Save in box displays the contents of the disk located in the A drive. Enter a desired filename or use the one that Word assigns for you in the File name text box, and click Save to save the document.

- You can save your document in a format other than Word by selecting Save as type and selecting a desired format (eg. WordPerfect,

Works, WordStar). Use this option if you intend to use your file with another software program.

- Once your document is named, the filename appears in the title bar.

- After saving your document for the first time, you can save the document again and continue working (updating it) by selecting Save from the File menu or by clicking the Save button 🖫 on the Standard toolbar. The Save As dialog box does not reappear; Word simply saves any changes you have made to your file. *Save often to prevent losing data.*

- Documents may also be saved by selecting Save As from the File menu. Use this command when you want to save your document under a different filename or in a different drive/directory (folder).

### Close a Document

- When a document has been saved, it remains on your screen. If you wish to clear the screen, you may close the document window by selecting Close from the File menu or double-clicking the Document Control button.

- If you attempt to close a document before saving it, Word will prompt you to save it before exiting. You may respond **Y** for Yes or **N** for No.

- If you make a mistake and would like to begin the document again, close the document window without saving the document.

- To begin a new document after closing the document window, you must select New from the File menu or click the New button 🗋 on the Standard toolbar. This will give you a new document window.

### Exit Word

- When you have finished working on your documents (saved and closed them), you will want to exit the Word application. To do so, select Exit from the File menu, or double-click the Program Control icon.

Document Control button

---

*In this exercise, you will create and save a document.*

---

# EXERCISE DIRECTIONS

1. Create a new document.

   *Note: The exercises in this book have been created using a 12-point font size. To have your work appear like the book exercises, you will need to change your default font size. To do so, follow the steps listed in the keystroke section on page 22. (Changing font style and size will be covered in detail in Exercise 15.) However, because printers and available fonts vary, your line endings may not appear exactly like the exercises shown in this text.*

2. Hide the Office Assistant.

3. Keyboard the paragraphs below, allowing the text to word wrap to the next line. Ignore the red and green wavy lines if they appear.

4. Begin the exercise at the top of your screen. Press the Enter key twice to start a new paragraph.

5. Correct immediately detected errors using the Backspace key.

6. Save the document; name it **TRY**.

7. Hide and then display the Standard toolbar.

8. Close the document window.

---

As you type, notice the Col indicator on your status bar change as the position of your insertion point changes.

The wraparound feature allows the operator to decide on line endings, making the use of Enter unnecessary except at the end of a paragraph or short line. Each file is saved on a disk or hard drive for recall. Documents must be given a name for identification.

# KEYSTROKES

## START WORD

### - USING THE TASKBAR -

1. Click **Start** .............................. `Ctrl` + `Esc`
2. Highlight **Programs** ...................... `P`
3. Select Microsoft Word.

**OR**

a. Click **Start** .............................. `Ctrl` + `Esc`
b. Click **New Office Document** ......... `▣`
c. Click **Blank Document** ................ `W`
d. Click **OK** ................................ `Enter`

### - USING THE SHORTCUT BAR -

1. Click **Start a New Office document**
   button. ..................................... `▣`
2. Double-click **Blank Document** ........ `W`

## CREATE A NEW DOCUMENT

*CTRL + N*

Click **New Document** button ............... `▯`

**OR**

1. Click **File** .............................. `Ctrl` + `F`
2. Click **New** ............................. `N`
3. Click **OK** .............................. `Enter`

## TO CHANGE DEFAULT FONT SIZE

1. Click **Format** ........................ `Alt` + `O`
2. Click **Style** ......................... `S`
3. Click **Modify** ....................... `Alt` + `M`
4. Click **Add to template** .......... `Alt` + `A`
   check box if necessary.
5. Click **Format** ....................... `Alt` + `O`
6. Click **Font** ......................... `F`
7. Click **Font** ......................... `Alt` + `N`
8. Click **Size** ......................... `Alt` + `S`
9. Type 12 ................................. `1` `2`
10. Press Enter ....... `Enter`, `Enter`, `Enter`
    three times

## SAVE A NEW DOCUMENT

*CTRL + S*

1. Click **Save** button ...................... `▣`

**OR**

a. Click **File** ...................... `Alt` + `F`
b. Click **Save** ...................... `S`
2. Click **Save in** text box ............ `Alt` + `I`
   to select drive or folder.
3. Select desired ...................... `↓`, `Enter`
   drive or folder.
4. To select ................... `Tab`, `↓`, `Enter`
   subfolder, if necessary,
   double-click folder.
5. Double-click **File** ............... `Alt` + `N`
   **name** text box.
6. Type filename ........................ filename
7. Click **Save** ............. `Alt` + `S` or `Enter`

## CLOSE DOCUMENT WINDOW

1. Double-click **Document control**
   button ..................................... `▣`
2. Click **Yes** ............................ `Y`
   to save changes.

**OR**

Click **No** .................................. `N`
to abandon changes.

**OR**

1. Click **File** ...................... `Alt` + `F`
2. Click **Close** .......................... `C`
3. Click **Yes** ........................... `Y`
   to save changes.

**OR**

Click **No** .............................. `N`
to abandon changes.

## EXIT WORD

1. Double-click **Program Control**
   button ..................................... `W`
2. Click **Yes** ........................... `Y`
   to save changes.

**OR**

Click **No** .............................. `N`
to abandon changes.

**OR**

1. Click **File** ...................... `Alt` + `F`
2. Click **Exit** .......................... `X`
3. Click **Yes** to save changes .......... `Y`

**OR**

Click **No** .............................. `N`
to abandon changes.

## HIDE OR DISPLAY STANDARD AND FORMATTING TOOLBARS

1. Click **View** ...................... `Alt` + `V`
2. Click **Toolbars** ..................... `T`
3. Select **Standard** ............... `↓`, `Enter`
   to display or hide.

**OR**

Select **Formatting** ............... `↓`, `Enter`
to display or hide.
4. Select remaining toolbars ... `↓`, `Enter`
   to turn on/off, if necessary.

## HIDE OR DISPLAY RULER

1. Click **View** ...................... `Alt` + `V`
2. Click **Ruler** ......................... `R`

## Exercise 2

- **AutoCorrect** - **Automatic Spell Checking**
- **Spelling** - **Grammar Check** - **Properties**

*Standard Toolbar*

Spell check

# NOTES

## AutoCorrect

- The AutoCorrect feature automatically replaces common spelling errors and mistyped words with the correct text as soon as you press the spacebar.

- There are numerous words already in the AutoCorrect dictionary. However, you can enter words that you commonly misspell into the AutoCorrect dictionary by selecting AutoCorrect from the Tools menu.

- If you find this feature annoying, you can deselect the Replace text as you type option in the AutoCorrect dialog box.

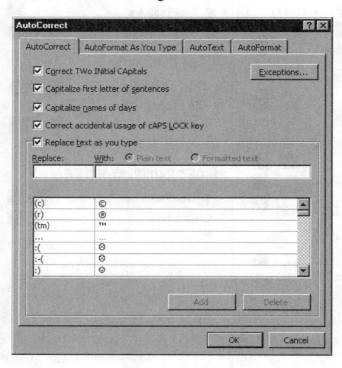

- You can specify other types of corrections in the AutoCorrect dialog box:

    - Correct TWo INitial CApitals automatically converts two initial capital letters of a word to an initial capital letter and a lowercase second letter.

    - Capitalize first letter of sentences automatically capitalizes the first letter of a sentence.

    - Capitalize names of days automatically capitalizes names of days of the week.

    - Correct accidental usage of cAPS LOCK key automatically assigns the proper case if CAPS LOCK key was set to ON.

    - **Replace text as you type** automatically replaces text as you type.

## Automatic Spell Checking

- The **Automatic Spell Checking** feature underlines spelling errors with a red wavy line as you type. To correct a misspelled word, point to the underlined error with your mouse and click the *right* mouse button. A shortcut menu displays with suggested corrections. Click the correctly spelled word in the menu and it will replace the incorrectly spelled word in the document.

- You can also add the word you misspelled (if Word provides a suggestion for the correct spelling) to the AutoCorrect dictionary by selecting AutoCorrect, then selecting the correctly spelled word.

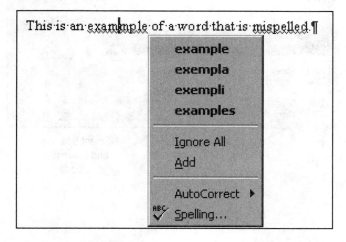

- A book icon 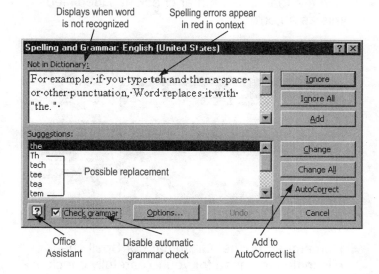 appears in the lower right of the Status bar. As you type, a check mark moves from page to page on the book. When you stop typing, a red check mark remains, indicating that no spelling errors were detected by Automatic Spell Checking. If an X appears, it indicates that errors exist in your document. Double-click the book icon and Word will advance you to an error and open a shortcut menu with suggested corrections.

## Spelling

- Word's Spelling feature checks the spelling of a word, a block of text, or an entire document. Occurrences of double words will also be flagged.

- The Speller compares the words in your document with the words in the Word for Windows dictionary. Proper names and words not in Word's dictionary will be identified as errors. When an error is detected, Word will supply a list of suggested spellings. You may accept Word's suggestions or ignore them.

- Spelling may be accessed by selecting Spelling and Grammar from the Tools menu or by clicking the Spelling button on the Standard toolbar. The following dialog box will appear:

- Words may be added to the custom dictionary before, after, or during the spell check session.

- To avoid having proper names flagged as incorrect spellings during the spell check session, add them to the custom dictionary by clicking on the Add button.

## Grammar Check

- In addition to checking spelling, Word automatically checks for correct word usage and style. Grammatical errors are underlined with a green wavy line. If you right-click anywhere on the underlined sentence, Word will display grammar errors and offer suggestions based on the selected Writing style (Standard, Casual, Formal, Technical, Custom).

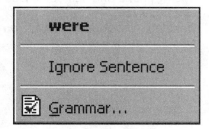

■ You can now accept the suggestion, ignore it (there may be times when you want the incorrect phrase to remain intact), or select Grammar to go to the Grammar dialog box. You can then see the reason Grammar check has identified this as an error.

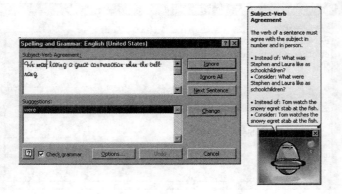

■ Remember, neither Grammar nor Spell check eliminates the need for you to carefully check a document.

## Grammar Check Limitations

■ Grammar check, just like Spell check, is not always correct and can be misleading. Since language is complex, it is difficult for a program to identify everything that is incorrect in a document. In fact, Grammar check can be totally wrong. Note the following example of a grammatically incorrect sentence that was not flagged by Word's Grammar check feature.

> *Running down the hall my books fell on the floor.*

- Grammar check didn't flag the dangling modifier or the missing comma.

- To turn off automatic grammar check:
  - Click Tools menu.
  - Click Options and select the Spelling & Grammar tab.
  - Deselect *Check grammar as you type* and *Check grammar with spelling*.

Type of error displays here

Grammar errors in green in context

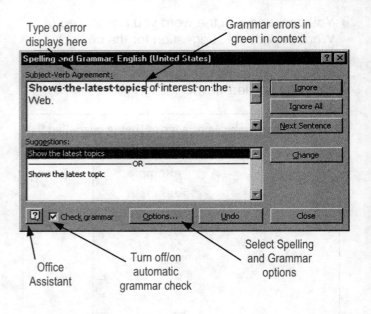

Office Assistant

Turn off/on automatic grammar check

Select Spelling and Grammar options

## Properties (Document Summary)

■ The Properties feature allows you to save summary information with each document. The information includes a document title, subject, author, keywords, and comments.

■ You can create, display, and edit summary information at any time by selecting Properties from the File menu.

■ To see a statistical summary of your document, click the Statistics tab. It lists the number of pages, paragraphs, lines, words, characters, and bytes in your document.

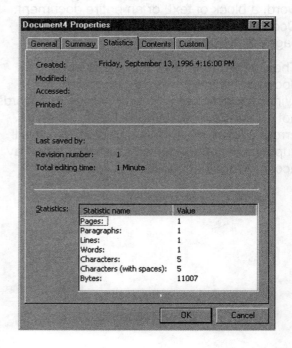

- You may also see a statistical summary of your document by selecting <u>W</u>ord Count from the <u>T</u>ools menu. It lists the number of pages, words, characters, paragraphs, and lines in your document.

- Statistical summaries are particularly useful if you are required to submit a report with a specified word or page count.

- You may specify that Word display the Properties dialog box each time you save a document. To do so, select Options in the Save As dialog box and select Prompt for document properties.

---

*In this exercise, you will type two short paragraphs using word wrap. The paragraphs contain misspelled words and a grammatically incorrect sentence. After typing the paragraphs, you will note that AutoCorrect corrected some of the words. You will use the Automatic Spelling and the Grammar features to correct the other errors.*

---

# EXERCISE DIRECTIONS

1. Create a new document.

2. Begin the exercise at the top of your screen.

3. Access the AutoCorrect feature. Be sure Replace Text as You Type has been selected.

4. Keyboard the paragraphs below exactly as shown, including the circled, misspelled words. Allow the text to word wrap to the next line.

5. Press the Enter key twice to begin a new paragraph.

   - Use the Spelling or Automatic Spelling feature to correct the spelling errors in the document.

   - Use the Grammar feature to correct the grammatically incorrect sentence. Accept Word's suggestion.

6. Using the Properties feature, fill out the following summary information about your document:

   | | |
   |---|---|
   | Title: | Word for Windows Information |
   | Subject: | Ease of use |
   | Author: | Your name |
   | Manager: | Your supervisor or teacher's name |
   | Company: | Your company or school name |
   | Category: | Advertising |
   | Keywords: | simple, margins, tabs |
   | Comments: | first try |

7. Save the exercise using the Save button on the toolbar; name it **TRYAGAIN**.

8. Close the document window.

---

Word 97 for Windows is simple to use since you can begin typing as soon as you enter the program.

THe Word 97 for Windows program sets the way text will lay out or "format" on a page. For example, margins are set for 1.25" on the left and 1.25" on the right; line spaceing is automatic; tabs are set to advance the insersion point ½ inch each time the Tab key is pressed. Formats may be changed at any time and as many times as desired throughtout the document.

# KEYSTROKES

## TAB

Press **Tab** ............................................ `Tab`

## AUTOCORRECT

1. Click **T**ools ............................ `Alt`+`T`
2. Click **A**utoCorrect ........................... `A`
3. Select Replace text as you type option.

   **To add words to AutoCorrect Dictionary:**

   - Click **R**eplace text box ........ `Alt`+`A`
   - Type commonly misspelled word to include.
   - Click **W**ith text box .............. `Alt`+`W`
   - Type correct version of word.

4. Click **A**dd ............................... `Alt`+`A`
5. Click **OK**.................................... `Enter`

## TURN GRAMMAR CHECK ON/OFF

> ✓ *If automatic grammar check is activated and you start checking a document for spelling, Word will flag the first item it perceives as an error (spelling or grammar). Since grammar check is not covered in this book, disable automatic grammar check for the exercises in this book.*

1. Click **T**ools ............................ `Alt`+`T`
2. Click **O**ptions.............................. `O`
3. Click Spelling & Grammar tab.
4. Select/Deselect desired options.

   - **Check grammar as you type**........................... `Alt`+`G`
     *Marks errors as you work.*

   - **Hide grammatical errors**.... `Alt`+`E` **in this document**
     *Green wavy line under possible errors will be hidden when this is selected.*

   - **Check grammar with** ......... `Alt`+`H` **spelling**
     *Select this option to check spelling and grammar. Not available if the grammar checker is not installed.*

   - **Show readability** ............... `Alt`+`R` **statistics**
     *Shows Readability Statistics dialog box after you run the grammar checker.*

5. Click **OK**.................................... `Enter`

## GRAMMAR

By default, spelling will be checked as you check grammar. If you want to just check Grammar, deselect **Check spelling as you type** in the Spelling & Grammar options dialog box.

Be sure that **Check grammar with spelling** is selected in the Spelling and Grammar dialog box (see steps above).

1. Place insertion point where grammar check will begin.

   **OR**

   Select block of text to check.

2. Click **Spelling** button...................... `ABC`

**Check grammar** should be selected.

Word will stop on the first error it finds (spelling or grammar). Grammar errors are underlined with a green wavy line. You can skip or change spelling errors as you go through a document looking for grammar errors.

When you encounter a grammar error, select one of the following options:

- Click **I**gnore ........................ `Alt`+`I` to reject suggested change and continue grammar check.

   **OR**

   a. Select desired suggestion if more than one suggestion appears.

   b. Select **C**hange .................. `Alt`+`C` to accept highlighted suggestion and make suggested correction in document.

   > ✓ *If no suggestions are made, the Change button will be dimmed. You can edit the text in the Spelling and Grammar window.*

3. Continue checking the rest of the document.

   **OR**

   Click **Cancel** ................................. `Esc` to return to document.

## 🌐 SPELLING

*F7*

1. Place insertion point where spell check should begin.

   **OR**

Select a word or block of text to spell check.

2. Click **Spelling** button ...................... `ABC`

   **OR**

   a. Click **T**ools ....................... `Alt`+`T`

   b. Click **S**pelling and Grammar ...... `S`

   > ✓ *When the system encounters a word not found in its dictionary, the word is displayed in red in the Not in Dictionary box; the insertion point will appear after the word(s).*

3. Click **I**gnore ......................... `Alt`+`I` to proceed without changing the word.

   **OR**

   Edit the word in the **Not in Dictionary** box.

4. Click **C**hange.......................... `Alt`+`C`

   **OR**

   a. Click **S**uggestions box ...... `Alt`+`E` and select (highlight) desired suggestion.

   b. Click **C**hange ................... `Alt`+`C`

   **To add to AutoCorrect:**

   Click **AutoCorrect** ............... `Alt`+`R`

5. Click **Close**.................................. `Esc` to discontinue spell check.

## AUTOMATIC SPELLING

1. Place mouse on word underlined with wavy red line.
2. Click right mouse button.
3. Click correctly spelled word (if Word offers one).

   **OR**

   a. Double-click book icon on status bar.

   b. Click correct spelling on shortcut menu.

## PROPERTIES (DOCUMENT SUMMARY)

1. Click **F**ile.............................. `Alt`+`F`
2. Click **P**roperties............................ `I`
3. Click **Summary** tab.
4. Enter relevant information.
5. Click **OK** ................................... `Enter`

## Exercise 3

- ■ **Insertion Point Movements**  ■ **Create a Business Letter**
- ■ **The Date and Time Feature**

## NOTES

### Insertion Point Movements

- ■ The arrow keys on the numeric keypad or the separate arrow keys located to the left of the keypad are used to move the insertion point in the direction indicated by the arrow. The insertion point will only move through text, spaces, or codes. The insertion point cannot be moved past the beginning or the end of your document.

- ■ To move the insertion point quickly from one point in the document to another, you may use express insertion point movements. *(Note the keystroke procedures on page 30.)*

### Create a Business Letter

- ■ There are a variety of letter styles for business and personal use.

- ■ The parts of a **business letter** and the vertical spacing of letter parts are the same regardless of the style used.

- ■ A business letter is comprised of eight parts: 1. **date**, 2. **inside address** (to whom and where the letter is going), 3. **salutation**, 4. **body**, 5. **closing**, 6. **signature line**, 7. **title line**, and 8. **reference initials** (the first set of initials belongs to the person who wrote the letter; the second set belongs to the person who typed the letter). Whenever you see "yo" as part of the reference initials in an exercise, substitute *your own* initials.

- ■ The letter style illustrated in this exercise is a full-block business letter: since the date, closing, signature, and title lines begin at the left margin.

- ■ A letter generally begins 2.5" from the top of a page. If the letter is long, it may begin 2" from the top of the paper. If the letter is short, it may begin 3" or more from the top.

- ■ Margins and the size of the characters may also be adjusted to make correspondence fit more appropriately on the page.

    ✓ Note: Changing margins and font size will be covered in a later lesson.

### The Date and Time Feature

- ■ The **Date and Time feature** lets you insert the current date and/or time into your document automatically.

- ■ To insert the date, select Date and Time from the Insert menu. In the Date and Time dialog box that follows, select the desired date format from the list of available formats.

- ■ To update the date each time the document is opened, click the Update automatically check box.

*Date and Time Dialog Box*

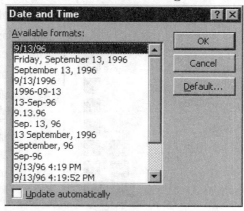

---

*In this exercise, you will create a full-block letter and practice moving the insertion point through the document.*

---

# EXERCISE DIRECTIONS:

✓ *Note: Directions are given for a 12-point font setting. Change your default font to 12 point (see keystrokes in Exercise 1); otherwise, there will be discrepancies between your document and the one shown in the exercise.*

1. Create a new document.

2. Keyboard the letter on the following page exactly as shown.

3. Use the default margins.

4. Access the AutoCorrect feature. Be sure Replace text as you type has been selected.

5. With your insertion point at the top of the screen, press the Enter key eight times. Use the date feature to insert the current date 2.5" from the top of the page.

6. Press the Enter key between parts of the letter as directed in the exercise.

7. Spell check using both the Automatic Spell Checking and Spelling features.

8. Correct the grammatical error in the third paragraph. Accept Word's first suggestion.

9. After completing the exercise, move the insertion point to the top of the screen (Ctrl+Home) and back to the end of the document (Ctrl+End).

10. Save the document; name it **LETTER**.

11. Close the document window.

# KEYSTROKES

### EXPRESS INSERTION POINT MOVEMENTS

**TO MOVE:**                            **PRESS:**

1. One character left ........................... ⬅

2. One character right........................ ➡

3. One line up ................................... ⬆

4. One line down ............................... ⬇

5. Previous word ..................... Ctrl + ⬅

6. Next word.......................... Ctrl + ➡

7. Top of screen ..................... Ctrl + Page Up

8. Top of next page............... Ctrl + Page Down

9. Beginning of document..... Ctrl + Home

10. End of document................ Ctrl + End

11. Top of pg. .... F5 , number, Enter , Esc

12. Beginning of line ...................... Home

13. End of line ................................. End

14. Top of previous section...................... Alt + Ctrl + Page Up

15. Top of next section...... Alt + Ctrl + Page Down

### INSERT CURRENT DATE

1. Click **Insert** .......................... Alt + I

2. Click **Date and Time** ...................... T

3. Click desired format................ ⬆ ⬇

4. Click **OK** ................................... Enter

*8x*                    *=2.5"*

October 1, 199-

            *4x*

Ms. Renee S. Brown
54 Williams Street
Omaha, NE  68101
   ↓ *2x*
Dear Ms. Brown:
   ↓ *2x*
Thank you for your $150 contribution to the American Art Institution.
This contribution automatically makes you a member in our arts program.
   ↓ *2x*
As an active member, you can participate in our many educational
activities.
   ↓ *2x*
For example, you can take part in our monthly art lectures, our semi-annual
auctions and our frequent art exhibits.  Admission to all these events are free.
   ↓ *2x*
We look forward to seeing you at our next meeting.  We know you will
enjoy speaking with our other members and participating in very
stimulating conversation.

Sincerely,

      *4x*

Alan Barry
President
   ↓ *2x*
ab/yo

## Exercise 4

■ **Create a Modified-Block Business Letter** ■ **Set Tabs**
■ **Print** ■ **Preview a Document** ■ **Full Screen View**
■ **Uppercase Mode** ■ **Change Case**

*Standard Toolbar*

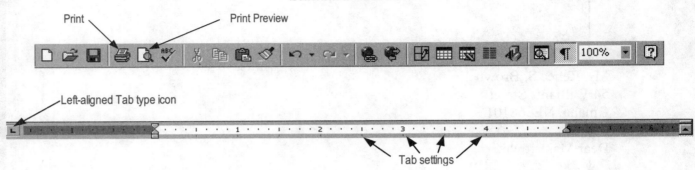

Print     Print Preview

Left-aligned Tab type icon

Tab settings

## NOTES

### Create a Modified-block Business Letter

■ The letter style in this exercise is called **modified-block**: since the date, closing, signature and title lines begin at the center point of the page.

    ✓ *Note: Since the Ruler measures only 6" of work area, the center of the page is 3".*

### Set Tabs

■ The Tab key indents a single line of text. Default tabs are set .5" apart. When the Tab key is pressed once, text advances ½ inch; when the Tab key is pressed twice, text advances 1 inch, etc.

■ It is possible to change the location or the number of tabs. For example, if you desire to advance .8" each time the Tab key is pressed, or eliminate all preset tabs except one, you can do so.

■ Tabs may be changed on the Ruler or by selecting <u>T</u>abs from the F<u>o</u>rmat menu. When you change tab settings in a document, changes take effect from that point forward.

### Set Tabs on the Ruler

■ Tab settings are displayed on the bottom of the Ruler as gray dots set .5" apart.

■ Default settings are left aligned. This means that text typed at such a setting will align at the left and move text to the right of the tab as you type.

> This is an example of left aligned text. Note that the text on the left edge is aligned, while text at the right edge is jagged.

■ The left-aligned tab type icon, located at the left of the Ruler, is displayed as an **L**.

■ **To set a new left-aligned tab**, click anywhere on the Ruler where a new tab is desired; a new tab marker is inserted. When a new tab is set, the preset tabs that precede it are deleted.

■ **To delete a tab setting**, drag the tab marker off the Ruler.

## Set Tabs in the Dialog Box

- Tabs may also be set using the Tabs dialog box (Format, Tabs, or double-click the Ruler). This method lets you set and clear tab positions in one operation. You cannot, however, see the result of your changes on text until all settings have been made.

## Print

- Word allows you to print *part* or *all* of a document that is on your screen. You can print a page of the document, selected pages of the document, one or more blocks of text within the document, or the entire document. You may also print a single document or multiple documents from a disk without retrieving them to the screen. In this exercise, you will print a complete document from a window on your screen.

- Check to see that your printer is turned on and that paper is loaded.

- There are three ways to print an entire document in Word:

  - Click the Print button ![Print button], or
  - Select File, Print from the menu bar and click OK in the Print dialog box, or
  - Click the Print button ![Print button] in Print Preview mode.

## Preview a Document

- The **Print Preview** feature allows you to see how a document will look on paper before you print it.

- To preview a document, select Print Preview from the File menu, or click the Print Preview button ![Print Preview button] on the Standard toolbar.

*Print Preview Screen*

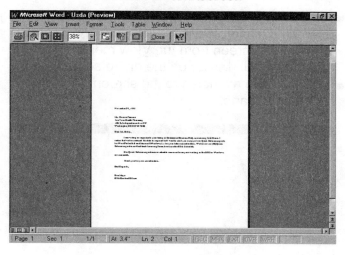

*Print Preview Toolbar*

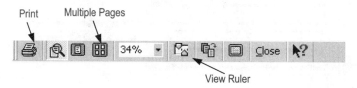

- Note the Print Preview toolbar above.

- Clicking the **Multiple Pages** button ![] allows you to view either one page or several pages at a time.

- Clicking the **View Ruler** button ![] allows you to display or hide the Vertical and Horizontal rulers. It is suggested that you keep both rulers visible because they are very useful in viewing and adjusting margin settings. In later lessons, you will learn how to easily adjust margin settings and page breaks in Print Preview mode using the mouse.

- You may scroll backward or forward through your document in Print Preview mode by pressing the Page Up or the Page Down key on the keyboard or by clicking on the scroll bar using the mouse. Exit Print Preview by pressing the Escape key or by clicking Close.

- You can also use the wheel on the IntelliMouse to scroll through a multiple-page document in Print Preview. The automatic pan feature, however, will not work in Print Preview.

## Full Screen View

- To see your document without the screen elements (Ruler, toolbars, Title bar, and Taskbar) select F<u>u</u>ll Screen from the <u>V</u>iew menu.  Your document will display on the entire screen.
- To return the elements to the screen, click <u>C</u>lose or press Escape.

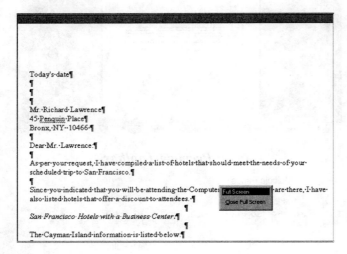

## Uppercase Mode

- Pressing the Caps Lock key once will allow you to type all capital letters without holding down the Shift key. Only *letters* are changed by Caps Lock. To end uppercase mode, press the Caps Lock key again.

✓ Note:  It's easy to forget to turn off CAPS LOCK and start typing with results like this:

dON'T fORGET tO tURN oFF cAPS lOCK.

> *Word will automatically correct this common error if Correct accidental usage of cAPS LOCK key is selected in the AutoCorrect options.*

## Change Case

- The Change Case feature lets you change an existing block of text to sentence case, lowercase, uppercase, title case, or toggle case (which changes uppercase to lowercase and lowercase to uppercase in all selected text).
- To change case, select the text, select Change Cas<u>e</u> from the F<u>o</u>rmat menu, and choose the desired case in the Change Case dialog box. The dialog box selections illustrate the way the case will appear.

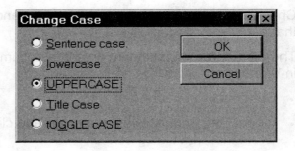

---

*In this exercise, you will create a modified-block letter and print one copy of the document.*

# EXERCISE DIRECTIONS

1. Create a new document.
2. Use the default margins.
3. Keyboard the letter on the following page as shown.
4. Set a tab stop at 3".
5. Access the AutoCorrect feature. Be sure Replace Text as You Type has been selected.
    - With the insertion point at the top of the screen, press the Enter key eight times.
    - Press the Tab key once.
    - Use the automatic Date feature to insert the date 2.5" from the top edge of the page.
6. Press the Enter key between parts of the letter as directed in the exercise.
7. Change case of Annual Awards Dinner to Title Case.
8. Spell check.
9. Display your document on the Full Screen.
10. Return the elements to the screen.
11. Change case of Annual Awards Dinner to uppercase.
12. Print one copy either:
    - from the Print Preview screen, or
    - using the Print button on the toolbar, or
    - by selecting File, Print on the menu bar.
13. Save the document; name it **BLOCK**.
14. Close the document window.

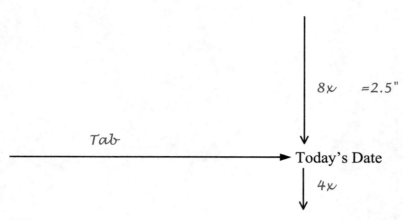

8x    ≈2.5"

*Tab* → Today's Date

↓ 4x

Mr. Thomas Walen
Updike Mechanics Company
23 Clogg Avenue
Atlanta, GA  30315

↓2x

Dear Mr. Walen:

↓2x

CONGRATULATIONS!  You have been nominated as the outstanding office employee
of the month beginning November 4, 1997 through November 30, 1997.

↓2x

The Committee that made your selection requires that you submit a photograph of
yourself  to your supervisor so that we can display your picture in the company's
executive offices.

↓2x

Updike Mechanics is proud of your accomplishments.  We look forward to honoring
you at our ANNUAL AWARDS DINNER on December 3.

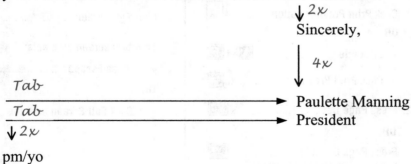

↓ 2x

Sincerely,

↓ 4x

*Tab* → Paulette Manning
*Tab* → President

↓2x

pm/yo

# KEYSTROKES

## CHANGE TAB SETTINGS

1. Click **F̲ormat**..........................Alt+O

2. Click **T̲abs** ...................................T

3. Click **Clear A̲ll** ....................Alt+A

   • Click **T̲ab stop position** ..Alt+T

   • Type new position

   **OR**

   • Click **De̲fault tab**
     **stops**...............................Alt+F

   • Type distance between tabs

4. Click **OK**..............................Enter

## UPPERCASE MODE

1. Press **Caps Lock** ..........................Caps

2. Type text ...........................................*text*

3. Press **Caps Lock** ..........................Caps
   to end uppercase mode.

## CHANGE CASE

1. Select text to change .......................*text*

2. Click **F̲ormat**..........................Alt+O

3. Click **Change Case**..........................E

4. Select a desired case.

## ⊕ PRINT A DOCUMENT

*CTRL + P*

Click **Print** button ...............................🖨

**OR**

1. Click **F̲ile** ..........................Alt+F

2. Click **P̲rint** ...............................P

3. Click **OK** ....................................Enter

## ⊕ PRINT PREVIEW

1. Click **Print Preview** button ............🔍
   **OR**

   a. Click **F̲ile** ..........................Alt+F

   b. Click **Print Preview** ...................V

2. Press **Page Up** ..............................Page Up
   **OR**
   Press **Page Down** ......................Page Down
   to page through the document.

3. Click **Close** ...................................Esc
   to exit Print Preview mode.

## PRINT A DOCUMENT FROM THE PRINT PREVIEW SCREEN

Click **Print** button ...............................🖨

## SET NUMBER OF PAGES TO DISPLAY IN PRINT PREVIEW

1. Click **Print Preview** button............🔍
   to enter Print Preview mode.

2. Click **Multiple Pages** button ...........▦

3. Drag to indicate desired number of
   pages to view.

## FULL SCREEN

1. Click **V̲iew**..........................Alt+V

2. Click **F̲ull Screen** ...........................U

   **To return screen elements:**

   • Press **Escape** ........................Esc

   **OR**

   • Click **Full Screen** button .........▣

<table>
<tr><td>**Exercise**<br>**5**</td><td>■ **Create a Personal Business Letter**</td></tr>
</table>

## NOTES

■ A **personal business letter** is written by an individual representing him/herself, not a business firm.

■ A personal business letter begins 2.5" down from the top of the page (same as the other letter styles) and includes the writer's return address (address, city, state, and zip code), which precedes the date. However, if personalized letterhead is used, keying the return address is unnecessary.

■ Personal business letters may be formatted in full-block or modified-block style. Operator's initials are not included. Depending on the style used, the writer's return address will appear in a different location on the letter. A full-block format appears below. Note that the return address is typed below the writer's name.

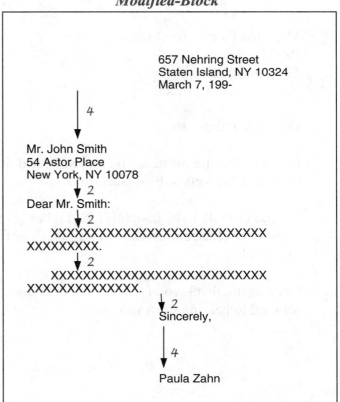

### *Full-Block*

```
March 7, 199-
        4

Mr. John Smith
54 Astor Place
New York, NY 10078
        2
Dear Mr. Smith:
        2
XXXXXXXXXXXXXXXXXXXXXXXX
XXXXXXXXXXX.
        2
XXXXXXXXXXXXXXXX
XXXXXXXXXXXXXXXXXXXX.
        2
Sincerely,
        4

Paula Zahn
765 Nehring Street
Staten Island, NY 10324
```

### *Modified-Block*

```
                  657 Nehring Street
                  Staten Island, NY 10324
                  March 7, 199-
              4

Mr. John Smith
54 Astor Place
New York, NY 10078
        2
Dear Mr. Smith:
        2
    XXXXXXXXXXXXXXXXXXXXXXXX
XXXXXXXXX.
        2
    XXXXXXXXXXXXXXXXXXXXXXXX
XXXXXXXXXXXXX.
              2
            Sincerely,
              4

            Paula Zahn
```

---

*In this exercise, you will create a modified-block personal business letter and use the automatic Date feature. You will also set tabs.*

# EXERCISE DIRECTIONS

1. Create a new document.
2. Display the Office Assistant. Read the tip if light bulb displays.
3. Keyboard the personal business letter below in modified-block style as shown.
4. Use the default margins.
5. Set a tab stop at 3".
6. Access the AutoCorrect feature. Be sure Replace text as you type has been selected.
7. Begin the exercise At 2.5".

   *Note: Set one tab stop at 3" and press the Tab key once to type the return address and closing.*

8. Spell check.
9. After completing the exercise, scroll your page up.
10. Display your document on the Full Screen, then return all the elements by closing the full screen.
11. Preview your work.
12. Print one copy.
13. Save the exercise; name it **PERSONAL**.
14. Close the document window.

---

765 Robeling Street
Teaneck, NJ 07666
[Date Feature]


Ms. Gina Palmisaro, Associate
PRC Securities, Inc.
50 Wall Street
New York, NY 10260


Dear Ms. Palmisaro:


It was a pleasure meeting you last week and discussing my summer internship prospect in Global Markets at PRC Securities.


I found our talk to be insightful, and it has given me a new focus on a possible career in sales.  The chance to work on a trading floor for the summer, therefore, would be invaluable.


Once again, thank you for your time and the opportunity to meet with you.  I look forward to hearing from you soon.


Sincerely,


Karen Winn

## Exercise 6

■ **Summary**

## EXERCISE DIRECTIONS

1. Create a new document.

2. Access the AutoCorrect feature. Make sure Replace text as you type has been selected.

3. Use the default margins.

4. Set a tab stop at 3".

5. Display the Office Assistant. Read the tip if a lightbulb displays.

6. Keyboard the letter below exactly as shown, including the circled grammatical error, in modified-block style.

7. Use the automatic date feature to insert the current date.

8. Change the case of the last paragraph to uppercase.

9. Spell and grammar check. Accept Word's first grammar correction.

10. Change the case of the last paragraph to sentence case.

11. Preview your document and print one copy from the print preview screen.

12. Save the file; name it **OPEN**.

13. Close the document window.

---

Today's date Mr. Martin Quincy 641 Lexington Avenue New York, NY 10022
Dear Mr. Quincy: We are pleased to announce the opening of a new subsidiary of our
company. We specialize in selling, training and service of portable personal
computers. ⌗This may be hard to believe, but we carry portable personal computers
that can (does) everything a conventional desktop can. Our portables can run all of the
same applications as your company's conventional PCs. With the purchase of a
computer, we will train two employees of your firm on how to use an application of
your choice. ⌗For a free demonstration, call us at 212-555-9876 any day from 9:00
a.m. to 5:00 p.m. Sincerely, Theresa Mann President tm/yo

| Exercise **7** | ■ **Open and Revise a Document** ■ **Open a Recently Saved Document** ■ **Open a Document Not Recently Saved** ■ **Open a Document Outside the Word Program** ■ **Insert Text** ■ **Overtype Mode** ■ **Save Changes to a Document** |
| --- | --- |

*Standard Toolbar*

# NOTES

## Open and Revise a Document

■ A document is revised when corrections or adjustments need to be made. **Proofreaders' marks** are symbols on a printed copy of a document that indicate changes to be made. As each proofreaders' mark is introduced in an exercise in this text, it will be explained and illustrated.

■ Before a document can be revised or edited, it must be opened from the disk to the screen.

## Open a Recently Saved Document

■ Word lists the four most recently opened documents at the bottom of the File menu. To open a recently opened document, select the desired filename on the list of recently opened documents.

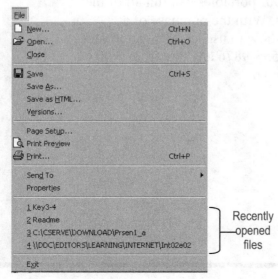

## Open a Document Not Recently Saved

■ After you select Open from the File menu or click the Open button 📂 on the Standard toolbar, the Open dialog box appears. In the Open dialog box, double-click the filename from the list of documents displayed. If the desired file is not listed, click the list arrow next to the Look in text box and select the desired drive and/or folder. Note the Open dialog box below:

## Open a Document Outside the Word Program

■ If you want to open a Word document when you begin working at your computer, you may open a document outside the Word Program. Doing so will launch the Word Program *and* display the Open dialog box.

- You may open a Word document before launching the program using any one of the following procedures:

  - Using the Shortcut bar: Click *Open Office Document*, and select the drive, folder, and document filename from the Open dialog box.

  - Using the Windows 95 Taskbar:

    - Click *Start*, highlight *Documents*, click one of your last 15 documents.

    - Click *Start*, click *Open Office Document*, select the drive, folder and document filename from the Open dialog box.

    - Click *Start*, highlight *Programs*, select *Windows Explorer*, select the drive and folder, double-click the document filename.

## Insert Text

- To make corrections, you can move through the document to the point of correction using the insertion point movement keys. These keys include End, Home, Page Up, Page Down, and the arrow keys. You have already had some practice moving the insertion point through your document in previous exercises.

- To insert text, place the insertion point to the left of the character that will follow the inserted material. When you type inserted text, the existing text moves to the right. When you insert a word, the space following the word must also be inserted.

- To create a new paragraph in existing text, place the insertion point immediately to the left of the first character in the new paragraph and press the Enter key twice.

## Overtype Mode

- Another way to edit text is to put Word into **Overtype mode** so you can type over the existing text with new text. In Overtype mode, existing text does not move to the right; it is typed over. By default, Word is in Insert mode. You may switch to Overtype mode by double-clicking the OVR indicator on the status bar. When Word is in Overtype mode, the **OVR** mode indicator is highlighted in the status bar.

  - ✓ Note: *If you cannot activate OVR by clicking on it on the Status bar, open the Tools, Options dialog box and be sure that Overtype mode is checked on the Edit tab. Check this option if you want to toggle between Insert and Overtype by checking on OVR on the Status bar.*

- To switch back to Insert mode double-click the OVR indicator in the Status bar. For most editing, it is recommended that you work in Insert mode.

## Save Changes to a Document

- You may save your changes as you are working or you may save your changes after all corrections have been made. Click the Save button 🖫 on the Standard toolbar, or select Save from the File menu. Your file will be updated, and the document will remain on the screen for you to continue working.

- When a document is opened and revisions are made, the revised or updated version must be resaved or replaced. When a document is resaved, the old version is replaced with the new version.

- It is recommended that you save often to prevent loss of data.

- The proofreaders' mark for insertion is: ∧

- The proofreaders' mark for a new paragraph is: ⁋

> *In this exercise, you will open a previously saved document and insert new text.*

# EXERCISE DIRECTIONS

1. Open 📠**TRY**, or open 💾**07TRY**.

2. Make the insertions indicated in the exercise below.

3. Use the Overtype mode to insert the word "determine" in the second paragraph. Return to Insert mode immediately following this step.

4. Save your work.

5. Spell check.

6. Print one copy.

7. Close the file.

8. Close the document window.

---

As you type, *you will* notice the Col indicator on your status bar change as the position of your insertion point changes.

The "wraparound" feature allows the *computer* operator to ~~decide on~~ *determine* line endings, making the use of *the* Enter unnecessary except at the end of a paragraph or short line.  ¶Each file is saved on a disk or hard drive for recall.  Documents must be given a name for identification. *or number*

key · data

---

# KEYSTROKES

### 🌐 OPEN A DOCUMENT

*CTRL + O*

1. Click **Open** button ......................... 📂
2. Double-click desired filename.

   **OR**

   a. Click **File** ........................... Alt + F
   b. Click **Open** ............................. O
   c. Select or type desired filename.
   d. Click **OK** ............................... Enter

   **OR**

   a. Click **File** ........................... Alt + F
   b. Select desired filename ............... ⬇️
      from list of recently opened files.

## OPEN A DOCUMENT OUTSIDE WORD PROGRAM

### – USING THE SHORTCUT BAR –

1. Click **Open Office** ........................... 📂
   **Document** button
2. Click **Look in** text box ............ Alt + I
   list arrow.
3. Select desired drive and folder.
4. Double-click desired document from
   those listed.

   **OR**

   a. Click **File name** text box .... Alt + N
   b. Enter desired filename.

**If document was not saved as a Word file:**

   a. Click **Files of type** .............. Alt + T
      list arrow
   b. Select desired file type (if other than a
      Word file).
   c. Click **Open** ............................. Enter

### – USING THE TASKBAR –

1. Click **Start** ............................. Ctrl + Esc
2. Highlight **Documents** ..................... D
3. Select one of the last 15 displayed
   documents.

   **OR**

   a. Click **Start** ........................ Alt + Esc
   b. Click **Open Office Document**.
   c. Select drive and folder.
   d. Double-click document filename.

   **OR**

   a. Click **Start** ........................ Ctrl + Esc
   b. Highlight **Programs** ..................... P
   c. Select **Windows Explorer**. .......... 🔍
   d. Select drive and folder.
   e. Double-click document filename.

## USE OVERTYPE

1. Double-click the OVR indicator in the
   Status bar.
2. Type text ........................................ *text*
3. Double-click the OVR indicator in the
   Status bar.

### 🌐 RESAVE A DOCUMENT

1. Click **Save** button ........................... 💾

   **OR**

   a. Click **File** ........................... Alt + F
   b. Click **Save** ............................. S

   **OR**

   a. Click **File** ........................... Alt + F
   b. Click **Close** ............................. C

   c. Click **Yes** ............................. Y
      when prompted to save changes.

## INSERT TEXT

1. Place insertion point to left of character
   that will immediately follow inserted text.
2. Type text ........................................ *text*

■ **Open a Document as Read Only** ■ **Save As** ■ **Undo** ■ **Redo**

*Standard Toolbar*

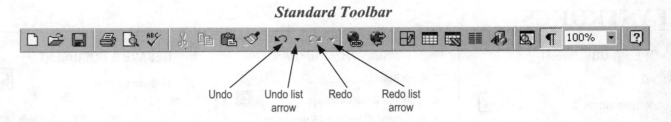

Undo    Undo list    Redo    Redo list
        arrow                arrow

## NOTES

### Open a Document as Read Only

■ If you wish to open a document but not make changes to it, you may open the document as Read Only. This option requires you to save your file with a different filename, preventing you from accidentally affecting the file.

■ To open a file as Read Only, point to the file you wish to open in the Open dialog box and click the *right* mouse button. Select Open Read Only from the choices. Or you may select the file you wish to open, then click the Commands and Settings button, and choose Open Read-Only.

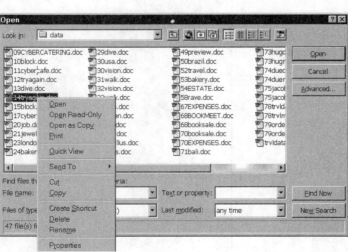

■ If you wish to save or edit a document that you opened using the Read Only option, Word automatically displays the Save As dialog box for you to give the file another name, thus leaving the original document intact.

### Save As

■ If you wish to save any document under a different filename or in a different location, you may select Save As from the File menu. When any document is saved under a new filename, the original document remains intact.

### Undo

■ The **Undo** feature lets you undo the last change you made to the document. Word remembers up to 300 actions in a document and allows you to undo any or all of them. You can undo all your recent actions by repeatedly clicking the Undo button ⟲ on the Standard toolbar, or you can undo a selected action by clicking the Undo list arrow next to the Undo button ▾ and choosing the action to undo from the list presented.

## Redo

■ The **Redo** feature allows you to reverse the last undo. Like Undo, Redo allows you to reverse up to 300 actions in a document. You can redo an action by repeatedly clicking the Redo button ⟳ on the Standard toolbar, or you can redo a selected action by clicking the Redo list arrow next to the Redo button ▾ and choosing the action to redo.

---

*In this exercise, you will insert text at the top of the page and create a modified-block letter. To do so, set a tab stop at 3". Then, insert the date, press the Enter key nine times to bring the At indicator to 2.6". Move the insertion point up so the At indicator reads 2.5", and then press the Tab key once to begin the date and closing at the middle of the page. Remember to use the automatic Date feature.*

*After inserting the date, you will continue inserting the inside address and salutation. Text will adjust as you continue creating the letter.*

---

# EXERCISE DIRECTIONS:

1. Open 🖮 **TRYAGAIN** as a Read Only file, or open 💾 **08TRYAGAIN** from the data disk as a Read Only file.

2. Set a tab stop at 3".

3. Access the AutoCorrect dialog box. Deselect Capitalize first letter of sentences.

4. Make the indicated insertions. Follow the spacing for a modified-block letter illustrated in Exercise 3.

5. Use the automatic Date feature to insert today's date.

6. Use Overtype mode to insert the word "start" in the second paragraph; return to Insert mode immediately.

7. After typing the initials (jo/yo), use Undo. Retype them in all caps.

8. After typing the initials in all caps, use Undo.

9. Use Redo to return the initials to all capitals.

10. Preview your work.

11. Modify the document summary information (Properties) as follows:

    Subject:   Inquiry about software programs

    Manager:  Jerry O'Brien

    Category: Customer Relations

12. Access the Statistics Tab in the Properties dialog box and note the number of words in this document.

13. Print one copy.

14. Use Undo to return the initials to lowercase.

15. Close the file; save as **TRYIT.**

# KEYSTROKES

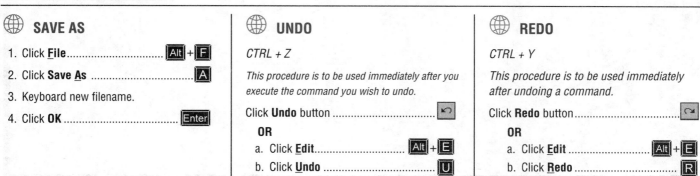

🌐 **SAVE AS**

1. Click **File** ............................. Alt + F
2. Click **Save As** .............................. A
3. Keyboard new filename.
4. Click **OK** ............................................ Enter

🌐 **UNDO**

*CTRL + Z*

*This procedure is to be used immediately after you execute the command you wish to undo.*

Click **Undo** button .................................. ↺

   **OR**
  a. Click **Edit** ............................ Alt + E
  b. Click **Undo** ................................. U

🌐 **REDO**

*CTRL + Y*

*This procedure is to be used immediately after undoing a command.*

Click **Redo** button .................................. ⟳

   **OR**
  a. Click **Edit** ......................... Alt + E
  b. Click **Redo** .............................. R

Today's Date

*Insert* {

Ms. Donna Applegate
Consultants Unlimited, Inc.
45 East 45 Street
New York, NY 10022

Dear Ms. Applegate:

In response to your inquiry about software programs, I have outlined some of the merits of Word 97 for Windows.

Word 97 for Windows is simple to use since you can ~~begin~~ typing as soon as you enter the program.

*start*

The Word 97 for Windows program sets the way text will lay out or "format" on a page. For example, margins are set for 1.25" on the left and 1.25" on the right; line spacing is automatic; tabs are set to advance the insertion point ½ inch each time the Tab key is pressed. #Formats may be changed at any time and as many times as desired throughout the document.

Yours truly,

*automatically*

*Insert* {

Jerry O'Brien
Sales Manager

jo/yo

## Exercise 9

■ **Delete Text** ■ **Select Text** ■ **Show/Hide Codes**

*Standard Toolbar*

Cut    Paste    Show/Hide

# NOTES

## Delete Text

- The **Delete** feature allows you to remove text, graphics, or codes from a document.

- Procedures for deleting text vary depending upon what is being deleted: a character, previous character, word, line, paragraph, page, remainder of page, or a blank line.

- The Backspace key may be used to delete characters and close up spaces to the left of the insertion point.

- To delete a character or a space, place the insertion point immediately to the left of the character or space to delete, then press the Delete (Del) key (located on the right side of your keyboard).

- A block of text (words, sentences, or paragraphs) may be deleted by selecting (highlighting) it and either:

  - pressing the Delete key, or

  - selecting Clear from the Edit menu, or

  - clicking the Cut button 🗒 on the toolbar.

- When text is deleted using the Cut button, it disappears from the screen and is moved to the Clipboard. The Clipboard is a temporary storage area in the computer's memory. The text most recently sent to the Clipboard may be retrieved by pressing Shift + Insert or by clicking the Paste button 📋 on the toolbar.

## Select Text

- Text may be highlighted or selected in several ways:

  - **Using the keyboard** by holding down the Shift key while pressing the insertion point movement keys.

  - **Using the keyboard in combination with the mouse**, by clicking where the selection should begin, holding down the Shift key, and clicking where the selection will end.

  - **Using the mouse** by dragging the mouse pointer over desired text.

  - **Using the F8 selection extender key**, which anchors the insertion point and allows you to use the insertion point movement keys to highlight or select text in any direction from the position of the insertion point. When in Extend mode (the letters EXT appear in the status bar), you may extend the selection to any character or symbol by pressing that character or symbol on the keyboard. Word will instantly highlight from the insertion point to the next occurrence of that character or symbol. Press Esc to cancel Extend Mode.

  - **Using the mouse with the selection bar** by clicking in the selection bar. The **selection bar** is a vertical space alongside the left edge of the Word screen. Note the illustration of the selection bar on the following page.

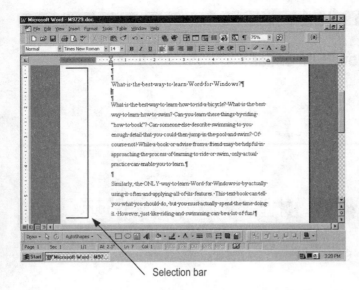

Selection bar

- When you move the mouse pointer into the selection bar, the mouse pointer changes to the shape of an arrow pointing upward toward the top right of the screen.

- Clicking the left mouse button while the pointer is in the selection bar will highlight the entire line of text opposite the pointer. Holding the left mouse button and dragging the mouse pointer up or down in the selection bar will allow you to highlight or select as many lines of text as you wish. To abandon any selection process, release the mouse button and click once anywhere on the Word screen.

### Show/Hide Codes

- As a document is created in Word, codes are inserted.

- When you select the **Show/Hide** button ¶ on the Standard toolbar, codes for paragraph marks (¶), tabs (→), and spaces (•) are visible in your document. These symbols will *not* appear, however, when the document is printed.

- To combine two paragraphs into one, delete the returns that separate the paragraphs. Returns are represented on the screen by paragraph symbols (¶). Therefore, deleting the symbol will delete the return.

- To delete a tab, place the insertion point to the left of the tab symbol (→), and press the Delete key.

- It is recommended that you keep paragraph marks visible when editing a document because:

  - It is easier to combine and separate paragraphs by deleting and inserting the actual paragraph symbols, and

  - Each paragraph symbol contains important information about the format of the paragraph preceding it (type size and style, indentation, borders, etc.).

  ✓ Note: *You will learn more about this feature in a later lesson.*

- Common proofreaders' marks for deleting or moving text are: deletion ℒ

  moving text to the left is ⌐ or ⟵{

---

*In this exercise, you will use various deletion methods to edit a document. Use block highlighting procedures to delete sentences, words, or blocks of text.*

---

# EXERCISE DIRECTIONS

1. Create a new document.
2. Use the default margins and tabs.
3. Disable the grammar check feature,
4. Create the exercise as shown in Part I, or open ▭**09DIVE** and begin At 1".
5. Click the Show/Hide button on the Standard toolbar to display codes.

6. Using the selection and deletion procedures indicated in Part II of the exercise, make the revisions.
7. After deleting the last paragraph, undelete it.
8. Using another deletion method, delete the last paragraph again.
9. Spell check.
10. Print one copy.
11. Close the file; save as **DIVE**.

## Part I

DIVING VACATIONS
DIVING IN THE CAYMAN ISLANDS

Do you want to see sharks, barracudas and huge stingrays?  Do you want to see gentle angels, too?

The Cayman Islands were discovered by Christopher Columbus in late 1503. The Cayman Islands are located just south of Cuba.  The Caymans are the home to only about 125,000 year-round residents.  However, they welcome approximately 200,000 visitors each year.  Each year, more and more visitors arrive.  Most visitors come with colorful masks and flippers in their luggage ready to go scuba diving.

Because of the magnificence of the coral reef, scuba diving has become to the Cayman Islands what safaris are to Kenya.  If you go into a bookstore, you can buy diving gear.

Now, you are ready to jump in.

Recommendations for Hotel/Diving Accommodations:

Sunset House, Post Office Box 4791, George Towne, Grand Cayman; (809) 555-4767.

Coconut Harbour, Post Office Box 2086, George Towne, Grand Cayman; (809) 555-7468.

Seeing a shark is frightening at first; they seem to come out of nowhere and then return to nowhere.  But as soon as the creature disappears, you will swim after it.  You will just want to keep this beautiful, graceful fish in view as long as you can.

**Part II**

| Line | DIVING VACATIONS |
| DIVING IN THE CAYMAN ISLANDS |

Word

Do you want to see sharks, barracudas and huge stingrays?  Do you want to see gentle angels, too?

Word
Character

Sentence
Remainder
of line

The Cayman Islands were discovered by Christopher Columbus in late 1503. The Cayman Islands are located just south of Cuba.  The Caymans are the home to only about 125,000 year-round residents.  However, they welcome approximately 200,000 visitors each year.  Each year, more and more visitors arrive.  Most visitors come with colorful masks and flippers in their luggage ready to go scuba diving.

Paragraph

Because of the magnificence of the coral reef, scuba diving has become to the Cayman Islands what safaris are to Kenya.  If you go into a bookstore, you can buy diving gear.

Now, you are ready to jump in.

Words

Recommendations for Hotel/Diving Accommodations:

Part of
word/
Character

Sunset House, Post Office Box 4791, George Towne, Grand Cayman; (809) 555-4767.

Coconut Harbour, Post Office Box 2086, George Towne, Grand Cayman; (809) 555-7468.

Remainder
of page

Seeing a shark is frightening at first; they seem to come out of nowhere and then return to nowhere.  But as soon as the creature disappears, you will swim after it.  You will just want to keep this beautiful, graceful fish in view as long as you can.

# KEYSTROKES

 **DELETE**

**Character:**

1. Place insertion point to the left of character to delete.

2. Press **Delete** ............................... [Del]

   **OR**

   a. Place insertion point to the right of character to delete.

   b. Press **Backspace** ............. [Backspace]

**Word:**

1. Double-click desired word.

2. Press **Delete** ............................... [Del]

   **OR**

   a. Place insertion point to the left of word to delete.

   b. Press **Ctrl + Delete** ........... [Ctrl] + [Del]

   **OR**

   a. Place insertion point to the right of word to delete.

   b. Press ...................... [Ctrl] + [Backspace]

      **Ctrl+Backspace**

**Block of Text:**

1. Select (highlight) block to delete using procedures described on the right.

2. Click **Cut** [✂] button to place text on clipboard.

   **OR**

   Press **Delete** ............................... [Del]

   **OR**

   Press **Shift+Delete** ............. [Shift] + [Del]
   to move block to clipboard.

   ✓ *The **clipboard** is a temporary storage area in computer memory. The text most recently sent to the clipboard may be retrieved by pressing **Shift** + **Insert** or by clicking the **Paste** button on the toolbar.*

## REPLACE DELETED TEXT WITH TYPED TEXT

1. Select text to replace using procedures described on the right.

2. Type new text ................................*text*

## SELECT (HIGHLIGHT) BLOCKS OF TEXT

### – USING THE KEYBOARD –

Place insertion point where highlight is to begin.

| TO HIGHLIGHT: | PRESS: |
|---|---|
| One character to the left ................ | [Shift] + [←] |
| One character to the right ................ | [Shift] + [→] |
| One line up ................................ | [Shift] + [↑] |
| One line down ................................ | [Shift] + [↓] |
| To end of a line ................................ | [Shift] + [End] |
| To beginning of a line ................ | [Shift] + [Home] |
| To end of a word ................ | [Shift] + [Ctrl] + [→] |
| To beginning of a word ........... | [Shift] + [Ctrl] + [←] |
| To end of a paragraph ............. | [Shift] + [Ctrl] + [↓] |
| To beginning of a paragraph ................ | [Shift] + [Ctrl] + [↑] |
| To end of document ............. | [Shift] + [Ctrl] + [End] |
| To beginning of document ................ | [Shift] + [Ctrl] + [Home] |
| Entire document ................ | [Ctrl] + [A] |

 **– USING THE HIGHLIGHT EXTENDER KEY (F8) –**

1. Place insertion point where block highlighting is to begin.

2. Press **F8** ................................ [F8]
   *EXT appears on the status bar.*

3. Press any character, punctuation, or symbol to highlight to the next occurrence of that key.

   **OR**

   Press any of the insertion movement keys to extend the highlighting.

   **OR**

   Press **F8** repeatedly ...................... [F8]
   until desired block is selected.

4. Press **Escape** ............................... [Esc]
   to cancel Extend mode.

### – USING THE MOUSE –

1. Place insertion point where block highlighting is to begin.

2. Hold down the left mouse button and drag the insertion point to desired location.

3. Release the mouse button.

   **OR**

   a. Place insertion point where block highlighting is to begin.

   b. Point to where selection should end.

   c. Press **Shift** ............................ [Shift]
      and click left mouse button.

### Mouse Selection Shortcuts

**To select a word:**

1. Place insertion point anywhere in word.

2. Double-click left mouse button.

**To select a sentence:**

1. Place insertion point anywhere in sentence.

2. Hold down **Ctrl** ............................ [Ctrl]
   and click left mouse button.

**To select a paragraph:**

1. Place insertion point anywhere in paragraph.

2. Triple-click left mouse button.

**To select a line of text:**

1. Place mouse pointer in **selection bar** opposite desired line.
   *Mouse pointer will point to the right when you're in the selection bar area.*

2. Click left mouse button once.

**To select an entire document:**

1. Place mouse pointer anywhere in selection bar.

2. Hold down **Ctrl** ............................ [Ctrl]
   and click with left mouse button.

**To cancel a selection:**

Click anywhere in text.

**Exercise 10**
- Track Changes ■ Mark Changes
- Customize the Way Revisions Display
- Accept/Reject Revisions ■ Shortcut menu

# NOTES

## Track Changes

- Making edits and changes to a document is relatively easy. Figuring out what changes were made and by whom can be more difficult. With the Track Changes feature on, you can view all edits (including formatting changes) that are made to a document. Later, you can accept or reject any revisions. You can also see who made the suggested edits.

    ✓ *Note:* *If By author is selected in the Track Changes options window, Word will assign a unique color to the first eight people who revise a document. (See **Customize the Way Revisions Display** on the following page for more information.) If more than eight people revise a document, the colors start over with the first color assigned. In addition, when you point to a revision, the name of the person making the edit will appear if the screen tips option is turned on (see illustration on the following page).*

- You can also determine how the revisions will display on screen and whether or not they will print.

## Mark Changes

- Make a copy of the original document before you begin making changes. Having a copy of the original makes it easier to compare documents, which is another way to keep track of revisions. Before you begin to edit an existing document, turn on Track Changes. To do so, select Track Changes, Highlight Changes from the Tools menu or double-click TRK on the status bar.

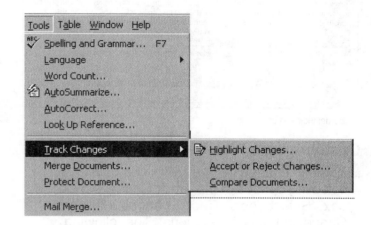

## To turn on Track changes:

- Double-click TRK on the status bar.

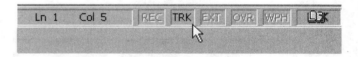

**OR**

- Click Tools
- Select Track Changes.
- Click Highlight Changes.
- Click Track changes while editing.

- In the Highlight Changes dialog box that follows, select Track changes while editing.

- To view the changes as you make them, be sure that Highlight changes on screen is selected.

- To have the changes print in a document, be sure that Highlight changes in printed document is selected.

- Below is a sample of how edits will appear in your document.

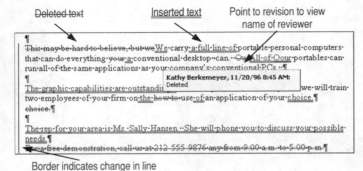

Deleted text   Inserted text   Point to revision to view name of reviewer

Border indicates change in line

## Customize the Way Revisions Display

- You can change the way revisions display by selecting options in the Track Changes dialog box. Select Tools, Track Changes, Highlight Changes; then click Options. The following dialog box appears.

  ✓ Note:   You can also access this dialog box by selecting the Track Changes tab in the Tools, Options dialog box.

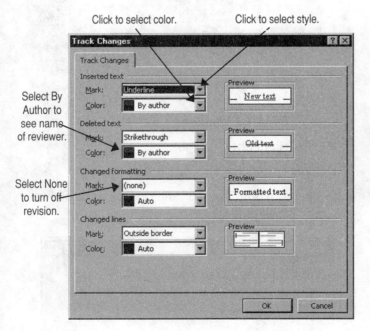

Click to select color.     Click to select style.

Select By Author to see name of reviewer.

Select None to turn off revision.

## Accept/Reject Revisions

- There are several ways you can accept or reject changes made to the document. You may use the Reviewing toolbar (select View, Toolbars, Reviewing), the Accept or Reject Changes dialog box, or the shortcut menu.

- Open the document containing the revisions that you want to evaluate. If the revision marks do not appear in the document, be sure that Highlight changes on screen is selected in the Highlight Changes dialog box. Select Track Changes, Accept or Reject Changes from the Tools menu.

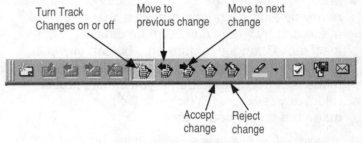

Turn Track Changes on or off   Move to previous change   Move to next change

Accept change   Reject change

- In the Accept or Reject Changes dialog box that follows, click the appropriate button.

## Accept or Reject Changes Dialog Box

- To use the Accept or Reject Changes dialog box, do the following:

  - Click Tools.

  - Select Track Changes.

  - Click Accept or Reject Changes.

  - You can leave the dialog box open while you make various selections.

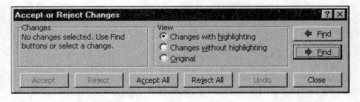

- You can accept or reject individual changes or accept or reject all of the edits in a document. You can also change the way the edits appear on screen without deleting them from the document. As you click on individual edits, the name of the author will appear on the left in the dialog box.

## Shortcut menu

- Point to an edit on screen and right-click. Select the desired action, or click Accept or Reject Changes to see more options.

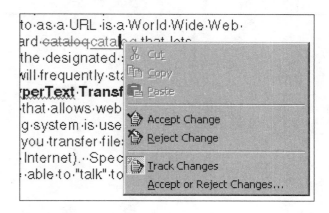

---

*In this exercise, you will edit a previously created letter.*

---

# EXERCISE DIRECTIONS

1. Open 🖨**LETTER**, or open 💾**10LETTER**.
2. Print one copy.
3. Access the Track Changes feature.
   - Track the changes while editing the document text.
   - Highlight the changes on screen.
   - Highlight changes in the printed document.
   - Turn on Show/Hide Symbols.
4. Make the indicated word and sentence deletions.
5. Print one copy.
6. Save the edited document as **LETTERA**.
7. Accept all changes.
8. Turn off the Track Change feature.
9. Print one copy.
10. Close the file; save as **LETTER**.

---

# KEYSTROKES

## TURN TRACK CHANGES ON/OFF

1. Double-click TRK on the Status bar

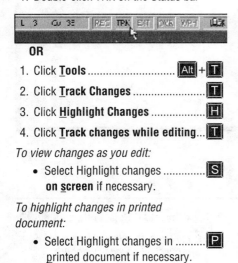

**OR**

1. Click **Tools** .............................. Alt + T
2. Click **Track Changes** .................. T
3. Click **Highlight Changes** ............. H
4. Click **Track changes while editing**... T

*To view changes as you edit:*

- Select Highlight changes ............. S
  **on screen** if necessary.

*To highlight changes in printed document:*

- Select Highlight changes in .......... P
  printed document if necessary.

## CUSTOMIZE THE WAY CHANGES DISPLAY

1. Click **Tools** .............................. Alt + T
2. Click **Track Changes** .................. T
3. Click **Highlight Changes** ............. H
4. Click **Options** ............................. O
5. Select desired **Mark** and **Color** options for the way changes will display.
   - Inserted text
   - Deleted text
   - Changed formatting
   - Changed lines

*Note that you can turn individual options off/on in this dialog box.*

## ACCEPT OR REJECT INDIVIDUAL CHANGES

### -USING THE TOOLBAR-

1. Turn on the Reviewing toolbar.
2. Point to change to accept/reject.
3. Click **Accept** button ..................... 🖘

**OR**

Click **Reject** button ....................... 🖘

4. Move to next change.

### -USING SHORCUT MENU-

1. Point to change and right-click.
2. Click **Accept Change** ................... E
   **OR**
   Click **Reject Change** .................... R

### -USING STATUS BAR-

1. Click once on a change.
2. Right-click on **TRK**.
3. Click **Accept or Reject Changes** ...... A
4. Click **Accept** ............................... A
   **OR**
   Click **Reject** ................................ R
5. Click **Close** to return to document .. Esc

*(continued on next page)*

October 1, 199-

Ms. Renee S. Brown
54 Williams Street
Omaha, NE 68101

Dear Ms. Brown:

Thank you for your $150 contribution to the American Art Institution. This contribution ~~automatically~~ makes you a member in our arts program.

As an active member, you can participate in our many ~~educational~~ activities.

For example, you can take part in ~~our~~ monthly art lectures, ~~our~~ semi-annual auctions and ~~our~~ frequent art exhibits. Admission to ~~all these~~ events is free.

We look forward to seeing you at our next meeting. ~~We know you will enjoy speaking with our other members and participating in very stimulating conversation.~~

Sincerely,

Alan Barry
President

ab/yo

# KEYSTROKES (continued)

## ACCEPT OR REJECT ALL CHANGES
### -USING THE MENU-

1. Click **Tools** .......................... Alt + T
2. Click **Track Changes** ....................... T
3. Click **Accept or Reject Changes** ...... A
4. Click **Accept All/Reject All** ....... C / J

If message appears asking if you really want to accept/reject all changes without reviewing them:

Click **Yes/No** .............................. Y / N

5. Click **Close** to return to document .. Esc

### -USING THE STATUS BAR-

1. Right-click on **TRK**.
2. Click **Accept or Reject Changes** ...... A

3. Click **Accept All/Reject All** ....... C / J

If message appears asking if you really want to accept/reject all changes without reviewing them:

Click **Yes/No** ............................. Y / N

4. Click **Close** to return to document . Esc

## Exercise 11

### ■ Non-breaking Spaces

## NOTES

### Non-breaking Spaces

- To prevent two or more words from splitting during word wrap, a **non-breaking space** can be inserted between the words. This is a particularly useful feature when keying first and last names, names with titles, dates, equations, and time. When you insert a non-breaking space, it is necessary to delete the original space, or the non-breaking space will have no effect.

- To add a non-breaking space, type the first word, press Ctrl+Shift+Spacebar, then type the second word.

- The proofreaders' mark for non-breaking space is: △.

- The proofreaders' mark for moving text to the right is: ]→ or →].

- The proofreaders' mark for capitalization is: ═══════ .

> *In this exercise, you will insert and delete text in a previously created letter.*

## EXERCISE DIRECTIONS

1. Open ⌨**BLOCK**, or open 💾**11BLOCK**.

2. Print one copy.

3. Access the Track Changes feature.

   - Track the changes while editing the document text.

   - Highlight the changes on screen.

   - Highlight the changes in the printed document.

4. Make the indicated revisions, inserting a non-breaking space where you see the triangular symbol (△).

5. After all revisions are made, undo the last deleted sentence.

6. Spell check.

7. Save the edited document as **BLOCKA**.

8. Print one copy.

9. Accept all changes.

10. Turn off the Track change feature.

11. Preview your work.

12. Print one copy.

13. Close the file; save as **BLOCK**.

## KEYSTROKES

**NON-BREAKING SPACE**

1. Type the first word.

2. Press.................. `Ctrl` + `Shift` + `Space`
   **Ctrl + Shift + Spacebar**.

3. Type next word...............................*word*
   **OR**
   a. Delete the normal space between words.

   b. Press ................ `Ctrl` + `Shift` + `Space`
      **Ctrl + Shift + Spacebar**
      to insert a non-breaking space.

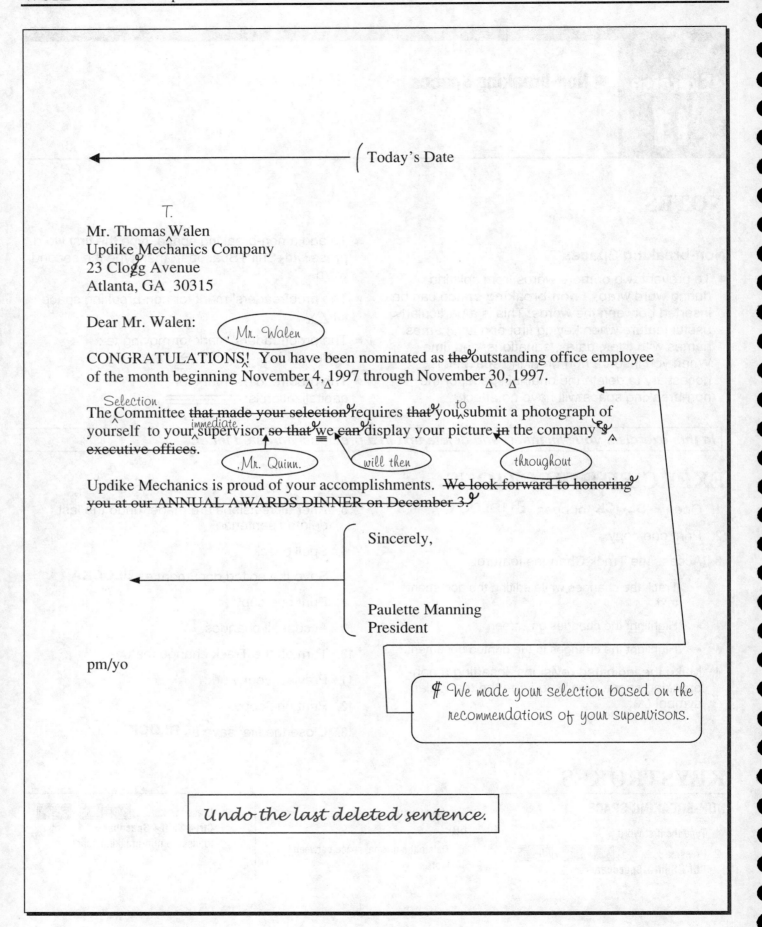

Today's Date

T.
Mr. Thomas Walen
Updike Mechanics Company
23 Clogg Avenue
Atlanta, GA  30315

Dear Mr. Walen:

, Mr. Walen

CONGRATULATIONS!  You have been nominated as the outstanding office employee
of the month beginning November 4, 1997 through November 30, 1997.

Selection
The Committee that made your selection requires that you submit a photograph of
yourself  to your immediate supervisor so that we can display your picture in the company
executive offices.

,Mr. Quinn.        will then        throughout

Updike Mechanics is proud of your accomplishments.  We look forward to honoring
you at our ANNUAL AWARDS DINNER on December 3.

                Sincerely,


                Paulette Manning
                President

pm/yo

¶ We made your selection based on the
  recommendations of your supervisors.

Undo the last deleted sentence.

**Exercise**
**12**

- **Preview a File** ▪ **Print a File without Opening**
- **Print Multiple Files** ▪ **Find Files**

# NOTES

## Preview a File

- The Open dialog box contains options for previewing or printing a file without retrieving it to the screen. These options are important for locating files, particularly when you do not remember the name of a file or the nature of its contents.

- **To preview a file**, select the drive and folder from the Look in drop-down list in the Open dialog box. Select the file you wish to view and click the Preview button 🖿 on the top of the dialog box. The first part of the document displays in the preview window. If this is the document you want to open, click the Open button.

Preview        Commands and Settings

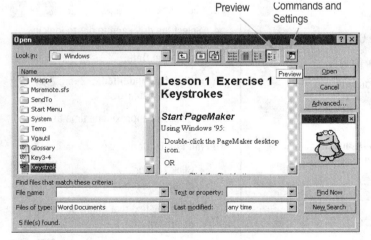

## Print a File without Opening

- **To print a file without opening it**, point to or select the file you wish to print in the Open dialog box, and click the *right* mouse button. Select Print from the drop-down menu. Or, you may click the Commands and Settings button at the top of the dialog box and select Print.

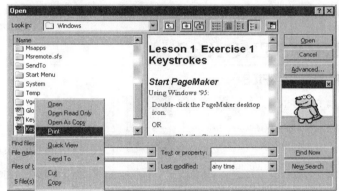

## Print Multiple Files

- **To print multiple files**, click the first file, then hold down the Ctrl key as you click another file.

## Find Files

- The Open dialog box also contains options for **finding files**. A file may be searched by its type, by its contents, or by the date it was created.

  - **To find a file by date**, click the list arrow next to the Last modified text box. Select an approximate time you last worked on the file and click the Find Now button.

- **To find a file by contents**, enter text that might be contained in the document, such as the addressee's name or a subject, in the Te<u>x</u>t or property text box and click the <u>F</u>ind Now button.

- **To find a file by type**, click the list arrow next to the Files of <u>t</u>ype text box. Select a file type to search and click the <u>F</u>ind Now button.

- When you begin a search, remember that Word is searching the current folder. If you wish to expand your search to include subfolders, choose C: in the Look-in drop-down list. Then click the Commands and Settings button and select Searc<u>h</u> Subfolders.

---

*In this exercise, you will insert text into a letter created previously.*

---

# EXERCISE DIRECTIONS

1. Use the Open dialog box to view ⌨**PERSONAL**, ⌨**TRYIT**, and ⌨**OPEN** or view 💾**12PERSON**, 💾**12TRYIT**, and 💾**12OPEN**. Select one file at a time to preview.

2. Open the file (your own or from the data disk) containing the text illustrated in the exercise.

3. Make the indicated revisions.

4. Spell check.

5. Close the file; save as **OPEN**.

6. Use the Open dialog box to print one copy each of **OPEN** and **PERSONAL**.

# KEYSTROKES

## PREVIEW A FILE

1. Click **File** .............................. `Alt`+`F`
2. Click **Open** .............................. `O`
3. Click **Look in** .......................... `Alt`+`I`
4. Select the drive and folder to look in.
5. Select the file to preview.
6. Click **Preview** button .................... 🔳

## PRINT A FILE WITHOUT OPENING

1. Click **File** .............................. `Alt`+`F`
2. Click **Open** .............................. `O`
3. Click **Look in** .......................... `Alt`+`I`
4. Select the drive and folder to look in.
5. Point to or select the file you wish to print.

**OR**

**To print multiple files:**

- Select the first file.
- Hold down the Ctrl key.
- Click additional files.

6. Click the right-mouse button.

7. Click **Print** .............................. `P`

**OR**

- Click **Commands and Settings** button .................... 🔳
- Click **Print** .............................. `P`

## FIND FILES

1. Click **File** .............................. `Alt`+`F`
2. Click **Open** .............................. `O`
3. Click **Look in** .......................... `Alt`+`I`
4. Select the drive and folder to look in.

**To Find File by Date:**

- Click **Last modified** ........... `Alt`+`M` text box list arrow.
- Select an approximate time to search.

**To Find File by Contents:**

- Click **Text** or ...................... `Alt`+`X` **property** text box.
- Type any text that might be contained in document.
- Click **Find Now** .................. `Alt`+`F`

**To Find File by Type:**

- Click **Files of type** ............... `Alt`+`T` text box list arrow.
- Select type of file to search.

January 22, 199-

~~Arnco Industries~~

T.      , President

Mr. Martin Quincy

641 Lexington Avenue

New York, NY  10022

Dear Mr. Quincy:

We are *very* pleased to announce the opening of a new subsidiary of our company, *COMPSELLTRAIN* We specialize in ~~selling~~, training and ~~service~~ of portable personal computers.

*service*          *selling*

~~This may be hard to believe, but~~ we carry *a full line of* portable personal computers that can do everything *your* ~~a~~ conventional desktop can. Our portables can run all of  the same applications as your company's conventional PCs. With the purchase of a computer, we will train two employees of your firm on ~~how to~~ use *the* an application of your choice. *of*          *All of*

~~For a free demonstration, call us at 212 555-9876 any day from 9:00 a.m. to 5:00 p.m.~~

*Very truly yours,*

~~Sincerely,~~

The rep for your area is Ms. Sally Hansen. She will phone you to discuss your possible needs.

The graphic capabilities are outstanding.

Theresa Mann
President

tm/yo

*Restore the deleted paragraph.*

# Exercise 13

■ **Summary**

## EXERCISE DIRECTIONS

1. Create a new document.

2. Keyboard the exercise as shown in Part I, or open 🖫**13REGRET**. Format the document as a full-block letter.

3. Begin the exercise At 2.5".

4. Click the Show/Hide button on the Standard toolbar to display codes.

5. Using the Properties feature, enter the following document summary information:

| | |
|---|---|
| Title: | Regrets about job opening |
| Subject: | No vacancies |
| Author: | Your name |
| Company: | Your company or school name |
| Manager: | Your supervisor or teacher's name |
| Category: | Personnel |
| Keyword: | resume, openings |

6. Turn on Track Changes and make the revisions shown in Part II on page 61.

7. Spell check.

8. Save as **REGRETSA**.

9. Review and accept edits individually.

10. Preview your work.

11. Print one copy.

12. Save the file; name it **REGRETS ABOUT JOB OPENINGS**.

13. Close the document window.

**PART I**

Today's date  Ms. Kristin Paulo  765 Rand Road  Palatine, IL  60074  Dear Ms. Paulo: Thank you for your inquiry regarding employment with our firm. ⨍We have reviewed your qualifications with several members of our firm.  We regret to report that we do not have an appropriate vacancy at this time. ⨍We will retain your resume in our files in the event that an opening occurs in your field. ⨍Your interest in our organization is very much appreciated.  We hope to be able to offer you a position at another time.  Very truly yours, Carol B. Giles  PERSONNEL MANAGER  cbg/yo

Today's date ⟩————————————→ 3"

                    Turner
Ms. Kristin ^ Paulo
765 Rand ~~Road~~ Avenue
Palatine, IL  60074

Dear Ms. Paulo:
                        recent                                    Quartz Industries, Inc.
Thank you for your ^ inquiry regarding employment with ^ ~~our firm?~~
                                    the various Quartz-affiliated companies, and
We have reviewed your qualifications with ^ ~~several members of our firm.~~ We regret to
report that we do not have an appropriate vacancy at this time.
      are, however, taking the liberty of                    of future
We ^ ~~will~~ retain your resume in our files in the event ^ ~~that an~~ opening ~~occurs~~ in your field.
            ing                        active                                    s
Your interest in our organization is very much appreciated ^ ~~We~~ hope to be able to offer
you a position at ^ ~~another time.~~                    and            sincerely
            a later date
Very truly yours,

                                ⟩————————————→ 3"


Carol B. Giles
~~PERSONNEL MANAGER~~

cbg/yo

**Exercise 14**

■ **Text Alignments** ■ **Vertical Centering**

*Formatting Toolbar*

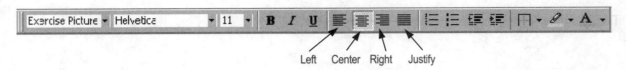

Left   Center   Right   Justify

# NOTES

## Text Alignments

■ Word lets you align all text that follows the alignment code until another justification code is entered. Word provides four alignment options:

- **Left** - all lines are even at the left margin but are ragged at the right margin (the default).

- **Right** - all lines are ragged at the left margin and even at the right margin.

- **Center** - all lines are centered between the margins.

- **Justify** - all lines are even at the left and right margins, except for the last line of the paragraph.

■ Alignments may affect blocks of text as well as individual lines.

■ Alignments may be changed before or after typing text.

■ Word applies left justification to your text by default.

■ A line of text or a paragraph may be aligned by positioning the insertion point anywhere within the paragraph and clicking an alignment button on the Formatting toolbar.

## Vertical Centering

■ Text may be centered vertically between the top and bottom margins or between the top and bottom edges of the page.

■ To vertically center text, select File, Page Setup from the menu. In the Page Setup dialog box that displays, click the Layout tab.

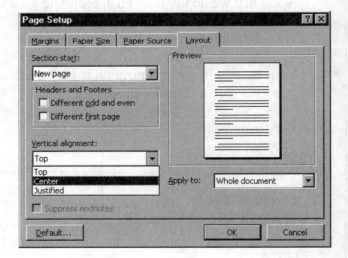

■ Click the Vertical alignment list arrow, choose Center from the choices, and select OK. *(Note illustration above.)*

■ In order to see the position of the vertically centered material on the page, switch to Page Layout view by selecting Page Layout from the View menu.

■ The proofreaders' mark for centering is: ] [.

# EXERCISE DIRECTIONS

1. Create a new document.

2. Display the Office Assistant.

3. Use the default margins and tabs.

4. Center the page from top to bottom.

5. Type each section of text shown in the exercise, changing the alignment appropriately.

6. Preview your work.

7. Change the case of the last block of text to sentence case.

8. Print one copy.

9. Change case of the last block of text to uppercase.

10. Print one copy.

11. Save the file; name it **COMPANY**.

12. Close the document window.

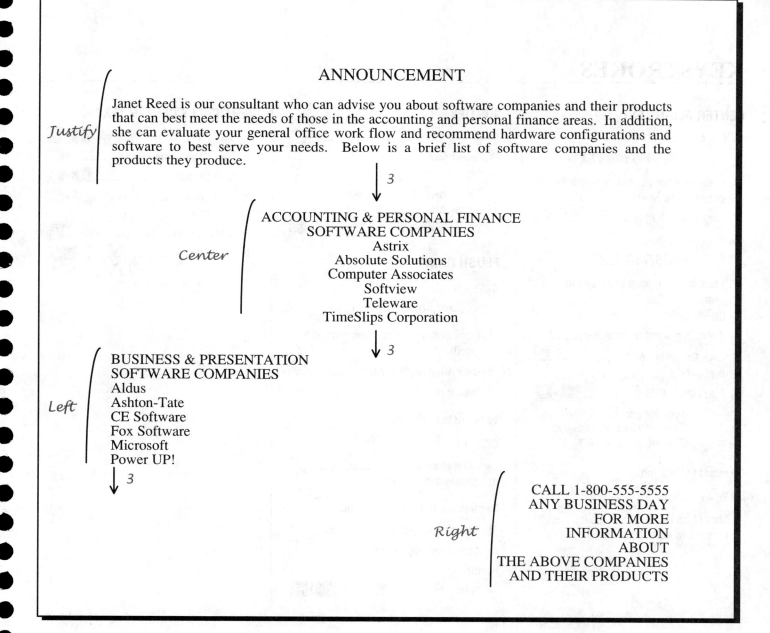

ANNOUNCEMENT

*Justify* Janet Reed is our consultant who can advise you about software companies and their products that can best meet the needs of those in the accounting and personal finance areas. In addition, she can evaluate your general office work flow and recommend hardware configurations and software to best serve your needs. Below is a brief list of software companies and the products they produce.

*3*

*Center*
ACCOUNTING & PERSONAL FINANCE
SOFTWARE COMPANIES
Astrix
Absolute Solutions
Computer Associates
Softview
Teleware
TimeSlips Corporation

*3*

*Left*
BUSINESS & PRESENTATION
SOFTWARE COMPANIES
Aldus
Ashton-Tate
CE Software
Fox Software
Microsoft
Power UP!

*3*

*Right*
CALL 1-800-555-5555
ANY BUSINESS DAY
FOR MORE
INFORMATION
ABOUT
THE ABOVE COMPANIES
AND THEIR PRODUCTS

# KEYSTROKES

## CENTER ALIGN TEXT

*CTRL + E*

### -BEFORE TYPING TEXT-

1. Place insertion point anywhere in line or paragraph to center.
2. Click **Center** button .......................... 🖫
3. Type text .......................................... *text*

### -EXISTING TEXT-

1. Place insertion point in paragraph to center.

   **OR**

   Select (highlight) block of text to center.
2. Click **Center** button .......................... 🖫

   **OR**

   Press **Ctrl + E** ....................... `Ctrl` + `E`

   ✓ *If you are centering a single line, there must be a paragraph mark (¶) at the end of the line.*

**To return to flush left:**

*CTRL + L*

Click **Flush Left** button....................... 🖫
to return to flush left mode.

## JUSTIFY

*CTRL + J*

1. Select paragraphs to justify.

   **OR**

   Place insertion point in desired paragraph.
2. Click **Justify** button.......................... 🖫

## FLUSH RIGHT

*CTRL + R*

### -BEFORE TYPING TEXT-

1. Place insertion point where text will be typed.
2. Click **Align Right** button ................... 🖫
3. Type text as necessary. ....................*text*

**To return to flush left:**

*CTRL + L*

Click **Align Left** button.......................... 🖫
to return to flush left mode.

**To align existing text flush right:**

1. Select (highlight) text to right align.
2. Click **Align Right** button ................... 🖫

   **OR**

   Press **Ctrl + R** ....................... `Ctrl` + `R`

## VERTICALLY CENTER TEXT

1. Click **File** ............................. `Alt` + `F`
2. Click **Page Setup** .......................... `U`
3. Click **Layout** .......................... `Alt` + `L`
4. Click **Vertical alignment** ........ `Alt` + `V`
   list arrow.
5. Select **Center** .................................. `↓`
6. Click **OK** ................................... `Enter`

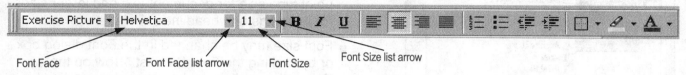

**Exercise 15**

## ■ Fonts ■ Font Faces ■ Font Style ■ Font Size

*Formatting Toolbar*

| Exercise Picture ▾ | Helvetica ▾ | 11 ▾ | **B** *I* <u>U</u> | ☰ ☰ ☰ ☰ | ⋮≡ ≡ 筆 筆 | ⬚ ▾ ✎ ▾ **A** ▾ |

Font Face      Font Face list arrow    Font Size    Font Size list arrow

## NOTES

### Fonts

- A **font** is a complete set of characters in a specific face, style, and size. Each set includes upper- and lowercase letters, numerals, and punctuation. A font that might be available to you in Word is Arial.

- A **font face** (often called **typeface** or just **font**) is the design of a character. Each design has a name and is intended to convey a specific feeling.

- You should select typefaces that will make your document attractive and communicate its particular message. As a rule, use no more than two or three font faces in any one document.

### Font Faces

- There are basically three types of font faces: serif, sans serif, and script. A **serif** face has lines, curves, or edges extending from the ends of the letter (**T**), while a **sans serif** face is straight-edged (**T**), and **script** looks like handwriting (*T*).

**Serif Font Face:**

| Times New Roman |

**Sans Serif Font Face:**

| Helvetica |

**Script Font Face:**

| *Freestyle Script* |

- A serif font face is typically used for document text because it is more readable. Sans serif is often used for headlines or technical material. Script typefaces are used for formal invitations and announcements.

- Font faces may be changed by selecting <u>F</u>ont from the F<u>o</u>rmat menu, then selecting the desired font listed in the Font dialog box.

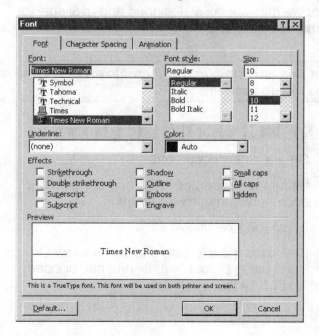

- Font faces may also be changed by clicking the Font Face list-arrow on the Formatting toolbar (which drops down a list of font choices).

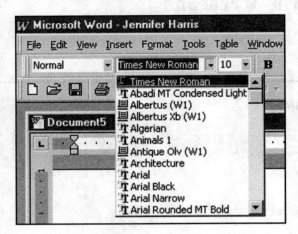

- The Font dialog box may also be accessed by clicking the *right* mouse button anywhere in the document window and selecting <u>F</u>ont.

## Font Style

- **Font style** refers to the slant and weight of letters, such as bold and italic.

> Times New Roman Regular
> *Times New Roman Italic*
> **Times New Roman Bold**
> ***Times New Roman Bold Italic***

- Note the Font dialog box illustrated on the previous page. The F<u>o</u>nt style box lists the styles or weights specially designed and available for the selected font.

## Font Size

- **Font size** generally refers to the height of the font, usually measured in points.

> Bookman 8 point
>
> Bookman 12 point
>
> **Bookman 18 point**

There are 72 points to an inch. Use 10- to 12-point type size for document text and larger sizes for headings and headlines.

- Font size may be changed in the Font dialog box or by clicking the Font Size list arrow on the Formatting toolbar (which drops down a list of font sizes).

- The currently selected font, style, and size are displayed in the Preview window and described at the bottom of the Font dialog box.

- You can change fonts *before* or *after* typing text. Existing text must be selected before changing font.

---

*In this exercise, you will create an advertisement and apply text alignments and enhancements to the document.*

# EXERCISE DIRECTIONS

1. Create a new document.

2. Using the Properties feature, enter relevant document summary information.

3. Begin the exercise At 2".

4. Keyboard the exercise exactly as shown in Part I using proper text alignments, or open
   📁**15ESTATE**

5. Change the font face, font size, and font style as shown in Part II, on page 68.

6. Vertically center the exercise.

7. Spell check.

8. Preview your work.

9. Print one copy.

10. Close the file; save as **ESTATE**

*At 2"*

PINEVIEW ESTATES.
↓2
The country home
that's more like a country club.

↓3

Far from the crowds, on the unspoiled North Fork of Long Island, you'll find a unique country home.  PineView Estates.  A condominium community perfectly situated between Peconic Bay and Long Island Sound on a lovely wooded landscape.  And like the finest country club, it offers a community club house, tennis court, pool and a golf course.

↓2

Models Open Daily 11 to 4
PineView Estates
Southhold, New York
(516) 555-5555
↓2

The complete terms are in an offering plan available from the sponsor.

**PART II**

**PINEVIEW ESTATES.** ⟩ *Sans serif*
*18 point*
*(Braggadocio)*

*The country home*
*that's more like a country club.* ⟩ *Script*
*22 point*

Far from the crowds, on the unspoiled North Fork of Long Island, you'll find a unique country home.  PineView Estates.  A condominium community perfectly situated between Peconic Bay and Long Island Sound on a lovely wooded landscape.  And like the finest country club, it offers a community club house, tennis court, pool and a golf course. ⟩ *Sans serif*
*10 point*

⟩ *Sans serif*
*10 point*

Models Open Daily 11 to 4
PineView Estates
Southhold, New York ⟩ *Sans serif*
(516) 555-5555 *9 point*

The complete terms are in an offering plan available from the sponsor. ⟩ *Sans serif*
*6 point*

# KEYSTROKES

## CHANGE FONT FACE

✔ *If all text in a paragraph will be in the same font, it is recommended that you include the paragraph mark at the end of the paragraph in your selection (highlighting) before changing the font.*

1. Select text for which font is to be changed.

   **OR**

   Place insertion point where new font is to begin.

2. Click **font list arrow** on the Formatting toolbar and click desired font.

   **OR**

   a. Click **Format** ..................... Alt + O
   b. Click **Font** .............................. F
   c. Select **Font** ........................ Alt + F
   d. Click desired font ............ ↓ or ↑
   e. Click **OK** ................................. Enter

## CHANGE FONT SIZE

1. Select text for which font size is to be changed.

   **OR**

   Place insertion point where new font size is to begin.

2. Click **point size list arrow** on the Formatting toolbar and click desired point size.

   **OR**

   a. Click **Format** ..................... Alt + O
   b. Click **Font** ................................. F
   c. Select **Size** ........................ Alt + S
   d. Click or type ..................... ↓ or ↑ desired point size.
   e. Click **OK** ................................. Enter

**Exercise 16**

■ **Emphasis styles: Bold, Underline, Italics, Highlight, Strikethrough, and Small Caps** ■ **Remove Emphasis Styles** ■ **Font Color**

*Formatting Toolbar*

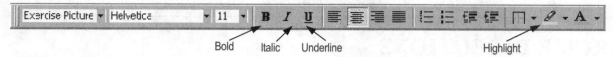

Bold    Italic    Underline                                    Highlight

# NOTES

## Emphasis Styles

■ **Bold**, <u>underline</u>, *italic*, and highlight are features used to emphasize or enhance text.

■ Text may be emphasized before or after it is typed.

■ To emphasize text *after* typing, select the text to be affected, then click the desired emphasis button on the Formatting toolbar. To emphasize text *before* typing, click the emphasis button to turn on the feature, type the text, then click the emphasis button to turn off the feature.

■ Highlighted text will appear yellow on the screen, but will appear gray when printed (unless you have a color printer). To change the highlight color, click the list arrow next to the highlight button on the Formatting toolbar and choose a different color.

■ There are numerous underline emphasis styles. Select <u>F</u>ont from the F<u>o</u>rmat menu. In the Font dialog box (right), click the <u>U</u>nderline box and select an underline style.

■ As indicated in the previous exercise, font styles also include bold and italic versions of a font face, but not all font faces have these styles.

■ In addition to bold and various underline styles, Word provides other effects. These include small caps, all caps, shadow, outline, emboss, engrave, and strikethrough. The strikethrough effect is used to indicate that text has been added, deleted, or moved, and is useful when comparing the current document with a different version of the same. Note examples above right:

SMALL CAPS              ALL CAPS
**Strikethrough**      ~~double strikethrough~~
**Shadow**              outline
emboss                  engrave

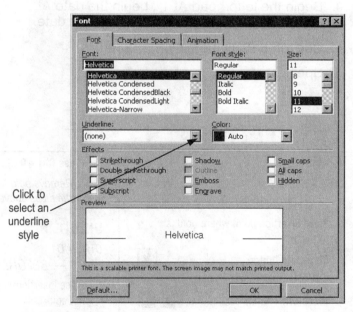

Click to select an underline style

■ Like the other appearance changes, these may be applied before or after typing text. They may be accessed by selecting one of the Effects in the Font dialog box.

■ Emphasis styles may be removed using the same procedure used when applying them.

■ You may remove emphasis styles individually, or you may remove all character formatting from a selected (highlighted) block of text by pressing the Ctrl key and the Spacebar.

## Font Color

- You may change the color of text by selecting the text to be affected, then clicking the list arrow below the color option in the font dialog box and selecting a desired font color.  You must have a color printer in order to output color.

- The proofreaders' mark for each style is:

bold  ～～～～

underline  ＿＿＿

double underline  ＝＝＝

italic  (ital)  *ital*

highlight  (highlight)  *hi*

---

*In this exercise, you will create and enhance a letter using various emphasis styles.*

---

# EXERCISE DIRECTIONS

1. Create a new document.

2. Keyboard the exercise as shown on the following page, using the appropriate alignments and enhancements indicated, or open 🖫**16GLOBAL** and format and enhance the text as shown in the exercise.

3. Begin the letterhead At 1"; begin the date At 2.5".  Use the Date feature to insert the date.

4. Use the default margins.

5. Spell check.

6. Justify paragraph text.

7. Highlight the first three hotels in yellow and the last three in green.

8. Preview your work.

9. Remove all highlighting; remove the dotted underlines.

10. Print one copy.

11. Close the file; save as **GLOBAL**.

# KEYSTROKES

## BOLD

*CTRL + B*

—BEFORE TYPING—

1. Place insertion point where bold is to begin.

2. Click **Bold** button .......................... `B`
   **OR**
   Press **Ctrl + B** .......................... `Ctrl`+`B`

3. Type text......................................*text*

4. Click **Bold** button .......................... `B`
   to discontinue bolding.
   **OR**
   Press **Ctrl + B** .......................... `Ctrl`+`B`
   to discontinue bolding.

—EXISTING TEXT—

1. Select (highlight) text to bold.

2. Click **Bold** button .......................... `B`
   **OR**

Press **Ctrl + B**.......................... `Ctrl`+`B`

✓ *Remove bold formatting by repeating the steps above.*

## UNDERLINE

*CTRL + U*

—BEFORE TYPING—

1. Place insertion point where underline is to begin.

2. Click **Underline** button...................... `U`
   **OR**
   Press **Ctrl + U** ...................... `Ctrl`+`U`
   **OR**
   a. Click **Format** ...................... `Alt`+`O`
   b. Click **Font** ...................... `F`
   c. Click **Font Tab**................... `Alt`+`N`
   d. Click **Underline** list arrow... `Alt`+`U`
   e. Select an underline style.
   f. Click **OK** ...................... `Enter`

3. Type text ...............................*text*

4. Click **Underline** button ................... `U`
   to discontinue underlining.
   **OR**
   Press **Ctrl + U**...................... `Ctrl`+`U`
   to discontinue underlining.

—EXISTING TEXT—

1. Select (highlight) text to underline.

2. Click **Underline** button ................... `U`
   **OR**
   Press **Ctrl + U** ...................... `Ctrl`+`U`
   **OR**
   Repeat steps a–f,left.

✓ *Remove underlining by repeating the steps above.*

*(Continued on page 72)*

*Set to blue*

**THE GLOBAL TRAVEL GROUP** ) *Sans serif 16 point bold*

485 Madison Avenue
New York, NY 10034 } *Sans serif 10 point italics*

PHONE: (212) 234-4566
FAX:  (212) 345-9877 } *Sans serif 10 point italics*

*Serif 12 point*

Today's Date

Mr. Astrit Ibrosi
45 Lake View Drive
Huntington, NY  11543

Dear Mr. Ibrosi:

*dotted underline*

Ms. Packer in our office has referred your letter to me.  You had asked her to provide you with a list of hotels in the San Francisco area that have a business center which offers laptop rentals, fax services, and teleconferencing capabilities.

Since I am the representative for the San Francisco area, I have compiled a list of hotels that offer the services you requested.  They appear below:

*Small caps 12 point*

REGENCY CENTRAL
SURRY HOTEL
FAIRMONT HOTEL
RENAISSANCE CENTER
MARRIOTT MARK
GRAND HYATT

*hi*

When you are ready to make your reservations, please call our office.  If you have any other travel needs, call GLOBAL.  Our experienced staff will give you prompt and courteous service and will answer all your travel questions.

*Serif 12 point*

Sincerely,

Marietta Dunn
Travel Representative

md/yo

# KEYSTROKES *(continued)*

## ITALICS

*CTRL + I*

### —BEFORE TYPING—

1. Place insertion point where italicizing is to begin.
2. Click **Italic** button ........................... `I`
   **OR**
   a. Click **Format** ..................... `Alt` + `O`
   b. Click **Font** ................................. `F`
   c. Click **Font Style** ................. `Alt` + `Y`
   d. Click **Italic** .......................... `↓` `↑`
   e. Click **OK** ............................. `Enter`
3. Type text ........................................ *text*
4. Click **Italic** button ........................... `I`
   to discontinue italicizing.
   **OR**
   Press **Ctrl + I** ........................ `Ctrl` + `I`
   to discontinue italicizing.

### —EXISTING TEXT—

1. Select (highlight) text to italicize.
2. Click **Italic** button ........................... `I`
   **OR**
   Press **Ctrl + I** ........................ `Ctrl` + `I`

   **OR**
   a. Click **Format** ..................... `Alt` + `O`
   b. Click **Font** ................................. `F`
   c. Click **Font Style** ................. `Alt` + `Y`
   d. Click **Italic** ........................ `↓` , `↑`
   e. Click **OK** ............................. `Enter`

   ✓ *Remove italics by repeating the steps above.*

## HIGHLIGHT

### —BEFORE TYPING—

1. Place insertion point where highlighting is to begin.
2. Click **Highlight** button ................. `🖉▾`
3. Type text ........................................ *text*
4. Click **Highlight** button ................. `🖉▾`

### —EXISTING TEXT—

1. Select (highlight) text to highlight.
2. Click **Highlight** button ................. `🖉▾`

   ✓ *Remove highlighting by repeating the steps above.*

## DOUBLE UNDERLINE

*CTRL + SHIFT + D*

1. Place insertion point where double underlining is to begin.
2. Press
   **Ctrl + Shift** + D ............ `Ctrl` + `Shift` + `D`
3. Type text ........................................ *text*
4. Press
   **Ctrl + Shift + D** ............ `Ctrl` + `Shift` + `D`
   to discontinue double underlining.

### —EXISTING TEXT—

1. Select (highlight) text to double underline.
2. Press
   **Ctrl + Shift + D** ............ `Ctrl` + `Shift` + `D`
   **OR**

   ✓ *Remove double underlining by repeating the steps above.*

## REMOVE CHARACTER FORMATTING

*CTRL + B, CTRL + U, CTRL + I, CTRL + SPACE*

1. Select (highlight) text containing the formatting to remove.
2. Click **Bold** button ........................... `B`
   to remove bolding.
   **OR**
   Click **Underline** button .................... `U`
   to remove underlining.
   **OR**
   Press **Ctrl + U** ...................... `Ctrl` + `U`
   to remove underlining.

**OR**
Click **Italics** button ........................ `I`
to remove italics.
**OR**
Press **Ctrl + I**. ........................ `Ctrl` + `I`
to remove italics.
**OR**
Press **Ctrl + Space** ......... `Ctrl` + `Space`
to remove *all* character formatting.

## EFFECTS (STRIKETHROUGH, SMALL CAPS, ALL CAPS)

1. Click **Format** ......................... `Alt` + `O`
2. Click **Font** ................................... `F`
3. Click desired Effects.
   - **Strikethrough** .................. `Alt` + `K`
   - **Small Caps** ..................... `Alt` + `M`
   - **All Caps** ......................... `Alt` + `A`
4. Click **OK** ................................ `Enter`

## CHANGE FONT COLOR

1. Select text for which font color is to be changed.
2. Click **Format** ......................... `Alt` + `O`
3. Click **Font** ................................... `F`
4. Click **Color** ........................... `Alt` + `C`
5. Select desired color.
6. Click **OK** ................................ `Enter`
   **OR**
   a. Click drop-down list arrow next to **Font Color** button .................. `A▾`
   b. Select desired color.

## Exercise 17

■ **Use Symbols**

## NOTES

■ **Wingdings** is an ornamental symbol font face collection that is used to enhance a document. Illustrated below is the Wingdings font collection.

■ A symbol font face must be available with your printer.

### *Wingdings Font Collection*

■ The upper- and lowercase of the letter and character key provide different Wingdings. To create a Wingding, press and then highlight the corresponding keyboard letter or character shown in the chart, and select Wingdings from the Font list. Or, select <u>S</u>ymbol from the <u>I</u>nsert menu and select a Wingding from the Symbol dialog box.

Click to select other symbols.

■ There are other ornamental fonts which may be accessed by clicking on the list arrow next to the <u>F</u>ont text box in the <u>S</u>ymbols dialog box.

■ Ornamental fonts and special character sets are also found as fonts. They can be accessed through the Font dialog box.

■ You may change the size of a symbol font face by changing the point size (as you would any other character).

■ Ornamental fonts can be used to:

- Separate items on a page:

| Wingdings |
|:---:|
| ◆❖◆❖◆ |
| Graphics |

- Emphasize items on a list:

| ✎dresses |
|---|
| ✎coats |
| ✎suits |

- Enhance a page:

| 📖📖📖📖📖 |
|:---:|
| BOOK SALE |
| 📖📖📖📖📖 |

> *In this exercise, you will create a menu and add a symbol font face to separate portions of it.*

# EXERCISE DIRECTIONS

1. Create a new document.
2. Keyboard the exercise as shown, using the alignments and enhancements indicated, or open 🖫 **17CAFE**, and format and enhance the text as shown in the exercise.
3. Use the default margins.

4. Enhance the document with symbols from the Wingdings font collection. Use any desired symbol.
5. Spell check.
6. Preview your work.
7. Vertically center the exercise.
8. Print one copy.
9. Close the file; save as **CAFE**.

# KEYSTROKES

## INSERT A SYMBOL

### —USING MENU—

1. Place insertion point where symbol will be inserted.
2. Click **Insert** ............................ Alt + I
3. Click **Symbol** ................................. S
4. Click **Symbols** tab ................ Alt + S
5. Click **Font** list arrow .............. Alt + F
6. Select desired font.................. ↑, ↓
7. Click left mouse button down to enlarge desired special character for viewing.

8. Double-click desired special character to insert it into document.

   **OR**

   a. Click ................................. Alt + P
      **Special Characters** tab.
   b. Select desired character ...... ↑, ↓
   c. Double-click desired special character to insert it into document.

### —USING SHORTCUT KEYS—

1. Position insertion point where you want to insert special character.

2. Click **Insert** ............................ Alt + I
3. Click **Symbol** ................................. S
4. Click **Special Characters** ........ Alt + P
5. Make note of the shortcut key(s) for the symbol you want to insert.
6. Close dialog box and type keyboard shortcut to insert symbol.

*Hint: Print out the list of keyboard shortcuts and place them near your keyboard for reference. You can also assign new keyboard shortcuts to special symbol(s) or character(s).*

# The ✆ Harbor ✆ Cafe

*Sans serif 26 pt bold*

125 Pine Hill Road
Fire Island, NY 11543
(516) 555-5555

*Sans serif 12 pt*

*Set to red*

*Double underline*

## BREAKFAST MENU

*Sans serif bold 14 pt*

### BEVERAGES

*Herbal Tea...$1.00*
*Coffee...$2.00*
*Cappuccino...$2.50*

● ❖ ◆ ⌘ ❖ ◆ ⌘ ●

*Set all headings to sans serif 12 pt bold*

### FRUITS

*Berry Refresher...$3.00*
*Sparkling Citrus Blend...$3.00*
*Baked Apples...$3.50*

● ❖ ◆ ⌘ ❖ ◆ ⌘ ●

### GRAINS

*Fruity Oatmeal...$3.50*
*Bran Muffins...$3.00*
*Whole Wheat Zucchini Bread...$3.00*
*Four-Grain Pancakes...$5.00*

*Set all menu items to serif 12 pt italics*

● ❖ ◆ ⌘ ❖ ◆ ⌘ ●

### EGGS

*Baked Eggs with Creamed Spinach...$6.50*
*Poached Eggs with Hollandaise Sauce...$6.00*
*Scrambled Eggs...$2.50*
*Sweet Pepper and Onion Frittata...$6.50*

*Willis Barton ◆ Proprietor*

*Script 16 pt bold*

# Exercise 18

## ■ Bullets and Numbering

*Formatting Toolbar*

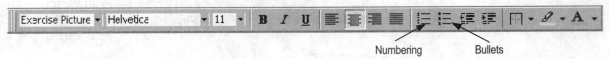

Numbering       Bullets

# NOTES

■ A bullet is a dot or symbol used to highlight points of information or to itemize a list that does not need to be in any particular order.

> • red     • apple
> • blue    • pear
> • green   • orange

■ Using the **Bullets and Numbering** feature, you can insert bullets automatically to create a bulleted list for each paragraph or item you type.

> ✓ *Note:* *Word will automatically start using the Bullet and Numbered List feature when it senses that you are creating lists. The Office Assistant will ask you if you do want to use the Bullet and Numbered List feature.*

■ The Bullets and Numbering feature also allows you to create numbered paragraphs for items that need to be in a particular order. The numbers you insert increment automatically.

> The Bullets and Numbering feature lets you:
>
> 1. Create numbered paragraphs.
>
> 2. Create bulleted paragraphs.
>
> 3. Use symbols instead of the traditional round dot or square bullet.

■ The Bullets and Numbering feature is accessed by selecting Bullets and Numbering from the Format menu.

■ In the Bullets and Numbering dialog box which follows, you may click the Bulleted tab and select the bullet style you desire. Or, you may click the Numbered tab and select the number style you desire.

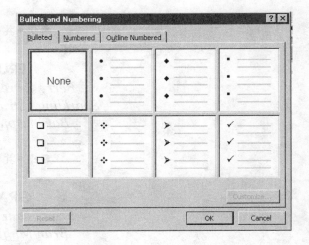

■ Once the bullet or number style is chosen, you may type your text. The bullet or number is entered automatically each time the Enter key is pressed.

■ Bullets and Numbering may also be accessed by clicking the Bullets or Numbering button on the Formatting toolbar.

- You can add bullets and numbers to existing text by selecting/highlighting the text and then choosing Bullets and Numbering from the Format menu or clicking the appropriate button on the Formatting toolbar.

- Symbols may also be used as bullets.

- When you use the Bullets and Numbering feature for numbered paragraphs, adding or deleting paragraphs will result in all paragraphs being automatically renumbered.

- To change the bullet style to a different symbol, select a bullet style to change in the Bullets and Numbering dialog box, and click Customize.

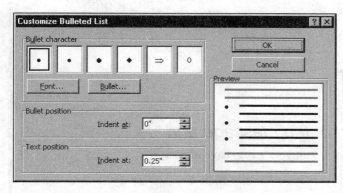

- Use the Font and Bullet buttons to select the desired font and symbol to use for the new bullet style.

## End Bullet or Numbered List

- Select the list from which you want to remove bullets or numbers.

  - Click the bullet button to remove bullets.

  - Click the numbered button to remove numbers.

## Interrupt Bullet or Numbered List

- To remove bullets from selected sections of numbered or bulleted lists, select the items you want to change and click the bullet or numbered list icon. Numbers in a list that is interrupted will automatically adjust.

- To resume numbering in a list that you have interrupted, select Bullets and Numbering on the Format menu. Select Continue previous list and click OK.

- To remove a single bullet or number, click between the number or bullet and press the Backspace key once.

---

*In this exercise, you will create a flyer and add a symbol face to separate portions of it.*

# EXERCISE DIRECTIONS

1. Create a new document.
2. Turn off the Grammar check feature.
3. Keyboard the exercise as shown, using the appropriate alignments and enhancements. Use any desired bullet style, or open 📄**18DESIGN**, then format and enhance the text as shown in the exercise.
4. Use the default margins.
5. Enhance the document with symbols from the Wingdings font collection. Use any desired symbols in this collection.

6. If you have a color printer, change the font color to blue for each bulleted heading (sans serif text). If you do not have a color printer, skip to step 7.
7. Spell check.
8. Preview your work.
9. Vertically center the exercise.
10. Print one copy.
11. Close the file; save as **DESIGN**.

36 point
and bold

*Create a*  ) Script
40 point
bold

**Design with Color** ) Serif
30 point
bold

④**Reasons Why** ) Sans serif
24 point

*The world is a colorful place.*
*So why not include color in all your* ) Serif
*processing?* 14 point italic

⇒*Color increases the visual impact of the message and* ) Sans serif
14 point
*makes it more memorable*. Don't you want your ads to have impact ) Serif 12 point
and be noticed?

⇒*Color creates a feeling and helps explain the subject*.
Greens and blues are cool, relaxing tones, while reds and oranges scream with
emphasis. Pastels communicate a gentle tone.

Use same
font face
and size
as first
item

⇒*Color creates a personality*. You can make your corporate forms and
brochures have their own identity and personality with color.

⇒*Color highlights information*. An advertisement or manual might have
warnings in red, explanations in black and instructions in blue.

◆  ◆  ◆ ) 12 point wingdings

Our color processing labs will take care of *all* your color processing needs. Just call ) Sans
*1-800-555-6666* for information. Our courteous staff is ready to assist you with any   serif
technical question. 12 point.

L◆ A◆ B◆ P◆ R◆ O
FOR ) Sans serif
COLOR PROCESSING 12 point

# KEYSTROKES

## BULLETS

1. Place insertion point where text will be typed.

   **OR**

   Select text to convert to a bulleted list.

2. Click **Bullet List** button ................... 🔳

   **OR**

   a. Click **Format**...................... `Alt`+`O`

   b. Click **Bullets and Numbering** ....... `N`

   c. Click **Bulleted**.................... `Alt`+`B`

   d. Click desired
      bullet style............... `Tab` `⇄` `↑↓`

   e. Click **OK** ................................ `Enter`

## REMOVE BULLETS

1. Select the part of the list from which bullets are to be removed.

2. Click **Bullet** button ......................... 🔳
   on Formatting toolbar.

## NUMBERING

1. Position insertion point where text will be typed or select (highlight) block of paragraphs to convert to a numbered list.

2. Click **Numbering List** button .......... 🔳

   **OR**

   a. Click **Format** ...................... `Alt`+`O`

   b. Click **Bullets and Numbering** ...... `N`

   c. Click **Numbered**................ `Alt`+`N`

   d. Click...................... `Tab`+ `⇄` `↑↓`
      desired numbering style.

   e. Click **OK** ................................. `Enter`

## END NUMBERING

1. Select the part of the list from which numbers are to be removed.

2. Click **Number List** button............... 🔳
   on Formatting toolbar.

## INTERRUPT BULLETS OR NUMBERS

1. Select the part of the list from which numbers or bullets are to be removed.

2. Click bullet or number icon.

   ✓ *Numbers in a list that is interrupted will automatically adjust.*

**To remove a single bullet or number:**

   a. Click between the number or bullet and the text.

   b. Press **Backspace** once ..... `Backspace`

**To resume numbering in an interrupted numbered list:**

   a. Click where numbering is to resume.

   b. Click **Format**..................... `Alt`+`O`

   c. Click **Bullets and Numbering** ..... `N`

   d. Click **Numbered** tab........... `Alt`+`N`

   e. Click **Continue** ................. `Alt`+`C`
      **previous list**

   f. Click **OK**................................. `Enter`

   g. Continue with numbered list.

## Exercise 19   ■ Summary

*In this exercise, you will create a flyer using text alignments, enhancements, bullets, and numbers.*

## EXERCISE DIRECTIONS

1. Create a new document.
2. Turn off the grammar check feature.
3. Keyboard the exercise as shown, using the appropriate alignments and enhancements. Use any desired bullet style for the bulleted items, or open 🖫**19COLOR**, then format and enhance the text as shown in the exercise.
4. Use the default margins.

5. Enhance the document with any desired symbols from the Wingdings font collection.
6. Set the font color for all occurrences of the word Color in Color Masters to Green.
7. Spell check.
8. Preview your work.
9. Vertically center the exercise.
10. Print one copy.
11. Close the file; save as **COLOR**.

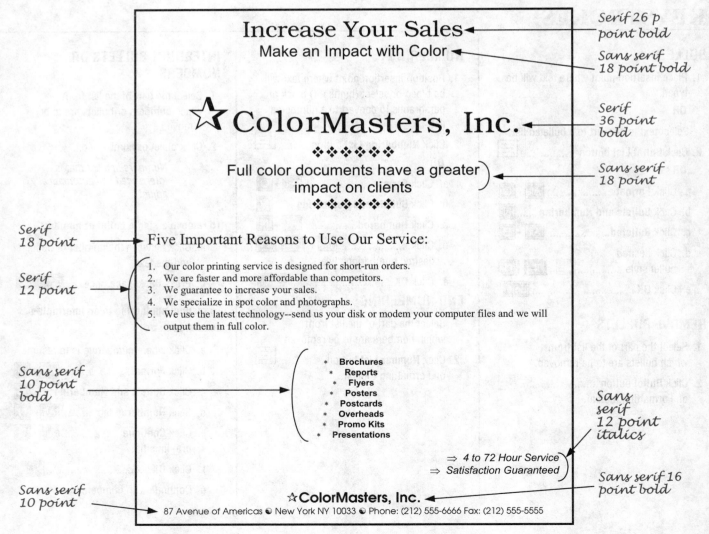

- Increase Your Sales — *Serif 26 p point bold*
- Make an Impact with Color — *Sans serif 18 point bold*
- ☆ColorMasters, Inc. — *Serif 36 point bold*
- Full color documents have a greater impact on clients — *Sans serif 18 point*
- Five Important Reasons to Use Our Service: — *Serif 18 point*
- *Serif 12 point*
  1. Our color printing service is designed for short-run orders.
  2. We are faster and more affordable than competitors.
  3. We guarantee to increase your sales.
  4. We specialize in spot color and photographs.
  5. We use the latest technology--send us your disk or modem your computer files and we will output them in full color.
- *Sans serif 10 point bold*
  * Brochures
  * Reports
  * Flyers
  * Posters
  * Postcards
  * Overheads
  * Promo Kits
  * Presentations
- ⇒ *4 to 72 Hour Service*
  ⇒ *Satisfaction Guaranteed* — *Sans serif 12 point italics*
- ☆**ColorMasters, Inc.** — *Sans serif 16 point bold*
- 87 Avenue of Americas ❂ New York NY 10033 ❂ Phone: (212) 555-6666 Fax: (212) 555-5555 — *Sans serif 10 point*

# EXERCISE 20

- Line Spacing ■ Paragraph Spacing ■ Indent Text
- Hanging Indent ■ First-Line Indents

## NOTES

### Line Spacing

- Use **line spacing** to specify the spacing between lines of text. A line spacing change affects text in the paragraph that contains the insertion point. Line spacing may also be applied to selected text.

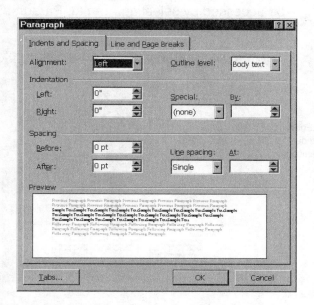

- Line spacing is measured in lines or in points. When line spacing is measured in points, it is referred to as leading (pronounced *ledding*). Reducing leading amounts can reduce the text's readability, while increasing leading can aid its readability.

### Leading Examples

> To make text easy to read, fonts that are measured in points usually use leading that is 120% of the font's point size. For example, a 10-point font usually uses 12-point leading. This is the default.

> The paragraph text in this box has been set to a specific amount (exactly) using 16 point. Note that the lines appear to be double spaced. They are not.

> The paragraph text in this box has been set to a specific amount (exactly) using 9 point. Note that the lines get less readable as the point size decreases.

- Line spacing may also be changed to single, double, or one and a half lines. The quickest way to change line spacing is to press Ctrl + 2 for double, Ctrl + 1 for single, and Ctrl + 5 for 1.5 lines. Other methods for changing line spacing are outlined in the keystrokes.

### Paragraph Spacing

- The paragraph spacing option allows you to add additional space between paragraphs, headings, or subheadings as you type your document. You may choose to add extra space before each paragraph, after each paragraph, or before and after each paragraph.

- To set paragraph spacing, select Paragraph from the Format menu. In the Paragraph dialog box which follows, click the Indents and Spacing Tab. Enter a spacing amount in the Before and/or After text box. The amount you enter may be in lines (2 li) or in points (2 pt). If you enter an amount in lines, Word will convert it to points.

## Indent Text

■ The indent feature sets a temporary left, right, or left and right margin for paragraph text. The indent feature may also be used to set a first-line indent for paragraphs.

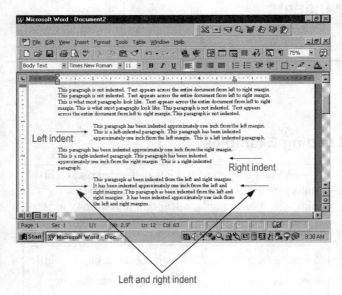

Left indent

Right indent

Left and right indent

■ There are several ways to indent text. You can:

• **Drag the indent markers on the Ruler.**

### *Page Layout View Ruler*

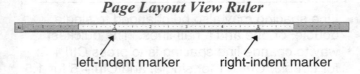

left-indent marker          right-indent marker

This is the most convenient way of setting left *and* right indents. To change indents, drag the left and/or right indent marker to the desired position. Note that the marker consists of three parts. Be sure to drag the correct part to achieve the desired indent.

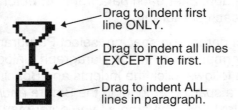

Drag to indent first line ONLY.

Drag to indent all lines EXCEPT the first.

Drag to indent ALL lines in paragraph.

• **Click the Increase Indent button** ![icon] **on the toolbar.**

Increase indent

Decrease indent

• This is the most convenient way of setting a *left* indent. Clicking the Increase Indent button indents text to a tab setting. Therefore, clicking Increase Indent once will indent text .5"; clicking it twice will indent text 1", etc.

• Left indents may be removed by selecting the indented text and clicking the Decrease Indent button ![icon].

• **Use the Paragraph Dialog Box** (which may be accessed by selecting Format, Paragraph, and the Indents and Spacing Tab).

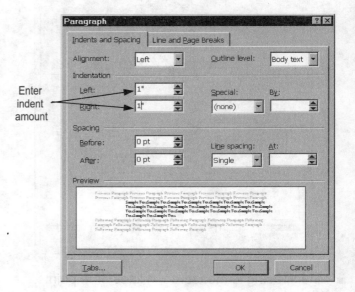

Enter indent amount

• This option allows greater precision for setting left and right indents. Enter the amount of indentation (or click the increment arrows) in the Left and/or Right indent text box.

## Hanging Indent

■ When all lines in a paragraph are indented except the first line, a **hanging indent** is created. Note the effect of a hanging indented paragraph.

> The way text will lay out or format on a page is set by the Word for Windows program. For example, margins are set for 1.25" on the left and 1.25" on the right.

■ There are several ways to create a hanging indent. You can:

● **Drag the hanging indent marker on the ruler.**

This method allows you to see the change as you make it. To set a hanging indent, drag the hanging indent marker where the hanging indent is to begin. Note the ruler position of the hanging indent marker below:

*Paragraph with a Hanging Indent*

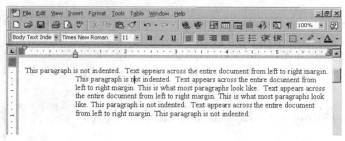

● **Press Ctrl + T.**

This method indents all paragraph text, except the first line, to the next tab stop. It is the quickest way to achieve a hanging indent.

Pressing Ctrl + Shift + T will undo indents created with Ctrl + T.

● **Use the Paragraph Dialog Box** (which is opened by selecting Format, Paragraph, and the Indents and Spacing Tab).

This option allows greater precision for setting a hanging indent. Enter the left indent amount in the Left text box. Select Special and choose Hanging. Then, select By and enter the desired measurement for the hanging indent.

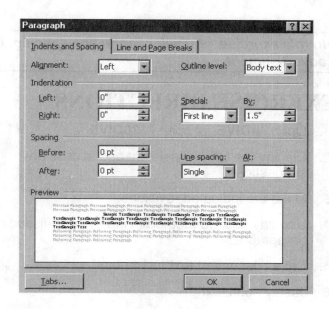

## First-Line Indent

■ A first-line indent lets you set the amount of space the first line of each paragraph indents. Each time you press Enter, the insertion point automatically begins at the indented setting. This eliminates the need to use the Tab key to indent each new paragraph.

■ To set a first-line indent, you may use either the Ruler or the Paragraph dialog box.

■ Using the Ruler, drag the first-line indent marker to the desired position. Using Indents and Spacing in the Paragraph dialog box, select Special, choose First line, and enter the amount you wish the paragraph to indent in the By text box.

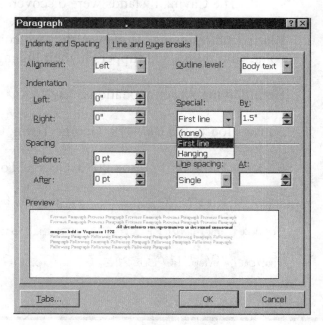

---

*In this exercise, you will change line spacing, indent text, and change fonts to create an advertisement.*

---

# EXERCISE DIRECTIONS

1. Open ⌨**DIVE**, or open 💾**20DIVE**.

2. Display the Office Assistant and access any suggestions.

3. Make the indicated revisions.

4. Use any desired method to indent hotel listings paragraphs.

5. Set all document text to 14 point.

6. Justify hotel text.

7. Set Hotel text to italic.

8. Double space paragraph text.  Set paragraph spacing to 10 point before and after each paragraph.

9. Spell check.

10. Preview your work.

11. Print one copy.

12. Reformat the indented paragraphs to hanging indented paragraphs. Leave the first line of each paragraph where it is; set an additional .5" indent for the remaining lines.

13. Print one copy.

14. Close the file; save as **DIVE**.

---

*Center and set to 18 pt sans serif bold*

DIVING IN THE CAYMAN ISLANDS

*and angelfish*

Do you want to see sharks, barracudas, and stingrays? ~~Do you want to see angels, too?~~

The Cayman Islands were discovered by Christopher Columbus in 1503. *and* ~~The Cayman Islands~~ are located south of Cuba.  The Caymans are home to only about 25,000 year-round residents.  However, they welcome 200,000 visitors each year.  Most visitors come with masks and flippers in their luggage.  ~~Now, you are ready to jump in.~~

Hotel/Diving Accommodations: *set to sans serif 14 pt bold*

Sunset House, PO Box 479, George Town, Grand Cayman; (809) 555-4767.

Coconut Harbour, PO Box 2086, George Town, Grand Cayman; (809) 555-7468.

Red Sail Sports, PO Box 1588, George Town, Grand Cayman; (809) 555-7965.

Cayman Diving Lodge, PO Box 11, East End, Grand Cayman; (809) 555-7555.

Anchorage View, PO Box 2123, George Town, Grand Cayman; (809) 555-4209.

# KEYSTROKES

## LINE SPACING

1. Place insertion point where new line spacing is to begin.

   **OR**

   Select the paragraphs in which line spacing is to be changed.

2. Select desired line spacing option:

   a. Press **Ctrl + 2** .................... `Ctrl`+`2`
      to change to double space lines.

   b. Press **Ctrl + 1** .................... `Ctrl`+`1`
      to change to single space lines.

   c. Press **Ctrl + 5** .................... `Ctrl`+`5`
      to change to 1.5 space lines.

   **OR**

   a. Click **Format** .................... `Alt`+`O`

   b. Click **Paragraph** .................... `P`

   c. Click **Indents and Spacing** `Alt`+`I`

   d. Click **Line Spacing** .......... `Alt`+`N`

   e. Click desired option .......... `↓` , `↑`

   **OR**

   To choose a fixed line spacing:

   a. Click **Line Spacing** text box. `Alt`+`N`

   b. Select **Exactly** .......................... `↓`

   c. Click **At** text box ............... `Alt`+`A`

   d. Type desired amount.

3. Click **OK** .................................... `Enter`

## PARAGRAPH SPACING

1. Position insertion point in the paragraph you want to format or select paragraphs to be formatted.

2. Click **Format** .................... `Alt`+`O`

3. Click **Paragraph** .................... `P`

4. Click **Indents and Spacing** tab `Alt`+`I`

5. Click **Before**/ .................... `Alt`+`B`
   **After** text box .................... `Alt`+`E`

6. Enter a before and/or after amount.

7. Click **OK** .................................... `Enter`

## INDENT TEXT FROM THE LEFT MARGIN

1. Place insertion point in paragraph to block indent.

   **OR**

   Place insertion point where block indenting will begin.

   **OR**

   Select paragraphs to block indent.

2. Click **Increase Indent** button.......... `⧉`
   on toolbar to indent text
   to desired tab stop.

   **OR**

   Click **Decrease indent** button ........ `⧉`
   on toolbar to move
   text back to left.

   **OR**

   Drag **left-indent marker** .................... `⧗`
   to desired position on Ruler.

## INDENT PARAGRAPHS FROM LEFT AND RIGHT MARGINS

1. Place insertion point in paragraph to block indent.

   **OR**

   • Place insertion point where block indent will begin.

   **OR**

   • Select paragraphs to block indent.

2. Drag left-indent marker .................... `⧗`
   to desired position on ruler.

3. Drag right indent marker .................... `△`
   to desired position on ruler.

   **OR**

   a. Click **Format** .................... `Alt`+`O`

   b. Click **Paragraph** .................... `P`

   c. Click **Indents and Spacing**
      tab .................... `Alt`+`I`

   d. Click **Left** text box ............ `Alt`+`L`

   e. Key distance from ................ *number*
      **Left** margin.

   f. Click **Right** text box .......... `Alt`+`R`

   g. Key distance from ................ *number*
      **Right** margin.

   h. Click **OK** ............................. `Enter`

## HANGING INDENT

1. Place the insertion point in paragraph to be affected.

   **OR**

   Select (highlight) the desired paragraphs.

2. Drag **hanging indent marker** ............ `△`
   to desired position.

   **OR**

   *– USING KEYBOARD SHORTCUTS –*

   a. Press **Ctrl + T** .................... `Ctrl`+`T`

   b. Press
      **Ctrl + Shift + T** ........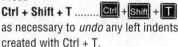
      as necessary to *undo* any left indents created with Ctrl + T.

   **OR**

   *– USING THE FORMAT PARAGRAPH COMMAND ON THE MENU BAR –*

1. Click **Format** .................... `Alt`+`O`

2. Click **Paragraph** .................... `P`

3. Click **Indents and** .................... `Alt`+`I`
   **Spacing** tab

4. Click **Special** .................... `Alt`+`S`

5. Click **Hanging** .................... `↓`

6. Click **By** .................... `Alt`+`Y`

7. Type distance that all lines, except the first, will be indented.

8. Click **OK** .................................... `Enter`

## ■ Format a One-Page Report ■ Set Margins and Tabs

## NOTES

- A **report** or manuscript generally begins 2" from the top of the page and is prepared in double space. Each new paragraph begins .5" or 1" from the left margin. The title of a report is centered and keyed in all caps. A quadruple space follows the title.

- Margins vary depending on how the report is bound. For an unbound report, use margins of 1" on the left and right.

### Set Margins

- Word measures margins in inches.

- The default margins are 1.25" on the left and right and 1" margins on the top and bottom of the page.

- There are three ways to change left and right margins. You can:

  • **Drag a margin marker on the ruler.** This method is the most convenient to adjust margins for the *entire document*. Changing margins in Page Layout view allows you to adjust margins as you work and see the immediate effect on text.

- To change margins, position the mouse pointer on the left or right margin marker. When the pointer changes to a left/right pointing arrow, drag the margin boundary to the desired position. If you hold down the Alt key as you drag, the margin measurements will display on the Ruler.

- The numbers in the white area of the Ruler represent the measurement of the text area in the document; the gray areas represent the margins between the text and the edges of the page.

  • **Drag margin marker in Print Preview mode.** This method allows you to see the effects of margin changes on the entire document as you make them.

- To change margins, drag the left or right margin marker on the horizontal Print Preview ruler. If the ruler is not displayed, click the View Ruler button.

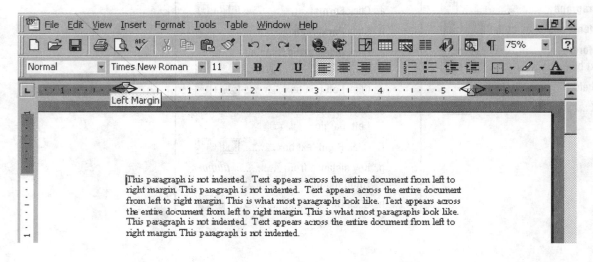

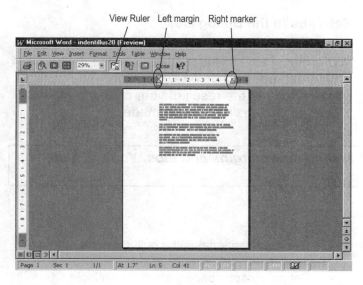

View Ruler    Left margin    Right marker

- A Vertical ruler also displays in this view, allowing you to change top and bottom margins.

- **Use the File, Page Setup Command**, which accesses the Page Setup dialog box. This method allows greater precision and permits you to limit margin changes to sections of your document.

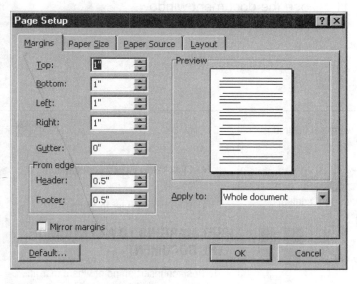

- To set margins in the dialog box, click the Margins Tab and enter the margin amount in the Left and Right text boxes or use the increment arrows to select a margin amount. Remember, margins are measured in inches.

- You may apply margin changes to the Whole Document (the default) or from This Point Forward. If you choose This Point Forward, the margin changes begin at the insertion point.

- If you wish to apply a margin change to a portion of the document, you must first break the page into sections. To do this, select Break from the Insert menu and choose Continuous at the point at which your margin is to change. Then apply the desired margin change. Repeat this procedure each time you wish to apply a new margin change.

  ✓ Note: You can use left and right indents to change margins to part of a document.

## Set Tabs

- The Tab key indents a single line of text. Default tabs are set .5" apart. When the Tab key is pressed once, text advances .5"; when the Tab key is pressed twice, text advances 1", etc.

- It is possible to change the location or the number of tabs. For example, if you desire to advance .8" each time the Tab key is pressed, or eliminate all preset tabs except one, you can do so.

- Tabs may be changed on the Ruler or by selecting Tabs from the Format menu. When you change tab settings in a document, changes take effect from that point forward.

## Set Tabs on the Ruler

- Tab settings are displayed on the bottom of the Ruler as vertical gray tick marks set .5" apart.

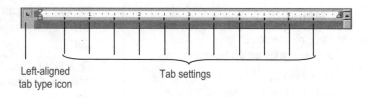

Left-aligned tab type icon                    Tab settings

- Default settings are left-aligned. This means that text typed at such a setting will align at the left and move to the right of the tab as you type.

> This is an example of left-aligned text. Note that the text on the left edge is aligned, while text at the right edge is jagged.

- The left-aligned tab type icon, located at the left of the Ruler, is displayed as an **L**.

■ **To set a new left-aligned tab**, click anywhere on the Ruler where you want a new tab; a new tab marker is inserted and all preset tabs to the left are deleted.

■ **To delete a tab setting**, drag the tab marker off the ruler.

**Set Tabs in the Dialog Box**

■ Tabs may also be set using the Tabs dialog box (Format, Tabs).  This method lets you set and clear tab positions in one operation.  You cannot, however, see the result of your changes on text until all settings have been made.

---

*In this exercise, you will create a one-page report, setting new margins and tabs. You will also review line spacing and indent procedures.*

---

# EXERCISE DIRECTIONS

1. Create a new document.
2. Set 1" left and right margins and .5" top and bottom margins.
3. Clear all tab stops.
4. Set the first tab stop at 1".
5. Keyboard the report on the next page:
   - Begin the title At 1". Use any desired Wingdings before and after the heading as shown.
   - Center and set the title to sans serif 14-point bold.
   - Set the side headings to sans serif 12-point bold.
   - Set the body text to serif 11 point.
   - Double space the first and last two paragraphs.
   - Single space and indent the middle paragraphs 1" from the left and right margins.
   - Use the telephone as the bullet symbol before each middle paragraph.
   - Set paragraph spacing after each middle paragraph to 6 point. (This eliminates the need to press the Enter key twice after these paragraphs).
6. Justify paragraph text.
7. Spell check.
8. Preview your work.
9. Print one copy.
10. Save the file; name it **CONNECT**.
11. Close the document window.

# KEYSTROKES

## SET MARGINS

1. Place mouse pointer over the desired margin marker on the horizontal ruler.
2. Hold down **Alt** ............................ `Alt` and drag marker to desired position.

## SET MARGINS USING PAGE SETUP DIALOG BOX

1. Click **File** .............................. `Alt`+`F`
2. Click **Page Setup** ........................... `U`
3. Click **Margins** tab .................. `Alt`+`M`
4. Click increment arrows to set **Left** margin.
   **OR**
   Click **Left** ................ `Alt`+`F`, *number* and type distance from left edge of paper.

5. Click increment arrows to set desired **Right** margin.
   **OR**
   Click **Right** .............. `Alt`+`G`, *number* and type distance from right edge of paper.
6. Click **Apply to** ...................... `Alt`+`A`
7. Click **This point forward** ......... `↓`, `↑`
   **OR**
   Click **Whole document** ........... `↓`, `↑`
8. Click **OK** ..................................... `Enter`

## CHANGE DEFAULT TAB SETTINGS

1. Click **Format** ........................ `Alt`+`O`
2. Click **Tabs** ................................... `T`
3. Click **Default Tab Stops** ........ `Alt`+`F`
4. Type distance between tabs.

5. Click **OK** ..................................... `Enter`
   **OR**
   - Click below ruler where tab is to be set.
   - Drag tab off ruler to delete it.

## SET MARGINS TO A SECTION OF THE DOCUMENT

1. Position insertion point where margin change is to begin.
2. Click **Insert** ........................... `Alt`+`I`
3. Click **Break** ................................... `B`
4. Click **Continuous** .................. `Alt`+`T`
5. Click **OK** ..................................... `Enter`
6. Set margins as desired (follow steps 1-8 in SET MARGINS USING PAGE SETUP DIALOG BOX).

# 📖 📖 📖 THE INTERNET 📖 📖 📖

The Internet is a global collection of computers and computer networks that exchange information. Networks range from small personal computers to large corporate systems. Colleges, universities, libraries, government bodies, businesses and special interest groups all over the world are part of the Internet. No one knows how many computer networks are linked together to form the Internet.

## INTERNET SERVICES INCLUDE

☎ Electronic Mail. E-mail is probably the most widely used service on the Internet. You can send and receive messages from anyone on the Internet. In addition to sending messages, you can also send a text or graphics file.

☎ Chat. This service allows you to type and send messages instantly to another person or several people. The other person can type their responses and transmit it back to you. The word "chat" is misleading; you are actually doing a good bit of typing!

☎ World Wide Web. This service is made up of documents around the world which are linked to each other through hypertext links. Click on one document which is located in New York, and another document (which may be located in Singapore) appears. The documents may contain pictures, sounds and animation. Reviewing documents that are linked to one another is sometimes referred to as "surfing the web."

## GAINING INTERNET ACCESS

There are several ways to gain Internet access. Your college will provide you with an Internet account, and it is usually without cost. Or, your company has an Internet connection--this, too, is without cost. To gain Internet access from home, you need to sign up with an online service provider such as The Microsoft Network (MSN), America Online, CompuServe, Prodigy or Erol's. Do not be confused. An online service provider is not the Internet--it will, however, allow you to gain access to it.

## THE BASIC COST OF INTERNET ACCESS

Service providers charge a monthly fee to subscribe and then charge you based on the amount of time you are online. Some providers charge a flat monthly rate so that you can "surf the web" as long as you like. College access is free--but then, again, that's really part of the tuition fee. Millions of computer terminals are connected to the Internet, with over 1000 computers being added each day.

## Exercise 22

# ■ Cut and Paste  ■ Drag and Drop  ■ Format Painter

*Standard Toolbar*

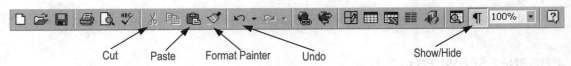

Cut    Paste    Format Painter    Undo    Show/Hide

## NOTES

- **Cut and Paste** and **Drag and Drop** are features that let you move a block of text (a sentence, paragraph, page, or column) within a document or to another document.

### Cut and Paste

- The **Cut** procedure allows you to cut or delete selected text from the screen and temporarily place it on the Clipboard (temporary storage buffer).  The **Paste** procedure allows you to retrieve text from the Clipboard and place it in a desired location in the document.

- There are several procedures to cut and paste text.  *(See keystrokes on page 91.)*

- Information remains on the Clipboard until you cut or copy another selection (or until you exit Windows).  Therefore, you can paste the same selection into many different locations, if desired.

### Drag and Drop

- The **Drag and Drop** method of moving text allows you to move selected text using your mouse. This method is convenient for moving text from one location to another within a document.

- Once text to be moved is selected, place the mouse pointer anywhere on the selected text and click and hold the *left* mouse button as you **drag** the highlighted text to the new location. The mouse pointer changes to a box with a dotted shadow 🖑 to indicate that you are dragging text.

*Hint:  If you hold down the Ctrl key as you drag a selection, you can copy the selection to a new location.*

- When you reach the new location, release the mouse button to **drop** the text into place. Be sure to remove the selection highlight before pressing any key, so that you do not delete your newly moved text.

- When moving a word or sentence, be sure to move the space following the word or sentence. Before you paste the moved text, always place the insertion point immediately to the left of where the text will be reinserted.

- If text was not reinserted at the correct point, you can undo it (Edit, Undo).  It is sometimes necessary to insert or delete spaces, returns, or tabs after completing a move.

- A paragraph is followed by a **paragraph mark** (¶). All paragraph formatting instructions, such as indents and tabs, are stored in the paragraph mark.  Therefore, it is essential that you move the paragraph mark along with the paragraph; otherwise, you will lose the formatting.

- To insure that you include the paragraph mark when moving (or copying) text, click the Show/Hide button ¶ so the paragraph marks are visible in your document.

## Format Painter

- The **Format Painter** feature allows you to copy formatting, such as font face, style, and size, from one part of text to another.

- To copy formatting from one location to another, select the text that contains the format you wish to copy. Then click the **Format Painter** button ⬚ on the Standard toolbar (the I-beam displays a paintbrush) and select the text to receive the format. To copy formatting from one location to several locations, select the text that contains the format you wish to copy, then *double-click* the Format Painter button ⬚. Select the text to receive the format, release the mouse button and select additional text anywhere in the document. To turn off this feature and return the mouse pointer to an I-beam, click the Format Painter button.

- The proofreaders' mark for moving text is: ↩ or ↻.

---

*In this exercise, you will move paragraphs, then format them using the Format Painter feature.*

---

# EXERCISE DIRECTIONS

1. Create a new document.
2. Keyboard the exercise shown in Illustration A, or open 🖫**22TIPS**.
3. Use the default margins and tabs.
4. Begin the exercise At 1".

*To create the Desired Result:*

5. Center the heading, and set the text to sans serif 20-point bold. Press Enter after the heading.
6. Move the paragraphs in alphabetical order (according to the first word in each tip). Use any desired move procedure.
7. Insert a Number and a Tab before each tip.
8. Press the Enter key once at the beginning of each tip explanation. If a number appears, press The Backspace Key. Word assumes you want autonumbering and is turning it on for you. Set a 1" indent from the left and right margin for text below each tip.
9. Set the text for the first tip, CARE FOR YOURSELF, to sans serif 14-point bold.
10. Using Format Painter, select the entire paragraph and copy the character formatting (font size and bolding) to the remaining tips.
11. Set the text below the first tip to italics.
12. Using Format Painter, copy the character formatting to the remaining text below each tip.
13. Spell check.
14. Center the page vertically.
15. Preview your work.
16. Print one copy.
17. Close the file; save as **TIPS**.

---

# KEYSTROKES

## MOVE

**Cut and Paste:**

1. Select text to move.

2. Click **Cut** button ............................ ✂

   **OR**

   Press **Shift + Delete** ........... `Shift` + `Del`

3. Place insertion point where you want text inserted.

4. Click **Paste** button ......................... 📋

   **OR**

   Press **Shift + Insert** ............... `Shift` + `Ins`

**Using the Keyboard:**

1. Select text to move.

2. Press **F2** ......................................... `F2`

3. Position insertion point where you want text inserted.

4. Press **Enter** ................................. `Enter`

**Drag and Drop:**

1. Select text to move.

2. Point to selected text.

3. Hold down left mouse button .......... and drag text to new location.

4. Release mouse button.

✓ *Clicking the Undo icon (Ctrl + Z) immediately after a move operation will restore moved text to its original location.*

## FORMAT PAINTER

1. Select (highlight) paragraph mark containing the formatting you wish to copy.

2. Click Format Painter button .............. ⬚

3. When mouse pointer assumes shape of paintbrush, select paragraphs to receive the new formatting.

## ILLUSTRATION A

SIX TIPS FOR THE WORKAHOLIC

SLOW DOWN.  Make a conscious effort to eat, talk, walk and drive more slowly.  Give yourself extra time to get to appointments so you are not always rushing.

DRAW THE LINE. When you are already overloaded and need more personal time, do not take on any other projects.  You will be just causing yourself more stress.

LEARN TO DELEGATE.  Let others share the load--you don't have to do everything yourself.  You will have more energy and the end result will be better for everyone.

TAKE BREAKS.  Take frequent work breaks:  short walks or meditating for a few minutes can help you unwind and clear your head.

CARE FOR YOURSELF.  Eat properly, get enough sleep and exercise regularly.  Do what you can so that you are healthy, both mentally and physically.

CUT YOUR HOURS.  Be organized, but do not let your schedule run your life.  Also, try to limit yourself to working eight hours a day--and not a minute more.

**DESIRED RESULT**

## SIX TIPS FOR THE WORKAHOLIC

1. **CARE FOR YOURSELF**.

   *Eat properly, get enough sleep and exercise regularly.  Do what you can so that you are healthy, both mentally and physically.*

2. **CUT YOUR HOURS**.

   *Be organized, but do not let your your life.  Also, try to limit yourself to eight hours a day--and not a minute*

3. **DRAW THE LINE**.

   *When you are already overloaded and need more personal time, do not take on any other projects.  You will be just causing yourself more stress.*

4. **LEARN TO DELEGATE**.

   *Let others share the load--you don't have to do everything yourself.  You will have more energy and the end result will be better for everyone.*

5. **SLOW DOWN**.

   *Make a conscious effort to eat, talk, walk and drive more slowly.  Give yourself extra time to get to appointments so you are not always rushing.*

6. **TAKE BREAKS**.

   *Take frequent work breaks:  short meditating for a few minutes can unwind and clear your*

# Exercise 23

## ■ Move Text ■ Shrink to Fit

## NOTES

### Move Text

■ You can use a shortcut key combination to move entire paragraphs up or down. To move a paragraph up, press and hold the Alt+Shift keys and tap the Up Arrow key. To move an entire paragraph down, press and hold the Alt+Shift keys and tap the Down Arrow key. Repeat the keystrokes as necessary to move the paragraph to the desired location.

### Shrink to Fit

■ The **Shrink to Fit** feature lets you shrink a document to fill a desired number of pages.

■ If, for example, your document fills 1¹/₄ pages, but you would like it to fit on one page, Shrink to

Fit automatically adjusts margins, font size, and/or line spacing so that the text will shrink to one page.

■ You may return your document to the original number of pages by selecting Undo Shrink to Fit from the Edit menu.

■ Shrink to Fit may be accessed by selecting Print Preview from the File menu and clicking the Shrink to Fit button 🔳 on the Print Preview toolbar.

*Print Preview Toolbar*

Shrink to fit

---

*In this exercise, you will gain more practice moving text. You will also use the Format Painter feature to format side headings.*

---

## EXERCISE DIRECTIONS

1. Open 📟**CONNECT**, or open 💾**23CONNECT**.

2. Set 1.5" left and right margins for the document.

3. Move the paragraphs as indicated. Use any procedure you desire to move the paragraphs.

4. Change the first side heading to serif 14-point bold italic.

5. Using Format Painter, change the remaining side headings to serif 14-point bold italic.

6. Make the remaining revisions.

7. Preview your work.

8. Use Shrink to Fit to keep all text on one page.

9. Print one copy.

10. Close the file; save the changes.

   ✓ *Note:*   *If your document runs onto a second page, change the line spacing to 1.5".*

## KEYSTROKES

### MOVE AN ENTIRE PARAGRAPH UP OR DOWN

1. Place insertion point in desired paragraph.

2. Press **Alt** + **Shift** + **Up** .. Alt + Shift + ↑

   **OR**

   Press **Alt** + **Shift** + **Down** ........................ Alt + Shift + ↓

3. Repeat steps above, as necessary, to move paragraph to desired location.

### SHRINK TO FIT

1. Click **File** ............................... Alt + F

2. Click **Print Preview** ........................ V

3. Click **Shrink to Fit** button ................. 🔳 on toolbar.

4. Click **Close**

## 📖 📖 📖 THE INTERNET 📖 📖 📖

The Internet is a global collection of computers and computer networks that exchange information. Networks range from small personal computers to large corporate systems. Colleges, universities, libraries, government ~~bodies~~ *agencies*, businesses and special interest groups all over the world are part of the Internet. No one knows how many computer networks are linked together to form the Internet.

### INTERNET SERVICES INCLUDE

☎ Electronic Mail. E-mail is probably the most widely used service on the Internet. You can send and receive messages ~~from anyone on the Internet. In addition to sending messages, you can also~~ *as well as* send a text or graphics file.

☎ Chat. This service allows you to type and send messages instantly to *one* ~~another~~ person or several people. The other person can type their responses and transmit it back to you. The word "chat" is misleading; you are actually doing a good bit of typing!

☎ World Wide Web. This service is made up of documents around the world which are linked to each other through hypertext links. Click on one document which is located in New York, and another document (which may be located in Singapore) appears. The documents may contain pictures, sounds and animation. Reviewing documents that are linked to one another is sometimes referred to as "surfing the web."

*move*

### GAINING INTERNET ACCESS

There are several ways to gain Internet access. Your college will provide you with an Internet account, and it is usually without cost. Or, your company ~~has~~ *might have* an Internet connection--this, too, is without cost. To gain Internet access from home, you need to ~~sign up with~~ *subscribe to* an online service provider such as The Microsoft Network (MSN), America Online, CompuServe, Prodigy or Erol's. Do not be confused. An online service provider is not the Internet--it will, however, allow you to gain access to it.

### THE BASIC COST OF INTERNET ACCESS

Service providers charge a monthly fee to subscribe and then charge you based on the amount of time you are online. Some providers charge a flat monthly rate so that you can "surf the web" as long as you like. College access is free--but then, again, that's really part of the tuition fee. Millions of computer terminals are connected to the Internet, with over 1000 computers being added each day.

# Exercise 24

- **Copy and Paste**
- **Drag and Drop**

## Standard Toolbar

Copy    Paste    Show/Hide

# NOTES

- **Copy and Paste** and **Drag and Drop** are features that let you copy text from one location to another.

- Copying leaves text in its original location while placing a duplicate in a different location in the same document or in another document. (Copying text to another document will be covered in a later lesson.) In contrast, moving removes text from its original location and places it elsewhere.

## Copy and Paste

- The procedure for copying text is similar to the procedure for moving text. (*See keystrokes on page 96.*) Remember, text to be copied must first be highlighted.

- Text may be copied by:

  - Selecting the text to copy, clicking the **Copy** button on the toolbar, placing the insertion point in the desired location, and clicking the **Paste** button on the toolbar, or

  - Selecting the text to copy, pressing Ctrl+C to copy the text, then pressing Ctrl+V to paste the text.

- When text is copied, it remains on the screen while a copy of it is placed on the Clipboard.

- Text remains on the Clipboard until you copy another selection (or until you exit Windows). Therefore, you can paste the same selection into many different locations, if desired.

## Drag and Drop

- Use the drag-and-drop method to copy selected text using your mouse.

- Once text to be copied is selected, place the mouse pointer anywhere on the selected text, and press the Ctrl key while **dragging** text to the new location.

  Then, **drop** a copy of the text into its new location by releasing the mouse button. Be sure to release the mouse button before releasing the Ctrl key.

- As with the Move feature, if text was not copied properly, you can undo it.

- When moving or copying paragraphs with indent formatting, be sure to include the paragraph mark along with the moved or copied text. To ensure that you do, click the Show/Hide button ¶ so the paragraph marks are visible in your document.

> *In this exercise, you will enhance a flyer created earlier using the copy procedure. In addition, you will gain practice using the Format Painter feature.*

# EXERCISE DIRECTIONS

1. Open ⌨️**TIPS**, or open 💾**24TIPS**.

2. Set top and bottom margins to .5".

3. Change the first tip and number to serif 14-point italics.

4. Using Format Painter, change the remaining tips to serif 14-point italics.

5. Press the tab key and insert a diamond symbol to the right of the first tip. Copy the symbol to create a line of diamonds.

6. Click the Show/Hide icon to display your symbols.

7. Copy the line of diamonds from the first tip (including the tab symbol preceding the diamonds and the paragraph mark following the diamonds), and paste it next to the remaining tips.

   ✓ *Note:   If an unwanted number appears, backspace to delete it.*

8. Type and center **To summarize:** in serif 14-point bold at the bottom of the document as shown.

9. Copy each tip as shown.

10. Center-align all tips.

11. Set font to serif 11 point.

12. Add a bullet preceding each tip (use any desired bullet symbol).

13. Set the title to 25 point.

14. Spell check.

15. Preview your work.

16. Print one copy.

17. Close the file; save as **TIPS**.

# KEYSTROKES

### COPY AND PASTE TEXT

1. Select text to copy.

2. Click **Copy** button .......................... 📋
   **OR**
   Press **Ctrl + C**

3. Place insertion point where text will be inserted.

4. Click **Paste** button .......................... 📋
   **OR**
   Press **Ctrl + V**

### DRAG AND DROP

1. Select text to copy.

2. Hold down Ctrl ................................ `Ctrl`
   and point to selected text.

3. Hold down mouse button ............... 🖱️
   and drag text to new location.

4. Release mouse button.

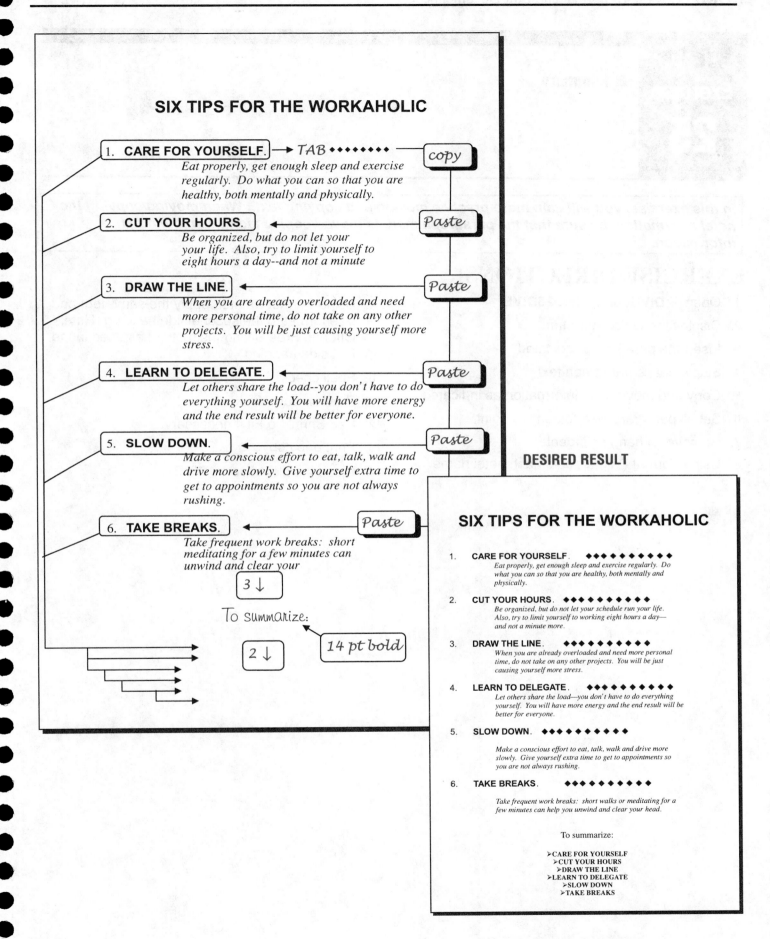

# SIX TIPS FOR THE WORKAHOLIC

1. **CARE FOR YOURSELF.** → *TAB* ♦♦♦♦♦♦♦♦ → copy

   *Eat properly, get enough sleep and exercise regularly. Do what you can so that you are healthy, both mentally and physically.*

2. **CUT YOUR HOURS.** ← Paste

   *Be organized, but do not let your your life. Also, try to limit yourself to eight hours a day--and not a minute*

3. **DRAW THE LINE.** ← Paste

   *When you are already overloaded and need more personal time, do not take on any other projects. You will be just causing yourself more stress.*

4. **LEARN TO DELEGATE.** ← Paste

   *Let others share the load--you don't have to do everything yourself. You will have more energy and the end result will be better for everyone.*

5. **SLOW DOWN.** ← Paste

   *Make a conscious effort to eat, talk, walk and drive more slowly. Give yourself extra time to get to appointments so you are not always rushing.*

6. **TAKE BREAKS.** ← Paste

   *Take frequent work breaks: short meditating for a few minutes can unwind and clear your*

   3 ↓

To summarize:

2 ↓     14 pt bold

## DESIRED RESULT

### SIX TIPS FOR THE WORKAHOLIC

1. **CARE FOR YOURSELF.** ♦♦♦ ♦ ♦ ♦ ♦ ♦ ♦
   *Eat properly, get enough sleep and exercise regularly. Do what you can so that you are healthy, both mentally and physically.*

2. **CUT YOUR HOURS.** ♦♦♦ ♦ ♦ ♦ ♦ ♦ ♦
   *Be organized, but do not let your schedule run your life. Also, try to limit yourself to working eight hours a day— and not a minute more.*

3. **DRAW THE LINE.** ♦♦♦ ♦ ♦ ♦ ♦ ♦ ♦
   *When you are already overloaded and need more personal time, do not take on any other projects. You will be just causing yourself more stress.*

4. **LEARN TO DELEGATE.** ♦♦♦ ♦ ♦ ♦ ♦ ♦ ♦
   *Let others share the load—you don't have to do everything yourself. You will have more energy and the end result will be better for everyone.*

5. **SLOW DOWN.** ♦♦♦ ♦ ♦ ♦ ♦ ♦

   *Make a conscious effort to eat, talk, walk and drive more slowly. Give yourself extra time to get to appointments so you are not always rushing.*

6. **TAKE BREAKS.** ♦♦♦ ♦ ♦ ♦ ♦ ♦

   *Take frequent work breaks: short walks or meditating for a few minutes can help you unwind and clear your head.*

To summarize:

➢CARE FOR YOURSELF
➢CUT YOUR HOURS
➢DRAW THE LINE
➢LEARN TO DELEGATE
➢SLOW DOWN
➢TAKE BREAKS

## Exercise
## 25

■ **Summary**

*In this exercise, you will gain more practice moving and copying text.  When moving/copying the hotel information, be sure that the paragraph mark is moved/copied along with the hotel information.*

# EXERCISE DIRECTIONS

1. Open 🖮**DIVE**, or open 💾**25DIVE**.
2. Display the Office Assistant.
3. Insert the paragraphs indicated.
4. Single space paragraph text.
5. Copy and move hotel information as indicated.
6. Set all paragraph text to serif 12 point.
7. Remove all hanging indents.
8. Using Format Painter, bold each hotel name.

9. Using Format Painter, apply the same font and size format to the second side heading (Hotels Offering Free Diving Instruction) as used in the first side heading.
10. Spell check.
11. Preview your work.
12. Use Shrink to Fit if necessary.
13. Print one copy.
14. Close the file; save as **DIVE**.

**Single space**

# DIVING IN THE CAYMAN ISLANDS

Do you want to see sharks, barracudas, stingrays and angelfish?

The Cayman Islands were discovered by Christopher Columbus

in 1503 and are located south of Cuba.  The Caymans are home to about 25,000

year-around residents.  However, they welcome 200,000 visitors each year.

Most visitors come with masks and flippers in their luggage.

**Insert**

## Hotel/Diving Accommodations:

*Move hotels into alphabetical order*

*Sunset House*, PO Box 479, George Town, Grand Cayman; (809) 555-4767.    **Copy**

*Coconut Harbour*, PO Box 2086, George Town, Grand Cayman; (809) 555-7468.

*Red Sail Sports*, PO Box 1588, George Town, Grand Cayman; (809) 555-7965.

*Cayman Diving Lodge*, PO Box 11, East End, Grand Cayman; (809) 555-7555.    **Copy**

*Anchorage View*, PO Box 2123, Grand Cayman; (809) 555-4209.

¶Before you descend the depths of the ocean, it is very important that you have a few lessons on the don'ts of diving.  Don't touch that coral.  Don't come up to the surface too fast holding your breath.  If you do, your lungs will explode.
¶Now, you are ready to jump in!
¶Here are some hotel suggestions.

Hotels Offering Free Diving Instruction:

## Exercise 26 ■ Thesaurus

## NOTES

### Thesaurus

■ The **Thesaurus** feature lists the meanings, synonyms, and antonyms (if any) of a desired word and also indicates the part of speech of each meaning.

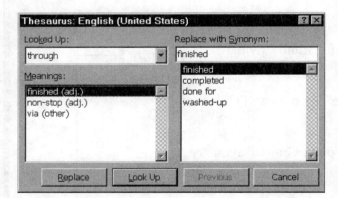

■ Note the Thesaurus dialog box in which the word "through" was looked up. You may replace a word in your document with a word listed in the thesaurus by clicking the desired meaning, then selecting the desired synonym (or antonym) and clicking the Replace button. It is sometimes necessary to edit the new word so it fits properly in the sentence *(EXAMPLE: Singular/Plural endings).*

■ Select the word you want to look up and press Shift+F7 to open the Thesaurus dialog box.

■ You can also select the Tools menu, select Language, then Thesaurus to open the dialog box.

✓ *Note: If Thesaurus does not appear on the Language submenu, you will have to install the Thesaurus.*

*In this exercise, you will format a report and use the Thesaurus feature to substitute highlighted words.*

## EXERCISE DIRECTIONS

1. Create a new document.

2. Keyboard the exercise on the right, or open 🖫**26SOD**.

3. Set 1" left and right margins.

4. Set a 1" first-line indent.

5. Begin the exercise At 1".

6. Keyboard the exercise exactly as shown, including the circled misspelled words and usage errors.

7. Set line spacing to double after typing the title.

8. Center and bold the main title in serif 12-point bold. Set the body text to serif 10 point.

9. Use Format Painter to bold and italicize text throughout the document.

10. Use the Grammar Check feature to grammar and spell check the document. Make the necessary corrections.

11. Use the Thesaurus feature to substitute the highlighted words.

12. Preview your work.

13. Print one copy.

14. Close the file; save as **SOD**.

**GREENTHUMB LANDSCAPE SERVICE**
OPERATING EXPENSE ANALYSIS
199-

We have seen many changes at Greenthumb Landscape Service this year.  An explanation of the Quarterly Income Statement for 199- is worthwhile. After much analysis we have decided to place our advertising with our local radio station, WDOV.  We have developed a comprehensive advertising program that runs year-round in an effort to develop business during our lighter winter months.

***The lower expense and income figures for the first quarter*** reflects ***the closing of our service center*** during the month of February.  The policy to close in February is under review for this winter, since we hae developed and sold additional contracts for snow removal. The executive committee will be meeting to develop a vacation system for full-time employees so that the center is staffed at all times.  For ***winter services***, we are contemplating the purchase of another snow removal vehicle to increase our capabillity. We are aware that our snow handling equiptment must be keep in good repair to avoid the breakdowns we experienced last winter. These factors will cause increases in repair and depreciation expenses for next year which should be offset by our increased revenues.

Our ***salaries expenses*** varies with the season.  We are continuing the practice of maintaining a core full-time staff while hiring additional part-time staff for the peak service periods of the year.  This has worked well in the past; however, we are being pressured to increase benifits for our full-time employees.

The high expenses for ***supplies*** in the third quarter reflect the increase in our full landscaping service.

We are always striving to improve our service to our customers and community, and continue to monitor our expenditures while increasing our client base.

# KEYSTROKES

**THESAURUS**

1. Place insertion point on word to look up.
   **OR**
   Select desired word.
2. Press **Shift+F7** ..................... `Shift`+`F7`
   **OR**
   a. Click **Tools** ........................ `Alt`+`T`

b. Click **Language** ........................... `L`
c. Click **Thesaurus** ......................... `T`
3. Select .......................... `Alt`+`M`, `↓`
   desired meaning.
4. Select .......................... `Alt`+`S`, `↓`
   desired synonym.
   **OR**

Click **Look Up** ........................ `Alt`+`L`
to list synonyms for selected meaning.
   **OR**
   Select **Antonyms**.
5. Select desired synonym or antonym.
6. Click **Replace** ........................ `Alt`+`R`

# Exercise 27

■ **Find and Replace Text** ■ **Hyphenate Text**
■ **Select Browse Object**

## NOTES

### Find Text

■ The **Find** feature scans your document and searches for occurrences of specified text, symbols, or formatting. Once the desired text or formatting is found, it can be edited or replaced.

■ Find may be accessed by selecting <u>F</u>ind from the <u>E</u>dit menu. When you first access the Find feature, the following Find and Replace dialog box appears.

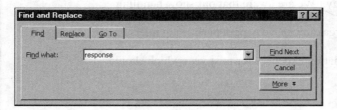

■ This abbreviated version of the Find and Replace dialog box is useful for a quick search. Click the <u>M</u>ore button to access additional Find options that will let you customize your search.

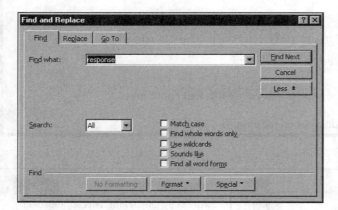

■ Find can also be accessed by clicking the Select Browse Object button on the vertical scroll bar and clicking the Find icon.

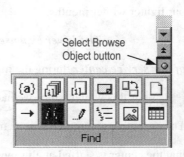

Select Browse Object button

Find

■ Word can be instructed to find separate, whole words rather than characters embedded in other words by selecting the Find whole words onl<u>y</u> option. For example, if this option is *not* selected, a search for the word "and" would find not only "and" but also ***sand, cand**y, **Sand**usky, **and**roid*, etc. It can be helpful to select the Find whole words onl<u>y</u> option, particularly when searching for short words.

■ The Sounds li<u>k</u>e check box looks up different homonyms (words that sound alike, but are spelled differently) of a word. If you search for the word *sight*, you will also find *cite* and *site*.

■ The Find all word for<u>m</u>s check box looks for all the different grammatical forms of a word.

■ The <u>S</u>earch text box contains options for the direction of the search. Word can search a document from the insertion point Down or Up, or it can search the entire document—All.

### Replace Text

■ The **Replace** feature allows you to locate all occurrences of certain text and *replace* it with different text. In addition to text, you may also search for and replace occurrences of special characters such as tab symbols or paragraph marks.

- Replace may be accessed by selecting Replace from the Edit menu or by clicking the Replace tab in the Find and Replace dialog box. Click More to view all Replace options. In this dialog box, indicate what you wish to find and what you wish to replace.

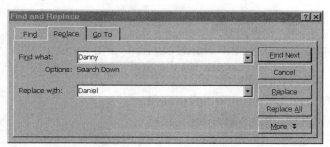

- To replace all occurrences of text or special characters without confirmation, click Replace All. To find the next occurrence, click Find Next, then click Cancel or Replace.

- To search for and replace special characters, click the Special button in the Find and Replace dialog box, and select the desired character from the pop-up list *(see below)*.

- Turn on the Show/Hide codes feature ¶ to assist you when searching for and replacing special characters.

## Hyphenate Text

- **Hyphenating** text produces a tighter right margin. If justified text is hyphenated, the sentences will have smaller gaps between words. Turn on the hyphenation feature when you justify text.

- To automatically hyphenate your document, select Language, Hyphenation from the Tools menu. In the Hyphenation dialog box which follows, click the Automatically hyphenate document check box.

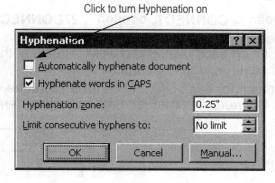

- You may change the width of the space a word must span before hyphenation divides it by changing the Hyphenation zone. *Increase* the percentage of the zone to hyphenate *fewer* words; decrease to hyphenate *more* words.

- If you wish to limit the number of consecutive hyphens, indicate the desired number in the Limit consecutive hyphens to text box.

- Word adds hyphens according to its rules without asking for confirmation from the user.

- To insert manual hyphens, click the Manual button. In the Manual Hyphenation dialog box which follows, you will be able to:
  - accept the suggested hyphenation
  - adjust where it will appear in the word, or
  - cancel and return to the document

  - **Regular**—Inserted with the Hyphen key. Use for words in which the hyphen should *always* appear in the word. A compound word like "sister-in-law" should always retain the hyphen.

  - **Optional hyphen**—Inserted by pressing Ctrl+Hyphen. Use for words that should be hyphenated *only* when they must be divided at the end of a line.

  - **Non-breaking hyphen**—Inserted by pressing Ctrl+Shift+Hyphen. Use when parts of the word connected by the hyphen are *never* to be *separated* at the end of a line. Examples of this kind of word include hyphenated surnames (Alice Harris-Gomez) and negative numbers.

*In this exercise, you will search for the highlighted words. The Find feature will quickly place the insertion point on those words so you can substitute them using the Thesaurus feature. You will use the Replace feature to find and replace words in the document and you will use the hyphenate feature to produce a tighter right margin.*

# EXERCISE DIRECTIONS

1. Open ⌨**CONNECT**, or open 💾**27CONNECT**.
2. Use the Find feature to place your insertion point on each highlighted word. Then use the Thesaurus feature to replace each word.
3. Search for each occurrence (except for the title) of the word "Internet" and replace with *Internet*.

4. Search for the word "service" and replace with "feature" (except for the first word of the last paragraph).
5. Hyphenate the document.
6. Print one copy.
7. Close the file; save as **CONNECT**.

---

### 📖 📖 📖 THE INTERNET 📖 📖 📖

The Internet is a global collection of computers and computer networks that exchange information. Networks range from small personal computers to large corporate systems. Colleges, universities, libraries, government agencies, businesses and special interest groups all over the world are part of the Internet. No one knows how many computer networks are linked together to form the Internet. Millions of computer terminals are connected to the Internet, with over 1000 computers being added each day.

### *INTERNET SERVICES INCLUDE*

☎Chat. This service allows you to type and send messages instantly to one person or several people. The other person can type their responses and transmit it back to you. The word "chat" is misleading; you are actually doing a good bit of typing!

☎Electronic Mail. E-mail is probably the most widely used service on the Internet. You can send and receive messages as well as send a text or graphics file.

☎World Wide Web. This service is made up of documents around the world which are linked to each other through hypertext links. Click on one document which is located in New York, and another document (which may be located in Singapore) appears. The documents may contain pictures, sounds and animation. Reviewing documents that are linked to one another is sometimes referred to as "surfing the web."

### *GAINING INTERNET ACCESS*

There are several ways to gain Internet access. Your college will provide you with an Internet account, and it is usually without cost. Or, your company might have an Internet connection--this, too, is without cost. To gain Internet access from home, you need to subscribe to an online service provider such as The Microsoft Network (MSN), America Online, CompuServe, Prodigy or Erol's. Do not be confused. An online service provider is not the Internet--it will, however, allow you to gain access to it.

### *THE BASIC COST OF INTERNET ACCESS*

Service providers charge a monthly fee to subscribe and then charge you based on the amount of time you are online. Some providers change a flat monthly rate so that you can "surf the web" as long as you like. College access is free--but then, again, that's really part of the tuition fee.

# KEYSTROKES

## FIND TEXT

*CTRL + F*

1. Click **Select Browse Object** ............... 🔘
2. Click **F**ind ................................... 🔍

   **OR**

   a. Click **E**dit ........................... `Alt`+`E`
   b. Click **F**ind ........................... `F`
3. Click **Fi**nd what ..................... `Alt`+`N`
4. Type desired search text ................. *text*
5. Click **More** ........................... `Alt`+`M`
   if necessary, to display the following options.
6. Select desired Search options:
   - **Match case** ...................... `Alt`+`H`
   - **Find whole words only** ...... `Alt`+`Y`
   - **Use wildcards** ................. `Alt`+`U`
   - **Sounds like** ..................... `Alt`+`K`
   - **Find all word forms** .......... `Alt`+`M`
7. Select a search direction ............................. `Alt`+`S`
   - Click **All** ........................... `A`
     to search entire document.

   **OR**

   - Click **Up** ........................... `U`
     to search from insertion point to beginning of document.

   **OR**

   - Click **Down** ........................... `D`
     to search from insertion point to end of document.
8. Click **F**ind **Next** ..................... `Alt`+`F`

   **OR**

   Press **Enter** ........................... `Enter`
   to find next occurrence of search text.
9. Click **Cancel** ........................... `Esc`
   to return to document at point where most recently located search text appears.

## REPLACE TEXT OR SPECIAL CHARACTERS

*CTRL + H*

1. Click **E**dit ........................... `Alt`+`E`
2. Click **R**eplace ........................... `E`
3. Click **More** ........................... `Alt`+`M`
   if necessary, to display all the Replace options.
4. Click **Fi**nd what ..................... `Alt`+`N`
5. Type desired search text ................. *text*

   **OR**

   Click **Special** ........................... `Alt`+`E`

   Select special character .......... `↓`, `↑`
6. Select **No Formatting** ............ `Alt`+`T`
   if necessary, so Word does not search for formatting.
7. Click **Replace with** ................. `Alt`+`I`
8. Type replacement text ..................... *text*

   **OR**

   a. Click **Special** ..................... `Alt`+`E`
   b. Select special character .......... `↓`, `↑`
9. Click one of the following.
   - **Match case** ...................... `Alt`+`H`
   - **Find whole words only** ...... `Alt`+`Y`
   - **Use wildcards** ................. `Alt`+`U`
   - **Sounds like** ..................... `Alt`+`K`
   - **Find All Word forms** .......... `Alt`+`M`
10. Click **F**ind **Next** ..................... `Alt`+`F`
    to find next occurrence.
11. Click **R**eplace ........................ `Alt`+`R`
    to replace this occurrence.

    **OR**

    Click **Replace All** .................. `Alt`+`A`
    to replace all occurrences of search text.
12. Click **F**ind **Next** ..................... `Alt`+`F`
    as necessary to search through entire document.
13. Click **Cancel** ........................... `Esc`
    to return to document at point where most recently located search text appears.

## HYPHENATE (AUTOMATIC OR MANUAL)

1. Select text to hyphenate.

   **OR**

   Place insertion point where hyphenation will begin.
2. Click **Tools** ........................... `Alt`+`T`
3. Click **Language** ........................... `L`
4. Click **Hyphenation** ........................... `H`
5. Do one of the following:
   a. Click **Automatically** ........... `Alt`+`A`
      **hyphenate document** check box.
   b. Click **OK** ........................... `Enter`

   **OR**

   a. Click **Manual** ..................... `Alt`+`M`
      to have Word prompt for each hyphen.
   b. Click **Yes** ........................... `Alt`+`Y`
      to accept suggested hyphen.

   **OR**

   Click **No** ........................... `Alt`+`N`
   to reject suggested hyphen.

   **OR**

   a. Place the insertion point where you want hyphen inserted.
   b. Click **Yes** ........................... `Alt`+`Y`
6. Press **Cancel** ........................... `Esc`
   to end hyphenation process.

   **OR**

   Click **OK** ........................... `Enter`
   when hyphenation is complete.

## Exercise 28

- **The Outline Feature**  ■ **Create an Outline**
- **Enter Outline Text**  ■ **Edit an Outline**

*Outlining Toolbar*

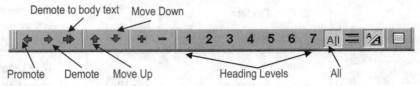

Demote to body text  Move Down

Promote    Demote  Move Up        Heading Levels        All

## NOTES

### The Outline Feature

- A **traditional outline** is used to organize information about a subject before you begin writing a report or delivering a speech.

- An outline contains many topics and subtopics, or levels. The **Outline Feature** automatically formats each level of topic and subtopic differently. Some levels are bolded, some are italicized, and some appear in different font size. Word allows up to nine different levels.

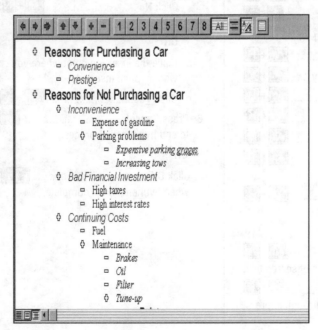

### Create an Outline

- **To create an outline**, Select Outline from the View menu or click the Outline View button 🗒. Outline view allows you to see your document

in an outline format and provides an Outlining toolbar to make outlining tasks easier.

### Enter Outline Text

- Type an outline in Outline view as you would normally. Level formatting styles are applied as you type. Use the Tab key to advance from level to level. Each level is preceded by a heading symbol, ➕ or ➖.

- To number and letter the topics and subtopics as you would in a traditional outline, you must use a separate procedure. Select Bullets and Numbering from the Format menu, then click the Outline Numbered tab. Select the desired numbering style, and click OK.

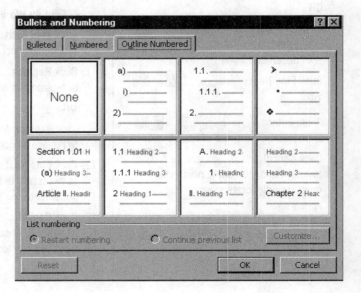

## Edit an Outline

■ To select a topic and its associated paragraph, position your insertion point on the **heading symbol** until it changes to a four-headed arrow, and click the left mouse button.

■ To move a heading in an outline without affecting the level or rank, click the Move Up button 🔼 or the Move Down button 🔽 on the Outlining toolbar. When you use this procedure, only the heading itself moves up or down; any subheadings or subtext under the heading will remain in their original positions.

■ To move all information under a heading (subheadings and subtext), select the heading symbol, then click the Move Up or Move Down button. Or you may select the heading symbol and drag the text to its new location. When you drag text, the mouse pointer changes to a double-headed arrow, and a guideline moves with the mouse to assist you in positioning the heading.

■ You may change the level of text by **promoting** or **demoting** it. To convert text to a lower level subheading (for example, from level II to level B), you must click the *Demote* button ➡ on the Outlining toolbar. To return the heading to a higher level (for example from level B, to level II), you must click the *Promote* button ⬅ on the Outlining toolbar.

## Collapse and Expand Outlines

■ You may collapse (hide) or expand (display) as many levels of headings as you desire by clicking the appropriate heading button on the Outlining toolbar. Clicking the All button displays all heading levels, the default in Word.

| 1 | 2 | 3 | 4 | 5 | 6 | 7 | All |
|---|---|---|---|---|---|---|-----|

---

*In Part I of this exercise, you will create a topic outline. The outline you create will contain five levels. The keystroke procedures are provided in the exercise directions for this first outline exercise. In Part II of this exercise, you will edit the outline.*

---

# EXERCISE DIRECTIONS

**Part I**

1. Create a new document.

2. Display the Office Assistant.

3. Set the left margin to 1.75". Begin the exercise at the top of your screen.

4. Click the Outline View button 🔲, or select View, Outline to change to Outline view.

5. Create the topic outline shown on the following page.

6. Key first level heading, *Reasons for Purchasing a Car*.

   ✓ Note: Do not type the numbers or letters that precede the headings; you will use the automatic Numbering feature to add them after completing the outline.

7. Press the Enter key, then the Tab key.

8. Key the second level heading, *Convenience*.

9. Press the Enter key.

10. Key the next second level heading, *Prestige*.

11. Press the Enter key.

12. Click the Promote button ⬅.

13. Key the next level heading, *Reasons for Not Purchasing a Car*. Press the Enter key.

14. Key the remaining headings, promoting or demoting as necessary. *Do not* press the Enter key after the last heading, *Timing*.

15. Insert numbers and letters in the outline using the format shown in Part I. (Highlight the text to receive the numbers and letters. Select Format, Bullets and Numbering. Click Outline Numbered Tab, select the desired format, and click OK.)

16. Click the Heading Level button ② that will display only two levels of headings. Click each Heading Level icon from 3 through 5 to see the effect on your outline. Click the All button ⓐ to reset the default to display all headings.

17. Spell check.

18. Using the Properties feature, fill out the following summary information about your document:

    Title: .. Purchasing vs. Not Purchasing a Car
    Subject: ....................... Comparison of each
    Author:............................................Your name
    Manager: ....................... Your supervisor or
    teacher's name
    Company:......Your company or school name
    Category....................................Economics
    Keyboards: .........Brakes, Oil, Inconvenience
    Comments:         Headings were numbered
    and lettered

19. Preview your work. (The document will display as 2 or 3 pages.)

20. Print one copy from Outline view.

21. Save the file; name it **CARS**.

22. Do not close the document window.

**Part II**

1. Move heading B. Hazards and the numbered items below it after the items in heading D. Continuing Costs.

2. Print one copy.

3. Close the file; save the changes.

4. Close the document window.

# KEYSTROKES

## CREATE AN OUTLINE

**To switch to Outline view:**

  a. Click **View** ......................... `Alt`+`V`

  b. Click **Outline**............................... `O`

  **OR**

Click **Outline** view button................ 🗏

1. Type topic or sentence heading.

2. Press **Enter**................................... `Enter`

3. Type next heading.

4. Press **Enter**................................... `Enter`
   to keep new heading at same
   level as previous heading.

  **OR**

Click **Demote** button...................... ➡
to create a lower level heading.

  **OR**

Click **Promote** button...................... ⬅
to create a higher level heading.

## NUMBER AN OUTLINE

1. Switch to **Outline** view ...... `Alt`+`V`, `O`
   if necessary.

2. Highlight text to receive number and letters.

3. Click **Format**........................... `Alt`+`O`

4. Click **Bullets and Numbering** .......... `N`

5. Click **Outlined Numbered**....... `Alt`+`U`

6. Click desired format.

7. Click **OK** .................................... `Enter`

## REMOVE NUMBERS FROM ALL HEADINGS

1. Switch to **Outline** view... `Alt`+`V`, `O`
   if necessary.
   *(See **CREATE AN OUTLINE**, left.)*

2. Place insertion point in section from which numbering will be removed.

3. Click **Format** ......................... `Alt`+`O`

4. Click **Bullets and Numbering**.......... `N`

5. Click **Outlined Numbered** ...... `Alt`+`U`

6. Click **None**.

## REMOVE NUMBERS FROM A SINGLE HEADING

1. Select the heading.

2. Click **Demote to Body Text** ............ ➡
   button on Outlining toolbar.

## HIDE OR DISPLAY HEADING LEVELS

1. Switch to **Outline** view ... `Alt`+`V`, `O`
   if necessary.

2. Click appropriate **Heading Level** button to display desired number of levels.

  **OR**

Click **All** button ............................. `All`
to display all heading levels.

## EDIT HEADINGS AND TEXT

1. Switch to **Outline** view ... `Alt`+`V`, `O`
   if necessary.

2. Drag heading symbol........... ✛ or ▭
   to desired location.

  **OR**

Select heading, subheadings and text to move.

3. Click **Move Up** button ..................... ⬆

  **OR**

Click **Move Down** button................. ⬇
as often as necessary to move heading to desired location.

I.  **Reasons for Purchasing a Car**
  A. *Convenience*
  B. *Prestige*
II. **Reasons for Not Purchasing a Car**
  A. *Inconvenience*
    1. Expense of gasoline
    2. Parking problems
      a) **Expensive parking garages**
      b) **Increasing tows**
  B. *Hazards*
    1. Possibility of accidents
    2. Unpredictable weather
  C. *Bad Financial Investment*
    1. High taxes
    2. High interest rates
  D. *Continuing Costs*
    1. Fuel
    2. Maintenance
      a) **Brakes**
      b) **Oil**
      c) **Filter**
      d) **Tune-up**
        (1) Points
        (2) Plugs
        (3) Timing

I.  **Reasons for Purchasing a Car**
  A. *Convenience*
  B. *Prestige*
II. **Reasons for Not Purchasing a Car**
  A. *Inconvenience*
    1. Expense of gasoline
    2. Parking problems
      a) **Expensive parking garages**
      b) **Increasing tows**
  B. *Hazards*
    1. Possibility of accidents
    2. Unpredictable weather
  C. *Bad Financial Investment*
    1. High taxes
    2. High interest rates
  D. *Continuing Costs*
    1. Fuel
    2. Maintenance
      a) **Brakes**
      b) **Oil**
      c) **Filter**
      d) **Tune-up**
        (1) Points
        (2) Plugs
        (3) Timing

**Exercise**

**29**

■ **Styles** ■ **Create a Style/Edit a Style**

## NOTES

### Styles

■ A style is a collection of formats you can assign to selected text. When you created your outline in the last exercise, Word assigned the styles available in Word. Click the Style list box to see the styles that Word provides.

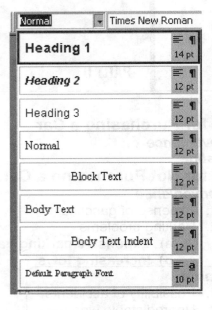

■ Heading 1 applies a 14-point Arial bold and left aligned font; Heading 2 applies a 12-point Arial bold italics font; Heading 3 applies a 12-point Arial font. Normal applies the default font in the default font size.

### Create a Style/Edit a Style

■ Suppose you want to create a style which contains a 16-point *script* font. You can do so by selecting the text on which you wish to base your style, clicking the Style list box in the Formatting toolbar, and replacing the current style name with one you provide. Pressing Enter will add that name to the Style list. Whenever you subsequently want to apply this new style to text, select the text, click the Styles list, and select the new name.

■ To keep the same indents for your headings, you must edit a Word style; that is, change the characteristics of Heading 1, Heading 2, or Heading 3, but not their names.

■ To make these changes, select Style from the Format menu. In the Style dialog box that follows, select the style you wish to modify and click Modify.

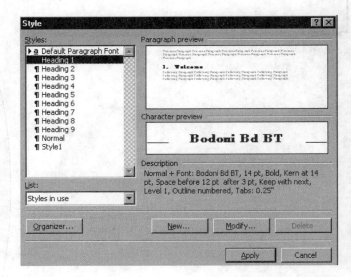

- In the Modify Style dialog box that follows, click Format and select Font from the pop-up list. Make the desired changes to the font, style and/or size. Click OK to return to the exercise. All headings based on the Heading 1 style will change to reflect the new style.

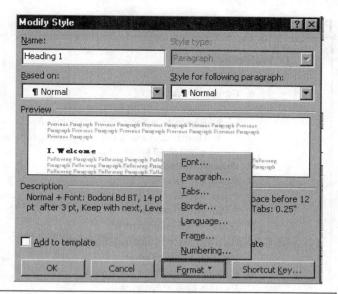

*In Part I of this exercise, you will apply a new heading style and gain more practice creating a topic outline. In Part II of this exercise, you will edit the outline. This outline will eventually be used to create a presentation in PowerPoint.*

# EXERCISE DIRECTIONS

## Part I

1. Create a new document.

2. Set the left margin to 1.5". Begin the exercise at the top of the screen.

3. Switch to Outline view.

4. Create the topic outline shown in Part I on the next page.

   ✓ Note: Do not type the numerals or letters that precede the headings; you will use the automatic Numbering feature to add them after completing the outline.

5. Use the Bullets and Numbering feature to insert numbers and letters in the outline using the format shown.

6. Spell check.

7. Preview your work.

8. Print one copy.

9. Save the file; name it **GREEN.**

10. Do not close the document window.

## Part II

1. Move IV. information (Company Mission) to become III.

2. Change Heading 1 style to Britannic Bold, 14-point bold.

3. Print one copy.

4. Close the file; save the changes.

5. Close the document window.

# KEYSTROKES

### EDIT A WORD STYLE

1. Click the Styles list box and select the style you wish to change.

2. Click **F**ormat ..........................

3. Click **Style** ..................................... S

4. Click **Modify** .......................... Alt + M

5. Click **Format** ........................... Alt + O

6. Click **Font** ..................................... F

7. Make desired changes.

8. Click **OK** ..................................... Enter

**PART I**

I.  **Welcome**

II.  **Overview**

    *A. Company history*

        1.  Started by Peter Moss in 1965

        2.  Began as a snow removal company

        3.  Diversifying into a full landscaping service with a year-round advertising program.

    *B. Organizational structure*

    *C. Company mission*

    *D. Sales trends*

    *E. Employee benefits*

    *F. Questions and answers*

III.  **Greenthumb Landscaping Service**

    *A. John Moss, President*

    *B. Wendy Hynes, Vice President*

    *C. Pamela Leigh, Finance*

    *D. Matt Chasin, Customer Service*

IV. **Company Mission**

    *A. To design quality landscapes in this city*

    *B. To maintain quality landscapes of all customers*

V.  **Sales Trends**

VI. **Employee Benefits**

    *A. Health Benefits*

        1.  Life Insurance

        2.  Medical, dental, optical

            a)  **GHI**

            b)  **Major Medical**

    *B. Commissions and Bonus*

    *C. Vacation and Sick Leave*

        1.  Vacation:  2 weeks after 12 months

        2.  Sick leave:  2.5 days earned each month

        3.  Extra provisions for employees who work winters

VII. **Questions and Answers**

**PART II**

I.  **Welcome**

II.  **Overview**

    *A. Company history*

        1.  Started by Peter Moss in 1965

        2.  Began as a snow removal company

        3.  Diversifying into a full landscaping service with a year-round advertising program.

    *B. Organizational structure*

    *C. Company mission*

    *D. Sales trends*

    *E. Employee benefits*

    *F. Questions and answers*

III.  **Greenthumb Landscaping Service**

    *A. John Moss, President*

    *B. Wendy Hynes, Vice President*

    *C. Pamela Leigh, Finance*

    *D. Matt Chasin, Customer Service*

IV. **Company Mission**

    *A. To design quality landscapes in this city*

    *B. To maintain quality landscapes of all customers*

V.  **Sales Trends**

VI. **Employee Benefits**

    *A. Health Benefits*

        1.  Life Insurance

        2.  Medical, dental, optical

            a)  **GHI**

            b)  **Major Medical**

    *B. Commissions and Bonus*

    *C. Vacation and Sick Leave*

        1.  Vacation:  2 weeks after 12 months

        2.  Sick leave:  2.5 days earned each month

        3.  Extra provisions for employees who work winters

VII. **Questions and Answers**

## Exercise 30

### ■ Summary

*In this exercise, you will create a one-page report. You will also gain practice using the Thesaurus, Grammar Check, and Find/Replace features.*

## EXERCISE DIRECTIONS

1. Create a new document.

2. Use the default margins and tabs.

3. Create a report from the text shown below. Keyboard the exercise exactly as indicated, including the circled usage errors, or open 💾**30BRANCH**.

4. Center and bold the main title in serif 14 point bold. Set the secondary titles to 12 point and center them.

5. Use the Grammar Check feature to grammar and spell check the document. Make the necessary corrections. In the first sentence, do not add the hyphen Word suggests, since three quarters here is not a fraction. Accept Word's *second* suggestion in correcting "Companys."

6. Use the thesaurus feature to replace the highlighted words.

7. Search for each occurrence of James and replace it with Jim.

8. Hyphenate the document.

9. Preview your work.

10. Print one copy.

11. Close the file; save as **BRANCH**.

---

WOODWORKS FURNITURE COMPANY
COMPENSATION SUMMARY
Today's date
A review of the first three quarters of this year for the Oxford branch indicates the addition of a new employee, James Thompson. #The addition of James Thompson increases our expenses at a difficult economic juncture of WoodWorks Furniture Company. However, it is expected that there will be an increase in sales because of numerous community contracts that have just been signed. Since community-based projects are now within James Thompson's sales territory, it is expected that his total compensation will increase considerably by the end of the year, which will offset the increase in salary expense. #The process of compiling expense data from all the Woodworks Furniture Companys stores will aid in long-term planning for our organization. #Early indications shows that total sales has picked up in the corporate sector. A detailed data analyses report will be forthcoming in the next quarter.

## Exercise 31

- ■ **Hard vs. Soft Page Breaks** ■ **Section Breaks**
- ■ **Headers/Footers** ■ **Page Numbers**

## NOTES

### Hard vs. Soft Page Breaks

- Word assumes you are working on a standard page measuring 8.5" wide x 11" long. Remember, Word is defaulted to leave a 1" top and 1" bottom margin. Therefore, there are 9" of vertical space on a standard page for entering text.

- The At indicator indicates how far you are from the top of the page. When you are working At 9.6", you are working on the last line of the page. Therefore, when you enter text beyond 9.7", Word automatically ends one page and starts another.

- When Word ends the page automatically, it is referred to as a **soft page break**. To end the page before 9.7", you can enter a hard page break by pressing Ctrl+Enter. In Normal view, a hard page break is indicated by a dotted horizontal line across the screen with the words *Page Break* in the center. In Page Layout view, the **hard page break** looks like a solid gray horizontal line of paper. When you insert a hard page break, Word automatically adjusts the soft page breaks that follow.

- Once the insertion point is below the page break line, the Page indicator on the status line displays Page 2 and the At indicator displays At 1".

### Section Breaks

- By default, a document contains one section. But Word allows you to break your document into multiple sections, so you can format each section differently.

For example, if you wish to apply different margin settings to different parts of your document, you can create a section break, change the margins for that section, then create another section break and return your margins to another setting after the break. Creating section breaks is like creating a document within a document.

- To create a section break, position the insertion point where you want the break and select <u>B</u>reak from the <u>I</u>nsert menu. In the Break dialog box which follows, select a desired section break option. Each option will create a break in a different location of your document.

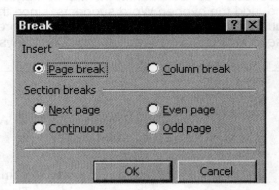

- <u>N</u>ext Page creates a new section on the next page.

- Con<u>t</u>inuous creates a new section at the insertion point.

- <u>E</u>ven Page creates a new section on the next even-numbered page (usually a left-facing page).

- <u>O</u>dd Page creates a new section on the next right-facing page.

- Since section break marks store section formatting (the same way paragraph marks store paragraph formatting), removing a section break may also remove all section formatting for the section that precedes the break. To remove a section break, position the insertion point on the section break and press the Delete key.

- A hard page break may be deleted, which will allow text below the hard page break to flow into the previous page, as room allows. You may also select a hard page break and drag it to a new position.

## Headers and Footers

- A multiple-page letter requires a heading on the second and succeeding pages. The heading should include the name of the addressee (to whom the letter is going), the page number, and the date. To include the heading on the second and succeeding pages, a header may be created.

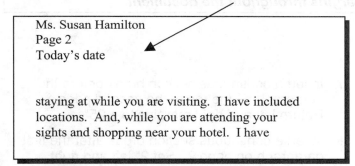

Header with page number and date

Ms. Susan Hamilton
Page 2
Today's date

staying at while you are visiting. I have included locations. And, while you are attending your sights and shopping near your hotel. I have

- A **header** is the same text appearing at the top of every page or every other page, while a footer is the same text appearing at the bottom of every page or every other page.

- After you type the desired header or footer once, the Header/Footer feature will automatically insert it on every page or on specific pages of your document.

- To see headers, footers, or page numbers on your screen, you must be in either Page Layout view or Print Preview. Although headers, footers, and page numbers do not appear on screen in Normal or Outline views, they will print.

- The header is defaulted to print .5" from the top of the page; the footer is defaulted to print .5" from the bottom of the page. The header/footer printing position may be changed, if desired.

  ✓ Note: Headers, footers, and page numbers usually appear on the second and succeeding pages of a letter or report; they generally do not appear on the first page.

- To add headers or footers, select <u>H</u>eader and Footer from the <u>V</u>iew menu. The Header box and the Header and Footer Dialog box display. Enter your header in the Header box. (*See below.*)

- If you wish to include a date or the time as header/footer text, use the Date button 🗓 and/or Time button 🕐 on the Header and Footer toolbar to insert these items.

- Page numbers and total numbers of pages can be added to headers or footers by clicking the Page Number button and/or the Insert Number of Pages button on the Header and Footer toolbar. Page numbers may be positioned in the header or footer by pressing Tab to get to the center tab and pressing Tab again to get to the right alignment tab.

*Header and Footer Toolbar*

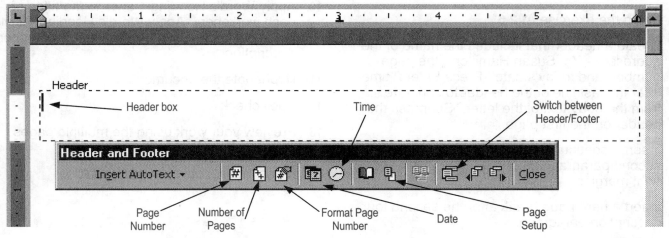

- To suppress the header, footer, or page number on the first page, select the Page Setup button 📖 on the Header and Footer toolbar, select the Layout tab, and click the Different first page check box.

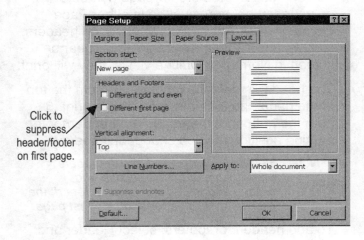

Click to suppress header/footer on first page.

**Page Numbers**

- The Page Numbering feature allows you to insert page numbers independent of headers and footers and indicate where on the printed page the page number should appear: in the upper or lower corners (left or right) or centered at the top or bottom of the page. *(See Page Numbering Placement, Exercise 34.)*

- If you plan to use only page numbers (not headers or footers), use the separate Page Numbering feature. If you plan to insert a header or a footer and a page number, it is easier to use the Header and Footer feature to enter the header/footer along with the page numbers.

- Headers, footers, and page numbers may be inserted before or after the document is typed.

*In this exercise, you will create a two-page letter and insert a header as the second-page heading. You will also create section breaks and change margins throughout the document.*

# EXERCISE DIRECTIONS

1. Create a new document.

2. Keyboard the exercise on the following page as shown, or open 🖫**31SEMINA**.

   - Use the default margins and tabs.

   - Type the company name at 1". Set it to 30-point bold. (Change the font size to 10 point before pressing the Enter key.)

   - Set the address information to serif 10 point italics. Insert any Wingding symbol in the address as shown.

3. Begin the exercise At 2.6".

4. Create a header that includes the name of the addressee (Ms. Susan Hamilton), the page number, and today's date. Press Enter 2 times after the last line of the header to separate it from the body text of the letter. Suppress the header on the first page.

5. Insert a continuous section break after the second paragraph as shown. Set 2" left and right margins.

6. Insert a hard page break after the second tour description paragraph.

7. Insert a continuous section break before the paragraph on the top of the second page. Return left and right margins to 1.25".

8. Insert a continuous section break after the first paragraph on page 2. Set 2" left and right margins for the two remaining workshop descriptions.

9. Insert a continuous section break after the tour descriptions and return left and right margins to 1.25".

10. Apply Word's Heading 1 style to the titles of each workshop. Apply Word's Heading 4 style to the second paragraphs below the workshop description.

11. Hyphenate the document.

12. Spell check.

13. Preview your work using the multiple pages option of Print Preview.

14. Close the file; save as **SEMINAR**.

# Time To Travel Tours

↓ *2x*

*777 Islington Street ✈ Portsmouth, NH 03801 ✈ Phone: (555) 555-5555 ✈ Fax: (555) 555-5555*

Today's date

Ms. Susan Hamilton
110 Sullivan Street
New York, NY  10012

Dear Ms. Hamilton:

Thank you for your inquiry about our summer and fall 1997 travel workshops.  These programs tend to fill to capacity, so it is best to enroll as soon as possible.  Some of the dates have not yet been finalized, so we will be sending you an update by the end of next week to keep you informed.

This year's week-long workshops will be held in Peru and Egypt.

*Insert continuous section break*

**POWER PLACES SEMINAR AND TOUR IN EGYPT:
July 14- July 21.  $2,199.**
Journey with others to one of the world's most sacred sites—the Great Pyramid.  You will have special access into the Great Pyramid not available to other tourists.  Experience a three-hour  private tour (closed to the general public) of all three chambers.  Learn about the teachings and technologies of ancient Egypt, taught by modern practitioners of these ancient sacred arts.  You may choose the optional three-day Nile cruise following the conference.

*Apply heading 4 style*

*Price includes airfare from New York, hotel accommodations, 30 meals, entrance into the Great Pyramid, most transportation within Egypt, luggage handling, conference fees and events.*

**POWER PLACES SEMINAR AND TOUR IN PERU:
June 14- June 22. $2,299.**
This conference has been specifically planned to culminate in Machu Picchu during the summer solstice, the holiest time of the year for the Incas.  You will travel through the sacred valley of the Incas, nestled in the serene Urubamba Valley.  You will meet native shamans, who will lead a special ceremony on the solstice, and provide insights on Peru's present-day culture, places and people.

*Price includes airfare from Miami, hotel accommodations (double occupancy), 30 meals, train and bus transportation within Peru, extensive sightseeing, entrances into Machu Picchu, conference fees and events.*

Ms. Susan Hamilton
Page 2
Today's date

This year's weekend panels, lectures and workshops will be held in Sonoma and Napa Valley, California.  Unless otherwise announced, the price will include three days and two nights of hotel accommodations, six meals, conference fees and special events.

**WOMEN'S RETREAT AT THE SONOMA MISSION INN.  (Date to be announced).  $425.**
This workshop will focus on women examining their individual power, spirituality, and self-image.  In addition to panel discussions and intensive group workshops, there will be plenty of relaxation and therapies at the natural hot springs.

**HOLISTIC HEALTH SEMINAR AT THE ST. HELENA HOSPITAL AND HEALTH CENTER.  September 20 - September 22.  $325.**
Open to health professionals and all those interested in health-related issues.  The weekend includes seminars and lectures on holistic approaches to western medicine in the areas of diet, exercise, herbal remedies, preventative medicine, and chronic illness.

Some of the lectures will be available to the general public.  If you are unable to attend for the entire weekend, please call us to inquire about the dates and times of free lectures.

You may also sign up by phone.  Please have a credit card available when you call.

Sincerely,

Angela Bacci
Tour Coordinator

ab/yo

# KEYSTROKES

### DELETE A HARD PAGE BREAK
#### -IN NORMAL VIEW-

1. Position insertion point on hard page break.
2. Press **Delete** ................................. `Del`

### MOVE A HARD PAGE BREAK
#### -IN NORMAL VIEW-

1. Select hard page break.
2. Drag it to the desired position.

### CREATE HEADERS/FOOTERS

1. Click **View** ............................. `Alt`+`V`
2. Click **Header and Footer** ................ `H`
   to display the Header and Footer dialog box.
3. Click **Header and Footer** button .... 
   to set header or footer as desired.
4. Type and format header or footer text as desired.
   - ✓ Header/footer text may be bolded, italicized, centered, right aligned, etc., just like normal text.
5. Click **Close** .............................. `Close`

### VIEW HEADERS/FOOTERS

1. Click **View** ............................. `Alt`+`V`
2. Click **Page Layout** ........................ `P`
3. Scroll to header/footer location.

### ADD PAGE NUMBERS, DATE, OR TIME TO A HEADER/FOOTER

1. Click **View** ............................. `Alt`+`V`
2. Click **Header and Footer** ................ `H`
   to display the Header and Footer toolbar.
3. Click **Header/Footer** button ..........
   to view header or footer as desired.
4. Click **Page Number** button ............
   to add page numbering to header/footer.
   **OR**
   Click **Date** button ...........................
   to add date to header/footer.
   **OR**
   Click **Time** button...........................
   to add time to header/footer.
5. Click **Close** ............................ `Close`

### SUPPRESS HEADER/FOOTER ON FIRST PAGE

1. Click **View**.............................. `Alt`+`V`
2. Click **Header and Footer** ................ `H`
   to display the Header and Footer toolbar.
3. Click **Page Setup** button .................
4. Click **Different first page** ....... `Alt`+`F`
5. Click **OK**................................ `Enter`

### DELETE HEADERS/FOOTERS

1. Click **View**.............................. `Alt`+`V`
2. Click **Header and Footer** ................ `H`
3. Click **Header/Footer** button ..........
   to view header or footer as desired.
4. Select header or footer text to delete.
5. Press **Delete**............................. `Del`
6. Click **Close** ............................ `Close`

### INSERT PAGE NUMBERS ONLY

1. Click **Insert**............................ `Alt`+`I`
2. Click **Page Numbers** ...................... `U`
3. Click **Position** list arrow ........ `Alt`+`P`
4. Select **Bottom of**.................... `↓`, `↑`
   **Page (Footer)**
   **OR**
   **Top of Page (Header)** ............ `↓`, `↑`
5. Click **Alignment** list arrow ...... `Alt`+`A`
6. Select desired location:
   - **Right**............................. `↑`, `↓`
   - **Left** ............................. `↑`, `↓`
   - **Center**........................... `↑`, `↓`
   - **Inside** .......................... `↑`, `↓`
   - **Outside** ......................... `↑`, `↓`
7. Click **OK** ............................... `Enter`

### INSERT SECTION BREAK

1. Position insertion point where you want break to begin.
2. Click **Insert**............................ `Alt`+`I`
3. Click **Break**.............................. `B`
4. Click desired section break:
   - **Next Page**.................... `Alt`+`N`
   - **Continuous**.................. `Alt`+`T`
   - **Even Page** .................. `Alt`+`E`
   - **Odd Page**.................... `Alt`+`O`
5. Click **OK** .............................. `OK`

# Exercise
# 32

■ **Letters with Special Notations**
■ **Print Specific Pages** ■ **Bookmarks**

## NOTES

### Letters with Special Notations

■ Letters may include special parts in addition to those learned thus far. The letter in this exercise contains a mailing notation, a subject line, an enclosure, and copy notations.

■ When a letter is sent by a **special mail service** such as Express mail, Registered mail, Federal Express, Certified mail, or By Hand (via a messenger service), it is customary to include an appropriate notation on the letter. This notation is placed two lines below the date and typed in all caps.

■ The **subject** identifies or summarizes the body of the letter. It is typed two lines below the salutation. One blank line follows it (press the Enter key twice). It may be typed at the left margin or centered in modified-block style. *Subject* may be typed in all caps or in upper- and lowercase. *Re* (in reference to) is often used instead of *Subject*.

■ An **enclosure** (or attachment notation) is used to indicate that something else besides the letter is included in the envelope. The enclosure or attachment notation is typed two lines below the reference initials and may be typed in several ways (the number indicates how many items are enclosed in the envelope):

| | | |
|---|---|---|
| ENC. | Enclosure | Enclosures (2) |
| Enc. | Encls. | Attachment |
| Encl. | Encls (2) | Attachments (2) |

■ If copies of the document are sent to others, a **copy notation** is typed two lines below the enclosure/attachment notation (or the reference initials if there is no enclosure/attachment).

A copy notation may be typed in several ways:

Copy to:   c:        pc: (photocopy)

### Print Specific Pages

■ You may choose to print the entire document, a specific page, several pages, selected (highlighted) text, or the current page. You may also specify the number of copies you wish to print. To do so, select <u>P</u>rint from the <u>F</u>ile menu and make your selection. (*See keystrokes on page 123.*)

✓ *Note: When working with multiple-page documents, it is convenient to use Print Preview to edit text and insert page breaks, because you can see the effect on several pages at once.*

### Bookmarks

■ The **Bookmark** feature allows you to return quickly to a desired location in a document. This is a convenient feature if, for example, you are editing a large document and have to leave your work for a time. You could set a bookmark to keep your place. When you return to work, you can open your file, find the bookmark in your document, and quickly return to the place you marked. Or, you might not have all the information needed to complete your document when you begin. Setting bookmarks will enable you to return to those sections of the document which need development or information inserted.

- To create a bookmark, position your insertion point where you wish to insert the bookmark. Then, select Bookmark from the Insert menu, enter the Bookmark name in the Bookmark dialog box, and click Add. To return to your bookmark, press F5 to display the Go To dialog box and then type the name of your bookmark.

- Your insertion point may be anywhere in the document when finding the bookmark.

- You can have several bookmarks in a document; however, each bookmark must be named for easy identification. The bookmark name can be the first line of the paragraph or a one-word or character name.

---

*In this exercise, you will create a two-page letter and insert a header as the second-page heading. You will insert a hard page break to create a second page.*

---

# EXERCISE DIRECTIONS

1. Create a new document.

2. Keyboard the exercise on the following page, or open 🖫**32PREVIEW**.

3. Use the default margins.

4. Begin the letterhead At 1" and the exercise At 2.5".

5. Create the letterhead in the point sizes shown in the exercise. Use the book symbol found in the Wingdings font collection.

6. Create a header which includes the name of the addressee, the page number, and today's date. Be sure to suppress the header on the first page.

7. Set bookmarks where indicated; name the first one INDENT1; the second, INDENT3; and the third, COPYTO.

8. Save the file as **PREVIEW**. **Do not close the document.**

9. Go To the first bookmark, INDENT1. Insert the following sentence at the bookmark location:

   *Furthermore, they have captured the objects on film so true to life that anyone watching them is captivated.*

10. Go To the second bookmark, INDENT3. Insert the following sentence as the third indented paragraph:

    *I will institute a program which will make schools throughout the country aware of their vocational potential.*

11. Go To the third bookmark, COPYTO, and insert a copy notation to Tien Lee.

12. Hyphenate the document. Limit the consecutive hyphens to 1.

    ✓ Note: *Limiting the number of consecutive hyphens is an option within the Hyphenation dialog box.*

13. In Print Preview mode, set the display for two pages, and insert a hard page break to end the first page where indicated.

    ✓ Note: *You may have to change the location of the hard page break from that shown in the illustration depending upon the printer you are using.*

14. Spell check.

15. Preview your work.

16. Print one copy of the entire document and two copies of page 2.

17. Close the file; save the changes.

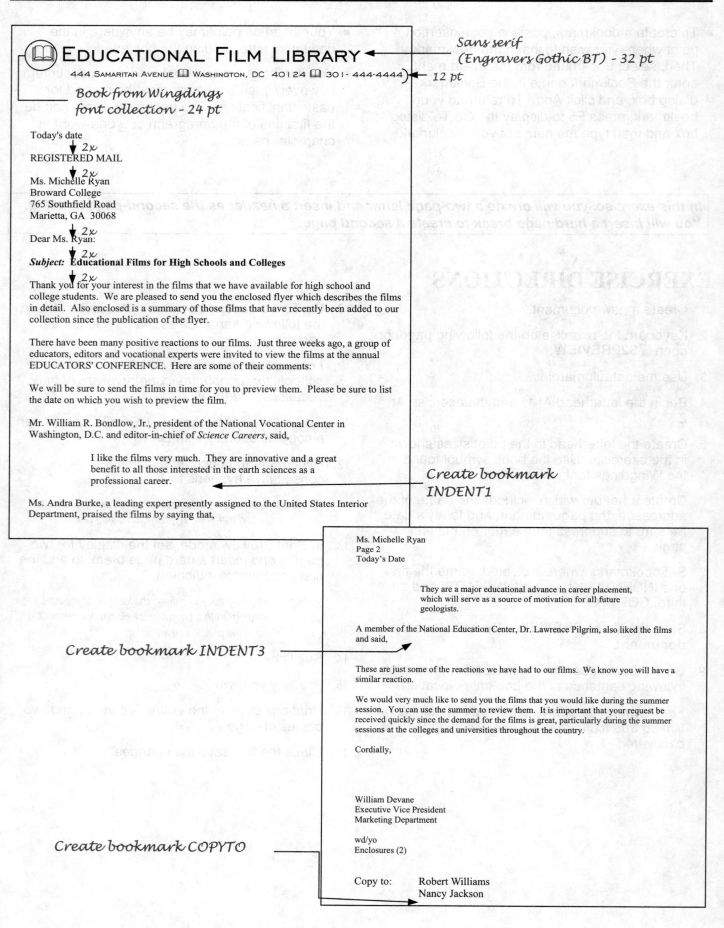

📖 EDUCATIONAL FILM LIBRARY ◄——— *Sans serif (Engravers Gothic BT) - 32 pt*

444 SAMARITAN AVENUE 📖 WASHINGTON, DC  40124 📖 301-444-4444 )◄— *12 pt*

*Book from Wingdings font collection - 24 pt*

Today's date

↓ *2x*

REGISTERED MAIL

↓ *2x*

Ms. Michelle Ryan
Broward College
765 Southfield Road
Marietta, GA  30068

↓ *2x*

Dear Ms. Ryan:

↓ *2x*

*Subject:* **Educational Films for High Schools and Colleges**

↓ *2x*

Thank you for your interest in the films that we have available for high school and
college students.  We are pleased to send you the enclosed flyer which describes the films
in detail.  Also enclosed is a summary of those films that have recently been added to our
collection since the publication of the flyer.

There have been many positive reactions to our films.  Just three weeks ago, a group of
educators, editors and vocational experts were invited to view the films at the annual
EDUCATORS' CONFERENCE.  Here are some of their comments:

We will be sure to send the films in time for you to preview them.  Please be sure to list
the date on which you wish to preview the film.

Mr. William R. Bondlow, Jr., president of the National Vocational Center in
Washington, D.C. and editor-in-chief of *Science Careers*, said,

> I like the films very much.  They are innovative and a great
> benefit to all those interested in the earth sciences as a
> professional career.

*Create bookmark INDENT1*

Ms. Andra Burke, a leading expert presently assigned to the United States Interior
Department, praised the films by saying that,

*Create bookmark INDENT3*

Ms. Michelle Ryan
Page 2
Today's Date

> They are a major educational advance in career placement,
> which will serve as a source of motivation for all future
> geologists.

A member of the National Education Center, Dr. Lawrence Pilgrim, also liked the films
and said,

These are just some of the reactions we have had to our films.  We know you will have a
similar reaction.

We would very much like to send you the films that you would like during the summer
session.  You can use the summer to review them.  It is important that your request be
received quickly since the demand for the films is great, particularly during the summer
sessions at the colleges and universities throughout the country.

Cordially,

William Devane
Executive Vice President
Marketing Department

wd/yo
Enclosures (2)

*Create bookmark COPYTO*

Copy to:      Robert Williams
              Nancy Jackson

# KEYSTROKES

## PRINT SPECIFIC PAGES OF A DOCUMENT

*CTRL + P*

**Print Entire Document:**

Click **Print** button ..................... 🖨

**Print Multiple Copies:**

1. Click **File** ........................... `Alt`+`F`
2. Click **Print** ........................... `P`
3. Type desired **Number** ............... *number of copies*.
4. Click **OK** ........................... `Enter`

**Print Specific Pages:**

1. Click **File** ........................... `Alt`+`F`
2. Click **Print** ........................... `P`
3. Click **Pages** ........................... `Alt`+`G`
4. Do one of the following:
   - Type non-sequential page numbers separated by commas.

   *EXAMPLE: 3,7,9*

   - Type range of pages separated by a hyphen.

   *EXAMPLE: 3-9*

   - Type a combination of non-sequential pages and a range of pages.

   *EXAMPLE: 2,5,7-10*

5. Click **OK** ........................... `Enter`

**Print Selected Text:**

1. Select (highlight) text to print.
2. Click **File** ........................... `Alt`+`F`
3. Click **Print** ........................... `P`
4. Click **Selection** ........................... `Alt`+`S`
5. Click **OK** ........................... `Enter`

## Print Current Page:

1. Click **File** ........................... `Alt`+`F`
2. Click **Print** ........................... `P`
3. Click **Current Page** ........................... `Alt`+`E`
4. Click **OK** ........................... `Enter`

## INSERT A HARD PAGE BREAK

1. Place insertion point where you would like page break.
2. Press **Ctrl + Enter** ............ `Ctrl`+`Enter`

   **OR**

1. Click **Insert** ........................... `Alt`+`I`
2. Click **Break** ........................... `B`
3. Click **Page Break** ........................... `Alt`+`P`
4. Click **OK** ........................... `Enter`

## EDIT TEXT IN PRINT PREVIEW MODE

1. Click **Print Preview** button............. 🔍 on the Standard toolbar.

   **OR**

   a. Click **File** ........................... `Alt`+`F`
   b. Click **Print Preview** ........................... `V`
2. Select and drag the **Multiple Pages** button 🔲 to set display for the number of pages desired.
3. Click **Magnifier** button................... 🔍 to enter Edit mode.
4. Edit text and page breaks as usual.
5. Click **Magnifier** button to exit Edit mode or press Esc to return to document.

## CREATE A BOOKMARK

1. Position insertion point where bookmark is to be inserted.
2. Click **Insert** ........................... `Alt`+`I`
3. Click **Bookmark** ........................... `B`
4. Type **Bookmark name** ........................... `Alt`+`K`
5. Click **Add** ........................... `Alt`+`A`

## GO TO BOOKMARK

1. Press **F5** ........................... `F5`

   **OR**

   - Click **Edit** ........................... `Alt`+`E`
   - Click **Go To** ........................... `G`
2. In **Go to what** list box, .......... `Alt`+`O` click Bookmark.
3. Click **Enter Bookmark name** .. `Alt`+`E`
4. Type bookmark name................... *name*
5. Click **Go To** ........................... `Alt`+`T`

## Exercise 33

■ **Footnotes** ■ **Endnotes** ■ **Comments** ■ **Widow/Orphan Lines**

# NOTES

### Footnotes/Endnotes

- A **footnote** is used to give information about the source of quoted material in a document. The information includes the author's name, the publication, the publication date, and the page number from which the quote was taken.

- There are several footnoting styles. Traditional footnotes are printed at the bottom of a page. A separator line separates footnote text from the text on the page.

- A reference number appears immediately after the quote in the text, and a corresponding footnote number or symbol appears at the bottom of the page.

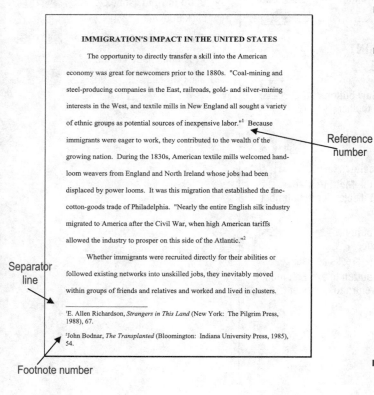

- An **endnote** contains the same information as a footnote but is typed on the last page of a report.

- The Footnote feature automatically inserts the reference number after the quote, inserts the separator line, numbers the footnote, and formats your page, so that the footnote appears on the same page as the reference number. If you desire endnotes instead of footnotes, Word will compile the endnote information on the last page of your document.

- The actual note may be viewed in Page Layout view if you scroll to the bottom of the page. In Normal view, you must double-click the footnote number or reference mark to view the footnote in a pane at the bottom of the screen.

- Footnotes may be inserted by selecting Foot<u>n</u>ote from the <u>I</u>nsert menu.

- After selecting <u>F</u>ootnote or <u>E</u>ndnote in the Footnote/Endnote dialog box that follows, a footnote screen appears, ready for you to type the text of the first footnote.

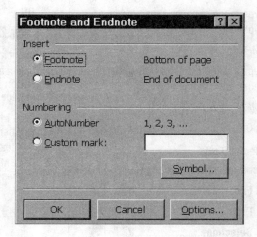

- To create a blank line between each footnote, you must press the Enter key once after typing the footnote.

- It is possible to have both footnotes and endnotes in the same document. In this exercise, however, you will create only footnotes.

- When a footnote or endnote is inserted or deleted, Word automatically renumbers all existing footnotes or endnotes as necessary.

- Footnote text will not conform to font changes made within the document. To modify the font used in footnote text, you must modify the style associated with it.

## Comments

- Comments are hidden notes or annotations that you or a reviewer can add to a document. These comments can be read on screen, hidden when the document is printed, printed with the document, or even incorporated into a document. Each comment is numbered and includes the initials of the person making the comment. By default, Word uses information in the User Information profile to identify the author of the comments inserted into a document.

- Inserting comments in a document is similar to inserting footnotes and endnotes. Position the cursor where you want to insert a comment, or highlight a block of text you want to comment on. Open the Insert menu and select Comment. Enter your comment in the comment pane at the bottom of the screen.

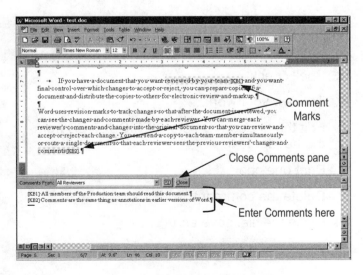

- Any text that you highlight before you insert a comment will appear in yellow in the document. The initials and the number of the comment will appear in yellow in square brackets.

- You can continue to add comments with the comment pane open, or you can click the Close button in the Comment pane to return to the document.

- To view the comment on screen, simply move the mouse pointer over any part of the highlighted text or the initials of the reviewer. The comment will appear under the name of the person making the comment.

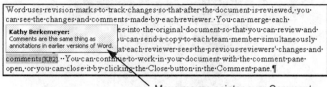

Move mouse pointer over Comments to view comment on screen.

- You can edit or delete comments easily. Right-click while pointing to the comment and select the desired option.

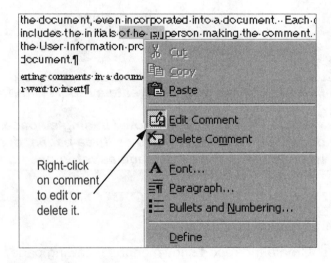

Right-click on comment to edit or delete it.

- By default, comments will not print.

- To print comments with a document:
  - Select File, Print.
  - Click Options in the lower-left corner of the Print dialog box.

Click here to print Comments

- Click Comments in the Include with document section of the Print options dialog box.

- Click OK and print the document.

## Widow and Orphan Lines

- A widow line occurs when the last line of a paragraph is printed by itself at the top of a page. An orphan line occurs when the first line of a paragraph appears by itself on the last line of the page. Widow and orphan lines should be avoided.

- The Widow/Orphan Control feature eliminates widows and orphans in a document and may be accessed by selecting Paragraph, Line and Page Breaks, Widow/Orphan Control from the Format menu.

*In this exercise, you will create a report with footnotes, a header, comments, and page numbers.*

✓ *While the exercise is shown in single space, you are to use double space. Your printed document will result in two or three pages, depending on the selected font, and footnotes will appear on the same page as reference numbers.*

## EXERCISE DIRECTIONS

1. Create a new document.

2. Create the report shown on the following page, or open ⊞**33VOYAGE**.

3. Begin the exercise At 2".

4. Use the default margins. Set line spacing to double after typing the title.

5. Create the header: DIFFICULTIES COMING TO AMERICA. Include a right-aligned page number as part of the header. Suppress the header and page number on the first page.

6. Insert the comment where shown.

7. Use widow and orphan control.

8. Spell check.

9. Preview your work.

10. Edit the header. Delete DIFFICULTIES from the header text.

11. Print one copy.

12. Delete the comment.

13. Close the file; save as **VOYAGE**.

## IMMIGRATION TO THE UNITED STATES
## IN THE NINETEENTH CENTURY

The United States is sometimes called the "Nation of Immigrants" because it has received more immigrants than any other country in history. During the first one hundred years of US history, the nation had no immigration laws. Immigration began to climb during the 1830s. "Between 1830-1840, 44% of the immigrants came from Ireland, 30% came from Germany, 15% came from Great Britain, and the remainder came from other European countries."[1]

The movement to America of millions of immigrants in the century after the 1820s was not simply a flight of impoverished peasants abandoning underdeveloped, backward regions for the riches and unlimited opportunities offered by the American economy. People did not move randomly to America but emanated from very specific regions at specific times in the nineteenth and twentieth centuries. "It is impossible to understand even the nature of American immigrant communities without appreciating the nature of the world these newcomers left."[2]

The rate of people leaving Ireland was extremely high in the late 1840s and early 1850s due to overpopulation and to the potato famine of 1846. "By 1850, there were almost one million Irish Catholics in the United States, especially clustered in New York and Massachusetts."[3]

Germans left their homeland due to severe depression, unemployment, political unrest, and the failure of the liberal revolutionary movement. It was not only the poor people who left their countries, but those in the middle and lower-middle levels of their social structures also left. "Those too poor could seldom afford to go, and the very wealthy had too much of a stake in the homelands to depart."[4]

*Add comment:* Insert additional paragraph on Italian immigration

Many immigrants came to America as a result of the lure of new land, in part, the result of the attraction of the frontier. America was in a very real sense the last frontier--a land of diverse peoples that, even under the worst conditions, maintained a way of life that permitted more freedom of belief and action than was held abroad. "While this perception was not entirely based in reality, it was the conviction that was often held in Europe and that became part of the ever-present American Dream."[5]

---

[1]Lewis Paul Todd and Merle Curti, *Rise of the American Nation* (New York: Harcourt Brace Jovanovich, Inc., 1972), 297.

[2]John Bodner, *The Transplanted* (Bloomington: Indiana University Press, 1985), 54.

[3]E. Allen Richardson, *Strangers in This Land* (New York: The Pilgrim Press, 1988), 6.

[4]Richardson, 13.

[5]Richardson, 72.

# KEYSTROKES

## FOOTNOTES/ENDNOTES

1. Place insertion point where footnote reference number will appear.
2. Click **Insert** ............................. `Alt` + `I`
3. Click **Foot__n__ote** ................................. `N`
4. Click **__F__ootnote** ........................... `Alt` + `F`

   **OR**

   Click **__E__ndnote** ........................... `Alt` + `E`
5. Click **OK** ............................... `Enter`
6. Type footnote/endnote information.

   *– IN NORMAL VIEW –*

7. Press **Shift + F6** ..................... `Shift` + `F6`
   to leave footnote pane open and return to where you were working in the document.

   **OR**

   Click **__C__lose** to close footnote pane and return to where you were working in the document.

   *– IN PAGE LAYOUT VIEW –*

   Press **Shift + F5** ......................... `Shift` + `F5`
   as often as necessary to return to where you were working in the document.

## VIEW FOOTNOTES/ENDNOTES

*– IN NORMAL VIEW –*

Double-click the footnote reference mark.

**OR**

1. Click **__V__iew** ............................. `Alt` + `V`
2. Click **__F__ootnotes** ........................... `F`

*– IN PAGE LAYOUT VIEW –*

Double-click the footnote reference mark.

**OR**

Scroll to footnote location.

## DELETE FOOTNOTES/ENDNOTES

1. Select the footnote reference mark.
2. Press **Delete** ............................. `Del`

   **OR**

   a. Click **__E__dit** ........................... `Alt` + `E`
   b. Click **Cu__t__** .................................... `T`

## INSERT COMMENTS

1. Click anywhere in document where comment will appear.

   **OR**

   Highlight text about which you want to comment.
2. Click **Insert** ........................... `Alt` + `I`
3. Click **Co__m__ment** ........................... `M`
4. Type comment in Comment pane.
5. Click **__C__lose** ................. `Alt` + `Shift` + `C`
   in Comments pane.

## DELETE COMMENTS

1. Right-click anywhere in comment area.
2. Click **Delete Co__m__ment** ................... `M`

## EDIT COMMENTS

1. Right-click anywhere in comment area.
2. Click **__E__dit Comment** ........................ `E`
3. Make desired edits.
4. Click **__C__lose** ................. `Alt` + `Shift` + `C`
   in Comments pane.

## WIDOW AND ORPHAN CONTROL

1. Click **F__o__rmat** ......................... `Alt` + `O`
2. Click **__P__aragraph** ........................... `P`
3. Click **Line and __P__age Breaks** ... `Alt` + `P`
   tab.
4. Click **__W__idow/Orphan Control** .. `Alt` + `W`
   check box to turn Widow/Orphan Control off or on.

## Exercise 34 ■ Page Numbering Placement and Formats

## NOTES

### Page Numbering Placement

- As indicated in Exercise 31, page numbers may be included independent of the header/footer text by selecting Page Numbers from the Insert menu.

- Word provides numerous page numbering position options. Numbers may be positioned at the top or bottom, left, center, or right of the page and aligned left, center, right, inside, or outside. The Page Numbers dialog box (which appears after Insert, Page Numbers is selected) displays the page numbering position you select in the preview window.

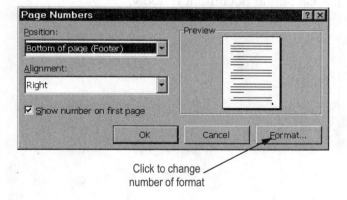

Click to change number of format

### Number Formats

- Word provides five different number formats.

  | | |
  |---|---|
  | Numbers | 1, 2, 3, 4, 5, etc. |
  | Lowercase Letters | a, b, c, d, e, f, etc. |
  | Uppercase Letters | A, B, C, D, E, F, etc. |
  | Lowercase Roman | i, ii, iii, iv, v, etc. |
  | Uppercase Roman | I, II, III, IV, V, etc. |

- To change Number formats, click the Format button on the Page Numbers dialog box (shown left).

- In the Page Number Format dialog box which follows, click the Number format list arrow and select a desired format.

Click to select number format

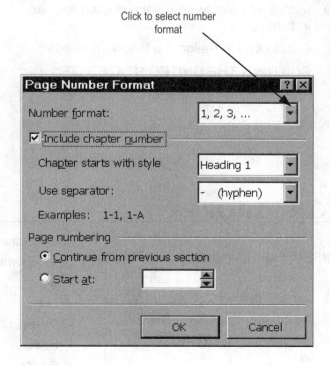

> *In this exercise, you will create a report with footnotes, a header, and bottom centered page numbers. Remember to suppress headers and page numbers on the first page.*
>
> ✓ *When a quotation is longer than two sentences, it is single spaced and indented. In this exercise, you will indent the quoted material, as directed.*
>
> ✓ *While the exercise is shown in single space, you are to use double line spacing. Your printed document will result in two or three pages, depending on the selected font, and footnotes will appear on the same page as reference numbers.*

# EXERCISE DIRECTIONS

1. Create a new document.

2. Create the report on the next page, or open 🖫**34USA**.

3. Begin the exercise At 2".

4. Set line spacing to double.

5. Use a serif 13-point font for the document.

   ✓ *To set the footnote reference number and footnote text to 13 point, you must modify the footnote style.*

6. Set 1.5" left and right document margins.

7. Set the title to 14-point bold.

8. Use widow and orphan control.

9. Indent and single-space the quoted text, as indicated.

10. Create and left-align the following header:

    BUILDING THE UNITED STATES OF AMERICA

11. Include an Uppercase Roman page number on the bottom center of the second and succeeding pages.

12. Spell check.

13. Edit the header to read: BUILDING THE U. S. A.

14. Preview your work.

15. Print one copy.

16. Delete the comment.

17. Save the file; name it **USA**.

18. Close the document window.

# KEYSTROKES

**INSERT PAGE NUMBERS**

1. Click **Insert** ............................ `Alt`+`I`

2. Click **Page Numbers** ...................... `U`

3. Click **Position** ......................... `Alt`+`P`

4. Click **Bottom of Page (Footer)**. `↓`, `↑`
   OR
   Click **Top of Page (Header)** ...... `↓`, `↑`

5. Click **Alignment** ................... `Alt`+`A`

6. Select desired location:

   • **Right** ................................. `↑`, `↓`

   • **Left** .................................. `↑`, `↓`

   • **Center** ............................... `↑`, `↓`

   • **Inside** ............................... `↑`, `↓`

   • **Outside** ............................. `↑`, `↓`

**To Change Format:**

   a. Click **Format** ..................... `Alt`+`F`

   b. Click ................................... `Alt`+`F`
      **Number format** drop-down list box.

   c. Select desired format.

7. Click **OK** ................................ `Enter`

# IMMIGRATION'S IMPACT IN THE UNITED STATES

The opportunity to directly transfer a skill into the American economy was great for newcomers prior to the 1880s. "Coal-mining and steel-producing companies in the East, railroads, gold- and silver-mining interests in the West, and textile mills in New England all sought a variety of ethnic groups as potential sources of inexpensive labor."[1] Because immigrants were eager to work, they contributed to the wealth of the growing nation. During the 1830s, American textile mills welcomed hand-loom weavers from England and North Ireland whose jobs had been displaced by power looms. It was this migration that established the fine-cotton-goods trade of Philadelphia. "Nearly the entire English silk industry migrated to America after the Civil War, when high American tariffs allowed the industry to prosper on this side of the Atlantic."[2]

Whether immigrants were recruited directly for their abilities or followed existing networks into unskilled jobs, they inevitably moved within groups of friends and relatives and worked and lived in clusters.

As the Industrial Revolution progressed, immigrants were enticed to come to the United States through the mills and factories who sent representatives overseas to secure cheap labor. An example was the Amoskeag Manufacturing Company, located along the banks of the Merrimack River in Manchester, New Hampshire. In the 1870s, the Amoskeag Company recruited women from Scotland who were expert gingham weavers. Agreements were set specifying a fixed period of time during which employees would guarantee to work for the company.[3] ← *Add Comment: Check Insert for Amoskeag Manufacturing*

In the 1820s, Irish immigrants did most of the hard work in building the canals in the United States. In fact, Irish immigrants played a large role in building the Erie Canal. American contractors encouraged Irish immigrants to come to the United States to work on the roads, canals, and railroads, and manufacturers lured them into the new mills and factories.

"Most German immigrants settled in the middle western states of Ohio, Indiana, Illinois, Wisconsin and Missouri."[4] With encouragement to move west from the Homestead Act of 1862, which offered public land free to immigrants who intended to become citizens, German immigrants comprised a large portion of the pioneers moving west. "They were masterful farmers and they built prosperous farms."[5]

---

[1] E. Allen Richardson, *Strangers in This Land* (New York: The Pilgrim Press, 1988), 67.

[2] John Bodnar, *The Transplanted* (Bloomington: Indiana University Press, 1985), 54.

[3] Bodnar, 72.

[4] David A. Gerber, *The Making of An American Pluralism* (Chicago: University of Illinois, 1989), 124.

[5] Bodnar, 86.

## Exercise 35

- **Move Text From One Page to Another**
- **Document Map**
- **Full Screen View**

## NOTES

### Move Text From One Page to Another

- The procedure for moving blocks of text from one page to another is the same as for moving blocks of text on the same page. However, if text is to be moved from one page to another, the **Go To** key (F5) or the Select Browse Object button on the vertical scroll bar may be used to quickly advance to the page where you want to insert the text.

- When you move text from one page to another within two or three pages of each other, it is helpful to work in Print Preview mode using the drag-and-drop technique.

- If a hard page break was inserted, delete the break, then move the text. Word will then insert a soft page break. If the soft page break is not in a satisfactory location, insert a hard page break in the desired location.

### Document Map

- Word provides several ways for you to view your documents on screen. You may be used to viewing a document in Normal, Page Layout, or Outline views. You can also use Document Map to navigate long documents.

- Document Map appears as a separate pane on the left of the document. To quickly jump to a new location in the document, click on the heading in the Document Map pane. You access Document Map by clicking on the Document Map button 🔍 on the Standard toolbar, or by selecting Document Map on the View menu.

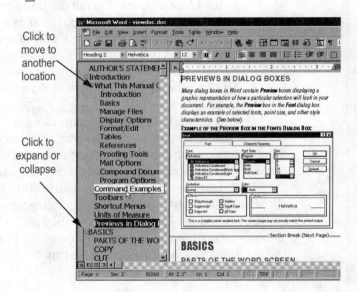

Click to move to another location

Click to expand or collapse

- The level of the displayed headings can be changed in the same way you change how Outline levels display. Right-click in the Document Map pane and select the level of heading that you want to display.

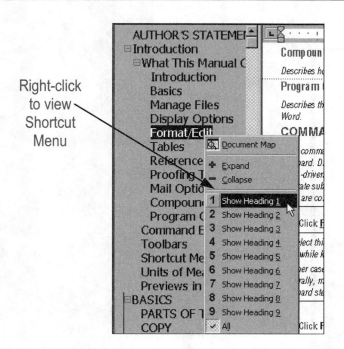

Right-click to view Shortcut Menu

You can also click on the expand and collapse buttons in the Document Map pane.

- If you do not see many heading levels when you activate Document Map, it is probably because you have not used the heading styles that Word looks for to create the map. If Word does not find Heading levels, it will look for paragraphs that resemble headings and use those to create a map. The Document Map will be empty if Word cannot find Headings or paragraphs that seem to function as headings.

- Close Document Map by clicking the Document Map button on the Standard toolbar or by clicking Document Map on the View menu.

---

*In this exercise, you will edit two different documents and gain practice moving text from one page to another. In addition, you will use the Thesaurus and other editing features.*

# EXERCISE DIRECTIONS

## PART I

1. Open 🖳PREVIEW, or open 🖫35PREVIEW.

2. Set Widow/Orphan Control to off.

3. Display the Document Map. Select each item on the document map.

4. Using the Thesaurus, replace highlighted words in brackets. Be sure replacement words maintain the same tense/endings as the original words.

5. Access Print Preview mode and set the display for two pages; make the indicated revisions in Print Preview or Page Layout mode.

6. Return to Page Layout view.

7. Change EDUCATORS' CONFERENCE to lowercase with initial capitals.

8. Preview your document.

9. Close the Document Map.

10. Print one copy.

11. Close the file; save as **PREVIEW**.

## PART II

✓ Note: *Moving paragraphs in this exercise will not affect footnote placement. Word automatically readjusts footnote placement.*

1. Open 🖳USA, or open 🖫35USA.

2. Display the Document Map.

3. Using the Thesaurus, replace the highlighted words. Be sure replacement words maintain the same tense/endings as the original words.

4. Access Print Preview mode and set the display for two (or three) pages; make the indicated revisions in this mode.

5. Return to Page Layout view.

6. Justify and hyphenate the document.

7. Preview your document.

8. Print one copy.

9. Close the file; save as **USA**.

**PART I**

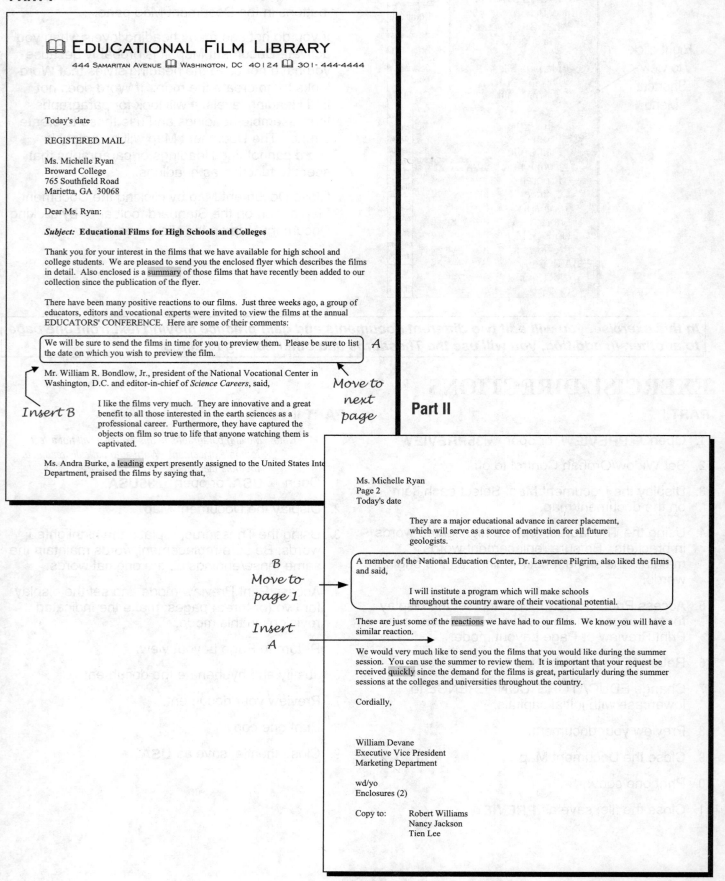

📖 EDUCATIONAL FILM LIBRARY

444 SAMARITAN AVENUE 📖 WASHINGTON, DC 40124 📖 301- 444-4444

Today's date

REGISTERED MAIL

Ms. Michelle Ryan
Broward College
765 Southfield Road
Marietta, GA 30068

Dear Ms. Ryan:

*Subject:* **Educational Films for High Schools and Colleges**

Thank you for your interest in the films that we have available for high school and college students. We are pleased to send you the enclosed flyer which describes the films in detail. Also enclosed is a summary of those films that have recently been added to our collection since the publication of the flyer.

There have been many positive reactions to our films. Just three weeks ago, a group of educators, editors and vocational experts were invited to view the films at the annual EDUCATORS' CONFERENCE. Here are some of their comments:

We will be sure to send the films in time for you to preview them. Please be sure to list the date on which you wish to preview the film.                                                      *A*

Mr. William R. Bondlow, Jr., president of the National Vocational Center in Washington, D.C. and editor-in-chief of *Science Careers*, said,

*Insert B*

I like the films very much. They are innovative and a great benefit to all those interested in the earth sciences as a professional career. Furthermore, they have captured the objects on film so true to life that anyone watching them is captivated.

Ms. Andra Burke, a leading expert presently assigned to the United States Inte... Department, praised the films by saying that,

*Move to next page*

**Part II**

Ms. Michelle Ryan
Page 2
Today's date

They are a major educational advance in career placement, which will serve as a source of motivation for all future geologists.

A member of the National Education Center, Dr. Lawrence Pilgrim, also liked the films and said,

*B*
*Move to page 1*

I will institute a program which will make schools throughout the country aware of their vocational potential.

*Insert*
*A*

These are just some of the reactions we have had to our films. We know you will have a similar reaction.

We would very much like to send you the films that you would like during the summer session. You can use the summer to review them. It is important that your request be received quickly since the demand for the films is great, particularly during the summer sessions at the colleges and universities throughout the country.

Cordially,

William Devane
Executive Vice President
Marketing Department

wd/yo
Enclosures (2)

Copy to:     Robert Williams
             Nancy Jackson
             Tien Lee

*Single space and indent quotation.*

# IMMIGRATION'S IMPACT IN THE UNITED STATES

The opportunity to directly transfer a skill into the American economy was great for newcomers prior to the 1880s. "Coal-mining and steel-producing companies in the East, railroads, gold- and silver-mining interests in the West, and textile mills in New England all sought a variety of ethnic groups as potential sources of inexpensive labor."[1] Because immigrants were eager to work, they contributed to the wealth of the growing nation. During the 1830s, American textile mills welcomed hand-loom weavers from England and North Ireland whose jobs had been displaced by power looms. It was this migration that established the fine-cotton-goods trade of Philadelphia. "Nearly the entire English silk industry migrated to America after the Civil War, when high American tariffs allowed the industry to prosper on this side of the Atlantic."[2]

Whether immigrants were recruited directly for their abilities or followed existing networks into unskilled jobs, they inevitably moved within groups of friends and relatives and worked and lived in clusters.

---

[1] E. Allen Richardson, *Strangers in This Land* (New York: The Pilgrim Press, 1988), 67.

[2] John Bodnar, *The Transplanted* (Bloomington: Indiana University Press, 1985), 54.

*Insert A*

BUILDING THE U. S. A.

As the Industrial Revolution progressed, immigrants were enticed to come to the United States through the mills and factories who sent representatives overseas to secure cheap labor.  An example was the Amoskeag Manufacturing Company, located along the banks of the Merrimack River in Manchester, New Hampshire.  In the 1870s, the Amoskeag Company recruited women from Scotland who were expert gingham weavers.  Agreements were set specifying a fixed period of time during which employees would guarantee to work for the company.[3]

In the 1820s, Irish immigrants did most of the hard work in building the canals in the United States.  In fact, Irish immigrants played a large role in building the Erie Canal.  American contractors encouraged Irish immigrants to come to the United States to work on the roads, canals, and railroads, and manufacturers lured them into the new mills and factories.

*A*
*Move to*
*page 1*

"Most German immigrants settled in the middle western states of Ohio, Indiana, Illinois, Wisconsin and Missouri."[4]  With encouragement to move west from the Homestead Act of 1862, which offered public land free to immigrants who intended to become citizens, German immigrants comprised a large portion of the pioneers moving west. "They were masterful farmers and they built prosperous farms."[5]

[3]Bodnar, 72.

[4]David A. Gerber, *The Making of An American Pluralism* (Chicago:  University of Illinois, 1989), 124.

[5]Bodnar,  86.

II

# KEYSTROKES

## GO TO

- Click Select Browse Object button on vertical scroll bar.
- Click **Go to** button.

**OR**

1. Press **F5**............................................. `F5`
2. In **Go To What list** .................`Alt`+`O` box select **Page**.
3. Click in **Enter Page Number**...`Alt`+`E` box.
4. Type page number .....................*number*

## SWITCH TO DOCUMENT MAP

1. Click **Document Map** button 🔲 on Standard toolbar.

   **OR**

   a. Click **View**...........................`Alt`+`V`
   b. Click **Document Map** ...................`D`

   *Document Map pane will appear on the left of the document.*

2. Click heading where you want to go.

   **To turn off Document Map:**

   Right-click in Document Map pane and click **D**ocument Map.

   **OR**

   a. Click **View**...........................`Alt`+`V`
   b. Click **Document Map** .................`D`

## CHANGE LEVEL OF HEADING IN DOCUMENT MAP VIEW

1. Right-click in Document Map pane.
2. Select desired level of heading level to view.

   **OR**

   Click **Expand** or **Collapse** buttons next to heading levels in Document Map pane.

# Exercise
# 36

## ■ Summary

*In this exercise, you will create a report with footnotes. This report will be bound on the left. Therefore, you will need to place the footer and page number accordingly.*

## EXERCISE DIRECTIONS

1. Keyboard the exercise on the following page, or open 🖫**36BRAZIL**.

2. Set a 2" left margin and a 1.5" right margin.

3. Begin the exercise At 2.5" down from the top of the page.

4. Create a right-aligned footer on the second and succeeding pages in a sans serif 12-point bold font which reads, BRAZIL: Investment Opportunities.

5. Include a page number at the top right corner of the page.

6. Set line spacing to double.

7. Use a serif 13-point font for the document; center and set the title to 16-point bold.

8. Use widow and orphan control.

9. Edit the footer to read BRAZIL.

10. Justify and hyphenate the document. Limit hyphenation to two consecutive lines.

11. Add a comment where shown.

12. Spell check.

13. Preview your work.

14. Print one copy.

15. Save the file; name it **BRAZIL**.

## BRAZIL

Brazil is often viewed as the economic giant of the Third World. Its economy and territory are larger than the rest of South America's and its industry is the most advanced in the developing world. Brazilian foreign debt is also the Third World's largest. The problem of foreign debt has plagued the Latin American economies since the 1960s when foreign borrowing was the only way for Latin American nations to sustain economic growth. However, when international interest rates began to rise in the 1980s, the debt these nations accumulated became unmanageable. In Brazil, the debt crisis of the 1980s marked the decline of an economy that had flourished since 1967 when foreign borrowing enabled the nation to develop its own productive industries and lessen its dependence on foreign manufactured goods. "Similar to other Latin American nations, Brazilian overseas borrowing between 1967 and 1981 became a drain on the economy when international interest rates rose; by 1985, its excessive borrowing resulted in economic disaster, political dissension and protest, and the rise of an opposition government in Brazil."[1]

Throughout the beginning of the twentieth century, growth of the Brazilian economy remained dependent upon agricultural exports. The twentieth century witnessed a decline in the export of sugar from the northeast of Brazil and a rise in the export of coffee from the southeast of Brazil. This concentrated economic growth and political power in the developed southeast part of the nation, particularly in the states of Rio de Janeiro and Sao Paulo. Industrial growth in this region progressed gradually and by 1919, domestic firms supplied over 70% of the local demand for industrial products and employed over 14% of the labor force."[2]

However, by the 1980s, Brazil accumulated massive foreign debt which ultimately caused the government to cut foreign spending and investment, drove interest rates so high that businesses could not borrow money for investment and expansion, and precipitated the bankruptcy of numerous companies, the unemployment of wage laborers, and growing social unrest. Between 1979 and 1982, the debt amassed by Brazilian banks increased from $7.7 billion to $16.1 billion. "By 1982, debt-service payments were equivalent to 91% of Brazil's merchandise exports, up from 51% in 1977."[3] In mid-1988, inflation in Brazil ran above 500% and the value of the foreign debt Brazil has to repay remains the largest in the Third World.

Brazil's financial situation is improving. Currently, Brazil has been able to sustain a 5% economic growth rate and is encouraging expanded foreign investment. Inflation in Brazil has fallen to 1.5% a month while United States exports to Brazil jumped by 35% last year."[4] ◄——————— *Add comment:* Double-check economic growth rate.

Rising international trade which may culminate in a South American free trade zone has enabled the Brazilian economy to flourish once again. Brazil's huge foreign debt, however, remains outstanding and continues to loom over its recent economic success.

---

[1] Jeffrey A. Frieden, *Debt, Development and Democracy: Modern Political Economy and Latin America, 1965-1985* (Princeton: Princeton University Press, 1991), 98.
[2] Frieden, 118.
[3] Frieden, 128.
[4] Barry Eichgreen and Peter H. Lindert, *The International Debt Crisis in Historical Perspective* (Cambridge, MA: The MIT Press, 1989), 130.

## Exercise 37

- ■ **Switch Among Open Documents** ■ **Display Multiple Documents**
- ■ **Copy/Move Text From One Document to Another**
- ■ **Close/Maximize a Document Window**

# NOTES

### Switch among Open Documents

- ■ It is often convenient to work with more than one document at once. Word allows you to have as many documents as you wish open at the same time. To switch (cycle) among open documents and view one document at a time, press Ctrl + F6.

### Display Multiple Documents

- ■ If you wish to copy or move information from one document to another, it is convenient to display more than one document on your screen. Multiple documents may be displayed by opening the documents you wish to view, then selecting Arrange All from the Window menu.

- ■ The document that contains the insertion point is known as the **active document.** To make a document active, press Ctrl+F6 and click in the desired document, or select the document name from the Window menu.

### Copy/Move Text from One Document to Another

- ■ The procedure for copying or moving text from one document to another is the same as copying/moving text within the same document. With your insertion point in the active document, select the text you wish to move or copy. Use whatever copy/move procedure you desire (cut/copy and paste for clarity or drag and drop). Click the document to receive the copied/moved text to make it active, and complete the copy/move procedure.

### Close and Save Multiple Documents

- ■ As you close each document window, you can save its contents. To close a window, double-click the Document Control button to the left of the title bar. Or click the document you wish to close and select Close from the File menu.

- ■ You can close all open documents at once by holding down the Shift key, opening the File menu, and selecting Close All. Similarly, you can save all open documents by holding down the Shift key, opening the File menu and selecting Save All.

- ■ To return a document to the full screen size, click the Maximize button to the right of the document title bar.

- ■ After closing one of your open documents, you may rearrange the remaining documents on the screen by selecting Arrange All from the Window menu.

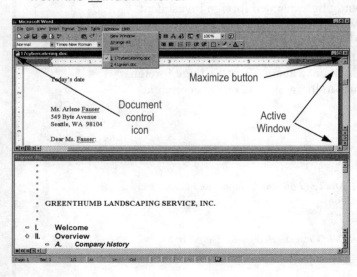

*In this exercise, you will open and display several documents and copy some text from each to create a new document. This procedure may also be used for moving text from one document to another.*

*Reminder: Copying text leaves text in its original location and pastes a copy in a new location.*

# EXERCISE DIRECTIONS

1. Create a new document.

2. Display the Office Assistant.

3. Keyboard the letter named "Hotels" exactly as shown on the following page, or open 🖫**37HOTELS**.

4. Use the default margins; begin the date at approximately 3". (Adjust the dateline after copying the letterhead.)

5. Open ⌨**GLOBAL** and ⌨**DIVE** if you completed them in a previous exercise, or open 🖫**37GLOBAL** and 🖫**37DIVE**.

6. Display all documents by selecting Arrange All from the Window menu.

7. Copy the letterhead from **GLOBAL** to the top of the new document.

   - Copy the remaining indicated text in each document into the new document.
   - Double space before and after each insert.
   ✓ *Note: The document to be copied from must be the active document. When you are ready to place the text, the new document must become the active document. Follow keystrokes carefully.*

8. Close all documents except the new document.

9. Maximize the new document window.

10. Change text in small caps to normal.

11. Insert an appropriate page 2 heading as a header in the new document.

12. Make any necessary adjustments to the text. Avoid awkward paragraph breaks.

13. Spell check the new document.

14. Print one copy of the new document.

15. Close and save the new document; name it **HOTELS**.

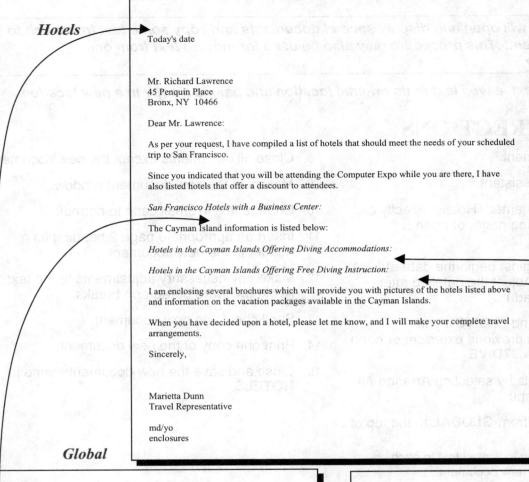

*Hotels*

Today's date

Mr. Richard Lawrence
45 Penquin Place
Bronx, NY  10466

Dear Mr. Lawrence:

As per your request, I have compiled a list of hotels that should meet the needs of your scheduled trip to San Francisco.

Since you indicated that you will be attending the Computer Expo while you are there, I have also listed hotels that offer a discount to attendees.

*San Francisco Hotels with a Business Center:*

The Cayman Island information is listed below:

*Hotels in the Cayman Islands Offering Diving Accommodations:*

*Hotels in the Cayman Islands Offering Free Diving Instruction:*

I am enclosing several brochures which will provide you with pictures of the hotels listed above and information on the vacation packages available in the Cayman Islands.

When you have decided upon a hotel, please let me know, and I will make your complete travel arrangements.

Sincerely,

Marietta Dunn
Travel Representative

md/yo
enclosures

*Global*

THE GLOBAL TRAVEL GROUP

485 Madison Avenu
New York, NY  1003

PHONE: (212) 234-4566
FAX: (212) 345-9877

Today' Date

Mr. Astrit Ibrosi
45 Lake View Drive
Huntington, NY  11543

Dear Mr. Ibrosi:

Ms. Packer in our office has referred your letter to me.  You had asked her to provic with a list of hotels in the San Francisco area that have a business center which offe laptop rentals, fax services, and teleconferencing capabilities.

Since I am the representative for the San Francisco area, I have compiled a list of h that offer the services you requested.  They appear below:

REGENCY CENTRAL
SURRY HOTEL
FAIRMONT HOTEL
RENAISSANCE CENTER
MARRIOTT MARK
GRAND HYATT

When you are ready to make your reservations, please call our office.  If you have other travel needs, call GLOBAL.  Our experienced staff will give you prompt and courteous service and will answer all your travel questions.

Sincerely,

Marietta Dunn
Travel Representative

md/yo

*Dive*

## DIVING IN THE CAYMAN ISLANDS

Do you want to see sharks, barracudas, stingrays and angelfish?

The Cayman Islands were discovered by Christopher Columbus in 1503 and are located south of Cuba.  The Caymans are home to about 25,000 year-around residents. However, they welcome 200,000 visitors each year.  Most visitors come with masks and flippers in their luggage.

Before you descend the depths of the ocean, it is important that you have a few lessons on the don'ts of diving.  Don't touch the coral.  Don't come up to the surface too fast holding your breath.  If you do, your lungs will explode.

Now, you are ready to jump in!

Here are some hotel suggestions:

### Hotel/Diving Accommodations:

*Anchorage View*, PO Box 2123, Grand Cayman; (809) 555-4209.

*Cayman Diving Lodge*, PO Box 11, East End, Grand Cayman; (809) 555-7555.

*Coconut Harbour*, PO Box 2086, George Town, Grand Cayman; (809) 555-7468.

*Red Sail Sports*, PO Box 1588, George Town, Grand Cayman; (809) 555-7965.

*Sunset House*, PO Box 479, George Town, Grand Cayman; (800) 555-4767.

### Hotels Offering Free Diving Instruction:

*Cayman Diving Lodge*, PO Box 11, East End, Grand Cayman; (809) 555-7555.

*Sunset House*, PO Box 479, George Town, Grand Cayman; (800) 555-4767.

# KEYSTROKES

## OPEN MULTIPLE DOCUMENTS

*CTRL + O*

1. Click **File**................................ `Alt` + `F`
2. Click **Open** ............................................ `O`
3. Hold down **Ctrl**................................. `Ctrl`
   and click each file to open.
   **OR**
   a. Hold down **Shift** ...................... `Shift`
   b. Click first file to open.
   c. Click last file to open.
4. Click **Open** .................................... `Enter`

   ✓ To use the second procedure, you
     must be selecting adjacent files

## MAKE A DOCUMENT ACTIVE

Press **Ctrl + F6** ............................ `Ctrl` + `F6`
until desired document is active.
   **OR**
   a. Click **Window** ................... `Alt` + `W`
   b. Click document ....... `↓`, `↑`, `Enter`
      name or number to switch
      to desired document.

## DISPLAY MULTIPLE DOCUMENTS

1. Open desired documents.
2. Click **Window**...................... `Alt` + `W`
3. Click **Arrange All**............................ `A`

## RETURN TO SINGLE DOCUMENT DISPLAY

1. Make desired document active.
2. Click **Maximize** button........... `Ctrl` + `F10`

## COPY TEXT FROM ONE DOCUMENT TO ANOTHER

1. Open both documents.
2. Make source document the active file.
3. Select (highlight) text to copy.

   *– USING TOOLBAR –*

   a. Click **Copy** button...................... 🗐
   b. Make the destination
      document active.
   c. Place insertion point where
      text will be inserted.
   d. Click **Paste** button ..................... 📋
   **OR**
   Press **Shift+Insert**............ `Shift` + `Ins`

   *– USING KEYBOARD –*

   a. Press **Shift + F2** ............... `Shift` + `F2`
   b. Make the destination document active.
   c. Press **Enter** ........................... `Enter`

   *– USING MOUSE –*

   a. Display both documents.
   b. Hold down **Ctrl**........................ `Ctrl`
      and point to selected text.
   c. Hold down left mouse button
      and drag text to new location.
   d. Release left mouse button.

## MOVE TEXT FROM ONE DOCUMENT TO ANOTHER

1. Open both documents.
2. Make the source document the active file.
3. Select (highlight) text to be moved.
4. Do one of the following:
   a. Click **Cut** button......................... ✂
   b. Click destination document.
   **OR**
   Press **Ctrl + F6**................. `Ctrl` + `F6`
   **OR**
   a. Click **Window** ................... `Alt` + `W`
   b. Select name of destination document
      to make it active.
5. Place insertion point where copied
   text will be inserted.
6. Click **Paste** button....................... 📋
   **OR**
   Press **Shift + Insert**............. `Shift` + `Ins`

## SAVE OR CLOSE ALL OPEN DOCUMENTS

1. Hold down **Shift** ......................... `Shift`
2. Click **File**...................................... `F`
3. Click **Save All**............................... `L`
   **OR**
   Click **Close All** ............................... `C`

## Exercise 38

■ **Insert a File**

## NOTES

### Insert a File

■ When you insert a file into a document, the inserted file is made part of the current document window. This is quite different from opening a document. When you open a document, each new, opened document is layered over the previous one.

■ The file which has been inserted will remain intact. You may insert it into another document when needed.

■ A file may be inserted by selecting File from the Insert menu.

■ In the Insert File dialog box that follows, you must select the drive and folder containing the file you wish to insert. *(Files may be accessed from the Insert dialog box using the same techniques used to open files in the Open dialog box. See Lesson 2, Exercise 7.)*

*In this exercise, you will create a memo and insert a previously created file into it.*

## EXERCISE DIRECTIONS

1. Create a new document.

2. Keyboard the letter shown on the next page in a serif 10-point font, or open 🖫**38HOMES**.

3. Use the default left and right margins; set .5" top and bottom margins.

4. Begin the letterhead At 1".

5. Set the letterhead title to sans serif 14-point bold; set the address and phone number information to sans serif 10-point italics. Use a Wingdings flag symbol where shown in 14-point bold.

6. Begin the date At 2".

7. Insert ⌨**ESTATE** or 🖫**38ESTATE** where indicated. Leave a double space before and after the insert.

8. Spell check.

9. Print one copy.

10. Close the file; name it **HOMES**.

## KEYSTROKES

### INSERT A FILE

1. Place insertion point where you want file inserted.

2. Click **Insert** ..................... `Alt` + `I`

3. Click **File** .......................... `L`

4. Select document to insert.

5. Click **OK** ................................... `Enter`

## ⚐ ⚐ **FLAGSHIP REALTY** ⚐ ⚐

*111 Center Street*
*Southhold, NY 11555*

*Phone: (516) 555-5555*
*Fax: (516) 666-6666*

Today's date


Ms. Rebecca Mondale, Branch Manager
Flagship Realty
98 Fire Lane
Southhampton, NY 11557

Dear Ms. Mondale:

We just received notice that we have been given the exclusive listing for PineView Estates, the country condominium residences located on the North Fork. The builder placed an advertisement for this new development in several local newspapers. The ad ran last Sunday and will run again next Sunday; a copy appears below:

As a result of this local exposure, you should have considerable activity on these properties. Keep me apprised of all activity.

Sincerely,



Jawanza Hughes
Vice President

jh/yo


*Insert the ESTATE file*

**Exercise**

# 39

## ■ AutoText

## NOTES

### AutoText

■ The **AutoText** feature allows you to save standard or repetitive text and insert it into a document when needed. For example, creating an AutoText entry for a letter closing eliminates the need to retype a closing each time a letter is generated. In a Last Will and Testament, many of the paragraphs are standard and used for all clients. Only those paragraphs that relate to specific items or names are changed. An AutoText entry may be created to save the repetitive paragraphs.

■ An unlimited amount of text or graphics may be stored in an AutoText entry. You may use up to 31 characters in naming AutoText entries, and you may include spaces, but it is recommended to use short names that are easy to remember.

■ To create an AutoText entry, keyboard or highlight the text (or graphics) that you want to become an AutoText entry. Open the Insert menu, select AutoText and then select New from the submenu.

*Hint: If you want to preserve the format of the AutoText entry, be sure to include the paragraph mark when selecting the text.*

■ In the Create AutoText dialog box that follows, type the name of your AutoText entry in the name text box, and click the OK button to create the entry. Use a one-letter abbreviation as your AutoText name if you use the entry frequently.

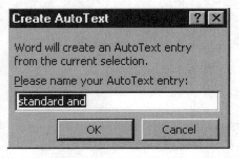

■ To insert an AutoText entry into a document:

• Type the name (or abbreviation) of the AutoText entry and press F3. As you begin to type the name of your entry, a pop-up box will display suggesting the entry name. Press Enter to accept Word's suggestion. This feature is active only when the AutoComplete Check box in the AutoText dialog box is on. You can access the AutoText dialog box by selecting Insert, AutoText, AutoText.

*AutoText Dialog Box*

AutoComplete check box

• If you are not certain of the name or content of the AutoText entry, open the Insert menu, select AutoText, then select Normal from the submenu. By default, all AutoText entries are stored in the Normal option. View the entries, then select the desired entry. You can also select AutoText from the submenu, select the desired entry from the list in the AutoText dialog box, and then click OK.

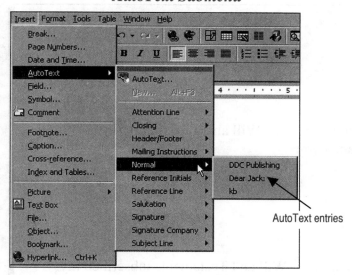

*AutoText Submenu*

- If you use the AutoText feature frequently, you may want to display the AutoText toolbar. Select Show Toolbar in the AutoText dialog box, or right-click on the Standard toolbar and select AutoText.

*AutoText Toolbar*

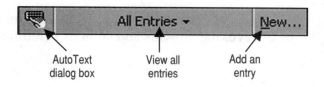

AutoText dialog box      View all entries      Add an entry

---

*In Part I of this exercise, you will create AutoText entries for several paragraphs that are standard for a Last Will and Testament and save each entry under a different filename. In Part II of the exercise, you will assemble a Last Will and Testament, inserting the appropriate standard paragraph files. Other AutoText entries will be used in subsequent exercises.*

# EXERCISE DIRECTIONS

## Part I

1. Create a new document.
2. Display the Office Assistant.
3. Use the default margins.
4. Keyboard the first standardized paragraph as shown in Part I on the next page, including the asterisks (*). (Do not include the AutoText name in the paragraph.)
5. Spell check.
6. Create an AutoText entry using the AutoText name indicated above the paragraph.
7. Keyboard the remaining paragraphs.
8. Spell check.
9. Highlight each paragraph and create an AutoText entry using the name indicated above it.
10. Close the document window without saving.

## Part II

1. Create a new document.
2. Keyboard the Last Will and Testament as shown in Part II on page 149, or open 🖫**39WILL**
3. Use the default margins.
4. Begin the exercise At 2".
5. Set the title to a serif 14-point bold font; set the body text to serif 12 point.
6. Set a first line indent of 2" for the first, second, and third paragraphs.
   (Alt + O, P, Alt + S, First Line, Alt + Y).
7. Insert the AutoText entries indicated.
8. Using the Find feature, locate each asterisk and insert the information indicated.
9. Spell check.
10. Preview your work.
11. Use the Shrink-to-Fit feature to shrink text to one page. Make any necessary adjustments to the text.
12. Print one copy.
13. Close the file; save as **WILL**

**PART I**

*Auto Text Name:  Will1*

I, *, of *, do make, publish and declare this to be my Last Will and Testament, hereby revoking all wills and codicils heretofore made by me.

*AutoText Name:  Will2*

IN TESTIMONY WHEREOF, I have to this my Last Will and Testament, subscribed my name and affixed my seal, this * day of * , 1997.

·········································································

*

Signed, sealed, published and declared by the above-named testator, as and for his Last Will and Testament, in our presence, and we at his request, in his presence and in the presence of each other, do hereunto, sign our names and set down our addresses as attesting witnesses, all on this * day of *, 1997.

·················································residing at··························································

·················································residing at··························································

·················································residing at··························································

*AutoText Name:  PSA*

*PsA* Micro**Computer** Systems, Inc.

*AutoText Name:  CO*

*Computer Technology Group, Inc.* ◄——— Turn off italics

**LAST WILL AND TESTAMENT
OF
JOHN RICHARD ADAMS**

# Insert WILL1    4    * 105 Oakland Lane
Goshen, NY

* John Richard Adams

FIRST:    I direct that all my just debts, the expenses of my last illness and funeral and the expenses of administering my estate be paid as soon as convenient.

SECOND:    I give all my articles of personal, household or domestic use or adornment, including automobile and boats, to my wife, Mary Adams, or, if she does not survive me, to my children, Thomas Adams and Betsy Adams, as shall survive me, in shares substantially equal as to value.

THIRD:    I give and devise all my residential real property, and all my interest in any policies of insurance thereon, to my wife, Mary Adams, if she survives me or if she does not survive me, to my surviving children, to be held by them jointly.

# Insert WILL2    * third    * January
* John Richard Adams

# KEYSTROKES

## CREATE AN AUTOTEXT ENTRY

1. Select (highlight) text/graphics to store as an AutoText entry.
2. Click **I**nsert............................ Alt + I
3. Click **A**utoText............................... A
4. Click **N**ew..................................... N
5. Type name for AutoText entry.
6. Click **OK**.

## DELETE AN AUTOTEXT ENTRY

1. Click **I**nsert............................ Alt + I
2. Click **A**utoText............................... A
3. Click **A**utoTe**x**t.............................. X
4. Select AutoText name to delete.
5. Click **D**elete ......................... Alt + D
6. Click **OK** ...................................... Enter

## INSERT AN AUTOTEXT ENTRY

### –USING KEYBOARD SHORTCUT–

1. Place insertion point where AutoText entry will be inserted.

2. Type name of AutoText entry.
3. Press **F3**............................................ F3

**OR**

(If AutoComplete is turned on)

Press **Enter** when Word suggests the desired AutoText entry.

### –USING THE INSERT MENU–

1. Place insertion point where AutoText entry will be inserted.
2. Click **A**utoText................................ A
3. Click **A**utoText................................ X
4. Select or type desired AutoText name.
5. Click **I**nsert............................ Alt + I

### –USING THE AUTOTEXT TOOLBAR–

1. Right-click on Standard (or any) toolbar and select AutoText to turn on toolbar.

2. Place insertion point where AutoText entry will be inserted.

3. Click **All Entries**.
4. Click template where AutoText entry is stored.

*(By default, all AutoText entries are stored in Normal template unless you select another template where you want to store them.)*

5. Select desired entry from list.

## EDIT AN AUTOTEXT ENTRY

1. Insert AutoText into document.
2. Edit as desired.
3. Select (highlight) the edit text/graphics.
4. Click **A**utoText ............................... A
5. Click **A**utoTe**x**t .............................. X
6. Select or type desired AutoText name.
7. Click **A**dd ............................... Alt + A
8. Click **Y**es ............................... Alt + Y
   when asked if you want to redefine the AutoText entry.

## Exercise 40

### ■ Record a Macro

## NOTES

- A **macro** is a saved series of commands and keystrokes which may be played with a single keystroke or mouse click. It is different from an AutoText entry in that it may contain commands and mouse actions in addition to text.

- For example, a macro may be used to automate a particular task, like changing margins or line spacing. Rather than press many keys to access a feature, you can record the process and play it with one keystroke.

- To record a macro, select Record New Macro from the Macro submenu on the Tools menu.

- In the Record Macro dialog box which follows, keyboard the name of your macro in the Macro name text box. Macro names may be up to 82 characters in length. Macro names may include letters and numbers, but they may not contain any spaces or special characters.

- It is important to type a Description of what each macro accomplishes. This will enable others to use them. Also, because macro names are easy to forget, you will always be reminded of what each macro does by its description.

- You can assign your macro to become a toolbar button or a keystroke on the keyboard.

- After entering the name and description of your macro, click OK.

  ✓Note:   To create a toolbar button for a particular macro, you must customize the toolbar. See Office documentation to customize toolbars.

- For the exercises in this text, click Keyboard to assign the keystroke(s) for each macro you record. After you enter and assign keystroke(s) for the macro and click Close, the Macro Control box appears on the screen and any key you press will be captured into the macro.

- To stop recording, click the Stop button on the Macro control box.

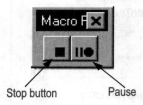

Stop button       Pause

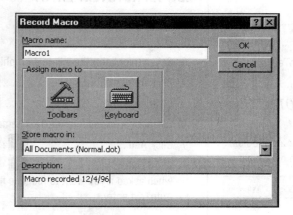

*In this exercise, you will create three macros to automate tasks. One of the macros will contain a closing in addition to task automation. In the next exercise, you will run the macros.*

# EXERCISE DIRECTIONS

1. Create a new document.

2. Close the Office Assistant (if it is displayed).

3. Create macro #1 (a closing, and print); name it **CLOSING** and use **Alt + Shift + S** as the shortcut keys.

4. Create macro #2 (font size and margin change); name it **BEGIN** and use **Alt + C** as the shortcut keys.

5. Create macro #3 (line spacing change); name it **LINE** and use **Alt + L** as the shortcut keys.

6. Close the document window.

---

**Macro #1**
*Name:* **CLOSING**
*Shortcut keys:*
**Alt + Shift + S**

Sincerely,


David Altmann, Esq.

da/yo

1. Click File.
2. Click Print.
3. Click OK.
4. Stop Recording.

---

**Macro #2**
*Name:* **BEGIN**
*Shortcut keys:*
**Alt + C**

1. Click font size button on Toolbar.
2. Select 14 point.
3. Click File.
4. Click Page Setup.
5. Click Margins tab.
6. Change left and right margins to 1".
7. Click OK.
8. Stop Recording.

---

**Macro #3**
*Name:* **LINE**
*Shortcut keys:*
**Alt + L**

1. Click Format.
2. Click Paragraph.
3. Click in At text box (line spacing).
4. Enter 1.3" as line spacing amount.
5. Click OK.
6. Stop Recording.

---

# KEYSTROKES

## RECORD A MACRO

1. Click **Tools** ............................ `Alt`+`T`

2. Click **Macro** ................................. `M`

3. Click **Record New Macro**.............. `R`

4. Type a name for the macro.

5. Click **Description**................. `Alt`+`D`

6. Type a description of the macro's function.

7. Click **Keyboard** ..................... `Alt`+`K`

8. Press **Alt** plus a desired shortcut key.

✓ *Do not use a key that is assigned to another function. Word will indicate whether each key you suggest is unassigned.*

9. Click **OK**................................... `Enter`

10. Type keystrokes to store in the macro.

✓ *Mouse actions in menus and dialog boxes may be used in a macro, but mouse actions that select text or position the insertion point may not be stored in a macro.*

## STOP RECORDING A MACRO

Click **Stop** button ................................... `▪`
on **Macro Control Box**

   **OR**

a. Click **Tools**............................ `Alt`+`T`

b. Click **Macro** ................................. `M`

c. Click **Stop Recording**........... `Alt`+`R`

## DELETE A MACRO

*ALT + F8*

1. Click **Tools**............................ `Alt`+`T`

2. Click **Macro**................................. `M`

3. Click **Macros**................................ `M`

4. Select desired macro name...... `↓`,`↑`

5. Click **Delete** ......................... `Alt`+`D`

6. Click **Yes**..................................... `Y`

7. Click **Close**................................ `Esc`

<table>
<tr><td>Exercise<br>**41**</td><td>■ **Run a Macro**</td></tr>
</table>

## NOTES

■ Once a macro has been recorded and saved, it can be *run* (or played) into your document whenever desired.

■ To run a macro, press the keystroke(s) assigned to the macro, or open the Tools menu, select Macro, then select Macros on the submenu. Select the name of the macro and click Run.

   ✓*Note:  You can also use this dialog box to create, delete, or edit macros.*

■ If you select Word Commands from the Macros in list box, numerous macros that you did not create will be listed in the macro window. Word has provided you with numerous macros to automate a variety of tasks. To determine what each macro does, click the macro and note the description at the bottom of the dialog box.

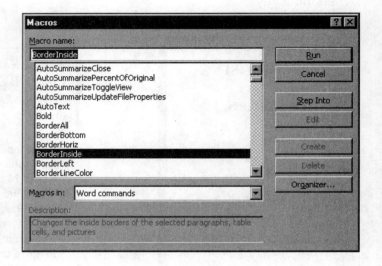

---

*In this exercise, you will create a legal letter, and, where indicated, play two AutoText entries, as well as two macros you created earlier. You will note that this document contains a Re line, which is commonly used in legal correspondence. "Re" means "in reference to" or "subject." Press the Enter key twice before and after typing the "re" line.*

---

## EXERCISE DIRECTIONS

1. Create a new document.

2. Run the BEGIN macro (Alt + C) to change font size and margins.

3. Keyboard the letter shown on the next page.

4. Begin the exercise At 2.5".

5. Justify paragraph text.

6. Play the PSA and CO AutoText entries wherever they appear in the text.

7. Run the CLOSING macro (Alt + Shift + S) to add a closing and print your letter.

8. Print one copy.

9. Close the file; save as **SETTLE**.

Today's date


Thomas Wolfe, Esq.
Wolfe, Escada & Yates
803 Park Avenue
New York, NY  10023

Dear Mr. Wolfe:

Re:          **[AutoText PSA]** vs. ABC Manufacturing Company

I am faxing a copy of the Bill of Sale that transfers all Gordon's assets to **[AutoText PSA]**.

In addition, you asked us to represent **[AutoText CO]** in their $200,000 payment to **[AutoText PSA]**.  Because of this payment, **[AutoText CO]** became subrogated to the claim made by **[AutoText PSA]**, and **[AutoText PSA]** cannot settle this matter without the approval of **[AutoText CO]**.

**[AutoText CO]** would also be entitled to recover some portion of any judgment recovered by **[AutoText PSA]**, in the above action.  In order to get a settlement in this matter, we will need to obtain a release of ABC Manufacturing Company by **[AutoText CO]**.

Let's discuss this so that we can quickly settle this matter.



*Insert CLOSING macro.*

# KEYSTROKES

**RUN A MACRO**

*ALT + F8*

1. Click **Tools** ............................ Alt + T

2. Click **Macro** .................................. M
3. Click **Macros** ................................. M
4. Select desired macro name ..... ↓ , ↑

5. Click **Run** ............................... Alt + R
   **OR**
   Press shortcut keys for desired macro.

**Exercise**

# 42

■ **Summary**

## EXERCISE DIRECTIONS

1. Create the following AutoText entry; name it **AD**.
   **RideTheTrack** Exerciser.

2. Close the document window.

3. Create the advertisement shown below. Play the macros and AutoText entries where indicated.

4. Center and bold the title beginning at 2". Use the default font face and size.
   ✓ *Note: Press the Enter key twice after the bulleted items.*

5. Begin At 2".

6. Spell check.

7. Preview your document.

8. Print one copy.

9. Save the file; name it **WORKOUT**.

10. Close the document window.

---

### DISCOVER AN EXCITING NEW WAY TO ACHIEVE
### WELLNESS OF BODY AND MIND

**[Line]**

According to medical fitness experts, regular aerobic exercise is essential for achieving all-around wellness. Aerobic exercise helps you prevent illness, feel better physically and mentally, boost your energy level, and increase the years of your life. That's why you need the **[AUTOTEXT AD]**.  **[AUTOTEXT AD]** will provide you with the following benefits:

**[Return to single space.  Left indent text 1" from left margin.  Use the bullet feature.]**

- You can burn more fat than on other exercisers and burn up to 1,100 calories per hour!
- You can improve your cardiovascular fitness and lower your overall cholesterol level.
- You'll feel more mentally alert, relaxed, positive and self-confident.

**[Line]**

With regular workouts on a **[AUTOTEXT AD]**, you'll feel wonderful because you're doing something positive for yourself.

Seven out of ten **[AUTOTEXT AD]** owners use their machines an average of three times per week.

Call your **[AUTOTEXT AD]** representative today at 1-800-555-4444 to receive a FREE video and brochure.

**[AUTOTEXT AD]**

---

**Lesson 8:** Clip Art and Templates; Envelopes and Labels

**Exercise 43**

- ■ **Work with Clip Art** ■ **Import Clip Art into a Document**
- ■ **Size Clip Art Images** ■ **Text Boxes** ■ **Wrap Text**

***Drawing Toolbar***

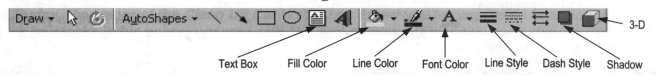

Draw ▾   AutoShapes ▾   3-D

Text Box   Fill Color   Line Color   Font Color   Line Style   Dash Style   Shadow

# NOTES

### Work with Clip Art

- ■ You can include, pictures (clip art and photos), sound clips, and even video clips in a document. Several clip art images are installed when you install Office 97. If you have a connection to the Internet, you can download additional images from Microsoft. The ability to combine pictures and text can help you communicate your message more effectively.

- ■ Word provides the Microsoft Clip Gallery, which contains numerous images covering a wide range of topics. Each clip art image has its own filename and contains the extension .WMF (Windows Metafile Format).

- ■ To insert a clip art image into a Word document, select Picture from the Insert menu. Then select Clip Art on the Picture submenu.

- ■ In the Microsoft Clip Gallery which follows, a list of categories appears on the left side of the Gallery window, and images relating to the category are displayed on the right. A description of the picture and its filename displays at the bottom of the window. Select the image you want to appear in your document and click Insert.

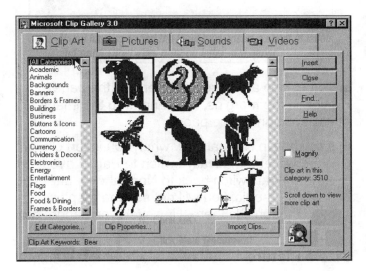

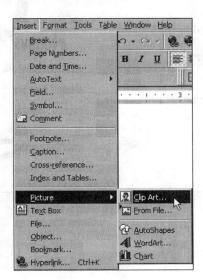

## Import a Picture

- By default, when a picture is imported into Word, it is aligned at the left margin. However, the horizontal alignment may be changed so the graphic is right-aligned or centered by

  - selecting the picture

  - selecting P̲icture from the F̲ormat menu

  - clicking the Position tab

  - deselecting Float over t̲ext

  - clicking the alignment buttons on the Standard toolbar, just as you would align text.

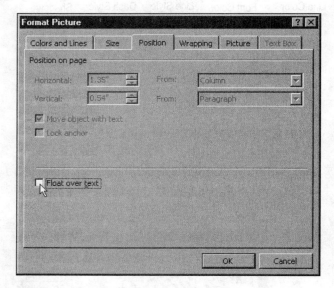

- To position a picture anywhere on the page, even in the margins, click and drag the image to any position on the page.

- If you are in Normal view when you insert clip art, Word will automatically switch to Page Layout view. If you switch back to Normal view after you insert a graphic, you will not see the graphic, even though it is there. However, you cannot do this if Float over t̲ext has been selected.

## Size a Picture

- When a graphic is imported, Word determines its size. However, after a graphic is imported, you may make it smaller, larger, stretch it into exaggerated shapes, move it, or delete it.

- To change the size of a graphic, move it, or delete it, you must first select it by clicking the image. A selected image appears below. Note the **sizing handles** that appear once the graphic is selected. When the mouse pointer is placed on one of the sizing handles, the pointer changes to a double-headed arrow. You may then change the size or shape of the image by simply dragging the sizing handle.

*Selected Graphic*

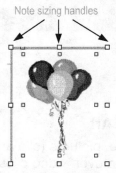

- When any of the four corner handles are dragged, the size of the entire image changes (becomes smaller or larger), and the picture retains its proportions. When any of the four middle handles are dragged, only the height or the width changes, thus changing the proportions or **scale** of the image and giving it a different appearance. Note the stars below.

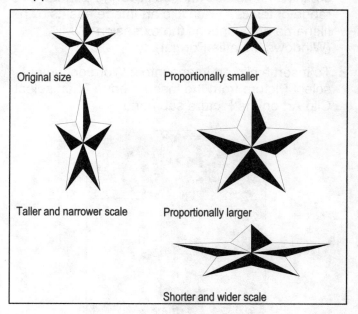

- You can also adjust the image by an exact amount. Select the picture, then select Picture from the Format menu. In the Format Picture dialog box, click the Size tab and enter the Size in the Width and Height text boxes.

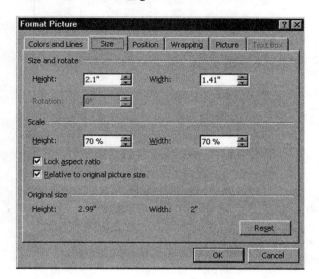

- You can return the graphic to its original size by clicking the Reset Picture button 🔳 on the Picture toolbar. The Picture toolbar can be displayed by selecting Toolbars, Picture from the View menu. You can also select Picture on the Format menu, click the Picture tab, select Reset and click OK.

- To delete a graphic, select it and press Delete.

## Text Boxes

- Text within a box is typically used to set off special text such as tables, charts, sidebars, and callouts.

- Text boxes can be used to enclose text or graphics.

- To create a text box, click the Text Box button 📄 on the Drawing toolbar. The insertion point changes to a crossbar +. Drag the crossbar to the desired text box size and type your text.

- Text in a text box can be sized, moved and positioned almost anywhere in a document. The text direction within the box can also be changed.

- Word automatically places a border around a text box. You can change the line style or line color of the border, add shading to the contents of the text box or change the font color within the text

box. In addition, you can create a shadow or 3D effect on the text box.

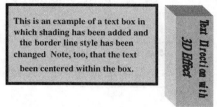

- **To change the line style** or **line color**, select the text box (so handles appear); then click the Line Style button and/or the Line Color list arrow on the Drawing toolbar and choose a desired line style and/or line color.

- **To shade the contents of the text box**, select the text box, then click the Fill Color list arrow on the Drawing toolbar and choose a desired fill.

- **To create a shadow or 3D effect**, select the text box, then click the Shadow or 3D button on the Drawing toolbar and select a shadow or 3D style to apply from the pop-up menu.

- You can also change line styles, line colors, and fill colors by selecting the text box, then selecting Text Box from the Format menu. In the Format Text Box dialog box that follows, select the Colors and Lines tab and make the desired changes.

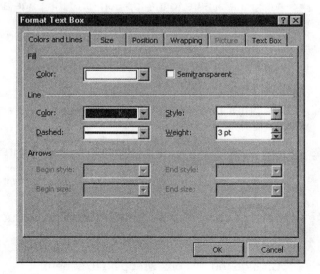

- **To change the font color**, select the text box, then click the Font Color list arrow on the Drawing toolbar and choose a desired font color.

- **To change text direction,** draw the text box and type the text. Then click the Text Direction button on the Text Box dialog box until the desired direction is achieved. You can display the Text Box toolbar by selecting Toolbars, Text Box from the View menu.

### Wrap Text

- Word provides several options for wrapping text around a picture (or text box).

- To wrap text around a picture, select the picture, then select Picture from the Format menu. In the Format Picture dialog box that follows, select the Wrapping Tab and select a desired text wrap option.

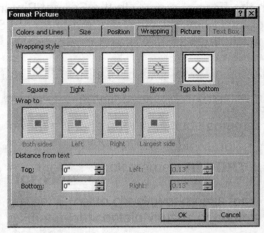

- When using text wrapping, carefully proofread the text that flows around the picture. You may need to adjust the picture position to avoid awkward word breaks.

*In this exercise, you will create an advertisement in which you insert a text box and anchor pictures.*

# EXERCISE DIRECTIONS

1. Create a new document.

2. Set .5" top and bottom margins.

3. Begin the exercise at the top of the screen.

4. Insert any relevant graphic:
   - Size it to 4" high by 5" wide.
   - Drag the picture to the top center of the page as illustrated.
   - Anchor the graphic to stay in this position. (Go to the Format Text Box dialog box, select the Position tab, then select Lock anchor and deselect Move object with text.)

5. Press Enter to move down to where the text will begin.

6. Center and bold the headline text in any desired font. Size it to 20 points.
   - ✓ *Note: If necessary, adjust the point size or change the font so the heading will fit on two lines.*

7. Insert a text box below the headline and do the following:
   - ✓ *Note: You can adjust the size of the text box at any time.*
   - Change the text box wrapping to square.

- Enter the text in a 10-point sans serif font.
- Center and bold the heading.
- Use any bullet other than the round dot.
- Use a dotted border.
- Shade the frame to a light gray.
- Position the text box in the middle of the page as shown. Use a tight text wrapping option.
- Adjust the size of the frame to fit the text.

8. Enter the text in serif 12 point. Set the line spacing to 1.5".

9. Set Coastal Electronics and the phone number to 9 point bold.

10. Insert another relevant graphic:
    - Size it to 1" x 1".

11. Spell check.

12. Preview your work.

13. Save the file; name it **COASTAL**.

14. Close the document window.

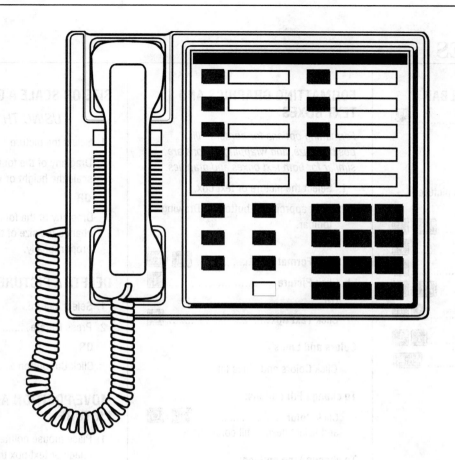

# Send and Receive Computer Data and Faxes from Wherever You Happen to Be.

With Phone/Data Link, you constraints of your office, but Phone/Data Link is a new Electronics that gives you the communicate anytime for allows you to connect your or fax machine to a portable the ability to send and receive anywhere that cellular service **Coastal Electronics 1-800-555-5555.**

**Phone/Data Link Advantages**

☑ Connects any modem-equipped computer or fax machine to a portable cellular telephone.
☑ Enables you to send and receive computer data or faxes via your cellular phone
☑ Compatible with your existing software.
☑ Compact design.
☑ Features simple two-cable connection.

can leave behind the physical never really lose touch.  The business tool from Coastal freedom to compute and anywhere.  Phone/Data Link modem-equipped computer cellular telephone and have data and faxes from virtually is available.

# KEYSTROKES

## DISPLAY DRAWING TOOLBAR

Click Drawing button ............................ 🖉
on Standard toolbar.

## INSERT A PICTURE

1. Place insertion point where picture
   is to be inserted.
2. Click **I**nsert ........................... `Alt` + `I`
3. Click **P**icture .............................. `P`
4. Click **C**lip Art .............................. `C`
5. Click **C**lip Art tab ................... `Alt` + `C`
6. Select desired category ............ `↑` `↓`
7. Click desired image. ................. `↑` `↓`
8. Click **I**nsert ............................. `Enter`

## SELECT A GRAPHIC

Click anywhere in the picture.

**To deselect a graphic:**

   Click anywhere in the picture.

## DISPLAY PICTURE TOOLBAR

Right-click on any toolbar and select
**Picture**.

## CREATE A TEXT BOX

1. Click Text box button 🔲 on Drawing
   toolbar.
   **OR**
   a. Click **I**nsert ......................... `Alt` + `I`
   b. Click Te**x**t Box.................... `Alt` + `X`
   *Mouse pointer assumes shape of
   crossbar.*
2. Position crossbar pointer where you
   want top left corner of text box to
   appear.
3. Hold down left mouse button and drag
   down and to the right until desired text
   box size is created.
4. Release the mouse.
5. Size, scale, reposition, or format text
   box as desired.

## FORMATTING GRAPHICS AND TEXT BOXES

*Formatting options for borders, fills,
position, size, and wrapping options are
similar for both text boxes and graphics.*

1. Select the picture or text box.
2. Click appropriate button on Drawing
   toolbar.
   **OR**
   a. Click **F**ormat ......................... `Alt` + `O`
   b. Click P**i**cture .............................. `I`
   **OR**
   Click Text B**o**x........................... `O`

### Colors and Lines

   Click Colors and Lines tab.

**To change Fill options:**

   Click **C**olor ............................. `Alt` + `C`
   and select desired fill color/shade.

**To change Line options:**

3. Select line **C**olor.................... `Alt` + `O`
4. Select **D**ashed style .............. `Alt` + `D`
5. Select **S**tyle.......................... `Alt` + `S`
6. Select **W**eight ...................... `Alt` + `W`
7. Click **O**K .............................. `Enter`

### Size

   Click **Size** tab.

**To change Size options:**

   a. Enter **H**eight measurement. `Alt` + `E`
   b. Enter **Wi**dth measurement .. `Alt` + `D`

**To change Scale options:**

1. Enter **H**eight measurement..... `Alt` + `H`
2. Enter **Wi**dth measurement ..... `Alt` + `W`
3. Click **O**K.................................... `Enter`

## SIZE OR SCALE A GRAPHIC

   *- USING THE MOUSE -*

1. Select the picture.
2. Drag any of the four middle handles to
   scale the height or width of the picture.
   **OR**
   Drag any of the four corner handles to
   change the size of the entire picture
   proportionally.

## DELETE A PICTURE

1. Select picture.
2. Press **Delete**............................. `Del`
   **OR**
   Click **Cut** button.............................. ✂

## MOVE/POSITION A TEXT BOX OR PICTURE

1. Place mouse pointer on any side of the
   image or text box until four-arrow shape
   appears at end of mouse pointer.
2. Drag framed image to desired location.

## ALIGN TEXT WITHIN A TEXT BOX

1. Place insertion point in desired
   paragraph.
   **OR**
2. Select desired text.
3. Click **Left Align** button ................... ▤
   **OR**
   Click **Right Align** button ................. ▤
   **OR**
   Click **Center** button ........................ ▤

# Exercise 44

## ■ Drop Capital ■ Draw Lines ■ Create a Newsletter

### Drawing Toolbar

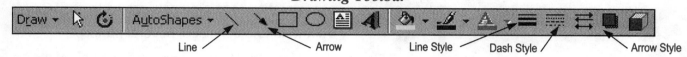

Line ——— Arrow ——— Line Style ——— Dash Style ——— Arrow Style

# NOTES

## Drop Capital

■ A **drop capital** is an enlarged capital letter that drops below the first line of body text. It is usually the first letter of a paragraph. It is often used to draw the reader's attention to chapter beginnings, section headings, and main body text.

> **D**rop capitals are large decorative letters often used to mark the beginning of a document, section, or chapter. Drop caps are set to a much larger font than the text, and often span the height of three or four lines.

■ To create a drop capital, place the insertion point in the paragraph where the drop cap will appear. Then select Drop Cap from the Format menu to open the Drop Cap dialog box.

■ If you want to include several letters, highlight the letters you want to include in the drop cap style, then open the Drop Cap dialog box.

■ In the Drop Cap dialog box, select the desired options for the Drop Cap. You can have the text wrap under the large letter (or letters) or let the text wrap to the right of the letter.

## Draw Lines

■ You can create horizontal and vertical lines in your document, in headers, or in footers.

■ Lines are used to create designs, to separate parts of a document, or to draw attention to a particular place.

■ You may adjust the position, length, and thickness of lines. You may select decorative line styles, such as dotted or dashed lines. You can also create lines with arrowheads.

■ To create a line, click the Line button ◹ on the Drawing toolbar. The insertion point changes to a crosshair. Drag the crosshair to create the desired horizontal or vertical line. Then, click the Line Style ▤ or Dash Style ▥ button on the Drawing toolbar and select a Line Style. Or, select More Lines to choose a different line style.

### Line Style

### Dash Style

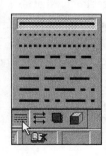

- To create a line of a particular thickness, size, or style, you can create a custom line in the Format AutoShape dialog box. Select the line and click Format, AutoShape. Select C**o**lor, **S**tyle, and **W**eight (thickness) options as desired.

- Line thickness is measured in point size.

*Format Autoshapes Dialog Box*

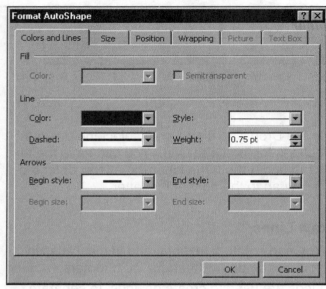

- Lines may be repositioned by dragging the whole object, just as you did with picture, or they may be reshaped and sized by dragging the sizing handle.

### Create a Newsletter

- A newsletter is a document used by an organization to communicate information about an event, news of general interest, or information regarding new products.

- Newsletters consist of several parts:

  - Nameplate - may include the name of the newsletter, the organization publishing the newsletter, and/or the logo (a symbol or distinctive type style used to represent the organization).

  - Dateline - may include the volume number, issue number, and date.

  - Headline - title preceding each article.

  - Body Text - the text of the article.

- Newsletters may also be created using a template.

# KEYSTROKES

### CREATE A DROP CAP

1. Place insertion point in paragraph where drop cap will appear.

2. Click **Format** ........................... Alt + O

3. Click **Drop Cap** ........................... D

4. Click desired position:

   **None** ........................................... N

   **Dropped** ...................................... D

   **In Margin** .................................... M

5. Select **Font** ................................. F
   (if different from rest of text)

6. Click **Lines to Drop** ............... Alt + L

7. Select increase or decrease ..... ↑, ↓ arrows to set desired number of lines.

8. Click **Distance from Text** ........ Alt + X

9. Select increase or decrease ..... ↑, ↓ arrows to set desired distance from text.

10. Click **OK** .................................. Enter

---

✓ *The Drawing toolbar must be visible on your screen for all of the following procedures. Click the Draw icon* 🖉 *on the Formatting toolbar to bring the Drawing toolbar to the screen.*

### DRAW A LINE

1. Click **Line Draw** button ................... ◇

2. Place crosshairs where line will begin.

3. Click and drag to point where line will end.

✓ *To create a straight line, hold down Alt as you drag the mouse.*

### WRAP TEXT

1. Click text box or picture.

2. Click **Format** ......................... Alt + O

3. Click **Text Box** ........................... O

   **OR**

   Click **Picture** ............................. I

   **OR**

   Click **Object** ............................. O

4. Click **Wrapping** tab.

---

5. Select desired Wrap option.

✓ *Options not available for the current situation will be dimmed.*

6. Click **OK** ...................................... Enter

### SET LINE STYLE

1. Select existing line.

2. Click **Line Style** button ................... ☰
   on Drawing toolbar.

3. Click desired line style.

### REPOSITION A LINE

1. Place mouse pointer on edge of line until a four-headed arrow is added to the end of the mouse pointer.

2. Drag object to desired position.

### RESIZE A LINE

1. Select the line.

2. Drag side handles to the desired length.

# EXERCISE DIRECTIONS

1. Create a new document.

2. Set left and right margins to 1". Set top and bottom margins to .5".

3. Type the nameplate as shown using serif 30-point bold for "American" and 48 point for "Traveler."

4. Move the insertion point to the end of "Traveler" and change font to sans serif 10 point.

5. Press Enter three times.

6. Enter dateline information as shown. Left align Volume 3, Number 3; use a center tab to center A Publication of Carl's Travel Network, and use a right tab to right-align Summer 1997.

7. Draw a 2-point horizontal line before and after nameplate and dateline information.

8. Position insertion point after Summer 1997 and press Enter three times.

9. Format the remainder of the document for 3 columns (Format, Columns).

   ✓ *Be sure to choose This point forward from the Apply to option in the Column dialog box.*

10. Keyboard the newsletter as shown; note the following:

    • Center the headlines; set them to sans serif 14-point bold.

    • Create drop caps as shown.

    • Set all paragraph text to serif 12 point.

    • Insert a text box and type TRAVEL TRIVIA text in sans serif 12 point as shown. Use the Top and Bottom Wrapping option. Add a Shadow to the text box as shown.

    • Insert a text box and type TRAVEL HIGHLIGHT OF THE SEASON text. Use sans serif 8 point bold for the text and 10-point bold for the title. Full Justify the text. Shade the text box using a 3D effect as shown.

    • Hyphenate the document. Limit consecutive hyphens to one.

    ✓ *Adjust the size of the framed text box as appropriate.*

11. Insert a relevant picture where shown. Size it to 1" wide by 1.25" high. Position it between columns. Use a Tight text wrapping option.

12. Insert any relevant picture and position it as part of the Newsletter Name as shown. Size it to fit next to American Traveler. Make sure you select through on the wrapping tab when formatting the picture.

13. Spell check.

14. Preview your work.

15. Save the file; name it **JOURNEY**.

16. Close the document window.

# AMERICAN
# TRAVELER

Volume 3, Number 3          A Publication of Carl's Travel Network          Summer 1997

## SMOKERS MEET NEW RESTRICTIONS DURING TRAVEL

Travelers should be aware of increased constraints on the ability to smoke in public places. About five years ago, smoking was prohibited on all domestic airline flights.

### Travel Trivia:

**Q.** What city is said to take its name from a Huron word meaning "meeting Place of the Waters?"
**A.** Toronto

Now, the Dallas-Fort Worth Airport recently declared the entire passenger terminal off limits to smokers. Those wishing to smoke will

now have to leave the airport premises to do so. Perhaps more far reaching is the law passed in Los Angeles and New York that makes cigarette smoking illegal in restaurants. Violators face a $50 fine for the first offense, $100 fine for the second offense within a year and $250 fine for every offense after that. Be cautious when traveling not to violate unexpected smoking laws!

## CRUISING ON THE RHINE

Strasbourg, the capital of French Alsace, is a wonderful city to begin or end a cruise. Its pink sandstone Cathedral and a well-preserved old town are enchanting attractions for vacationing tourists.
The cost of a three-day cruise including two evening meals, two breakfasts, two luncheons

and coffee and cakes will cost approximately $567 a person. The view from the middle of the river is more dramatic than the glimpses of the same scenery that a passenger sees on the train ride along the river bank from Cologne to Frankfurt. For further information, contact your local travel agent and request the "RIVER CRUISES TO EUROPE PACKAGE" or the "SILLIA TOURS PACKAGE."

### TRAVEL HIGHLIGHT OF THE SEASON

#### The Greek Islands

There are over 3,000 islands that comprise what are commonly referred to as "The Greek Islands." However, only 170 of these islands are inhabited, each with its own character and terrain. This summer, Sunshine Travel Network is offering special fares on cruises to many of these charming islands. A four-day cruise to Rhodes, Heraklion, Santorini, and Piraeus costs $799 per person.

Since the prices include fabulous meals and breathtaking land tours, this package is definitely the buy of the season! Call today. (201) 555-5555

## Exercise 45

### ■Create a Memo Using a Template

*Standard Toolbar*

New

## NOTES

■ A **template** is a skeleton document that may contain formatting, pictures, and/or text. It may be used to create documents that are used over and over again.

■ Using Word's predesigned templates, you can create documents such as memos, faxes, letters, and résumés (as well as other documents).

■ To use a template, select <u>N</u>ew from the <u>F</u>ile menu. In the New dialog box that follows, select the desired tab and template style.

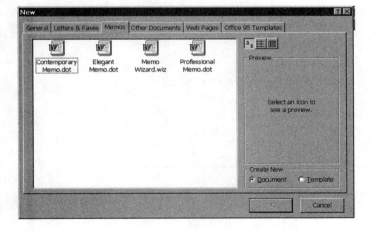

■ For each template, there are usually several styles from which to choose. The memo group, for example, provides three styles: Contemporary, Elegant, and Professional. To view a style, select the template and a sample will appear in the Preview window.

■ Many templates also offer a Wizard option *(Wizards will be covered in exercise 46.)*

■ If you select Professional Memo as your desired template, a predesigned memo form appears. The date is pulled from the computer's memory and automatically inserted in the proper location. Highlight the bracketed information (including the company name) and enter the relevant information for your memo.

■ Press Enter to automatically double-return at the end of a paragraph.

## KEYSTROKES

### ACCESS TEMPLATES

1. Click **<u>F</u>ile**.............................. `Alt` + `F`
2. Click **<u>N</u>ew**.................................... `N`

3. **Click tab for desired template**:
   Publications
   General
   Letters and Faxes
   Memos
   Reports
   Web Pages
   Legal Pleadings

Other Documents

4. Click desired template style.
5. Click **OK** ..................................... `Enter`

*In this exercise, you will use a template to create a memorandum.*

# EXERCISE DIRECTIONS

1. Create a new document.

2. Use the Professional Memo template to create the memo illustrated below.

3. Highlight the bracketed prompts, and enter the following relevant information:

   | | |
   |---|---|
   | Company Name: | MicroProducts, Inc. |
   | To: | Janice Smith |
   | From: | Your name |
   | CC: | Latifa Jones |
   | Re: | New Product Announcement |

4. Type the memo text as shown.

5. Print one copy.

6. Save the file; name it **ANNOUNCE**.

7. Close the document window.

---

**MicroProducts, Inc.**

# Memo

| | |
|---|---|
| **To:** | Janice Smith |
| **From:** | Your name |
| **CC:** | Latifa Jones |
| **Date:** | February 6, 1997 |
| **Re:** | New Product Announcement |

---

The new Product Development Committee will be meeting on Thursday at 10 a.m. to discuss the details of the MicroForm announcement.

We will need to prepare a press release later this month and plan for promotion.  Please bring development files with you.

• Page 1

## Exercise 46

### ■ Use a Template Wizard to Create a Fax Cover Sheet

## NOTES

### Use a Template Wizard

■ Some templates contain a option (such as Memo Wizard, Letter Wizard, Fax Wizard, etc.) as one of the template styles listed in the New dialog box.

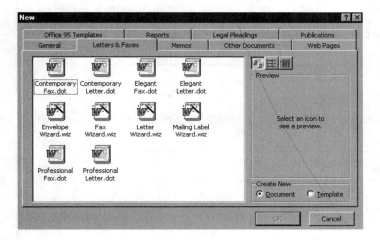

■ **Wizards** walk you through the steps for creating and sending a document.

■ A **fax cover sheet** is used as the first page of several to be faxed.  Its purpose is to identify the recipient and the sender of the faxed pages. You can also use the fax cover sheet to type a message.

■ When you access Fax Wizard, for example, the following dialog box appears in which you can start creating a fax.

■ After clicking the Next button, follow the prompts to complete your fax cover sheet.

■ The Fax Wizard will ask you to fill in the recipient's name, phone, fax, copies to, remarks, etc.  When you click Finish, the fax cover sheet will appear with the information you entered. You can then enter any other information you want to include on the fax cover sheet.

---

*In this exercise, you will create a Fax Cover Sheet using the Fax Wizard.*

---

## EXERCISE DIRECTIONS

1. Create a new document.

2. Use the Fax Wizard to create the fax cover sheet illustrated on the following page.

3. Use portrait orientation and any desired cover sheet style.

4. Use the information shown in the exercise to fill in the prompted information as well as recipient's name and comment information.

5. Print one copy.

6. Save the file; name it **FAX**.

7. Close the document window.

1504 Broadway
New York, NY  10024
Phone: (212) 555-5555
Fax: (212) 444-4444

# facsimile transmittal

**To:**     Brittany Williams                    **From:**   Your name

**Fax:**    (516)  777-7777                      **Date:**   June 5, 1997

**Phone:**  (516) 888-8888                       **Pages:**  1

**Re:**     June 5 Meeting Cancelled             **CC:**     Janice Polo

☐ **Urgent**     x **For Review**     ☐ **Please Comment**     ☐ **Please Reply**     ☐ **Please Recycle**

**Notes:**  Please make note that the June 5 meeting, scheduled in my office, has been cancelled until

further notice.

**CONFIDENTIAL**

## Exercise 47

### ■ Envelopes and Labels

## NOTES

■ To create envelopes and labels independent of templates or merging, select Envelopes and Labels from the Tools menu.

■ In the Envelopes and Labels dialog box that follows, select the Envelopes or Labels tab as desired.

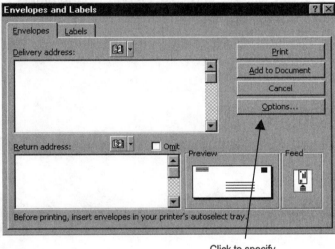

Click to specify
envelope size

### Envelopes

■ If a document is on screen (in the current document window), Word automatically retrieves its mailing address into the Delivery address window. If not, type the mailing address in manually.

■ You may also type a return address in the Return address window. To insure that the return address is printed, make sure the Omit check box is de-selected.

■ Clicking the Add to Document button appends the envelope file to the beginning of the document so you can print it with the document at any time (providing you name and save the document). The Print button allows you to print your envelope without appending it to the document.

■ To specify an envelope size, select the Options button in the Envelope and Labels dialog box and then the Envelope Options tab in the Envelope Options dialog box.

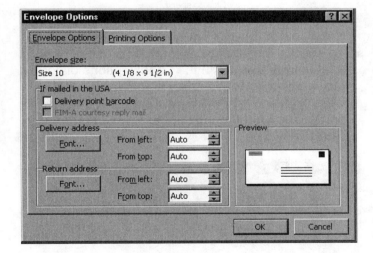

■ To change the appearance of the return or mailing address text, you may select a desired font face and size by clicking one of the Font buttons in the Envelope Options dialog box.

■ The Printing Options tab provides envelope feed options. You must select the feed method that is compatible with your printer.

## Labels

- The Label feature allows you to create mailing labels, file folder labels, or diskette labels.

- To create labels, you must select the Labels tab in the Envelopes and Labels dialog box. In the dialog box that follows, set label specifications.

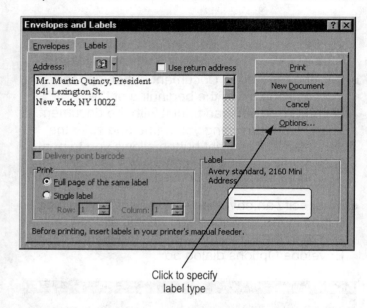

Click to specify
label type

- To specify the label type you will be using, click the Options button. In the Label Options dialog box which follows, you may select the type of label on which you will be working from the predefined Label products and Product number lists.

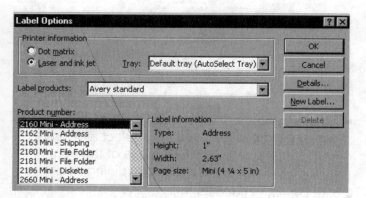

- For each label type you highlight, information about the label and sheet size is displayed in the Label information area of the dialog box.

- Once you specify the label format and click OK, you will be brought back to the previous dialog box. Click New Document and blank labels will display, ready for you to start keyboarding text onto them. Press the Tab key to advance from label to label.

- To see the labels as they will be arranged when printed, use Print Preview.

- When you are ready to print, load your printer with the proper size and type of label paper you specified, and then print. When you print a single page, the entire physical page is printed.

- If you desire to print a sheet of labels with the same information, enter the information in the Address window and select the Full page of the same label radio button in the Envelope and Labels dialog box.

> *In Part I of this exercise, you will create an envelope for a previously created letter. In Part II of this exercise, you will create labels for three addresses.*

# EXERCISE DIRECTIONS

## PART I

1. Open 🖳**REGRETSABOUTJOBOPENINGS**, or open 💾**47REGRET**.

2. Create an envelope for this letter (the inside address will automatically display in the Delivery address window).

3. Use the default envelope size.

4. Append the envelope file to the document.

5. Print one copy of the letter and the envelope.

6. Close the file; save the changes.

## PART II

1. Create a new document.

2. Create three labels using the addresses below.

Ms. Margie Zana
2399 Santiago Lane
Denver, CO 80333

Mr. Michael Chen
Acme Design Studio, Inc.
80 Plaza A
Milwaukee, WI 53212

Mr. Tom Polanski
Holistic, Inc.
777 Westgate Road
San Antonio, TX 76888

3. Use Avery Standard 5660 Address as your label type.

4. Print one copy of the page.

   ✓ *If you have specified the label type, insert a sheet of labels and print. Otherwise, print on letter-size paper.*

5. Save the file; name it **LABEL**.

# KEYSTROKES

## CREATE AN ENVELOPE

1. Click **Tools** ......................... `Alt`+`T`

2. Click **Envelopes and Labels** ............ `E`

3. Click **Envelopes tab** .............. `Alt`+`E`

4. Type mailing address ........... `Alt`+`D`
   in **Delivery address** window.

   ✓ *If a document containing an inside address is on the screen, the mailing address will automatically be retrieved into the Delivery address window.*

5. Type return address .............. `Alt`+`R`
   in **Return address** window.

6. Select a print option:

   • **Add to Document** .............. `Alt`+`A`

   • **Print** .................................. `Alt`+`P`

## CREATE A LABEL

1. Click **Tools** ............................ `Alt`+`T`

2. Click **Envelopes and Labels** ........... `E`

3. Click **Labels** tab .................... `Alt`+`L`

4. Click **Options** ........................ `Alt`+`O`

5. Select a label type.

6. Click **OK** .................................. `Enter`

7. Click **New Document** ............. `Alt`+`D`

8. Keyboard address for first label.

9. Press **Tab** to advance to the next label tab.

10. Repeat steps 8 and 9 for each additional address.

11. Load labels into printer.

12. Print as you would a normal document.

## Exercise

## 48

■ **Summary**

*In this exercise, you will create a newsletter and include pictures, a text box with a 3D effect, and a drop capital.*

# EXERCISE DIRECTIONS

1. Create a new document.

2. Set left and right margins to 1". Set top and bottom margins to .5".

3. Type the nameplate as shown using serif 30 point bold for "Cablecom," 48 point for "News Briefs," and 9 point for A Monthly Publication of CableCom…"

4. Press Enter three times.

5. Format the remainder of the document for 3 columns (Format, Columns).

6. Keyboard the newsletter as shown; note the following:

   • Center the headlines; set them to sans serif 14 point bold.

   • Create the drop cap as shown.

   • Set paragraph text to serif 11 point.

   • Full justify column text.

   • Create a text box with a 3D effect and insert the Please Note text. Hyphenate the document. Limit consecutive hyphens to 2.

7. Insert an appropriate graphic at the top of the newsletter and size it as desired.

8. Insert another appropriate graphic at the bottom of the newsletter as shown. Size it to 1.34" wide by 2" high. Position it between columns and use a Tight text wrapping option.

9. Spell check.

10. Preview your work.

11. Save the file; name it **CABLE**.

12. Close the document window.

# CABLECOM

# News Briefs

A Monthly Publication of CableCom ■ December 1997

## Senior Vice President of Human Resources Named

**D**avid Duffy has been named Senior Vice President of Human Resources for CableCom. He is being promoted from General Manager, and will assume his new position on April 1. In his new role, David will report directly to Chief of Corporate Operations.

David has been with CableCom for 12 years and has held a variety of positions of increasing responsibility in Human Resources.

## Employee Health Club Construction Update

The men's upstairs locker room will be closed through April 19, at which time construction is expected to be completed. As soon as the men's room is finished, construction will begin in the women's locker room and is expected to last four weeks.

## Fire Procedures

All employees should take notice of the new fire procedures posted on each floor. Please become familiar with the fire exits located in the same area on every floor:

- **Exit A** is located in the back freight elevator lobby.

- **Exit B** is the outside fire escape located at the end of the main hallway.

- **Exit C** is located in the front elevator lobby.

In the event that a fire alarm does sound on your floor, please wait for an announcement from the Fire Warden who will instruct you as to which exit to use.

## Computer Workshops

The Information Services department is conducting the following monthly workshops. These workshops will be offered during lunch hours and will be open to all employees.

⇒ *Now Up To Date 3.0.* This calendar program lets you schedule appointments and "to do" items for one or more people. The workshop will address creating a new calendar, scheduling events, using categories and reminders, customizing and printing schedule views. *Thursday, January 9, 12-2.*

⇒ *Windows 95 Upgrade.* This workshop will present the new features of Windows 95. *Thursday, January 16, 12-2.*

**Please Note:**
Workshops have limited seating capacity, so sign up early if you wish to attend. Call Mary Rizzo at Extension 444.

## Achievement Awards Dinner

This year's annual CableCom Achievements Awards Dinner will be held at the Marriott Hotel on Thursday, April 25. Cocktails will be served at 6:30 p.m. followed by dinner at 8:00 p.m.

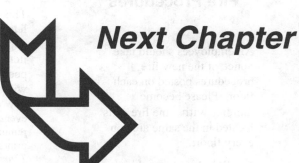

# Microsoft Excel 97

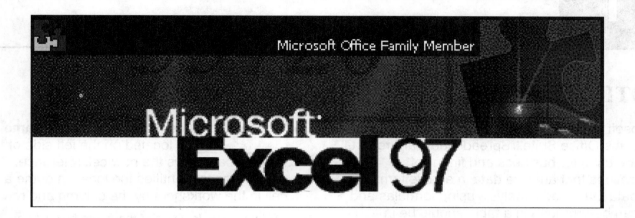

**Lesson 1:** Create, Save, and Exit a Worksheet

**Lesson 2:** Use Formulas; Format; Copy; Print

**Lesson 3:** Use Formulas and Functions; Edit; Print Options

**Lesson 4:** Additional Formatting and Editing; Working with Workbooks

**Lesson 5:** Logical Functions; Autoformat; Protecting and Hiding Data

**Lesson 6:** Charting

<table>
<tr><td rowspan="2">Exercise<br>1</td><td>■ Start Excel ■ The Excel Window ■ Excel Menu and Toolbars</td></tr>
<tr><td>■ Exit Excel ■ Explore the Worksheet Using the Mouse and Keyboard</td></tr>
</table>

# NOTES

Microsoft Excel 97 is the spreadsheet application tool in the Office Suite.  Spreadsheets are reports that are used for business and financial applications that analyze data in a table format.  Any data that needs analysis using formulas and that can be arranged in a table should be in spreadsheet.

## Start Excel

■ Excel may be started in the following ways:
   (*See Office Basics, Exercise 1, page 3.*)

   • Click **Start**, highlight **Programs**, highlight and select **Microsoft Excel** from the Windows 95 Taskbar.

   • Click **Start**, highlight and select **New Office Document**, select **Blank Workbook** from the Windows 95 Taskbar.

   • Select **Start a New Document**, select **Blank Workbook**, from the Shortcut bar.

## The Excel Window

■ The Microsoft Excel 97 window that displays when the program is first started appears.
   (*See Illustration A on the following page.*)

   • The default workbook contains three sheets that contain rows and columns made up of cells.

   • The active cell is the cell that is ready to receive data or a command.  You can change the active cell in a worksheet by using the mouse or keyboard.

■ When you change the active cell, the **name box** located on the left side of the formula bar shows the new cell reference.  The cell reference identifies the location of the active cell in the worksheet by the column and row.

   ✓ Note:   *The location of the name box with an active reference displayed.*

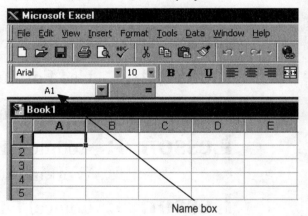

Name box

■ Excel highlights the row numbers and column letters of selected cells in a worksheet.  This makes it easier to identify your worksheet selection with a quick glance.

## Excel Menu and Toolbars

■ As shown in Illustration A on the following page, the default Excel window contains the Menu bar, Standard toolbar, Formatting toolbar, Formula bar, and the Status bar.  Except for the Formula bar, the use and functions of these bars are similar to those discussed in Exercise 1 of the Word section of this text.

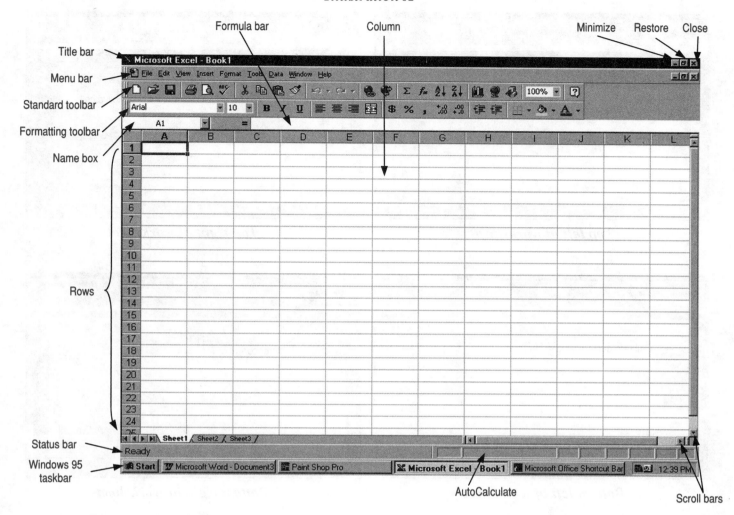

**Illustration A**

## Explore the Worksheet
## Using the Mouse and Keyboard

- The workbook window displays a limited portion of the worksheet. It is possible to view other portions of the worksheet by **scrolling** to the desired location.

- You can scroll to different areas in a worksheet using the mouse or keyboard. Scrolling does not change the active cell.

- Microsoft has introduced a new pointing device to replace your mouse, called the IntelliMouse, which makes it easier to scroll and zoom your view of a worksheet or expand and collapse data in special formats.

- There are 256 columns and 65,536 rows in a worksheet.

✓ Note the illustrations of the outer edges of a worksheet in Illustration B on the following page.

- You can change the active cell in a worksheet by selecting the <u>G</u>o To command on the <u>E</u>dit menu or by pressing F5.

✓ Note the Go To dialog box that appears when Go To is selected or F5 is pressed.

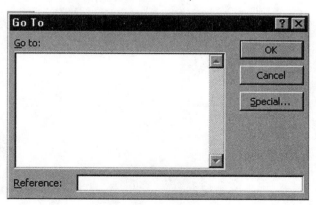

## Illustration B

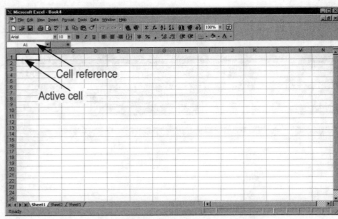

*Top left of worksheet*

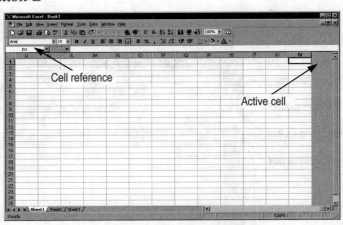

*Top right of worksheet*

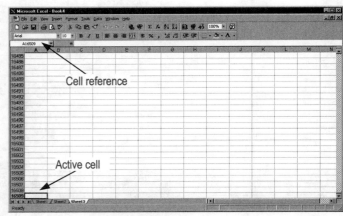

*Bottom left of worksheet*

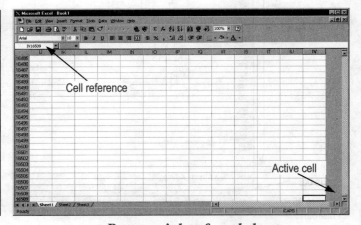

*Bottom right of worksheet*

*In this exercise, you will start Excel and practice changing the active cell using the mouse, the GoTo command and the name box.*

# EXERCISE DIRECTIONS

1. Start Excel from the Windows 95 Taskbar using the procedure below:
   a. Click Start, highlight and select New Office Document.
   b. Select Blank Workbook.

2. Click cell E5 to make it active.
   ✓ *Note the cell reference in the name box.*

3. Press the left arrow key until cell C5 is selected.
   ✓ *Note the cell reference in the name box.*

4. Select cell C9.
   ✓ *Note the cell reference in the name box.*

5. Use the arrow keys to select the following cells:
   - A6
   - R19
   - Z365
   - AA45

6. Click the down scroll arrow on the vertical scroll bar.
   ✓ *Note the worksheet moves down by one row.*

7. Click the right scroll arrow on the horizontal scroll bar.
   ✓ *Note the worksheet moves right by one column.*

8. Click the scroll bar below the scroll box on the vertical scroll bar.
   ✓ *Note the worksheet moves down by one screen.*

9. Click the scroll bar to the right of the scroll box on the horizontal scroll bar.
   ✓ *Note the worksheet moves right by one screen.*

10. Drag the horizontal scroll box all the way to the right on the scroll bar.
    ✓ *Note how the view of the worksheet has changed.*

11. Drag the vertical scroll box all the way down on the scroll bar.
    ✓ *Note how the view of the worksheet has changed.*

12. Use the scroll bars to move to the following parts of the worksheet:
    - Down one screen
    - Up one screen
    - Right one screen
    - Left one screen
    - Lower left of worksheet
    - Top right of worksheet

13. Select Edit on the menu bar.

14. Select Go To.

15. Type A10 in the Reference text box.

16. Click OK.
    ✓ *Note the active cell is A10.*

17. Using the Go To command, change the active cell to the following:
    - AB105
    - BG200
    - DB65000
    - A1 (Home)
    ✓ *Note the Go to list box displays the last four references you chose to go to.*

18. Click in the name box on the left side of the formula bar.
    ✓ *Note A1 becomes highlighted.*

19. Type C6 and press Enter.
    ✓ *Note C6 is now the active cell.*

20. Using the name box, change the active cell to the following:
    - P365
    - IV56
    - Lower left of worksheet (A65536)
    - Top right of worksheet (IV1)
    - Bottom right of worksheet (IV65536)
    - Left of worksheet (A1)

21. Place the mouse pointer under every icon on the Standard and Formatting toolbar.
    ✓ *Note each ToolTip under the icon and the explanation of the icon on the Status Bar.*

22. Use the Close button to exit Excel.

# KEYSTROKES

## RUN EXCEL

1. Click **Start** ............................`Ctrl` + `Esc`
2. Point to **Programs** .......................... `P`
3. Click **Microsoft Excel** ............. `↓` , `↵`

## CHANGE ACTIVE CELL USING THE KEYBOARD

One cell right ........................................ `→`

One cell left.......................................... `←`

One cell down ....................................... `↓`

One cell up ........................................... `↑`

One screen up........................................ `Page Up`

One screen down .................................... `Page Down`

One screen right ...................... `Alt` + `Page Down`

One screen left............................ `Alt` + `Page Up`

First cell in current row .................... `Home`

Last cell in current row ................. `Ctrl` + `→`

First cell in worksheet............. `Ctrl` + `Home`

Last occupied cell ...................... `Ctrl` + `End`
in worksheet.

## CHANGE ACTIVE CELL USING THE MOUSE

- Click desired cell.
- ✓ *If desired cell is not in view, use the scroll bars to move area of worksheet containing cell into view, then click the cell.*

## SCROLL USING THE MOUSE

*The vertical scroll bar is located on the right side of the workbook window.  The horizontal scroll bar (illustrated below) is located on the bottom of the workbook window.*

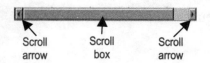

Scroll     Scroll     Scroll
arrow      box        arrow

## To scroll one column left or right:

- Click left or right scroll arrow.

## To scroll one row up or down:

- Click up or down scroll arrow.

## To scroll one screen up or down:

- Click vertical scroll bar above or below the scroll box.

## To scroll one screen right or left:

- Click horizontal scroll bar to left or right of the scroll box.

## To scroll to the beginning columns:

- Drag horizontal scroll box to the extreme left of the scroll bar.

## To scroll to the beginning rows:

- Drag vertical scroll box to the top of the scroll bar.

## To scroll quickly to an area in worksheet:

- Drag scroll box to desired position on the scroll bar.
- ✓ *The limits of the scrolling area will depend on the location of data in the worksheet.*

## To scroll quickly to the last row where data was entered:

- Press Ctrl and drag vertical scroll box to the bottom of the scroll bar.

## SCROLL USING THE KEYBOARD

One screen up....................................... `Page Up`

One screen down................................... `Page Down`

One screen right ...................... `Alt` + `Page Down`

One screen left.......................... `Alt` + `Page Up`

To active cell ...................... `Ctrl` + `Backspace`

## CHANGE ACTIVE CELL USING GO TO

1. Press **F5** ........................................... `F5`
   **OR**
   a. Click **Edit**............................ `Alt` + `E`
   b. Click **Go To** ................................ `G`
2. Type cell reference........... *cell reference*
   in **Reference** text box.
   - ✓ *The **Go to** list box displays the last four references you chose to go to*
3. Click `OK` ................................. `Enter`

## CHANGE ACTIVE CELL USING THE NAME BOX

1. Click in name box on left side of formula bar.
2. Type cell reference............ *cell reference*
3. Press **Enter**................................`Enter`

## 🌐  EXIT EXCEL

- Click Close Button................. `Alt` + `F4`

**Exercise 2**

- ■ **Open a Blank Workbook** ■ **Enter Labels**
- ■ **Make Simple Corrections** ■ **The View Menu**
- ■ **Save a Workbook** ■ **Close a Workbook** ■ **Exit Excel**

## NOTES

### Open a Blank Wordbook

- ■ If you use the New Office Document or Start a New Document methods to open Excel (see exercise 1), you will open a blank workbook. However, if you start Excel using Programs, Microsoft Excel, you may need to use the File menu to open a new workbook. A new file may be opened using the New file button 🗋 on the Standard toolbar.

### Enter Labels

- ■ The **status** of a cell is determined by the first character entered.

- ■ When an alphabetical character or one of the following symbols (` ~†!†# % ^ & * ( ) _ \ | [ ] { } ; : ' " < > , ?) is entered as the first character in a cell, the cell contains a **label**. A label is generally text data.

- ■ By default, each cell is approximately nine (9) characters wide; however, it is possible to view an entered label that is longer than the cell width if the cell to the right is blank. Excel 97 now supports up to 32,000 characters in a cell entry.

- ■ As you enter a label into a cell, it appears in the cell and on the formula bar. The formula bar displays the entry and three buttons, (Cancel, Enter, Edit Formula), as shown below:

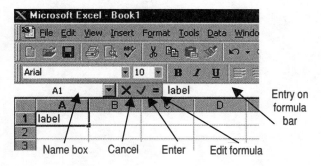

- ■ A label is entered in the cell after you do one of the following:
  - Press the Enter key, or
  - Press an arrow key, or
  - Click another cell, or
  - Click the Enter box ☑ on the formula bar.

- ■ The contents in a label will automatically align to the left of the cell, making it a left-justified entry.

### Make Simple Corrections

- ■ Before data is entered, the Backspace key may be used to correct an error. To delete the entire entry, press the Escape key or click the Cancel box ☒ on the formula bar. After text is entered, a correction may be typed directly over the existing text. This is referred to as the **strikeover** method of correction.

### The View Menu

- ■ A quick way to view or hide the Formula or Status Bars is to select or deselect these items from the View menu.

- ■ Note the check marks on the View menu below which indicate that the Formula Bar and the Status Bar are selected:

- The <u>T</u>oolbars command on the <u>V</u>iew menu displays a submenu that contains the list of available toolbars, which are checked if they are displayed. You may select a toolbar to display it and deselect the toolbar to hide it.

- The <u>V</u>iew menu contains a new option called F<u>u</u>ll Screen that expands the worksheet to fill the screen. As you will note in the illustration below, the toolbars are hidden and only the menu bar is displayed for commands. A <u>C</u>lose Full Screen box appears, which can be used to return to the default view. You may also use the <u>V</u>iew menu and deselect F<u>u</u>ll Screen to close this view.

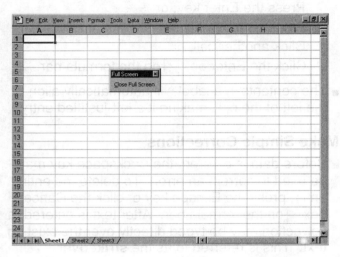

- The <u>V</u>iew menu also contains a <u>Z</u>oom option that allows you to set the magnification of cells in a worksheet. When <u>Z</u>oom is selected, the following dialog box appears:

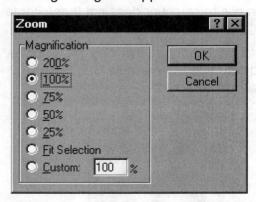

By clicking an option button, you can display the cells at <u>25</u>%, <u>50</u>%, <u>75</u>%, <u>100</u>% or <u>200</u>% of the normal display. The <u>C</u>ustom option sets the zoom percentage anywhere from 10% - 400%. The <u>F</u>it Selection option sizes a selected range to the current window size.

## Save a Workbook

- Each workbook may be saved on a data disk or hard drive for future recall and must be given a name for identification. A saved workbook is called a **file**.

- Prior to Windows 95, filenames were limited to eight characters. Now filenames may be more descriptive, since the limit for the name, drive and path is 255 characters. When you save a file, Excel automatically adds a period and a **filename extension** (usually .XLS) to the end of the filename. Because Excel identifies file types by their extension, you should not type the filename extension.

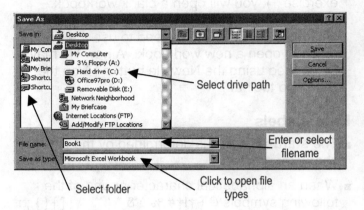

## Close a Workbook

- A workbook must be saved before you close it or all current or updated entries will be lost. If you attempt to close a workbook or exit Excel before saving, you will be asked if you want to save the changes.

  ✓ *Note:* *If you make a mistake and want to begin again, you may choose to close the workbook without saving it.*

- If you have more than one file open and wish to close and save them all, Excel 97 lets you quickly exit Excel and save all files. To do this, just click Yes to <u>A</u>ll after selecting the <u>F</u>ile and E<u>x</u>it commands.

---

*In this exercise, you will begin to create a worksheet for the Sunny Superette by entering labels. Numeric data will be entered in a later exercise.*

---

# EXERCISE DIRECTIONS

1. Open Excel and a new worksheet.

2. Go to cell B2.

3. Type your name and look at the formula bar.

   ✓ *See location of Cancel and Enter boxes to the left of the formula bar.*

   ✓ *If the Formula is not visible, see SET VIEW PREFERENCES, page 184, and follow steps to select the Formula Bar option.*

4. Cancel the entry by pressing the Escape key or by clicking the Cancel box ▨.

5. Create the worksheet below.

6. Enter the labels in the exact cell locations shown in the illustration.

7. Correct errors using the Backspace or strikeover method.

8. Click the View menu.

9. Select Full Screen and note the new view.

10. Close the full screen display.

11. Click View, Zoom.

12. Set the zoom percentage to 50%

13. Return the workbook to 100% sizing.

14. Save the workbook; name it **SALES**.

15. Close the workbook.

|    | A    | B            | C    | D     | E   | F     | G          | H   |
|----|------|--------------|------|-------|-----|-------|------------|-----|
| 1  |      | SUNNY SUPERETTE |   |       |     |       |            |     |
| 2  |      | DAILY SALES REPORT |  |    |     |       |            |     |
| 3  | DATE: |             |      |       |     |       |            |     |
| 4  |      |              |      |       |     |       |            |     |
| 5  | CODE | DEPARTMENT   |      | SALES | TAX | TOTAL | % OF SALES |     |
| 6  |      |              |      |       |     |       |            |     |
| 7  | A    | GROCERIES -TAX |    |       |     |       |            |     |
| 8  | B    | CANDY        |      |       |     |       |            |     |
| 9  | C    | CARDS        |      |       |     |       |            |     |
| 10 | D    | HEALTH AIDS  |      |       |     |       |            |     |
| 11 | E    | DELI         |      |       |     |       |            |     |
| 12 | F    | DAIRY        |      |       |     |       |            |     |
| 13 | G    | PRODUCE      |      |       |     |       |            |     |
| 14 | H    | OTHER-NT     |      |       |     |       |            |     |

# KEYSTROKES

### 🌐 OPEN A NEW WORKBOOK

Click **New** file button.................................... 🗋

**OR**

1. Click **File** ................................ Alt + F
2. Click **New** ............................... Alt + N
3. Double-click Workbook.

**OR**

Highlight workbook
and click  OK  ........... ⬆⬇ , Enter

### 🌐 SAVE A NEW WORKBOOK

1. Click **Save** button .......................... 💾
2. Click **File name** ....................... Alt + N
3. Type in desired name ............... *filename*
4. Click  Save  ................................ ⏎

### ENTER A LABEL

*Labels are left aligned and cannot be calculated.*

1. Click cell.................................. ↔↕
   to receive label.
2. Type label text......................... *label text*
3. Press **Enter** ............................... Enter

   **OR**

   Click Enter box ✓ ................... Enter
   on the formula bar.

   **OR**

   Press any arrow key to enter label and move to next cell.

### CLOSE A WORKBOOK

1. Click **File**............................... Alt + F
2. Click **Close**............................. C

   If a save changes in workbook message appears:

   Click  Yes  ............................... Y
   to save changes to the workbook.

   If you have not previously saved the workbook, the Save As dialog box appears.  (See *SAVE A NEW WORKBOOK*.)

   If you have more than one file open and wish to close and save them all, click

   **Yes to All** ....................................... A

   **OR**

   Click  No  ............................... N
   to close without saving the changes.

### SET VIEW PREFERENCES

Click **View**................................ Alt + V

**To view formula bar:**

Click **Formula Bar**........................... F

**To view status bar:**

Click **Status Bar** ............................. S

**To add toolbars:**

a. Click **Toolbars**........................... T
b. Select toolbar name ..... ↓ , Space
c. Click  OK  ............................ Enter

**To set zoom options:**

a. Click **Zoom**............................... Z
b. Set percentage ............. ↓ , Space
c. Click  OK  ........................ Enter

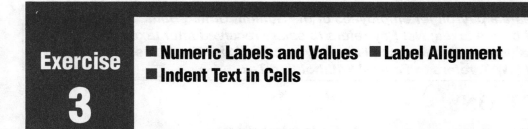

**Exercise 3**

- ■ **Numeric Labels and Values** ■ **Label Alignment**
- ■ **Indent Text in Cells**

*Formating Toolbar*

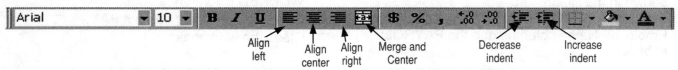

# NOTES

## Numeric Labels and Values

- ■ When a number or one of the following symbols (+-.=$) is entered as the first character in a cell, the cell contains a **value**.

- ■ A value is entered after you do one of the following:
  - • Press the Enter key, or
  - • Press an arrow key, or
  - • Click another cell, or
  - • Click the Enter box ☑ on the formula bar.

- ■ Excel 97 will accept up to eleven numbers in a cell by automatically widening the cell. If a value is longer than eleven characters, Excel displays the number in scientific notation or number signs (######) appear in the cell. In this case, the column width must be reset. (*Setting column width will be covered in Exercise 11.*)

- ■ A **numeric label** is a number that will not be used in calculation. Examples of numeric labels are social security numbers or identification numbers. To indicate that such numbers are to be treated as labels (text) and not values, it is necessary to begin the entry with a **label prefix**, an apostrophe (').

- ■ The label prefix is not displayed on the worksheet but is shown on the formula bar.

- ■ Numbers may also be formatted as text or labels by using the Format, Cells, Number Text commands.

## Label Alignment

- ■ A value automatically aligns to the right of the cell, making it a right-justified entry.

- ■ Since labels are left-justified and values are right-justified in a cell, column titles (which are labels) will not appear centered over numeric data. Column title labels above numeric data may be centered or right-aligned to improve the appearance of the worksheet.

  ✓ *Note the illustration of how data is aligned in cells.*

| Text | | left-justified label |
|---|---|---|
| 123 | | right-justified value |
| 123 | | left-justified numeric label |

- ■ You can align a label by using the alignment buttons on the Formatting toolbar. (*See illustration above.*)

- ■ Labels may also be aligned by selecting the cells containing the label(s) to align and choosing an alignment through the Format, Cells menu system.

## Indent Text in Cells

- ■ Excel 97 has a new horizontal alignment option: Indent. Indent lets you align text away from the left edge of a cell. You can indent cell text quickly using the Indent buttons on the Formatting toolbar, as illustrated above. You can also set the indent of text in cells using the Format, Cells, Alignment commands.

---

*In this exercise, you will create a payroll for employees of the Summit United Bank. Gross Pay refers to total salary earned before taxes; Net Pay refers to salary received after taxes are deducted; Soc. Sec. Tax is a designation for social security tax; Medicare Tax is the mandatory deduction for Medicare and F.W.T. refers to Federal Withholding Tax.*

# EXERCISE DIRECTIONS

1. Create the worksheet below.
2. Enter the labels in the exact cell locations shown in the illustration.
3. Indent the second line of the Card Number and Employee Name columns and the PAYROLL subtitle.
4. Correct any errors.
5. Right-align the HOURLY RATE and HOURS WORKED column headings.
6. Save the workbook; name it **PAY**.
7. Close the workbook.

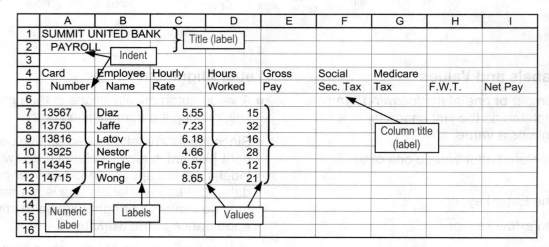

| | A | B | C | D | E | F | G | H | I |
|---|---|---|---|---|---|---|---|---|---|
| 1 | SUMMIT UNITED BANK | | | | | | | | |
| 2 | PAYROLL | | | | | | | | |
| 3 | | | | | | | | | |
| 4 | Card | Employee | Hourly | Hours | Gross | Social | Medicare | | |
| 5 | Number | Name | Rate | Worked | Pay | Sec. Tax | Tax | F.W.T. | Net Pay |
| 6 | | | | | | | | | |
| 7 | 13567 | Diaz | 5.55 | 15 | | | | | |
| 8 | 13750 | Jaffe | 7.23 | 32 | | | | | |
| 9 | 13816 | Latov | 6.18 | 16 | | | | | |
| 10 | 13925 | Nestor | 4.66 | 28 | | | | | |
| 11 | 14345 | Pringle | 6.57 | 12 | | | | | |
| 12 | 14715 | Wong | 8.65 | 21 | | | | | |
| 13 | | | | | | | | | |
| 14 | | | | | | | | | |
| 15 | | | | | | | | | |
| 16 | | | | | | | | | |

Title (label)
Indent
Column title (label)
Numeric label
Labels
Values

# KEYSTROKES

## ENTER A NUMERIC LABEL

✓ *Numbers entered as numeric labels are left-aligned and cannot be calculated.*

1. Click cell.................................
   to receive numeric label.

2. Press ' (label prefix) .......................

3. Type number ............................. *number*

4. Press **Enter**.................................Enter

## ENTER A VALUE

✓ *Numbers entered as values are right-aligned and can be calculated.*

1. Click cell.................................
   to receive value.

2. Type number ............................ *number*

✓ *Begin entry with a number from zero to nine or a decimal point. Precede a negative number with a minus sign (-) or enclose it within parentheses().*

3. Press **Enter**.................................Enter

✓ *If Excel displays number signs (######) or the number in scientific notation, the column is not wide enough to display the value. Excel stores the value in the cell but cannot display it. To see the entry, double-click the right border of the column heading. If the value has more than nine decimal places, Excel automatically rounds it to nine places.*

## SELECT (HIGHLIGHT) A RANGE OF CELLS USING THE MOUSE

1. Point to interior of first cell to select. **Pointer** *becomes a* ⬩.

2. Drag through adjacent cells until desired cells are highlighted.

## SELECT (HIGHLIGHT) A RANGE OF CELLS USING THE KEYBOARD

1. Click first cell.................................

2. Press **Shift + arrow** ............Shift + 
   to select adjacent cells.

## ALIGN LABELS USING THE TOOLBAR

1. Select cell(s) containing label(s) ....

   —*FROM FORMATTING TOOLBAR*—

2. Click **Align Left** button .....................
   **OR**
   Click **Center** button .........................
   **OR**
   Click **Align Right** button ..................

## INDENT TEXT IN CELLS

**To increase indent:**

1. Select cells containing text to indent.

2. Click **Increase Indent** button...........

**To decrease indent:**

1. Select cells containing indented text.

2. Click **Decrease Indent** button ..........

# Exercise 4

## ■ Summary

*Mr. Sudsy, the owner of the Clean Up Car Wash, has asked you to prepare an inventory listing the items he stocks in his accessory area with the item numbers, unit cost, and selling price of each item.*

## EXERCISE DIRECTIONS

1. Using the data below, create the worksheet. Include an appropriate two-line worksheet title.  Leave a blank column (column C) between ITEM and UNIT COST.  Enter item numbers as numeric labels.  Right-align column labels where appropriate.

| ITEM NUMBER | ITEM | UNIT COST | SELLING PRICE |
|---|---|---|---|
| 142 | Car Fresh | 1 | 2 |
| 162 | spray freshener | 2 | 4 |
| 175 | vinyl cleaner | 2 | 4 |
| 321 | chamois cloth | 4 | 10 |
| 393 | car wax | 2 | 5 |
| 421 | car caddy | 12 | 22 |
| 572 | front mats | 18 | 28 |
| 574 | back mats | 12 | 18 |
| 580 | mat sets | 28 | 42 |
| 932 | fan belt | 15 | 25 |

2. Save the workbook; name it **INVEN**.

## Exercise 5

### ■ Use Formulas

## NOTES

### Use Formulas

- A **formula** is an instruction to calculate a number.

- A formula is entered in the cell where the answer should appear. As you type the formula, it appears in the **cell** and in the **formula bar**. After a formula is entered, the answer is displayed in the cell, and the formula is displayed in the formula bar.

- **Cell references** and **mathematical operators** are used to develop formulas. The cell reference can be typed or inserted into a formula. An equal sign (=) must precede a formula. For example, the formula =C3+C5+C7 results in the addition of the values in these cell locations. Therefore, any change to a value made in these cell locations causes the answer to change automatically.

  ✓ *Note: If you are using the number pad and enter the formula (+C3+C5+C7) using a plus sign as the first character, Excel will substitute the equal sign.*

- The standard mathematical operators used in formulas are:

  | | | | |
  |---|---|---|---|
  | + | Addition | - | Subtraction |
  | * | Multiplication | / | Division |
  | ^ | Exponentiation | | |

- It is important to consider the **order of mathematical operations** when preparing formulas. Operations enclosed in parentheses have the highest priority and are executed first; exponential calculations are executed second. Multiplication and division operations have the next priority and are completed before any addition and subtraction operations.

- Excel 97 automatically corrects many common mistakes (such as omitting a parenthesis) in formula entry. The Office Assistant provides help as you build a formula, as well.

- All operations are executed from left to right in the order of appearance. For example, in the formula =A1*(B1+C1), B1+C1 will be calculated before the multiplication is performed. If the parentheses were omitted, A1*B1 would be calculated first and C1 would be added to that answer. This would result in a different outcome.

- Multiplication and division formulas may result in answers with multiple decimal places. These numbers can be rounded off using a formatting feature. *(See Format Data, Exercise 8.)*

- When using a **percentage** as a numeric factor in a formula, you can enter it with a decimal or with the percent symbol. For example, you may enter either .45 or 45% to include 45 percent in a formula.

*In this exercise, LIST PRICE refers to the manufacturer's suggested retail price; DISCOUNT refers to a reduction from the list price. The SALES TAX percentage for this exercise will be 8%. Note the formula used to calculate SALES TAX: 8% has been changed to .08.*

# EXERCISE DIRECTIONS

1. Create the worksheet below.

2. Enter the labels and values in the exact cell locations shown in the illustration.

3. Enter the formula illustrated in the SALE PRICE column to calculate the list price less the discount.

4. Enter formulas for the remaining products in the SALE PRICE column using appropriate cell references.

5. Enter the formula illustrated in the SALES TAX column, multiplying the sale price by 8%
   ✓ *The answer may need formatting, which will be done in the next exercise.*

6. Enter SALES TAX formulas for the remaining products.

7. Enter the formula illustrated in the TOTAL PRICE column, adding the sale price and sales tax.

8. Enter TOTAL PRICE formulas for the remaining products.

9. Save the workbook; name it **PRICE**.

10. Close the workbook.

|   | A | B | C | D | E | F | G |
|---|---|---|---|---|---|---|---|
| 1 |   |   | LIST | DIS- | SALE | SALES | TOTAL |
| 2 | PRODUCT |   | PRICE | COUNT | PRICE | TAX | PRICE |
| 3 |   |   |   |   |   |   |   |
| 4 | OVEN |   | 745 | 185 | =C4-D4 | =E4*.08 | =E4+F4 |
| 5 | REFRIGERATOR |   | 985 | 265 |   |   |   |
| 6 | WASHER |   | 395 | 98 |   |   |   |

# KEYSTROKES

**ENTER A FORMULA USING MATHEMATICAL OPERATORS**

1. Click cell ........................... [↔]
   to receive formula.

2. Press **Equal** ........................... [=]

3. Type formula ........................... *formula*
   using cell references and mathematical operators.

   *Example: =A1*(B2+B10)/2*

✓ *You can select cells instead of typing references to tell Excel which cells you wish the formula to reference.*

**To insert cell references by selecting cells:**

a. Click formula where cell reference will be inserted.

   ✓ *If necessary, type preceding operator or parenthesis.*

b. Select cell(s) you want formula to reference.

   ✓ *Reference appears in formula.*

c. Type desired operator or parenthesis.

d. Repeat steps a-c as needed.

e. Press **Enter** ........................... [Enter]

## Exercise 6

- ■ **Open Files**  ■ **Check for Virus**
- ■ **Save Files**  ■ **Format Data**  ■ **Use Ranges**

# NOTES

## Open Files

- ■ To open a workbook that has been saved and closed, go to the same drive designation and filename used during the saving process. The Open dialog box contains a drop-down list with the drives or folders and a box containing a list of the files in that directory. In addition to opening a previously saved file, you may preview it, search for the file, and list details or properties about the file. Note the illustration of the Open dialog box below.

### *Open Dialog Box*

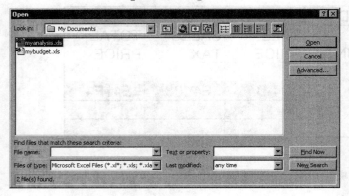

- ■ When the File menu is accessed, a list of the last four files used is provided. Clicking the filename of one of these recently used files is a quick way to open a file.

- ■ A newly opened workbook becomes the active workbook and hides any other open workbook. A previously opened workbook will not be closed automatically and can be made the active workbook.

## Check for Virus

- ■ You can set Excel to check workbooks for macros that might contain viruses or commands that perform unwanted actions. When you enable **Macro virus protection**, Excel will display a warning message whenever you open a workbook that contains macros. The setting is made using the Tools, Options commands. Excel cannot determine if a macro contained in a workbook is a virus. Therefore, you must decide about the safety of opening a workbook (considering the source of the workbook) before opening it with its macros enabled.

## Save Files

- ■ When you resave a workbook, the **Save** command overwrites the previous version.

- ■ The **Save As** option allows for the changing of the filename as well as other save conditions. A new version of a previously saved workbook may be saved under a new name in order to keep both files.

### *Save As Dialog Box*

Click to open a list of drives on your computer

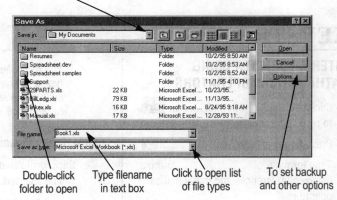

Double-click folder to open | Type filename in text box | Click to open list of file types | To set backup and other options

- It is also possible to backup all workbooks as they are being saved. This setting can be made using the Options dialog box, and will create backup files with a .BAK extension. Note the illustration below of the Save Options dialog box with the Always create backup option checked.

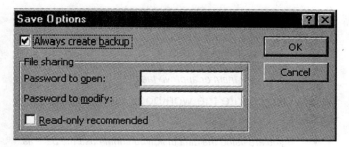

## Format Data

- You can change the appearance of data to make it more attractive and readable by formatting it. Some available number formats are currency, percent, date, time, and scientific notation.

- The following formats may be used for formatting money values:

    **Number** Displays number with or without decimal places and commas (1000 separator).

    **Currency** Displays number with currency symbols: dollar signs, commas, and decimals.

    ✓ *Note: Other formats will be introduced in later exercises.*

- You can format data by selecting it and clicking the appropriate button on the Formatting toolbar or by selecting Format, Cells. Note the illustration of the Format Cells dialog box.

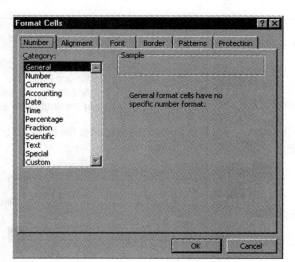

## Use Ranges

- A **range** is a defined area of a worksheet. For example, selecting the cells F4, F5, and F6 can be indicated as F4:F6. You can format data in a column or row by selecting the range of cells containing the data to format.

- A **block of cells** may be defined as a range. For example, A1:G2 includes all the cells in columns A through G in rows one and two.

- Cell contents may be formatted or aligned before or after data is entered.

- As noted in Exercise 3, since label text is left-aligned while values are right-aligned in a cell, column headings may need to be aligned to the right. The alignment buttons on the Formatting toolbar or the alignment settings in the Format Cells dialog box may be used to align a column title in a single cell or all the column titles in a selected range.

*In this exercise, you will create a tabular document in which ranges of data will be formatted using number and alignment formats.*

# EXERCISE DIRECTIONS

1. Open 📖PRICE, or open 💾06PRICE.

   ✓ *If you are using the data disk, files should be opened using the Read Only feature.  See WORD, Lesson 2, Exercise 8.*

2. Select the range of data in columns C, D, E, and F.

3. Using the Number formatting option, format the data for two decimal places.

4. Select the range of data in column G and format the data for Currency.

5. Select and center all column titles using the Center button on the Formatting toolbar.

6. Enable check for viruses:

   • Click Tools, click Options; click General tab.

   • Select Macro virus protection; click OK.

   ✓ *Hereafter, any files that contain macros will not open unless you disable them or approve the file.*

7. Save/overwrite the workbook file, or save as Price.

   ✓ *If you are using the data disk, you should use the Save as instrument to save the file under a new name.*

8. Create a backup file by checking the Always create a backup box in the Save Options dialog box.

9. Close the workbook.

|   | A | B | C | D | E | F | G | H | I |
|---|---|---|---|---|---|---|---|---|---|
| 1 |   |   | LIST | DIS- | SALE | SALES | TOTAL |   |   |
| 2 | PRODUCT |   | PRICE | COUNT | PRICE | TAX | PRICE |   |   |
| 3 |   |   |   |   |   |   |   |   |   |
| 4 | OVEN |   | 745 | 185 | 560 | 44.8 | 604.8 |   |   |
| 5 | REFRIGERATOR |   | 985 | 265 | 720 | 57.6 | 777.6 |   |   |
| 6 | WASHER |   | 395 | 98 | 297 | 23.76 | 320.76 |   |   |
| 7 |   |   |   |   |   |   |   |   |   |
| 8 |   |   |   |   |   |   |   |   |   |
| 9 |   |   |   |   |   |   |   |   |   |

Range C1:G2

Range C4:F6

# KEYSTROKES

## OPEN A WORKBOOK FILE

1. Click Open button on the Standard toolbar.

   OR

   a. Click **File** ... Alt+F
   b. Click **Open** ... O

**To select a drive:**

   a. Click **Look in** ... Alt+I
   b. Select desired drive ... , ↵

   *Files in current directory of selected drive appear in File Name list box.*

**To select a folder in the drive:**

Double-click folder name in list box ... ↵

   ✓ *Files in selected folder appear in File Name list box.*

**To list files of a different type:**

   a. Click **Files of type:** ... Alt+T
   b. Click file type to list ... , ↵

   ✓ *Only files of specified type appear in File Name list box.*

   ✓ *This option to change the kinds of files displayed in the File Name list box. For example, if you want to open a Lotus file into Excel, you would select the Lotus 1-2-3 Files (\*.wk\*) item in the drop-down list.*

2. Click file to open in File Name list box.

   OR

   a. Select **File Name** list box ... Alt+N
   b. Type filename ... *filename* to open.

3. Click **Open** ... Alt+O

## RESAVE/OVERWRITE A WORKBOOK FILE

Click **Save File** button ........................ [💾]
on Standard toolbar.

**OR**

1. Click **File** ............................... [Alt]+[F]
2. Click **Save** ................................ [S]

## SAVE AS

*Saves and names the active workbook.*

1. Click **File** ............................... [Alt]+[F]
2. Click **Save As** ........................... [A]

**To select a drive:**

   a. Click **Save in** ................... [Alt]+[I]
   b. Select desired drive .......... [,] [↵]

**To select a folder in the drive:**

   Double-click folder name
   in list box ........................... [,] [↵]

3. Click **File name** ...................... [Alt]+[N]
4. Type filename ...........................*filename*

**To set Excel to always create a backup of previous version when saving:**

   a. Click **Options** ................... [Alt]+[P]
   b. Click **Always create**
      **backup** ........................... [Alt]+[B]
   c. Click **OK** .......................... [Enter]

5. Click **OK** .......................... [Enter]

## SELECT (HIGHLIGHT) A RANGE OF CELLS USING THE KEYBOARD

  ✓ *A range of cells is two or more cells. Cells in a selected range are highlighted and the active cell within the selection is white.*

**To select a range of adjacent cells:**

1. Press **arrow** keys ..........................
   until first cell to select is highlighted.
2. Press **Shift** + **arrow**
   keys ................................... [Shift]+

**To select entire row containing active cell:**

Press **Shift** + **Space** ............. [Shift]+[Space]

**To select entire column containing active cell:**

Press **Ctrl** + **Space** ................. [Ctrl]+[Space]

**To select adjacent rows:**

1. Press **arrow** keys ..........................
   until a cell in first row to select is outlined.
2. Press and hold **Shift** ................. [Shift]
   then press **Space** ................. [Space]
   to highlight first row to select.
3. Still pressing **Shift**,
   press **up** or **down** key ...................
   to highlight adjacent rows to select.

## FORMAT NUMBERS USING THE MENU

1. Select cell(s) to format.
2. a. Click **Format** menu ........... [Alt]+[O]
   b. Click **Cells**... ......................... [E]
   **OR**
   a. Right-click a selected cell.
   a. Click **Format Cells** ................... [F]
3. Select Number tab ................. [Ctrl]+[Tab]
4. Click desired category
   in Category list ............. [Alt]+[C] ,

  ✓ *Category list items include: General, Number, Currency, Accounting, Date, Time, Percentage, Fraction, Scientific, Text, special, and Custom.*

5. Click Number ................................. [↓]

## To set decimal places:

   a. Click **Decimal places** ........ [Alt]+[D]
   b. Set number of places...............

6. Click **OK** ................................. [Enter]

## FORMAT NUMBERS USING THE TOOLBAR

*Applies commonly used number formats.*

Select cell(s) to format.

   *-USE THE FORMATTING TOOLBAR-*

**To apply currency style:**

Click **Currency Style** button................. [$]

**To apply percent style:**

Click **Percent Style** button.................. [%]

**To apply comma style:**

Click **Comma Style** button................... [,]

**To increase or decrease decimal places:**

Click **Increase Decimal** button............. [.00]
**OR**
Click **Decrease Decimal** button............ [.00]

## ENABLE OR DISABLE CHECK FOR VIRUSES

1. Click **Tools** ............................. [Alt]+[T]
2. Click **Options**................................. [O]
3. Click the **General** tab.
4. Select or deselect **Macro virus protection** ........................... [Alt]+[T]
5. Click **OK** ................................. [Enter]

## Exercise 7

- **Copy Data**
- **Print a Worksheet**

# NOTES

### Copy Data

- Formulas may be **copied**:
  - Horizontally or vertically, or
  - To another cell or range of cells, or
  - To another worksheet or workbook.

- When a formula is copied, the cell references change relative to their new location.

- If you are copying a formula across a row or down a column, you can use the fill button in the bottom right corner of the cell to drag the formula to fill the cells.

| Employee Name | Hourly Rate | Hours Worked | Gross Pay | Social Sec. Tax |
|---------------|-------------|--------------|-----------|-----------------|
| Diaz          | 5.55        | 15           | 83.25     |                 |

fill handle

- You can copy a range of data to a new location using the Edit menu.  Highlight the range to be copied, click Edit, Copy, select the destination cell or range and click Edit, Paste.  You may also use the Copy and Paste buttons on the toolbar.

### Print a Worksheet

- The workbook, the selected worksheet(s), or the selected range of data may be printed using the Print command.  When the Print command is accessed, Excel allows you to select various print options.  One way you can preview the print output is by selecting the Print Preview button in the Print dialog box (see below), or by clicking the Print Preview button on the Standard toolbar.

*Print Dialog Box*

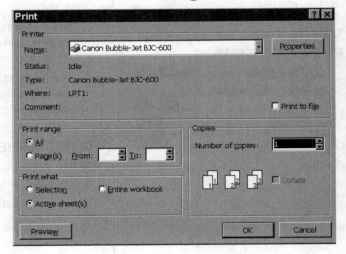

- Excel uses the default page size (usually 8 1/2" x 11") of the installed printer.  The page size settings can be accessed by selecting the Page tab from the Page Setup option found on the File menu, as illustrated on the next page.

- The top and bottom default page margins are set at 1" and the right and left default page margins are set at 0.75".  The margin page settings can be accessed by selecting the Margins tab from the Page Setup option on the File menu.

194

## Page Setup Dialog Box with the Page and Margins Tabs Selected

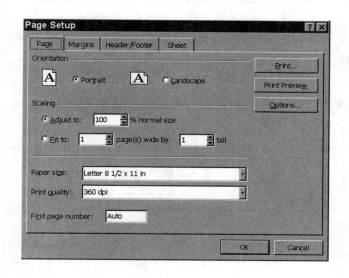

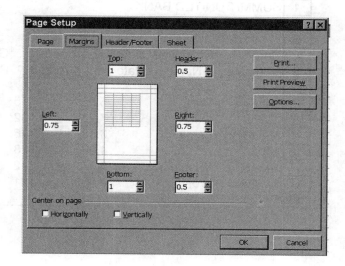

In this exercise, you will prepare and print a payroll where Federal Withholding Tax is calculated using a fixed percentage.

NOTE: F.W.T. is actually determined using a table where the tax varies according to your salary and number of exemptions.

# EXERCISE DIRECTIONS

1. Open ⌨PAY, or open 💾07PAY.

2. Enter a formula to calculate GROSS PAY for the first employee.

3. Copy the GROSS PAY formula for each employee.

4. Enter a formula to compute Soc. Sec. Tax at 6.2% of Gross Pay.

5. Copy the Soc. Sec. Tax formula for each employee.

6. Enter a formula to compute Medicare Tax at 1.45% of Gross Pay.

7. Copy the Medicare Tax formula for each employee.

8. Enter a formula to calculate F.W.T. at 20% of Gross Pay.

9. Copy the F.W.T. formula for each employee.

10. Enter a formula to calculate NET PAY.

11. Copy the NET PAY formula for each employee.

12. Format columns E, F, G, H and I for two decimal places using Number format.

13. Center all column labels.

14. Print one copy of the worksheet.

15. Close and save the workbook, or save as PAY.

✓ If your file is PAY, when you close the workbook you are prompted to save changes to update the file. If you are using the data disk, you must use the Save As command to create a PAY file.

| | A | B | C | D | E | F | G | H | I |
|---|---|---|---|---|---|---|---|---|---|
| 1 | SUMMIT UNITED BANK | | | | | | | | |
| 2 | PAYROLL | | | | | | | | |
| 3 | | | | | | | | | |
| 4 | Card | Employee | Hourly | Hours | Gross | Social | Medicare | | |
| 5 | Number | Name | Rate | Worked | Pay | Sec. Tax | Tax | F.W.T. | Net Pay |
| 6 | | | | | | | | | |
| 7 | 13567 | Diaz | 5.55 | 15 | | | | | |
| 8 | 13750 | Jaffe | 7.23 | 32 | | | | | |
| 9 | 13816 | Latov | 6.18 | 16 | | | | | |
| 10 | 13925 | Nestor | 4.66 | 28 | | | | | |
| 11 | 14345 | Pringle | 6.57 | 12 | | | | | |
| 12 | 14715 | Wong | 8.65 | 21 | | | | | |
| 13 | | | | | | | | | |

# KEYSTROKES

## COPY USING THE MENU

*Copies the data once and overwrites existing data in the destination cells.*

1. Select cell(s) to copy.

2. Click **Edit** ............................... `Alt`+`E`

3. Click **Copy** ....................................... `C`

   ✓ *A flashing outline surrounds selection.*

4. Select destination cell(s).

✓ *Select the destination range or select the upper left cell in the destination cell range. The destination can be in the same worksheet, another sheet, or another workbook.*

5. Click **Edit** ............................... `Alt`+`E`

6. Click **Paste** ..................................... `P`

## PRINT A WORKSHEET

*Prints worksheet data using the current page settings.*

✓ *When printing a worksheet, Excel will only print the print area, if you defined one.*

Click **Print** button ............................ 🖨
on Standard toolbar.

**OR**

1. Click **File** ............................... `Alt`+`F`

2. Click **Print** .................................... `P`

3. Select **Acti̲ve Sheet(s)** ........... `Alt`+`V`

4. Click ` OK ` .......................... `Enter`

**Exercise 8**

- Copy a Formula (Absolute Reference)
- Format Data (Percent, Fonts and Font Size)

# NOTES

## Copy Formulas (Absolute and Relative Reference)

- When formulas are copied, the cell references change relative to their new locations. Cells in these formulas are called **relative** references. If a formula with relative references is copied, a zero (0) appears if the formula is referring to empty cells.

- In some cases, a value in a formula must remain constant when copied to other locations. This is referred to as an **absolute reference.**

- To identify a cell as an absolute value, you must place a dollar sign ($) before column and row references for that cell.

- In this exercise, we must divide each department's sales by the total to find each department's percentage of total sales. Therefore, the total sales amount is a constant value in each line's formula. Note the formula indicated in the exercise on page 199. When this formula is copied, the total sales remains as a constant in every formula.

## Format Data

### Percent

- Formatting may be used to change decimal answers into a percentage format. Select the data to be formatted and use the Percentage button % on the Formatting toolbar or the Format Cells dialog box.

### Fonts and Font Size

- Excel lets you apply desktop publishing features to create a more attractive screen view and printout. Your monitor and printer, however, must be able to support these features.

- Worksheet enhancements such as changing the **font** and **font size** can be accomplished using the Formatting toolbar.

- A **font** is a set of characters that share a design and name. Since Windows TrueType fonts are scalable, a single TrueType font can be set to a variety of sizes. The currently active font name (usually Arial) is displayed in the Font box, and the current font size is displayed in the Font Size box.

- The **font size** is an attribute that sets the height of characters in a scalable font. This size is measured in **points**. A point is 1/72 of an inch. When the size of a font is changed, Excel automatically adjusts the row height but does not adjust the column width.

- The easiest way to apply a new font or font size is to select the cells to format, then select the font or font size in the **Font** or **Font Size** box on the Formatting toolbar. Excel immediately formats the text in the selected cells. You can also change the font or font size for only those characters you select while editing a cell. Note the illustration on the next page.

■ The default or standard font Excel uses may be changed as well.  To do this, select Options from the Tools menu. Then, from the General tab in the Options dialog box, set the Standard font and font Size.

*Example Showing use of the Formatting Toolbar to Change Font and Font Size*

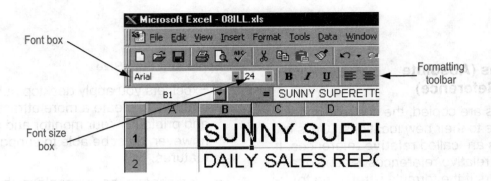

*In this exercise, you will complete the Sunny Superette daily sales report by calculating sales, tax, and total sales.  Some items are not taxed, as indicated in the illustration.  To analyze departmental sales, the owner is requesting an analysis showing the percent each department's sales is of the total sales.*

# EXERCISE DIRECTIONS

1. Open 🖩**SALES**, or open 🖫**08SALES**.

2. Enter sales data, as shown.

3. Enter a formula to calculate a 5% TAX on Groceries-Tax.

4. Copy the TAX formula for each department *except* DELI, DAIRY, PRODUCE, and OTHER-NT.

5. Enter a formula to determine TOTAL for Groceries-Tax by adding sales and tax.

6. Copy the TOTAL formula for each department.

7. Enter the indented label TOTALS in cell B16.

8. Enter a formula in cell D16 to calculate TOTAL for the SALES column.

9. Copy the TOTALS formula to cells E16 and F16.

10. Enter the formula in G7, as illustrated, using an absolute reference in the % OF SALES column.

11. Copy the % OF SALES formula for each department.

12. Copy the TOTALS formula to find the total of the % OF SALES column.

13. Using the Number formatting option, format the money columns (D, E and F) for two decimal places.

14. Using the Percentage formatting option, format the % OF SALES column for percentages with two decimal places.

15. Center column D, E, and F labels.

16. Make the font changes indicated below:
    - Main title:  Arial 24 point
    - Secondary title: Arial 18 point
    - Column titles:  Arial 12 point
    - Data in rows: MS San Serif 10 point
    - TOTALS row: Arial 10 point
    ✓ *If your system does not have these fonts, choose your default font and one other selection.*

17. Print one copy of the worksheet.

18. Close and save the workbook, or save as **SALES**.

|   | A | B | C | D | E | F | G | H |
|---|---|---|---|---|---|---|---|---|
| 1 |   | SUNNY SUPERETTE |   |   |   |   |   |   |
| 2 |   | DAILY SALES REPORT |   |   |   |   |   |   |
| 3 | DATE: |   |   |   |   |   |   |   |
| 4 |   |   |   |   |   |   |   |   |
| 5 | CODE | DEPARTMENT |   | SALES | TAX | TOTAL | % OF SALES |   |
| 6 |   |   |   |   |   |   |   |   |
| 7 | A | GROCERIES -TAX |   | 1345.32 |   |   | =D7/$D$16 |   |
| 8 | B | CANDY |   | 254.76 |   |   |   |   |
| 9 | C | CARDS |   | 145.33 |   |   |   |   |
| 10 | D | HEALTH AIDS |   | 232.43 |   |   |   |   |
| 11 | E | DELI |   | 548.98 |   |   |   |   |
| 12 | F | DAIRY |   | 197.87 |   |   |   |   |
| 13 | G | PRODUCE |   | 218.55 |   |   |   |   |
| 14 | H | OTHER - NT |   | 453.65 |   |   |   |   |
| 15 |   |   |   |   |   |   |   |   |
| 16 |   | TOTALS |   |   |   |   |   |   |

# KEYSTROKES

## ENTER FORMULAS FOR ABSOLUTE CONDITIONS

1. Select cell to receive formula.

2. Press **Equal** .......................... ▣

3. Type formula.............................*formula* using absolute references and mathematical operators.

   *Example of a formula using absolute references:  =$A$1\*($B$2+$B$10)/2*

   ✓ *You can select cells instead of typing absolute references to tell Excel which cells you wish the formula to reference.*

### To insert cell references by selecting cells:

a. Double-click formula where cell reference will be inserted.

   ✓ *If necessary, type preceding operator or parenthesis.*

b. Select cell(s) you want formula to reference.

   *Reference appears in formula.*

c. Press **F4** .................................. F4 until absolute reference appears.

d. Type desired operator or parenthesis.

e. Repeat steps a-d as needed.

4. Press **Enter** ................................ Enter

## CHANGE FONT USING THE FONT BOX

1. Select cells or characters in cells to format.

2. Click **Font box** ,....... [Arial] drop-down arrow on Formatting toolbar.

3. Select desired font ............... ⬇ , ↵

## CHANGE FONT SIZE USING THE SIZE BOX

1. Select cells or characters in cells to format.

2. a. Click **Font Size** box ............... [10 ▾] drop-down arrow on Formatting toolbar.

   b. Select a number in list ....... ⬇ , ↵

   **OR**

   a. Click **Font Size** box ............... [10 ▾] on Formatting toolbar.

   b. Enter desired number.

3. Press **Enter** ................................ Enter

## FORMAT VALUES FOR PERCENT

1. Select value or range of values.

2. Click Percent button %

   **OR**

   a. Click **Format** .................... Alt + O

   b. Click **Cells** ............................... E

   c. Select **Number** tab. .......... Ctrl + Tab

   d. Click **Percentage**.

   e. Click **Decimal places** .......... Alt + D

   f. Set number of places.

   g. Click **OK** ............................. Enter

## Exercise 9     ■ Summary

You are employed by the RED WAGON MANUFACTURING CO. and need to prepare a summary of the number of employees located in branches throughout the United States.

# EXERCISE DIRECTIONS

1. Create an appropriate title for your worksheet.

2. Create a listing of each STATE and the number of EMPLOYEES at each location.

    | | |
    |---|---|
    | Arizona | 1060 |
    | California | 120 |
    | Montana | 450 |
    | New Mexico | 695 |
    | Oregon | 543 |
    | South Dakota | 267 |

3. At the bottom of the list, enter a label and find:

    - TOTAL EMPLOYEES

4. Create a new column heading and find for each state:

    - The PERCENT of the (total) firm's employees employed at each location.

5. Format values in the EMPLOYEES column for commas with no decimal places.

6. Format PERCENT column for two-place percents.

7. Right-align all column titles over numeric data.

8. Use font and font size changes to enhance the spreadsheet.

9. Print one copy of the worksheet.

10. Save the workbook; name it **WAGON**.

11. Close the workbook.

## Exercise 10

- **Use Functions** ■ **Formula Bar and Palette**
- **Paste Function** ■ **AutoCalculate**

# NOTES

## Use Functions

- A **function** is a built-in formula that performs a special calculation automatically. For example, the SUM function can be used with a range of cells to add all values in the range specified. When you add the values in A4, A5, and A6, the function appears in the formula as follows: =SUM(A4:A6).

- Functions appear in formulas in the following order: first the function name (in either uppercase or lowercase) followed by an open parenthesis, then the number, cell, or range of cells to be affected; followed by a closed parenthesis.

- A function may be used by itself, or it may be combined with other functions.

- Excel provides functions that are used for statistical and financial analysis or for database operations:

| | |
|---|---|
| **AVERAGE ( )** | Averages values in a range of cells. |
| **COUNT ( )** | Counts all the non-blank cells in a range. Cells containing values as well as labels are counted. |
| **MAX ( )** | Indicates the highest value in a range of cells. |
| **MIN ( )** | Indicates the lowest value in a range of cells. |
| **SUM ( )** | Adds all values in a range of cells. |

- The data the functions require you to supply are called **arguments.** For example, in =MAX(A1:A5) the range of cells is the argument.

- You can type or insert functions into formulas. If you are typing a function and you wish to start the formula with a function, first type an equal sign (=).

## Formula Bar and Palette

- You can enter or edit a function using the Edit Formula button. If you click on the Edit Formula button (=) in the Formula Bar, a drop-down list of functions appears to the left of the formula bar, as illustrated below. You can select the desired function and then enter the arguments using the dialog boxes that appear.

- The Formula Palette is a tool that appears below the formula bar when you click the Edit Formula button. The palette provides information about the selected function in your formula and the result of the function for editing purposes.

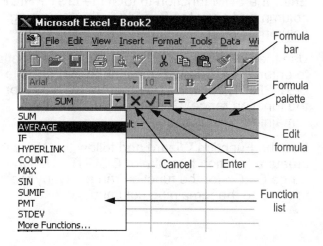

## Paste Function Wizard

- The **Paste Function** button $f_x$, located on the Standard toolbar or active formula bar, lets you insert functions into formulas by selecting the function from a list.  It provides steps that prompt for required and optional arguments.

- When you use the Paste Function Wizard to insert a function at the beginning of a formula, do not type an equal sign; the Function Wizard enters one for you.

## AutoCalculate

- AutoCalculate is a new feature that automatically provides the Average, Count, Count Nums, Max, Min, or Sum for a selected range.  After selecting the range to be calculated, you can right-click on the AutoCalculate section of the Status bar, which is at the right side of the Status bar at the bottom of the screen.  Select the desired function

from a pop-up list of automatic functions and the answer will appear on the Status bar as indicated in the illustration.  This result is for your use and cannot be transferred to the worksheet.

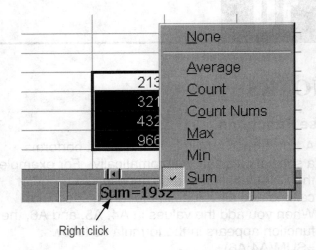

Right click

---

*In this exercise, you will enter summary labels and find summary data using the AVERAGE, COUNT, MAX and MIN functions with the Edit Formula button, the Function Wizard, AutoCalculate and by entering formulas to complete the PRICE worksheet.*

---

# EXERCISE DIRECTIONS

1. Open 🖮**PRICE**, or open 💾**10PRICE**.

2. Enter new labels in column A, as indicated.

3. Enter the SUM function to total the LIST PRICE column and copy the formula to the remaining columns.

4. Use the Edit Formula button and formula palette to enter the AVERAGE function to average the LIST PRICE column.  Use the range C4:C6 for the function range. Copy the formula to the remaining columns.

5. Use the Function Wizard and follow the steps to create a function formula for COUNT.  Use the range C4:C6 for the function range.  Copy the formula to the remaining columns.

6. Preview the answer to the MAXIMUM column by using AutoCalculate as follows:
   - Select the values in the List Price column.
   - Point to the AutoCalculate box at the right end of the Status Bar.
   - Click right mouse to view the pop-up list of functions.
   - Select Max.
   - View the answer on the Status bar.

7. Enter the MAX and MIN function formulas to complete the worksheet.  Copy formulas to the remaining columns.

8. Format summary data money amounts for two decimal places.

9. Close and save the workbook, or save as **PRICE**.

| | A | B | C | D | E | F | G |
|---|---|---|---|---|---|---|---|
| 1 | | | LIST | DIS- | SALE | SALES | TOTAL |
| 2 | PRODUCT | | PRICE | COUNT | PRICE | TAX | PRICE |
| 3 | | | | | | | |
| 4 | OVEN | | 745.00 | 185.00 | 560.00 | 44.80 | $ 604.80 |
| 5 | REFRIGERATOR | | 985.00 | 265.00 | 720.00 | 57.60 | $ 777.60 |
| 6 | WASHER | | 395.00 | 98.00 | 297.00 | 23.76 | $ 320.76 |
| 7 | | | | | | | |
| 8 | *TOTALS* | | | →————————————————————→ | | | |
| 9 | *AVERAGE* | | | →————————————————————→ | | | |
| 10 | *COUNT* | | | →————————————————————→ | | | |
| 11 | *MAXIMUM* | | | →————————————————————→ | | | |
| 12 | *MINIMUM* | | | →————————————————————→ | | | |
| 13 | | | | | | | |

# KEYSTROKES

## INSERT A FUNCTION USING FUNCTION WIZARD

1. Click cell.......................................... [⇵⇵]
   to contain formula.
   **OR**
   a. Double-click cell
      containing formula ...................... [F2]
   b. Place insertion point within
      formula where............................ [⇆⇉]
      function will be inserted.
2. Click **Paste Function** button............
   on Standard toolbar or formula bar.
   **OR**
   a. Click **Insert**........................ [Alt]+[I]
   b. Click **Function** ............................. [F]
      – *FUNCTION WIZARD – STEP 1 OF 2–*
3. Select a category.......... [Alt]+[C], [⇵⇵]
   in **Function Category** list.
4. Select a function .......... [Alt]+[N], [⇵⇵]
   in **Function Name** list.
5. Click **OK**.......................................... [↵]
   – *FUNCTION WIZARD – STEP 2 OF 2–*
6. Click desired argument box............. [Tab]
7. Type data ......................................... *data*

*Depending on the function, enter the following kinds of data:*

- **numbers (constants)** – type numbers (integers, fractions, mixed numbers, negative numbers) as you would in a cell.
- **references** – type or insert cell references.
- **named references or formulas** – type or insert named references or formulas.
- **functions** – type a function or click the Paste Function [*fx*] button to insert a function into an argument (nest functions).

*The Function Wizard describes the current argument, indicates if the argument is required, and shows you the result of the values you have supplied.*

8. Repeat steps 6 and 7, as needed.
9. Click **OK** ....................................... [Enter]
10. Type or insert remaining parts of formula.
    **OR**
    Press **Enter**................................ [Enter]

## INSERT A FUNCTION IN A CELL

1. Select cell to receive formula.
2. Press Equal ................................. [=]
3. Type function name.
4. Type open parenthesis ................... [(]
5. Type range or data range or data.
6. Type close parenthesis ................. [)]
7. Press Enter................................. [Enter]

## EDIT FORMULA USING FORMULA PALETTE

1. Select cell containing formula.
2. In formula bar, place insertion point in part of formula containing function to edit.
3. Click [=] (Edit Formula button).
   ✓ *Formula Palette appears below formula bar.*
4. Follow prompts provided by Formula Palette.

**Exercise**
# 11

## ■ Change Column Width ■ Create a Series
## ■ Natural Language Formulas ■ AutoComplete ■ Comma Format

## NOTES

### Change Column Width

■  All worksheets in a workbook are set for a **standard column width** (default setting).  This number represents the number of characters displayed in a cell using the standard font.

■ It is sometimes desirable to change (widen or narrow) the column widths so text or values can fit or have a better appearance.  Only the width of an entire column or a group of columns may be changed, not the width of a single cell.  You can use the Column, AutoFit Selection command on the Format menu or the mouse to set the column width to fit the longest entry.  A quick way to set the column to AutoFit is to double - click the right edge of the column heading. You can set a specific column width by using the Format, Column, Width commands to enter a number that represent the number of characters to be displayed.

■ In Excel 97, when you use the mouse to drag the column to a new width, the column setting appears above and to the right of the column and changes as you widen the column.

■ When you enter long labels, the text flows into the next column if the cell to the right is empty.  If the next cell is not empty, text that exceeds the column width is covered by the data in the cell to the right.

■ Unlike label text, numeric values do not flow into the next column once you have entered the limit of the cell.  If the column is not wide enough to display a numeric value, Excel displays the number in scientific notation to indicate a need to widen the column.

■ If you wish to shrink text to fit in a cell, Excel 97 will automatically adjust the point size to fit the column width.  You can set the Shrink to fit option on the Alignment tab by selecting the Format, Cells commands.

### Create a Series

■ You can use the Fill, Series command on the Edit menu to quickly enter sequential values in a range of cells.  You can enter sequential numbers, dates, or times in any increment (e.g., 2, 4, 6, 8 or 5, 10, 15, 20 or January, February, March, April).

■ Another way to fill a range with a series is to drag the **fill handle** of a selection containing the first or first and second series values over a range into which you want the series to be entered.  Excel completes the series based on the value(s) in the selected cell(s).

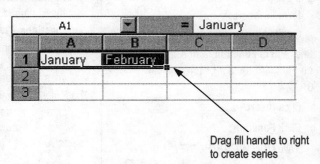

Drag fill handle to right
to create series

## Natural Language Formulas

■ In formulas, Excel 97 lets you refer to data using column or row headings instead of typing a reference to range of cells. For example, you can type =SUM(BASE SALARY) to add up all the values in a column containing the text label *BASE SALARY*. If more than one label of that name exists, Excel will prompt you to choose the range needed for your calculation.

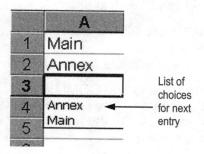

List of choices for next entry

## AutoComplete

■ A new feature, AutoComplete, allows you to enter labels automatically after making repetitive entries. For example, if several labels are entered in a list and the next items are repeated, you may use the right mouse and the quick menu to Pick from list, which allows you to select the next label from a list.

## Comma Format

■ To make large numbers more readable, formatting may be used to include commas. When you format for commas, the number of decimal places to display may also be set.

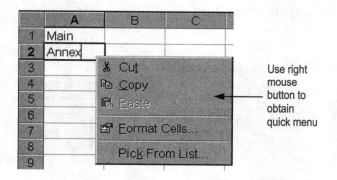

Use right mouse button to obtain quick menu

In this exercise, you will create a worksheet for the Colonial Furniture Gallery showing employees' quarterly SALES and COMMISSION earned. Each employee receives a 5% commission on sales.

# EXERCISE DIRECTIONS

1.  Create the worksheet on the following page, or open 🖫**11REPORT**.

2.  Set column widths as follows:

    Column A: 4    Column B: 15    Column C: 10
    Column E: 12   Column F: 12    Column G: 12

3.  Shrink text in the column B heading to fit into the cell.

4.  Practice using the Fill, Series option as follows:
    *   Using the Edit menu, enter employee numbers starting with 110 and stopping at 114.
    *   Delete the employee numbers.

5.  Enter 1 and 2 as employee numbers for the first two employees. Select the numbers and use the fill handle to extend the series.

6.  Practice using the AutoComplete feature as follows:
    *   Enter BUILDING as the column heading for column C.
    *   Enter Main for Judy Belis and Annex for Peter Hirsch.
    *   Place mouse cursor in the next cell (C9) for Kelly Miner.
    *   Right-click to display a quick menu.
    *   Select Pick from list...
    *   Select Main for Kelly Miner.
    *   Use this procedure to enter Annex for Sweet and Main for Tables.

- Delete all the data and column heading in column C.
- Set column C width to 6.

7. Copy BASE SALARY to the remaining employees.

   ✓ *Note: All employees have the same base salary.*

8. Enter a formula to find COMMISSION for the first employee. The commission rate is 5% of sales. Copy the formula to the remaining employees.

9. Enter a formula to find QUARTERLY SALARY for the first employee by adding BASE SALARY and COMMISSION for the quarter. Copy the formula to the remaining employees.

10. Enter a formula to find TOTALS for the BASE SALARY column using =SUM(SALARY) as the formula.

11. Enter formulas to calculate AVERAGES, HIGHEST, and LOWEST values.

12. Copy the formulas to each column.

13. Center column title labels.

14. Format numeric data to include commas and two decimal places.

15. Save the workbook; name it **REPORT**.

16. Print one copy.

17. Close the workbook.

| | A | B | C | D | E | F | G |
|---|---|---|---|---|---|---|---|
| 1 | | | COLONIAL FURNITURE GALLERY | | | | |
| 2 | | QUARTERLY SALES AND SALARY REPORT-JANUARY-MARCH | | | | | |
| 3 | | | | | | | |
| 4 | EMP. | | | BASE | | 5% | QUARTERLY |
| 5 | NO. | SALES ASSOCIATE | | SALARY | SALES | COMMISSION | SALARY |
| 6 | | | | | | | |
| 7 | | BELIS, JUDY | | 1500 | 113456.67 | | |
| 8 | | HIRSCH, PETER | | | 150654.87 | | |
| 9 | | MINER, KELLY | | | 234765.36 | | |
| 10 | | SWEET, LETOYA | | | 89765.43 | | |
| 11 | | TABLES, TONY | | | 287987.76 | | |
| 12 | | | | | | | |
| 13 | | TOTALS | | | | | |
| 14 | | AVERAGES | | | | | |
| 15 | | HIGHEST | | | | | |
| 16 | | LOWEST | | | | | |

# KEYSTROKES

## CHANGE COLUMN WIDTHS USING THE MENU

1. Select any cell(s) in column(s) to change.

2. Click **Format** ......................... Alt + O

3. Click **Column** ................................. C

4. Click **Width** ...................................... W

5. Type number (0-255) ............... *number* in Column Width text box.

   ✓ *Number represents number of characters that can be displayed in cell using the standard font.*

6. Click [ OK ] ............................. Enter

## CHANGE COLUMN WIDTHS USING THE MOUSE

### Change One Column Width

1. Point to right border of column heading to size.

2. Pointer *becomes a* ←→.

3. Drag ←→ left or right.

   ✓ *Excel displays width on left side of formula bar.*

### Change Several Column Widths

1. Select columns to size.

2. Point to right border of any selected column heading.

   ✓ Pointer becomes a ←→.

3. Drag ←→ left or right.

   ✓ Excel displays width on left side of formula bar.

### Use Right Mouse Button

1. Highlight column by clicking on label.

2. Right-click mouse.

3. Click **Column Width** ...................... C

4. Type in width ........................... *number*

5. Click [ OK ] ............................. Enter

## SET COLUMN WIDTH TO FIT LONGEST ENTRY

Double-click right border of column heading.

**OR**

1. Select column

   to size..................... ⬍, Ctrl + Space

2. Click **Format** ......................... Alt + O

3. Click **Column**.............................. C

4. Click **AutoFit Selection** ................... A

## SET STANDARD COLUMN WIDTH

*Changes column widths that have not been previously adjusted in a worksheet.*

1. Click **Format** ......................... Alt + O

2. Click **Column**.............................. C

3. Click **Standard Width**.................. S

4. Type new number (0-255) .........*number* in Standard Column Width text box.

   ✓ *Number represents number of characters that can be displayed in cell using the standard font.*

5. Click OK .............................. Enter

## CREATE A SERIES OF NUMBERS, DATES, OR TIMES USING THE MENU

1. Enter first series value in a cell to create a series from a **single value** .

   **OR**

   Enter first and second series values in consecutive cells to create a series from multiple values.

2. Select cell(s) containing series value(s) and cells to fill.

   ✓ *Select adjacent cells in rows or columns to fill.*

3. Click **Edit**.............................. Alt + E

4. Click **Fill**.............................. I

5. Click **Series** .......................... S

**To change proposed step value:**

- Type step value .....................*number* in Step Value text box.

---

**To change proposed direction of series:**

Select desired Series in option:

- **Rows**.............................. Alt + R
- **Columns** .......................... Alt + C

**To change proposed series type:**

Select desired Type option:

- **Linear** .............................. Alt + L
  to increase/decrease each value in series by number in Step Value text box.

- **Growth** .............................. Alt + G
  to multiply each value in series by number in Step Value text box.

- **Date** .............................. Alt + D
  to set increment by days, weekdays, months, or years.

- **AutoFill**.............................. Alt + F
  to fill cells based on values in selection.

**If Date was selected:**

Select desired Date Unit option:

- **Day** .............................. Alt + A
- **Weekday**.......................... Alt + W
- **Month** .............................. Alt + M
- **Year** .............................. Alt + Y

**To set stop value for series:**

   ✓ *Type a stop value if you want series to end at a specific number.*

   a. Click **Stop Value**:.............. Alt + O

   b. Type stop value .................... number

6. Click OK .......................... Enter

## CREATE A SERIES OF NUMBERS, DATES, OR TIMES USING THE MOUSE

*Creates a series by dragging the fill handle of a cell selection containing the first or first and second series value(s).*

   ✓ *The fill handle is a small square in the lower right corner of a selection.*

**Create a Series from a Single Value:**

1. Enter first series value in a cell.

2. Select cell containing the first series value.

---

3. Point to fill handle.

   ✓ *Pointer becomes a + when positioned correctly.*

4. Press Ctrl and drag + over adjacent cells to extend border in rows or column to fill.

   ✓ *Drag border down or to the right to create an ascending series. Drag border up or to the left to create a series decreasing in value.*

**Create a Series from Multiple Values:**

1. Enter first and second series values in consecutive cells.

2. Select cells containing series values.

3. Point to fill handle.

   ✓ *Pointer becomes a + when positioned correctly.*

4. Drag + over adjacent cells to extend border in rows or columns to fill.

   ✓ *Drag border down or to the right to create an ascending series. Drag border up or to the left to create a series decreasing in value.*

## AUTOCOMPLETE - ENTER TEXT

*Select text to enter in a cell from a list of entries you have made in the current column.*

1. Right-click cell to receive text.

2. Click **Pick From List** ........................ K

3. Click desired entry.

## SHRINK TEXT TO AUTOMATICALLY FIT COLUMN WIDTH

1. Select cells containing text to shrink.

2. Click **Format**........................ Alt + O

3. Click **Cells**. .............................. E

4. Select **Alignment** tab.

5. Select **Shrink to fit**................ Alt + K

6. Click **OK**................................ Enter

## Exercise 12

# ■ Print Options  ■ Edit Data  ■ Comments

## NOTES

### Print Options

■  When the Print command is accessed, Excel allows you to set various print options.  You can choose to print a range of cells, use the Properties button to access page setting options for printing, and use the Print Preview button to preview, on screen, the output your settings will yield.

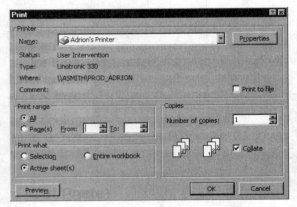

■ You can select File, Page Setup and then select the Sheet tab to set various print options for the sheet, such as gridlines and row and column headings.

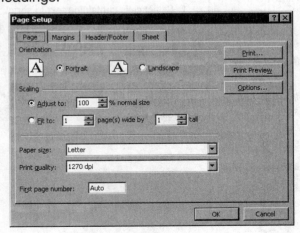

■ In the dialog boxes, you can also select the Print Preview button to review, on screen, the output your settings will yield.

### Edit Data

■ Data may be changed either before or after it has been entered in a cell.

■ Before data is entered, the Backspace key may be used to correct a keystroke.

■ To clear a cell's content before it is entered:

• Press the Escape key, or

• Click the Cancel box on the formula bar.

■ After data is entered, there are several methods of correction:

• Replace the entire entry with new data, or

• Edit part of an entry by enabling cell editing, or

• Erase a single cell entry, or

• Erase a range of cell entries.

■ Excel's Range Finder feature makes it easier to troubleshoot or adjust references in formulas. When you edit a formula, Excel provides color controls (outlines and extend boxes) that indicate in the worksheet the cells or cell ranges contained in the formula. You can use these controls to change the references in the formula instead of retyping the references.

## Comments

- It is possible to attach a text note to a cell that displays or plays when the cursor is placed on the cell. This feature is useful to document formulas or assumptions built into the worksheet. A note is entered using the Insert, Comment commands. Note the illustration of a completed text cell comment. A red triangle will appear in the top right corner of a cell with a comment as shown on the next page.

| SUMMIT UNITED BANK | | | | | | | | |
| PAYROLL | | | | | | | | |
| | | | | | | | | |
| Card | Employee | Hourly | Hours | Gross | Social | Medicare | | |
| Number | Name | Rate | Worked | Pay | Sec. Tax | Tax | F.W.T. | Net Pay |
| | | | | | | Tax calculated at 6.2% | | |
| 3567 | Diaz | 5.55 | 15 | 83.25 | 5.16 | | | 60.23 |
| 3750 | Jaffe | 7.23 | 32 | 231.36 | 14.34 | | | 167.39 |
| 3816 | Latov | 6.18 | 16 | 98.88 | 6.13 | | | 71.54 |
| 3925 | Nestor | 4.66 | 28 | 130.48 | 8.09 | | | 94.40 |

*In this exercise, you will complete the payroll for the Summit United Bank for the week ending April 7, 199-. You will then copy the entire worksheet to a new location and edit data to create another payroll for the week ending April 14, 199-. Notes will be entered on the first line of the payroll to document the tax rates used for the payroll.*

# EXERCISE DIRECTIONS

1. Open 🖬 PAY, or open 🖫 12PAY.

2. Edit the first line of the title, as illustrated.

3. Erase the second line of the title. Replace it, as indicated.

4. Enter the new row labels, as indicated.

5. Find TOTALS and AVERAGES for Gross Pay, Soc. Sec. Tax, Medicare Tax, F.W.T. and Net Pay columns.

6. Format TOTALS and AVERAGES for two decimal places.

7. Edit formulas using the Range Finder feature:

   a. Double-click TOTALS formula for Gross Pay.
      ✓ Note the color controls that indicate the cells in the formula.
   b. Change cell range by dragging extend box of range to E13.
   c. Press ENTER.

8. Enter comments cell notes as follows:
   - In F7: Tax calculated at 6.2%
   - In G7: Tax calculated at 1.45%
   - In H7: Tax calculated at 20%

9. View the comments.

10. Copy the range of data shown to a new location on the worksheet.
    ✓ Select the range and specify only the first position in the destination range for the paste operation.

11. THE FOLLOWING STEPS ARE FOR THE BOTTOM PAYROLL —

    a. Edit the title to read:

## FOR THE WEEK ENDING APRIL 14, 199-

    b. Edit the HOURS WORKED as follows:

| | | |
|---|---|---|
| Diaz, 20 | Jaffe, 31 | Latov, 23 |
| Nestor, 22 | Pringle, 15 | Wong, 25 |

12. Preview the printout of this file.

13. Print one copy of the April 14 payroll.

14. Close and save the workbook, or save as PAY.

|    | A | B | C | D | E | F | G | H | I |
|----|---|---|---|---|---|---|---|---|---|
| 1 | SUMMIT UNITED BANK ← *PAYROLL* | | | | | | | | |
| 2 | ~~PAYROLL~~ ← *FOR THE WEEK ENDING APRIL 7, 199-* | | | | | | | | |
| 3 | | | | | | | | | |
| 4 | Card | Employee | Hourly | Hours | Gross | Social | Medicare | | |
| 5 | Number | Name | Rate | Worked | Pay | Sec. Tax | Tax | F.W.T. | Net Pay |
| 6 | | | | | | | | | |
| 7 | 13567 | Diaz | 5.55 | 15 | 83.25 | 5.16 | 1.21 | 16.65 | 60.23 |
| 8 | 13750 | Jaffe | 7.23 | 32 | 231.36 | 14.34 | 3.35 | 46.27 | 167.39 |
| 9 | 13816 | Latov | 6.18 | 16 | 98.88 | 6.13 | 1.43 | 19.78 | 71.54 |
| 10 | 13925 | Nestor | 4.66 | 28 | 130.48 | 8.09 | 1.89 | 26.10 | 94.40 |
| 11 | 14345 | Pringle | 6.57 | 12 | 78.84 | 4.89 | 1.14 | 15.77 | 57.04 |
| 12 | 14715 | Wong | 8.65 | 21 | 181.65 | 11.26 | 2.63 | 36.33 | 131.42 |
| 13 | | | | | | | | | |
| 14 | *TOTALS* | | | | | | → | | |
| 15 | *AVERAGES* | | | | | | → | | |
| 16 | | | | | | | | | |
| 17 | | Copy | | | | | | | |
| 18 | | | | | | | | | |
| 19 | | | | | | | | | |

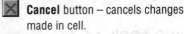

# KEYSTROKES

## EDIT CELL CONTENT AFTER IT IS ENTERED (ENABLE CELL EDITING)

1. Double-click cell to edit.

   **OR**

   a. Select cell to edit. ...................... [↔↕]

   b. Press F2 ..................................... [F2]

*An insertion point appears in the active cell and these buttons appear on the formula bar:*

   [X] **Cancel** button – cancels changes made in cell.

   [✓] **Enter** button – accepts changes made in cell.

2. Click desired data position............. [↕]

   in cell or in formula bar.

3. Type new data ................................*data*

   **OR**

   Press **Backspace** ................. [Backspace]

   to delete character to left of insertion point.

   **OR**

   Press **Delete**................................. [Del]

   to delete character to right of insertion point.

   **To accept changes:**

   Press **Enter**................................... [↵]

### OR

• Click **Enter** button ........................ [✓]

on the formula bar.

**To cancel changes:**

• Press **Escape** ........................... [Esc]

**OR**

Click **Cancel** button ........................ [X]

on the formula bar.

## EDIT CELL CONTENTS WHILE TYPING

**To delete character to the left of insertion point:**

• Press **Backspace** ............. [Backspace]

**To cancel all characters:**

• Press **Escape** ........................... [Esc]

## ERASE CONTENTS OF CELL OR RANGE

1. Select cell or range containing contents to erase.

2. Press **Delete**................................. [Del]

## CREATE TEXT COMMENTS

1. Select cell to attach note to.

2. Click **Insert** .......................... [Alt]+[I]

3. Click **Comment**............................. [M]

4. Type note in box.

5. Click outside box.

*Excel marks each cell containing a note with a note marker (small red triangle in upper right corner).*

*Point to the cell containing the note to view it.*

### 🌐 PRINT PREVIEW

1. Click **Print Preview** button ............. [🔍]

   on Standard toolbar.

   **OR**

   a. Click **File** ........................... [Alt]+[F]

   b. Click **Print Preview**..................... [V]

   *– FROM PREVIEW WINDOW –*

**For multiple page worksheets:**

   **To view next page:**

   • Click [ Next > ] ................... [Alt]+[N]

## To view previous page:

- Click `Previous` .............. `Alt` + `P`

## To view a magnified portion of the page:

a. Click area of page .............. `Alt` + `Z` to magnify.

b. Click any area of page ........ `Alt` + `Z` to return to full page view.

2. Click `Close` ...................... `Alt` + `C` to exit Print Preview.

##  PRINT RANGE OF CELLS

*Prints data in range using the current page settings.*

> ✓ *When you print a range, this procedure will override a print area, if you defined one.*

1. Select range of cells to print.
2. Click **File** .............................. `Alt` + `F`
3. Click **Print** .................................. `P`
4. Click **Selection** ..................... `Alt` + `N`
5. Click `OK` ......................... `Enter`

## SET PRINT OPTIONS FOR WORKSHEET

*Sets a print area and shows or hides gridlines on printed sheet.*

1. Click **File** .............................. `Alt` + `F`
2. Click **Page Setup** ......................... `U`
3. Select **Sheet** tab .................. `Ctrl` + `Tab`

### To set a print area:

> ✓ *Use this option to print a specific area of a worksheet each time you print.*

a. Click in **Print Area**: ............ `Alt` + `A`

b. Select range of cells in worksheet to print.

**OR**

Type cell reference(s) .............. *references* of area to print.

> ✓ *To remove a print area, delete the reference.*

### To show or hide gridlines:

- Select or deselect **Gridlines** .......................... `Alt` + `G`

4. Click `OK` ......................... `Enter`

## CHANGE FORMULA REFERENCES WITH RANGE FINDER

- Double-click formula.

*Excel adds a colored border and extend box on each worksheet cell or cell range contained in formula.*

### To change location of cell range:

a. Drag border to desired location.

> ✓ *Pointer becomes an arrow when positioned correctly.*

b. Press Enter to complete the change.

### To change size of cell range:

a. Drag extend box of range.

> ✓ *Pointer becomes a cross hair ⊹ when positioned correctly.*

b. Press Enter to complete the change.

## Exercise 13

# ■ Page Setup ■ Multiple Undo and Redo

# NOTES

## Page Setup

- Excel 97 uses the default page size (usually 8 1/2" x 11") of the installed printer. To change the page size, use the Page Setup option on the File menu, then select the Page tab.

- Use the Page Setup option to control the print output for the selected page size. The Page Setup dialog box (see below) may be accessed directly from the File menu or from the Print Preview option. The Page Setup dialog box has several tabs. Each tab contains options that control the print output.

### *Page Setup Dialog Box with Page Tab Selected*

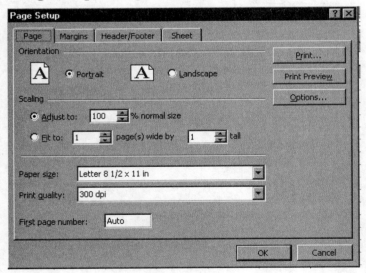

- Page Setup options include:

**Page Tab**

- **Orientation** The worksheet data may be printed in either **Portrait** (vertical) or **Landscape** (horizontal) paper orientation.

- **Scaling** The printed worksheet can be enlarged or reduced. The scaling options are: Adjust to % of normal size or Fit to pages wide by pages tall. Both scaling options proportionally scale the worksheet.

- ✓ *Note: Scaling is often needed when you want a printed worksheet to fit on a page. You can use the Print Preview option to check how it will fit before printing.*

- **Paper Size** The paper size options include letter, legal, and other size options.

- **First Page Number** The starting page number for the pages on the current sheet.

**Margins Tab**

- **Margins** The page margins, the distance of the worksheet data to the Top, Bottom, Left, or Right edge of the page, may be set in inches. The Header and Footer margins, the distance of the header and footer data from the top and bottom edges of the worksheet, can be set in inches.

- **Center on Page** The worksheet data can be Horizontally and/or Vertically centered within the page margins.

### Header/Footer Tab

- **Header/Footer** A line of text may be included above or below the worksheet. This may be used to include a title, a date, or a page number. *(See Exercise 14.)*

### Sheet Tab

- **Print Area** Only define this area if you always want to print the same range of cells when printing a worksheet.

- **Print Titles** Descriptive information from designated Rows that will print on the top of each page and/or Columns that will print on the left of each page. *(See Exercise 15.)*

- **Print** Includes the following print options: Gridlines, Comments, Draft Quality, Black and White, and Row and Column Headings.

- **Page Order** The setting that determines the printed page order: Down, then Across or Across, then Down.

### Multiple Undo and Redo

- As with the Word program, any edit activity can be reversed using Edit, Undo. You can undo up to 16 previous actions, not just your last action, with the Edit, Undo command or the Undo button ⌂ ▾.

- The Undo feature specifically names the last edit to be undone. This feature lets you work with greater safety and confidence.

- You can also redo undone actions (again, up to 16) with the Redo command or button ↰ ▾.

---

*In this exercise, you will open the quarterly sales worksheet for the Colonial Furniture Gallery and expand the worksheet to include quarterly data.*

## EXERCISE DIRECTIONS

1. Open 🖩**REPORT**, or open 🖫**13REPORT**.

2. Edit the second line of the title. Replace MARCH with JUNE.

3. In row 4, replace QUARTERLY with JAN-MAR.

4. Change column widths as follows:

   | | |
   |---|---|
   | Column C: | 3 |
   | Columns H, I, J: | 12 |

5. Copy column titles SALES, 5% COMMISSION, and SALARY to columns H, I, and J. Insert the label APR-JUN over SALARY in column J.

6. Center all new labels where necessary.

7. Undo last edit by pressing Ctrl+Z.

8. Quickly redo last undone action.

9. Enter new sales data in column H.

10. Copy the COMMISSION formula for the first associate in column F to column I.

11. Copy the COMMISSION formula down for each associate.

12. Enter a formula in column J to compute BASE SALARY + COMMISSION for the second quarter.

13. Copy the BASE SALARY + COMMISSION formula in column J down for each employee.

14. Find TOTALS, AVERAGES, HIGHEST, and LOWEST for the second quarter. (Copy formulas using ranges and one copy operation.)

15. Format numeric data for commas and two decimal places.

16. Change the scale setting to fit worksheet on one page.

17. Check your scale setting using Print Preview.

18. Print one copy.

19. Close and save the workbook, or save as **REPORT**.

| | A | B | C | D | E | F | G | H | I | J |
|---|---|---|---|---|---|---|---|---|---|---|
| | | | | | | | | ←—12—→ | ←—12—→ | ←—12—→ |
| 1 | | | | COLONIAL FURNITURE GALLERY | | | | | | |
| 2 | | QUARTERLY SALES AND SALARY REPORT-JANUARY-MARCH | | | | ◄ | JUNE | | | |
| 3 | | | | | | | JAN-MAR ◄ | | | |
| 4 | EMP. | | | BASE | | 5% | QUARTERLY | | | APR-JUN |
| 5 | NO. | SALES ASSOCIATE | | SALARY | SALES | COMMISSION | SALARY | → | → | → |
| 6 | | | | | | | | → | | |
| 7 | 1 | BELIS, JUDY | | 1,500.00 | 113,456.67 | 5,672.83 | 7,172.83 | **114342.87** | | |
| 8 | 2 | HIRSCH, PETER | | 1,500.00 | 150,654.87 | 7,532.74 | 9,032.74 | **143276.65** | | |
| 9 | 3 | MINER, KELLY | | 1,500.00 | 234,765.36 | 11,738.27 | 13,238.27 | **187956.76** | | |
| 10 | 4 | SWEET, LETOYA | | 1,500.00 | 89,765.43 | 4,488.27 | 5,988.27 | **93984.69** | ↓ | ↓ |
| 11 | 5 | TABLES, TONY | | 1,500.00 | 287,987.76 | 14,399.39 | 15,899.39 | **254768.64** | | |
| 12 | | | | | | | | | | |
| 13 | | TOTALS | | 7,500.00 | 876,630.09 | 43,831.50 | 51,331.50 | → | | |
| 14 | | AVERAGES | | 1,500.00 | 175,326.02 | 8,766.30 | 10,266.30 | → | | |
| 15 | | HIGHEST | | 1,500.00 | 287,987.76 | 14,399.39 | 15,899.39 | → | | |
| 16 | | LOWEST | | 1,500.00 | 89,765.43 | 4,488.27 | 5,988.27 | → | | |
| 17 | | | →  3  ◄ | | | | | | | |

# KEYSTROKES

## CHANGE SCALE OF PRINTED DATA

1. Click **File** ............................... Alt + F
2. Click **Page Setup** .......................... U
3. Select **Page** ...................... Ctrl + Tab

**To reduce or enlarge data on printed sheet:**

a. Click **Adjust to:** .................. Alt + A
b. Type percentage
   (10-400) ............................... *number*

✓ *You can also click the increment box arrows to select a percentage.*

4. Click  OK  ........................... Enter

**To fit worksheet on a specified number of pages:**

a. Click **Fit to** .................................. F
b. Type number of pages or use increment box arrows.
c. Click **OK**.

## UNDO LAST ACTION

Press **Ctrl+Z** ........................... Ctrl + Z
**OR**

Click Undo button [↶▾] on Standard toolbar.

## UNDO LAST ACTION USING MENU

1. Click **Edit** .............................. Alt + E
2. Click **Undo** action name .................. U

## REDO LAST UNDONE ACTION

Press **Ctrl+Y** ........................... Ctrl + Y
**OR**

Click Redo button [↷▾] on Standard toolbar.

## REDO LAST UNDONE ACTION USING MENU

1. Click **Edit** .............................. Alt + E
2. Click **Redo** action name .................. R

## UNDO SELECTED ACTIONS

1. Click **Undo** arrow ...................... [↶▾]
2. Drag through actions to undo, then click.

✓ *You can only undo consecutive actions, starting with the last action at the top of the list.*

## Exercise 14

■ **Page Breaks** ■ **Page Break Preview**
■ **Headers and Footers** ■ **Spell Check**

## NOTES

### Page Breaks

■ Before printing, you may set page breaks and add headers and footers.

■ When the **Page Break** option is set, Excel stops printing on the current page and starts printing on the top of a new page.

■ Excel inserts **automatic page breaks** based on the current paper size, scaling, and margin settings. Automatic page breaks appear as dashed lines on the worksheet. To view automatic page breaks, you must select the A_utomatic Page Breaks check box on the View tab in the Options dialog box. You can override the automatic page breaks by inserting **manual page breaks** in your worksheet. Manual page breaks appear as bold dashed lines.

### Page Break Preview

■ When you switch from **Normal** view to **Page Break Preview**, you can adjust page breaks, resize the print area, and edit the worksheet. You can switch between Normal view and Page break preview using the _V_iew menu, or from Print preview.

■ When you move a page break, Excel automatically scales the worksheet to fit on the page or pages. Initially, page breaks are automatically defined based on the size of your worksheet and the current page settings. Automatic page breaks appear as dashed lines. When you move an automatic page break, its appearance changes to a solid line. If you drag a page break off the worksheet, Excel resets the page breaks.

### Headers and Footers

■ **Headers** and **footers** are used when you want to repeat the same information at the top (header) or bottom (footer) of every page.

■ With Excel, you can select from built-in headers and footers, or you can customize one. These print enhancements can be set in the Page Setup dialog box from the Header/Footer tab.

■ Headers/footers are limited to a single line of text. Header/footer text may, however, be separated into segments. Selected header/footer text can be formatted.

■ When you create a custom header, text entered in the left-most section will be left-justified. Text entered in the middle section will be centered, and text entered in the right-most section will be right-justified.

■ You may insert **codes** to print the current date, current time, page number, and/or workbook filename as part of the header/footer text by clicking a code button representing the desired item.

✓Note the illustration on the next page.

### Spell Check

■ The spelling of the text in a worksheet may be checked by using the Spell Check button on the Standard toolbar, by pressing F7, or by selecting _S_pelling from the _T_ools menu. If mistakes are found, replacement words are suggested and can be used to correct the text.

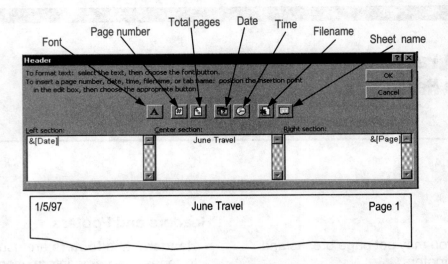

In this exercise, you will create a travel expense report for one of the salespeople at the Wilmot Chemical Company. The June travel report will include two trips, each printed on a separate page with a header. The reports will be spell checked.

# EXERCISE DIRECTIONS

1. Create the top worksheet shown on the next page including bold styles, or open ⊟**14EXPENSE**.

   ✓ *Enter the days of the month as numeric labels.*

2. Use the Spell Check feature to check your worksheet.

3. Set column widths as follows:

   Column A:          15
   Column B:          3

4. Find for Car (miles):
   - Total Miles (add daily mileage)
   - Total Travel Expense (mileage * .29).

5. Find:
   - TOTALS for each day (which include the dollar amount rows in the TRANSPORTATION section).
   - Total of Total Travel Expenses column (which includes the DAILY EXPENSES and the TRANSPORTATION costs).

6. Format all money columns for two decimal places.

7. Center all column titles.

8. Copy the entire top worksheet to cell A34.

9. Create a page break at cell A31.

10. Edit or delete data in the DATES, PURPOSE, TRANSPORTATION and DAILY EXPENSES areas on the second page to display the data for the next trip, as indicated.

11. In the Total Travel Expenses column find:
    - Total of the Car Rental expenses
    - Total of the Plane expenses
    - Copy the formula to each expense item.

12. Set a custom header that includes a left-justified date, a centered title that reads JUNE TRAVEL, and a right-justified page number.

13. Set the footer to none.

14. Switch to Page Break view of the worksheet.
    a. Drag page break to A33.
    b. Check that print area border (dark outline) includes both expense reports.

15. Switch to normal view of the worksheet.

16. Print the file to fit to the page.

17. Save the workbook file; name it **EXPENSE**.

18. Close the workbook.

◀ 15 ▶

**WILMOT CHEMICAL COMPANY**
**TRAVEL EXPENSE REPORT**

▶3◀

| NAME: | Rudy McDermott | | | | | |
|---|---|---|---|---|---|---|
| **DATES:** | 6/3-6/6/9- | **PURPOSE:** | | Madison, WI Plant | | |

enter as numeric labels

| | | | | | Total Miles @ $.29 | Total Travel Expenses |
|---|---|---|---|---|---|---|
| | Jun 3 | Jun 4 | Jun 5 | Jun 6 | | |
| **TRANSPORTATION** | | | | | | |
| Car (miles) | 168 | 55 | 43 | 175 | | |
| | | | | | | |
| Car Rental | | | | | | |
| Plane | | | | | | |
| Train | | | | | | |
| | | | | | | |
| **DAILY EXPENSES** | | | | | | |
| Hotal | 125.65 | 125.65 | 125.65 | 125.65 | | |
| Breakfast | 0.00 | 5.59 | 15.95 | 7.55 | | |
| Lunch | 15.60 | 12.95 | 45.95 | 43.55 | | |
| Dinner | 39.35 | 95.86 | 135.85 | 0.00 | | |
| Tolls | 0.00 | 1.50 | 2.00 | 0.00 | | |
| Parking | 0.00 | 15.00 | 12.00 | 7.00 | | |
| Tips | 6.00 | 18.00 | 22.00 | 11.00 | | |
| Phone | 3.25 | 7.53 | 8.52 | 4.76 | | |
| Misc. | 0.00 | 12.00 | 15.00 | 3.00 | | |
| | | | | | | |
| **TOTALS** | | | | | | |

copy

enter page break

**WILMOT CHEMICAL COMPANY**
**TRAVEL EXPENSE REPORT**

| NAME: | Rudy McDermott | | | | | |
|---|---|---|---|---|---|---|
| **DATES:** | 6/14-6/16/9- | **PURPOSE:** | | LosAngeles, CA Plant | | |

| | | | | | Total Miles @ $.29 | Total Travel Expenses |
|---|---|---|---|---|---|---|
| | June 14 | June 15 | June 16 | | | |
| **TRANSPORTATION** | | | | | | |
| Car (miles) | | | | | | |
| | | | | | | |
| Car Rental | 65.00 | 65.00 | 65.00 | | | |
| Plane | 375.89 | | | | | |
| Train | | | | | | |
| | | | | | | |
| **DAILY EXPENSES** | | | | | | |
| Hotal | 135.65 | 135.65 | 135.65 | | | |
| Breakfast | 0.00 | 6.68 | 5.76 | | | |
| Lunch | 35.55 | 13.64 | 43.32 | | | |
| Dinner | 88.75 | 145.76 | 0.00 | | | |
| Tolls | 3.50 | 4.50 | 4.00 | | | |
| Parking | 18.50 | 22.15 | 16.75 | | | |
| Tips | 10.00 | 25.00 | 15.00 | | | |
| Phone | 8.95 | 9.95 | 6.25 | | | |
| Misc. | 0.00 | 16.50 | 0.00 | | | |
| | | | | | | |
| **TOTALS** | | | | | | |

# KEYSTROKES

## INSERT MANUAL PAGE BREAKS

✓ *After you insert a manual page break, Excel adjusts the automatic page breaks that follow it. To display automatic page breaks, see **SHOW AUTOMATIC PAGE BREAKS**, right.*

### Insert a Horizontal Page Break:

1. Select row where new page will start.
2. Click **I**nsert ............................. `Alt`+`I`
3. Click Page **B**reak ........................... `B`

### Insert a Vertical Page Break:

1. Select column where new page will start.
2. Click **I**nsert ............................. `Alt`+`I`
3. Click Page **B**reak ........................... `B`

### Insert a Horizontal and Vertical Page Break:

1. Click cell ................................. `↕↔`
   where new pages will start
2. Click **I**nsert ............................. `Alt`+`I`
3. Click Page **B**reak ........................... `B`

## REMOVE MANUAL PAGE BREAKS

✓ *After you remove a manual page break, Excel adjusts the automatic page breaks that follow it. To display automatic page breaks, see **SHOW AUTOMATIC PAGE BREAKS**, right.*

### Remove a Horizontal Page Break:

1. Select a cell immediately below page break.
2. Click **I**nsert ............................. `Alt`+`I`
3. Click **R**emove Page **B**reak .............. `B`

### Remove a Vertical Page Break:

1. Select a cell immediately to the right of page break.
2. Click **I**nsert ............................. `Alt`+`I`
3. Click **R**emove Page **B**reak .............. `B`

### Remove All Manual Page Breaks:

1. Click blank button at top left corner of worksheet grid.
2. Click **I**nsert ............................. `Alt`+`I`
3. Click **R**eset All Page **B**reaks .......... `B`

## SHOW PAGE BREAKS

1. Click **T**ools ............................. `Alt`+`T`
2. Click **O**ptions… .......................... `O`
3. Select **View** tab ................... `Ctrl`+`Tab`
4. Click Page Brea**k**s ...................... `Alt`+`K`
5. Click `OK` ................................. `↵`

## 🌐 SET HEADER AND FOOTER OPTIONS

*Adds text or special codes to top or bottom of each page.*

1. Click **F**ile .............................. `Alt`+`F`
2. Click Page Set**u**p ........................ `U`
3. Select **Header/Footer** tab ....... `Ctrl`+`Tab`

### To select a built-in header:

a. Click **H**eader ...................... `Alt`+`A`
   drop-down list.
b. Select desired header type ......... `↕↔`

### To select a built-in footer

a. Click **F**ooter ...................... `Alt`+`F`
   drop-down list.
b. Select desired footer type ......... `↕↔`

### To customize selected header or footer:

a. Click `Custom Header...` ............ `Alt`+`C`

**OR**

Click `Custom Footer...` ................. `Alt`+`U`

b. Click in section to change:
   - **L**eft ...................... `Alt`+`L`
   - **C**enter ................... `Alt`+`C`
   - **R**ight ..................... `Alt`+`R`

c. Type or edit text ........................ *text*
   to appear in header or footer section.

### To change font of header or footer text:

a. Select text to format.
b. Click Font button `A` ........ `Tab`+`↵`
   ✓ *Press **Tab** until **Font** button is highlighted.*
c. Select desired font options.
d. Click `OK` ............................. `↵`

## To insert a header or footer code:

a. Place insertion point where code will appear.
b. Click desired ...................... `Tab`+`↵`
   code button from the following choices:
   ✓ *Press **Tab** until desired code button is highlighted.*

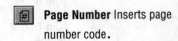 **Page Number** Inserts page number code.

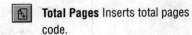 **Total Pages** Inserts total pages code.

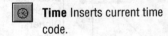 **Date** Inserts current date code.

🕐 **Time** Inserts current time code.

💲 **Filename** Inserts filename code.

⌨ **Sheet Name** Inserts active sheet name code.

c. Repeat steps b and c for each custom header or footer to change.
d. Click `OK` ............................. `↵`
4. Click `OK` ............................. `↵`

## SPELL CHECK

1. Select any cell .......................... `↕↔`
2. Click Spell Check button ................. `✓`

**OR**

1. Click **T**ools ............................. `Alt`+`T`
2. Click **S**pelling .......................... `S`

*The Spelling dialog box appears and Excel shows the first word not found in dictionary above the Change To text box.*

## SWITCH TO PAGE BREAK VIEW OF WORKSHEET

**From Worksheet:**

1. Click **V**iew ............................ `Alt` + `V`
2. Click **P**age Break Preview .............. `P`

OR

**From Print Preview:**

Click Page Break Preview command.

✓ *Automatic page breaks appear as dashed lines. Page breaks you have inserted appear as thick lines. Excel also labels page numbers. If you defined a print area, it appears asa thick outline.*

**To return to normal view:**

a. Click **V**iew: ........................ `Alt` + `V`
b. Click **N**ormal ............................. `N`

## MOVE HORIZONTAL OR VERTICAL PAGE BREAK

1. Switch to Page break preview.
2. Drag page break (dashed or solid line) to desired location.

   ✓ *Automatic page breaks change to hard page breaks (solid lines) when you move them.*

   ✓ *If you drag the page break outside the print area, Excel restores the automatic page break.*

## RESET (REMOVE) ALL PAGE BREAKS

✓ *This procedure does not remove automatic page breaks, which are determined by the size of your worksheet and page settings, such as margins and scale.*

4. Switch to Page break preview
5. Right-click any cell.
6. Click **Reset All Page Breaks** on shortcut menu.

## ADJUST PRINT AREA

1. Switch to Page break preview.
2. Drag print area border (dark outline) to define a new area.

## RESET PRINT AREA

1. Switch to Page break preview.
2. Right-click any cell.
3. Click **Reset Print Area** on shortcut menu.

## SWITCH TO NORMAL VIEW OF WORKSHEET

**From Worksheet:**

1. Click **V**iew ............................ `Alt` + `V`
2. Click **N**ormal ................................. `N`

OR

**From Print Preview:**

Click Normal **V**iew command.

## EXERCISE 15

- **Print Titles**
- **Range Entry Using Collapse Button**

# NOTES

### Print Titles

- As a print option, you may print **column and row titles**, which are the column or row labels for data.  Column and row titles are set on the Sheet tab of the Page Setup dialog box by selecting the columns or rows for titles using the collapse button.  Note the illustration below with a setting for column titles.

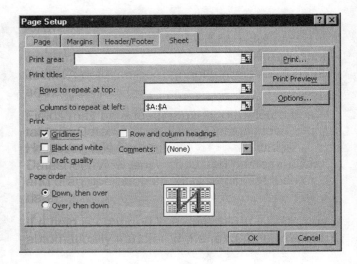

- Column and row titles are used in the following situations.

    - Titles may be useful when printing a range that is too wide or too long to fit on one page.  Titles on the second page would clarify the data. The column or row titles you select, will repeat beginning on the second page when an extra wide or extra long worksheet is set up as the print range.

- You can also print titles when printing a part of a columnar series of data that does not have column or row titles adjacent to the number values. If you set print titles and wish to print part of a worksheet, you should not include the row or column titles in the print range.

- Note Illustration A below.  It shows the first and second pages of a worksheet that was too wide for one page (using 100% sizing).  Since column titles were set for column A, both pages show the labels contained in column A.

### Illustration A

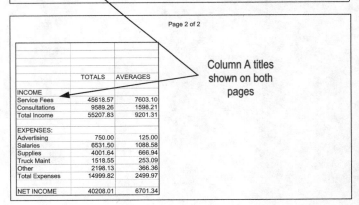

Column A titles shown on both pages

## Range Entry Using Collapse Button

- As in previous versions of Excel, you may need to enter cells or ranges in dialog boxes. In Excel 97, dialog boxes that prompt for cell references contain a collapse button on the right side of the text box. When you click the collapse button, the dialog box collapses to a smaller size, providing access to the worksheet so you can highlight the range.

- Note Illustration B showing the collapse button on the Page Setup dialog box, which is being used to set column and row titles. Illustration C shows how the dialog box collapses when clicked, allowing you to select the columns to be included as repeating titles.

*Illustration B*

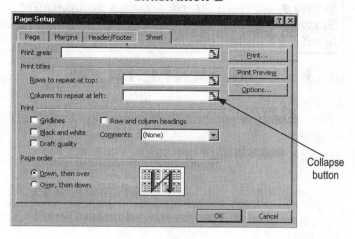

*Illustration C*

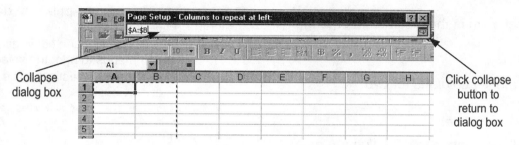

# KEYSTROKES

## SET REPEATING PRINT TITLES FOR WORKSHEET

*Sets titles to print on current and subsequent pages.*

1. Click **File**............................. `Alt`+`F`
2. Click **Page Setup** ........................ `U`
3. Select **Sheet** tab.................. `Ctrl`+`Tab`

   **To set columns as repeating print titles:**

   a. Click **Columns to repeat at left**:............... `Alt`+`C`
   b. Click collapse button ................. 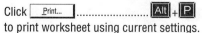 and select columns.

   **OR**

   Type column reference ................... *column reference*

   EXAMPLE: *The cell reference $A:$A indicates column A.*
   ✓ *Columns must be adjacent. To remove print titles, delete the reference.*

**To set rows as repeating print titles:**

a. Click **Rows to repeat at** top `Alt`+`R`
b. Click collapse button.................... and select rows.

**OR**

Type row reference ...........*row reference*

EXAMPLE: *The cell reference $1:$4 indicates rows 1 through 4.*

✓ *Rows must be adjacent. To remove print titles, delete the reference.*

4. Click `OK` ......................... `Enter` to return to the worksheet.
   **OR**
   Click `Print...` ..................... `Alt`+`P` to print worksheet using current settings.

## RANGE ENTRY USING THE COLLAPSE BUTTON

**In a dialog box:**

1. Click collapse button at the right of the text box ............

   *Dialog box shrinks to provide a better view of worksheet.*

2. Select desired cells.
3. Press Enter ................................ `Enter`
   **OR**
   Click collapse button ......................

   *Dialog box returns to full size and worksheet reference is inserted into text box.*

In this exercise, you will create a comparative income statement for Wilson's Better Gardening Service. To print data for only the last three months, you must set repeating print titles for the labels in the first column.

# EXERCISE DIRECTIONS

1. Create the worksheet below and enter the months by dragging the fill handle to create the series, or open 🖫**15INCOME**.

2. Set column widths as follows:
   - Column A:    15
   - Column B:    3
   - Column C-J:  12

3. Find for each month:
   - Total Income
   - Total Expenses
   - NET INCOME

4. Find for each item in the income statement:
   - TOTALS
   - AVERAGE

5. Format all money columns for two decimal places.

6. Center all column titles.

7. Use the collapse button to set column A as a repeating print title on the Page Setup dialog box.

8. Create a header that includes the page number and total pages centered on the page. Set the footer to none.

9. Set the print area for the entire worksheet on the Sheet tab of the Page Setup dialog box and be sure that scaling is set to 100% of normal size. Preview both pages of the worksheet by clicking Next on the Print Preview toolbar.
   - ✓ *Page one will show column A with JANUARY through MAY data. Page two will show column A with JUNE through AVERAGES data. This may vary according to printer.*

10. Print one copy of the two-page report.

11. Change columns C-J back to the standard width.

12. Print one copy of the April-June data with column titles:
    - Highlight the April-June columns. Enter commands to print the selection.
    - Preview the print selection. (The column border was set previously.)
    - ✓ *The April-June data will be shown with the column titles in column A.*
    - Print the selection.

13. Save the workbook file; name it **INCOME**.

14. Close the workbook.

| | A | B | C | D | E | F | G | H | I | J |
|---|---|---|---|---|---|---|---|---|---|---|
| 1 | | | WILSON'S BETTER GARDENING SERVICE | | | | | | | |
| 2 | | | COMPARATIVE INCOME STATEMENT | | | | | | | |
| 3 | | | | | | | | | | |
| 4 | ←—15—→ | →3← | ←—12—→ | ←—12—→ | ←—12—→ | ←—12—→ | ←—12—→ | ←—12—→ | ←—12—→ | ←—12—→ |
| 5 | | | JANUARY | FEBRUARY | MARCH | APRIL | MAY | JUNE | TOTALS | AVERAGES |
| 6 | | | | | | | | | | |
| 7 | INCOME | | | | | | | | | |
| 8 | Service Fees | | 5342.87 | 5543.65 | 6165.87 | 8343.84 | 9862.89 | 10359.45 | | |
| 9 | Consultations | | 1564.98 | 1654.76 | 1689.76 | 1893.65 | 1498.62 | 1287.49 | ↓ | ↓ |
| 10 | Total Income | | | | | | | | | |
| 11 | | | | | | | | | | |
| 12 | EXPENSES | | | | | | | | | |
| 13 | Advertising | | 55.00 | 65.00 | 150.00 | 150.00 | 165.00 | 165.00 | | |
| 14 | Salaries | | 754.65 | 754.65 | 1255.55 | 1255.55 | 1255.55 | 1255.55 | | |
| 15 | Supplies | | 154.76 | 245.65 | 589.53 | 769.54 | 965.62 | 1276.54 | | |
| 16 | Truck Maint | | 95.00 | 125.54 | 243.98 | 185.87 | 543.51 | 324.65 | | |
| 17 | Other | | 143.43 | 43.54 | 231.65 | 326.43 | 654.65 | 798.43 | | |
| 18 | Total Expenses | | | | | | | | ↓ | ↓ |
| 19 | | | | | | | | | | |
| 20 | NET INCOME | | | | | | | | | |
| 21 | | | | | | | | | | |

# Exercise 16

■ **Summary**

*Your teacher, Mr. Harry Cooper, has asked you to help him set up a worksheet to organize his grades. He plans to administer three major examinations this term for his Business Marketing 110 class.*

# EXERCISE DIRECTIONS

1. Create a worksheet file that summarizes student exam grades. *Use a format similar to the illustration below.* Provide each student with a consecutive ID number. Begin with the number 300 for Adamson.

   The students and their exam grades for Test 1, 2 and 3 are:

   ✓ Note: *Some of the students were absent for some of the exams. Leave the cell blank for absent grades. Line spacing was created to make it easier to copy data. Therefore, do not leave blank rows between data.*

   Adamson: 78, 96, 80
   Barnes: 71, 89, 80
   Costello: 67, 79, 80
   Dionesios: 88, absent, 80
   Eckert: 90, 70, 73
   Falstaff: 76, 90, 90
   Garcia: 84, 91, 76
   Hamway: 87, 68, 80
   Ianelli: 98, absent, 70
   Jae Woo: absent, 80, 70
   Kelly: 75, 90, 93

2. Find for each student:
   • NUMBER OF TESTS TAKEN
   • TEST AVERAGE

3. Change column widths to fit the widest entries.

4. Find for each test:
   • NO. OF PAPERS
   • CLASS AVERAGE
   • HIGHEST GRADE
   • LOWEST GRADE

5. Format all averages to one decimal place.

6. Center all column titles.

7. Print one copy that is 75% of the actual worksheet size. (Your teacher wants to insert the printout into a notebook.)

8. Edit the names and adjust column width to include a first initial for each student as follows:
   Adamson, M.
   Barnes, F.
   Costello, A.
   Dionesios, A.
   Eckert, S.
   Falstaff, L.
   Garcia, H.
   Hamway, R.
   Ianelli, J.
   Jae Woo, K.
   Kelly, G.

9. Save the file; name it **MKTG**.

| BUSINESS MARKETING 110 | | | | | MR. HARRY COOPER | |
| EXAM GRADES | | | | | | |
| | | | | | | |
| | | | | | NO. OF TESTS | TEST |
| ID# | STUDENT | TEST1 | TEST2 | TEST3 | TAKEN | AVERAGE |

**Exercise 17**

■ **Insert and Delete Columns and Rows**  ■ **Move (Cut/Paste)**
■ **Drag and Drop**  ■ **Undo a Command**

# NOTES

## Insert and Delete Columns and Rows

- It is recommended that you save a worksheet before you insert, delete, move, or copy data so you can retrieve the original worksheet in the event of an error.

- Columns and/or rows may be inserted or deleted to change the structure of a worksheet.

- When a column or row is **inserted**, a blank area is created. Existing columns or rows shift to allow for the newly created space. To insert a column or row, select the column or row location and click Insert, Columns or Insert, Rows.

- When a column or row is **deleted**, all data in that column or row is eliminated. Existing columns or rows shift to fill in the space left by the deletion.

## Move (Cut/Paste)

- When you **move** data, the data is removed (cut) from one location and reinserted (pasted) into another location. You may choose to overwrite existing data or to insert the data and shift existing data.

## Drag and Drop

- You can move data using a combination of cutting and pasting as discussed above, or by selecting the range and dragging it to the paste location (known as **drag and drop**). To drag and drop data, drag the border of the range selection to its new location.

- If data is dragged and dropped, it is pasted in the new location and cut from the previous location. If data is dragged to a cell where data exists, you will be asked if you wish to overwrite existing data. If you want to insert dragged data between cells or rows without deleting the existing data, you can press Control + Shift and drag the insertion outline onto the row or column insertion point on the gridline. This is essentially a copy, paste procedure.

- Inserting, deleting, moving, or copying data can affect formulas. Be sure formulas are correct after an insert, delete, move, or copy operation.

- The format of the data will be moved or copied along with the data.

## Undo a Command

- As discussed in Exercise 13, any edit activity can be reversed using Edit, Undo. For example, if you drag and drop data and find it did not move correctly, you would use this feature. As shown in the illustration, the Undo feature specifically names the last edit to be undone. The Undo/Repeat buttons on the Standard toolbar have the same functions and either method may be used to undo a series of edits.

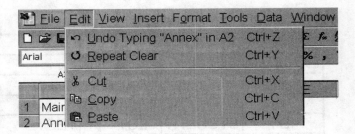

*In this exercise, you will insert, delete, and move columns and rows to include additional information in the Summit United Bank payroll worksheet. In addition, a new payroll worksheet will be created below the existing one for the new pay period.*

# EXERCISE DIRECTIONS

1. Open ⌨ **PAY**, or open 💾 **17PAY**.

2. Make the following changes on the top payroll as shown in the illustration on the following page:

   - Insert a new column A. (Select column A and click Insert, Column.)

   - Move all the data in the EMPLOYEE NAME column to column A. (Try using drag and drop. Use Edit Undo if the move is not correct.) Adjust column width.

   - Set column width for column C to 11 and enter and center the label Social Sec. No. as the column title.

   - Enter social security numbers as follows:

     | | |
     |---|---|
     | Diaz | 069-65-4532 |
     | Jaffe | 123-75-7623 |
     | Latov | 107-53-6754 |
     | Nestor | 103-87-5698 |
     | Pringle | 127-78-0045 |
     | Wong | 043-67-7600 |

   - Copy the Social Security Number column title and data from the April 7 to the April 14 payroll.

   - Copy the entire April 14 payroll, including the title, to a new location below the existing worksheet.

3. Make the following changes on the bottom payroll:

   - Edit the title to read:
     FOR THE WEEK ENDING APRIL 21, 199-

   - Delete the row containing data for JAFFE.

   - Insert a row where necessary to maintain alphabetical order for a new employee named Suraci.

   - Enter the following information for Suraci.

     | | |
     |---|---|
     | Card Number: | 14967 |
     | S.S. No: | 146-93-0069 |
     | Hourly Rate: | 6.25 |

   - Edit the HOURS WORKED as follows:

     | | |
     |---|---|
     | Diaz | 22 |
     | Latov | 33 |
     | Nestor | 21 |
     | Pringle | 16 |
     | Suraci | 18 |
     | Wong | 28 |

   - Copy payroll formulas to complete SURACI's data.

4. Format data if necessary.

5. Print one copy of all three payrolls to fit on a page.

6. Close and save the workbook file, or save as **PAY**.

| | A | B | C | D | E | F | G | H | I |
|---|---|---|---|---|---|---|---|---|---|
| 1 | SUMMIT UNITED BANK PAYROLL | | | | Insert new | | | | |
| 2 | FOR THE WEEK ENDING APRIL 7, 199- | | | | column A | | | | |
| 3 | | Move | | | | | | | |
| 4 | Card | Employee | Hourly | Hours | Gross | Social | Medicare | | |
| 5 | Number | Name | Rate | Worked | Pay | Sec. Tax | Tax | F.W.T. | Net Pay |
| 6 | | | | | | | | | |
| 7 | 13567 | Diaz | 5.55 | 15 | 83.25 | 5.16 | 1.21 | 16.65 | 60.23 |
| 8 | 13750 | Jaffe | 7.23 | 32 | 231.36 | 14.34 | 3.35 | 46.27 | 167.39 |
| 9 | 13816 | Latov | 6.18 | 16 | 98.88 | 6.13 | 1.43 | 19.78 | 71.54 |
| 10 | 13925 | Nestor | 4.66 | 28 | 130.48 | 8.09 | 1.89 | 26.10 | 94.40 |
| 11 | 14345 | Pringle | 6.57 | 12 | 78.84 | 4.89 | 1.14 | 15.77 | 57.04 |
| 12 | 14715 | Wong | 8.65 | 21 | 181.65 | 11.26 | 2.63 | 36.33 | 131.42 |
| 13 | | | | | | | | | |
| 14 | TOTALS | | | | 804.46 | 49.88 | 11.66 | 160.89 | 582.03 |
| 15 | AVERAGES | | | | 134.08 | 8.31 | 1.94 | 26.82 | 97.00 |
| 16 | | | | | | | | | |
| 17 | | | | | | | | | |
| 18 | FOR THE WEEK ENDING APRIL 14, 199- | | | | | | | | |
| 19 | | | | | | | | | |
| 20 | Card | Employee | Hourly | Hours | Gross | Social | Medicare | | |
| 21 | Number | Name | Rate | Worked | Pay | Sec. Tax | Tax | F.W.T. | Net Pay |
| 22 | | | | | | | | | |
| 23 | 13567 | Diaz | 5.55 | 20 | 111.00 | 6.88 | 1.61 | 22.20 | 80.31 |
| 24 | 13750 | Jaffe | 7.23 | 31 | 224.13 | 13.90 | 3.25 | 44.83 | 162.16 |
| 25 | 13816 | Latov | 6.18 | 23 | 142.14 | 8.81 | 2.06 | 28.43 | 102.84 |
| 26 | 13925 | Nestor | 4.66 | 22 | 102.52 | 6.36 | 1.49 | 20.50 | 74.17 |
| 27 | 14345 | Pringle | 6.57 | 15 | 98.55 | 6.11 | 1.43 | 19.71 | 71.30 |
| 28 | 14715 | Wong | 8.65 | 25 | 216.25 | 13.41 | 3.14 | 43.25 | 156.46 |
| 29 | | | | | | | | | |
| 30 | TOTALS | | | | 894.59 | 55.46 | 12.97 | 178.92 | 647.24 |
| 31 | AVERAGES | | | | 149.10 | 9.24 | 2.16 | 29.82 | 107.87 |
| 32 | | | | | | | | | |
| 33 | | Copy | | | | | | | |
| 34 | | | | | | | | | |

# KEYSTROKES

## INSERT COLUMNS/ROWS

*Inserts blank columns or rows and shifts existing columns or rows to make room for the insertion.*

1. Select as many adjacent columns or rows as you want to add to worksheet.

   ✓ *Be sure to select the entire column or row. New columns will be placed to the left of the highlighted columns. New rows will be placed above the highlighted rows.*

2. Click **Insert**.......................... `Alt` + `I`

3. Click **Columns**.............................. `C`

   **OR**

   Click **Rows** ................................ `R`

## INSERT COLUMNS/ROWS USING THE MOUSE

*Inserts blank columns or rows and shifts existing columns or rows to make room for the insertion.*

1. Select as many columns/rows as you want inserted.

2. Right-click any part of selection.

   *A pop-up menu appears.*

3. Click **Insert**................................. `I`

4. Select option from Insert dialog box.

5. Click **OK** ............................... `Enter`

## DELETE COLUMNS/ROWS

*Deletes columns or rows and the data they contain. Existing columns or rows shift to fill in the space left by the deletion.*

1. Select column(s) or row(s) to delete.

   ✓ *Be sure to select the entire column or row. When deleting more than one row or column, select adjacent columns or rows.*

2. Click **Edit**............................... `Alt` + `E`

3. Click **Delete** ............................... `D`

---

 **MOVE (CUT/PASTE) USING THE MENU**

*Moves data in a cell or a range of cells to another area.*

1. Select cell or range to move.

2. Click **Edit** .............................. `Alt` + `E`

3. Click **Cut** ................................... `T`

4. Select cell or range to receive data.

   ✓ *You only have to specify the top left cell. The destination range can be in another workbook or worksheet.*

**To move and <u>overwrite</u> existing data in destination cells:**

- Press **Enter** ......................... `Enter`

**To move and <u>insert</u> between existing cells:**

a. Click **Insert**...................... `Alt` + `I`

b. Click **Cells** .............................. `E`

c. If prompted, select **Insert Paste** option:

   - **Shift cells <u>right</u>**.................. `R`
   - **Shift cells <u>down</u>**................. `D`

 **MOVE (DRAG AND DROP)**

*Moves data in a cell or range of cells to another area.*

1. Select cell or range to cut.

2. Move mouse pointer to edge of range.

   *Pointer becomes a* ⬚.

**To move and <u>overwrite</u> existing data in destination cells:**

a. Drag border outline to new location.

b. Click ` OK ` .................... `Enter`

**To move and <u>insert</u> between existing cells:**

a. Press **Shift** and drag........ `Shift` +*drag* insertion outline onto row or column gridline.

---

   ✓ *If you drag the insertion outline onto a column gridline, cells are shifted right; if you drag onto a row gridline, cells are shifted down.*

b. Release mouse button, then the key.

 **COPY (DRAG AND DROP)**

*Copies data in a cell or range of cells to another area.*

1. Select cell or range to copy.

2. Move mouse pointer to edge of range.

   *Pointer becomes a* ⬚.

**To copy and <u>overwrite</u> existing data in destination cells:**

a. Press **Ctrl** and drag ......... `Ctrl` +*drag* border outline to new location.

b. Release the key, then mouse button.

c. Click ` OK ` .................... `Enter`

**To copy and <u>insert</u> between existing cells:**

a. Press **Ctrl + Shift** and drag insertion outline.................. `Ctrl` + `Shift` +*drag* onto row or column gridline.

   ✓ *If you drag the insertion outline onto a column gridline, cells are shifted right; if you drag onto a row gridline, cells are shifted down.*

b. Release mouse button, then the key.

## UNDO A COMMAND

   ✓ *To successfully undo a command, select Undo before another command is selected. Not all commands can be undone.*

Click **Undo** button........................... ↺ on Standard toolbar.

**OR**

Press **Ctrl+Z** ......................... `Ctrl` + `Z`

**OR**

a. Click **Edit** ....................... `Alt` + `E`

b. Click **Undo**............................... `U`

## Exercise 18

■ **Copy and Paste Special** ■ **Transpose Data** ■ **AutoCorrect**

# NOTES

### Copy and Paste Special

■ Paste Special is a feature that gives you added control over the pasting process when data is copied. As shown in the illustration of the Paste Special Dialog box below, you can:
  • Specify which characteristics of the selection should be copied (Paste Options).
  • Specify how data should be combined when the paste area contains data (Operation Options).
  • Skip blanks.
  • Transpose data.
  • Create a Pasted Link.

*Paste Special Dialog Box*

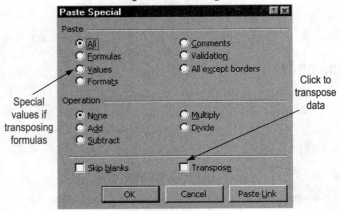

### Transpose Data

■ You can transpose data to copy and rearrange data. For example, data in rows can be copied to columns and vice versa.
  ✓ *Note the example above right. The labels in column B, when transposed, are copied to row 5.*

|   | A | B | C | D | E | F | G |
|---|---|---|---|---|---|---|---|
| 1 |   |   |   |   |   |   |   |
| 2 |   |   |   |   |   |   |   |
| 3 |   | JAN |   |   |   |   |   |
| 4 |   | FEB |   |   |   |   |   |
| 5 |   | MAR |   | JAN | FEB | MAR |   |

■ To transpose formulas, select the Paste Values option and the Transpose box in the Paste Special dialog box. This selection ensures that only the values are transposed to the new location, not the formulas. The formulas cannot be transposed with a simple paste command, since the cell references are not valid for the new location.

### AutoCorrect

■ The AutoCorrect feature automatically changes text as you type if the incorrectly spelled word is in the dictionary or if you, in advance, add words that you often type incorrectly. This feature also automatically corrects capitalization of days of the week, accidental use of the Caps Lock key, capitalization of the first letter of a sentence and the case of incorrectly capitalized letters in the first two positions in a word. Note the illustration of the AutoCorrect dialog box (right).

*AutoCorrect Dialog Box*

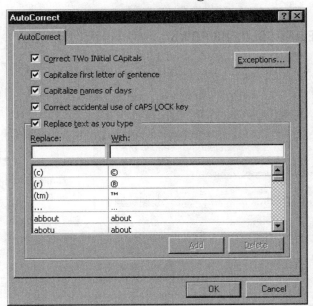

In this exercise, you will insert a new expense item in the Wilson's Better Gardening Service worksheet and practice using the AutoCorrect feature. In addition, you will use transposed data from the income statement to prepare an income statement analysis.

# EXERCISE DIRECTIONS

1. Open ⬚INCOME, or open ⬚18INCOME.

2. Delete column B.

3. Set column widths for columns B through H to 10.

**To include a monthly interest expense of $25:**

- Insert a row between Truck Maintenance and Other.
- Enter the label: Interest.
- Enter $25 for each month.
- Copy the TOTALS and AVERAGES formulas to the interest line.
- Format the interest line for two decimal places.

4. Enter new title and column labels below the existing worksheet, as illustrated.

5. Center column labels.

6. Practice using the AutoCorrect feature by doing the following:
- In cell A24 type saturday. Note the correction to Saturday.
- In cell A25 type FRiday. Note the correction to Friday.
- In cell A26 type INcome. Note the correction to Income.
- Delete data in A24, A25, and A26.

7. Practice entering a word into the AutoCorrect replace list as follows:
   ✓ *If you always type advertising as advertsing, you could place that correction in the automatic replace box.*
- Select the AutoCorrect feature from the Tools menu.
- In the Replace box enter the misspelled version of the word (advertsing).
- In the With box enter the correct version of the word (advertising).
- Click OK.
- In A13 type Advertsing using the incorrect version.
- Note the correction to Advertising.

8. Transpose the column titles JANUARY through JUNE, including TOTALS and excluding AVERAGES, to become row titles in column A in the range A31:A37.

9. Transpose Total Income data for JANUARY through JUNE, including TOTALS and excluding AVERAGES, to become row data for column B in the range B31:B37.
   ✓ *Be sure to select the Paste Values option when transposing formulas.*

10. Transpose Total Expenses data for JANUARY through JUNE, including TOTALS, and excluding AVERAGES, to become row data for column D in the range D31:D37
    ✓ *Be sure to select the Paste Values option when transposing formulas.*

11. Transpose NET INCOME data for JANUARY through JUNE, including TOTALS, and excluding AVERAGES, to become row data for column F in the range F31:F37.
    ✓ *Be sure to select the Paste Values option when transposing formulas.*

12. Enter formulas in the % OF TOTAL columns to find what percent each item is of the six-month total.
    *Hint: Use absolute reference in the formula.*

13. Use AutoSum to total the % of TOTAL columns, which should equal 100%.

14. Format % OF TOTAL columns for percentage with one decimal place.

15. Print one copy of the entire worksheet to fit on a page.

16. Close and save the workbook file, or save as **INCOME**.

| | B | C | D | E | F | G | H | I | J | K |
|---|---|---|---|---|---|---|---|---|---|---|
| 1 | | WILSON'S BETTER GARDENING SERVICE | | | | | | | | |
| 2 | | COMPARATIVE INCOME STATEMENT | | | | | | | | |
| 3 | | | | | | | | | | |
| 4 | | | | | | | | | | |
| 5 | | JANUARY | FEBRUARY | MARCH | APRIL | MAY | JUNE | TOTALS | AVERAGES | |
| 6 | | | | | | | | | | |
| 7 | INCOME | | | | | | | | | |
| 8 | Service Fees | 5342.87 | 5543.65 | 6165.87 | 8343.84 | 9862.89 | 10359.45 | 45618.57 | 7603.10 | |
| 9 | Consultations | 1564.98 | 1654.76 | 1689.76 | 1893.65 | 1498.62 | 1287.49 | 9589.26 | 1598.21 | |
| 10 | Total Income | 6907.85 | 7198.41 | 7855.63 | 10237.49 | 11361.51 | 11646.94 | 55207.83 | 9201.31 | |
| 11 | | | | | | | | | | |
| 12 | EXPENSES: | | | | | | | | | |
| 13 | Advertising | 55.00 | 65.00 | 150.00 | 150.00 | 165.00 | 165.00 | 750.00 | 125.00 | |
| 14 | Salaries | 754.65 | 754.65 | 1255.55 | 1255.55 | 1255.55 | 1255.55 | 6531.50 | 1088.58 | |
| 15 | Supplies | 154.76 | 245.65 | 589.53 | 769.54 | 965.62 | 1276.54 | 4001.64 | 666.94 | |
| 16 | Truck Maint | 95.00 | 125.54 | 243.98 | 185.87 | 543.51 | 324.65 | 1518.55 | 253.09 | |
| 17 | Interest | 25.00 | 25.00 | 25.00 | 25.00 | 25.00 | 25.00 | 150.00 | 25.00 | |
| 18 | Other | 143.43 | 43.54 | 231.65 | 326.43 | 654.65 | 798.43 | 2198.13 | 366.36 | |
| 19 | Total Expenses | 1227.84 | 1259.38 | 2495.71 | 2712.39 | 3609.33 | 3845.17 | 15149.82 | 2524.97 | |
| 20 | | | | | | | | | | |
| 21 | NET INCOME | 5680.01 | 5939.03 | 5359.92 | 7525.10 | 7752.18 | 7801.77 | 40058.01 | 6676.34 | |
| 22 | | | | | | | | | | |
| 23 | | WILSON'S BETTER GARDENING SERVICE | | | | | | | | |
| 24 | | INCOME STATEMENT ANALYSIS | | | | | | | | |
| 25 | | | | | | | | | | |
| 26 | | | | | | | | | | |
| 27 | MONTH | | TOTAL | % OF | TOTAL | % OF | NET | % OF | | |
| 28 | | | INCOME | TOTAL | EXPENSES | TOTAL | INCOME | TOTAL | | |
| 29 | | | | | | | | | | |
| 30 | | | | | | | | | | |
| 31 | | | | | | | | | | |
| 32 | | | | | | | | | | |
| 33 | | | | | | | | | | |
| 34 | | | | | | | | | | |
| 35 | | | | | | | | | | |
| 36 | | | | | | | | | | |
| 37 | | | | | | | | | | |

Delete column B

Transpose

Insert data row for Interest

# KEYSTROKES

## SET AN AUTOCORRECT REPLACEMENT

1. Click **Tools** ........................... `Alt`+`T`
2. Click **AutoCorrect** ..................... `A`
3. Click **Replace** ........................ `Alt`+`R`
4. Type abbreviation or commonly misspelled word.
5. Click **With** .............................. `W`
6. Type replacement text.
7. Click **Add** ............................... `A`
8. Click `OK` ....................... `Enter`

## TRANSPOSE DATA

*Copies and transposes data from horizontal to vertical arrangement and vice versa.*

1. Select range to transpose.
2. a. Click **Edit** ......................... `Alt`+`E`
   b. Click **Copy** ............................ `C`
   **OR**
   a. Right-click a cell in selection to open shortcut menu.
   b. Click **Copy** ............................ `C`
3. Click upper-left cell ...................... `↕↔` to receive transposed data.
4. a. Click **Edit** ......................... `Alt`+`E`
   b. Click **Paste Special** ................... `S`

**OR**

c. Right-click destination cell to open shortcut menu.
d. Click **Paste Special** .................. `S`
5. Click **Transpose** ......................... `E` check box.

**To paste transposed data as values, not formulas:**

- Click **Values** ........................... `V`
6. Click `OK` ....................... `Enter`
7. Press **Escape** ........................... `Esc` to end copying.

## Exercise 19

- **Freeze Titles** ■ **Split Panes** ■ **Scroll Tips**
- **Create New Workbook** ■ **Select Workbook**
- **Copy and Paste Special (Extract Data)**

## NOTES

- Excel provides two methods for working with large worksheets: freezing titles to keep titles in view and splitting the window into two panes or four panes.

### Freeze Titles

- To keep headings or titles in view at the left or top edge of the worksheet when scrolling, you must hold, or **freeze**, them in place. Select the row below or the column to the right of the data to be frozen and then select <u>W</u>indow, <u>F</u>reeze Panes. To remove the freeze, click <u>W</u>indow, Un<u>f</u>reeze Panes.

### Split Panes

- To view different parts of a large worksheet at one time, you may **split** the worksheet horizontally or vertically so data may be viewed through all of the windows at the same time. To split the worksheet into panes, click <u>W</u>indow, <u>S</u>plit; use <u>W</u>indow, Remove <u>S</u>plit to remove the split.

  - When you split a window *vertically* (by placing the cursor at a location in Row 1), the panes scroll together when you scroll up or down, but they scroll independently when you scroll left or right.

  - When you split a window *horizontally* (by placing the cursor at a location in column A), the panes scroll together when you scroll left or right, but they scroll independently when you scroll up or down.

  - If you place the cursor in the middle of the worksheet, the worksheet will split into four panes that will scroll like a horizontal split.

- When you freeze a split worksheet, the top and/or left pane locks when you scroll through the worksheet.

### Scroll Tips

- You can move through a large worksheet by moving the scroll box on the horizontal or vertical scroll bar. When you move the scroll box, Excel displays the row or column numbers near the scroll box as you move through the worksheet. Note the illustration below:

| L | L | M | N | O | |
|---|---|---|---|---|---|
| | | | | | |
| | | | | | |
| | | | | Row: 3 | |

### Create New Workbook

- New workbooks can be created to store new or extracted data by using the <u>F</u>ile, <u>N</u>ew commands.

### Select Workbook

- When working with more than one open workbook at a time, you can use the Window menu to select the name of the workbook you want to make active.

### Copy and Paste Special

- You can use the <u>C</u>opy and Paste <u>S</u>pecial commands to copy part of a worksheet into another workbook.

- Paste options allow you to select what part of the cell contents should be pasted. The options are:

  **All** Replaces paste area cells with all formulas, formats, and notes contained in copied cells.

  **Formulas** Pastes data that exists in formula bar of copied cells (the formulas).

✓Note:  *Relative cell references in formulas will adjust.*

**Values**   Pastes data as it appears in copied cells (results of formulas).

**Formats**   Pastes only the formats of cells.

**Comments**   Pastes only comments cells may contain

**Validation**   Pastes the validation rules from the copied cells.

**All except borders**   Pastes all cell contents and formats except for borders.

■  In the Paste Special dialog box, the Formulas and Values paste options affect the paste result. Select Formulas to extract values, labels and formulas *exactly as they exist.*  Select Values to extract values, labels *and the results of the formulas.* You should select Values if the range to be extracted contains formulas that refer to cells outside the copy area.

---

*In this exercise, you will divide the data into quarterly information.  To do this, you must insert and delete columns.  However, because inserting or deleting columns from the top portion of the worksheet will affect the bottom portion, you will extract the bottom portion of the worksheet, save it to another file, and delete it from the original.  The top portion of the worksheet will then be expanded and edited.*

---

# EXERCISE DIRECTIONS

1. Open ⌨INCOME, or open 🖫19INCOME.

2. Open a new blank workbook and use the Window menu to switch back to the INCOME workbook.

3. To use the Copy and Paste Special commands to extract the Income Statement Analysis portion of the worksheet to a new workbook:
   • Select the Income Statement Analysis section of the worksheet.
   • Click Edit, Copy.
   • Switch to new workbook.
   • Click Edit, Paste Special, Values.
   • Save the new workbook file as **ISANA**.
   ✓ *Select the Values option in the Paste Special dialog box to ensure that the results of the formulas are copied, not the formulas themselves*

4. Switch back to the INCOME workbook and delete the Income Statement Analysis portion from the INCOME worksheet.

5. Insert a column between MARCH and APRIL and enter the centered column title:
   1ST QTR.
   TOTALS

6. Insert a column between JUNE and TOTALS and enter the centered column title:
   2ND QTR.
   TOTALS

7. Edit column title TOTALS to read:
   COMBINED
   TOTALS

8. Delete the AVERAGES column.

9. Find 1ST QTR. TOTALS, and format for two decimal places.

10. Copy the formula to the remaining items.

11. Copy the formulas for 1ST QTR. TOTALS to the column for 2ND QTR. TOTALS.

12. Edit the formula in the COMBINED TOTALS column to add 1ST QTR. TOTALS and 2ND QTR. TOTALS.

13. Freeze titles in column A.

14. Practice using the scroll bar and scroll tips by moving the horizontal scroll box to bring the worksheet into position to enter data in column K.

15. Enter third quarter data and column headings indicated on the next page beginning in the next available column of your worksheet.

|   | A | K | L | M |
|---|---|---|---|---|
| 1 | | | | |
| 2 | | | | |
| 3 | | | | |
| 4 | | | | |
| 5 | | JULY | AUGUST | SEPTEMBER |
| 6 | | | | |
| 7 | INCOME | | | |
| 8 | Service Fees | 11986.45 | 11050.65 | 10573.87 |
| 9 | Consultations | 1343.27 | 1186.87 | 965.78 |
| 10 | Total Income | | | |
| 11 | | | | |
| 12 | EXPENSES: | | | |
| 13 | Advertising | 165.00 | 165.00 | 150.00 |
| 14 | Salaries | 1255.55 | 1255.55 | 1255.00 |
| 15 | Supplies | 1887.98 | 1667.09 | 1654.98 |
| 16 | Truck Maint | 486.98 | 245.90 | 327.65 |
| 17 | Interest | 25.00 | 25.00 | 25.00 |
| 18 | Other | 674.79 | 543.87 | 476.98 |
| 19 | Total Expenses | | | |
| 20 | | | | |
| 21 | NET INCOME | | | |

16. Copy and edit formulas, where necessary, to complete the worksheet.

17. Find 3RD QTR. TOTALS.

18. Copy the formula to the remaining items.

19. Center column title labels.

20. Format numeric data for two decimal places.

21. Save the file, or save as **INCOME**.

22. Print one copy of INCOME to fit on a page.

23. Switch to the **ISANA** workbook.

24. Center column titles, format percent data for percentages with one decimal place and adjust column width as needed.

25. Resave **ISANA**, then print one copy.

26. Close both workbook files.

|   | A | B | C | D | E | F | G | H | I |
|---|---|---|---|---|---|---|---|---|---|
| 1 | | WILSON'S BETTER GARDENING SERVICE | | | *Insert column 1st QTR. TOTALS* | | *Insert column 2nd QTR. TOTALS* | | *Delete column* |
| 2 | | COMPARATIVE INCOME STATEMENT | | | | | | | |
| 3 | | | | | | | | | |
| 4 | | | | | | | | | |
| 5 | | JANUARY | FEBRUARY | MARCH | APRIL | MAY | JUNE | TOTALS | AVERAGES |
| 6 | | | | | | | | | |
| 7 | INCOME | | | | | | | | |
| 8 | Service Fees | 5342.87 | 5543.65 | 6165.87 | 8343.84 | 9862.89 | 10359.45 | 45618.57 | 7603.10 |
| 9 | Consultations | 1564.98 | 1654.76 | 1689.76 | 1893.65 | 1498.62 | 1287.49 | 9589.26 | 1598.21 |
| 10 | Total Income | 6907.85 | 7198.41 | 7855.63 | 10237.49 | 11361.51 | 11646.94 | 55207.83 | 9201.31 |
| 11 | | | | | | | | *delete column* | |
| 12 | EXPENSES: | | | | | | | | |
| 13 | Advertising | 55.00 | 65.00 | 150.00 | 150.00 | 165.00 | 165.00 | 750.00 | 125.00 |
| 14 | Salaries | 754.65 | 754.65 | 1255.55 | 1255.55 | 1255.55 | 1255.55 | 6531.50 | 1088.58 |
| 15 | Supplies | 154.76 | 245.65 | 589.53 | 769.54 | 965.62 | 1276.54 | 4001.64 | 666.94 |
| 16 | Truck Maint | 95.00 | 125.54 | 243.98 | 185.87 | 543.51 | 324.65 | 1518.55 | 253.09 |
| 17 | Interest | 25.00 | 25.00 | 25.00 | 25.00 | 25.00 | 25.00 | 150.00 | 25.00 |
| 18 | Other | 143.43 | 43.54 | 231.65 | 326.43 | 654.65 | 798.43 | 2198.13 | 366.36 |
| 19 | Total Expenses | 1227.84 | 1259.38 | 2495.71 | 2712.39 | 3609.33 | 3845.17 | 15149.82 | 2524.97 |
| 20 | | | | | | | | | |
| 21 | NET INCOME | 5680.01 | 5939.03 | 5359.92 | 7525.10 | 7752.18 | 7801.77 | 40058.01 | 6676.34 |
| 22 | | | | | | | | | |
| 23 | | | | | | | | | |
| 24 | | WILSON'S BETTER GARDENING SERVICE | | | | | | | |
| 25 | | INCOME STATEMENT ANALYSIS | | | | | | | |
| 26 | | | | | | | | | |
| 27 | MONTH | TOTAL | % OF | TOTAL | % OF | NET | % OF | *Extract to new workbook and save new workbook as ISANA* | |
| 28 | | INCOME | TOTAL | EXPENSES | TOTAL | INCOME | TOTAL | | |
| 29 | | | | | | | | | |
| 30 | JANUARY | 6907.85 | 12.5% | 1227.84 | 8.1% | 5680.01 | 14.2% | | |
| 31 | FEBRUARY | 7198.41 | 13.0% | 1259.38 | 8.3% | 5939.03 | 14.8% | | |
| 32 | MARCH | 7855.63 | 14.2% | 2495.71 | 16.5% | 5359.92 | 13.4% | | |
| 33 | APRIL | 10237.49 | 18.5% | 2712.39 | 17.9% | 7525.1 | 18.8% | | |
| 34 | MAY | 11361.51 | 20.6% | 3609.33 | 23.8% | 7752.18 | 19.4% | | |
| 35 | JUNE | 11646.94 | 21.1% | 3845.17 | 25.4% | 7801.77 | 19.5% | | |
| 36 | TOTALS | 55207.83 | 100.0% | 15149.82 | 100.0% | 40058.01 | 100.0% | | |
| 37 | | | | | | | | | |

# KEYSTROKES

## COPY AND PASTE SPECIAL (EXTRACT DATA)

*Copies a portion of the current worksheet to a new workbook.*

1. Copy range to extract to the clipboard:

   a. Select range of worksheet to extract.

   b. Click **Edit**............................ `Alt`+`E`

   c. Click **Copy** ................................. `C`

2. Open a new workbook:

   a. Click **File**............................ `Alt`+`F`

   b. Click **New** ................................. `N`

   **OR**

   Click **New Workbook** button ............ 🗋

   – FROM NEW WORKBOOK –

3. Use Paste Special command:

   a. Click **Edit** ........................ `Alt`+`E`

   b. Click **Paste Special** ................... `S`

c. Click **Values**..............................[V]
to copy data as it appears in cells
(results of formulas).

**OR**

Click **Formulas**..........................[F]
to copy data as it exists in formula
bar (formulas).

✓ *Only relative cell references in*
*formulas will adjust.*

d. Click [ OK ] ........................[Enter]

4. Save and name the new workbook.

a. Click **File**...........................[Alt]+[F]

b. Click **Save As**........................[A]

c. Type new filename .............. *filename*

✓ *The filename you type replaces default*
*name of the workbook.*

d. Click [ OK ] ........................[Enter]

## CREATE NEW WORKBOOK

Opens a new workbook based on the default
template.

• Click **New Workbook** button ............[□]
on Standard toolbar.

**OR**

1. Click **File**...........................[Alt]+[F]

2. Click **New** ..............................[N]

## SELECT WORKBOOK

✓ *When more than one workbook is open,*
*the workbook you want may be hidden*
*or reduced to an icon. In order to use*
*the workbook, you must select the*
*workbook window or open the workbook*
*icon.*

**To select a workbook window:**

• Click anywhere on workbook window.

**OR**

1. Click **Window** ........................[Alt]+[W]

2. Select name of workbook......[↑↓], [↵]
near bottom of the menu.

**To open a workbook icon:**

• Double-click workbook icon.

**OR**

1. Click **Window** ........................[Alt]+[W]

2. Select name of workbook......[↑↓], [↵]
near bottom of the menu.

## SPLIT WORKSHEET INTO PANES USING SPLIT BOXES

Provides simultaneous scrolling of up to four
panes. You can freeze panes (see right) to
prevent top, left, or both panes
from scrolling.

✓ *If the scroll bars are not displayed in*
*panes, see SET VIEW PREFERENCES,*
*page 184.*

1. Point to horizontal split box ⊏⊐ or
vertical split box [] on scroll bar.
Pointer becomes a ↕ or ↔.

2. Drag ↕ or ↔ along scroll bar until
split bar is in desired position.

## SPLIT WORKSHEET INTO PANES USING THE MENU

*Provides simultaneous scrolling of up to four*
*panes. You can freeze panes (see right) to*
*prevent top, left ,or both panes*
*from scrolling.*

1. Select row below which horizontal split
will occur.

**OR**

Select column to right of which vertical
split will occur.

**OR**

Select cell below and to the right of
which horizontal and vertical split will
occur.

2. Click **Window**........................[Alt]+[W]

3. Click **Split** ......................................[S]

## REMOVE SPLIT BARS

• Double-click any part of split bar.

**OR**

1. Click **Window**........................[Alt]+[W]

2. Click **Remove Split** ..........................[S]

## ADJUST WORKSHEET PANES

1. Point to horizontal split box ⊏⊐ or
vertical split box [] on scroll bar.
Pointer becomes a ↕ or ↔.

2. Drag ↕ or ↔ along scroll bar until
split bar is in desired position.

## MOVE BETWEEN WORKSHEET PANES

• Click desired pane.

**OR**

Press **F6** ...........................................[F6]
until active cell is in desired pane.

## FREEZE PANES ON SPLIT WORKSHEET

Locks top and/or left pane when scrolling.

1. Click **Window** .......................[Alt]+[W]

2. Click **Freeze Panes**........................[F]

## UNFREEZE PANES

1. Click **Window** .......................[Alt]+[W]

2. Click **Unfreeze Panes**......................[F]

## FREEZE TITLES

*Locks display of title row and/or title column*
*on the screen. This procedure is for a*
*worksheet that has not been split into panes.*

1. Select row below horizontal titles to
freeze.

**OR**

Select column to right of vertical titles to
freeze.

**OR**

Select cell below and to the right of
horizontal and vertical titles to freeze.

2. Click **Window** .......................[Alt]+[W]

3. Click **Freeze Panes**........................[F]

## UNFREEZE TITLES

1. Click **Window** .......................[Alt]+[W]

2. Click **Unfreeze Panes**......................[F]

## SCROLL TIPS

1. Click on horizontal or vertical scroll bar.

2. Move bar as desired.

3. Note row or column Scrolltip.

## SET WINDOW OPTIONS

1. Click **Tools** .........................[Alt]+[T]

2. Click **Options**..................................[O]

3. From the View tab, select desired option.

4. Click [ OK ] ........................[Enter]

# Exercise 20

## ■ Workbook Sheets ■ Group Sheets ■ Print Workbook
## ■ Print Worksheet on Specified Number of Pages

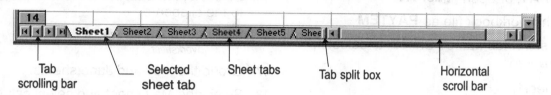

Tab scrolling bar     Selected sheet tab     Sheet tabs     Tab split box     Horizontal scroll bar

# NOTES

## Workbook Sheets

■ By default, each new workbook contains three worksheets labeled Sheet1 through Sheet3. **Sheet tabs** show the names of the sheets *(see illustration above)*.

■ Excel provides a tab split box between the sheet tabs and the horizontal scroll bar. You can drag this split box left or right to show more or fewer sheet tabs.

■ You can use the **tab scrolling buttons** to scroll hidden sheet tabs into view. If no sheet tabs are visible, you can tell Excel to show them by selecting Sheet tabs from the Tools, Options dialog box. If you right-click the scroll buttons, you will be able to select the sheet you wish to access. Note the illustration below:

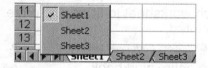

• Excel lets you work with sheets in many ways. To delete, insert, rename, move, copy, or select all sheets, right-click on the worksheet tab and select the desired action from the shortcut menu. Note the illustration of the menu that appears when a sheet tab is right-clicked:

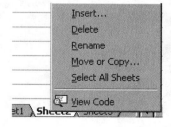

• You can also move sheets by using the drag and drop method.

• When you need to insert a new sheet tab, you may use the Insert command on the right-click menu or select Insert, Worksheet from the menu bar.

## Group Sheets

■ You can select multiple sheets (grouping) to work on several sheets simultaneously. To group consecutive sheets, select the first and last sheet in the group, pressing Shift between selections. Press Ctrl between sheet selections to select non-consecutive sheets.

■ When sheets are grouped, any entries and formats made in the top sheet are simultaneously made in all grouped sheets. In a group selection **selected sheet tabs** are white and the **active sheet tab** name is in bold.

## Print Workbook

■ You can tell Excel on how many pages you want a worksheet to print. Then Excel will automatically scale the worksheet to fit on the specified number of pages.

*In this exercise, you will create a payroll template for future use. To do this you will insert and rename sheet tabs and work with grouped sheets to quickly edit data on more than one worksheet at a time.*

# EXERCISE DIRECTIONS

1. Open 🖳**PAY**, or open 🖳**20PAY**.

2. Resave the workbook file as **PAYTEM**.

3. Click the sheet tab named Sheet2 to select it.
   - ✓ *Sheet2 is empty.*

4. Select Sheet1.

5. Select Sheet3.

6. Use tab split box to increase, then decrease, the amount of space for sheet tabs.

7. Select Sheet2 through Sheet3.
   - ✓ *Selected sheet tabs are white and [Group] appears on the title bar.*

8. Delete the grouped worksheets using the right-click menu.
   - ✓ *Only Sheet1 remains.*

9. Rename Sheet1 to April.

10. Insert a new worksheet; name it May.

11. Move the May sheet to the right of April.

12. Insert a new worksheet; name it June.

13. Use drag and drop to move the June sheet to the right of May.

14. Select the April sheet and edit the titles in each week's payroll to read:
    FOR THE WEEK ENDING
    - ✓ *Delete the dates.*

15. To make payrolls uniform on the April sheet:
    - Jaffe has left our employment; delete the Jaffe rows in the top two payrolls.
    - Copy the Suraci information from the last payroll to the first two payrolls in the correct order.

16. Select all the data in the April sheet and copy it to the clipboard.
    - *HINT:  You can click the Select All button to select the entire worksheet.*

17. Group the May and June sheets.

18. Select the May sheet and select cell A1.

19. Use the Paste command to copy the April worksheet data to A1 in the grouped sheets (May and June).

20. Click cell A1 to deselect the range.

21. Select the April sheet.

22. Click cell A1 to deselect the range.

23. Group all the sheets in the workbook (April through June).

    —WHILE ALL SHEETS ARE GROUPED—
    Clear the data in the cells containing the hours worked for each employee in each payroll week.  (Do not delete the column.)
    *Note that this action clears all calculated data. This is now a template file with formulas ready for new hourly data.*

24. Deselect grouped sheets and check that each sheet contains identical data.

25. Set each worksheet to fit on one page when printed.
    - ✓ *You cannot set print page options for a group.*

26. Print the entire workbook.

27. Close and save the workbook file.

| | A | B | C | D | E | F | G | H | I | J | K | L |
|---|---|---|---|---|---|---|---|---|---|---|---|---|
| 1 | SUMMIT UNITED BANK PAYROLL | | | | | | | | | | | |
| 2 | FOR THE WEEK ENDING APRIL 7, 199- | | | | | | | | | | | |
| 3 | | | | | | | | | | | | |
| 4 | Employee | Card | Social Sec. | Hourly | Hours | Gross | Social | Medicare | | | | |
| 5 | Name | Number | No. | Rate | Worked | Pay | Sec. Tax | Tax | F.W.T. | Net Pay | | |
| 6 | | | | | | | | | | | | |
| 7 | Diaz | 13567 | 069-65-4532 | 5.55 | 15 | 83.25 | 5.16 | 1.21 | 16.65 | 60.23 | | |
| 8 | Jaffe | 13750 | 123-75-7623 | 7.23 | 32 | 231.36 | 14.34 | 3.35 | 46.27 | 167.39 | ← Delete row | |
| 9 | Latov | 13816 | 107-53-6754 | 6.18 | 16 | 98.88 | 6.13 | 1.43 | 19.78 | 71.54 | | |
| 10 | Nestor | 13925 | 103-87-5698 | 4.66 | 28 | 130.48 | 8.09 | 1.89 | 26.10 | 94.40 | | |
| 11 | Pringle | 14345 | 127-78-0045 | 6.57 | 12 | 78.84 | 4.89 | 1.14 | 15.77 | 57.04 | | |
| 12 | Wong | 14715 | 043-67-7600 | 8.65 | 21 | 181.65 | 11.26 | 2.63 | 36.33 | 131.42 | | |
| 13 | | | | | | | | | | | | |
| 14 | | TOTALS | | | | 804.46 | 49.88 | 11.66 | 160.89 | 582.03 | | |
| 15 | | AVERAGES | | | | 134.08 | 8.31 | 1.94 | 26.82 | 97.00 | | |
| 16 | | | | | | | | | | | | |
| 17 | | | | | | | | | | | | |
| 18 | FOR THE WEEK ENDING APRIL 14, 199- | | | | | | | | | | | |
| 19 | | | | | | | | | | | | |
| 20 | Employee | Card | Social Sec. | Hourly | Hours | Gross | Social | Medicare | | | | |
| 21 | Name | Number | No. | Rate | Worked | Pay | Sec. Tax | Tax | F.W.T. | Net Pay | | |
| 22 | | | | | | | | | | | | |
| 23 | Diaz | 13567 | 069-65-4532 | 5.55 | 20 | 111.00 | 6.88 | 1.61 | 22.20 | 80.31 | | |
| 24 | Jaffe | 13750 | 123-75-7623 | 7.23 | 31 | 224.13 | 13.90 | 3.25 | 44.83 | 162.16 | ← Delete row | |
| 25 | Latov | 13816 | 107-53-6754 | 6.18 | 23 | 142.14 | 8.81 | 2.06 | 28.43 | 102.84 | | |
| 26 | Nestor | 13925 | 103-87-5698 | 4.66 | 22 | 102.52 | 6.36 | 1.49 | 20.50 | 74.17 | | |
| 27 | Pringle | 14345 | 127-78-0045 | 6.57 | 15 | 98.55 | 6.11 | 1.43 | 19.71 | 71.30 | | |
| 28 | Wong | 14715 | 043-67-7600 | 8.65 | 25 | 216.25 | 13.41 | 3.14 | 43.25 | 156.46 | | |
| 29 | | | | | | | | | | | | |
| 30 | | TOTALS | | | | 894.59 | 55.46 | 12.97 | 178.92 | 647.24 | | |
| 31 | | AVERAGES | | | | 149.10 | 9.24 | 2.16 | 29.82 | 107.87 | | |
| 32 | | | | | | | | | | | | |
| 33 | | | | | | | | | | | | |
| 34 | FOR THE WEEK ENDING APRIL 21, 199- | | | | | | | | | | | |
| 35 | | | | | | | | | | | | |
| 36 | Employee | Card | Social Sec. | Hourly | Hours | Gross | Social | Medicare | | | | |
| 37 | Name | Number | No. | Rate | Worked | Pay | Sec. Tax | Tax | F.W.T. | Net Pay | | |
| 38 | | | | | | | | | | | | |
| 39 | Diaz | 13567 | 069-65-4532 | 5.55 | 22 | 122.10 | 7.57 | 1.77 | 24.42 | 88.34 | | |
| 40 | Latov | 13816 | 107-53-6754 | 6.18 | 33 | 203.94 | 12.64 | 2.96 | 40.79 | 147.55 | | |
| 41 | Nestor | 13925 | 103-87-5698 | 4.66 | 21 | 97.86 | 6.07 | 1.42 | 19.57 | 70.80 | | |
| 42 | Pringle | 14345 | 127-78-0045 | 6.57 | 16 | 105.12 | 6.52 | 1.52 | 21.02 | 76.05 | Copy A1:J47 | |
| 43 | Suraci | 14967 | 146-93-0069 | 6.25 | 18 | 112.50 | 6.98 | 1.63 | 22.50 | 81.39 | ← to May and | |
| 44 | Wong | 14715 | 043-67-7600 | 8.65 | 28 | 242.20 | 15.02 | 3.51 | 48.44 | 175.23 | June sheets | |
| 45 | | | | | | | | | | | | |
| 46 | | TOTALS | | | | 883.72 | 54.79 | 12.81 | 176.74 | 639.37 | | |
| 47 | | AVERAGES | | | | 147.29 | 9.13 | 2.14 | 29.46 | 106.56 | | |

# KEYSTROKES

## USE TAB SPLIT BOX

Lets you show more or fewer tabs.

1. Point to tab split box.

   Pointer becomes a ⇔.

2. Drag split box left or right.

## SELECT SHEETS

### Select One Sheet:

1. If necessary, click tab ....... 🔘🔘🔘🔘
   scrolling buttons to scroll a hidden
   sheet tab into view.

2. Click desired sheet tab ......... Sheet #

### Select All Sheets:

1. Right-click any sheet tab ...... Sheet #

2. Select **Select All Sheets** ........

## Select (Group) Consecutive Sheets

*IMPORTANT: When you group sheets, entries and formatting applied to one sheet are duplicated on all sheets in the group.*

1. If necessary, click tab ..... 🔘🔘🔘🔘
   scrolling buttons to scroll hidden sheet
   tabs into view.

2. Click first sheet tab ............... Sheet #
   to select.

3. If necessary, click tab.......
   scrolling buttons to scroll hidden sheet tabs into view.

4. Press **Shift** and click............ `Sheet #`
   last sheet tab to select.

5. [Group] appears in title bar.

### Select (Group) Non-Consecutive Sheets

*IMPORTANT: When you group sheets, entries and formatting applied to one sheet are duplicated on all sheets in the group.*

1. If necessary, click...........
   tab scrolling buttons to scroll hidden sheet tabs into view.

2. Click first sheet..................... `Sheet #`
   tab to select.

3. If necessary, click...........
   tab scrolling buttons to scroll hidden sheet tabs into view.

4. Press Ctrl and click.............. `Sheet #`
   each sheet tab to select.

5. [Group] appears in title bar.

## DESELECT GROUPED SHEETS

- Click.................................... `Sheet #`
  any sheet tab that is not in the group.
  **OR**
1. Right-click............................ `Sheet #`
   any sheet tab in group.

2. Click **Ungroup Sheets** .......... `↑↓` , `⏎`

## DELETE SHEETS

### Delete One Sheet:

1. Right-click............................ `Sheet #`
   sheet tab to delete.

2. Click Delete .......................... `↑↓` , `⏎`

3. Click `OK` ................................ `Enter`

### Delete Multiple Sheets:

1. Select sheet tabs to delete.

2. Right-click any ..................... `Sheet #`
   selected sheet tab.

3. Click **Delete**................................ `D`

4. Click `OK` .......................... `Enter`

## RENAME A SHEET

1. Double-click ......................... `Sheet #`
   sheet tab to rename.
   **OR**
   a. Right-click....................... `Sheet #`
      sheet tab.

   b. Select **Rename** ........................ `R`

2. Type new name ...........................*name*

3. Click `OK` .............................. `Enter`

## INSERT SHEETS

### Insert One Worksheet:

1. Right click sheet tab ........... `Sheet #`
   before which new sheet will be inserted.

2. Click **Insert**.................................. `I`

3. Select Worksheet......................... `↑↓`
   on General page.

4. Click `OK` .......................... `Enter`

*Excel inserts sheet and makes the new sheet active.*

### Insert Multiple Worksheets:

1. Highlight as many sheets as you wish to insert.

2. Right-click sheet tab............. `Sheet #`
   before which new sheets will be inserted.

3. Click **Insert**.................................. `I`

4. Select **Worksheet** ......................... `↑↓`
   on General page.

5. Click `OK` .......................... `Enter`

*Excel inserts sheets and makes the first new sheet active.*

## MOVE SHEETS WITHIN A WORKBOOK

### Move One Sheet:

1. If necessary, click.............
   tab scrolling buttons to scroll a hidden sheet tab into view.

2. Drag sheet tab to
   desired sheet tab position.

*Pointer becomes a ⍾, and black triangle indicates point of insertion.*

### Move Multiple Sheets:

1. If necessary, click .......
   scrolling buttons to scroll a hidden sheet tab into view.

2. Select sheets to move.

3. Drag selected sheet tabs to desired sheet tab position.

*Pointer becomes a ⍾, and black triangle indicates point of insertion.*

## 🌐 PRINT WORKBOOK

*Prints worksheet data using the current page settings.*

1. Click **File**............................ `Alt`+`F`

2. Click **Print**................................ `P`

3. Click **Entire Workbook** .......... `Alt`+`E`

4. Click `OK` .......................... `Enter`

## SET WORKSHEET TO PRINT ON SPECIFIED NUMBER OF PAGES

*Determines how much to scale printed data to fit on a specified number of pages.*

✓ *Excel ignores manual page breaks when this setting is selected.*

1. Click **File**............................ `Alt`+`F`

2. Click **Page Setup**........................ `U`

3. Select **Page** tab.................... `Ctrl`+`Tab`

4. Select **Fit to**: ........................ `Alt`+`F`

### To change settings for number of pages:

a. Type number of pages ..........*number*
   in **page(s) wide**.

b. Select **by tall** ........................ `Tab`

c. Type number of pages...........*number*

5. Click `OK` .......................... `Enter`

# Exercise 21

## ■ Named Ranges

## NOTES

### Named Ranges

■ Excel allows you to assign a **name** to a cell or range of cells rather than use the cell reference for identification.

■ Naming ranges makes formulas easy to read and understand and makes printing and combining ranges easier to accomplish.  For example, when you define a print area, you can type the defined name of a range (such as EMPS), rather than typing the cell reference (such as A1:D17).

■ You should keep range names short and descriptive.  Since spaces are not allowed, use an underscore to simulate a space character.  Do not use range names that could be interpreted as a number or a cell reference.  Range names may contain up to 255 characters and may consist of letters, numbers, underscores (_), backslashes (\), periods (.), and question marks (?).

■ You can define a named range by selecting the range and using the Insert, Name, Define commands or by naming the range in the Name Box.  The name box [_____] allows you to view a list of the named ranges you have created and to easily name or select a range.

■ A list of the named ranges you created and their corresponding cell references may be inserted into the worksheet by selecting Insert, Name, Paste and clicking the Paste List button.

■ It is possible to modify a named range by changing the range or the name.

■ As discussed in Exercise 11, formulas can contain natural language labels.  For example, =Sum(SALARY) will total the SALARY column.  If more than one label of that name exists, Excel will prompt you to choose the range needed for your calculation.  You can select label range names by using the Insert, Name, Label commands.

> *In this exercise, you will include third-quarter sales commission data and define named ranges in the report for printing and for later use in combining files.*

# EXERCISE DIRECTIONS

1. Open ⌨**REPORT**, or open 💾**21REPORT**.

2. Edit the title to read:

   QUARTERLY SALES AND SALARY REPORT – JANUARY– SEPTEMBER

3. Insert a row to include a new employee hired on July 1:  Employee Number, 6;  Name, THOMPSON, JIM;  Base Salary, $1500.

   ✓ *Note:    Format base salary to be consistent with other formatting.*

4. Freeze columns A-D for vertical titles.

5. Change column widths to 12 for columns K, L, and M.

6. Enter the following data in columns K, L, and M:

| | K | L | M |
|---|---|---|---|
| 1 | | | |
| 2 | | | |
| 3 | | | |
| 4 | | 5% | JULY-SEPT |
| 5 | SALES | COMMISSION | SALARY |
| 6 | | | |
| 7 | 112469.32 | | |
| 8 | 152643.36 | | |
| 9 | 215050.16 | | |
| 10 | 98463.14 | | |
| 11 | 246315.19 | | |
| 12 | 76451.13 | | |
| 13 | | | |
| 14 | | | |
| 15 | | | |

7. Format all data to be consistent with other formatting.

8. Copy the COMMISSION formulas to the new column.

9. Find JULY-SEPT SALARY using the BASE SALARY + COMMISSION.

10. Copy the formula to the remaining employees.

11. Copy the formulas for TOTALS, AVERAGES, HIGHEST, and LOWEST to the new columns.

12. Clear the freeze.

13. Check and edit the formulas for TOTALS, AVERAGES, HIGHEST, and LOWEST in the BASE SALARY column to include the new employee data, if necessary.

14. Copy the edited formulas to all columns.

15. Create the following named ranges using the name box method or the Insert, Name, Define commands:

    | | |
    |---|---|
    | EMPS | A1:D17 |
    | JAN_MAR | G1:G17 |
    | APR_JUNE | J1:J17 |
    | JUL_SEPT | M1:M17 |

16. Print one copy of the range EMPS.

17. In range beginning at cell B19, paste list of named ranges.

18. Close and save the workbook file, or save as **REPORT**

| | A | B | C | D | E | F | G | H | I | J | K | L | M |
|---|---|---|---|---|---|---|---|---|---|---|---|---|---|
| 1 | | COLONIAL FURNITURE GALLERY | | | | | | | | | | | |
| 2 | | QUARTERLY SALES AND SALARY REPORT-JANUARY-JUNE | | | | | | *SEPTEMBER* | | | ◄—12—► | ◄—12—► | ◄—12—► |
| 3 | | | | | | | | | | | | | |
| 4 | EMP. | | | BASE | | 5% | JAN-MAR | | 5% | APR-JUN | | | |
| 5 | NO. | SALES ASSOCIATE | | SALARY | SALES | COMMISSION | SALARY | SALES | COMMISSION | SALARY | | | |
| 6 | | | | | | | | | | | | | |
| 7 | 1 | BELIS, JUDY | | 1,500.00 | 113,456.67 | 5,672.83 | 7,172.83 | 114,342.87 | 5,717.14 | 7,217.14 | | | |
| 8 | 2 | HIRSCH, PETER | | 1,500.00 | 150,654.87 | 7,532.74 | 9,032.74 | 143,276.65 | 7,163.83 | 8,663.83 | | | |
| 9 | 3 | MINER, KELLY | | 1,500.00 | 234,765.36 | 11,738.27 | 13,238.27 | 187,956.76 | 9,397.84 | 10,897.84 | | | |
| 10 | 4 | SWEET, LETOYA | | 1,500.00 | 89,765.43 | 4,488.27 | 5,988.27 | 93,984.69 | 4,699.23 | 6,199.23 | | | |
| 11 | 5 | TABLES, TONY | | 1,500.00 | 287,987.76 | 14,399.39 | 15,899.39 | 254,768.64 | 12,738.43 | 14,238.43 | insert row | | |
| 12 | | | | | | | | | | | | | |
| 13 | | TOTALS | | 7,500.00 | 876,630.09 | 43,831.50 | 51,331.50 | 794,329.61 | 39,716.48 | 47,216.48 | | | |
| 14 | | AVERAGES | | 1,500.00 | 175,326.02 | 8,766.30 | 10,266.30 | 158,865.92 | 7,943.30 | 9,443.30 | | | |
| 15 | | HIGHEST | | 1,500.00 | 287,987.76 | 14,399.39 | 15,899.39 | 254,768.64 | 12,738.43 | 14,238.43 | | | |
| 16 | | LOWEST | | 1,500.00 | 89,765.43 | 4,488.27 | 5,988.27 | 93,984.69 | 4,699.23 | 6,199.23 | | | |

# KEYSTROKES

## NAME/MODIFY A RANGE USING THE MENU

1. Click **I**nsert ......................... `Alt`+`I`
2. Click **N**ame ............................. `N`
3. Click **D**efine .......................... `D`

*Active cell reference appears in **Refers to** text box.*

**To name a range:**

a. Type name for range ................ *name*
   in **Names in workbook** text box.
b. Click `Add` .................... `Alt`+`A`
c. Drag through existing
   reference .......................... `Alt`+`R`
   in **Refers to** text box.
d. Using collapse button, select cells in
   worksheet to name.
   **OR**
   Type reference of cells ......... *reference*
   to name.

**To delete a name:**

a. Click name ...................... `Tab` , `↑↓`
   to delete in list box.
b. Click `Delete` .................. `Alt`+`D`

**To change a name:**

a. Click name ...................... `Tab` , `↑↓`
   to change in list box.
b. Double-click in **Names in**
   **workbook** ....................... `Alt`+`W`
c. Type new name ....................... *name*
   for range.
d. Click `Add` .................... `Alt`+`A`
e. Click old name ................ `Tab` , `↑↓`
   to delete in list box.
f. Click `Delete` .................. `Alt`+`D`

## To change reference a name refers to:

a. Click name ...................... `Tab` , `↑↓`
   to edit in list box.
b. Drag through existing
   reference .......................... `Alt`+`R`
   in **Refers to** text box.
c. Using collapse button, select cells in
   worksheet to reference.
   **OR**
   Type new reference .................. *reference*
4. Click `OK` .......................... `Enter`

## NAME A RANGE USING THE NAME BOX

1. Select range to name.
2. Click in name box on left side of formula bar.
3. Type name of range ..................... *name*
   to create.
4. Press **Enter** ............................... `Enter`

## SELECT A NAMED RANGE

**Select a Named Range Using the Name Box:**

1. Click drop-down arrow in name box on
   left side of formula bar.
2. Click desired named range.

**Select a Named Range Using Go To:**

1. Press **F5** ........................................ `F5`
2. Type name ................................. *name*
   to select in **Reference** text box.
3. Click `OK` .......................... `Enter`

## INSERT LIST OF NAMED RANGES

*Inserts a list of named ranges and their corresponding references in current worksheet.*

1. Select upper-left cell in range to receive list.
2. Click **I**nsert ......................... `Alt`+`I`
3. Click **N**ame ............................. `N`
4. Click **P**aste ............................ `P`
5. Click `Paste List` ..................... `Alt`+`L`

✓ *Excel includes sheet names in references.*

6. Press any arrow key ..................... `↑↓`

## SET PRINT AREA FOR A NAMED RANGE

✓ *Use this option only when you want to print a specific area of a worksheet each time you print.*

1. Follow steps to **SET PRINT OPTIONS FOR WORKSHEET**, Exercise 12.
2. When you set the print area, type named range *name* in **Print Area** text box.
3. Follow steps to **PRINT A WORKSHEET**, Exercise 12.

## PRINT A NAMED RANGE

1. Follow steps to **SELECT A NAMED RANGE**, left.
2. Follow steps to **PRINT RANGE OF CELLS**, Exercise 12.

## Exercise 22

## ■ Copy and Paste Special (Extract and Combine Data)

## NOTES

### Copy and Paste Special

■ As described in previous exercises, the Paste Special command gives you added control on how data is pasted when copied.

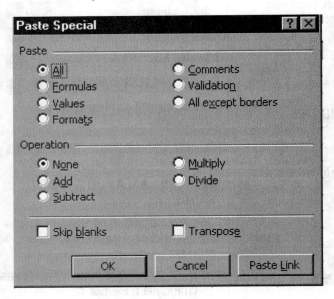

■ The Operation options in the Paste Special dialog box provide a variety of ways to combine data.

| | |
|---|---|
| **None** | Replaces paste cells with copied cells (default setting). |
| **Add** | Adds numeric data in copied cells to values in paste cells. |
| **Subtract** | Subtracts numeric data in copied cells from values in paste cells. |
| **Multiply** | Multiplies numeric data in copied cells by values in paste cells. |
| **Divide** | Divides numeric data in copied cells by values in paste cells. |

■ In this lesson you will use the Add operation option in the Paste Special dialog box to copy and paste data to a column in another workbook. The Add option will allow you to add the values from each quarter to obtain a total for all quarters.

*In this exercise, you will extract data in a named range to a new file. Then you will use the Paste Special command to combine (add) the quarterly totals (as values) in the new workbook file, thus creating a summary workbook.*

REMINDER:  *When you paste data using the **Add** and **Values** options in the **Paste Special** dialog box, the new combined data will not include formulas. Therefore, the summary data will be incorrect and will require that a new formula be entered to obtain the correct answers.*

## EXERCISE DIRECTIONS

1. Open 💻REPORT, or open 💾22REPORT.

2. Use the Copy and Paste Special commands to extract the named range EMPS to a cell A1 in a new workbook file using the Formulas option; save and name the new workbook **RPTSUM**.

3. Edit the second line of the **RPTSUM** workbook title to read:

    COMPENSATION SUMMARY - JANUARY-SEPTEMBER

4. Use the Window menu to switch to the **REPORT**  workbook.

5. To extract and combine named ranges into the **RPTSUM** workbook:
   - Use the Name box to select and copy the JAN_MAR named range.
   - Switch to the RPTSUM workbook.
   - Use Edit, Paste Special, Values, Add to add the values to cell F1.
   - Repeat this procedure for the ranges below:
   APR_JUNE
   JUL_ SEPT

   Note: *Each time you paste a range into F1, the values will be added to the contents, which results in the total of all three ranges.*

6. In column F of the REPTSUM workbook, enter the column title:
   TOTAL
   COMPENSATION

7. The combined summary data for AVERAGES, HIGHEST, and LOWEST is now incorrect. To correct this information, copy the formulas for TOTALS, AVERAGES, HIGHEST, and LOWEST from the BASE SALARY column to the TOTAL COMPENSATION column.

8. Format column F to show two decimal places.

9. Adjust column width to show all values.

10. Save **RPTSUM** and print one copy.

11. Close both workbook files.

| | A | B | C | D | E | F | G | H | I | J | K | L | M |
|---|---|---|---|---|---|---|---|---|---|---|---|---|---|
| 1 | | | | COLONIAL FURNITURE GALLERY | | | | | | | | | |
| 2 | | QUARTERLY SALES AND SALARY REPORT-JANUARY-SEPTEMBER | | | | | | | | | | | |
| 3 | | | | | | | | | | | | | |
| 4 | EMP. | | | BASE | | 5% | JAN-MAR | | 5% | APR-JUN | | 5% | JULY-SEPT. |
| 5 | NO. | SALES ASSOCIATE | | SALARY | SALES | COMMISSION | SALARY | SALES | COMMISSION | SALARY | SALES | COMMISSION | SALARY |
| 6 | | | | | | | | | | | | | |
| 7 | 1 | BELIS, JUDY | | 1,500.00 | 113,456.67 | 5,672.83 | 7,172.83 | 114,342.87 | 5,717.14 | 7,217.14 | 112469.32 | 5,623.47 | 7,123.47 |
| 8 | 2 | HIRSCH, PETER | | 1,500.00 | 150,654.87 | 7,532.74 | 9,032.74 | 143,276.65 | 7,163.83 | 8,663.83 | 152643.36 | 7,632.17 | 9,132.17 |
| 9 | 3 | MINER, KELLY | | 1,500.00 | 234,765.36 | 11,738.27 | 13,238.27 | 187,956.76 | 9,397.84 | 10,897.84 | 215050.16 | 10,752.51 | 12,252.51 |
| 10 | 4 | SWEET, LETOYA | | 1,500.00 | 89,765.43 | 4,488.27 | 5,988.27 | 93,984.69 | 4,699.23 | 6,199.23 | 98463.14 | 4,923.16 | 6,423.16 |
| 11 | 5 | TABLES, TONY | | 1,500.00 | 287,987.76 | 14,399.39 | 15,899.39 | 254,768.64 | 12,738.43 | 14,238.43 | 246315.19 | 12,315.76 | 13,815.76 |
| 12 | 6 | THOMPSON, JIM | | 1,500.00 | | | | | | | 76451.13 | 3,822.56 | 5,322.56 |
| 13 | | | | | | | | | | | | | |
| 14 | | TOTALS | | 7,500.00 | 876,630.09 | 43,831.50 | 51,331.50 | 794,329.61 | 39,716.48 | 47,216.48 | 901,392.30 | 45,069.62 | 54,069.62 |
| 15 | | AVERAGES | | 1,500.00 | 175,326.02 | 8,766.30 | 10,266.30 | 158,865.92 | 7,943.30 | 9,443.30 | 150,232.05 | 7,511.60 | 9,011.60 |
| 16 | | HIGHEST | | 1,500.00 | 287,987.76 | 14,399.39 | 15,899.39 | 254,768.64 | 12,738.43 | 14,238.43 | 246,315.19 | 12,315.76 | 13,815.76 |
| 17 | | LOWEST | | 1,500.00 | 89,765.43 | 4,488.27 | 5,988.27 | 93,984.69 | 4,699.23 | 6,199.23 | 76,451.13 | 3,822.56 | 5,322.56 |
| 18 | | | | | | | | | | | | | |

range A1:D17 named EMPS

# KEYSTROKES

## COPY AND PASTE SPECIAL (COMBINE DATA)

*Combines data copied to the paste area in the way you specify.*

1. Select range of worksheet to extract.

2. Click **Edit** .......................... `Alt`+`E`

3. Click **Copy** .......................... `C`

**To change destination workbook or worksheet:**

- Select workbook and/or sheet to receive data.

4. Select upper-left cell in destination area.

5. Click **Edit** .......................... `Alt`+`E`

6. Click **Paste Special**.......................... `S`

7. Select **Paste** option:
   - **All** .......................... `A`
   - **Formulas** .......................... `F`
   - **Values** .......................... `V`
   - **Formats** .......................... `T`
   - **Comments** .......................... `C`
   - To combine copied data with paste area data:

8. Select **Operation** option:
   - **None** .......................... `O`
   - **Add** .......................... `D`

- **Subtract** .......................... `S`
- **Multiply** .......................... `M`
- **Divide** .......................... `I`

**To prevent overwriting existing data with blank cells:**

- Click **Skip blanks** .......................... `B`

**To change orientation of data in paste area:**

- Click **Transpose** .......................... `E`

8. Click `OK` .......................... `Enter`

## Exercise 23

■ **Arrange Workbooks**  ■ **Drag and Drop Between Workbooks**

# NOTES

### Arrange Workbooks

■ If you are copying and pasting between workbooks, you may find it easier to arrange both workbooks on the screen using the Window, Arrange commands. The Arrange dialog box, as illustrated below, allows you to select the arrangement of data.

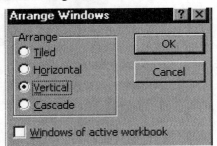

### Drag and Drop Between Workbooks

■ If you have workbooks arranged on the screen, as illustrated below, you can use drag and drop to copy the range to another workbook. Select the range, press CTRL and drag the border of the selection to the new workbook.

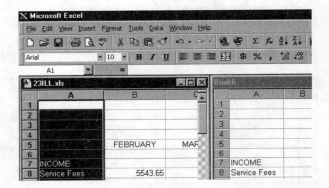

*In this exercise, you will update the Wilson's Better Gardening Service worksheet to include fourth-quarter data. In addition, you will create a new worksheet comparing quarterly data using drag and drop to copy titles and Copy and Paste Special to extract and combine file data.*

# DIRECTIONS

1. Open 🖫INCOME, or open 🖫23INCOME.

2. Delete the COMBINED TOTALS column.

3. Enter fourth-quarter data indicated at the right, beginning in the next available column of your worksheet.

4. Copy formulas, where necessary, to complete the worksheet.

5. Find 4TH QTR. TOTALS.

6. Copy the formula to the remaining items.

7. Center column title labels.

8. Format numeric data for two decimal places.

|    | N | O | P | Q |
|----|---|---|---|---|
| 4  |   |   |   | 4TH QTR. |
| 5  | OCT | NOV | DEC | TOTALS |
| 6  |   |   |   |   |
| 7  |   |   |   |   |
| 8  | 9968.54 | 6235.87 | 5256.78 |   |
| 9  | 1065.93 | 988.54 | 1054.32 |   |
| 10 |   |   |   |   |
| 11 |   |   |   |   |
| 12 |   |   |   |   |
| 13 | 150.00 | 55.00 | 55.00 |   |
| 14 | 1255.00 | 754.65 | 754.65 |   |
| 15 | 1435.62 | 567.87 | 102.54 |   |
| 16 | 95.87 | 325.65 | 627.89 |   |
| 17 | 25.00 | 25.00 | 25.00 |   |
| 18 | 546.87 | 325.87 | 95.87 |   |

9. Create the following named ranges (notice underscores) for each quarterly total column:

_1ST_QTR
_2ND_QTR
_3RD_QTR
_4TH_QTR

✓ Include blank cells in column, for example E1:E21 for _1ST_QTR.

10. Clear the freeze on Column A titles.

11. Save the file, or *save as* **INCOME**.

12. Open a new workbook.

13. Use the Window, Arrange commands to arrange the workbooks vertically.

14. Use the drag and drop method to copy column A data, rows 1 through 21, to cell A1 in the new workbook file; save and name the new workbook **INQTRS**.

15. In INQTRS workbook, enter a worksheet title beginning in cell C1 that reads:

WILSON'S BETTER GARDENING SERVICE
QUARTERLY INCOME STATEMENT COMPARISON

16. Switch to the INCOME workbook.

17. Use the Copy and Paste Special commands to copy the named range _1ST_QTR to the range beginning in C1 in the

INQTRS workbook. Select the named range using the Name box.

*IMPORTANT: Set the Paste option to **Values**, Operation option to **None**, and select **Skip Blanks**.*

18. Repeat step 15 for the _2ND_QTR, _3RD_QTR, and _4TH_QTR named ranges. Paste ranges in INQTRS workbook in columns D1, E1, and F1, respectively.

19. Maximize the INQTRS workbook.

20. Enter title in column G:
COMBINED
TOTALS

21. Find the combined total for Service Fees INCOME.

22. Copy the formula to the remaining items.

23. Format all numeric values for commas with two decimal places.

24. Right align column titles for numeric data.

25. Adjust column widths as needed.

26. Save the **INQTRS** workbook and print one copy.

27. Close both workbook files.

| | | | | | 1ST QTR. | | | | 2ND QTR. | COMBINED | |
| | WILSON'S BETTER GARDENING SERVICE COMPARATIVE INCOME STATEMENT | | | | | | | | | | |
| | JANUARY | FEBRUARY | MARCH | TOTALS | APRIL | MAY | JUNE | TOTALS | TOTALS | JULY |
|---|---|---|---|---|---|---|---|---|---|---|
| INCOME | | | | | | | | | | |
| Service Fees | 5342.87 | 5543.65 | 6165.87 | 17052.39 | 8343.84 | 9862.89 | 10359.45 | 28566.18 | 45618.57 | 11986.45 |
| Consultations | 1564.98 | 1654.76 | 1689.76 | 4909.50 | 1893.65 | 1498.62 | 1287.49 | 4679.76 | 9589.26 | 1343.27 |
| Total Income | 6907.85 | 7198.41 | 7855.63 | 21961.89 | 10237.49 | 11361.51 | 11646.94 | 33245.94 | 55207.83 | 13329.72 |
| | | | | | | | | | | |
| EXPENSES: | | | | | | | | | | |
| Advertising | 55.00 | 65.00 | 150.00 | 270.00 | 150.00 | 165.00 | 165.00 | 480.00 | 750.00 | 165.00 |
| Salaries | 754.65 | 754.65 | 1255.55 | 2764.85 | 1255.55 | 1255.55 | 1255.55 | 3766.65 | 6531.50 | 1255.55 |
| Supplies | 154.76 | 245.65 | 589.53 | 989.94 | 769.54 | 965.62 | 1276.54 | 3011.70 | 4001.64 | 1887.98 |
| Truck Maint | 95.00 | 125.54 | 243.98 | 464.52 | 185.87 | 543.51 | 324.65 | 1054.03 | 1518.55 | 486.98 |
| Interest | 25.00 | 25.00 | 25.00 | 75.00 | 25.00 | 25.00 | 25.00 | 75.00 | 150.00 | 25.00 |
| Other | 143.43 | 43.54 | 231.65 | 418.62 | 326.43 | 654.65 | 798.43 | 1779.51 | 2198.13 | 674.79 |
| Total Expenses | 1227.84 | 1259.38 | 2495.71 | 4982.93 | 2712.39 | 3609.33 | 3845.17 | 10166.89 | 15149.82 | 4495.30 |
| | | | | | | | | | | |
| NET INCOME | 5680.01 | 5939.03 | 5359.92 | 16978.96 | 7525.10 | 7752.18 | 7801.77 | 23079.05 | 40058.01 | 8834.42 |

extract to new file, INQTRS

# KEYSTROKES

## ARRANGE WORKBOOKS

1. Click **Window** ........................ `Alt`+`W`
2. Click **Arrange** ......................... `A`
3. Select:

   **Tiled** ................................. `Alt`+`T`

   **Horizontal** ...................... `Alt`+`O`

   **Vertical** ........................... `Alt`+`V`

   **Cascade** .......................... `Alt`+`C`

4. Click **OK** .................................. `Enter`

## DRAG AND DROP BETWEEN WORKBOOKS

1. Select range to copy.
2. Press CTRL and drag border of selection to location on new workbook.

# Exercise 24

## ■ Use Templates (Spreadsheet Solutions)

## NOTES

■ Excel provides **template spreadsheets** (model worksheet designs) for common business tasks. The formulas, formats, print ranges, layout, etc. are pre-set so that you only need to add your data. If data is added to a template file, the Save As option should be used to prevent changes in the template.

■ You can customize the template for your purposes and save it as a template file with a new filename. This will enable you to use a customized form that only requires new variable data. You may also create your own templates by saving them as template files.

■ The template spreadsheet solutions that are available in Excel are found on the Spreadsheet Solutions page of the File, New dialog box. Note the illustration of the New dialog box with the Spreadsheet Solutions tab selected.

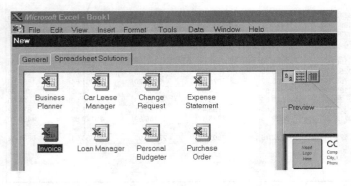

■ You can also download additional Microsoft Excel templates from Microsoft on the World Wide Web.

■ Each template workbook contains the **template worksheet** and a **customize worksheet** with data entry placeholders to customize the form for your use. In addition, a **Template toolbar** appears on the template when it is opened. Note the illustration of the Invoice toolbar with a ToolTip displayed.

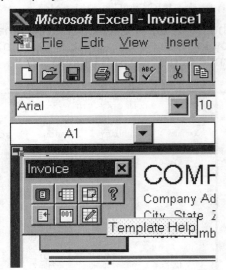

■ When you save a file as a template file, the file will have an .XLT extension. The files should be saved in the Excel or Spreadsheet Solutions folder in the Templates folder; this way they will appear on the Spreadsheet Solutions tab of the New dialog box.

■ Several of the templates provided by Excel have a database feature that allows you to track the forms created by producing a record of the data. For the purposes of this exercise, the template will be used without the database feature.

*In this exercise, you will explore a template and the Template toolbar. You will customize the invoice template for the Art Depot, save it as a template, and create an invoice.*

# EXERCISE DIRECTIONS

1. Click File, New on the main menu to create a new file.

2. Switch to the Spreadsheet Solutions page in the New dialog box.

3. Double-click the Invoice template.

   ✓ *Note: Since the templates contain macros, the virus protection installed earlier in the text will activate. You can open this file with macros enabled because the file source is known.*

4. Place the mouse pointer under every button on the Invoice toolbar to view the ToolTip.

5. Press the Size to Screen/Return to Size button (top left corner) to view the template. Press the button to return to size.

6. To view a cell tip, click on the Shipping Handling cell under the Total column.

7. Click on the Help ? button to view a help screen on the Invoice template. After looking at the screen, press the Close button.

8. Close the Invoice toolbar.

9. Switch to the Customize Invoice sheet.

10. Make the entries as shown on the form on the next page.

11. At the bottom of the Customize Your Invoice form, click the Select Logo button. Select an appropriate picture for a logo if you have these files installed. *Note: Clipart files may also be downloaded from the Internet.*

12. Switch to the Invoice sheet and check your input.

13. Click on the **Insert Fine Print Here** location at the bottom of the invoice and insert:

    *Please check merchandise carefully upon delivery.*

14. Click on the **Insert Farewell Statement Here** location and insert:

    *Thank you for your order.*

15. Save the file as **ARTINV** as a template file.

16. Close ARTINV.

17. Open a new workbook. Use the ARTINV template.

18. Enter information to complete an invoice for Sabrina Advertising as follows:

| | |
|---|---|
| **Customer:** | Sabrina Advertising |
| | 40 Scaran Road |
| | Peoria, IL 62543 |
| **Phone:** | 555-1234 |
| **Invoice Number:** | AD456 |
| **Order No.:** | MA25 |
| **Rep:** | Mary |
| **FOB** | Galesburg, IL |

| QTY | DESCRIPTION | UNIT PRICE |
|---|---|---|
| 6 | Toner Cartridges X-341 | 69.95 |
| 10 | Drawing Pads JJ4356 | 21.95 |
| 5 | Pencil Sets CA65763 | 5.43 |

**Payment Details:** Check

19. Print a copy of the invoice.

20. Save the invoice as **SABRINA**.

21. Close the file.

## CUSTOMIZE YOUR INVOICE

Hover Your Pointer
HERE for a Useful Tip!

**Type Company Information Here...**

| | | | |
|---|---|---|---|
| Company Name | Art Depot | Phone | 309-555-9000 |
| Address | 1254 Miller Road | Fax | 309-555-9001 |
| City | Galesburg | | |
| State | IL | | |
| ZIP Code | 61401 | | |

**Specify Default Invoice Information Here...**

Credit Cards Accepted

| | | |
|---|---|---|
| 1st Tax Name | IL | Master Plan |
| Rate | 6.00% | Discovery |
| ☑ | Apply tax on local purchases only. | American Presto |

2nd Tax Name

Rate

☐ Apply tax on local purchases only.

Shipping Charge  $7.50

☐ Share invoice numbers on network.

Counter Location

Template Wizard Database   c:\program files\microsoft office\office\library\invdb.xls

**Formatted Information**

# Art Depot
1254 Miller Road
Galesburg, IL  61401
309-555-9000 fax 309-555-9001

# KEYSTROKES

## USE AN EXCEL TEMPLATE

1. Click **File** ............................ `Alt`+`F`
2. Click **New** ................................. `N`
3. Click Spreadsheet Solutions tab.
4. Double-click on desired template.

## SAVE A FILE AS A TEMPLATE

1. Click **File** ............................ `Alt`+`F`
2. Click **Save As** ............................... `A`
   ✓ If you are saving from an Excel
   template, a message will be displayed
   about creating a database record.
   Click Cancel if the database feature will
   not be used.

3. Select drive in **Save in** box.
4. Double-click folder name in
   documents list.
5. Repeat step 4 until folder to receive
   template is current.
6. Click on **File name** box .................... `N`
7. Enter name
   of template ..................... *template name*
8. Click on **Save as type** box ............... `T`
9. Select **Template** option .................. `↓`
10. Click **Save** ...................................... `S`

## OPEN ORIGINAL TEMPLATE FILE

1. Click **Open** button ...........................
   on Standard toolbar.
   **OR**
   a. Click **File** ........................... `Alt`+`F`
   b. Click **Open** .................................. `O`
2. Select Templates (*.xlt)
   in **Files of type** .............................. `T`
3. Select folder containing template in
   **Look in** box.
4. Select  template file to open.
5. Press **Shift** and click **Open**.

## Exercise 25

■ **Original Templates** ■ **Link Workbooks**

# NOTES

## Original Templates

■ When you need to create several workbooks containing similar data and formulas that are not provided with the Excel program, you can create your own form and save the workbook as a template. When the file is saved as a template, it automatically saves to the Templates directory of Microsoft Office 97. Once the file is in that directory, you can move the file to the Spreadsheet Solutions folder to be able to view your template in the New dialog box as illustrated in the last exercise.

■ It is advisable to save a template file as a read-only file so that the format cannot be accidentally changed or overwritten.

   ✓ *Note: Template files have .XLT filename extensions.*

## Link Workbooks

■ **Linking workbooks** allows you to consolidate and merge data from several workbooks into one summary workbook. Linking allows the summary workbook to be automatically or manually updated when the linked data changes.

■ The workbooks that provide the data are referred to as **source workbooks**; the workbook that references the data is referred to as the **dependent workbook**. References to cells in other workbooks are called **external references**.

■ By default, links are set to automatically update. Excel updates links when you open the dependent workbook and also when source data is changed while the dependent workbook is open.

■ Linking differs from combining data (Copy and Paste Special) in that the combining of data merely copies, adds, or subtracts data to the dependent file. Changes in the source workbook are not reflected in the dependent workbook except by repeating the combining procedure.

■ There are three ways to link a file:

   • The copied data from the source workbook may be pasted into the dependent workbook as a pasted link, which automatically creates an external reference that links the workbooks.

   ✓ *Note: In this exercise, we will use the Paste Link method.*

   • An external reference may be typed in a formula using the following format: drive:\path\[file.xls]sheetname!reference

*EXAMPLES:*

=c:\excel\[PAT.xls]Sheet1!A1  creates a link to A1 in PAT workbook.

=sum([PAT.xls]Sheet1!A1:D1) + B3  finds sum of A1:D1 in PAT workbook and adds it to contents of B3 in current workbook.

   ✓ *Note: If the source file is in the same directory, you may omit the path.*

   • You can include an external reference in a formula by selecting cells in the source workbook while editing or creating a formula in the dependent workbook.

■ If the cell in an external reference includes a formula, only the formula result will be brought forward.

■ When possible, follow these guidelines for saving linked workbooks:

- Save linked workbooks in the same directory.

- Save the source workbooks before the dependent workbook.

- An illustration of the linking process appears below.

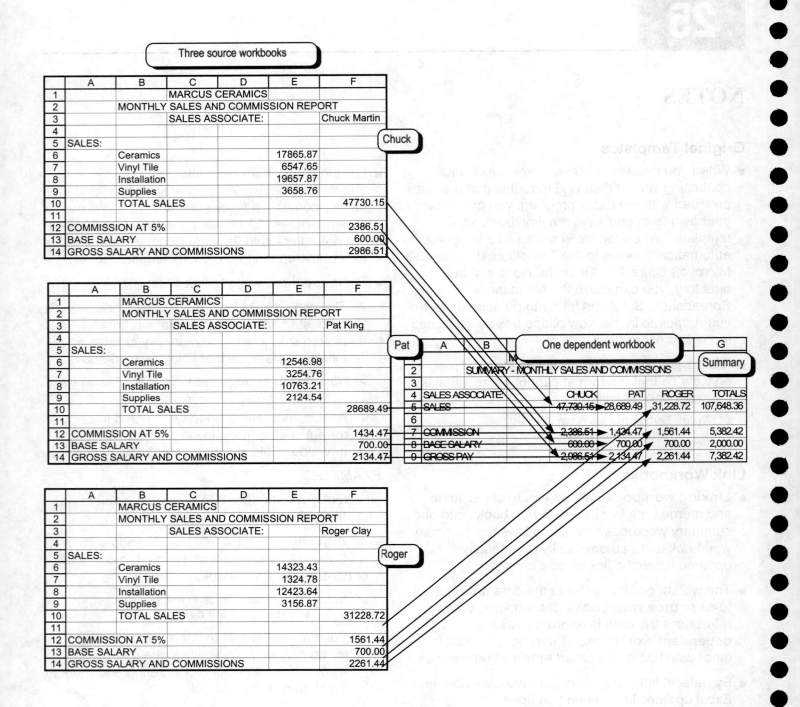

Three source workbooks

| | A | B | C | D | E | F |
|---|---|---|---|---|---|---|
| 1 | | | MARCUS CERAMICS | | | |
| 2 | MONTHLY SALES AND COMMISSION REPORT | | | | | |
| 3 | | | SALES ASSOCIATE: | | | Chuck Martin |
| 4 | | | | | | |
| 5 | SALES: | | | | | |
| 6 | | Ceramics | | | 17865.87 | |
| 7 | | Vinyl Tile | | | 6547.65 | |
| 8 | | Installation | | | 19657.87 | |
| 9 | | Supplies | | | 3658.76 | |
| 10 | | TOTAL SALES | | | | 47730.15 |
| 11 | | | | | | |
| 12 | COMMISSION AT 5% | | | | | 2386.51 |
| 13 | BASE SALARY | | | | | 600.00 |
| 14 | GROSS SALARY AND COMMISSIONS | | | | | 2986.51 |

Chuck

| | A | B | C | D | E | F |
|---|---|---|---|---|---|---|
| 1 | | MARCUS CERAMICS | | | | |
| 2 | | MONTHLY SALES AND COMMISSION REPORT | | | | |
| 3 | | | SALES ASSOCIATE: | | | Pat King |
| 4 | | | | | | |
| 5 | SALES: | | | | | |
| 6 | | Ceramics | | | 12546.98 | |
| 7 | | Vinyl Tile | | | 3254.76 | |
| 8 | | Installation | | | 10763.21 | |
| 9 | | Supplies | | | 2124.54 | |
| 10 | | TOTAL SALES | | | | 28689.49 |
| 11 | | | | | | |
| 12 | COMMISSION AT 5% | | | | | 1434.47 |
| 13 | BASE SALARY | | | | | 700.00 |
| 14 | GROSS SALARY AND COMMISSIONS | | | | | 2134.47 |

Pat

One dependent workbook

Summary

| | A | B | | CHUCK | PAT | ROGER | TOTALS |
|---|---|---|---|---|---|---|---|
| 1 | | M | | | | | |
| 2 | SUMMARY - MONTHLY SALES AND COMMISSIONS | | | | | | |
| 3 | | | | | | | |
| 4 | SALES ASSOCIATE | | | CHUCK | PAT | ROGER | TOTALS |
| 5 | SALES | | | 47,730.15 | 28,689.49 | 31,228.72 | 107,648.36 |
| 6 | | | | | | | |
| 7 | COMMISSION | | | 2,386.51 | 1,434.47 | 1,561.44 | 5,382.42 |
| 8 | BASE SALARY | | | 600.00 | 700.00 | 700.00 | 2,000.00 |
| 9 | GROSS PAY | | | 2,986.51 | 2,134.47 | 2,261.44 | 7,382.42 |

| | A | B | C | D | E | F |
|---|---|---|---|---|---|---|
| 1 | | MARCUS CERAMICS | | | | |
| 2 | | MONTHLY SALES AND COMMISSION REPORT | | | | |
| 3 | | | SALES ASSOCIATE: | | | Roger Clay |
| 4 | | | | | | |
| 5 | SALES: | | | | | |
| 6 | | Ceramics | | | 14323.43 | |
| 7 | | Vinyl Tile | | | 1324.78 | |
| 8 | | Installation | | | 12423.64 | |
| 9 | | Supplies | | | 3156.87 | |
| 10 | | TOTAL SALES | | | | 31228.72 |
| 11 | | | | | | |
| 12 | COMMISSION AT 5% | | | | | 1561.44 |
| 13 | BASE SALARY | | | | | 700.00 |
| 14 | GROSS SALARY AND COMMISSIONS | | | | | 2261.44 |

Roger

> In this exercise, the Marcus Ceramics company creates a monthly sales and salary statement for each sales associate. They would like a summary workbook consolidating the information about the associates' sales performance. Using the Linking feature, the data on the consolidated workbook will automatically update monthly as the consultant data changes.

# EXERCISE DIRECTIONS

1. Create template workbook A, as indicated on the next page, or open 🖫**25COMM**.

2. Add formulas to template to find:

   - TOTAL SALES
   - COMMISSION (5% of Sales)
   - GROSS SALARY AND COMMISSION (Commision+ Base Salary)

   ✓ *Note: Formulas will result in zero values.*

3. Format all money columns for two decimal places.

4. Save the file as a template and a read-only file; name it **COMM**. (*Save the file in the Templates folder.*)

5. Close **COMM**.

6. Reopen **COMM**. (*COMM is in the Templates folder and has an .XLT extension.*)

   HINT: *Since you just saved the file, you can select it from near the bottom of the* **File** *menu.*

7. Use the template to create a workbook for each sales consultant using the data below. When the data is entered, the formulas in the template will complete the workbook. After each workbook is completed, save and name each workbook file **CHUCK**, **PAT**, and **ROGER** respectively.

   ✓ *Do not close these files after saving.*

   | ASSOCIATE: | CHUCK MARTIN | PAT KING | ROGER CLAY |
   |---|---|---|---|
   | Ceramics | 17865.87 | 12546.98 | 14323.43 |
   | Vinyl Tile | 6547.65 | 3254.76 | 1324.78 |
   | Installation | 19657.87 | 10763.21 | 12423.64 |
   | Supplies | 3658.76 | 2124.54 | 3156.87 |
   | BASE SALARY | 600.00 | 700.00 | 700.00 |

8. Open a new workbook and create workbook B (dependent), as indicated on the next page, or open 🖫**25SUMM**. Save the workbook; name it **SUMM**.

9. Minimize all workbook windows except **CHUCK** and **SUMM**. Use the Window menu to arrange the open workbooks so data can be seen in both files.

10. Copy and Paste Link the range that includes TOTAL SALES, COMMISSION, BASE SALARY and GROSS PAY in the **CHUCK** workbook to cell D5 in **SUMM** workbook.

11. Minimize **CHUCK** workbook.

12. Open **PAT** workbook icon; arrange open workbooks.

13. Copy and Paste Link the F10:F14 range in the PAT workbook to cell E5 in the **SUMM** workbook.

14. Minimize **PAT** workbook.

15. Open **ROGER** workbook icon; arrange open workbooks.

16. Copy and Paste Link the F10:F14 range in the **ROGER** workbook to cell F5 in the **SUMM** workbook.

17. In the **SUMM** workbook, format all numbers for two place decimals and delete zeros in the blank row. Right-align column titles for numeric data.

18. Find all totals in **SUMM** workbook.

19. Save the **SUMM** workbook.

20. Print one copy of **SUMM** workbook.

21. Minimize all windows except **PAT** and **SUMM**; arrange open workbooks.

22. Select **PAT** workbook and change her Vinyl Tile sales to $8254.76.

23. Note the updated values in the **PAT** column of the **SUMM** workbook and the updated totals.

24. Close all workbook files *without* resaving.

**Workbook A –
source template file**

| | A | B | C | D | E | F |
|---|---|---|---|---|---|---|
| 1 | | | MARCUS CERAMICS | | | |
| 2 | | | MONTHLY SALES AND COMMISSION REPORT | | | |
| 3 | | | SALES ASSOCIATE: | | | |
| 4 | | | | | | |
| 5 | SALES: | | | | | |
| 6 | | Ceramics | | | | |
| 7 | | Vinyl Tile | | | | |
| 8 | | Installation | | | | |
| 9 | | Supplies | | | | |
| 10 | | TOTAL SALES | | | | 0 |
| 11 | | | | | | |
| 12 | COMMISSION AT 5% | | | | | 0 |
| 13 | BASE SALARY | | | | | |
| 14 | GROSS SALARY AND COMMISSIONS | | | | | 0 |

**Workbook B –
dependent file**

| | A | B | C | D | E | F | G |
|---|---|---|---|---|---|---|---|
| 1 | | | MARCUS CERAMICS | | | | |
| 2 | | SUMMARY - MONTHLY SALES AND COMMISSIONS | | | | | |
| 3 | | | | | | | |
| 4 | SALES ASSOCIATE: | | | CHUCK | PAT | ROGER | TOTALS |
| 5 | SALES | | | | | | |
| 6 | | | | | | | |
| 7 | COMMISSION | | | | | | |
| 8 | BASE SALARY | | | | | | |
| 9 | GROSS PAY | | | | | | |

# KEYSTROKES

## CREATE A TEMPLATE WORKBOOK

Saves and names the active workbook as a template file.

1. Click **File** ............................. Alt + F
2. Click **Save As** ................................. A
3. Click **Save as type** ................. Alt + T
4. Select **Template** file type ....... ↑↓ , ↵
5. Double-click in **File name** ...... Alt + N
6. Type filename ........................... *filename*
7. Click Save ............................. ↵

## ARRANGE WORKBOOK WINDOWS

1. Click **Window** ........................ Alt + W
2. Click **Arrange** ................................. A
3. Select desired **Arrange** option:
   - **Tiled** ...................................... T
   - **Horizontal** ............................. O
   - **Vertical** .................................. V
   - **Cascade** ................................. C
4. Click OK ...................... Enter

## ORIGINAL TEMPLATE FILE

Normally, Excel opens a copy of a template file. Use this procedure to open the original template file.

1. Follows steps 1 and 2 to **OPEN A WORKBOOK FILE**, page 192.
2. Press **Shift** and
   click Open ...................... Shift + ↵

## SAVE FILE AS A TEMPLATE WITH READ-ONLY RECOMMENDATION

1. Click **File** ............................. Alt + F
2. Click **Save As** ............................ A
3. Click **Save as type** ................. Alt + T
4. Select **Template** file type ....... ↑↓ , ↵
5. Double-click in **File name** ...... Alt + N
6. Type filename ........................... *filename*
7. Click Options... ............... Alt + O
8. Click **Read-only**
   **recommended** ...................... Alt + R
9. Click OK ...................... Enter
10. Click Save ......................... ↵

## LINK WORKBOOKS USING PASTE LINK

1. Open workbooks to link.
2. Arrange workspace so both workbooks are in view.
3. Select cell(s) to reference in source workbook.
4. Click **Edit** ............................. Alt + E
5. Click **Copy** ....................................... C
6. Select cell(s) to receive reference(s) in dependent workbook.

   ✓ *If referencing more than one cell, select upper-left cell in paste cell range.*

7. Click **Edit** ............................. Alt + E
8. Click **Paste Special** ........................ S
9. Click Paste Link ...................... Alt + L

   **OR**

   Press **Escape** ................................ Esc
   to end procedure.

## Exercise 26

- ■ 3-D Formulas ■ Workbook Sheets
- ■ Duplicate Workbook Window

# NOTES

## 3-D Formulas

- ■ If you wish to summarize the data from several sheets on a summary sheet, you can create a formula that references values in any sheet or range of sheets in a workbook. These references are often called **3-D references**.

- ■ Use the following rules when writing 3-D references:

  - In a 3-D reference, exclamation points (**!**) separate a sheet name from a cell reference.

  - For example, Sheet3!A2, refers to cell A2 on Sheet 3.

  - Use quotation marks if the worksheet name contains a space – for example, "April 1997": A3.

  - Colons (**:**) between worksheet names indicate a range of worksheets. For example, Sheet3:Sheet5!A1:D1 refers to cells A1 to D1 on Sheet3 through Sheet5.

  - Functions can be combined with 3-D references to create a formula that refers to data on different sheets, as illustrated on the right. You can type the 3-D reference in a formula, or you can insert it by selecting the cells in the worksheets you wish to reference while typing or editing a formula.

  Note the illustration of formulas and 3-D references on the following page.

## Workbook Sheets

- ■ You can use the sheet tabs or the menu to **copy sheets** and the data they contain.  You should copy a sheet when you need to create multiple sheets that contain similar or identical data arrangements.

## Duplicate Workbook Window

- ■ You can create **duplicate workbook windows** of the active workbook so that you can view more than one worksheet at a time in the same workbook.  Use the Window, New Window commands to open a duplicate workbook window.

  Consider the following when working with duplicate workbook windows:

  - Excel places the new workbook window in front of the active workbook window.

  - ✓ Note:  If the active workbook is maximized, you will not be able to see the new workbook.

  - Duplicate workbook windows are indicated in the title bar, which shows the workbook name followed by a colon and a number;  for example, BOOK1**:**2.

  - Your system memory determines the number of duplicate windows you can open.

  - Closing a duplicate window will not close the workbook.

  - You can add or edit data in the original or duplicate window.

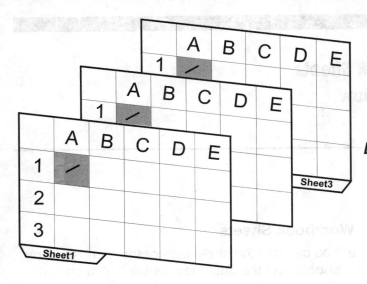

**EXAMPLE:**   *Using 3-D references to add the values in A1 in a range of sheets.*
*=SUM(**Sheet1:Sheet3!A1**) or*
*=**Sheet1!A1 + Sheet2!A2 + Sheet3!A3***

---

*In this exercise, you will recall the PAYTEMP payroll file and add a new worksheet (Totals) to it. In the new worksheet, you will enter formulas containing 3-D references to the April, May, and June worksheets. Finally, you will open a duplicate workbook window so you can view the Totals worksheet while you change test values in the April worksheet.*

---

# EXERCISE DIRECTIONS

1. Open ⌨**PAYTEMP**, or open 💾**26PAYTEM**.

2. Copy the June sheet.

3. Rename June (2) sheet; name it TOTALS.

4. Move the Totals tab to the right of June.

5. Group the April, May, and June worksheets.

6. Select April and, while worksheets are grouped, enter test values in the HOURS WORKED columns for each employee as shown:

   10  for each employee in first payroll week

   20  for each employee in second payroll week

   30  for each employee in third payroll week

7. Ungroup sheets and check that test values have been entered on each month's worksheet.

8. Select cell E7 in the TOTALS worksheet and enter a 3-D formula that adds the values in cell E7 in the April, May, and June worksheets.

   *HINT:  The completed formula should read: =April!E7+May!E7+June!E7 or =SUM(April:June!E7) and 30 (the sum of the test values) should appear in the cell.*

9. Repeat step 8 for each employee in each payroll week.

   ✓  *Note:   The formula may be copied from E7 to each employee.*

10. Open a duplicate workbook window and select the Totals worksheet in the duplicate window.

11. Arrange workbook windows so data in both workbook windows is in view.

12. Select the April worksheet in the original window and change the HOURS WORKED test values in the first payroll week to 50 for each employee.

   ✓  *Note that the Totals worksheet in the duplicate window shows updated values.*

13. Change the HOURS WORKED test values back to 10.

14. Close the duplicate workbook window.

15. Select the Totals worksheet and set it to fit on one page when printed.

16. Print the Totals worksheet.

17. Group the April, May, and June worksheets.

18. Select the April worksheet and delete all test values in HOURS WORKED.

19. Ungroup sheets and check that test values have been deleted on each month's worksheet.

20. Save **PAYTEMP** as a template file.

21. Close the workbook file.

# KEYSTROKES

## COPY SHEETS WITHIN A WORKBOOK

✓ *Excel will rename sheets that you copy.*

### Copy One Sheet by Dragging

- Press **Ctrl** and .................... `Sheet #`
  drag sheet tab you want to copy to desired sheet tab position.

  *Pointer becomes a ▨ and a black triangle indicates point of insertion.*

### Copy Multiple Sheets by Dragging

1. Select sheets to copy.

2. Press **Ctrl** and drag selected sheet tabs to desired sheet tab position.

   *Pointer becomes a ▨ and a black triangle indicates point of insertion.*

### Copy Sheets Using the Menu

1. Select sheets to copy.

2. Click **E**dit............................. `Alt`+`E`

3. Click **M**ove or Copy Sheet...... `Alt`+`M`

4. Select location to insert copied sheet in **B**efore Sheet list ... `↑↓`

5. Click **C**reate a Copy .............. `Alt`+`C`

6. Click `OK` ............................ `Enter`

## INSERT 3-D REFERENCE IN FORMULA

1. If necessary, type or edit formula.

2. Place insertion point in formula where reference will be inserted.

3. Select sheet containing cell(s) to reference.

   ✓ *When you click a sheet tab, its name appears in the formula bar.*

4. Select cell(s) to reference.

   ✓ *When you select the cell(s), the complete 3-D reference appears in the formula bar.*

### To enter a 3-D reference for a range of worksheets:

- Press **Shift** and click last worksheet tab to reference.

5. Type or insert remaining parts of formula.

6. Press **Enter** .............................. `Enter`

*When you press Enter, Excel returns to the starting worksheet.*

## TYPE A 3-D REFERENCE IN FORMULA

1. If necessary, type or edit formula.

2. Place insertion point in formula where reference will be typed.

3. Type the sheet name .............*sheetname*

   ✓ *If the sheet name contains a space, type single or double quotes before and after the sheet name.*

### To type a 3-D reference for a range of worksheets:

   a. Press **colon (:)**............................ `:`

   b. Type last sheet name ....... *sheet name* in range.

4. Press **exclamation (!)**...................... `!`

5. Type cell reference or range.....*reference*

   EXAMPLES:    Sheet1:Sheet5!A1:A5'
   'Total Sales'!A1:A5

## OPEN A DUPLICATE WORKBOOK WINDOW

Creates a new window for active workbook window.

1. Click **W**indow ........................ `Alt`+`W`

2. Click **N**ew Window ......................... `N`

## CLOSE A DUPLICATE WORKBOOK WINDOW

- Double-click workbook window control menu box........................ `✕`

**OR**

1. Select duplicate .................... `Ctrl`+`Tab` workbook.

2. Press **Alt + F4**........................ `Alt`+`F4`

**Exercise 27**

■ **Summary**

*Mr. Cooper has administered three additional exams plus a final examination to his class. He needs to revise the worksheet he prepared earlier to include new test data and two new students. In addition, Mr. Cooper's supervisor has requested a separate worksheet showing student names and final exam averages.*

# EXERCISE DIRECTIONS

✓ *Note: Freeze row labels to facilitate data entry.*

1. Open ⌨**MKTG**, or open 💾**27MKTG.**

2. Insert rows in alphabetical sequence for the following two new students: Goldstein, J., ID# 311 and Harris, M., ID# 312.

3. Insert the columns of data, as shown on the next page, for TESTS 4, 5, and 6 after the TEST 3 column.

4. Edit the formulas in the NO. TESTS TAKEN and TEST AVERAGE columns to include the new test data.

5. Create a new column after the TEST AVERAGE column and name it FINAL EXAM. Enter the exam grades below or as shown on the following page:

    Adamson, 72; Barnes, 85; Costello, 86; Dionesios, 70; Eckert, 65; Fallstaff, 91; Garcia, 71; Goldstein, 69: Hamway, 89; Harris, 71; Ianelli, 61; Jae Woo, 80; Kelly, 96

6. Create a new column after FINAL EXAM and name it FINAL AVERAGE.

7. Find the FINAL AVERAGE for each student. The final exam is worth 1/3 of the final average, while the tests are worth 2/3 of the final average.

    HINT: (FINAL EXAM+TEST AVERAGE+TEST AVERAGE)/3

8. Complete the summary data at the bottom of the workbook.

9. Format TEST AVERAGE, FINAL AVERAGE, and CLASS AVERAGE data to one decimal place.

10. Center new column titles.

11. Save the workbook file, or *save as* **MKTG.**

12. Print one copy to fit on a page.

13. Create named ranges as follows:

    Names     A1:B23

    Averages   L1:L23

14. Open a new workbook;

15. Using the Copy and Paste feature, copy the range Names to A1 in the new workbook.

16. Using the Copy and Paste Special feature, copy the range Averages to D1 in the new workbook. Paste only the values.

17. Edit the subtitle to read: MR. HARRY COOPER.

18. Format averages for one decimal place.

19. Format summary data, if necessary.

20. Save the new file; name it **MKTGSUM.**

21. Print one copy of **MKTGSUM.**

22. Close the workbook files.

Sheet1

| BUSINESS MARKETING 110 | | | | | MR. HARRY COOPER | | | | | | |
|---|---|---|---|---|---|---|---|---|---|---|---|
| EXAM GRADES | | | | | | | | | | | |
| | | | | | | | | NO. OF TESTS | TEST | FINAL | FINAL |
| ID # | STUDENT | TEST 1 | TEST 2 | TEST 3 | TEST 4 | TEST 5 | TEST 6 | TAKEN | AVERAGE | EXAM | AVERAGE |
| 300 | Adamson, M. | 78 | 96 | 80 | 75 | | 69 | | | 72 | |
| 301 | Barnes, F. | 71 | 89 | 80 | 85 | 79 | 82 | | | 85 | |
| 302 | Costello, A. | 67 | 79 | 80 | 83 | 84 | 76 | | | 86 | |
| 303 | Dionesios, A. | 88 | | 80 | 76 | 74 | 78 | | | 70 | |
| 304 | Eckert, S. | 90 | 70 | 73 | 52 | 61 | 70 | Edit formula for new tests. | | 65 | |
| 305 | Falstaff, S. | 76 | 90 | 90 | 84 | 88 | | | | 91 | |
| 306 | Garcia, H. | 84 | 91 | 76 | 72 | | 80 | | | 71 | |
| 311 | Goldstein, J | | | | 52 | 61 | 70 | | | 69 | |
| 307 | Hamway, R. | 87 | 68 | 80 | 82 | 85 | 81 | | | 89 | |
| 312 | Harris, M. | | | | 41 | 59 | 57 | | | 71 | |
| 308 | Ianelli, J. | 98 | | 70 | 72 | 76 | 79 | | | 61 | |
| 309 | Jae Woo, K. | | 80 | 70 | | 84 | 73 | | | 80 | |
| 310 | Kelly,G. | 75 | 90 | 93 | 91 | 94 | 84 | | | 96 | |
| | | | | | | | | | | | |
| NO. OF PAPERS | | 10 | 9 | 11 | | | | | | | |
| CLASS AVERAGE | | 81.4 | 83.7 | 79.3 | | | | | | | |
| HIGHEST GRADE | | 98 | 96 | 93 | | | | | | | |
| LOWEST GRADE | | 67 | 68 | 70 | | | | | | | |

27ill

## Exercise 28

■ **Insert IF Functions** ■ **Use the Paste Function Feature**

# NOTES

## Insert IF Functions

■ An **IF statement** is a logical function which sets up a condition to test data. The results of the statement depend on whether the condition is true or false.

■ The format for an IF statement is:

=IF(CONDITION,X,Y)

The condition is a True/False question.

If the condition is true, the function results in X; if the condition is false, the function results in Y.

■ For example, in this exercise, the teacher uses an IF statement to determine the student's final grade based on his or her final average. The passing grade is 65; therefore, an IF statement can be used to test whether the student's final average is greater than 64.9. If so, the student passes and the word PASS is entered in the function location. If not (if the average is not greater than 64.9), the word FAIL is entered in the function location.

✓ *Note the breakdown of one of the IF statement formulas used in this problem:*

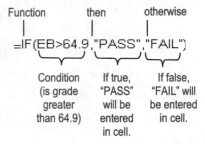

Function        then         otherwise

=IF(EB>64.9,"PASS","FAIL")

Condition       If true,     If false,
(is grade       "PASS"       "FAIL" will
greater         will be      be entered
than 64.9)      entered      in cell.
                in cell.

✓ *Note: Since PASS and FAIL are labels, you must enclose them in quotation marks (").*

■ IF statements may use the conditional operators below to state the condition:

| = | Equals | <= | Less than or equal to |
| > | Greater than | >= | Greater than or equal to |
| < | Less than | <> | Not equal to |
| & | Used for joining text | | |

✓ *Note: IF statements may be used in combination with OR, AND, and NOT statements to evaluate complex conditions.*

## Use Paste Function Feature

■ IF functions may be entered using the keyboard or by using the Paste Function feature. Press the Paste Function *fx* button to view the list of functions available in Excel. Select the IF function and complete the dialog box illustrated below. The first section is used to enter the condition or logical test. The second line is for the value or action to be done if the test is true. The third line is for the value or action to be done if the test is false. Each line has a collapse box at the end so that ranges can be selected from the workbook.

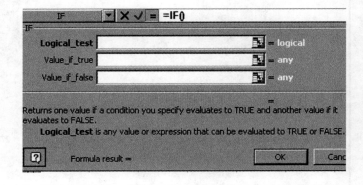

*In this exercise, you will calculate the FINAL GRADE and CREDITS GRANTED for Harry Cooper's class based on a 65% passing grade by using IF statements.*

# EXERCISE DIRECTIONS

1. Open ⌨MKTGSUM, or open 💾28MKTGSU.

2. Insert the following columns after FINAL AVERAGE, as illustrated:
FINAL      CREDITS
GRADE     GRANTED     NOTES:

3. Enter an IF statement for the first student in the FINAL GRADE column that will produce the word PASS if the final average is greater than 64.9 and FAIL if it is not.
*Hint: See notes.*

4. Copy the formula to the other students.

5. Use the Paste Function button to enter an IF statement for the first student in the CREDITS GRANTED column that will produce the number three if the final average is greater than 64.9 and zero if it is not.

*Hint:* Logical_test: D6>64.9
Value_if_true: 3
Value_if_false: 0

6. Copy the formula to the other students.

7. Center all new entries.

8. Enter an if statement in the NOTE: column to enter "Register for Marketing 120." for those who passed the course and "See Dr. Martin." for those who failed.

9. Delete the row containing NO. OF PAPERS.

10. Print one copy of the worksheet.

11. Close and save the workbook file, or *save as* **MKTGSUM**.

|  | A | B | C | D | E | F | G |
|---|---|---|---|---|---|---|---|
| 1 | BUSINESS MARKETING 110 | | | | | | |
| 2 | MR. HARRY COOPER | | | | | | |
| 3 | | | | | | | |
| 4 | | | | FINAL | *FINAL* | *CREDITS* | |
| 5 | ID # | STUDENT | | AVERAGE | *GRADE* | *GRANTED* | *NOTE:* |
| 6 | 300 | Adamson, M. | | 77.1 | | | |
| 7 | 301 | Barnes, F. | | 82.3 | | | |
| 8 | 302 | Costello, A. | | 80.8 | | | |
| 9 | 303 | Dionesios, A. | | 76.1 | | | |
| 10 | 304 | Eckert, S. | | 67.9 | | | |
| 11 | 305 | Falstaff, S. | | 87.4 | | | |
| 12 | 306 | Garcia, H. | | 77.4 | | | |
| 13 | 311 | Goldstein, J | | 63.7 | | | |
| 14 | 307 | Hamway, R. | | 83.3 | | | |
| 15 | 312 | Harris, M. | | 58.6 | | | |
| 16 | 308 | Ianelli, J. | | 73.0 | | | |
| 17 | 309 | Jae Woo, K. | | 77.8 | | | |
| 18 | 310 | Kelly,G. | | 90.6 | | | |
| 19 | | | | | | | |
| 20 | NO. OF PAPERS | | | 13 | | | |
| 21 | CLASS AVERAGE | | | 76.6 | | | |
| 22 | HIGHEST GRADE | | | 90.6 | | | |
| 23 | LOWEST GRADE | | | 58.6 | | | |
| 24 | | | | | | | |

# KEYSTROKES

### INSERT AN IF FUNCTION USING FUNCTION WIZARD

*You can also type a function to insert it.*

1. Click cell.................................... ⬍

2. Click **Function Wizard** button........... 𝑓ₓ on Standard toolbar.

3. Select **Logical**.............................. 📐 in **Function category** list.

4. Select **IF** function in ..... Alt + N , 📐 **Function name** list.

5. Click **OK** ..................................... Enter

6. Type condition........................*condition* in **Logical_test** box.

   ✓ *You can click cells in worksheet to insert cell references.*

7. Click **Value_if_true** box................. Tab

8. Type the argument ................. *argument* if condition is true.

9. Click **Value_if_false** box ............... Tab

10. Type the argument ................ *argument* if condition is false.

11. Click **OK**..................................... Enter

**Exercise**

**29**

**■ IF Function**

## NOTES

■ An IF statement may be created to perform one calculation if the condition is true and another calculation if the condition is false.

■ When creating a condition using the **greater than** operator (>), you must take care to use the correct value. In this problem, when testing if the years of seniority are more than 5, you must use >5 or >=6 in the formula so that a value of 5 is interpreted as a false condition.

---

*The Conway Manufacturing Company has decided to give salary increases based on seniority. Employees who have more than five years of service will receive a 7.25% raise; those who have fewer will receive a 4.5% raise. As a bonus, employees who have 10 or more years of service will receive an additional 1% raise.*

---

## EXERCISE DIRECTIONS

1. Create the worksheet on the next page exactly as shown, or open 🖫**29SALARY**.

2. Using YEARS OF SENIORITY as a condition, create an IF statement to enter the percent of the raise in the % INCREASE column.

   Employees who have worked more than 5 years get a 7.25% raise, while others get a 4.5% raise.

   *HINT:  Enter 7.25% and 4.5% as labels using quotes in the IF statement. Use either >5 or >=6 as the condition.*

3. Enter a formula to find the 1998 RAISE by multiplying the SALARY 1997 by the % INCREASE.

4. Using YEARS OF SENIORITY as a condition, create an IF statement to calculate a 1% bonus on SALARY for employees who have worked for 10 years or more, and no bonus for those who do not meet the condition.

5. Enter a formula to calculate SALARY 1998 by including SALARY 1997, RAISE 1998, and SENIORITY BONUS.

6. Format all money columns for commas with two decimal places and all percent columns for two-place percents.

7. Copy the formulas to the remaining employees.

8. Total all money columns.

9. Set column widths, as necessary.

10. Save the file; name it **SALARY**.

11. Print one copy to fit on a page.

12. Close the file.

|   | A | B | C | D | E | F | G | H |
|---|---|---|---|---|---|---|---|---|
| 1 | | | | CONWAY MANUFACTURING COMPANY | | | | |
| 2 | | | | ANALYSIS OF SALARY INCREASES | | | | |
| 3 | | | | | | | | |
| 4 | | | | | | | | |
| 5 | | | YEARS OF | SALARY | % | RAISE | SENIORITY | SALARY |
| 6 | EMPLOYEE | | SENIORITY | 1997 | INCREASE | 1998 | BONUS | 1998 |
| 7 | | | | | | | | |
| 8 | Miller, John | | 16 | 49000.00 | | | | |
| 9 | Vantnor, Link | | 11 | 35000.00 | | | | |
| 10 | Barrow, Wilson | | 5 | 17500.00 | | | | |
| 11 | Abrahams, Larry | | 3 | 20000.00 | | | | |
| 12 | Nunex, Maria | | 15 | 23000.00 | | | | |
| 13 | Tse, Sandra | | 4 | 27000.00 | | | | |
| 14 | D'Agostino, Joe | | 8 | 30000.00 | | | | |
| 15 | Harrison, Reggie | | 9 | 35000.00 | | | | |
| 16 | Wingate, George | | 2 | 27000.00 | | | | |
| 17 | Ingold, Terry | | 10 | 41500.00 | | | | |
| 18 | | | | | | | | |
| 19 | TOTALS | | | | | | | |

# KEYSTROKES

## INSERT AN IF FUNCTION USING FUNCTION WIZARD

*You can also type a function to insert it.*

1. Click cell..................................... 〔↗↓〕

2. Click **Function Wizard** button.......... 〔*f*ₓ〕
   on Standard toolbar.

3. Select Logical............................... 〔↗↓〕
   in **Function category** list.

4. Select **IF** function in...... 〔Alt〕+〔N〕, 〔↗↓〕
   **Function name** list.

5. Click 〔Next >〕 ............................ 〔↵〕

6. Type condition .........................*condition*
   in **logical_test** box.

   ✓ *You can click cells in worksheet to insert cell references.*

7. Click **Value_if_true** box................. 〔Tab〕

8. Type the argument .................*argument*
   if condition is true.

9. Click perform **Value_if_false** box .. 〔Tab〕

10. Type the argument .................*argument*
    if condition is false.

11. Click 〔Finish〕 ......................... 〔Enter〕

**Exercise**
# 30

■ **Enter a Date as Numerical Data** ■ **Format Numerical Dates**
■ **AutoFormat** ■ **Color Buttons**

## NOTES

### Enter Date as Numerical Data

■ Excel recognizes the number format you desire based on how you enter data. For example, if you enter 25%, the entry is recognized as a value with a percent format. Similarly, if you enter 12/24/96 without a label prefix, the entry is recognized as numerical data in date format.

■ Dates can be entered as label data (with a label prefix), but when there is a need to add or subtract dates, they must be entered as numerical data (without a label prefix). Dates entered in one of the standard formats are automatically recognized as dates and assigned a **serial value**. The serial value is the number of days the date represents counting from January 1, 1900. Thus, 1/1/1900 is given a serial value of 1 and 3/28/1905 is given a serial value of 1914. This system allows you to add or subtract dates and obtain the correct value. See the examples at the bottom of this page.

### Format Numerical Dates

■ Illustrated below are a number of standard date formats that Excel recognizes as numerical date values. Notice that the format represents the way the date looks and is entered. The formula bar entry is the full date that appears on the formula bar after you make the entry. If you enter 00 as a year, the software will assume that you mean the year 2000. The serial values are the

values assigned to the date for mathematical purposes and represent the number of days the date is from January 1, 1900. To view the serial value for a date, you can format the date as a number.

■ Once you enter a date as a numerical value, you may change the date format by using the Format, Cells, Number commands.

### AutoFormat

■ Excel provides built-in formats which can be applied to a range of data. These formats, called **AutoFormats**, include number formats, fonts, borders, patterns, colors, alignments, row heights, and column widths. They give the worksheet a professional, organized appearance.

■ The AutoFormat dialog box provides a selection of table formats that may be applied to a range of data. (*See the illustration on the following page.*) Any of the AutoFormats may be customized through the Options dialog box.

| Formats: | Example Entries | Formula Bar: | Serial values: |
|---|---|---|---|
| mm/d/yy | 12/24/00 | 12/24/1900 | 359 |
| d-mmm-yy | 12/24/00 | 12/24/2000 | 36884 |
| d-mmm | 25-Jul | 07/25/1997 | 35636 |
| mmm-yy | Jul-97 | 07/25/1997 | 35636 |
| mm/d/yy hh:mm | 12/24/00 6:30 | 12/24/2000 6:30 AM | 36884 |

## Color Buttons

- The Color buttons on the Formatting toolbar provide a palette of colors that can be used to set the Fill Color or the Font Color in a selected cell. (See the illustration on the right.)

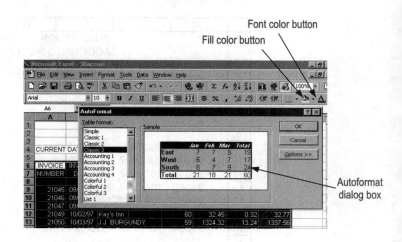

Font color button
Fill color button
Autoformat dialog box

---

*Accounts Receivable are records for customers who owe money to a company. Aging of accounts receivable is done to determine how many days the customers' payments are overdue.*

*In this exercise, your supervisor has asked you to determine how many days, as of today (December 1, 1997), the accounts receivable invoices have been unpaid. In addition, she wants you to calculate a late fee of 1% on unpaid amounts that are outstanding for more than 30 days.*

# EXERCISE DIRECTIONS

1. Create the worksheet on the following page, or open 🖫**30ACCREC**.

   ✓ *Note: Enter the dates in the format illustrated.*

2. Find the DAYS UNPAID and format for numbers.

   *HINT: DAYS UNPAID = CURRENT DATE-INVOICE DATE*

   ✓ *Note: The reference to the current date should be an absolute reference.*

3. Use an IF statement to find a 1% LATE FEE *only* if the days unpaid are greater than 30. Otherwise, enter 0 in the LATE FEE column.

4. Format for two decimal places.

5. Copy the formula to the remaining invoices.

6. Find AMOUNT DUE and copy to all invoices.

7. Total all money columns and format totals for two decimal places.

8. Select the range A6 to H21 and choose the Classic 3 table format in the AutoFormat dialog box.

   ✓ *Note: As you highlight each table format, an example of the style appears in the Sample box.*

9. Select the heading range A1 to H4 and do the following:

   - Format the text for bold type.
   - Change the background color to dark blue.
   - Change the text color to white.

10. Save the file; name it **ACCREC**.

11. Print one copy so that it all fits on one page.

12. Close the workbook file.

|    | A | B | C | D | E | F | G | H |
|----|---|---|---|---|---|---|---|---|
| 1  |   |   | KITCHEN KING STORES | | | | | |
| 2  |   |   | ACCOUNTS RECEIVABLE AGING REPORT | | | | | |
| 3  |   |   | | | | | | |
| 4  | CURRENT DATE: | | 12/01/97 | | | | | |
| 5  |   |   | | | | | | |
| 6  | INVOICE | INVOICE | | | DAYS | | | AMOUNT |
| 7  | NUMBER | DATE | CUSTOMER | | UNPAID | AMOUNT | LATE FEE | DUE |
| 8  |   |   | | | | | | |
| 9  | 21045 | 09/22/97 | Martha Schef | | | 475.43 | | |
| 10 | 21046 | 09/23/97 | Red's Restaurant | | | 321.43 | | |
| 11 | 21047 | 09/24/97 | Martha Schef | | | 543.98 | | |
| 12 | 21049 | 10/02/97 | Kay's Inn | | | 32.45 | | |
| 13 | 21050 | 10/03/97 | Marvin Diamant | | | 1324.32 | | |
| 14 | 21052 | 10/06/97 | Red's Restaurant | | | 124.98 | | |
| 15 | 21054 | 10/15/97 | George Lopez | | | 564.12 | | |
| 16 | 21056 | 10/18/97 | Kay's Inn | | | 187.65 | | |
| 17 | 21062 | 10/28/97 | Marvin Diamant | | | 454.56 | | |
| 18 | 21079 | 11/05/97 | Sam Hopkins | | | 308.21 | | |
| 19 | 21087 | 11/20/97 | Red's Restaurant | | | 163.28 | | |
| 20 |   |   | | | | | | |
| 21 | TOTALS | | | | | | | |
| 22 |   |   | | | | | | |

# KEYSTROKES

## ENTER DATE AS NUMERICAL DATA

✓ *Dates entered as numerical data are right-aligned and can be calculated.*

1. Select cell to receive date.

**To enter current date:**

- Press **Ctrl + ;**
  (semicolon) ........................ `Ctrl` + `;`

**To enter a specific date:**

- Type date ................................... *date*
  in valid format.

  *You may use the following formats:*

- **m/d/yy** ........................ (e.g. 6/24/96)
- **d-mmm** .......................... (e.g. 24-Jun)
- **d-mmm-yy** .............. (e.g. 24-Jun-96)
- **mmm-yy** ...................... (e.g. Jun-96)

2. Press **Enter** ................................ `Enter`

✓ *If Excel displays number signs (######), the column is not wide enough to display the date.  To see the entry, double-click the right border of the column heading.*

## FORMAT NUMERICAL DATES

1. Select cells containing numerical dates to format.

2. a.  Click **Format** ...................... `Alt`+`O`
   b.  Click **Cells** .................................. `E`
   **OR**
   a.  Right-click any selected cell.
   b.  Click **Format Cells** ...................... `F`

3. Select **Number** tab ................ `Ctrl`+`Tab`

4. Select date ................... `Alt`+`C`, `↑↓`
   in **Category** list.

5. Select desired format... `Alt`+`T`, `↑↓`
   in **Type** list:

   - **m/d/yy**
   - **d-mmm-yy**
   - **d-mmm**
   - **mmm-yy**
   - **mm/d/yy h:mm**

6. Click `OK` .......................... `Enter`

## APPLY AUTOFORMAT

1. Select range of data to be formatted.

2. Click **Format** ......................... `Alt`+`O`

3. Click **AutoFormat** ...................... `A`

4. Select desired **Table format** .......... `↑↓`

5. Click `OK` ................... `Enter`

## APPLY COLOR TO CELL FOREGROUND

1. Select object or range of cells.

2. Click on Fill Color Button arrow.

3. Select color.............................
**OR**
1. Select object or range of cells.

2. Click **Format** ........................ `Alt`+`O`

3. Click **Cells** .................................. `E`

4. Select **Patterns** tab .............. `Ctrl`+`Tab`

5. Click **Color** ........................ `Alt`+`C`

6. Select color.

7. Click `OK` ........................... `Enter`

## APPLY COLOR TO TEXT

1. Select range of data.

2. Click on Font Color......................
   Button arrow

3. Select color.
**OR**
1. Select object or range of cells.

2. Click **Format** ........................ `Alt`+`O`

3. Click **Cells** .................................. `E`

4. Select **Font** tab ..................... `Ctrl`+`Tab`

5. Click **Color** ........................ `Alt`+`C`

6. Select color.

7. Click `OK` ........................... `Enter`

**Exercise**

# 31

## ■ What-If Data Tables ■ Payment Function

## NOTES

### What-If Data Tables

■ A **What-if worksheet** is used to answer a question based on one or more factors that might influence the outcome.

■ You can create a **data table** (what-if table) to evaluate a series of possible answers for values you supply in the first row and left-most column of the table. These values are called **substitution values**.

■ The data table created in a what-if problem may be used to evaluate different situations based on certain variables and to find the best solution.

■ For example, if you wanted to purchase a home and could only afford to spend $1,000 per month on your mortgage payment, you might want to determine the maximum mortgage amount you can afford to borrow and the number of loan payment years for which you should apply. A data table should be created showing the mortgage payments for various loan amounts and loan payment periods. Then you could determine what you could afford.

■ When you use the Data, Table commands, Excel uses the formula in the upper-left corner of the table to calculate the substitution values. Data tables that require two sets of substitution values (a row and a column) are called **two-input data tables**. The input cells data are placed at the bottom of the table and are the first row data item and the first column data item. Note the illustration below:

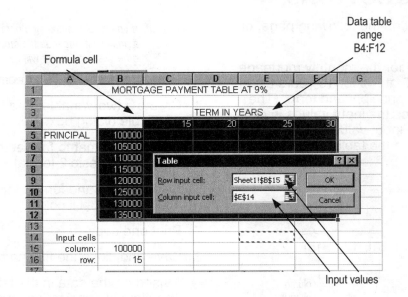

■ The format of a two-input data table must meet the following criteria:

• The **column and row input values** that the formula will refer to must be outside the table.

• The **formula** must be in the top-left cell of the table range and must refer to the column and row input values.

• The **substitution values** for the table must be arranged in the first row and column of the table as shown in the illustration on the following page.

■ To create the table values, you will select the data table range (which includes the formula), then indicate the row and column input cells (the cells that contain the column and row input values) from the Table dialog box.

### Payment Function

■ The **PMT** (payment) **function** can be applied to calculate a loan payment amount using principal, interest rate, and number of payment periods. The PMT function uses the following format and contains three parts, which are defined on the right.

The arguments for the PMT function are:

| | |
|---|---|
| **=PMT** | (rate,nper,pv) |
| **rate** | Interest rate per period (for example, interest/12). |
| **nper** | Number of payment periods (for example, term*12). |
| **pv** | Present value – total amount that a series of future payments is worth now (for example, the principal). |

✓ Note:  The rate and the number of payment periods (nper) must be expressed in the same manner.  For example, if you wish to calculate a _monthly_ payment at a 9% rate of interest for 25 years, both the interest and time are expressed in years.  You must, therefore, enter .09/12 as the rate to determine a monthly rate and enter 25*12 to get the number of monthly payment periods (nper) per year.

In this exercise, you will create a mortgage payment table to determine payment amounts at 9% for various principal amounts and for various numbers of years.

## EXERCISE DIRECTIONS

1. Create the worksheet on the following page, or open ⊟**31PAYMEN**.

2. Enter a formula in B4 for the monthly mortgage payment for $100,000 at 9% for 15 years using the input cell data for principal and term. (The formula must reference the input values in cells B15 and B16.  These input values will not affect the computed values in the table when it is generated.)

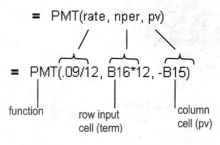

= PMT(rate, nper, pv)

= PMT(.09/12, B16*12, -B15)

function    row input    column
            cell (term)  cell (pv)

HINT:    =PMT (rate, nper, pv)

✓ Note: If you type a minus sign before the principal, Excel finds a positive number as the monthly mortgage payment; otherwise, the result will be a negative number.

3. Format answer for two decimal places.

4. Create a two-variable data table by completing the Table dialog box.

5. Use AutoFormat to format the range A4:F12 range for Classic 2 format.

6. Select A1:F3 and format for Bold, Dark Blue font and Gray-25% fill color.

7. Print one copy.

8. Save and close the file; name it **PAYMENT**.

❷ Based on the data in the table, what would be the highest principal you could borrow with a payment of approximately $1000 a month?

Formula location

| | A | B | C | D | E | F |
|---|---|---|---|---|---|---|
| 1 | MORTGAGE PAYMENT TABLE AT 9% | | | | | |
| 2 | | | | | | |
| 3 | | | | TERM IN YEARS | | |
| 4 | | | 15 | 20 | 25 | 30 |
| 5 | PRINCIPAL | 100000 | | | | |
| 6 | | 105000 | | | | |
| 7 | | 110000 | | | | |
| 8 | | 115000 | | | | |
| 9 | | 120000 | | | | |
| 10 | | 125000 | | | | |
| 11 | | 130000 | | | | |
| 12 | | 135000 | | | | |
| 13 | | | | | | |
| 14 | Input cells | | | | | |
| 15 | column: | 100000 | | | | |
| 16 | row: | 15 | | | | |

Row substitution values

Column substitution values

Data table range B4:F12

# KEYSTROKES

## TWO-INPUT DATA TABLES (WHAT-IF TABLES)

Data tables generate values that change based on one or two values in a formula. For example, a two-input table displays the result of changing two values in a formula.

The row input cell is used to indicate an initial input value that the formula will reference.

The column input cell is used to indicate an initial input value that the formula will also reference.

✓ *Because Excel uses a table function to generate answers for each pair of substitution values, you cannot edit or delete any single value in the answer set. You can, however, delete all the answers in the generated data table.*

*Although instructions listed below are for a two-input data table, you could also create a one-input data table that would find answers for a single row or column of substitution values.*

### CREATE A TWO-INPUT DATA TABLE

1. Enter initial value........................*number* in row input cell.

2. Enter initial value........................*number* in column input cell.

3. Enter series of substitution ......*numbers* values in a column.

4. Enter series of substitution.......*numbers* values in a row.

   ✓ *The first value in row and column will contain a single formula.*

5. Click upper-left cell........................ 🔀 in table.

6. Type formula ............................ *formula*

   ✓ *Formula must refer to row and column input cells.*

7. Select all cells in data table range.

   ✓ *Select cells containing formula and substitution values and cells where results will be displayed.*

8. Click **Data**............................ Alt + D

9. Click **Table** ............................ T

10. Click row input cell in worksheet.
    **OR**
    Type reference ........................*reference* of input cell in **Row input cell** text box.

11. Click **Column input cell**: ........ Alt + C

12. Click column input cell in worksheet.
    **OR**
    Type reference........................*reference* of column input cell.

13. Click OK ............................ Enter

## USE THE PMT FUNCTION

Applies the PMT function to find the monthly payment for a principal amount for a specific number of years.

1. Click cell ........................................ 🔀 where answer should appear.

2. Press **Equal** .................................... =

3. Type *PMT*........................... P M T

4. Press **(** (open parenthesis) .............. (

5. Type rate */12* ...............*rate* / 1 2

   ✓ *The rate is a percentage. You can type the percentage or type the cell reference containing the percentage.*

6. Press **,** (comma) ........................... ,

7. Type term *\*12* ............ *term* \* 1 2

   ✓ *The term is the number of years. You can type the number or type the cell reference containing the number.*

8. Press **,** (comma) ........................... ,

9. Type principal .........................*principal*

   ✓ *The principal is the amount of the loan. You can type the amount or type the cell reference containing the amount. If you want the answer expressed as a positive number, type a minus sign before the principal.*

10. Press **)** (close parenthesis).............. )
    EXAMPLES
    =PMT(.06/12,20*12,-100000)
    =PMT(A1/12,A2*12,-A3)

11. Press **Enter** .............................. Enter

## Exercise 32

# ■ Insert Lookup Functions

## NOTES

- The **lookup functions** (VLOOKUP and HLOOKUP) select a value from a table and enter it into a location on the worksheet. For example, the VLOOKUP function may be used to look up taxes on a tax table to create a payroll or to look up postage rates to complete a bill of sale.

- The table containing the data to be looked up must be created in a blank or empty location on the worksheet. The mortgage payment table below, created in Exercise 31, may be used for a lookup function Table.

| | A | B | C | D | E | F | G | H |
|---|---|---|---|---|---|---|---|---|
| 1 | | MORTGAGE PAYMENT TABLE AT 9% | | | | | | |
| 2 | | | | | | | | |
| 3 | | | | TERM IN YEARS | | | | |
| 4 | | 1014.27 | 15 | 20 | 25 | 30 | | |
| 5 | PRINCIPAL | 100000 | 1014.27 | 899.73 | 839.20 | 804.62 | | |
| 6 | | 105000 | 1064.98 | 944.71 | 881.16 | 844.85 | | |
| 7 | | 110000 | 1115.69 | 989.70 | 923.12 | 885.08 | | |
| 8 | | 115000 | 1166.41 | 1034.68 | 965.08 | 925.32 | | |
| 9 | | 120000 | 1217.12 | 1079.67 | 1007.04 | 965.55 | | |
| 10 | | 125000 | 1267.83 | 1124.66 | 1049.00 | 1005.78 | | |
| 11 | | 130000 | 1318.55 | 1169.64 | 1090.96 | 1046.01 | | |
| 12 | | 135000 | 1369.26 | 1214.63 | 1132.92 | 1086.24 | | |
| 13 | | 1 | 2 | 3 | 4 | 5 | | |
| 14 | input cells | | | | | | | |
| 15 | column: | 100000 | | | | | | |
| 16 | row: | 15 | | | | | | |

*table range B5:F12* (pointing to F5)

*column positions* (pointing to row 13)

- The lookup function is entered in the location on the worksheet that requires data from a table. (*Note the illustration at the end of this exercise.*)

- There are two ways to look up data, depending on the way the data is arranged: **vertically** or **horizontally**.

  - **VLOOKUP** (vertical lookup) looks up data in a particular *column* in the table, while

  - **HLOOKUP** (horizontal lookup) looks up data in a particular *row* in the table.

- The VLOOKUP function uses the following format and contains three arguments (parts), defined below and on the following page:

  **=VLOOKUP(item,table-range,column-position)**

  - **ITEM** is text, a value, or the cell reference of the item you are looking for (search item) and should be in the first column of the VLOOKUP table. Numerical search items should be listed in ascending order.

  - **TABLE-RANGE (ARRAY)** is the range reference or range name of the lookup table in which the search is to be made. If the lookup function is to be copied, the range should be expressed as an absolute reference.

  - **COLUMN-INDEX-NUMBER** is the column number in the table from which the matching value should be returned. The far left column has a position number of one; the second column has a position number of two, etc.

    ✓ *Note:*   *Column numbers are counted from the left column in the range, not from the left column of the worksheet.*

- For example, note the outlined lookup table on this page. To look up the mortgage payment for a mortgage amount of $105,000 for 25 years at 9%, a lookup formula would be created as follows:

  Item  Table range  Column position

  **=VLOOKUP(105000,B5:F12,4)**

- When looking up numeric data, the lookup function returns to the formula location: The value from the table (in this case 881.16) or the largest value that is less than or equal to the search item.

- If you need to look up more than one item and need to copy the lookup formula, the formula should use the cell reference (not the value) as the search item. In addition, the range should be absolute so the table range remains constant.

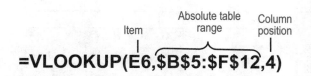

=VLOOKUP(E6,$B$5:$F$12,4)

*In this exercise, you will retrieve the mortgage table created earlier and create a worksheet for the DREAM HOME MORTGAGE CO. to calculate the mortgage amount and the customer's monthly mortgage payment for 25 or 30 years. Use the VLOOKUP function to enter mortgage payments depending upon the mortgage amount.*

# EXERCISE DIRECTIONS

1. Open ⌨PAYMENT, or open 💾32PAYMENT.

   *REMINDER:  The values in cells B4, B15, and B16 are needed to compute the values in the table. Do not delete or change these values.*

2. Create the DREAM HOME MORTGAGE CO. worksheet below the MORTGAGE PAYMENT TABLE, as indicated.

3. Center all column titles.

4. Find MORTGAGE AMOUNT by subtracting the DOWN PAYMENT from the CONTRACT PRICE.

5. Copy the formula to the remaining customers.

6. Using the VLOOKUP function, find the monthly payment for the first customer (for 25 years) based on the amount to be mortgaged.

   ✓ *Note the outlined range and column position which have been illustrated. Use an absolute reference for the table range.*

7. Copy the formula to the remaining customers.

8. Using the VLOOKUP function, find the monthly payment for the first customer (for 30 years) based on the amount to be mortgaged.

   ✓ *Note the range and column position illustrated. Use an absolute reference for the table range.*

9. Copy the formula to the remaining customers.

10. Format all numeric data in the bottom worksheet for commas and two decimals.

11. Adjust column width, as necessary.

12. AutoFormat the bottom portion of the worksheet, range A19:H27, using the Classic 2 format.

13. Format the title for Gray-25% fill color, bold with a Violet font.

14. Save the workbook file; name it **DREAM**.

15. Print one copy of the bottom portion of the worksheet to fit on one page.

16. Close the workbook file.

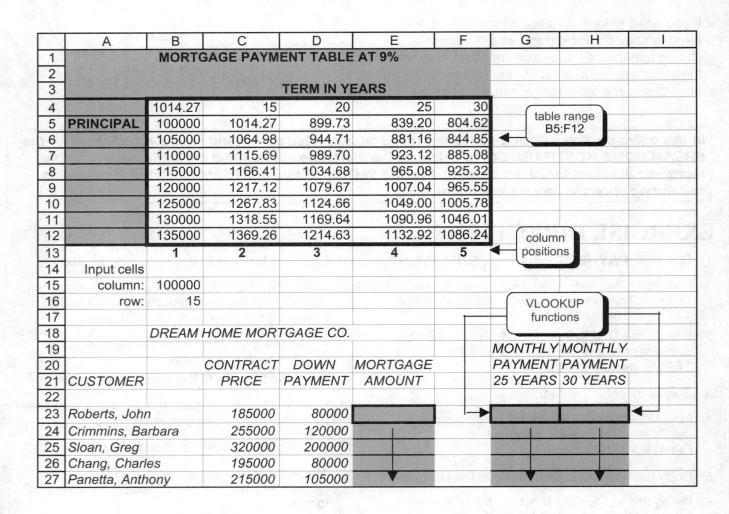

| | A | B | C | D | E | F | G | H | I |
|---|---|---|---|---|---|---|---|---|---|
| 1 | | **MORTGAGE PAYMENT TABLE AT 9%** | | | | | | | |
| 2 | | | | | | | | | |
| 3 | | | | **TERM IN YEARS** | | | | | |
| 4 | | 1014.27 | 15 | 20 | 25 | 30 | | | |
| 5 | **PRINCIPAL** | 100000 | 1014.27 | 899.73 | 839.20 | 804.62 | | | |
| 6 | | 105000 | 1064.98 | 944.71 | 881.16 | 844.85 | | | |
| 7 | | 110000 | 1115.69 | 989.70 | 923.12 | 885.08 | | | |
| 8 | | 115000 | 1166.41 | 1034.68 | 965.08 | 925.32 | | | |
| 9 | | 120000 | 1217.12 | 1079.67 | 1007.04 | 965.55 | | | |
| 10 | | 125000 | 1267.83 | 1124.66 | 1049.00 | 1005.78 | | | |
| 11 | | 130000 | 1318.55 | 1169.64 | 1090.96 | 1046.01 | | | |
| 12 | | 135000 | 1369.26 | 1214.63 | 1132.92 | 1086.24 | | | |
| 13 | | 1 | 2 | 3 | 4 | 5 | | | |
| 14 | Input cells | | | | | | | | |
| 15 | column: | 100000 | | | | | | | |
| 16 | row: | 15 | | | | | | | |
| 17 | | | | | | | | | |
| 18 | | *DREAM HOME MORTGAGE CO.* | | | | | | | |
| 19 | | | | | | | *MONTHLY* | *MONTHLY* | |
| 20 | | | *CONTRACT* | *DOWN* | *MORTGAGE* | | *PAYMENT* | *PAYMENT* | |
| 21 | *CUSTOMER* | | *PRICE* | *PAYMENT* | *AMOUNT* | | *25 YEARS* | *30 YEARS* | |
| 22 | | | | | | | | | |
| 23 | *Roberts, John* | | 185000 | 80000 | | | | | |
| 24 | *Crimmins, Barbara* | | 255000 | 120000 | | | | | |
| 25 | *Sloan, Greg* | | 320000 | 200000 | | | | | |
| 26 | *Chang, Charles* | | 195000 | 80000 | | | | | |
| 27 | *Panetta, Anthony* | | 215000 | 105000 | | | | | |

Callouts: table range B5:F12; column positions; VLOOKUP functions

# KEYSTROKES

### INSERT A VLOOKUP OR HLOOKUP FUNCTION USING PASTE FUNCTION

✓ *You can also type a function to insert it.*

1. Click cell ........................................ 🔁
   to receive function.

2. Click **Paste Function** button ............. *fx*
   on Standard toolbar.

3. Select **Lookup & Reference** .......... 🔼
   in **Function category** list.

4. Select **VLOOKUP** .......... Alt + N , 🔼
   or **HLOOKUP** in **Function name** list.

5. Click [ OK ] ........................... Enter

6. Type item ........................................ *item*
   in **Lookup_value** box.

   ✓ *Item can be an actual column item or a reference to a cell containing the column item. You can click a cell in the worksheet to insert the cell reference.*

7. Click **Table_array** box .................... Tab

8. Type reference ........................ *reference*
   to table range.

   ✓ *You can select range in worksheet to insert cell references.*

9. Click **Row** or **Col_index_num** box ... Tab

10. Type the row or
    column position ........................ *number*

11. Click [ OK ] ........................... Enter

**Exercise 33**

■ **Protect a Sheet** ■ **Lock Cells in a Worksheet**

## NOTES

■ In Exercise 32, you created lookup formulas using the cell references of the table range. It is possible to use a named range rather than the cell reference of the table. When you copy a formula containing a named range, the reference will not change (that is, it will always refer to the original table location).

### Protect a Sheet, Lock Cells

■ It is possible to protect, or lock, an entire workbook, a worksheet, individual cells, or a range of cells from accidental changes or unauthorized use. The protection feature locks the cells so that they cannot be changed.

■ All cells in a workbook are in a locked status as the default setting. The locked status, however, only becomes effective when protection is put on the workbook. Therefore, if you wish to keep certain cells accessible in a protected worksheet, these cells must be unlocked before the worksheet is protected. To lock or unlock cells in a worksheet, use the Format, Cells commands and the Protection tab.

■ A worksheet is protected using the Tools, Protection, Protect Sheet commands. The Protect Sheet dialog box, illustrated below, allows you to protect the contents, objects (graphic objects), or scenarios (defined variations for the worksheet), and to set a password.

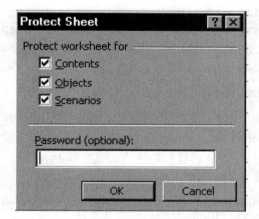

■ When a worksheet is protected, the message "Locked cells cannot be changed" will appear when you try to change the contents of protected cells.

*IMPORTANT:* *If you set a password when protecting a worksheet and you forget the password, you will not be able to make changes to the worksheet.*

*In this exercise, Kitchen King Stores is updating its accounts receivable aging report as of 2/1/98. Paid invoices will be deleted from this new report, while new outstanding invoices will be added.*

*In addition, Kitchen King has changed its late fee policy. It will now determine late fees based on the number of days the account is unpaid. Using Lookup, you will determine the late fee to charge.*

# EXERCISE DIRECTIONS

1. Open ⌨**ACCREC**, or open 💾**33ACCREC**.

2. Delete rows for invoices marked on the illustration.

3. Delete column D.

4. Insert rows below remaining invoices and enter the following new invoices.

   | | | | |
   |---|---|---|---|
   | 21093 | 12/10/97 | Carl Clinton. | 169.42 |
   | 21106 | 12/16/97 | Kay's Inn. | 396.16 |
   | 21142 | 12/29/97 | Red's Restaurant | 84.96 |
   | 21179 | 01/04/98 | Andrea Billela | 1490.14 |
   | 21205 | 01/10/98 | George Lopez | 354.75 |
   | 21246 | 01/25/98 | Kay's Inn | 742.15 |

5. Change the CURRENT DATE to 2/1/98.

6. Copy the Days Unpaid formula for the new invoices.

7. Create the LATE FEE TABLE below the worksheet.

8. Name the LATE FEE TABLE range, containing days and interest values, LATETABLE.

9. Insert a column between AMOUNT and LATE FEE, and enter the label INTEREST RATE.

10. Delete only the values in the LATE FEE and AMOUNT DUE columns.

11. Format INTEREST RATE column for three decimal places.

12. Protect the LATE FEE TABLE:
    - Unlock all cells in entire worksheet.
    - Select cells in LATE FEE TABLE and lock them.
    - Turn worksheet protection on.

13. Using VLOOKUP, find INTEREST RATE (based on the days unpaid).

14. Copy the function to the remaining items.
    - ✓ *If you did not use the LATETABLE range name in the function, you must set the table range to absolute before copying.*

15. Find:
    - LATE FEE
    - AMOUNT DUE

15. Copy formulas to the remaining items.

16. Format all remaining money columns for two decimal places.

17. Center column titles.

18. Edit the TOTAL formulas.

19. Disable worksheet protection.

20. Change the interest rate for one unpaid day to be 0.005.

21. Protect the worksheet.

22. Print one copy of the top portion of the worksheet.

23. Close and save the workbook file, or save as **ACCREC**.

## KITCHEN KING STORES
## ACCOUNTS RECEIVABLE AGING REPORT

Insert INTEREST RATE column

CURRENT DATE:          ~~12/01/97~~ 2/1/98

| INVOICE NUMBER | INVOICE DATE | CUSTOMER | DAYS UNPAID | AMOUNT | LATE FEE | AMOUNT DUE |
|---|---|---|---|---|---|---|
| 21045 | 09/22/97 | Martha Schef | 70 | 475.43 | 4.75 | 480.18 |
| ~~21046~~ | ~~09/23/97~~ | ~~Red's Restaurant~~ | ~~69~~ | ~~321.43~~ | ~~3.21~~ | ~~324.64~~ |
| ~~21047~~ | ~~09/24/97~~ | ~~Martha Schef~~ | ~~68~~ | ~~543.98~~ | ~~5.44~~ | ~~549.42~~ |
| ~~21049~~ | ~~10/02/97~~ | ~~Kay's Inn~~ | ~~60~~ | ~~32.45~~ | ~~0.32~~ | ~~32.77~~ |
| ~~21050~~ | ~~10/03/97~~ | ~~Marvin Diamant~~ | ~~59~~ | ~~1324.32~~ | ~~13.24~~ | ~~1337.56~~ |
| ~~21052~~ | ~~10/06/97~~ | ~~Red's Restaurant~~ | ~~56~~ | ~~124.98~~ | ~~1.25~~ | ~~126.23~~ |
| ~~21054~~ | ~~10/15/97~~ | ~~George Lopez~~ | ~~47~~ | ~~564.12~~ | ~~5.64~~ | ~~569.76~~ |
| 21056 | 10/18/97 | Kay's Inn | 44 | 187.65 | 1.88 | 189.53 |
| ~~21062~~ | ~~10/28/97~~ | ~~Marvin Diamant~~ | ~~34~~ | ~~454.56~~ | ~~4.55~~ | ~~459.11~~ |
| 21079 | 11/05/97 | Sam Hopkins | 26 | 308.21 | 0.00 | 308.21 |
| 21087 | 11/20/97 | Red's Restaurant | 11 | 163.28 | 0.00 | 163.28 |
| **TOTALS** | | | | 4500.41 | 40.29 | 4540.70 |

LATE FEE TABLE

| UNPAID DAYS | INTEREST |
|---|---|
| 1 | 0.000 |
| 30 | 0.010 |
| 60 | 0.015 |
| 90 | 0.020 |
| 120 | 0.025 |
| 150 | 0.030 |

Name range LATETABLE

# KEYSTROKES

## PROTECT A SHEET

Prevents changes to locked cells, graphic objects, embedded charts in a worksheet or chart items in a chart sheet.

1. Lock or unlock cells as desired.

   ✓ By default, all cells and objects in a worksheet are locked.

2. Click **Tools** .......................... `Alt` + `T`

3. Click **Protection** .................... `Alt` + `P`

4. Click **Protect Sheet**... ................ `P`

**To password protect sheet:**

- Type password ....................password in Password (optional) text box.

**To protect cell contents and chart items:**

- Click **Contents** .................. `Alt` + `C`

**To protect graphic objects:**

- Click **Objects** ...................... `Alt` + `O`

**To protect scenarios:**

- Click **Scenarios** ................. `Alt` + `S`

5. Click | OK | .......................... `Enter`

**If a password was typed:**

   a. Retype password ............... password in text box.

   b. Click | OK | ........................ `Enter`

## UNPROTECT A SHEET

1. Click **Tools** .......................... `Alt` + `T`

2. Click **Protection** .................... `P`

3. Click **Unprotect Sheet**... .................. `P`

**If sheet is password protected:**

   a. Type password ................... password in Password text box.

   b. Click | OK | ........................ `Enter`

## LOCK/UNLOCK CELLS IN A WORKSHEET

Locks or unlocks specific cells. By default, all cells in a worksheet are locked.

Locking takes effect when a worksheet is protected.

1. If necessary, unprotect worksheet.

   ✓ You cannot lock or unlock cells if the worksheet is protected.

2. Select cell(s) to unlock or lock.

3. Click **Format** .......................... `Alt` + `O`

4. Click **Cells**... ..................................... `E`

   ✓ Press Ctrl + 1 to access Format options quickly.

5. Select **Protection** tab ............. `Ctrl` + `Tab`

6. Deselect or select **Locked** ...... `Alt` + `L`

   ✓ A gray check box indicates the current cell selection contains mixed (locked/unlocked) settings.

7. Click | OK | .......................... `Enter`

8. Repeat steps for each cell or object to lock or unlock.

9. Protect worksheet to enable locking.

## Exercise 34

■ **Summary**

*A national distributor of paper goods pays its sales personnel a commission on their total sales. To provide an extra incentive for the sales staff to be more productive, the company has adopted a graduated commission scale.  The more a person sells, the higher the commission percentage. Note the table on the following page.  Only those salespeople in Category 2 receive a flat salary of $200 per month in addition to their commissions.*

## EXERCISE DIRECTIONS

1. Create the worksheet and table as shown on the next page, or open 💾**34RATE**. Be sure to enter CATEGORY numbers as labels and use fill handle to create Commission Rate table.

2. Find:
   - COMMISSION RATE
     - ✓   *Use a Lookup function.*
   - COMMISSION
   - SALARY
     - ✓   *Use an IF statement. Only Category 2 salespeople receive a flat salary of $200 per month in addition to their commission.  Use quotation marks for the category number in your formula, since it is entered as a label.*
   - TOTAL EARNINGS.

3. Set column width, as necessary.

4. Format percents for two place percents and money values for commas.

5. Find TOTALS for each column, as indicated.

6. Unlock all cells except the COMMISSION RATE table, then turn worksheet protection on.

7. Print one copy of the top portion of the worksheet.

8. Save the workbook file; name it **RATE**.

9. Close the workbook file.

| | A | B | C | D | E | F | G | H |
|---|---|---|---|---|---|---|---|---|
| 1 | | | PAPYRUS PAPER COMPANY | | | | | |
| 2 | | | SALES STAFF EARNINGS REPORT | | | | | |
| 3 | | | MONTH ENDED MAY 31, 199- | | | | | |
| 4 | | | | | | | | |
| 5 | | | TOTAL | COMMISSION | | | TOTAL | |
| 6 | CATEGORY | NAME | SALES | RATE | COMMISSION | SALARY | EARNINGS | |
| 7 | | | | | | | | |
| 8 | 2 | Barton, R. | 11,545.00 | | | | | |
| 9 | 3 | Bond, P. | 26,876.00 | | | | | |
| 10 | 4 | Cards, M. | 31,575.00 | | | | | |
| 11 | 2 | Gross, C. | 28,231.00 | | | | | |
| 12 | 4 | Martin. P. | 26,090.00 | | | | | |
| 13 | 3 | Ragg, C. | 34,921.00 | | | | | |
| 14 | 2 | Vellum, G. | 22,100.00 | | | | | |
| 15 | | | | | | | | |
| 16 | | | | | | | | |
| 17 | | | | | | | | |
| 18 | COMMISSION RATE TABLE | | | | | | | |
| 19 | | | COMMISSION | | | | | |
| 20 | | SALES | RATE | | | | | |
| 21 | | | | | | | | |
| 22 | | 10000 | 7.00% | | | | | |
| 23 | | 11000 | 7.25% | | | | | |
| 24 | | 12000 | 7.50% | | | | | |
| 25 | | 13000 | 7.75% | | | | | |
| 26 | | 14000 | 8.00% | | | | | |
| 27 | | 15000 | 8.25% | | | | | |
| 28 | | 16000 | 8.50% | | | | | |
| 29 | | 17000 | 8.75% | | | | | |
| 30 | | 18000 | 9.00% | | | | | |
| 31 | | 19000 | 9.25% | | | | | |
| 32 | | 20000 | 9.50% | | | | | |
| 33 | | 21000 | 9.75% | | | | | |
| 34 | | 22000 | 10.00% | | | | | |
| 35 | | 23000 | 10.25% | | | | | |
| 36 | | 24000 | 10.50% | | | | | |
| 37 | | 25000 | 10.75% | | | | | |
| 38 | | 26000 | 11.00% | | | | | |
| 39 | | 27000 | 11.25% | | | | | |
| 40 | | 28000 | 11.50% | | | | | |
| 41 | | 29000 | 11.75% | | | | | |
| 42 | | 30000 | 12.00% | | | | | |
| 43 | | 31000 | 12.25% | | | | | |
| 44 | | 32000 | 12.50% | | | | | |
| 45 | | 33000 | 12.75% | | | | | |
| 46 | | 34000 | 13.00% | | | | | |
| 47 | | | | | | | | |
| 48 | | | | | | | | |

Unlock all cells, except cells in this table, then turn worksheet protection on.

EXERCISE
## 35

- **Chart Basics** ■ **Select Chart Data** ■ **Chart Elements**
- **Create Charts** ■ **Change Chart Types**
- **Select, Size, and Edit Embedded Chart**
- **Enable Chart Editing** ■ **Edit Chart Text**

# NOTES

## Chart Basics

- **Charts** are a way of presenting and comparing data in a graphic format.

- You can create **embedded charts** or **chart sheets**.

  - When you create an embedded chart, the chart exists as an *object* in the worksheet alongside the data. All illustrations in this exercise are embedded charts.

  - When you create a chart sheet, the chart exists on a separate sheet in the workbook. Excel names chart sheets Chart1, Chart2, etc. You can change these sheet names to better describe the chart.

- All charts are linked to the data they plot. When you change data in the plotted area of the worksheet, the chart also changes.

- To create a chart, you must first select the data to plot. Here are some guidelines for selecting data to chart:

  - The selection should be rectangular.

  - The selection should not contain blank columns or rows.

  - A non-adjacent selection is used to plot data separated by other data or blank columns or rows.

  - You can hide columns you do not wish to plot.

- The blank cell in the upper-left corner of a selection tells Excel that the data below and to the right of the blank cell contains labels for the values to plot.

- The selection determines the orientation (in columns or rows) of the data series. However, orientation may be changed as desired.

## Select Chart Data

- Typically the selection of worksheet data will include these parts of a chart:

| | |
|---|---|
| **Data series** | Values the chart represents. |
| **Series labels** | Labels identifying the charted values. These labels appear in the chart **legend** which identifies each data series in the chart. |
| **Category labels** | Labels identifying each data series shown on the horizontal or x-axis. |

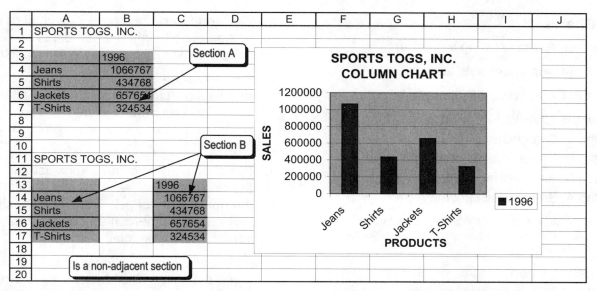

- The illustration above shows two selections that would result in the same displayed chart. Both selections are rectangular and contain a blank cell (outlined) in the upper-left corner. The second selection (B) contains non-adjacent ranges required because of the blank column between he data. Select non-adjacent columns using the Ctrl key between selections.

## Chart Elements

- The parts of a column chart are labeled in the illustration below. In Excel 97, as you move your mouse over each part of a chart, the name of the object displays.

- For charts which use axes (all except pie charts):

  - The y-axis typically represents the vertical scale. The scale values are entered automatically, based on the values being charted.

  - The x-axis is the horizontal scale and typically represents the data series categories.

  - The x-axis title describes the x-axis (horizontal) data. (PRODUCTS in the illustration below.)

  - The y-axis title describes the y-axis (vertical) data. (SALES in the illustration below.)

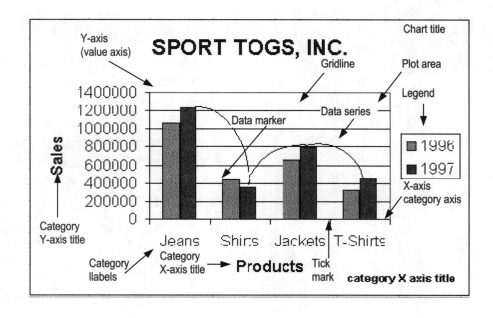

## Create Charts

- The basic steps to creating a chart are:

1. Select the worksheet data to chart.

2. Click the Chart Wizard Button 📖 .

3. Follow the ChartWizard prompts:
   Step 1: Select Chart Type
   Step 2: Check Chart Source Data
   Step 3: Select Chart Options
   Step 4: Select Chart Location

   ✓ *Note: Charts may be located on a separate chart sheet or as an embedded object on the worksheet.*

- In Excel 97, Chart Wizard contains tabbed dialog boxes that allow you to select and format chart types and elements with greater control and ease. As you make selections, Chart Wizard shows you exactly how the chart will look. You can thus select the format that is best suited to presenting your data.

## Change Chart Types

- Excel provides many chart types. In this exercise, we will discuss and explore three of them (illustrated below):

- **Column charts** compare individual or sets of values. The height of each bar is proportional to its corresponding value in the worksheet.

- **Line charts** are another way of presenting data graphically. Line charts are especially useful when you plot trends, since lines connect points of data and show changes over time effectively.

- **Pie charts** are circular graphs used to show the relationship of each value in a data range to the entire data range. The size of each wedge represents the percentage each value contributes to the total.

  - Only one numerical data range may be used in a pie chart. This data will be represented as pie slices.

  - Pie charts may be formatted to indicate the percentage each piece of the pie represents of the whole.

- A chart can be copied and then edited to produce a different chart that uses the same worksheet data.

  ✓ *Note: The contents of the clipboard remain unchanged until another item is copied. Therefore, you can paste a copied object more than once.*

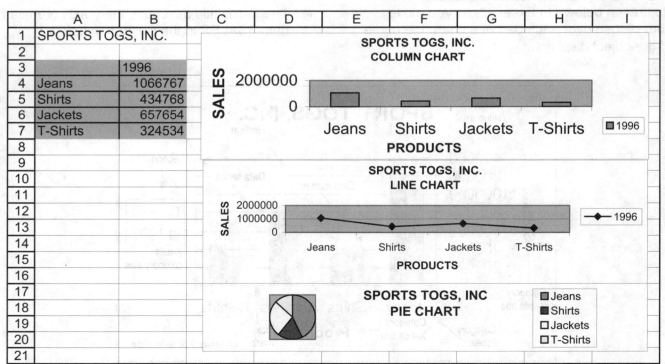

### Select, Size, and Edit Embedded Charts

- You can click an embedded chart once to select it or to enable chart editing. When you click it, **handles** (small squares) appear around its border. When selected in this way, a chart can be sized, moved, edited, or copied.

### Enable Chart Editing

- As discussed above, click the chart once to enable editing. To edit a chart sheet, just click the sheet tab of the chart you want to change.

- You can change or enhance all chart items, such as the **legend** and **data markers** *(illustrated on page 205)*, by clicking them and making the edit. When you right-click chart items, Excel displays a shortcut menu containing relevant commands.

- To edit a chart, Excel provides the following features:

  - **Menu bar options**

    Excel modifies the menu bar so that options specific to the chart type and selected chart item are available. For example:

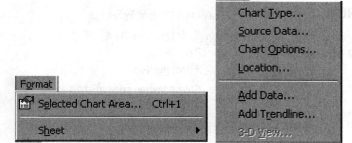

- **Shortcut menu options**

  Excel displays shortcut menus that are appropriate to the part of the chart you right-click: for example, the illustration below is the menu that appears when the data series is right-clicked.

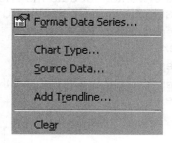

- **Name box**

  Displays the selected chart item.

- **Chart Toolbar**

  - There is a Chart toolbar that may be displayed. The toolbar will be discussed in the next exercise.

---

*In this exercise, you will create a column chart, a line chart, and a pie chart with labels showing manufacturing sales for Sports Togs, Inc.*

---

## EXERCISE DIRECTIONS

1. Create the worksheet as shown below, or open ⊟**35SPORTS**.

2. Create an embedded chart to show the 1996 sales for each product:

   - Select the non-adjacent ranges indicated by the shaded cells in the worksheet, using Ctrl between selections.
   - Follow the Chart Wizard steps and make the following selections:
     - Step 1: Note chart type selections. Since the Column type is the default, click Next.

   - Step 2: Check the data range and note the illustration of the data range selected.
   - Step 3: On the Titles tab, enter the following titles:

     SPORT TOGS, INC. -Chart title

     PRODUCTS - Category X axis

     SALES – Category Y axis
   - Click Next
   - Step 4: Locate the chart on Sheet1. Click Finish.

3. Size and move the chart, if necessary, so that the chart appears in D1:J15.

4. Copy the embedded chart to the worksheet range beginning at D16.

5. Enable chart editing for the copied chart and change the chart type to a line chart.

6. Reselect the worksheet data making the following selections in Chart Wizard:
   - Step 1: Select Pie Chart type. Click Next.
   - Step 2: Note the selection.
   - Step 3: Enter SPORT TOGS INC. as the title.
   - Step 4: Locate the chart as a new sheet on Chart1.

7. Select Chart1 sheet and edit the chart title to add a second line:
   MANUFACTURING SALES

8. Preview the pie chart on the chart sheet.
   ✓ *Note the chart will print on its own sheet.*

9. Select Sheet1 and deselect the worksheet data.

10. Preview Sheet1.
    ✓ *Note the column and line charts will print with the worksheet data.*

11. Save the workbook file; name it **SPORTS**.

12. Close the workbook file.

|   | A | B | C |
|---|---|---|---|
| 1 | SPORTS TOGS, INC. | | |
| 2 | MANUFACTURING SALES | | |
| 3 | | | 1996 |
| 4 | Jeans | | 1066767 |
| 5 | Shirts | | 434768 |
| 6 | Jackets | | 657654 |
| 7 | T-Shirts | | 324534 |

# KEYSTROKES

## SELECT NON-ADJACENT CELLS USING THE MOUSE

1. Click first cell.

2. Press **Ctrl** and click each additional cell.

   **AND/OR**

   Press **Ctrl** and drag through cells until desired cell ranges are highlighted.

## SELECT NON-ADJACENT CELLS USING THE KEYBOARD

1. Select the first cell of the first range you wish to use ............ [↕↔]

2. Press the Shift Key as you use the arrow keys to select the rest of the first range. .............................. [Shift]

3. Still holding the Shift Key, press **F8** ............................... [Shift] + [F8]

   ✓ *This locks the selection in place.*

4. Use the arrows to select the first cell of the next range you wish to use.

5. Repeat steps 2 and 3 for each range you wish to select.

## CREATE A CHART FROM WORKSHEET DATA

1. Select cells containing data to plot.

2. Click **Insert** ............................ [Alt] + [I]

3. Click **Chart** .................................... [H]

   ✓ *This brings you into Chart Wizard. (See below.)*

## CREATE CHART WITH CHART WIZARD

1. Select data to chart.

2. Click Chart Wizard button [⬜] on Standard toolbar.

   —*CHART WIZARD STEP 1 OF 4*—

3. Select a chart type:

   **To select a standard chart type:**

   From Standard tab:

   a. Select chart type in **Chart type** list box.

   b. Select sub-type for selected chart in **Chart sub-type** list box.

   c. If desired, press and hold **Press and hold to view sample** command.
      **OR**

a. Click Custom Types tab.

b. Select **User defined**
   **OR**
   Select **Built-in**

c. Select desired custom chart in **Chart type** list.

4. Click [ Next > ].

   —*CHART WIZARD STEP 2 OF 4*—

5. If desired, change data range options:

   From **Data Range** tab:

   **To change data range:**

   • Type or select new worksheet range in **Data range** text box.

   **To change orientation of data series:**

   • Select Series in **Rows**
     **OR**
   • Select Co**l**umns

6. If desired, click **Series** tab to change series options:

   **To add a series:**

   a. Click **Add** button.

   *Excel adds a series to Series list.*

b. Type new name for series in **Name** text box.

c. Type or select range for new series (just the data) in **Values** text box.

**To remove a series:**

a. Select series to remove in **Series** list.

b. Click **Remove**.

**To change range containing category labels:**

- Type or select range containing labels in **Category axis labels** text box.

7. Click [ Next > ].

—CHART WIZARD STEP 3 OF 4—

8. If desired, from **Titles** tab, type title text:

a. Type text for chart title in **Chart title** text box.

b. Type labels for category, series and value axis.
*(Axis label options will vary.)*

9. If desired, click **Axes** tab to set axes options:

**To set axis display options:**

- Select category, series and value axis display options.
*(Axis display options will vary.)*

10. If desired, click **Gridlines** tab to set gridline options:

- Select category, series, value, 2-D and 3-D gridline options.
*(Gridline options will vary.)*

11. If desired, click **Legend** tab to set gridline options:

a. Select **Show legend**.

b. Select one placement option:
- **Bottom**
- **Corner**
- **Top**
- **Right**
- **Left**

12. If desired, click **Data Labels** tab to set data label options:

**To set display of data labels:**

a. Select desired data label display option:
*Available options may include: **None, Show value, Show percent, Show label, Show label and percent, Show bubble sizes.***

b. Select or deselect **Legend key next to labels**.

13. If desired, click **Data Table** tab to set data table options:

**To show data table:**
- Select **Show data table**.

**To show legend keys:**
- Select **Show legend keys**.

14. Click [ Next > ].

—CHART WIZARD STEP 4 OF 4—

15. Place chart:

**To place chart as a new sheet:**
a. Select **As new sheet**.
b. Type name for sheet in **As new sheet** text box.

**OR**

**To place chart as an object in sheet:**
a. Select **As object in**.
b. Type name for sheet in **As object in** text box.

16. Click .

## ENABLE CHART EDITING

**Embedded Chart:**
- Click embedded chart.
*A border with handles surrounds the chart or, if the entire chart was not displayed on the sheet, the chart appears in a window.*

**Chart Sheet:**
- Select chart sheet.

## DISABLE CHART EDITING

**Embedded Chart:**
- Click any cell in worksheet.

**Chart Sheet:**
- Click another sheet tab.

## SIZE EMBEDDED CHARTS

1. Select chart.

2. Point to handle on side of border to size.

Pointer becomes a ....... ↔  ⤢⤢⇕⤡  when positioned correctly.
✓ *To size object proportionally, point to corner handle.*

**To size object without constraints:**
- Drag border outline until desired size is obtained.

**To size object and align to Worksheetgridlines:**
- Press **Alt** and drag border outline until desired size is obtained.

## CHANGE CHART TYPE FOR ENTIRE CHART

1. Select chart object or chart sheet.

2. Click **Chart**. ........................ Alt + C

3. Click **Chart Type**............................ T

4. Select a chart type:

**To select a standard chart type:**
From Standard tab:

a. Select chart type in **Chart type** list box.

b. Select sub-type for selected chart in **Chart sub-type** list box.

c. If desired, click and hold **Press and hold to view sample** command.

**OR**

a. Click Custom Types tab.

b. Select **User defined**
**OR**
Select **Built-in**

c. Select desired custom chart in **Chart type** list.

**To set current chart type as default:**
- Click **Set as default chart type**.

5. Click **OK** ...........................

## EDIT CHART TEXT IN CHART

*Edits unlinked chart text (such as axis and chart titles, text boxes, and trendline labels) and some linked text (data labels and tick mark labels).*

✓ *When you edit linked text in a chart, Excel removes the link to the worksheet data.*

1. Enable chart editing.

2. Double-Click chart item containing text.

**To replace existing text with new text:**

a. Type desired text .........................*text*
*Text appears in formula bar.*

b. Press **Enter**.............................. Enter

**To edit existing text:**

a. Click desired character position in chart text.

b. Insert and delete characters as desired.

✓ *To insert a line break, press **Enter**.*

c. Click anywhere outside of chart text.

## Exercise 36

■ **Change Chart Subtype** ■ **Custom Chart Types**
■ **Chart Toolbar** ■ **Delete an Embedded Chart** ■ **Chart Tips**
■ **Edit Chart in its Own Window** ■ **Change Legend Position**

# NOTES

## Change Chart Subtype

■ When you create a chart, you will want to select a chart type and format that best presents the worksheet data. Worksheet data may be charted using one of fifteen chart types: Area, Bar, Column, Line, Pie, Doughnut, Radar, XY (Scatter), Surface, Bubble, Stock, Cylinder, Cone, and Pyramid. Excel also provides **chart subtypes** which are variations on the selected chart type. Each chart type has at least two chart subtypes. Note the illustration below of the chart sub-types for the column chart.

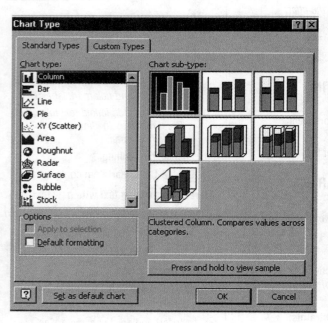

■ The **stacked column charts**, for example, the second and third charts in the chart sub-type illustration below, are chart subtypes. This chart is often used to show the total effect of several sets of data. Each bar consists of sections representing values in a range. For example, in the illustration below, each bar has two sections representing 1996 and 1997 sales values.

*Stacked Column Chart*

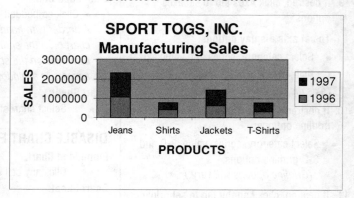

## Custom Chart Types

■ You can select customized chart types by selecting the Custom Types tab on the Chart Types dialog box. When each chart type is selected, Excel will plot your data with the customized type selection.

- The **combination chart** is a custom chart type that lets you plot each data series as a different chart type. For example, in the illustration of the Line-Column chart below, the line chart type is used to plot the 1997 data and the column chart type to plot the 1996 data.

*Combination Chart*

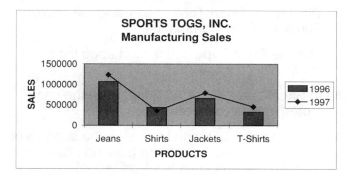

## Chart Toolbar

- You can display the Chart toolbar by selecting <u>V</u>iew, <u>T</u>oolbars, Chart. The toolbar illustrated below will appear.

- The Chart toolbar provides the following tools:

**Chart Objects** – displays the selected chart object. Allows you to select chart objects.

**Format Chart Area** – formats chart area (borders and background colors).

**Chart Type** – provides list of chart types from which you can select.

**Legend** – hides or displays the chart legend.

**Data Table** – hides or displays data table in the chart.

**By Rows** – changes orientation of data series to rows.

**By Column** – changes orientation of data series to columns.

**Angle Text Downward** – angles selected text downward.

**Angle Text Upward** – angles selected text upward.

## Edit Chart in its Own Window

- You can open an embedded chart in its own window so that you can edit the chart independently of the worksheet. After selecting the chart, use the <u>V</u>iew, C<u>h</u>art Window commands to open a chart window. Sizing or moving the window will change the appearance of the chart on the sheet after you close the window.

## Change Legend Position

- A chart **legend** is usually created automatically when the data is charted. Legend placement, font, and patterns may be changed or edited by using the Format Legend selection on the shortcut menu, and the Placement tab. Legend labels are changed by double-clicking the text and retyping the label.

*Chart Toolbar*

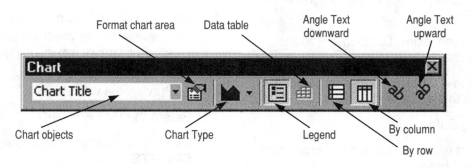

In this exercise, you will retrieve the Sports Togs, Inc. statistics, include additional data, delete charts and prepare several new charts. The owner wants to compare the sales in 1996 with 1997.

# EXERCISE DIRECTIONS

1. Open ⌨**SPORTS**, or open 💾**36SPORTS**.

2. Delete all embedded charts in Sheet1.

|   | A | B | C | D |
|---|---|---|---|---|
| 1 | SPORTS TOGS, INC. | | | |
| 2 | MANUFACTURING SALES | | | |
| 3 | | | 1996 | 1997 |
| 4 | Jeans | | 1066767 | 1235467 |
| 5 | Shirts | | 434768 | 354245 |
| 6 | Jackets | | 657654 | 789643 |
| 7 | T-Shirts | | 324534 | 453234 |

3. Enter new data in column D, as shown below. Enter 1997 as a numeric label.

4. Rename Sheet1; name it DATA.

5. To create an embedded column chart showing 1996 and 1997 sales in the DATA sheet:

6. Select the non-adjacent ranges indicated by the shaded cells in the worksheet.

   – *FROM CHARTWIZARD* –

7. Select the default chart type (Column)

8. Add the chart title: SPORT TOGS, INC.

9. Create axis titles as follows:
   Category (X): ................................... PRODUCTS
   Value (Y): ...................................SALES

10. Size the chart and place it in the range B10:G24.

11. Select and set the legend placement to the bottom of the chart.

12. Edit the chart in a Chart Window and add a second line to the chart title:

    Manufacturing Sales

13. Close the chart window. Select the chart and cut it to the clipboard.

14. In Sheet2, select cell A1 and paste the chart stored in the clipboard.

15. Select cell A17 and paste the chart stored in the clipboard again.

16. Display the Chart Toolbar by using the View, Toolbars, Chart commands.

17. Use the Chart Type button to change the chart in cell A17 to a line chart.

18. In Sheet2, select cell A33 and paste the chart stored in the clipboard.

19. Use the shortcut menu to change the subtype of this chart to stacked column (second chart pictured in the column Subtype group).

20. Place legend on right side of chart.

21. Select the column chart (first chart in Sheet2) and copy it to the clipboard.

22. In Sheet2, select cell A49 and paste the column chart stored in the clipboard.

23. Change the new chart to a combination chart:
    - Right-click the chart.
    - Select Chart Type on the shortcut menu.
    - Select the Custom Types tab.
    - Select the Lines-Column selection. *Note: Your data will be displayed. Make other selections to test the custom feature.*

24. Rename Sheet2; name it EMBEDDED CHARTS.

25. Rename Chart1; name it PIE CHART.
    To preview the embedded charts:
    - Select EMBEDDED CHARTS sheet.
    - Set it to print on one page.
    - Preview the worksheet.

26. Select the DATA sheet.

27. Close and save the workbook file, or save as **SPORTS**.

# KEYSTROKES

## DELETE AN EMBEDDED CHART

1. Select embedded chart as an object.
2. Press **Delete** ................................. `Del`

## CHANGE CHART SUBTYPE

1. Enable chart editing.
2. Click **Chart** ........................... `Alt`+`C`
3. Click **Chart Type** ...................... `T`
4. Select **Chart sub-type** .......... `Alt`+`T`
5. Select desired style ...................... `↹`
   in **sub-type** group.
6. Click `OK` ........................... `Enter`

## CREATE A COMBINATION CHART

*Change chart type for specified data series.*

1. Enable chart editing.
2. Select data series for which a new chart type will be selected.
3. Click **Chart** ........................... `Alt`+`C`
4. Click **Chart Type** ...................... `T`
5. Click **Custom Types** tab ....... `Alt`+`Tab`
6. Select Line-Column.
7. Click `OK` ........................... `Enter`

## POSITION LEGEND IN CHART

1. Enable chart editing.
2. Right-click legend.
3. Select **Format Legend** ................... `O`
4. Select **Placement** ................. `Ctrl`+`Tab`
5. Select desired position:

   **Bottom** ............................ `Alt`+`B`
   **Corner** ............................ `Alt`+`C`
   **Top** ............................... `Alt`+`T`
   **Right** ............................. `Alt`+`R`
   **Left** .............................. `Alt`+`L`
6. Click `OK` ........................... `Enter`

## SELECT CHART ITEMS

*Select chart items (such as the legend or a data series) prior to selecting commands to change the item in some way.*

> *Excel marks the currently selected chart item with squares and displays its name in the name box.*

> Enable chart editing, then perform the desired actions below.

**To select next or previous class of chart items:**

> Press **up** or **down** ...................... `↹`

**To select next or previous item for selected chart class:**

> Press **left** or **right** ...................... `↹`

**To select a specific item with the mouse:**

> Click chart item.

**To select a data series:**

> Click any data marker in data series.

**To select a data marker:**

1. Click any data marker in data series.
2. Click data marker in selected series.

**To select the chart area:**

> Click any blank area outside plot area.

**To select the plot area:**

> Click any blank area inside plot area.

**To select the legend or legend items:**

> *Legend items are the legend entry and key.*

1. Click legend.
2. Click item in legend.

**To deselect a selected chart item:**

> Press **Escape** ............................... `Esc`

## OPEN EMBEDDED CHART IN A WINDOW

1. Click chart to select it.
2. Click **View** ........................... `Alt`+`V`
3. Click **Chart Window** ...................... `A`

**To return to normal editing:**

> Click Close button `X` on window.

**To size window:**

> Drag border of window to increase or decrease size.

**To move window:**

> Drag window title bar.

## Exercise 37

# ■ Print Charts  ■ Print Embedded Chart Separately
# ■ Change Location of Chart  ■ Format Chart Area

## NOTES

### Print Charts

- Charts can be printed with the worksheet or as separate sheets. You can select an embedded chart to print it apart from the worksheet.

- You can use Print Preview to see how a worksheet or chart will print.

- From Print Preview, you can also:

  - View the Previous or Next page when more than one page will be printed.

  - Change the page margins by dragging the handles that appear when you select the Margins button.

  - Click the Setup button to access the Page Setup dialog box, from which you can change many page print settings, such as scaling.

  - Print the chart or worksheet.

### Print Embedded Chart

- When you print a selected embedded chart or a chart sheet:

  - Excel selects the page orientation (Portrait or Landscape) that best matches the shape of the chart. You can change the page orientation from the Page tab in the Page Setup dialog box.

  - The Sheet tab becomes a Chart tab in the Page Setup dialog box. You can set the chart print options, such as **Printing quality** and the **Printed chart size**, from the Chart tab. Note the illustration below.

- Chart components will be shown in different colors on your montitor. When you print these charts on a black and white printer, the colored text and lines are printed in black, the colored areas are printed in shades of gray, and the background color is ignored.

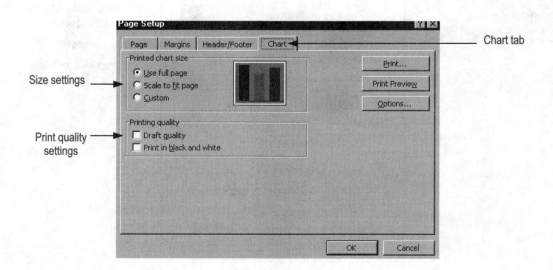

## Change Location of Charts

■ You can easily change the location of a chart on a Chart sheet or as an object on a sheet. Use the Chart, Location commands to move an embedded chart to a chart sheet or to place a chart as an object on a worksheet.

## Format Chart Areas

■ The chart area includes the chart patterns, font settings and properties of an embedded chart. There are tabs for each of these settings, which can be accessed by right-clicking the element and selecting the Format option.

■ Chart pattern options are extensive. They include borders, background area, and fill effects, such as gradients, textures, patterns or a picture.

■ The Font tab lets you set the font style, size and attributes of chart text.

■ The Properties tab allows you to decide how the chart can be moved or sized, whether the chart will print with the worksheet; and whether the chart is protected.

---

*In this exercise, you will change the location of a chart on a chart sheet, format chart areas and print the charts you created for Sport Togs, Inc.*

---

# EXERCISE DIRECTIONS

1. Open ⌨**SPORTS**, or open 💾**37SPORTS**.

2. Select the PIE CHART sheet.

3. Use Print Preview to note the orientation of the page.

4. Use Chart, Location to change the location of the chart so that is an object on the Embedded Charts sheet.

5. Place the chart to the right of the first chart on the Embedded Charts sheet in cell I1.

6. Edit the pie chart title so that the subtitle is in upper and lower case and add the year, as follows:

   Manufacturing Sales - 1996

7. Select the column chart and format the 1997 data series as follows:

   • Right-click the 1997 data series (click on any data marker in the 1997 range.)

   • Select Format Data Series.

   • In the Area section, click on Fill Effects.

   • On the Patterns tab, select the second box in the bottom row (90% dot).

   • Click OK twice.

8. Select the stacked bar chart and format the Font size of the main and subtitle to 14 point.

9. Select EMBEDDED CHARTS sheet and preview the worksheet.

10. From the print preview window, select the Setup button.

    *— FROM PAGE SETUP DIALOG BOX—*

    a. Click on the Sheet tab and turn printing of gridlines off.

    b. Click on the Page tab and set worksheet scale to one page wide by one page tall.

11. Return to the Preview screen and print the worksheet.

12. In the worksheet, select the line chart, then select Print Preview.

    ✓ *Note that only the line chart appears.*

13. Select the Setup button.

14. From the Chart tab, set the Printed chart size to scale to fit the page; set print quality to draft.

15. Return to Print Preview and print the chart.

16. Close and save the workbook file, or save as **SPORTS**

# KEYSTROKES

## PRINT CHARTS

*Print chart sheet or embedded chart as part of the worksheet.*

1. Select worksheet or chart sheet containing chart to print.

2. Follow steps to **PRINT A WORKSHEET**, Exercise 12.

## PRINT EMBEDDED CHART SEPARATELY

1. Enable chart editing for chart to print.

2. Follow steps to **PRINT A WORKSHEET**, Exercise 12.

## SET CHART PRINT OPTIONS

1. Double-click on chart to be printed.

*–FROM PRINT PREVIEW–*

2. Click `Setup...` ......................... `Alt`+`S`

**OR**

*–FROM WORKSHEET OR CHART SHEET–*

a. Click **File** ............................. `Alt`+`F`

b. Click **Page Setup** ....................... `U`

3. Select **Chart** tab .................... `Ctrl`+`Tab`

✓ *Available options depend upon the currently selected printer.*

**To set printed chart size:**

**Select desired fit:**

• **Use Full Page** .............. `Alt`+`U`

• **Scale to fit page** .......... `Alt`+`F`

• **Custom** ....................... `Alt`+`C`

✓ *With Custom selected, you can center the chart on the page from the Margins tab.*

**To set printing quality of chart:**

• Click **Draft quality** ........ `Alt`+`Q`

**To print chart in black and white:**

• Click **Print in black and white** ................... `Alt`+`B`

4. Click `OK` ........................... `Enter`
   to return to sheet or Print Preview.

## SET PAGE ORIENTATION OF PRINTED PAGE

*– FROM PRINT PREVIEW –*

1. Click **Page Setup** ................... `Alt`+`U`

2. Select **Page** tab .................... `Ctrl`+`Tab`

**OR**

*–FROM WORKSHEET OR CHART SHEET–*

a. Click **File** .......................... `Alt`+`F`

b. Click **Page Setup** ...................... `U`

3. Click **Portrait** ...................... `Alt`+`T`

**OR**

Click **Landscape** .................. `Alt`+`L`

4. Click `OK` .......................... `Enter`

to return to sheet or Print Preview.

## CHANGE LOCATION OF CHART

1. Click chart to select it.

2. Click **Chart** ............................. `C`

3. Click **Location** .......................... `L`

4. a. Select **As new sheet** ......... `Alt`+`S`

   b. If desired, type chart name in text box.

**OR**

a. Select **As object in** .......... `Alt`+`O`

b. Select sheet to place chart in drop-down list.

5. Click `OK` .......................... `Enter`

## FORMAT CHART AREA

1. Select chart.

2. Click format Chart Area button on Chart toolbar............................. 📊▾

**OR**

a. Click **Format** ...................... `Alt`+`O`

b. Click **Selected Chart Area** ........ `E`

3. Set chart area options as desired:

• **Patterns**

• **Border** – Automatic, None, Custom (Style, Color, Weight)

• **Shadow** ...................... `Alt`+`D`

• **Round corners** ................. `Alt`+`R`

• **Area** – Automatic, None, color, Fill Effects (Gradient, Texture, Patterns, Picture)

• **Font**

  Font, Font style, Size, Underline, Color, Background, Effects (Strikethrough, Superscript, Subscript), Auto scale, Color, Background

• **Properties** (embedded chart objects only)

• Move and size with cells, Move and don't size with cells, Don't move or size with cells

• Print object, Locked

4. Click **OK**.

## Exercise 38

- **Use Data Map Feature** ■ **Edit Map and Legend**
- **Data Map Toolbar**

## NOTES

### Use Data Map Feature

- Excel 97 has a mapping feature that will display geographic data, such as information about countries or states, on the appropriate map. To use the map feature, select the range of cells to be mapped, including the geographic data, and click the Map button 🌐 on the Standard toolbar. Excel then provides the crosshair ✛ mouse symbol to drag and size the map and finds the map that relates to the data selected. (If you do not have the Map button on your toolbar, rerun the Setup program to install the mapping feature.)

- This exercise will demonstrate several of the many options in the data mapping feature.

### Edit Map

- As with charts, click on the displayed map to enable editing. When the map is first created, you are in edit mode which includes a border around the map, the Data Map Control Box, menu bar that includes map commands, and the Data Map toolbar which replaces the Standard and Formatting toolbars. Note the illustration below of the data map menus, toolbars and the Data Map Control Box.

- The Data Map Control Box may be hidden or displayed. It is displayed when the map is created and may be used to format items on the map. The format buttons may be dragged onto the box area to change the format of the map. The Data Map Control box may be closed with the Close button or by clicking the Show/hide Data Map Control Box icon on the Map toolbar.

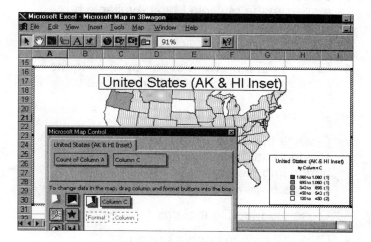

### Data Map Toolbar

- The Data Map toolbar, which appears as the toolbar when you enable editing for a map, contains buttons that enable you to edit the map and change map views. Note the illustration of the Data Map toolbar below:

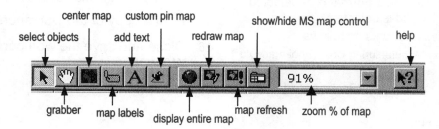

In this exercise, you will use the Red Wagon Manufacturing Co. worksheet to apply the map feature. The map and the legend will be edited, data labels will be added, and the map will be sized and moved for better appearance. Use the illustration of the solution to assist you in creating the desired result.

# EXERCISE DIRECTIONS

1. Open ⌨**WAGON**, or open 💾**38WAGON**.

2. Select the range to map, including the state names and the number of employees.

3. Click on the Map button 🌍 on the Standard toolbar.

4. Place the map in the range A16.I30.

5. Select the United States (AK and HI insert) map from the Multiple Maps Available box
   ✓ Note: The default map will appear with a legend, a Data Map Control box, and the map menus and toolbar.

6. Explore the Map Control box by moving the pointer over the format buttons to see the ToolTips.
   ✓ Note that the chart is using Value Shading.

7. Change the chart to Category Shading by clicking and dragging the Category Shading button into the box.
   ✓ Note that the map shading changes to colors.

8. Close the Map Control box.

9. Click the map to enable editing.

10. To hide the United States heading:
    • Click on the **United States (AK & HI inset)** title box.
    • Right-click and select Hide from the shortcut menu.

11. To edit the legend:
    • Click on the legend box.
    • Right-click and select Edit from the shortcut menu
    • Check that Use Compact Format is deselected and that Show legend is selected.
    • Change the titles and fonts as follows:
      Title: Red Wagon Manufacturing Co. (Bookman Old Style, 11 pt.)
      Subtitle: Employees by State (Bookman Old Style, 9 pt.)
    • Close the dialog box.

12. To label the map with state names and data:
    • Click the Map Labels button on the Map toolbar (in edit mode).
    • In the Map Labels dialog box, select Map feature names for state labels.
    • Point to each state that has data. You will note that the name of the state appears. Place the label in the topmost position within each state. Click to insert the label. Right-click to clear unwanted labels.
    • Click the Map Labels button on the Map toolbar.
    • In the Map Labels dialog box, select the Values from option and note that Column C or the column with the values is selected.
    • Point to each state and click to enter the value below the state name.
    • Click anywhere outside of map to exit labeling.

13. To change colors of the states:
    • Select the Map, Category Shading Options from the map menu bar.
    • Go to the values for Arizona (1060 - Red) and change it to white.
    • Go to the values for Montana (450 - Blue) and change it to light gray.
    • Click OK.

14. To move the map into view:
    • Change the Zoom % to 100% to bring the map closer for easier viewing.
    • Use the Grabber icon to move the map to the left of the map area.
    • Move the legend box to the bottom right corner of the map.
    (Use the illustration of the solution as a guide for moving the elements of the map.)

15. Print a copy of the worksheet.

16. Close and save the workbook file, or save as **WAGON**.

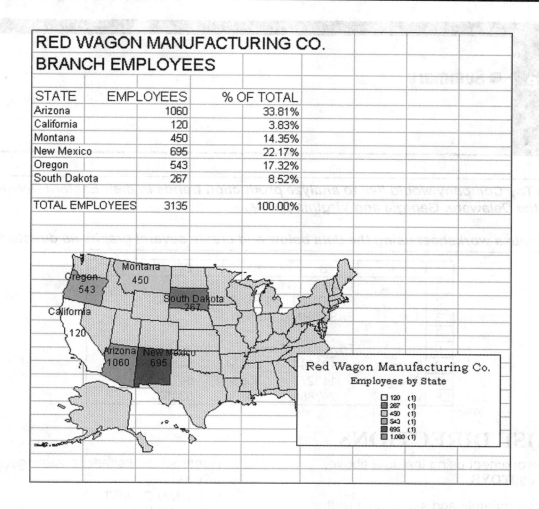

RED WAGON MANUFACTURING CO.
BRANCH EMPLOYEES

| STATE | EMPLOYEES | % OF TOTAL |
|---|---|---|
| Arizona | 1060 | 33.81% |
| California | 120 | 3.83% |
| Montana | 450 | 14.35% |
| New Mexico | 695 | 22.17% |
| Oregon | 543 | 17.32% |
| South Dakota | 267 | 8.52% |
| | | |
| TOTAL EMPLOYEES | 3135 | 100.00% |

# KEYSTROKES

### INSERT AND USE A MAP

1. Select cells containing geographic data.
2. Click 🌐.
   **OR**
   a. Click **Insert** ...................... Alt + I
   b. Click **Map** .................................... A
   *Pointer becomes a +.*
3. Drag rectangle to define map area.
4. If prompted, select desired map in list
5. Click OK ............................ Enter

### ENABLE MAP EDITING

• Double-click the map.
   *The Map Control window opens and the Map toolbar appears below the menu bar.*

### SHADING CHANGE CATEGORY

1. Click **Map** .............................. Alt + M
2. Click **Value Shading Options** .......... V
3. Select **Categories** on the Category Shading Options tab.
4. Select category .............................. ↓
5. Select **Color** .................................... O
6. Select new color ............................. ↓
7. Click **OK** .................................... Enter

## Exercise 39    ■ Summary

*The Tickle Toy Company would like to analyze production trends in their Eastern Division using data from the Delaware, Georgia and Virginia plants.*

*You will create a worksheet using the data below and create several graphs as directed.*

|   | A | B | C | D | E |
|---|---|---|---|---|---|
| 1 |   | TICKLE TOY COMPANY |   |   |   |
| 2 |   | PRODUCTION SUMMARY |   |   |   |
| 3 |   | EASTERN DIVISION |   |   |   |
| 4 |   |   |   |   |   |
| 5 |   | Toys | Games | Stuffed Toys |   |
| 6 | Delaware | 123344 | 89654 | 54888 |   |
| 7 | Georgia | 143277 | 95654 | 64733 |   |
| 8 | Virginia | 297888 | 135333 | 53456 |   |

# EXERCISE DIRECTIONS

1. Create a worksheet using the data above, or open 🖫**39TOYS**.

2. Format appropriately and set column widths where needed.

3. Create an embedded column graph comparing production for the products listed.

4. Include appropriate titles and legends, as well as horizontal gridlines.

5. Using the same data and titles above, create line and line-column charts.

6. Create an embedded pie chart of Virginia data by selecting the product labels and the Virginia data. Use subtype (2), which is the 3-D visual effect chart. Enter a title: TICKLE TOY CO. Virginia Production.

7. Use Edit, Cut and Edit, Paste to move each chart to a separate worksheet. Insert sheets as necessary.

8. Rename each sheet containing a chart as follows:
   COLUMN CHART
   LINE CHART
   LINE-COLUMN CHART
   PIE CHART

9. Rename Sheet1; name it DATA.

10. Select the States and toy data, range A6:B8, and create a data map below the worksheet.
    - Use the Data Map Control box to change the chart to Category shading.
    - Select and hide the title.
    - Edit the legend title to Tickle Toy Co, Inc.
    - Edit the legend subtitle to Toy Production.
    - Change the zoom percentage to 250%.
    - Use the grabber to bring the data into view.
    - Enter the map labels for states and data.

11. Copy the map to a new sheet. Name the sheet DATA MAP.

12. Save the workbook file, name it **TOYS**.

13. Close the workbook.

*Line Chart*

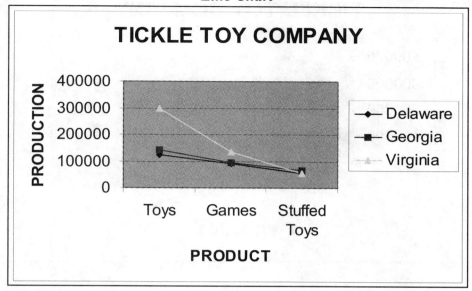

*Line-Column Chart*

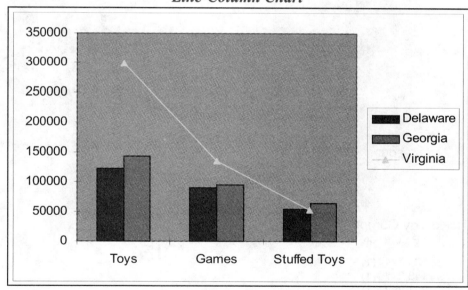

*Pie Chart*

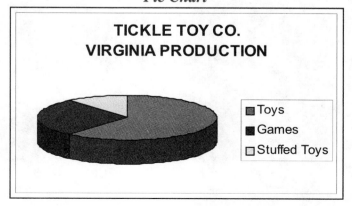

*Column Chart*

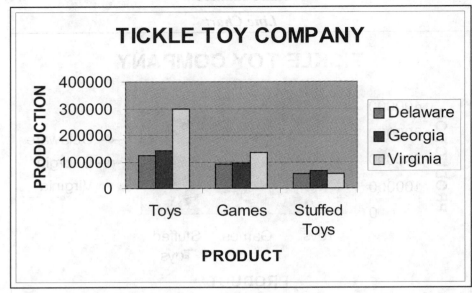

*Map*

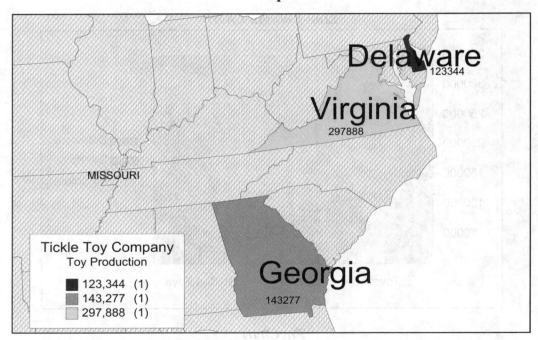

# Microsoft Access 97

**Lesson 1:** Create a Database Form

**Lesson 2:** Edit and Print a Database

**Lesson 3:** Search and Sort a Database

**Lesson 4:** Queries

**Lesson 5:** Reports

**Database Basics**

- ■ **What is Access?** ■ **What is a Database?**
- ■ **What is a Database Management System?**
- ■ **What are Database Objects?**
- ■ **How is an Access Database Organized?**
- ■ **What are Access Tables?** ■ **How are Access Tables Related?**

# NOTES

## What is Access?

■ Access is the **database management system** in Microsoft Office.  To understand what a database management system is and what it can do, you need to study the database basics information that follows.

## What is a Database?

■ A **database** is an organized collection of facts about a particular subject.  An address book or a library's card catalog is a database; an office filing cabinet can also contain a database.

■ Examples of manual databases are illustrated below.  To use and maintain them requires manual labor and a lot of time.  Suppose you have two hundred people listed in your address book.  To update the telephone number and address of a friend who just moved to Boise, you must page through the book, locate the entry, and make the change.

### Examples of Manual Database Records

| Name | Call Number |
|------|-------------|
| Address | Author |
| City    St  Zip | Title |
| Telephone | Subject |

**Address Book Entry**        **Card Catalog Entry**

■ An **Access database** is the electronic equivalent of a manual database.  It lets you organize the facts and provides a way for you to maintain the data electronically.  To update the telephone number of a friend who moved to Boise, you simply call up the friend's entry and make the change.

## What is a Database Management System?

■ If all you gained from an electronic database were ease of data update and maintenance, you would probably think it worth the trouble.  But Access is a database management system that provides a great many other functions besides data maintenance.

■ A database management system provides functions to store, search, filter, query, and report on the data in the database.  For example, suppose you wish to find all books about political science.  To do this manually, you must read the card catalog entries and write down those with a subject of political science.  Such a manual search could be quite time-consuming.  With an automated database management system like Access, however, you can locate all the political science books with its search function and a few simple keystrokes.

## What are Database Objects?

■ To help you use your database efficiently, modern database management systems, like Access, provide **database objects**.  Database objects are the tools you need to store, maintain, search, analyze, and report on the data in your database.

■ In the following Access exercises, you will learn about the four database objects listed in the table on the following page.

| | |
|---|---|
| **Table** | Also called a **datasheet**. Data is formatted in a table or spreadsheet format and provides information about a specific aspect of the database. Each row in a table represents one record in a database. |
| **Form** | A format that displays one record (one row from a table) at a time. Forms are used to enter or update data. |
| **Query** | A structured way to tell Access to retrieve data that meets certain criteria from one or more database tables. For example, a query may request that Access retrieve data on all printers sold within the last six months. |
| **Report** | A formatted way to display information retrieved from the database. A report formats and analyzes data you specify. |

- Two other database objects – macros and modules – are not covered in this text, but you may see them referred to as you use Access.

## How is an Access Database Organized?

- The Access database management system lets you maintain, in a single file, database objects that are displayed in the **database window**. The database window contains tabs for each object. You can select each tab to display lists of the named objects of that type.

Types of Database Objects

*Access Database Window*

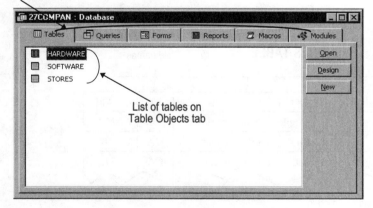

List of tables on Table Objects tab

- Using Access, you organize the data *itself* into separate electronic storage containers called **tables**. Each table contains data about a particular part of the entire subject.

Consider a company that sells computer hardware and software. The company database may contain one table that identifies customers, another that describes its hardware products, a third that tracks software, a fourth that maintains data about the sales force, and a fifth that tracks sales. These tables, along with others perhaps, form the database. By organizing its data into an electronic database of a number of tables, the company replaces filing cabinets with their electronic equivalent.

## What are Access Tables?

- An Access table is a group of rows and columns. Each row contains one **record**. A record is a set of details about a specific item. For example, one record in a company's hardware inventory table will contain details on one of its NEC printers, giving its product identifier, manufacturer, model number, cost, and purchase date. When data processing people ask about the "NEC printer record," they want to know the details in the table row where the printer is described.

- Each column in the table is a **field**, headed by a **field name**. Each row in the column contains specific data called the **field contents**. The field contains a detail. For example, the field MANUFACTURER in one of the hardware records would contain the entry NEC to identify the manufacturer of a piece of equipment. When data processing people ask, "What's in the manufacturer field?" they are asking about the field contents of the field name "manufacturer."

## How are Access Tables Related?

- When designing a database, you should provide at least one field in each Access table that is repeated from table to table. This field relates the tables to each other so that you can create queries from all the tables in the database. The field should be unique and not contain duplicate entries. In a library database, an obvious candidate for a field common to all tables is a book's call number. A company that has many stores can create one table that contains generalized information for each store (Stores) and other tables that contain information about Inventory, Hardware, and Software. These tables can be related to the Stores table by use of a Store identifier such as the Branch field.

<table>
<tr><td>Exercise<br>1</td><td>■ Database Basics  ■ Plan a Database<br>■ Create a Table (Datasheet) Design<br>■ Switch Between Table Views  ■ Save a Datasheet Design</td></tr>
</table>

# NOTES

## Database Basics

■ Access 97 is a **Relational Database Management System**.  A **database** is a collection of related information that is organized into separate tables (listings) or objects within a file.  This allows you to store related information in one place (the database).  Each table is created to contain data pertaining to a specific aspect of the database.  Each table in a database usually has one item of information in common with other tables to allow for access of information among tables.

■ An Access database file is like a filing cabinet of **related** information in which each drawer contains a specific aspect of that information.  Each drawer in the filing cabinet is like a **datasheet** or **table** and contains individual "index cards" called **records**.  A record contains information about an item in the table.  A table is a list of records about one aspect of the database.

For example:  A company that has many stores can create one table that contains generalized information for each store (Stores) and other tables that contain information about Inventory, Hardware, and Software.  These tables would be saved in the Company database.  Each table (or file drawer) contains information which is related to the other tables and which is accessible within the database.  Note the illustration below.

■ All the records in a table (file drawer) have data stored using the same category names.  Each category is referred to as a **field**.  There are two parts to a field:  the **field name** and the **field contents**.  In our example, the BRANCH field, on the record shown, can be the field used in all tables of the database to relate the tables.

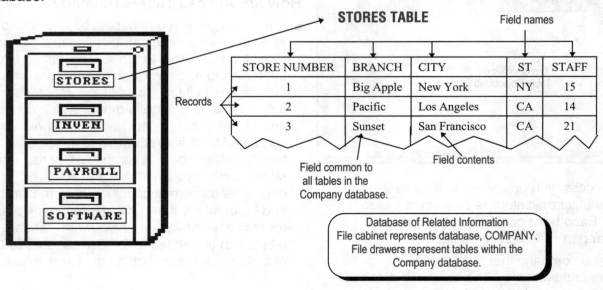

**STORES TABLE**                    Field names

| STORE NUMBER | BRANCH | CITY | ST | STAFF |
|---|---|---|---|---|
| 1 | Big Apple | New York | NY | 15 |
| 2 | Pacific | Los Angeles | CA | 14 |
| 3 | Sunset | San Francisco | CA | 21 |

Records

Field common to
all tables in the
Company database.

Field contents

Database of Related Information
File cabinet represents database, COMPANY.
File drawers represent tables within the
Company database.

## Plan the Database

■ Before creating a database, you should plan the fields you want to include in each datasheet or table—that is, what type of information the database should contain and how you wish it organized. Plan your database on paper first by writing the field names that would best identify the information entered as field contents.

■ If you are designing two or more datasheets, you should have these tables share a common field name. The linking field must be unique. If you decide to use a number as the unique field data, Access will automatically create unique record numbers using the AutoNumber feature. When your plan is complete, you are ready to enter your field names and data into the computer.

■ Text data can be used as the linking field; for example, if Branch is the common field between tables, two branches may never have the same name and each branch must have a unique name.

## Create a Database File

■ At the opening Access window (see below), you have three choices: to Create a new Database using a Blank Database, to Create a new Database using Database Wizard, or to Open an Existing Database.

*Opening Access Window*

■ When the Database Wizard is selected, a dialog box appears that contains over 20 sample database designs such as an Address Book or a Video Collection database. The Wizard assists you in creating all parts of the database with suggested fields and layouts. This feature will be discussed and used later in this text after database objects are practiced and understood.

■ When you select Blank Database, the File New Database dialog box appears (see the illustration below). The default database name of db1 should be changed to a name that is more appropriate for your database. Unless you choose to change its destination, the file will be stored in My Documents directory, with a **.MDB** extension for a database file.

*File New Database Dialog Box*

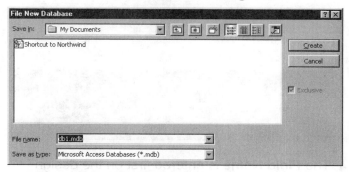

■ After you name your database file and click Create, a Database Object window appears with the file name on the title bar. The relational database objects are summarized in this window and can be accessed by using the object tabs. Database object categories are: Tables, Queries, Forms, Reports, Macros, and Modules.

*Database Object Window*

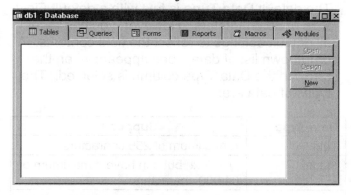

The best way to begin creating database objects is to create tables (the default option), which are also known as datasheets.

## Create a Table (Datasheet) Design

- A table can be created and customized in Table Design view where the Field Names, Data Types, Descriptions, and Field Properties are defined. After selecting the Tables tab and New in the Database Object window, you will be presented with a New Table dialog box where you select Design view. A Table Design view screen is shown below.

*Table Design View*

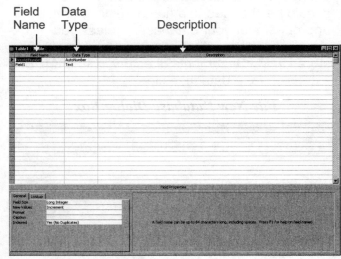

- The **Field Name** is entered first on the design screen and can contain a maximum of 64 characters. These characters can include letters, numbers, spaces (except leading spaces), and special characters except the period (.), exclamation mark (!), backquote ('), either the left or right brackets ( [ ] ), or printer control codes. After the field name is entered, the type of data must be defined.

- The default **Data Type** is text with a default Field Size of 50 characters. However, you can reset all default settings to reflect the field contents. A drop-down list of data types appears when the arrow in the Data Type column is selected. The types of data are:

| Data Type | Supports |
|-----------|----------|
| Text | A maximum of 255 characters |
| Memo | Like text, but can have a maximum of 64,000 characters |
| Number | Various forms of numerical data that can be used in calculations |
| Date/Time | Date and time entries in various formats |

| Data Type | Supports |
|-----------|----------|
| Currency | Currency values expressed in various formats |
| AutoNumber | A permanent identification number is entered that increases with each record. |
| Yes/No | A check box with an ☑ for Yes or blank ☐ for No |
| OLE Object | A linkage to an object in another file |
| Hyperlink | Stores a path to a file on your hard drive, a LAN server (UNC path), or a URL (Internet destination). |
| Lookup Wizard | Creates a lookup column which creates a list of values to choose from when entering data. |

- The field **Description** is optional, but it helps you describe the field and can be viewed by the user. The description can be up to 255 characters.

- After entering the Field Name and Data Type, you define the properties of the data, such as Field Size or Format. You may toggle to the Field Properties screen by pressing F6.

## Switch Views

- You can switch between Table Design view and Datasheet view by using the appropriate option on the View menu. Table Design view displays the format of the table, while Datasheet view shows the records entered into the table. Data can be entered or edited in Datasheet view.

## Save a Datasheet Design

- After a database object has been designed, it must be named and saved using the Save or Save As option on the File menu. If you close the table without saving it, you are prompted to save the file and asked about a primary key.

- To efficiently select information from different tables within the database, Access uses a **primary key**. The field used as a primary key must be unique to each record. Therefore, a field such as NAME cannot be a primary key since more than one person in a datasheet may have the same last name. A branch name or vendor number would be an appropriate choice for a primary key field. Access will ask if one should be created before saving the file. If you do not specify a primary key, Access will insert a primary key named ID, whose data type is AutoNumber.

*Bit-Byte Computer Stores, Inc. has opened numerous branches throughout the United States during the last several months. In order to keep track of the branches and the cities in which the branches are located, you have been asked to create a database file to organize information relating to these stores.*

# EXERCISE DIRECTIONS

1. Select Blank Database from the Access opening screen.

2. Replace the default file name, DB1, with **COMPANY**.

3. Select Create or press Enter.

4. Select New on the Tables tab.

5. Select Design view.

6. Create a table design using the data listed below:

| FIELD NAME | DATA TYPE | SIZE | DESCRIPTION |
|---|---|---|---|
| STORE NUMBER | Number | Integer | |
| BRANCH | Text | 16 | |
| CITY | Text | 13 | |
| ST | Text | 2 | |
| STAFF | Number | Integer | Number of employees |

*Note:* *The setting for data size does not appear on the top section of table design but on the General tab of the field properties at the bottom of the screen. Press F6 to switch to field properties.*

7. Save the table design; name it STORES. (Do not add a primary key.)

8. Switch to Datasheet view from the View menu. Note the field names at the top of the table.

9. Close the STORES datasheet.

10. Close the **COMPANY** database.

# KEYSTROKES

### ⊕ CREATE AND RENAME A NEW FILE

1. Click **F**ile ............................... Alt + F
2. Click **N**ew Database ....................... N
3. Choose **Blank Database** ................ ↓
4. Click **OK** ......................................... Enter
5. Replace file name ...................... *filename*
6. Click Create ................................ Create

### CREATE A TABLE DESIGN

1. Open a new file (see above) or open an existing file.

   In the database object dialog box:

2. Select **Table** tab .................... ▦ Tables
3. Click **N**ew .............................. Alt + N
4. Select **Design View** ....................... ↓

5. Click **OK** ................................... Enter
6. Type Field Name ..................... *fieldname*
7. Press **TAB** .................................... Tab
8. Use pull down list to select data type (default type is text).
9. Press **F6** ........................................ F6
   to switch to field properties.
10. Enter properties ......................*properties*
11. Press **F6** to switch to table ............. F6
12. Press **TAB** .................................... Tab
13. Enter description, if desired.
14. Press Enter ................................ Enter
15. Repeat steps 6-11 until table is complete.
16. Save table design (see right).

### SAVE TABLE DESIGN

1. Click **F**ile ............................... Alt + F
2. Click Save **A**s/Export ....................... A
3. Click Within the **C**urrent Database as: ........................ Alt + C
4. Type table name..................... *tablename*
5. Click **OK** ................................... Enter
6. Click **N**o ...................................... N
   to bypass creation of primary key.
   **OR**
   Click **Y**es to create a primary key ..... Y

### CHANGE FROM TABLE DESIGN TO DATASHEET VIEW

**When in Table Design view:**
1. Click **V**iew ........................... Alt + V
2. Click Data**s**heet View...................... S

**Exercise 2**

■ **Open a Database File** ■ **Create a Table in Datasheet View**
■ **Primary Key** ■ **Use Date/Time and Currency Data Types**
■ **Yes/No Data Type**

## NOTES

### Open a Database File

■ To open a saved database, select Open an Existing Database from the opening screen or select the Open Database command from the File menu.

### Create a Table in Datasheet View

■ In the first exercise, you created a table in Table Design view where you defined the fields, data type, and size. Although this is the recommended procedure, you can also create a table in Datasheet view. Access will interpret entries made in Datasheet view and determine data type and size. When you select New, Datasheet View, a blank datasheet with generic column headings appears. To enter field names in Datasheet view, you must double-click on the column heading and enter the field name.

*Datasheet View*

| ⊞ Table1 : Table | | | | _ □ ✕ |
|---|---|---|---|---|
| **Field1** | **Field2** | **Field3** | **Field4** | **Field5** |
| ▶ | | | | |
| | | | | |
| | | | | |
| | | | | |
| | | | | |
| | | | | |
| Record: ⚊⚊ ◀ 1 ▶ ▶⚊ ▶✳ of 30 | | | | |

■ A database may contain all the related data for a company. For example: In the COMPANY database, created in Exercise 1, you saved a datasheet for STORES containing information about each store. You will now create a datasheet for HARDWARE, listing hardware purchased for each store.

### Primary Key

■ When you save a table, Access asks if you wish to create a primary key. If you answer yes, the first field in the table will be established as the primary key. A Key icon ▧ appears next to the first field. If you wish to create a primary key, or linking field, in another field, select the row and the field and click the Key icon on the toolbar.

### Use Date/Time and Currency Data Types

■ The Date/Time and Currency data types do not allow you to set the field size; however, you can use field properties to select a format for each type. For example, the Date/Time setting offers a list of formats for the date, as shown below.

*Date/Time Data Types*

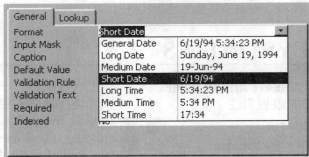

| General | Lookup | | |
|---|---|---|---|
| Format | | Short Date | ▼ |
| Input Mask | | General Date | 6/19/94 5:34:23 PM |
| Caption | | Long Date | Sunday, June 19, 1994 |
| Default Value | | Medium Date | 19-Jun-94 |
| Validation Rule | | Short Date | 6/19/94 |
| Validation Text | | Long Time | 5:34:23 PM |
| Required | | Medium Time | 5:34 PM |
| Indexed | | Short Time | 17:34 |

■ To accommodate dates for the year 2000 and beyond, Access 97 interprets dates entered in short format as described in the table below:

| Date range for abbreviated year format | Interpretation |
|---|---|
| 1/1/00 – 12/31/29 | 1/1/2000 – 12/31/2029 |
| 1/1/30 – 12/31/99 | 1/1/1930 – 12/31/1999 |

✓ *Note:* *Regardless of the format specified for the date Data Type, you can enter all four digits for the year. Thus, rather than typing 02/14/28 for a date, you can type 02/14/1928 to avoid confusion. The date will display as 2/14/28 but will be interpreted correctly.*

- When the Currency data type is selected, the format automatically sets to currency, which includes dollar signs and decimals. The format may be changed to Standard, which includes two decimal places and no dollar sign.

## Yes/No Data Type

- If you have data that represents a Yes/No or True/False condition, you may use the Yes/No data type. This setting will display a box in the field that can be checked if Yes or True and left blank if No or False. Note the Yes/No boxes on the datasheet below. You may use field properties to set the default for this field to Yes or No to minimize data entry.

*Yes/No Data Type*  Yes/No boxes

| G | MODEL | COST | PURDATE | WTY | ASSIGN |
|---|---|---|---|---|---|
| | PS2 | 1,348.50 | 6/1/95 | ☑ | Accounti |
| | ExecJet II | 335.00 | 6/1/95 | ☑ | Accounti |
| | Thinkpad 350C | 2,199.00 | 6/1/95 | ☑ | Accounti |
| | Thinkpad 500 | 1,399.00 | 6/1/95 | ☑ | Accounti |
| tum | LPS40 170MB | 199.00 | 6/1/95 | ☐ | Accounti |
| er | CFS4 210MB | 200.00 | 6/1/95 | ☐ | Purchas |
| h | Notebook 486 | 1,889.00 | 1/1/96 | ☑ | Shipping |

> *To track the equipment purchased by the Bit-Byte Computer Stores, Inc., your employer has asked you to create an inventory table for your COMPANY database. You will set BRANCH as the primary key in the STORES table and open the COMPANY database, and create a new table in Datasheet view. You will switch to Design view and practice defining the fields.*

# EXERCISE DIRECTIONS

1. Open the 💿COMPANY database, or open 💾02COMPAN.

   **IMPORTANT:** *To use the Access data files on the accompanying CD-ROM, you must first copy the files onto your hard drive. Then, before you open the file, right-click on the file and select Properties from the shortcut menu. In the dialog box that follows, deselect Read-only. If you do not deselect the Read-only option, you will be unable to make any changes to the database file.*

2. Open the STORES table in Design view.
3. Select the BRANCH field row.
4. Click the Key icon to create BRANCH as the primary key.
5. Save the design and close the table design.
6. Create a new table in Datasheet view by double-clicking on the Field1, Field2, etc. headings and entering the following field names: BRANCH, ITEM, MFG, MODEL, COST, PURDATE, WTY.
7. Save the table, name it HARDWARE. Do not create a primary key. *The BRANCH field is not unique in this Table.*

8. Switch to Table Design view using the View menu.

   ✓ Note: *The fields are assigned the default settings of a text data type with 50 characters. These settings would be adjusted as data is entered into the datasheet. Therefore, this table can be considered complete since it will adapt to the data entered.*

9. To practice making Table Design view settings, make the following Data Type and Size settings in Design view. Size and format settings are made in the field properties section.

| FIELD NAME | DATA TYPE | SIZE | FORMAT |
|---|---|---|---|
| BRANCH | Text | 16 | |
| ITEM | Text | 15 | |
| MFG | Text | 8 | |
| MODEL | Text | 15 | |
| COST | Currency | | Standard |
| PURDATE | Date/Time | | Short Date |
| WTY | Yes/No | | Yes/No (default value Yes) |

10. Switch to HARDWARE Datasheet view.

11. Close the HARDWARE datasheet and **COMPANY** database.

# KEYSTROKES

## 🌐 OPEN A FILE

1. Click **File** .............................. `Alt` + `F`
2. Click **Open Database** ...................... `O`
3. Select file in proper directory.
4. Click **Open** ........................ `Open`

## CREATE TABLE IN DATASHEET VIEW

1. Open a new file or open existing file.

**From the database object dialog box:**

2. Select **Table** tab ................ `⊞ Tables`
3. Click **New** .............................. `Alt` + `N`
4. Select Datasheet view.
5. Double-click on column heading.
6. Replace heading with field name.
7. Repeat steps 5-6 until all fields are entered.
8. Save table.

## CREATE A PRIMARY KEY

**In Table Design:**

1. If the first field is the primary key, answer yes when asked if you wish to create a primary key, when saving a table design.

   **OR**

   a. Select Primary Key row.
   b. Click **Key** icon on toolbar ............

<table>
<tr><td>Exercise<br><br>3</td><td>■ Open a Datasheet  ■ Enter Records  ■ Input Mask<br>■ Correct a Field Entry  ■ Change Datasheet Column Width<br>■ Security</td></tr>
</table>

# NOTES

## Open a Datasheet (Table)

■ When you create or open a database file, the Database Object window appears listing all previously created objects.

### *Database Object Window*

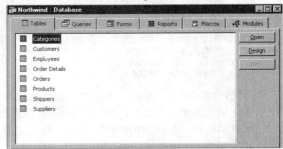

■ To open a saved **table** (datasheet) **design** and enter data, highlight the desired table name and select the Open option.  A row and column format, similar to a spreadsheet, is displayed with the previously entered field names as the column headings.  This **Datasheet view** gives you an efficient way to work with more than one record on the same screen.  In this view, each row contains the data of a single record.

### *Datasheet View*

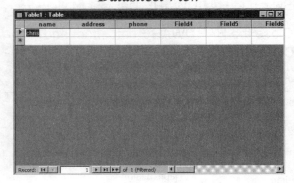

■ Once records have been added to a Datasheet, you can use the arrow-head buttons on the Datasheet scroll bar to scroll through the records.

### *Datasheet Scroll Bar*

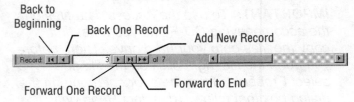

## Enter Records

■ To enter records in a Datasheet, type the data below each field name as you would in a spreadsheet.  Use the Tab key to advance from column to column.  To advance to the next row, click in the first column of the new row.  Use the Tab key or use the direction-arrow keys.  When you leave a record row, your data will automatically be saved in the table.

■ It is recommended you enter data in upper- and lowercase so that the data may be used in word processing files.  You may enter field names (column headings) in uppercase to distinguish them from field data.

■ You may use the Copy or Cut and Paste options to quickly enter repetitive data.  You can copy either one cell entry or an entire record.  To select an entire row, click the shaded area to the left of the first field in the row.

## Input Mask

- You can control how data is entered in a field by creating an **input mask** or field template. For example, you can set the format for a telephone number with parentheses and hyphens to reduce data entry keystrokes and check for valid data. You can set an Input Mask in the field properties section by clicking the Build button ... to start the Input Mask wizard.

## Correct a Field Entry

- Use the Backspace key to correct an error made while keyboarding an entry. If you have already advanced to another field, you can return to the field that needs correction by clicking in the field, pressing Shift+Tab, or by using the direction arrow keys. Retype the entry, or press F2, to access edit mode, make the correction, and then move to another field.

## Change Datasheet Column Width

- You may find that the default column width on your datasheet table is not appropriate for your entries, and/or the table is too wide to fit on one screen. You can change the column size on the datasheet at any time without affecting the field size specified in the table design.

## Security

- Access 97 provides several methods to secure your database. You can hide Tables or other database objects you do not want others to see, or you can assign a single password to control who can open a database. The User-Lever Security Wizard can assist in these tasks. These security measures will not be practiced in this text, but you should be aware of this feature.

---

*You are the president of HUG, a computer users' group. One of your responsibilities is to send announcements and annual reports to the members. To make your mailings easier, you have decided to create a name and address file for your computer users' group. In this exercise, you will create a database file, design a table, and enter data into the datasheet.*

# EXERCISE DIRECTIONS

1. Create a new database file; name it **HUGCLUB**.

2. Create a table in Table Design view using the Field Names and Field Size indicated below:

| Field Name | Data Type | Size |
|---|---|---|
| NUMBER | AutoNumber | Integer |
| LAST | Text | 10 |
| FIRST | Text | 8 |
| ADDRESS | Text | 20 |
| CITY | Text | 15 |
| PHONE | Text — Input Mask | 13 |

For the Phone field, press F6. In the Input Mask property, click the Build button and follow the wizard's instructions.

- Save the table; name it MEMBERS.
- Set Number as a primary key.

- Select Phone Number. Click Next.
- Do not select placeholder or change mask style. Click Next.
- Store the data *with* the symbols in the mask. Click Next. Click Finish.

3. Switch to Datasheet view.

4. From the notebook page illustrated on the next page, enter the information for each person into your table in the appropriate field.

5. Adjust column widths to accommodate the longest entry in each field.

6. Proofread data and correct errors.

7. Save and close the MEMBERS table.

8. Close the **HUGCLUB** database.

| 1 | Barnes | Leanne | 808 Summer Street | Anaheim | (213)555-4987 |
| 2 | Brown | Miles | 154 Newburg Road | Anaheim | (213)555-4837 |
| 3 | Griffith | Stuart | 1551 Dean Street | Beverly Hills | (213)555-3010 |
| 4 | Moon | Michael | 17 Pine Street | Beverly Hills | (213)555-9275 |
| 5 | Smith | Trina | 3954 Wood Avenue | Anaheim | (213)555-7283 |
| 6 | Smith | Sheila | 417 Specific Court | Anaheim | (213)555-7284 |
| 7 | Walker | Bette | 1584 F Street | North Hollywood | (213)555-9174 |
| 8 | Castillo | Carl | 1956 Park Avenue | North Hollywood | (213)555-5192 |
| 9 | Davis | John | P.O. Box 2333 | North Hollywood | (213)555-8129 |
| 10 | Dixon | Amy | 237 Albee Street | North Hollywood | (213)555-8917 |

# KEYSTROKES

## CHANGE FROM DATASHEET TO TABLE DESIGN VIEW

**In Datasheet view:**

1. Click **View** ............................. `Alt`+`V`
2. Click **Table Design** ......................... `D`

## CHANGE DATASHEET COLUMN WIDTH

**Keyboard:**

1. Click field selector for desired column.
2. Click **Format** ....................... `Alt`+`O`
3. Click **Column Width** ....................... `C`
4. Click **Best Fit** ........................ `Alt`+`B`
   **OR**
   a. Type column width ............. *number*
   b. Click **OK** ............................... `Enter`

**Mouse:**

1. Click right edge of the field name cell.
2. Click and drag border to desired size.

## ⊕ EDITING DATA

**Before data is entered, data may be edited by backspacing and  correcting the entry.**

**After data is entered:**

1. Press **Shift+Tab** .................. `Shift`+`Tab`
   to return to a field.
2. Press **F2** ..................................... `F2`
3. Make corrections.

## SET INPUT MASK PROPERTY

**In Table Design view:**

1. Select field.
2. Click **F6** ........................................... `F6`
3. Click Input Mask property.
4. Click Build button ....
5. Follow Input Mask wizard dialog boxes.
6. Click **Finish** when complete.

## Exercise 4

■ **Open an Existing Table** ■ **Enhance a Table (Datasheet)**

## NOTES

### Open an Existing Table

■ To open an existing table, you must first open the database file that contains the table. A listing of all the tables currently existing in that database file appears when the file is opened.

### Enhance a Table (Datasheet)

■ Access has established default settings for a datasheet. The default settings for items such as format and gridlines affect the entire datasheet and can be changed.

■ When you are in Datasheet view, a Format menu option is available.

*Datasheet Format Menu*

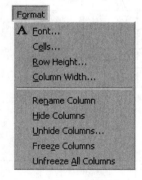

■ The Font option gives you a dialog box listing all available fonts, their size, and style options. A sample box allows you to preview your choices before making changes.

*Font Dialog Box*

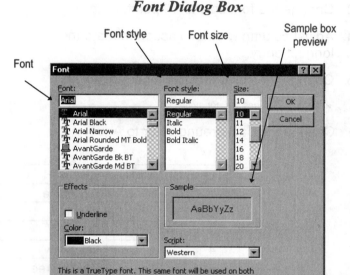

■ The Cells option gives you a dialog box with gridline, cell effects, and color options along with a sample box for viewing changes. The Gridlines Shown feature will only work with the flat cell effect as illustrated below:

*Cells Effects Dialog Box*

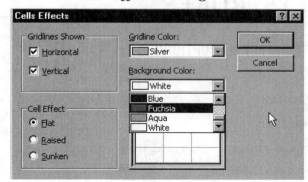

✓ *Note:* *All the format selections affect the datasheet display only and do not change any other table view.*

> *Your manager at Bit-Byte has just given you a list of the new branches and their locations. She has asked you to enter this information into your database table STORES. The datasheet will be enhanced using font, gridline, and color options.*

## EXERCISE DIRECTIONS

1. Open the 💾**COMPANY** database, or open 💾**04COMPAN**.

2. Open the STORES table and enter the data listed below.

3. Change the font size to 12 point, italics style.

4. Adjust column widths to accommodate the longest entry.

5. Change the cell effect to Raised.

   ✓ *Note: Gridlines are not available.*

6. Change the background color to Aqua.

7. Save and close the datasheet

8. Open the STORES table again.

9. Change the font size to 10, regular style.

10. Return cell effect to Flat.

11. Change gridline color to Blue.

12. Adjust column widths, if necessary.

13. Save and close the datasheet.

14. Close the **COMPANY** database.

| STORE NUMBER | BRANCH | CITY | ST | STAFF |
|---|---|---|---|---|
| 1 | Big Apple | New York | NY | 15 |
| 2 | Pacific | Los Angeles | CA | 14 |
| 3 | Sunset | San Francisco | CA | 21 |
| 4 | Lakeview | Chicago | IL | 15 |
| 5 | Peach Tree | Atlanta | GA | 9 |
| 6 | Bean Town | Boston | MA | 16 |
| 7 | Astro Center | Houston | TX | 8 |
| 8 | Twin Cities | St. Paul | MN | 7 |
| 9 | Wheatland | Topeka | KS | 12 |
| 10 | Oceanview | Providence | RI | 6 |

## KEYSTROKES

**SET FONT FORMAT OPTIONS**

1. Click **F**ormat........................... `Alt`+`O`

2. Click **F**ont....................................... `F`

**To select font:**

   a. Click **F**ont.......................... `Alt`+`F`

   b. Select desired font............... `↓` `↑`

**To select font style:**

   a. Click **Font Style** ................ `Alt`+`Y`

   b. Select desired style............... `↓` `↑`

**To select font size:**

   a. Click **S**ize ......................... `Alt`+`S`

   b. Select desired size ............... `↓` `↑`

**To underline text:**

   a. Click **U**nderline ................. `Alt`+`U`

**To change font color:**

   a. Click **C**olor ....................... `Alt`+`C`

   b. Select desired color ............. `↓` `↑`

## Exercise 5

- **Create a Form from an Existing Datasheet**  ■ **Enter Records**
- **Use Form Design View**  ■ **Undo Control Adjustments**
- **Change Form Data Area Width**  ■ **Repeat Data Entry**

# NOTES

### Create a Form from an Existing Datasheet

■ You may view a table in either Datasheet or Form view. **Datasheet view** displays the table in a column and row format, similar to a spreadsheet grid. Each row is a record and each column is a field.

*Datasheet View*

Fields

Records

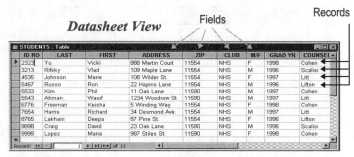

■ **Form view** displays your records one at a time as they would be on index cards in a file drawer.

*Form View*

Field

Record

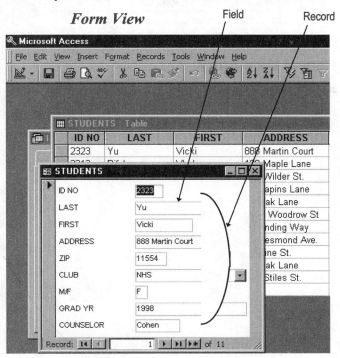

■ The **New Object** button on the Database toolbar automatically creates a Form view of the fields and data listed in an open table.

■ Once records have been added to either a datasheet or a form, you can use the arrow-head buttons on the Scroll bar to scroll through the records.

■ There is a Form Design view, which is discussed on the next page. To quickly switch between Form Design, Form, and Datasheet views, when using forms, use the appropriate option on the View menu or the View button and list box on the Standard toolbar.

View button

Drop-down list

Form with first record

Status line

Form scroll bar

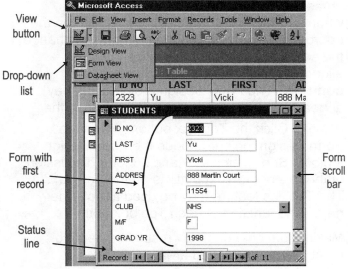

### Enter Records

■ It is easier to enter records in Datasheet view. Records added in either view will automatically be visible in the other. You enter data in Form view in the same manner as in Datasheet view. Pressing the Tab key after the last field brings up the next record form, and data is automatically saved as entered.

## Use Form Design View

- Form Design view can be used to change item width and to enhance the format of a form design.

- You can only make enhancement changes to a form in Form Design view.

### Form Design View

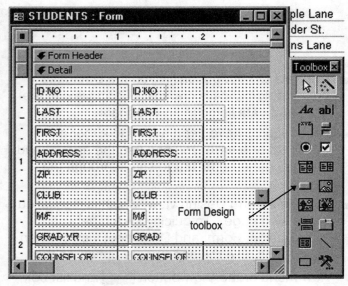

Form Design toolbox

- The enhancement options become available on an added Form Design toolbar that appears when a form item is selected. By clicking on the appropriate Form Design button, you can change the selected item's font type, size, style, or alignment. Access refers to form items as **controls**. The Form Design toolbox that may appear may be closed or used to enhance the design. Click the Toolbox button ⚒ on the Form Design toolbar to open the Form Design toolbox. See Exercises 9 and 26 for a discussion of the use of the Text buttons on the Toolbox. The Tooltips feature may be used to note the name and function of each Toolbox button.

- Making font changes may result in a need to reset the item's allotted area.

## Undo Control Adjustments

- You can undo all enhancement changes by selecting the control to be reset and using the Apply <u>D</u>efault option from the F<u>o</u>rmat menu.

## Change Form Data Area Width

- If you discover that the Form view data areas need adjusting, especially after making font size changes, you must use Form Design view to make desired changes. To resize a field control area, first click on the item, click and hold down the left mouse button on one of the handles, and move in the desired direction. Note the illustration of a selected control box ready to be sized.

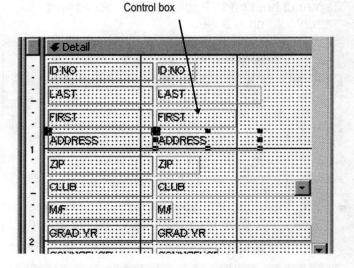

Selected
Control box

## Repeat Data Entry

- If you have data in a field that is the same as the previous record, you may quickly repeat the entry, in Datasheet view, by pressing Ctrl+apostrophe (').

> *Your school wants to create a database file that will keep track of students who apply for school activities and clubs. You will create the form for this database.*

# EXERCISE DIRECTIONS

1. Create a new database file; name it **CLUBS**.

2. Design a table in the CLUBS file in Table Design view using the information listed below. (All fields will be text.)

| FIELD NAME | FIELD SIZE |
|---|---|
| ID NO | 4 |
| LAST | 20 |
| FIRST | 15 |
| ADDRESS | 20 |
| ZIP | 5 |
| M/F | 1 |
| GRAD YR | 4 |
| COUNSELOR | 10 |

3. Save the table; name it STUDENTS. Set a primary key: ID NO.

4. Switch to Datasheet view.

5. Click the New Object button on the toolbar. (A form will be created for the table data.)

6. Save the created form; name it STFORM.

7. If the form is not open, select the FORM tab from the database objects window. (STFORM name will be highlighted.) Select Open. View the created form.

8. Close STFORM.

9. Open the STUDENTS table.

10. The information listed in the table at the bottom of this page was taken from the applications for membership in the NHS (National Honor Society) Club. Enter the first three records using the STUDENTS table.

11. Adjust column widths to accommodate the longest column entry.

12. Save the layout and close the STUDENTS datasheet.

13. Open the STFORM.

14. Scroll through all the records in form view.

15. Add the fourth, fifth, and sixth records from the listing in Form view.

16. Switch to Form Design view.

17. Select the LAST Field Name; change the font size to 12 point. Adjust item width and height, if necessary.

18. Select the LAST data area and make the following change:

    Font size - 10 point; style - bold

19. Save the Form.

20. Using the View button, switch to Form view.

21. View the results of your enhancements.

22. Switch to Form Design view.

23. Select each item that was changed; and apply default settings, which were 8 point font, normal style, left aligned. Resize the LAST Field Name area.

24. Save this Form design.

25. Close the form and the **CLUBS** database.

| ID NO. | LAST | FIRST | ADDRESS | ZIP | M/F | GRAD YR. | COUNSELOR |
|---|---|---|---|---|---|---|---|
| 4535 | Johnson | Marie | 108 Wilder St. | 11554 | F | 1997 | Litt |
| 7654 | Harris | Richard | 34 Desmond Ave. | 11554 | M | 1997 | Litt |
| 5467 | Russo | Ron | 22 Hapins Lane | 11554 | M | 1996 | Lifton |
| 8765 | Lakhani | Deepa | 87 Pine St. | 11554 | F | 1996 | Lifton |
| 9999 | Lopez | Maria | 987 Stiles Street | 11590 | F | 1998 | Cohen |
| 6776 | Freeman | Keisha | 5 Winding Way | 11554 | F | 1998 | Cohen |

# KEYSTROKES

## CREATE FORM VIEW FOR TABLE

1. Open database and table.

2. Press **New Object** button ...........

## ENTER DATA IN FORM VIEW

1. Type data in first field ..................... *data*
2. Press **Tab** ...................................... Tab
3. Repeat steps 1 and 2 until complete.

## CHANGE WIDTH OF FORM ITEM

1. Change to Form Design view (see right).

2. Click on the item to be sized.

3. When mouse pointer is an arrow, use right handle and drag to size.

## MOVE A FORM ITEM

1. Change to Form Design view (see below).

2. Click on the item to be moved.

3. When mouse pointer is a hand, drag and drop item to new location.

## SWITCH FROM FORM TO FORM DESIGN VIEW

1. Click **View** ............................. Alt + V
2. Click **Form Design** ......................... D

## DISPLAY FORM DESIGN TOOLBAR

1. Click **View** ........................... Alt + V
2. Click **Toolbars** ............................. T
3. Select **Form Design** ................. ↑ ↓
4. Press Spacebar.
5. Click **Close** .................

## FORMAT FORM DESIGN

1. Select item to be formatted.

2. Click button that applies from the Form Design toolbar.

## REPEAT DATA ENTRY

**In Datasheet view:**

Press Ctrl+' (apostrophe) for field data that is to be the same as in the previous record.

# Exercise 6

## ■ Summary

*Your department in the Bit-Byte Computer Co. is responsible for ordering and evaluating software products used at company stores. To keep track of the types of software you order, their price, and where they are stored, you have been asked to set up a new company database table for software.*

# EXERCISE DIRECTIONS

1. Open the ⌨COMPANY database, or open 💾06COMPAN.
2. Create a new table using the field data listed below:

| FIELD NAME | DATA TYPE | SIZE | DESCRIPTION |
|---|---|---|---|
| BRANCH | Text | 16 | Where currently in use. |
| TITLE | Text | 11 | |
| TYPE | Text | 17 | |
| PRICE | Currency | (Use Fixed Format) | |
| PURDATE | Date/Time | (Use Short Date Format). Use Input Mask. | |
| STORED | Text | 4 | Storage Drawer # |

3. Save the table design; name it SOFTWARE. Do not set a primary key for this table.
4. Switch to the SOFTWARE Datasheet.
5. Click the New Object button on the toolbar to create a form.
6. Save the created form; name it SOFTFORM.
7. Switch to Form view, if necessary

8. Enter the software listed at the bottom of the page.
9. In Form view, scroll through all the records to verify data.
10. Switch to Form Design view.
11. Select the BRANCH Field Name; change font size to 12.
12. Enlarge the BRANCH Field Name area to accommodate the larger font size.
13. Select the BRANCH data area; make the following changes: font size - 10 point; style - bold.
14. Save this design.
15. Change to Form view. Note the results of your enhancements.
16. Check the design elements; make any needed adjustments.
17. Switch to Datasheet view.
18. Change font size to 12 point; adjust column widths as necessary.
19. Save and close the datasheet.
20. Close the COMPANY database.

| BRANCH | SOFTWARE TITLE | TYPE | PRICE | PURCHASE DATE | STORED |
|---|---|---|---|---|---|
| Sunset | Word-O | Word Processing | 499.85 | 8/17/95 | D230 |
| Big Apple | Micro Words | Word Processing | 459.80 | 6/14/95 | D230 |
| Pacific | Word-O-2 | Word Processing | 499.85 | 5/18/95 | D235 |
| Lakeview | Word-O-2 | Word Processing | 499.85 | 2/20/95 | D235 |
| Lakeview | Tulip5 | Spreadsheet | 594.20 | 3/21/95 | D238 |
| Big Apple | Exceller | Spreadsheet | 475.50 | 3/21/95 | D238 |
| Pacific | Accessor | Database | 550.50 | 12/15/95 | A114 |
| Big Apple | InfoBase | Database | 488.88 | 1/20/96 | A114 |
| Bean Town | BBS | Communications | 111.50 | 3/15/96 | D230 |
| Wheatland | Officemate | Integrated | 479.95 | 3/15/96 | D238 |
| Sunset | Harwood | Graphics | 299.95 | 1/30/96 | D230 |
| Lakeview | Pagemaker | Desktop | 399.40 | 2/15/96 | A114 |

**Exercise 7**

■ **Add, Delete, and Move Fields in Design View**
■ **Add a Lookup Value List Field**

## NOTES

■ Fields may be added, moved, or deleted in a table in Datasheet or Table Design view. (*Modifying a table in Datasheet view will be covered in Exercise 8.*)

### Add, Delete, and Move Fields in Design View

■ Fields may be added in Table Design view by using the Insert, Rows commands. A field is deleted by using the Edit, Delete Row command or by selecting the row and pressing Delete. Moving a field can be done most efficiently by clicking the field's row selector and then dragging the triangular arrow head that appears to a new position. All changes made in Table Design view are reflected in the datasheet.

### Add a Lookup Value List Field

■ If there are several defined choices for a field of data, you may elect to add a value list that appears when a list box arrow is clicked. For example, if the choices for a field named Club are either NHS or AFP, a list box of these values can be displayed and the correct selection made instead of typing each entry. A value list field may be created in either Table Design or Datasheet view using the Lookup Wizard. The values in the value list are typed into the Lookup Wizard screen when the field is defined. Note the illustration of the value list field for this exercise:

| ID NO | LAST | FIRST | ADDRESS | ZIP | CLUB | M/F | GRAD YR | COUNSELOR |
|---|---|---|---|---|---|---|---|---|
| 2323 | Yu | Vicki | 888 Martin Court | 11554 | NHS | F | 1998 | Cohen |
| 3213 | Rifsky | Vlad | 109 Maple Lane | 11554 | NHS | M | 1996 | Scalisi |
| 4535 | Johnson | Marie | 108 Wilder St. | 11554 | NHS | F | 1997 | Litt |
| 5467 | Russo | Ron | 22 Hapins Lane | 11554 | NHS | M | 1996 | Lifton |
| 5533 | Kim | Phil | 11 Oak Lane | 11590 | NHS | M | 1997 | Cohen |
| 5543 | Ahman | Wasif | 1234 Woodrow St | 11590 | NHS ▾ | M | 1997 | Litt |
| 6776 | Freeman | Keisha | 5 Winding Way | 11554 | NHS | | 1998 | Cohen |
| 7654 | Harris | Richard | 34 Desmond Ave. | 11554 | AFP | | 1997 | Litt |
| 8765 | Lakhani | Deepa | 87 Pine St. | 11554 | NHS | F | 1996 | Lifton |
| 9898 | Craig | David | 23 Oak Lane | 11590 | NHS | M | 1996 | Scalisi |
| 9999 | Lopez | Maria | 987 Stiles St. | 11590 | NHS | | | |

Value list box created with Lookup Wizard.

List box arrow

✓ *The Lookup Wizard may also be used to look up data from a related table and place it into the field. In Access 97, data from the lookup field in another table is not automatically updated when the data in the other table changes. To update data in such a field, select the field and press the F9 key. This feature will not be practiced in this exercise.*

---

*You have been given student applications for the NHS Club which can now be entered into the Students table in the CLUB database. Using the Lookup Wizard, you will add a new lookup value list field to the table to list the names of the clubs to which students may apply.*

---

## EXERCISE DIRECTIONS

1. Open the 🖫**CLUBS** database, or open 🖫**07CLUBS**.
2. Open the STUDENTS Table Design view.
3. Insert a new field after ID NO.
   • Name the new field CLUB (Data type - Lookup Wizard).
   • After a pause, the Lookup Wizard dialog box will appear.

• Select **I will type in the values that I want**.
• The number of columns is one (default).
• Type the values below in the first two rows of the Col1 box, using the down arrow to enable you to type the second club.
   NHS
   AFP

4. Confirm the CLUB field name by clicking Finish.

5. Save the Design view layout.

6. Switch to Datasheet view.

7. Enter the data taken from the membership applications to the NHS Club into the appropriate fields.

   ✓Note: When the Club field is entered, click the list box arrow and select NHS for each record.

8. Adjust column widths to accommodate the longest column entry.

9. Save the STUDENTS datasheet.

10. Switch to Table Design view.

11. Move the CLUB field so that it is positioned after the ZIP column.

12. Save and close Table Design view.

13. Using AutoForm, create a new Form using this datasheet; save it and name it CLUBFORM.

14. Scroll through the records in the created form.

15. Save and close the form and the database **CLUBS**.

| ID NO | Club | LAST | Name | Address | Zip | M/F | Grad. Yr. | Counselor |
|-------|------|------|------|---------|-----|-----|-----------|-----------|
| 4535 | NHS | Johnson | Marie | 108 Wilder St. | 11554 | F | 1997 | Litt |
| 7654 | NHS | Harris | Richard | 34 Desmond Ave. | 11554 | M | 1997 | Litt |
| 5467 | NHS | Russo | Ron | 22 Hapins Lane | 11554 | M | 1996 | Lifton |
| 8765 | NHS | Lakhani | Deepa | 87 Pine St. | 11554 | F | 1996 | Lifton |
| 9999 | NHS | Lopez | Maria | 987 Stiles St. | 11590 | F | 1998 | Cohen |
| 6776 | NHS | Freeman | Keisha | 5 Winding Way | 11554 | F | 1998 | Cohen |
| 2323 | NHS | Yu | Vicki | 888 Martin Court | 11554 | F | 1998 | Cohen |
| 3213 | NHS | Rifsky | Vlad | 109 Maple Lane | 11554 | M | 1996 | Scalisi |
| 9898 | NHS | Craig | David | 23 Oak Lane | 11590 | M | 1996 | Scalisi |
| 5533 | NHS | Kim | Phil | 11 Oak Lane | 11590 | M | 1997 | Cohen |
| 5543 | NHS | Ahman | Wasif | 1234 Woodrow St. | 11590 | M | 1997 | Litt |

# KEYSTROKES

## ADD FIELDS
### In Table Design view:

1. Click **Insert**...........................`Alt`+`I`

2. Click **Rows**.............................`R`

3. Type new field name ............. *fieldname*
   ✓ Field names may be up to 64 characters long.

4. Press **Tab**................................`Tab`

5. Click drop-down arrow to reveal data type list ...........`Alt`+`↓`

6. Select **data type**.......................`↓``↑`

7. Press **Tab**................................`Tab`

8. Type description, if desired.

## DELETE A FIELD
### In Design view:

1. Click the field selector (left of field name) to highlight row.

2. Press **Delete**.................................`Del`

## MOVE A FIELD
### In Design view:

1. Click the field selector (left of field name).

2. When the mouse pointer looks like a box, click and drag field selector to new location. As you drag the field, Access displays a bold line below the field after which the moved field will be inserted.

## USE LOOKUP WIZARD FOR VALUE LIST
### In Design view:

1. Click **Insert**...........................`Alt`+`I`

2. Click **Lookup Field**..........................`L`

3. Select **I will type in the values that I want**.

4. Click **Next**.

5. Set number of columns..............*number*

6. Type list values in Col1 ...............*values* (Use down arrow to add values in new rows that appear.)

7. Click **Finish** to confirm field name.

<table>
<tr><td>Exercise<br>8</td><td>■ **Add, Delete, and Move Fields in Datasheet View**<br>■ **Simple Print** ■ **Hide Datasheet Fields**</td></tr>
</table>

# NOTES

## Add, Delete, and Move Fields in Datasheet View

■ You can add a new field by clicking on the column to the right of the location of the new field and by using the Insert, Column commands. A new column will be added to the left of the selected column.

■ To delete a field, select the field by highlighting the column and then use the Edit, Delete Column commands. You will be asked to confirm the deletion and the data will reposition itself. A deletion permanently removes the field and all its data.

■ Fields may be added, moved, or deleted in a table in Datasheet or Table Design view. However, it is better not to move a field in Datasheet view since copy and paste or click and drag operations may result in the loss of data.

■ If a field is changed in a datasheet, it does not automatically transfer to the related form. It is easier to delete the old form and use AutoForm to create a new form.

## Simple Print

■ You can get a printout of current screen data in either Datasheet or Form view. To print the current screen data, either choose the Print option from the File menu or click the Print button 🖶. The Print button causes the data to print immediately.

■ The Print dialog box appears only after you select File, Print. It provides selections for the Print Range, Properties, Number of Copies, and Setup options. Note the Print dialog box above right.

*Print Dialog Box*

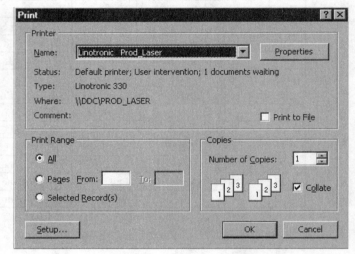

■ If you wish to set options for paper, graphics, fonts, or devices, click the Properties button on the Print dialog box.

■ If you wish to set options for orientation, margins, etc., click the Setup button on the Print dialog box.

■ Clicking the Print Preview button 🔍 on the Table Datasheet toolbar allows you to check your output before printing.

## Hide Datasheet Fields

■ You may display and/or print selected fields in a datasheet by hiding unwanted fields using the Hide Columns option in the Format menu. Columns may be redisplayed by using the Unhide Columns option. As mentioned earlier, this may be used as a security measure.

*The manager at Bit-Byte Computer Stores has asked you to add two more fields to your STORES table. Fields for sales and evening hours information will be included in datasheet view, columns will be hidden, and the datasheet and form view will be printed.*

# EXERCISE DIRECTIONS

1. Open the 🖿**COMPANY** database, or open 💾**08COMPAN**.

2. Select and open the STORES table.

3. Insert two blank columns before the STAFF field column.

4. Double-click on each new Field1 and Field2 column heading and replace with the new field names:
   First field - change to SALES
   Second field - change to EVE

5. Switch to Design view and note the new fields and the default type settings.

6. Edit the data type settings to reflect the following information:
   - SALES (Data type - number; Field size - long integer; Format - standard; Decimal places - 0)
   - EVE (Data type - Yes/No)

7. Save the new design

8. Switch to Datasheet view.

9. Delete the STORE NUMBER field.

10. From the list below, enter the information for each branch. Enter the EVE data into the checkbox format.

| BRANCH | SALES | EVE |
|---|---|---|
| Astro Center | 541,000 | ☐ |
| Bean Town | 682,450 | ☑ |
| Big Apple | 789,300 | ☑ |
| Lakeview | 755,420 | ☐ |
| Oceanview | 433,443 | ☑ |
| Pacific | 685,400 | ☐ |
| Peach Tree | 457,800 | ☑ |
| Sunset | 876,988 | ☐ |
| Twin Cities | 235,420 | ☑ |
| Wheatland | 352,415 | ☑ |

11. Adjust column widths to accommodate the longest entry.

12. Print Preview the datasheet.

13. Hide SALES field.

14. Print Preview the datasheet.

15. Print this datasheet display.

16. Unhide the SALES field.

17. Save the datasheet.

18. Use AutoForm to create a related Form view of this datasheet; name it STFORM.

19. Scroll through STFORM to locate the Lakeview form.

20. Print the selected record from Form view.

21. Close the database **COMPANY**.

# KEYSTROKES

## 🌐 PREVIEW FORM/TABLE

1. Click **Print Preview** button ............ 🔍
   **OR**
   a. Click **File** ........................ `Alt` + `F`
   b. Click **Print Preview** ................... `V`

## PRINT DATA IN A FORM

1. View form to print.
   **OR**
   Select form in Database window.
2. Click **File** ............................ `Alt` + `F`
3. Click **Print** ............................ `P`
4. Click a Print Range option to select:

   **All** ........................................ `Alt` + `A`
   **Pages** .................................... `Alt` + `G`
   **Selected Record(s)** ............... `Alt` + `E`
5. Select **Properties** ............... `Alt` + `P`
   if desired.

---

*Choose desired option tab: Paper, Graphics, Fonts, Device Options and select options.*

6. Click **OK** ................................... `Enter`
7. Type number ........... `Alt` + `C`, *number* in **Number of Copies** text box, if desired.
8. Click **OK** ................................... `Enter`

## PRINT DATA FROM DATASHEET TABLE

1. Click **File** ............................... `Alt` + `F`
2. Click **Print** ............................... `P`
3. Click **OK** ............................... `Enter`

## INSERT COLUMN (FIELD) IN DATASHEET

1. Place cursor on the column to the right of the insertion point
2. Click **Insert** ........................... `Alt` + `I`
3. Click **Column** ................................. `C`

---

## DELETE COLUMN (FIELD) IN DATASHEET

1. Click on column to be deleted.
2. Press **Delete** ................................ `Del`

## HIDE A COLUMN

**In Datasheet view:**

1. Click in column you would like to hide.
2. Click **Format** ...................... `Alt` + `O`
3. Click **Hide Columns** ................... `H`

## UNHIDE A COLUMN

1. Click **Format** ........................ `Alt` + `O`
2. Click **Unhide Columns** ................... `U`
3. Check column to unhide.
4. Click **Close** ......................... `Alt` + `C`

## Exercise 9

■ **Print Setup**  ■ **Form View Toolbox**
■ **Print with headers and Footers**

## NOTES

### Print Setup

■ You may select various print options, before printing a Datasheet or Forms, by selecting the Page Setup command. The Page Setup dialog box contains tabs for Page and Margins when accessed in Datasheet view and tabs for Page, Margins, and Layout when accessed in Form view.

■ In Datasheet view, you may make the following Page Setup settings:

PAGE TAB

- Print Orientation: Portrait (the default) or Landscape (to print sideways)
- Paper Size (Letter - the default, Legal, Envelope, User Defined Size)
- Printer

MARGINS TAB

- Margins
- Print Headings (check box)

■ In Form view, there are additional printing options that can be accessed by selecting the Columns tab in Page Setup. You can set the number of items to print across the page, the row and column spacing, the width and height of the items, and the layout of the items on a page.

■ The print Preview option allows you to check the layout before printing. Note the illustrations of the Print Preview screens for one column and two column print-outs:

*Print Preview with 1 Item Across*

*Print Preview with 2 Items Across*

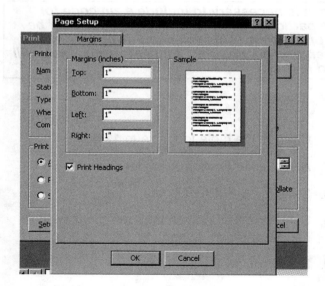

## Form View Toolbox

■ As mentioned in Exercise 5, the Toolbox that appears in Form Design view can be used to modify Form view items. Use the Tooltips feature to note the function of each button. The Label ![Aa] button can be used to create text for new data or for header or footer labels.

To create a label:

- Click the ![Aa] button.
- Click the desired location.
- Drag label box to size.
- Enter text and size box, as necessary.

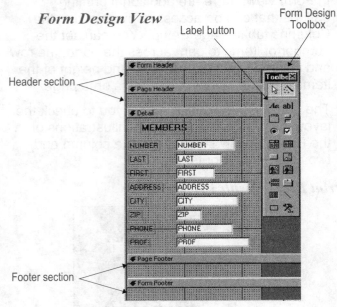

*Form Design View*

Form Design Toolbox

Label button

Header section

Footer section

## Print with Headers and/or Footers

■ Headers or footers cannot be customized in a datasheet printout; however, in Datasheet view by checking the Print Headings box on the Margins tab of the Page Setup dialog box, a default header will be included in the print-out. The header will include the table name and date of the printout. Customized headers or footers may be added in Report View, which will be discussed in Lesson 5.

■ In Form Design view, an upper section titled Form Header and a lower section titled Form Footer appears when Form Header/Footer is activated (✔) on the View menu. Once the section appears, form header or footer text may be added using the label button on the Form Design Toolbox. Double-click the header or footer label control and enter the text. These entries will appear on every form. Note the illustration of a Form Design with a form footer and the preparation for a header entry, on the left.

■ If you wish the print-out heading to be different from the header on each form, you may set a page header or footer by activating the Page Header/Footer command on the View menu and entering the desired information in the Page areas that display. The page header and footer areas appear on the Form Design and may be completed in the same manner as form header and footers.

---

*In order to use the HUG membership list for mailings, it is necessary to include a zip code for each member. Since certain mailings apply only to a particular professional group, it would be helpful to include a field that will identify a person's profession. This will enable you to send information to one particular group rather than to everyone on your list. In this exercise, you will add two new fields (ZIP and PROF) and print selected records.*

---

# EXERCISE DIRECTIONS

1. Open the ⌨**HUGCLUB** database, or open 💾**09HUGCLB**.

2. Open MEMBERS in Table Design view.

3. Add two new fields, ZIP and PROF, in the locations noted on the following page; set an appropriate field size. Both are text fields.

4. Save the design.

5. Add the data indicated for these new fields.

6. Change the table font size to 12 point.

7. Adjust column widths, as necessary.

8. Save the MEMBERS datasheet.

9. Use Page Setup to change the orientation to Landscape and margins to .5".

10. Print Preview the printout.

11. Print the datasheet. Create a form for the updated datasheet; name it MEMFORM.

12. Switch to Design view.

13. If the form footer is not displayed, use the View, Form Header/Footer option. Enter MEMBERS as the footer (create a label), using the label button on the Toolbox.

14. Select Page Header/Footer from the View menu.

15. In the new Page Header section that appears, enter the heading CALIFORNIA MEMBERS, using the Label button. Save the design.

16. Switch to Form view.

17. Set up for two column printing.

18. Print Preview.

19. Print the records.

20. Close and save **MEMFORM**.

21. Close the database.

| | LAST | FIRST | ADDRESS | CITY | ZIP | PHONE | PROF |
|---|---|---|---|---|---|---|---|
| 1 | Barnes | Leanne | 808 Summer Street | Anaheim | 92803 | (213)555-4987 | Student |
| 2 | Brown | Miles | 154 Newburg Road | Anaheim | 92803 | (213)555-4837 | Accountant |
| 3 | Griffith | Stuart | 1551 Dean Street | Beverly Hills | 90210 | (213)555-3010 | Lawyer |
| 4 | Moon | Michael | 17 Pine Street | Beverly Hills | 90210 | (213)555-9275 | Teacher |
| 5 | Smith | Trina | 3954 Wood Avenue | Anaheim | 92803 | (213)555-7283 | Student |
| 6 | Smith | Sheila | 417 Specific Court | Anaheim | 92803 | (213)555-7284 | Chiropractor |
| 7 | Walker | Bette | 1584 F. Street | North Hollywood | 91615 | (213)555-9174 | Lawyer |
| 8 | Castillo | Carl | 1965 Park Avenue | North Hollywood | 91615 | (213)555-5192 | Banker |
| 9 | Davis | John | P.O. Box 2333 | North Hollywood | 91615 | (213)555-8129 | Student |
| 10 | Dixon | Amy | 237 Albee Street | North Hollywood | 91615 | (213)555-8917 | Orthopedist |

# KEYSTROKES

## ADD HEADER TO FORM

1. View form design.
2. Click **View** ............................ Alt + V
3. Click desired option to select:
   **Page Header/Footer** ...................... A
   **Form Header/Footer** ...................... H

## DELETE HEADER

1. View form design.
2. Click **View** ............................ Alt + V
3. Click desired option to clear:
   **Page Header/ Footer** ...................... A
   **Form Header/Footer** ...................... H

## CREATE LABEL

1. View form design.
2. Click label [A] icon.
3. Click and drag label box to size at desired location.
4. Enter text.
5. Size box as necessary.

## PRINT SETUP FOR LANDSCAPE ORIENTATION

1. Click **File** ............................ Alt + F
2. Click **Page Setup** ...................... U
3. On **Page** tab, select an orientation:
   **Portrait** .............................. Alt + R
   OR
   **Landscape** ............................ Alt + L
4. Click **OK** ............................ Enter

## PRINT SETUP FOR MARGINS

1. Click **File** ............................ Alt + F
2. Click **Page Setup** ...................... U
3. On **Margins** tab, enter margins:
   **Top** .................................. Alt + T
   **Bottom** ............................... Alt + B
   **Left** ................................. Alt + F
   **Right** ................................ Alt + G
4. Click **OK** ............................ Enter

## PRINT SETUP FOR FORMS

1. Click **File** ............................ Alt + F
2. Click **Page Setup** ...................... U
3. On **Columns** tab, enter settings for:
   GRID SETTINGS
   **Number of Columns** ........ Alt + C
   **Row Spacing** .................. Alt + W
   COLUMN SIZE
   **Width** ............................... Alt + I
   **Height** .............................. Alt + E
   COLUMN LAYOUT
   **Down, then Across** .......... Alt + O
   **Across, then Down** .......... Alt + N
4. Click **OK** ............................ Enter

## Exercise 10

■ **Edit a Record** ■ **Add and Delete a Record**
■ **Remove Gridlines** ■ **Form Backgrounds**

# NOTES

### Edit a Record

■ To change data that has already been entered in a field, highlight the existing data and retype the new data. This may be done in either Datasheet view or Form view. You may also place the cursor at the location of data to be inserted and make the needed changes.

■ To delete the contents of a field, select the data, then press the Delete key or select Delete from the Edit menu.

### Add a Record

■ Records may be added in either Datasheet view or Form view but only at the end of the existing records. Records can be arranged in order through sorting which will be discussed in Lesson 3.

### Delete a Record

■ Records may be deleted in either Datasheet view or Form view by using the Select Record option from the Edit menu and the Delete key. Access will renumber the records when a new record is added or when a record is deleted.

### Remove Gridlines

■ If you wish to print a datasheet without gridlines, you may remove them by selecting the Off condition for the Gridlines Shown check box on the Format, Cells Effects dialog box. Both horizontal and vertical gridlines must be deselected to remove gridlines.

*Cells Effects Dialog Box*

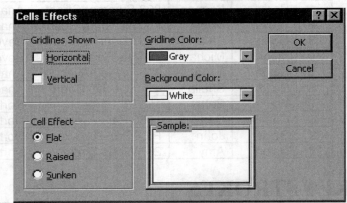

### Form Backgrounds

■ You can add a logo or other graphic to the background of a form to enhance its design. A picture created in Microsoft Paint, a worksheet from Excel, or a Word document can be added to a form. The Microsoft Office 97 CD-ROM contains a CLIPART folder containing graphics including photographs and background art.

■ To add a background to a form, use Form Design view. Open the Properties sheet by clicking View, Properties or by double-clicking the form selector. (Note the illustration of the form selector.)

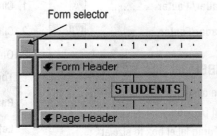

- On the property sheet, illustrated at the right, click in the Picture field and then double-click the Build button to locate the desired picture file. Note that when a background file picture is selected, it appears as a form background.

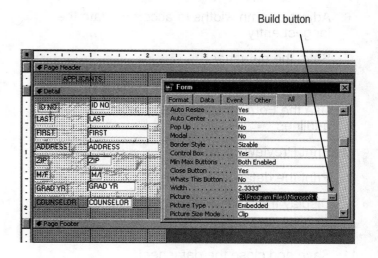

Several students are no longer being considered for membership in the National Honor Society (NHS), and several new students have just submitted applications. You have also discovered several errors in the records. You will need to edit your datasheet to reflect these changes. Applications have just been received for the Academy of Finance Program (AFP). You will need to add these to your datasheet.

# EXERCISE DIRECTIONS

1. Open the CLUBS database, or open 10CLUBS.

2. Open the STUDENTS table.

3. The students listed below have applied for admission to the Academy of Finance Program (AFP). Add their records to the database and select AFP in the list box Club field.

| ID NO | LAST | FIRST | ADDRESS | ZIP | M/F | GRAD YR. | COUNSELOR |
|-------|------|-------|---------|-----|-----|----------|-----------|
| 6661 | DeLorenzo | Kristen | 871 River Road | 11554 | F | 1997 | Litt |
| 9976 | Chasin | Matthew | 99 Bridle Lane | 11554 | M | 1996 | Lifton |
| 1212 | Wilkinson | Chad | 2 Token Court | 11554 | M | 1996 | Lifton |
| 5555 | Rivers | Ebony | 33 Pine St. | 11554 | F | 1997 | Litt |
| 8888 | Juliana | Jennifer | 78 Token Court | 11554 | F | 1997 | Litt |

4. Ron Russo is no longer being considered for membership in the NHS; delete his record.

5. The students listed below have applied for admission to the NHS; add their records to the datasheet and select NHS in the list box Club field.

| ID NO | LAST | FIRST | ADDRESS | ZIP | M/F | GRAD YR. | COUNSELOR |
|-------|------|-------|---------|-----|-----|----------|-----------|
| 5536 | Chou | Wendy | 9005 Hylan Blvd. | 11554 | F | 1997 | Cohen |
| 2234 | Smith | Rick | 9012 Hylan Blvd. | 11554 | M | 1997 | Cohen |

6. Adjust column widths to accommodate the longest entry.

7. Save the datasheet.

8. Hide the ADDRESS and ZIP columns.

9. Use the Format, Cells dialog box to remove gridlines.

10. Print Preview your page.

11. Print the datasheet.

12. Display the hidden fields.

13. Re-select gridlines.

14. Save and close the datasheet.

15. Open the STFORM design view.

16. From the View menu, activate Page Header/Footer.

17. In the new Page Header section that appears, enter the heading APPLICANTS.

18. Add a background to the form.

   a. Double-click the form selector button to display the Property sheet.

   b. Double-click the Build button on the Picture property box.

   c. Locate the Blocks background by selecting the following from the Office 97 CD-ROM: CLIPART\PHOTOS\BACKGRND\BLOCKS

   d. Close the Property sheet.

19. Save the design.

20. Switch to Form view.

21. Set the Page Setup for two column printing.

   *Note:    If the forms are too wide, resize them by moving fields until they fit.*

22. Print Preview.

23. Print the records.

24. Close the **CLUBS** database file.

# KEYSTROKES

## EDIT DATA

### Replace Data in a Field:

   ✓ *Access automatically saves changes to fields when you move to the next record. A pencil icon appears at left of the record in datasheet view and at the top left of the window in Form view to indicate that the changes have not yet been saved.*

1. Place insertion point............................. |
   in field to change.
   **OR**
   Press the **Down-Arrow** key.............. [↓]
   **OR**
   Click and drag to select field contents.

2. Type desired new value ................. *value*

## DELETE A RECORD

### In Form view:

1. Page to the record to be deleted.

2. Click **Edit** ........................... [Alt]+[E]

3. Click **Select record** ....................... [L]

4. Press **Delete** ............................... [Del]
   **OR**
   a. Click **Edit** ....................... [Alt]+[E]
   b. Click **Delete Record** ................. [D]

5. Click **OK** .................................... [Enter]

## DELETE A RECORD

### In Datasheet view:

1. Click the left edge of the record to be deleted.

2. Click **Edit** .............................. [Alt]+[E]

3. Click **Delete Record** ...................... [R]

4. Click **OK** .................................... [Enter]

## REMOVE GRIDLINES

### In Datasheet view:

1. Click **Format** ....................... [Alt]+[O]

2. Click **Cells** ................................. [E]

3. Deselect Gridlines Shown for

   **Horizontal** ........................... [Alt]+[H]

   **Vertical** ............................... [Alt]+[V]

4. Click **OK** .................................... [Enter]

## FORM BACKGROUNDS

### In Form Design view:

1. Click **View** ........................... [Alt]+[V]

2. Click **Properties** ........................... [P]

3. Select Format tab ............... [Format]

4. Scroll down to Picture field.

5. Click Build button when Picture field is selected.

6. Follow Wizard steps to insert a background picture.

# Exercise 11

- ■ **Window Between Objects**  ■ **Form AutoFormat**
- ■ **Lookup Field Values from Another Table**

## NOTES

### Window Between Objects

■ The <u>V</u>iew menu can be used to switch between Form view and Form Design view or between Table view and Table Design view.  However, when you are working with several objects at the same time (such as a form and a table) and have them all open, you can switch between the objects easily by selecting the <u>W</u>indow menu and the database object you desire from the list of open objects.  Note the illustration of the Window menu with a list of several open database objects.  The "clubs : Database" selection brings you to the Database Object window.  Tables are listed and labeled, and forms are listed by their heading. For example "STUDENTS" in the illustration below is the form.

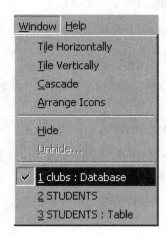

### Form AutoFormat

■ Since many firms use Form view for data entry, it may be desirable to format the screen with an interesting background.  Access provides an AutoFormat feature, in Form Design view, that allows you to provide background colors or patterns.  The F<u>o</u>rmat, Auto<u>F</u>ormat commands will display the AutoFormat dialog box with the Standard setting.  The setting in the AutoFormat box below is for the Clouds AutoFormat.

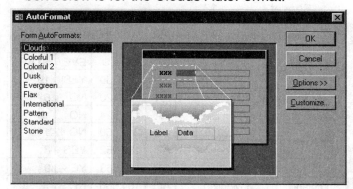

■ The <u>O</u>ptions settings in the box allow you to eliminate color, font, or border settings to your taste.

■ The Customize settings allow you to create your own format and use it as an AutoFormat.  The default setting in this dialog box brings your existing data into the new format.

### Lookup Field Values from Another Table

■ In Exercise 7 we used the Lookup Wizard to create a list of values for a field.  You can also use a lookup field to select values from another table.  If you are using a text primary key that will be entered on related tables, you run the risk of mistyping the text data and thus corrupting the link.  Instead of typing text linking fields, such as BRANCH, on related tables, use the Lookup Wizard to find the exact text from the primary key source table.

> *Bit-Byte has opened several new branches. In some branches there have been personnel changes. The datasheet STORES, therefore, will need to be updated. The branch fields in the hardware and software tables will be changed to lookup fields to make BRANCH entry more accurate.*

# EXERCISE DIRECTIONS

1. Open the ⌨**COMPANY** database, or open 💾**11COMPAN**.

2. Open the STORES table.

3. Add the following new branches to the datasheet.

4. Adjust column widths to accommodate the longest entry.

5. There have been changes in the number of employees in the following branches.
   - Make these changes in the datasheet:

     | | |
     |---|---|
     | Big Apple | 20 |
     | Wheatland | 11 |
     | Sunset | 13 |
     | Astro Center | 12 |
     | Peach Tree | 16 |

| BRANCH | CITY | ST | SALES | EVE. | STAFF |
|---|---|---|---|---|---|
| Liberty | Philadelphia | PA | 423,150 | YES | 19 |
| Seal City Center | Anchorage | AK | 185,420 | NO | 6 |
| Central States | San Diego | CA | 144,524 | NO | 14 |
| Federal Plaza | Washington | DC | 245,860 | NO | 11 |
| Desert View Mall | Phoenix | AZ | 189,252 | YES | 8 |
| Rocky Mountain | Denver | CO | 102,563 | YES | 9 |
| Southland | Mobile | AL | 104,566 | NO | 7 |
| River View Plaza | Atlanta | GA | 215,400 | NO | 6 |
| Dixieland | Atlanta | GA | 352,622 | YES | 14 |
| Iron City Plaza | Cleveland | OH | 543,233 | NO | 13 |

6. The Twin Cities branch closed; delete the record.

7. Remove the datasheet's gridlines.
   - ✓ *Note: Use the Format, Cells command and click Gridlines Shown off for both Horizontal and Vertical.*

8. Use the Window menu to switch to the Database Object window and open the HARDWARE table in Design view.

9. To change the BRANCH field using Lookup Wizard:
   - Select the BRANCH data type box and select Lookup Wizard.
   - Select **I want the lookup column to lookup values in a table or query**.
   - Click Next. Select STORES as the table to provide the values.
   - Click Next.
   - Click the arrow button to select BRANCH as the field that contains the values.
   - Click Next.
   - Adjust column width, if necessary.
   - Click Finish.

10. Save the design.

11. Repeat steps 9 and 10 for the SOFTWARE table.

12. Switch to the Database Object window and open the SOFTFORM form.

13. Switch to Design view. Use Autoformat to set the pattern design for the form.

14. Save and close the Form Design.

15. Close the SOFTFORM form.

16. On the STORES table, use Page Setup to set for Landscape orientation.

17. Print the datasheet.

18. Restore the datasheet's gridlines to the default setting.

19. Save and close the datasheet.

# KEYSTROKES

**FORM AUTOFORMAT**

**In Form Design view:**

1. Click **F**ormat.......................... `Alt`+`O`
2. Click Auto**F**ormat ..................... `F`
3. Select desired format ............... `↓` `↑`

**To select Options:**

1. Click **O**ptions........................ `Alt`+`O`
2. Deselect features as desired........................ `Tab` , `Space`

**To customize format:**

1. Click **C**ustomize ................... `Alt`+`C`
2. Select desired option..................... `Tab`

**Exercise**

**12**

**Part I**

■ **Summary**

In the past, computer equipment inventory records for your company were kept on "inventory cards." In an earlier exercise, you created an inventory datasheet design, HARDWARE. In this exercise, you will enter information from those cards into the database.

# EXERCISE DIRECTIONS

1. Open the ⌨COMPANY database, or open 💾**12COMPAN**.

2. Open the HARDWARE in Table Design view.

3. Add two text fields to the end of the existing design:

   ASSIGNED TO (Field size - 15);
   SERIAL # (Field size - 7).

4. Save the new design.

5. Change to Datasheet view.

6. The listing below represents "inventory card" data. Enter the field data in upper and lower case, except where names are represented by initials (NEC, IBM, etc.). Change the default WTY setting, where needed. The BRANCH field entries are now lookup values.

7. Adjust column widths.

8. Print the datasheet.

9. Save the datasheet; do not close the datasheet.

10. Create a Form view of this datasheet.

11. Save Form view; name it **HARDFORM**.

12. Use Page Setup from the File menu to make the following changes: Landscape orientation; all print margins to .5 "; set to print 3 items across. Adjust form layout, if necessary.

13. Print the form records.

14. Save and close Form view.

| BRANCH | ITEM | MFG | MODEL | COST | PUR DATE- | WTY | ASSIGNED TO | SERIAL |
|--------|------|-----|-------|------|-----------|-----|-------------|--------|
| Big Apple | Computer | IBM | PS2 | 1248.50 | 6/1/95 | Yes | Accounting | 651198 |
| Big Apple | Printer | IBM | ExecJet II | 335.00 | 6/1/95 | Yes | Accounting | 55211 |
| Sunset | Computer | IBM | Thinkpad 350C | 2199.00 | 6/1/95 | Yes | Accounting | AB2059 |
| Pacific | Computer | IBM | Thinkpad 500 | 1399.00 | 6/1/95 | Yes | Accounting | 671150 |
| Pacific | Hard Drive | Quantum | LPS40 170MB | 199.00 | 6/1/95 | Yes | Accounting | 54219 |
| Sunset | Hard Drive | Conner | CFS4 210MB | 200.00 | 6/1/95 | No | Purchasing | 12345 |
| Pacific | Printer | HP | Laserjet | 1479.00 | 7/1/95 | No | Accounting | 88842 |
| Bean Town | Computer | Canon | Notebook 486 | 1889.00 | 1/1/96 | Yes | Shipping | 1445A |

## Part II

*Your company has acquired new equipment. These new purchases must be added to the inventory. When checking the datasheet, you find several errors which need to be corrected.*

# EXERCISE DIRECTIONS

1. Open the **HARDWARE** table.

2. Add the data below to the table. The BRANCH field entries are now lookup values.

3. Adjust column widths if necessary.

4. The correct cost of the IBM PS2, purchased on 6/1/95, was $1348.50; make the correction.

5. The Quantum hard drive is not under warranty; make the correction.

6. The HP Laserjet printer, purchased on 7/1/95, is no longer in use; delete the record from the datasheet.

7. Change the datasheet font to Times New Roman, size 12.

8. Change the datasheet row height to 14.

9. Print Preview the datasheet. (The preview will have two pages.)

10. Change the print orientation to Landscape.

11. Preview this setup.

12. Return to the datasheet; adjust column widths, as desired.

13. Print one copy of the datasheet.

14. Reset the font to the default setting (MS Sans Serif, 10 point).

15. Reset the Row Height setting to Standard Height.

16. Save and close the database.

| BRANCH | ITEM | MFG | MODEL | COST | PUR DATE- | WTY | ASSIGNED TO | SERIAL |
|---|---|---|---|---|---|---|---|---|
| Wheatland | Printer | NEC | FGE/3V | 539.00 | 8/1/95 | No | Purchasing | 87098 |
| Lakeview | Printer | NEC | FGE/3V | 589.00 | 12/1/95 | No | Shipping | 11112 |
| Bean Town | Modem | Intel | PMCIA | 115.00 | 9/1/95 | No | Accounting | 098A |
| Bean Town | Printer | Okidata | ML320 | 295.00 | 8/1/95 | Yes | Shipping | 98983 |
| Sunset | Printer | HP | Deskjet | 429.00 | 11/1/95 | Yes | Accounting | 99911 |
| Pacific | Printer | HP | Deskjet | 429.00 | 11/1/95 | Yes | Purchasing | 22230 |
| Wheatland | Computer | Canon | Notebook | 2436.00 | 8/1/95 | Yes | Purchasing | 98763 |
| Lakeview | Computer | Canon | Notebook | 2436.00 | 8/1/95 | Yes | Shipping | 76666 |

## Exercise 13

■ **Find Records** ■ **Find Records and Replace Data**
■ **Search Using Wildcards**

## NOTES

### Find Records

■ The <u>E</u>dit menu contains options which assist in finding and replacing data. These options are available in both Datasheet and Form views.

■ You may wish to find a specific record for editing or informational purposes. You may find records by searching the entire datasheet or by selecting a specific field for the search. Searching for data in a specific field will expedite the search process. After opening either Datasheet or Form view of the records to be searched, select <u>F</u>ind from the <u>E</u>dit menu and the Find dialog box will appear:

*Find Dialog Box*

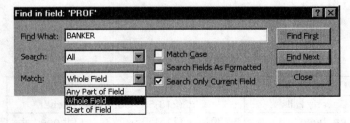

■ After making the appropriate entry in the Fi<u>n</u>d What box, set the Find window conditions:

**Sear<u>c</u>h -** drop-down list to search all, or below or above a selected record.

**Mat<u>c</u>h -** Match Whole Field, Any Part of Field, or Start of Field.

**Search only Curr<u>e</u>nt Field -** Search on a specific field to speed up the search.

**Match <u>C</u>ase -** Select to match exactly upper and lowercase entries or, if not selected, search will ignore case of entry.

**Search Fields As F<u>o</u>rmatted** (if data format in view is different from defined format) - Selected or not selected.

■ When all the appropriate conditions have been set, select Find Fir<u>s</u>t to begin the search. The first record, containing the search data, is presented with the search data highlighted. You can now view or edit the located record. To edit a record, close the Find window, make the needed changes, and reopen the Find window to continue.

■ To search for another record that contains the same data, select <u>F</u>ind Next. The next record containing the search data, or a message that no more records were found, is presented.

### Find and Replace

■ If you know that all records with the same field data should be replaced, you can use a Find and Replace option. After you select <u>R</u>eplace from the <u>E</u>dit menu, a Replace dialog box will appear, as shown below.

*Replace Dialog Box*

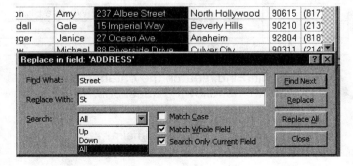

The Replace dialog box has many of the same options as the Find dialog box. In the Replace window, make the appropriate entries in the Find What and Replace With boxes. When all the appropriate conditions have been set, select Find Next to find each occurrence of your search entry. You may choose to make the replacement or find the next occurrence.

**OR**

Select Replace - to replace one occurrence of the search entry.

**OR**

Select Replace All - to automatically change all occurrences. Access will NOT ask you to confirm replacements.

## Search Using Wildcards

■ A wildcard is a symbol used in a search value to substitute for unknown characters. There are two wildcard symbols that broaden the Edit, Find command: the asterisk (*) and the question mark (?).

■ The asterisk (*) is used to indicate an unknown group of characters. For example: If you were searching for a particular name but were certain of only the last three letters, you would indicate the search value as *sky. This will find all records in which the last name ends with sky.

■ The question mark (?) is used to substitute for an unknown single character. If you were searching for a particular name but were uncertain of some characters in the spelling, the search value could be entered as, for example, Br?wn or Br?w? or B??wn. This would find records with any letter in the question mark location.

---

*Several new members have joined HUG, your computer users' group. In addition, you have been notified that several members' records need to be updated. After updating your records, you will be in a better position to generate membership information.*

---

# EXERCISE DIRECTIONS

1. Open the ▧**HUGCLUB** database, or open ▧**13HUGCLB**.

2. From the information below, add the new members to your current datasheet. Adjust column widths, if necessary.

| NUMBER | LAST | FIRST | ADDRESS | CITY | ZIP | PHONE | PROF |
|--------|------|-------|---------|------|-----|-------|------|
| 11 | Kendall | Gale | 15 Imperial Way | Beverly Hills | 90210 | (213)555-9888 | Teacher |
| 12 | Dagger | Janice | 27 Ocean Avenue | Anaheim | 92804 | (213)555-7777 | Orthopedist |
| 13 | Chow | Michael | 188 Riverside Drive | Culver City | 90311 | (213)555-7655 | Accountant |
| 14 | Wagner | David | 879 Beverly Drive | Beverly Hills | 90210 | (213)555-6676 | Banker |
| 15 | Smith | Cleo | 90 Rodeo Drive | Beverly Hills | 90210 | (213)555-2222 | Student |
| 16 | Anderson | Carolyn | 666 Santa Ana Drive | Culver City | 90312 | (213)555-9988 | Lawyer |
| 17 | Ramaz | Nadine | 9012 Wilshire Blvd. | Beverly Hills | 90210 | (213)555-2211 | Teacher |
| 18 | Yakar | Winston | 776 Prince Lane | North Hollywood | 91615 | (213)555-1584 | Student |
| 19 | Mancuso | Mary | 12 Pacific Court | North Hollywood | 91615 | (213)555-7773 | Banker |

3. Using Edit, Find, search the database for the answers to the following questions. Make note of the answers.

   a) Which members live in Anaheim?

   b) Which members live in Beverly Hills?

   c) Which members are Lawyers?

   d) How many members are Students?

   e) What is Trina Smith's profession?

4. Locate the record for Michael Moon. Make the following changes on his record:

   - His new address is 32 Oak Street, located in the same city and zip code.
   - His new phone number is (213)555-8750.

5. Locate the record for Bette Walker. Make the following changes on her record:

   - Her new name is Bette Walker-Sim.
   - Her new address is 1745 River Street, located in North Hollywood, 91615.
   - Her new phone number is (213)555-8520.

6. Locate the record for a member named Sheila Smith. We know she lives in Anaheim. Change her phone number to (213)555-5672.

7. Use a wildcard to search for a member whose last name begins with Ram to assist in reading a signature. Which member's signature begins with Ram?

8. Select the Address column in the table and find and replace all occurrences of Avenue with Ave.

   ✔ *Note:   Set Match Whole Field to Off.*

9. Adjust column widths, as necessary.

10. Save and close the datasheet.

11. Close the **HUGCLUB** database.

# KEYSTROKES

## FIND AND REPLACE DATA

1. Click field to match or, in Datasheet view, click field selector or any field in column.

2. Click **Edit** ............................... Alt + E

3. Click **Replace** ................................. E

4. Type data to replace ........................ *data* in **Find What** text box.

5. Type replacement data .................... *data* in **Replace With** text box.

6. Click **Search** list box to select desired option:

   **All**

   **Up**

   **Down**

   - Click **Match Case** ............... Alt + C to restrict search.

   - Click **Match Whole Field** .... Alt + W to restrict search.

   - Click **Search only Current Field** to restrict search ........ Alt + E

**To replace text in current field:**

7. Click **Replace** ....................... Alt + R

**To replace text in all matching fields at once:**

   Click **Replace All** .................... Alt + A

**To view next matching field:**

   Click **Find Next** ..................... Alt + F

8. Click **Close** when finished.

9. Click **OK** ................................... Enter to confirm changes.

## FIND RECORDS USING FIND OPTIONS

1. Click field to match or, in Datasheet view, click field selector or any field in column.

2. Click **Find** button. ........................... 🔍

   **OR**

   Click **Edit** ............................ Alt + E

   Click **Find** ............................. F

3. Type value in **Find What** ............... *value* text box.

4. Select **Match** .......................... Alt + H to desired part of field.

   **Any Part of Field**

   **Whole Field**

   **Start of Field**

5. Click **Search** list box to select desired option:

   **All**

   **Up**

   **Down**

   - Click **Match Case** ............... Alt + C to restrict search.

   - Click **Search only Current Field** to restrict search. ............... Alt + E

   - Click **Search Field as Formatted** to restrict search. ............... Alt + O

   ✔ *Matches formatting of number, date, currency, and yes/no field rather than data actually stored in table.*

6. Click **Find Next** ...................... Alt + F

   **OR**

   Click **Find First** ...................... Alt + S

## Exercise 14

■ **Sort Records** ■ **Quick Sort** ■ **Multiple Sorts**

# NOTES

## Sort Records

■ The order in which records are entered is frequently not appropriate to locate and update records. Sorting allows you to rearrange the information so that you can look at it in different ways.

■ Sorting a collection of records can provide the following:

- Data arranged in alphabetical or numerical order.

- Data arranged to see the largest or smallest number in a numerical field.

- Data arranged into groups. (Example: All clients who live in Washington.)

- A method to find duplicate entries.

■ Database records can be sorted in either Form or Datasheet view. However, it is easier to see the rearranged records in Datasheet view.

■ Sorting is accomplished in either ascending or descending order. Ascending order arranges data in alphabetical order from A to Z or in numerical order. Dates and time are sorted from earliest to latest. Descending order is the opposite.

## Quick Sort

■ A quick sort option is available on the Records menu in either the Datasheet or Form view. When Records, Sort is selected, the choice of ascending or descending is provided. The sort may also be accomplished using the ascending or descending sort buttons, on the Table Datasheet view and Form view toolbars.

### Sort Buttons

Ascending button ⟶ [ A↓Z  Z↓A ] ⟵ Descending button

✓ Note:   The selected column(s) will be *TEMPORARILY* sorted. The sorted records can be printed at this time. This version can become permanent only by saving the Table or form.

## Multiple Sorts

■ Several columns of data may be sorted at one time, and each column's sort order can be determined independently to provide a sort on multiple criteria. A datasheet may be sorted on multiple criteria by selecting two or more adjacent columns at the same time, and then sorting them all either in ascending or descending order. The leftmost column is sorted first. In Form view, you can only sort on one field at a time. If you wish to do a multiple sort, you must use features discussed later in this text.

■ To undo the sort, select Remove Filter/Sort on the Records menu.

> *Your company manager has requested the stores datasheet records to be sorted to make it easier to find information. In this exercise, you will sort records using one or more fields.*

# EXERCISE DIRECTIONS

1. Open the 🖥COMPANY database, or open 💾14COMPAN.

2. Open the HARDWARE table.

3. Sort the datasheet in each of the following ways:

    a. in ascending (alphabetical) order by ITEM.
      - How many computers are in inventory?
    b. in ascending order by ASSIGNED TO.
      - Which printer does the Accounting department have in the Sunset store?
    c. in descending order by COST.
      - Which hardware item was the most costly?
    d. in alphabetical order by ITEM and alphabetical order by MFG. Print one copy of this sort in Landscape orientation.

4. Open the SOFTWARE table.

5. Sort the datasheet in ascending order by TYPE and by PRICE.

6. Print one copy of this sort in landscape orientation.

7. Open HARDFORM.

8. Sort the forms in each of the following ways:

    a. in ascending (alphabetical) order by BRANCH.
    b. in descending order by PURDATE.
    c. in descending order by COST. Print the forms.

9. Close all database objects without saving.

10. Close the COMPANY database.

# KEYSTROKES

## USE SORT

1. Open the datasheet or form.
2. Select the column(s) to be sorted in Datasheet view or one field in Form view.
3. Click **Records**......................... Alt + R
4. Click **Sort** ........................................ S

5. Select **Ascending** or **Descending**.
  **OR**

  Click **Ascending** button ................. ⬇A↓

  or **Descending** button ................... Z↓A

## REMOVE SORT

1. Click **Records** ....................... Alt + R
2. Click **Remove Filter/Sort**................ R

## Exercise 15

■ **Filter a Record Subset** ■ **Sort a Record Subset**
■ **Edit a Record Subset** ■ **Shortcut Filters**

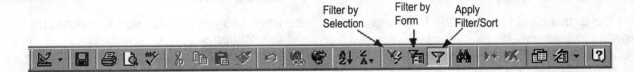

Filter by Selection    Filter by Form    Apply Filter/Sort

# NOTES

## Filter Records

■ There are times when the most efficient way to gather information from datasheet or form records is to isolate (filter out) only those records that satisfy a specific set of conditions into a **subset**.

■ The Standard toolbar contains three options that filter out a set of records:

- Filter by Form
- Filter by Selection
- Advanced Filter/Sort

These Filter by Form and by Selection options can also be accessed using the appropriate button on the Standard toolbar.  Note the labeled toolbar illustration above.

■ Filter by Selection and Filter by Form are two easy ways to filter records in a form or datasheet.

■ Filter by Selection is used when you wish to select one item or part of an item in a field and filter for all occurrences of that item.  For example, if you wish to select all members that live in Oradell, you would select one "Oradell" item from the CITY field and click on Filter by Selection.  All the members living in Oradell would be isolated in table format.

■ Filter by Form can be used in Datasheet or Form view when you want to set filters for data in more than one field or if you cannot find the selection you need for a filter by selection.  It allows you to enter the desired data into a sample form and to set "or" criteria using the Or tab.  In the illustration below of the Filter by Form dialog box, you are entering criteria to find members in zip code 90311 named Carl.  You would enter both criteria in the appropriate fields.

### *Filter by Form Dialog Box*

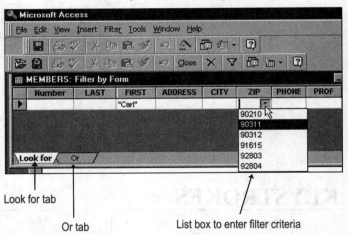

Look for tab

Or tab

List box to enter filter criteria

■ Another filtering option, available on the Records, Filter command Filter Excluding Selection, selects all records except those that contain the selection you specify.

- Advanced Filter/Sort is used when you have multiple filter and sort criteria. It will be discussed in Exercise 16.

- When a table is saved with a filter, the filter result can be used in a report. *(See Lesson 5, Reports.)*

### Shortcut Filters

- In Access 97, you can use the shortcut menus to make filtering even easier. If you right-click in a form or datasheet field, then select Filter For:, you can type in the exact value you are searching for in that field. You can also use Filter by Selection as discussed previously. Conversely, if you select all or part of a value in a field, then click Filter Excluding Selection, you will find all records that do not contain the selected value.

---

*The members datasheet of the Hugclub needs revision. Due to increasing population, the phone company has decided to revise telephone exchanges. Anaheim and North Hollywood will now have a different area code. You will use a filter to isolate the members in each city and make the needed correction. You will then print a sorted listing of the membership list.*

# EXERCISE DIRECTIONS

1. Open the 🖳HUGCLUB database, or open 🖫15HUGCLB.

2. Open the MEMBERS table in Design view.

3. Select the PHONE field and delete the Input Mask field property.
   ✓ Note: We will be using this field for the replace feature.

4. Switch to Datasheet view.

5. Select one Anaheim entry in the CITY field.

6. Select Filter, Filter by Selection from the Records menu or use the Filter by Selection button on the toolbar.
   ✓ Note: A filtered list of only Anaheim members will appear.

7. Highlight the PHONE field.

8. Select Replace from the Edit menu.

9. Make the following entries:
   - Find What        213        Replace With        818
   - Search All            Replace All
   - Match Whole Field Off
   - Say Yes to Unable to Undo
   ✓ Note: The replacements will be made.

10. Close the Replace window.

11. Select Remove Filter/Sort from the Records menu.

12. Select the Filter, Filter by Form option from the Records menu.

13. Click the list box arrow in the CITY field and select North Hollywood.

14. Select Apply Filter/Sort from the Filter menu.
    ✓ Note: A filtered list of only North Hollywood members will appear.

15. Use the Replace command to change the area code to 817 for North Hollywood.

16. Close the Replace window.

17. Select Remove Filter/Sort from the shortcut menu.

18. Right-click on any data item in the CITY field. Select Filter for Input. Type Culver City.

19. Change the Culver City Area Code to 214.

20. Create an alphabetical listing of members who live in Anaheim.

21. Print these records.

22. Switch to Design view and reset the input mask for the PHONE field.

23. Close and save the HUGCLUB database.

# KEYSTROKES

## FILTER RECORDS BY SELECTION

✓ *Filters and displays records that match a selected item.*

1. View desired form or datasheet.
2. Select the desired item in a field location.
3. Click **Filter by Selection** button ...... 🏷️
   **OR**
   a. Click **Records** ................... Alt + R
   b. Click **Filter** ....................... F
   c. Click **Filter by Selection** ........... S

✓ *The records that match the selected item will appear.*

## FILTER RECORDS BY FORM

✓ *Filters and displays records that meet selected criteria.*

1. View desired form or datasheet.
2. Click **Filter by Form** button ............ 🏷️
   **OR**
   a. Click **Records** ................... Alt + R
   b. Click **Filter** ............................. F
   c. Click **Filter by Form** .................. F
3. Enter the items required in the appropriate fields.
   **OR**
   a. Click on the desired field list box arrow.
   b. Select the desired data item.
4. Click **Filter** ........................... Alt + R
5. Click **Apply Filter/Sort** .................... Y

✓ *Result of the filter will appear.*

## FILTER EXCLUDING SELECTION

1. Select field data to be excluded.
2. Right-click.
3. Select **Filter Excluding Selection** .... X

✓ *Records that do not contain selected data will appear.*

## FILTER USING MOUSE

1. Right-click field in datasheet or form.
2. Select **Filter for**: ........................... F
3. Type search value ........................... *text*

✓ *Records that match will appear.*

## REMOVE A FILTER

1. Click **Records** ....................... Alt + R
2. Click **Remove Filter/Sort** ............... R

## Exercise 16

### ■ Advanced Filter/Sort ■ Filter Forms ■ Sort a Form Subset

## NOTES

### Advanced Filter/Sort

- Advanced Filter/Sort is used when you have multiple criteria to be defined and sorted. When you select Advanced Filter/Sort from the Records, Filter, an Advanced Filter/Sort dialog box will appear as shown below.

- Records are selected for the Filter/Sort dialog box by dragging the required field(s) to the lower pane's table. The sort instructions may be specified and additional criteria added using field information or relational operators.

- If you are including sort instructions and are sorting on more than one field, arrange the fields in the grid in the order you want the sorts performed. Access sorts on the left-most Sort field first, then on the next. For example, if you want a database sorted first by LAST and then by FIRST name, you would place the fields in that order. The last names would be in alphabetical order and the first names in order within each last name grouping.

- By adding criteria for a field, you can extract a more specific subset of records. Note the illustration of an Advanced filter Dialog box showing settings for COUNSELOR and M/F fields.

*Advanced Filter Dialog Box*

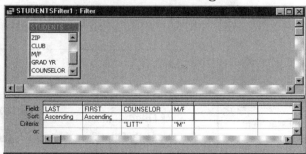

- You may remove a filter/sort by deselecting the Apply Filter button ▽ on the toolbar.

- The techniques applied for creating a subset of records are the same when working in Form view as they were in Datasheet view.

- A subset of a subset is called a **dynaset**. For example, if records are filtered out for students assigned to one counselor, you may then want another filter to view only female students graduating this year. Dynasets may be created from a subset by repeating the filtering process on the subset of records.

- You can further define those records that you wish to filter out of the complete set of records. In the Criteria area of the Filter Box, you can use any one of a number of **relational operators**:

| Use: | For Criteria: |
|---|---|
| = | is equal to (the default symbol can be left out) |
| < | is less than |
| <= | is less than or equal to |
| > | is greater than |
| >= | is greater than or equal to |
| <> | is not equal to |
| Like | to match a pattern of characters |
| And | to select records that satisfy 2 or more conditions |
| Or | to select records that satisfy any of the listed conditions |
| Between...And | to select a value in a given range |
| In | to select a value from a list of values |
| Is | to determine if a value is null |

For example: To filter students with ID numbers greater than 6000, you would use the appropriate field and a criteria setting of >6000 (greater than 6000) to select those records. Note the illustration at the right:

*Advanced Filter/Sort Dialog Box*

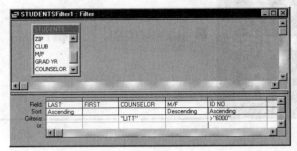

> You need to create subsets and dynasets of records from the STUDENTS records to answer requests for data. You decide to use student records in form view for your searches.

# EXERCISE DIRECTIONS

1. Open the 📖**CLUBS** database, or open 💾**16CLUBS**.

2. Open STFORM.

3. Search for the first form that lists Litt as the counselor. Select Litt's name on the form.

4. Select Filter by Selection from the Records, Filter menus.
   ✓ *Note: A notation appears on the form stating that this form is 1 of 6 filtered forms.*

5. Scroll through the presented record forms.

6. Create a dynaset of records for Mr. Litt that will contain an alphabetical collection of all his male students.
   a. Select Advanced Filter/Sort from the Records, Filter menus.
   b. Note the Counselor selection for Litt.
   c. Scroll to find the M/F field in the top pane. Drag the M/F field down to the table.
   d. Enter M in the Criteria box.
   e. If not already in place, drag the LAST field to the table.
   f. Select Ascending Sort for the LAST field.
   g. Select Apply Filter/Sort from the Filter menu.
   h. Scroll to check that the forms remaining are Males, in alphabetical order who have Mr. Litt as counselor.

7. Remove Filter/Sort from the forms.

8. Select Filter by Form from the Records, Filter menus. *Note that a form displays.*

9. Filter records for Mr. Litt or Mr. Lifton who are male. *HINT: Use the COUNSELOR field.*
   a. Enter M and Litt.
   b. Select OR.
   c. Enter M and Lifton.

10. Select Apply Filter/Sort from the Filter menus.

11. Scroll through the forms to check the filter process.

12. Switch to Datasheet view.

13. Use any filter method to create a record subset with the following features:
    Counselor - Mr. Litt
    Students in M/F order
    Students in alphabetical order by LAST name
    ID numbers greater than 6000

14. Print these records.

15. Close the **CLUBS** database.

# KEYSTROKES

## ADVANCED FILTER/SORT

✓ *Sorts and displays specified records in Form or Datasheet view and allows setting of sort and selection criteria.*

1. View desired form or datasheet.

2. Click **Advanced Filter/Sort** button.
   **OR**

a. Click **Records**................... `Alt`+`R`

b. Click **Filter** ................................ `F`

c. Click **Advanced Filter/Sort**......... `A`

3. Drag desired field from field list to field cell in lower part of window.

4. Click **Sort** and select sort direction.

5. Place pointer in Criteria cell *criteria*

6. Enter Criteria.

7. Repeat steps 3-6 for each additional field to search or sort.

8. Click **Filter**............................. `Alt`+`R`

9. Click **Apply Filter/Sort** .................... `Y`

**Exercise**

**17**

■ **Summary**

## Part I

*The owner of Jane's Boutique, a local clothing store, has hired you to create an inventory system for her store. The clothing is arranged by style number, type of garment, color, and size. This store specializes in junior sizes from 5 to 13. In this exercise, you will create a database to keep track of inventory and the number of garments on hand. You will then search it when customers call about availability of stock or when information is needed for reordering merchandise.*

# EXERCISE DIRECTIONS

1. Create a new database file; name it
   **JANESHOP**.

2. From the information listed below, create a datasheet design for your database. Use the column headings as field names. Determine the appropriate field properties from the information shown in the fields.

| STYLE | TYPE | COLOR | J5 | J7 | J9 | J11 | J13 | DATEORD |
|-------|------|-------|----|----|----|----|----|----|
| J8510 | SKIRT | BLACK | 4 | 4 | 2 | 4 | 2 | 10/18/96 |
| J5540 | BLOUSE | WHITE | 5 | 6 | 6 | 4 | 3 | 11/12/96 |
| J4309 | PANTS | TAN | 2 | 12 | 12 | 4 | 4 | 11/17/96 |
| J3254 | DRESS | BLUE | 4 | 15 | 16 | 3 | 14 | 7/16/96 |
| J7654 | SUIT | GREEN | 12 | 17 | 34 | 12 | 12 | 9/18/96 |
| J7455 | BLAZER | BLACK | 23 | 32 | 21 | 32 | 32 | 9/23/96 |
| J3280 | DRESS | YELLOW | 5 | 7 | 4 | 34 | 12 | 11/17/96 |
| J5532 | SKIRT | PURPLE | 12 | 21 | 32 | 5 | 21 | 10/19/96 |
| J4230 | PANTS | GRAY | 24 | 4 | 6 | 12 | 13 | 12/12/96 |
| J5550 | BLOUSE | ORANGE | 12 | 24 | 43 | 7 | 4 | 8/21/96 |
| J7676 | SUIT | WHITE | 9 | 6 | 5 | 25 | 7 | 8/21/96 |
| J7405 | BLAZER | YELLOW | 12 | 32 | 32 | 3 | 21 | 10/8/96 |
| J5555 | BLOUSE | GREEN | 13 | 32 | 45 | 6 | 9 | 6/19/96 |
| J3290 | DRESS | BLUE | 23 | 32 | 33 | 23 | 12 | 11/17/96 |
| J3317 | DRESS | WHITE | 3 | 6 | 7 | 3 | 4 | 1/7/96 |
| J2222 | PANTS | BLACK | 32 | 23 | 32 | 54 | 16 | 2/2/96 |
| J3290 | DRESS | RED | 17 | 21 | 35 | 32 | 18 | 10/8/96 |

3. Save the datasheet; name it STOCK. (Do not set a primary key.)

4. Enter the data for each item.

5. Adjust column widths to accommodate the longest field entry, where necessary.

6. Change the field name DATEMFG to DATEORD and save the design change.

7. Search the datasheet for answers to the following questions:
   a. What color is style number J7654?
   b. Which item is orange?
   c. What are the style numbers for black items?

8. Replace the type description of BLAZER with JACKET.

9. Save and close the database file.

## Part II

> *Jane Blackwell, your boss at Jane's Boutique, has asked you to enter new purchases into the computer inventory you created earlier, (STOCK). In addition, she would like you to enter one new field, delete sold inventory items, and then sort and print the records.*

# EXERCISE DIRECTIONS

1. Open the STOCK table, if necessary, or open 💾**17JANE**.

2. Add the highlighted information to your datasheet, in the positions indicated.

3. The following items are no longer in stock. Delete the records:  J3280, J7405, J2222.

| STYLE | TYPE | COLOR | J5 | J7 | J9 | J11 | J13 | PRICE | DATEORD |
|-------|------|-------|----|----|----|-----|-----|-------|---------|
| J8510 | SKIRT | BLACK | 4 | 4 | 2 | 4 | 2 | 26.00 | 10/18/96 |
| J5540 | BLOUSE | WHITE | 5 | 6 | 6 | 4 | 3 | 18.59 | 11/12/96 |
| J4309 | PANTS | TAN | 2 | 12 | 12 | 4 | 4 | 44.50 | 11/17/96 |
| J3254 | DRESS | BLUE | 4 | 15 | 16 | 3 | 14 | 61.99 | 7/16/96 |
| J7654 | SUIT | GREEN | 12 | 17 | 34 | 12 | 12 | 85.50 | 9/18/96 |
| J7455 | JACKET | BLACK | 23 | 32 | 21 | 32 | 32 | 50.99 | 9/23/96 |
| J3280 | DRESS | YELLOW | 5 | 7 | 4 | 34 | 12 | 59.44 | 11/17/96 |
| J5532 | SKIRT | PURPLE | 12 | 21 | 32 | 5 | 21 | 23.67 | 10/19/96 |
| J4230 | PANTS | GRAY | 24 | 4 | 6 | 12 | 13 | 49.99 | 12/12/96 |
| J5550 | BLOUSE | ORANGE | 12 | 24 | 43 | 7 | 4 | 23.99 | 8/21/96 |
| J7676 | SUIT | WHITE | 9 | 6 | 5 | 25 | 7 | 106.99 | 8/21/96 |
| J7405 | JACKET | YELLOW | 12 | 32 | 32 | 3 | 21 | 48.50 | 10/8/96 |
| J5555 | BLOUSE | GREEN | 13 | 32 | 45 | 6 | 9 | 19.99 | 6/19/96 |
| J3290 | DRESS | BLUE | 23 | 32 | 33 | 23 | 12 | 56.88 | 11/17/96 |
| J3317 | DRESS | WHITE | 3 | 6 | 7 | 3 | 4 | 62.65 | 1/7/96 |
| J2222 | PANTS | BLACK | 32 | 23 | 32 | 54 | 16 | 39.99 | 2/2/96 |
| J3290 | DRESS | RED | 17 | 21 | 35 | 32 | 18 | 48.25 | 10/8/96 |
| J2121 | SWEATER | BROWN | 40 | 4 | 6 | 6 | 7 | 29.99 | 2/7/97 |
| J2123 | SWEATER | OLIVE | 5 | 5 | 6 | 7 | 9 | 35.75 | 2/7/97 |
| J7699 | SUIT | NAVY | 12 | 10 | 10 | 8 | 7 | 110.10 | 2/7/97 |
| J9090 | VEST | RED | 23 | 22 | 22 | 25 | 25 | 20.00 | 2/7/97 |
| P214 | BLOUSE | RED | 5 | 6 | 8 | 9 | 9 | 25.50 | 2/10/97 |
| P232 | SKIRT | BLACK | 5 | 5 | 5 | 5 | 7 | 29.50 | 2/10/97 |
| P287 | JACKET | NAVY | 7 | 9 | 11 | 14 | 14 | 75.50 | 2/10/97 |
| P987 | SKIRT | BLACK | 3 | 4 | 5 | 6 | 7 | 30.75 | 2/10/97 |
| P998 | SKIRT | NAVY | 2 | 4 | 4 | 5 | 7 | 35.40 | 2/10/97 |
| P999 | VEST | NAVY | 6 | 6 | 7 | 7 | 7 | 25.50 | 2/10/97 |
| P765 | JACKET | RED | 7 | 9 | 11 | 11 | 11 | 60.99 | 2/10/97 |

4. Format the price so that the $ sign is included.

5. Search the datasheet for answers to the following questions:
   *HINT    Use filters. Write the answers to the following requests.*
   a. Which item costs $19.99?
   b. Which items cost more than $50?
   c. What are the style numbers for black jackets?
   d. Which skirts cost less than $40?
   e. How many items have more than 15 pieces on hand in size J13?  List these items so that the number of pieces are in descending order.
   f. Which items are black or white?  List these items in alphabetical order by color.
   g. Which items were ordered after 10/31/95 and have 13 or more J7 items in stock?

6. Filter and sort the datasheet records in each of the following ways:
   *HINT:    Use Advanced Filter/Sort and remove the sort between problems.*
   a. in alphabetical order by COLOR and ascending order by PRICE within each color
   b. skirts by COLOR and descending order by PRICE
   c. in alphabetical order by TYPE and COLOR and ascending order by PRICE
   d. in alphabetical order by COLOR, in alphabetical order by TYPE, and ascending order by STYLE

7. Use Page Setup, set the left and right margins to .5" and the top margin to 2.5"; set print orientation to Landscape.

8. Print one copy of the 6d (above) subset of records.

9. Close the database file.

# Exercise 18

■ **Create a Query** ■ **Change a Query Design** ■ **Save a Query**

## NOTES

■ As discussed in Lesson 3, Access allows you to find specific records, replace data, filter a subset of records, and print this subset in the original datasheet order with all fields included. Access also provides a more powerful searching tool called a **query**.

■ A **query** is a Database Object in which you can isolate a group of records, limit the fields to be included, and determine the order of presentation. It can even be created using data from more than one table within a database. Queries can be saved and used as a basis for a report. Filters by Form or Selection can also be saved as queries and used later for reports.

### Create a Query

■ Access provides Wizards to help you develop queries, however, in these exercises you will create queries without using the Query Wizard. After you open the database file to be queried and select the Query tab, and New, the following dialog box appears:

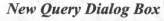

*New Query Dialog Box*

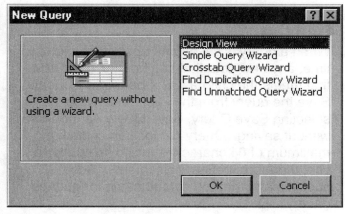

■ When you select Design view, two windows appear as shown below. The Show Table dialog box lists the database tables that may be used for the query. By allowing you to select all the tables from the database, you can create a customized query and report. The tables to be included can be highlighted and added to the query before closing the dialog box.

*Show Table Dialog Box*

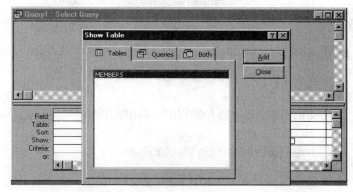

■ When the Show Table dialog box is closed, the Query Design window appears with the previously selected table(s). Note the illustration on the next page. It looks very much like the Filter screen, except for an added row option, Show. The Show box will be turned on, by default, whenever a field name is inserted into a column. You can click this box if you want a field to be involved in the query but do not want it to show in the resulting datasheet layout.

■ The fields may be selected in any order and will determine the column order of the resulting datasheet. The field's criteria or sorting condition should be entered.

### Query Design Window

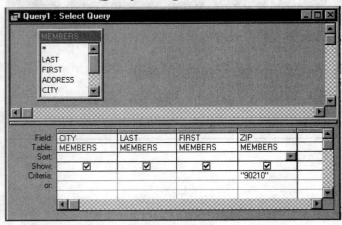

✓ Note:     The fields that are listed in the first row of the query design are joined using an implicit "AND". When you want to use multiple criteria for a field ("OR"), use the field's criteria row and those below it.

The data, in the illustrated Query, will be sorted by CITY and LAST NAME, in alphabetical order, will include only those names in zip code 90210, and print only the city, first and last names.

- To see the results of your Query Design), use:
  - the View menu, Datasheet option
    or
  - the Run option from the Query menu
    or
  - the Run button on the toolbar.

### Datasheet View of Query

| | CITY | LAST | FIRST |
|---|---|---|---|
| ▶ | Anaheim | Barnes | Leanne |
| | Anaheim | Brown | Miles |
| | Beverly Hills | Griffith | Stuart |
| | Beverly Hills | Moon | Michael |
| | Anaheim | Smith | Trina |
| | Anaheim | Smith | Sheila |
| | North Hollywood | Walker-Sim | Bette |
| | North Hollywood | Castillo | Carl |

- To return to the Query Design screen from the Datasheet view, use the View menu Query Design option.

## Change a Query Design

- You can change field entries or their order in a Query design in a number of different ways.

### To add a field to the design:

Drag a field name from the table window to the desired column. The fields to the right of this position will automatically be moved to the right to make room for this insertion.

### OR

Place the cursor into the column that is to receive the new field, and select the Column option from the Insert menu. A blank column will be inserted, and the existing fields to the right of this position will automatically be moved to the right. You can now either drag a new field name into the blank column or use the Copy, Cut, or Paste options of the Edit menu to move an existing entry.

- If two columns have the same field listed, you will have duplicate entries in your datasheet. Duplicate field columns should be deleted.

### To delete a field from the design:

Select the entire field column and press the Del key.

### OR

Place the cursor into the column that is to be deleted and select the Delete Column option from the Edit menu.

- Query datasheets can be changed or enhanced like other datasheets. Use the Format menu options of Font, Row Height, Column Width, Hide Columns, Unhide Columns, and Cells to customize the Query datasheet.

## Save a Query

- When a query is saved and opened at a later time, any new data that has been entered and that meets the criteria will appear in the query. Save the query from the File menu by either selecting Save Query, Save Query As, or Close without saving. Query names can contain a maximum of 64 characters including spaces and can, therefore, define the contents. Access supplies a numbered default name for queries (Query1, Query2, etc.).

As the secretary of the HUG Club, you have been asked to insert a title field in the MEMBERS datasheet. This field will be used for future mailings. You also have been asked to search the datasheet to find records that meet various criteria. To save time and effort, you will save some of the search conditions for later use.

# EXERCISE DIRECTIONS

1. Open the ⌨ HUGCLUB database or 💾 18HUGCLB.

2. Open the MEMBERS datasheet.

3. Add the title field and the field information, as listed on the next page.

4. Close the datasheet.

5. Select the Queries tab.

6. Select New.

7. Select Design View.

8. With the MEMBERS table highlighted, select Add on the Show Table window.

9. Select Close on the Show Table window.

10. Create a query to get a listing of all members in the club in City order.
    Select the fields listed below and add the indicated conditions:
    CITY Sort - Ascending
    LAST Sort - Ascending
    FIRST Sort - Ascending
    PROF

11. Switch to Datasheet view.

12. Select Save from the File menu; name the query MEMBERS BY CITY.

13. Switch to Query Design view.

14. Insert PROF into column 2 and sort in alphabetical order.
    Remember to delete any duplicate fields.

15. Add PHONE as the last field of the query.

16. Switch to Datasheet view.

17. Save the query as MEMBERS PROFESSION BY CITY and close the query.

18. Create a new query to list female members by profession.
    Include the fields: PROF, TITLE, FIRST, LAST, and PHONE.
    Sort PROF and LAST in alphabetical order.
    Set Criteria to select female members.

19. Switch to Datasheet view.

20. Switch to Query Design view.

21. Make the following changes:
    Set Show to off for the TITLE field.
    Add CITY between LAST and PHONE.

22. Switch to Datasheet view.

23. Save and close; name it FEMALE MEMBERS BY PROFESSION.

24. Create new or use existing queries to answer each of the following questions. After determining the needed information, close the query without saving.
    a. Which members live in Beverly Hills and are Teachers?
    b. Which members live in North Hollywood and are Bankers?
    c. Which members have a last name beginning with "D" and live in North Hollywood? Change John Davis' phone number to (817)555-8563.
    d. Which members have a last name beginning with "D" or "M" and live in North Hollywood?

25. Close the HUGCLUB database.

| NUMBER | TITLE | LAST | FIRST | ADDRESS | CITY | ZIP | PHONE | PROF |
|---|---|---|---|---|---|---|---|---|
| 1 | Ms. | Barnes | Leanne | 808 Summer Street | Anaheim | 92803 | (818)555-4987 | Student |
| 2 | Mr. | Brown | Miles | 154 Newburg Road | Anaheim | 92803 | (818)555-4837 | Accountant |
| 3 | Mr. | Griffith | Stuart | 1551 Dean Street | Beverly Hills | 90210 | (213)555-3010 | Lawyer |
| 4 | Mr. | Moon | Michael | 32 Oak Street | Beverly Hills | 90210 | (213)555-8750 | Teacher |
| 5 | Ms. | Smith | Trina | 3954 Wood Ave. | Anaheim | 92803 | (818)555-7283 | Student |
| 6 | Ms. | Smith | Sheila | 417 Specific Court | Anaheim | 92803 | (818)555-5672 | Chiropractor |
| 7 | Ms. | Walker-Sim | Bette | 1745 River St. | North Hollywood | 91615 | (817)555-8520 | Lawyer |
| 8 | Mr. | Castillo | Carl | 1956 Park Ave. | North Hollywood | 91615 | (817)555-5192 | Banker |
| 9 | Mr. | Davis | John | P.O. Box 2333 | North Hollywood | 91615 | (817)555-8563 | Student |
| 10 | Ms. | Dixon | Amy | 237 Albee Street | North Hollywood | 91615 | (817)555-8917 | Orthopedist |
| 11 | Ms. | Kendall | Gale | 15 Imperial Way | Beverly Hills | 90210 | (213)555-9888 | Teacher |
| 12 | Ms. | Dagger | Janice | 27 Ocean Ave. | Anaheim | 92804 | (818)555-7777 | Orthopedist |
| 13 | Mr. | Chow | Michael | 88 Riverside Drive | Culver City | 90311 | (214)555-7655 | Accountant |
| 14 | Mr. | Wagner | David | 879 Beverly Drive | Beverly Hills | 90210 | (213)555-6676 | Banker |
| 15 | Ms. | Smith | Cleo | 90 Rodeo Drive | Beverly Hills | 90210 | (213)555-2222 | Student |
| 16 | Ms. | Anderson | Carolyn | 666 Santa Ana Drive | Culver City | 90312 | (214)555-9988 | Lawyer |
| 17 | Ms. | Ramaz | Nadine | 9012 Wilshire Blvd. | Beverly Hills | 90210 | (213)555-2211 | Teacher |
| 18 | Mr. | Yakar | Winston | 776 Prince Lane | North Hollywood | 9615 | (817)555-1584 | Student |
| 19 | Ms. | Mancuso | Mary | 12 Pacific Court | North Hollywood | 9615 | (817)555-7773 | Banker |

# KEYSTROKES

### QUERIES - CREATE

1. Select **Queries** tab in Database Objects window.
2. Click **New** .............................. Alt + N
3. Select **Design View** ............. ↓ , Enter
4. Choose desired category to display:

   **Tables**

   **Queries**

   **Both**

5. Select **Table/Query** ......................... ↓
   to include.
6. Click **Add** ........................................ A
7. Repeat steps 4 and 5 for each table or query to add.
8. Click **Close** .................................... C

### QUERIES - SAVE

1. Click **Save** button ..........................
   **OR**

   a. Click **File** ...................... Alt + F

   b. Click **Save** ............................. S

2. Type query name ........................ *name*
   if saving query for the first time.

   ✓ *Don't give a query the same name as an existing table unless you want to replace the existing table.*

3. Click **OK** .................................... Enter

## Exercise 19

- ■ **Use All Fields of a Table for a Query**
- ■ **Reposition a Datasheet Column** ■ **Rename a Query**
- ■ **Print a Query Datasheet**

# NOTES

### Use All Fields of a Table for a Query

■ When a selected table appears in the top pane of a query design window, the first field option is an asterisk ( * ), which represents **all fields** of the selected table. If this is selected, only the table name shows in the lower pane and all fields will be in the query.

*Query Design with All Fields Selected*

■ To sort or set criteria for one or more fields when all fields are selected, you can add that field and set the desired conditions; but you must turn the Show condition off, or you will have duplicate entries. For example, if you select all fields in the Stores table and want to sort on ST, you must add that field to the query, set the sort order, and deselect the show condition. Since all fields are selected, the additional field would be a duplicate.

### Reposition a Datasheet Column

■ In Datasheet view of a query, columns can be repositioned as follows:

- • Select the column by clicking on the field name. (The column will be represented in reverse video, that is, with light text on a dark background.)

- • Click the field name again, holding down the mouse button. (The column will be represented by a thick line in reverse video.)

- • Drag the line to the vertical grid line that will become the new left boundary of the moved column.

- • Release the mouse button.

### Rename a Query

■ If you mistype or want to change an existing query name, you may highlight the name to be edited on the Queries tab list, click it again, and retype the name.

### Print a Query Datasheet

■ A query datasheet can be printed in the same manner used to print other database objects.

The print-out will include:

- • A header that contains the query name and the current date, and

- • A footer that contains the current page number on each page.

> *Your manager at Bit-Byte Computer Stores has many questions about the branch stores.  You can provide the answers by searching the company database you have developed.*

# EXERCISE DIRECTIONS

1. Open the ▧**COMPANY** database, or open ▭**19COMPAN**.

2. Create a New Query for all stores in the company.  Use the STORES Table.
   - All fields of the STORES table will be used.
   - ST and CITY fields are to be added and sorted in alphabetical order.  Be sure to deselect the Show box.

3. View the resulting datasheet.

4. Move the columns into the following order: ST, CITY, BRANCH, SALES, STAFF, EVE

5. Save the query as **Bit-Byte Stores in State Order**.

6. Change the Query Design to select only stores with evening hours.
   - ✓ Note:  The datasheet shows the EVE data as Yes or No, but the field data type is set as Yes/No and not Text. Therefore, internally the settings are **-1 for Yes** and **0 for No**.

7. View the resulting datasheet.

8. Switch to Design view toggle EVE Show condition to off.

9. Save As **Has Evening Hours**.

10. Change the Query Design to select stores that do not have evening hours.

11. Switch to Datasheet view.

12. Save and close the query; name it **Stores WITHOUT Evening Hours**.

13. Select **Has Evening Hours** and rename it to **Stores WITH Evening Hours**.

14. Create a new Query to locate stores that have sales of less than $400,000.

*Do not use dollar ( $ ) or comma ( , ) symbols in the Criteria setting.*
   - The Query should include the BRANCH names (in alphabetical order), CITY, STAFF, and SALES.
   - Save the query; name it **POOR PERFORMERS**.

15. Make the following changes in Datasheet view:
   - Font size to 12 point
   - Column widths to improve the general appearance
   - BRANCH column to the right of the CITY column

16. Print Preview the Datasheet view.
   - Return to the Datasheet if adjustments have to be made.

17. Print the Query Datasheet.

18. Save and close the Query.

19. Open the appropriate Query or create a new one to answer each of the following questions.
   - ✓ Note:  A Query Design may be temporarily changed to aid in a search.  DO NOT SAVE THE REVISIONS.
   a. What stores are located in Atlanta?
   b. In what city is the Federal Plaza Store located?
   c. Which store has sold exactly $245,860 worth of merchandise?
   d. Which stores have sold more than $400,000 worth of merchandise?
   e. Which stores have sold more than $400,000 worth of merchandise and are open evenings?
   f. Which stores have sold more than $400,000 worth of merchandise and have more than 10 employees?
   g. Which stores are in CA (California) or GA (Georgia)?

20. Return to the COMPANY database window.

21. Close the database.

# KEYSTROKES

## MOVE A COLUMN IN A QUERY

1. Click on the header bar of the column to move.

   The entire column will be highlighted.

2. Drag the header bar to the desired location.

   The column will be represented by a thick vertical line.

3. Release the mouse button.

## RENAME A QUERY

1. View Database object window.

2. Choose **Queries** tab

3. Select query to rename.

4. Click query name.

5. Retype query name.

## USE ALL FIELDS OF A QUERY

1. Double-click title bar of field list.

   **OR**

   Click asterisk ( * ) at top of table field list.

   - ✓ If asterisk is used, all fields in table will always be used in query even if table is later modified.

2. Drag group to QBE grid (lower pane).

## Exercise 20

- Change Field Format in Query Design
- Change Field Names in a Query Design

# NOTES

## Change Field Format in Query Design

- The data in a query datasheet contain the properties from the original table, as you experienced with the Yes/No data type in Exercise 19. However, some properties can be changed for the purposes of the query. For example: If a currency data type was set for a format that did not include the dollar ($) or comma (,) symbols, you could change your query datasheet to include them.

- To change a field format in Query Design view:

    - Click on the Field name box of the field to be revised.

    - Select the Properties option from the View menu.

    - Enter the desired Format name, in the Format row. *(The change can be seen in Datasheet view.)*

## Change Field Names in a Query Design

- You may wish to change a field name in a query for viewing results. Changing a field name in a query does not affect the Table or Form design. A field name may be changed in Design view as follows:

    - Click to the left of the first letter of the field name to be replaced in the lower pane of Design view.

    - Type a new name followed by a colon (:) before the field name. (*Your replacement will appear in the query's datasheet and may require a column width adjustment.*) Note the example below which shows the field name being changed from CITY to Store Location. The field name CITY remains on the same line since it is not being changed.

New Field Name.        Colon        Field Name

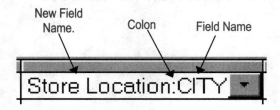

Store Location:CITY ▼

> *Your company is preparing to purchase new computer equipment. Before doing so, management needs to know information about the current inventory. Your supervisor has asked you to respond to a survey by searching the hardware table.*

# EXERCISE DIRECTIONS

1. Open the ⌨COMPANY database, or open 💾20COMPAN.

2. Create a new query for the HARDWARE table:
   - Include the BRANCH, ITEM, MFG, MODEL, COST, WTY, and PURDATE fields.
   - The first two fields are to be sorted in alphabetical order.
   - View the Datasheet.
   - Save the query; name it **All Hardware**.

3. Make the following changes on the query datasheet:
   a. The Quantum hard drive is under warranty.
   b. The correct model number for the Okidata printer is ML330RR.
   c. Return to Design view and make the following changes:
   d. Change the field name PURDATE to DATE OF PURCHASE.
   e. Change the format of the COST field to include dollar signs ($) and commas (,).

4. View the results of your changes in Datasheet view.

5. Save the new layout.

6. Print the ALL HARDWARE datasheet.

7. Create a new query for the HARDWARE table. Include the ASSIGNED TO, BRANCH, ITEM, MFG, MODEL, and COST fields.
   - The first three fields are to be sorted in alphabetical order.
   - View the Datasheet.
   - Save and close the query; name it **Department Hardware Assignments**.

8. Open the All Hardware query.

9. Make the following change to the Query Design to create a new query to isolate records that are under warranty:
   - Criteria for **WTY** set to **Yes**.
   - **Show** set for **off**.

   ✓ *Note:  The WTY field was set as: Data Type Yes/No (-1,0)*

10. View the datasheet.

11. Save As **Hardware Under Warranty**.

12. Return to Design view; change criteria for WTY to No.

13. Close and Save As **Hardware Not Under Warranty**.

14. Open the appropriate query to determine the purchase dates of computers which are under warranty and cost less than $2,000.  How many are there?

15. Close the query.

16. Close and save the database.

# KEYSTROKES

## EDIT FIELD NAMES

   ✓ *Query field name changes do not affect table design.*

**In Query Design view:**

1. Place cursor before field name to be changed.  (Do not highlight.)

2. Type new field name followed by a colon.

3. Press **Enter**................................. Enter

## CHANGE FIELD FORMAT

1. Highlight the field name to change.

2. Click **View**...........................

3. Click **Properties**.......................... P

4. Click **General** tab.

5. Click in format box.

6. Type custom format name..*formatname*
   **OR**
   Select from pull-down list.

7. Close Properties window .......

**Exercise**

**21**

- **Create a Query Using Data from Multiple Tables**
- **Print a Query Table**

# NOTES

### Create a Query Using Data from Multiple Tables

- You can create a query that contains field data from various datasheets or queries, which allows you to find data using information from the entire database. To query more than one object:

  - Select the Queries tab from the Database Object window.

  - Select Design view from the New Query window.

  - Select from the Show Table, accessing a list of database Tables, Queries, or Both. Note the illustration of the Show Table dialog box with the Both tab selected.

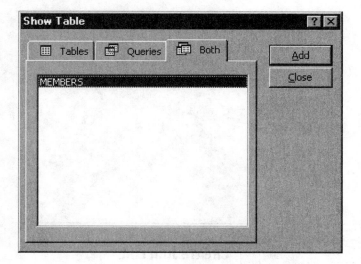

- Add each of the tables or queries you need before closing the Add Table window.

- Select the field names, from the field listings available, and drag them to the desired query design location.

- Draw a Join Line between the selected database objects to indicate the relationship between them. Note the illustration of a Query Design grid with a join line between the BRANCH fields.

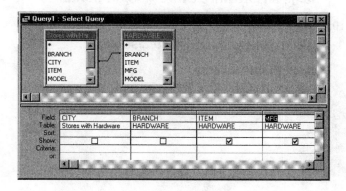

- Proceed, as previously discussed, naming, saving, and viewing the resulting datasheet.

Your manager at bit-byte computer stores has many questions about branch stores.  You can provide the answers by searching the company database objects that you have developed.

# EXERCISE DIRECTIONS

1. Open the ⌨COMPANY database, or open 💾21COMPAN .

2. Select the Queries tab screen.

3. Create a new Query Design.

4. From the Show Table dialog box add the STORES and HARDWARE tables and close the window.

5. Join the BRANCH fields, if not already joined by a line.

6. Create a query using the following fields: BRANCH, CITY, ST, ITEM, MODEL, and COST.

7. Sort the BRANCH, ST, and ITEM fields in alphabetical order.

8. View the query's datasheet.

9. Return to Design view and save this query; name it **Hardware Store Assignments**.

10. Change the format of COST field to Currency. *HINT: See NOTES - Exercise 20.*

11. View the query's datasheet.

12. Save this new layout.

13. Close the query.

14. Create a new query that will  list the branches that have equipment not under warranty.
    - Use the STORES table and **Hardware Not Under Warranty** query.
    - Join the BRANCH fields.
    - The query should contain BRANCH, CITY, ITEM, MODEL, COST, and DATE OF PURCHASE.
    - BRANCH and ITEM are to be sorted in alphabetical order.

15. Save this query as **Stores with Hardware Not Under Warranty**.

16. Print this datasheet, adding enhancements.

17. Save the query enhancements.

18. Close the query.

19. Close and save the database.

# KEYSTROKES

## QUERY MULTIPLE DATASHEETS OR QUERIES

1. View Database Object window.

2. Click **Queries** tab.

3. Click **New** ............................. `Alt`+`N`

4. Select **Design View**.

5. Select **Both** tab ...................... 🗐 Both

6. Highlight Table/Query to add.

7. Click **Add** ......................................... `A`

8. Repeat steps 6 and 7 until all desired Tables/Queries are added.

9. Click **Close** .................................... `C`

## CREATE JOIN LINE

*On Query Design table fields section, drag a field name in one listing and drop it on top of its related field in the other listing.*

## Exercise 22

■ **Summary**

You are being asked to gather information relating to all computer hardware and software. You will have to pull information from various tables in the company database.

# EXERCISE DIRECTIONS

1. Open the ⌨COMPANY database, or open ⊟22COMPAN.

2. Create a Query Design using SOFTWARE table fields:
   - TYPE (in alphabetical order)
   - TITLE (in alphabetical order)
   - PRICE, BRANCH, and PURDATE
   - Name it **Software by Type**.

3. Change:
   - PURDATE to PURCHASED
   - Format PURCHASED to Medium Date and PRICE to Currency

4. View the datasheet; adjust and enhance columns.

5. Print the query datasheet.

6. Close and save the query.

7. Create a Query Design using STORES and SOFTWARE.
   - Draw a join line between BRANCH fields, if necessary.
   - Use fields: BRANCH (in alphabetical order), CITY, TYPE (in alphabetical order), and TITLE. Name it **Software used in Cities**.
   - View the datasheet; adjust and enhance columns.

8. Create a Query Design using information from HARDWARE, Software by Type, and STORES. Draw join lines between BRANCH fields, if necessary.
   - Use fields:
     BRANCH (in alphabetical order)
     ST, TYPE (in alphabetical order)
     TITLE, PRICE, ITEM, MFG, and COST.
   - Name it **Branch Software and Hardware**.

9. Change the field names for the query: TYPE to SOFTWARE and ITEM to HARDWARE.

10. Change format of money columns to Currency, if necessary.

11. View the datasheet; adjust columns as necessary.

12. Change:
    - Font (your choice) - 10 point
    - Row height to 11
    - Print orientation to Landscape
    - All print margins to .5"

13. Preview the print-out; make changes as necessary.

14. Print the datasheet.

15. Save and close the query.

16. Select a query to answer each of the following questions in the most efficient manner:
    a. How many word processing programs are in use?
    b. How many word processing and spreadsheet programs are in use?
    c. How much was paid for Tulip5 software?
    d. Which software costs less than $470 and is a word processor?
    e. Which database programs cost less than $500?

17. Close and save the database.

# Exercise 23

■ **Reports** ■ **Create Reports with Report Wizard**
■ **Move Design View Items (Controls)**

## NOTES

### Reports

■ Reports allow you to present data in a customized way.

■ Reports can be presented in a number of ways using the fields of a table:

- Single column - Records are presented with selected fields listed below each other (like a form).

- Tabular form - Records are presented with fields in a grid (like a datasheet).

- Group/Totals - Field data is grouped with totals calculated for each group.

- Mailing label form

- Summary

- AutoReport - All records and their fields are presented in a single column.

- MS Word Mail Merge

■ Reports can include:

- Report headers and footers

- Page headers and footers

- Summary statistics

- Objects imported from other sources (such as graphics)

■ You can design a report from scratch using Report Design view (see illustration above right), which is similar in operation to Form Design view. The Report Design Toolbox illustrated on the right of the screen will be discussed in Exercise 26. However, you can let Access design a report for you by using a Report Wizard.

*Report Design View*

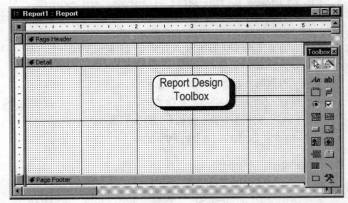

### Create Reports with Report Wizard

■ A Report Wizard will ask you to respond to some questions, create the report, and present you with a Sample Report screen. You can redesign the resulting report. Report Wizard has Grouping controls which allow you to create a report and do query-type selections at the same time. To create a report with a Report Wizard:

- Open the database that contains the table or query from which to select the report data.

- Select the Reports tab in the Database Object window.

- In the Report dialog box, select New.

- Select Report Wizard.

- Select the data source, either a table or a query name.

- Respond to a series of questions to select:

– Fields from the selected data source, in the order of desired presentation

- Grouping levels - subtotals or subsets
- Sort order, if any
- Layout, Orientation, and Column Width Setting
- Style for the report
- Report title and print options

### *Report Wizard Field Screen*

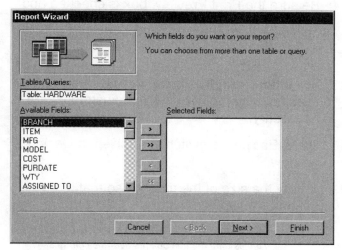

- A report will be created, and you will be presented with a zoomed-in version of the Print Preview screen.

- Press the Esc key to return to the report's Design view from any preview screen. All aspects of a report are controlled from the Design view. Note the labeled illustration below of Report Design view.

- The manner in which page numbers, totals, counts, etc., are included in a report will be discussed in another lesson.

## Move Design View Items (Controls)

- By default, numbers are right justified and text is left justified. This often makes adjustments in spacing and alignment necessary in a report. To move a report detail item in Report Design, click and hold down the mouse button within the item's boundary. The appearance of a hand indicates that the item can be moved. Drag the box to the desired position. The rulers at the top and left side of the screen should be used to help position the item.

- To change the size of a boundary box, click on the item and release the mouse button. Point to one of the square, black handles surrounding the box. When you see a double-headed arrow, drag it into position. Print Preview from the File menu may be used to see the results of your adjustments. You can then press the Esc key to return to Design view. You may have to repeat the adjustment routine a number of times.

- To change the size of the design sections, click on the bar of the section heading, release the mouse button, and then drag the design section title bar with the double-headed arrow that appears.

## Save a New Report

- Reports are automatically saved using the title of the form. You can save and name the report by using the Save As option on the File menu or you can edit the report title name assigned by Access. The report name will appear on the Database Object Reports tab.

### *Report Design View*

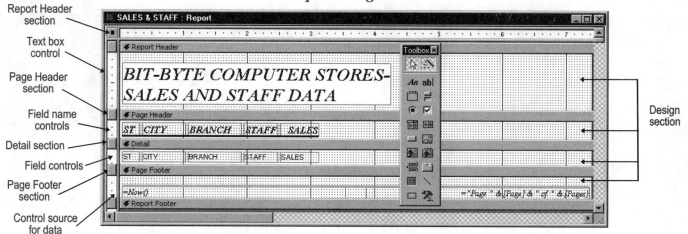

Your manager at Bit-Byte must submit reports to the president of the company.  You have been asked to create these reports from your available records.

# EXERCISE DIRECTIONS

1. Open the ⌨COMPANY database, or open 🖫23COMPAN.

2. Select Reports section in the Database Objects window.

3. Select New.

4. Select Report Wizard.

5. Click on the list box arrow and enter STORES for the selected table.

6. Select the fields in the order listed below:

    ST, CITY, BRANCH, STAFF, SALES.

    Click Next.

7. Pass the grouping screen by clicking Next.

8. Choose to sort first by ST and then by CITY in alphabetical order.  Click Next.

9. Set the print orientation to Portrait.

10. Click on Columnar and Tabular Layout choices to see the difference.  Leave the setting at a tabular layout.

11. The box should be checked to "Adjust field width so all fit on a page." Click Next.

12. On the style page, test all style formats to note the different designs.  Select the Corporate style for this report.

13. For the report title use **BIT-BYTE COMPUTER STORES - SALES AND STAFF DATA**.

14. Be sure the Print Preview  box is checked and choose Finish.

    ✓ Note:  A zoomed-in view of the report will appear on the screen.

15. Make note from the Print Preview screen what spacing, alignment, and size adjustments are necessary.

16. Press Esc key to switch to the Report Design window.

17. Modify the size of the title box so that it becomes a two-line heading.

    HINT:     Click on the title box, release the mouse, move the handles until the title box fits over the columns. Adjust the width of the box, and stretch the box vertically to fit the title on two lines.

18. Select Print Preview from the File menu.

19. Make any other desired adjustments.

20. Print the report.

21. Close the report.

22. Click on the report name on the Reports tab and change it to SALES & STAFF.

23. Close and save the database.

# KEYSTROKES

## CREATE NEW REPORT USING REPORT WIZARD

1. Click **Reports** tab in Database window.
   **OR**
   a. Click **View** ........................ `Alt`+`V`
   b. Click **Database Object.**
   c. Click **Reports**............................. `R`
2. Click **New** button................... `Alt`+`N`
3. Select **Report Wizard**...................... `↓`
4. Click drop-down arrow to select a table or query.
5. Select fields. ................`Alt`+`T`, `↓` to be included in report
6. Click on > to move field .................. `>`
7. Click **Next**....................................... `N`

### To choose a sort order:

   a. Click drop-down arrow to choose a field.
   b. Click **Sort** button for Ascending or Descending sort.
   c. Click **Next**.

### To set a format:

   a. Choose a Layout (**Columnar**, **Tabular**, or **Justified**).
   b. Choose an Orientation (**Portrait** or **Landscape**).
   c. Click **Next**.
3. Choose a style from the list provided and click **Next**.
4. Give the report a title in the provided text box, and choose to **Preview the report** or **Modify the report design**.
5. Click **Finish**.

## OPEN REPORT

1. Click **Reports** tab in Database Object window.
   **OR**
   a. Click **View**........................ `Alt`+`V`
   b. Click **Database Objects**.
   c. Click **Reports**............................. `R`
2. Select report................`↓` `↑`, `Enter`
3. Click **Design**................... `Alt`+`D`
   to view report Design view.
   **OR**
   Click **Preview** ........................ `Alt`+`P`
   to view report as it will appear when printed.

## RETURN TO DESIGN VIEW

- Press **Esc** ..................................... `Esc`
   **OR**
   a. Click **View**........................ `Alt`+`V`
   b. Click **Design View**. .................. `D`
   **OR**
   Click **Design View** button ............ `🖌 ▾`

## SELECT ITEMS (CONTROLS)

**In Design view:**

   Click control or attached label to select both.

**To select more than one control:**

   Press Shift .................................. `Shift`
   and click desired controls.
   **OR**
   Click outside of the controls and drag rectangle to touch desired controls to select.

## MOVE ITEMS (CONTROLS)

1. Select control or controls to move.
2. Place pointer on control border to move control and attached label.

   ✓ *Pointer will appear as a five-fingered hand.*

   **OR**

   Place pointer on upper left corner to move label or control only.

   ✓ *Pointer will appear as a pointing hand.*

3. Click and drag to new location.

   ✓ *Labels and controls must be moved together.*

## CHANGE CONTROL SIZE

1. Select control to change.
2. Place pointer on any of the three small corner handles.

   ✓ *Pointer will become a diagonal, two-headed arrow.*

3. Click and drag border to new size.

## CHANGE SECTION SIZE

1. Place pointer at bottom edge of section to change.

   ✓ *Pointer will become a line with a black, two-headed arrow.*

2. Click and drag to new size.

**Exercise**

**24**

■ **Change and Enhance a Report**
■ **Edit Report Sections and Controls** ■ **Change Item Order**

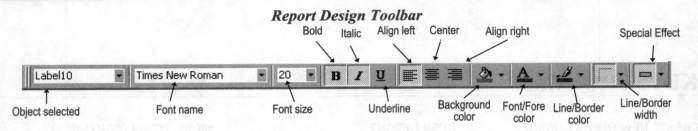

*Report Design Toolbar*

Bold    Italic    Align left    Center    Align right    Special Effect

| Label10 | Times New Roman | 20 | **B** *I* U | ≣ ≣ ≣ | 🎨▾ | **A**▾ | ✏▾ | ▾ | ▬▾ |

Object selected    Font name    Font size    Underline    Background color    Font/Fore color    Line/Border color    Line/Border width

# NOTES

## Change a Report

■ Creating a report using a Report Wizard simplifies creating a basic report structure. However, the result may include unwanted data and exclude desired items. Also, the general alignment and positioning of a column heading and its related data, its font, and style may not yield an attractive report.

## Edit Report Sections and Controls

■ A **control** is the term used to describe an item in a database form or report, such as a field name, data name, calculated field, summary field, etc. The **control source** is the field from a table that supplies data for the control. The **control label** is the text item used as a caption for the control. To edit control labels, click on the specific control until the insertion pointer is visible ( I ) and make changes.

■ To delete a control label, click on the item and, when the box handles appear, press the Del key.

## Change Item Order

■ Changing the order of report items or controls usually requires that you move some existing items to a temporary location. You can move controls to the right edge of the report, and the report will expand to accommodate the moved item. After you have repositioned controls, move the right edge of the report to the last item entry or you may get blank page(s) inserted into the report.

## Enhance a Report

■ To change a control's font, font size, alignment, or palette enhancement (color, border, or shading), you need to use the Report Design toolbar.

■ The Report Design toolbar, shown at the top of this page, displays on the Report Design screen. If it is not visible:

• Select the Tool**b**ar option from the **V**iew menu.

• Highlight Report Design option.

• Click Close.

■ To make a change or enhancement:

• Select an item, or control.

• Choose the appropriate button on the Report Design toolbar.

✓ *Note:*     *When a toolbar button has been selected, it will be highlighted. When changing fonts or font sizes, you often have to change an item's boundary box and items aligned with it to accommodate the change. To center the Report Heading, extend the heading's right boundary to the extent of the report width. Click on the center button on the Report Design toolbar.*

- If you wish to select a group of controls upon which the same condition is to apply:
  - Select the first item.
  - Hold down the Shift key when selecting the others.

- The Report Wizard adds two controls to its pre-formatted report form:

  **=Now()** - contains the date the report is printed.

  **=Page** - contains the printed page number.

---

*In order to prepare for a computer equipment inventory audit, you have been asked to prepare a report that will list specific information about this hardware.*

---

# EXERCISE DIRECTIONS

1. Open the 📠**COMPANY** database, or open 💾**24COMPAN**.

2. Select the Report tab of the COMPANY database.

3. Create a New report for the data from the HARDWARE table.
   - Respond to the Report Wizard as follows:
   - Select Fields in given order: ITEM, MFG, MODEL, PURDATE, COST.
   - Ignore grouping levels.
   - Sort by ITEM and MFG, in ascending order.
   - Select Compact style, Tabular layout and Portrait print orientation.
   - See all fields on one page.
   - Title the report: **BIT-BYTE COMPUTER STORES INC**

4. Switch to Design view.

5. Change Page Headers and reposition as necessary:
   MFG to MANUFACTURER
   PURDATE to PURCHASED

6. Move the =Now() item to the center of the Page Footer section. Adjust the size of the control if necessary.

7. Show the Report Design toolbar if it is not present.

8. Change both the Date and Page footers to bold, without italics.

9. Change the report title to **COMPUTER EQUIPMENT INVENTORY**.

10. Change the title font size to 18 point.

11. Use the Palette to shade the title (back color) light gray.

12. Change all Page Headers to 12 point.

13. Adjust report items to accommodate the decreases in font size.

14. Center the report header by moving it horizontally to the center of the section.

15. Print Preview your adjustments.

16. Print the report.

17. Save the report.

18. In the Database Object window, highlight the report name and edit it to **COMPUTER EQUIPMENT**.

19. In Design View, move headings and fields to interchange the ITEM and MFG fields.

20. Change the title to **COMPUTER EQUIPMENT by MANUFACTURER.**

21. Print Preview.

22. Adjust spacing and alignment.

23. Save this version as **COMPEQUIP by MFG**.

24. Close and save the database.

# KEYSTROKES

| DISPLAY REPORT DESIGN TOOLBAR |
| --- |
| 1. Click **View**.............................Alt + V |
| 2. Click **Toolbars** ...............................T |
| 3. Select **Report Design**. |
| 4. Click **Close**. |

**CHANGE REPORT TEXT FONT OR ALIGNMENT WITHIN CONTROL**

1. Select item to be changed.
2. Click appropriate item on Report Design toolbar.

# Exercise 25

## ■ Change Control Properties ■ Hide Duplicate Entries

# NOTES

## Change Control Properties

■ Each control, in every section of a report has properties that can be changed. The Properties window for an item is opened by selecting the control and either selecting the Properties option on the View menu or by clicking on the Properties button 🖼 on the Formatting toolbar.

■ The Properties window remains on the screen until you close it, which allows you to preview changes and return to make further changes without having to reopen this window. In addition, the Properties window will be updated for each new selected item.

*Properties Window for a Label Control*

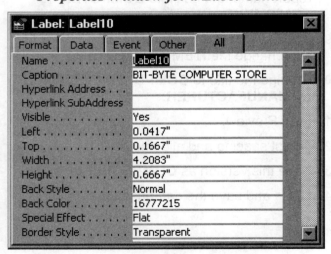

■ To change the format of field data for display purposes:

• Select the Detail Item, with the format to be changed.

• Open its Property box.

• Click on the desired tab (Format, Data, Event, or All).

• Select the property to be changed.

• Click on the drop-down list arrow, if it exists, **OR** Select the display format desired.

• Close the Property window.

## Hide Duplicate Entries

■ If you have duplicate column entries and would like to display only the first one, you can suppress the others by using the Properties dialog box for that detail element. For example: If you are listing your friends in order of their state of residence in a tabular listing, you can suppress all but the first state entry in each group.

To hide duplicate entries:

• Select the detail control for which duplicates should be suppressed.

• Open the Properties window for that item (View menu).

• Change the Hide Duplicates entry to Yes and close the Properties box.

*After taking inventory at Jane's boutique, your manager wants you to create a report that will list the type of items that the store has in stock.*

# EXERCISE DIRECTIONS

1. Open the 🖳JANESHOP database, or open 🖫25JANSHP

2. Create a New Report for the JANESHOP database using the STOCK table.

3. Create a Tabular Report using the STOCK table:
   - Include the fields TYPE, COLOR, PRICE, and STYLE, in the order listed.
   - Sort by TYPE, COLOR, and PRICE in ascending order.
   - Select Tabular layout, Portrait orientation, Casual style.
   - Name the report **STOCK ITEMS**.

4. Move the date function from the Page Footer to the Report Header as a subtitle.

5. Set the following items to Bold:

   Date function in the Report Header section

   Page function in the Page Footer section

6. Select the detail item TYPE and open its Properties window.

7. Change the Hide Duplicates option to Yes.

8. Print Preview the report and return to Design view.

9. Select the detail item COLOR and open its Properties window.

10. Change the Hide Duplicates option to Yes.

11. Print Preview the report and return to Design view.

12. Change the format of the PRICE detail item to fixed, with two decimals.

13. Center the Page Headers.

14. Change the font size of the subtitle to 10 point.

15. Print Preview and adjust the report layout, as necessary.

16. Print the report.

17. Save and close the report.

18. Close the database.

# KEYSTROKES

## CHANGE REPORT PROPERTIES

1. Select item or control on Report Design screen.

2. Click **Properties** button................. 🖻
   **OR**
   a. Click **View** ..................... `Alt`+`V`
   b. Click **Properties** ..................... `P`
   **OR**
   Double-click the control.

3. Click desired property text box.

4. Click drop-down arrow.

5. Select desired option.

6. Click **Properties** button to close...... 🖻
   **OR**
   Double-click control menu box to close.

## SET REPORT TO HIDE DUPLICATES

1. Select text box control in Report Design view.

2. Display property sheet.

3. Click **Format** tab.

4. Click Hide Duplicates text box.

5. Click drop-down list arrow.

6. Select **Yes** ..................................... `Y`

7. Click Properties button to close. ..... 🖻
   **OR**
   Double-click control menu box to close.

## SET DATA FORMAT IN REPORT

1. Select item or control in Report Design.

2. Click **Properties** button ...................
   **OR**
   a. Click **View** ..................... `Alt`+`V`
   b. Click **Properties** ..................... `P`

3. Click **Format** tab.

4. Click drop-down list arrow.

5. Select desired format.

6. Click **Properties** button to close ...... 🖻
   **OR**
   Double-click control menu box to close.

## Exercise
# 26

■ **Create a Report from a Query**   ■ **Add Report Sections and Controls**
■ **Group Controls and Headers and Footers**   ■ **Add Report Statistics**

## NOTES

### Create a Report from a Query

■ You can select a previously created query as a report reference. A query that includes all the data necessary for a needed report has already isolated the data necessary and is easier to work with than the source table. Only those fields and records that belong to the query will be included in the report.

### Add Report Sections and Controls

■ If you wish to add a control to a report design section, you need to open the Toolbox. This is done by selecting the Toolbox option from the View menu or from the Report Design toolbar. The Toolbox will appear and remain visible until you close it. The function of each button in the Toolbox is described on the Status bar when the mouse pointer is resting on the button. Note the illustration of the toolbox below.

*Report Design Toolbox*

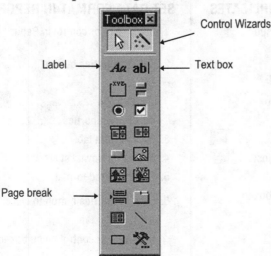

### Group Controls and Headers and Footers

■ Controls can be sorted and grouped in Report Design view to improve the readability of the report.

■ To group data, you may use the Report Wizard grouping page or open the Sorting and Grouping dialog box from the View menu. The current settings are reflected in the upper pane. You can control all the report's group settings from this window, but groupings can only be applied to sorted fields. In the upper pane, you can add or change field entries and sort settings. Note the illustration of the dialog box below.

■ The Toolbox ![Aa] button is used to add a label and the ![abl] button is used to add a text box to display data and calculation results. Click the appropriate icon; then move the mouse pointer to the proper location and draw a box to receive the data. Once the item box (control) has been created, you can enter the appropriate label identifier.

*Sorting and Grouping Dialog Box*

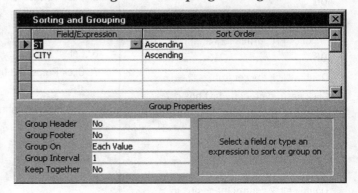

- The lower pane options are:

**Group Header and/or Footer** - A Yes selection is necessary to create a group and open a header or footer section for the selected control.

**Group On** - Yields an option list related to the selected field's data type that is to be grouped.

**Group Interval** - 1 is the default setting. Indicates the number of characters in text used to determine group breaks.

**Kept Together** options:

**No** - Page breaks may split the group.

**Whole group** - Group must print on the same page.

**With first detail** - Group header and at least the first record must print on the same page.

- You may use the Report Wizard grouping page to group data and give group items a header or footer as well. For example, if you have many duplicate entries for BRANCH and ASSIGNED TO data, it would improve the report to group all the records for the same branch and the assigned to data within each branch. The branch name would be the group header, the assigned to data would be the sub-header and then the data controls would be listed. See the illustration below.

*Report Wizard Grouping Page*

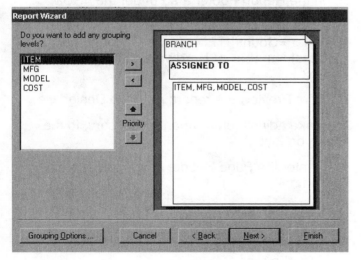

## Add Report Statistics

- When a footer is added to a group, Access automatically creates a summary formula. In Report Wizard, you can select the summary options for the data. You can add or edit a text box on the report design to explain the total such as "Number of Members" for a =Count formula. The formulas can calculate:

| | |
|---|---|
| Count of field data items | **=Count**([field detail name]) |

For numerical field data:

| | |
|---|---|
| Sums | **=Sum**([field detail name]) |
| Averages | **=Avg**([field detail name]) |
| Maximum values (Highest) | **=Max**([field detail name]) |
| Minimum  values (Lowest) | **=Min**([field detail name]) |

(For other options, use Access Help to research "functions.")

> *Before your company orders more software, they want to determine which products have been assigned to each department, the cost of the package they have purchased, etc. You have been asked to prepare a report so that your manager can make an analysis.*

# EXERCISE DIRECTIONS

1. Open the 🖳**COMPANY** database, or open 🖳**26COMPAN**.

2. Create a New Report for the COMPANY database using the Report Wizard.

   a. Use the Department Hardware Assignments query for the report.

   b. Include the fields, in the order listed: BRANCH, ASSIGNED TO, ITEM, COST

   c. Group first by BRANCH, then by ASSIGNED TO).

   d. Sort by ITEM.

   > ✓ Note: The Branch and Assigned to fields are not available for sort since they are grouped.

   e. Click on Summary Options and select the Sum option for Cost. Be sure Show Detail and Summary is checked.

   f. Report should be set for Portrait orientation with Stepped layout.

   g. Select Bold style.

   h. Title report: HARDWARE ASSIGNMENTS.

3. Preview the report.

4. Switch to Design view.

5. Increase the Page Header height by moving the Branch Header title bar down .5".

6. Increase the size of the framing boxes to accept two lines of text for the four field headings.

7. Change the column headings to read:

   | BRANCH | DEPARTMENT | HARDWARE | HARDWARE |
   |--------|------------|----------|----------|
   | OFFICE | ASSIGNMENT | ITEM     | COST     |

   (Adjust width of controls as necessary and be sure line is below the headers.)

8. Select Page Header; open and view the Sorting and Grouping window from the View menu.

9. Note the settings. Close the window.

10. Select the Assigned To control in the Assigned To Header and select the properties icon or menu item.

11. Change the Special Effect item to Shadowed. Close the Properties dialog box.

12. Print Preview the report; return to Design view.

13. Select the Summary box in the Assigned To Footer and delete it. Leave the SUM controls in place.

14. Select the Summary box in the Branch Footer and delete it. Leave the SUM controls in place.

15. Open the Toolbox using the Toolbox icon or by using the View menu.

16. Click on the **ab**l icon; draw a text box in the Assigned To Footer above the =SUM entry.

   > ✓ Note   An unbound box for a formula and a text box will appear.

17. Enter =Count([ITEM]) in the Unbound box.

   > ✓ Note:   This entry will yield a count of hardware items in each branch.

18. In the text box created enter **Number of Items**:. Adjust the alignment of the new entries.

19. Move to the area at the bottom of the Report Footer and click at the bottom of the grid to extend the area.

20. Click on the abl icon to create another text box in the Report Footer area under the =SUM entry.

21. Enter =Count([ITEM]) in the Unbound box and **Total Number of Hardware Items** in the Text box.

22. Print Preview the report; return to Design view.

23. Make adjustments, where necessary, to the report layout.

24. Center the Page Header labels within each control.

25. Add other report enhancements, as desired.

26. Print Preview the report; return to Design view.

27. Print the report.

28. Save and close the report; it should be named **HARDWARE ASSIGNMENTS**.

29. Close and save the database.

# KEYSTROKES

## USE QUERY TO CREATE A REPORT

Select a previously created query as the source of the new report on the New Report screen.

## CHANGE SIZE IN REPORT

1. Place pointer at bottom edge of section to change.

   *Pointer will become a line with a black, two-headed arrow.*

2. Click and drag to new size.

## GROUP REPORT DATA

1. View report in Design view.

2. Click **Sorting and Grouping** button . 〔≣〕

   **OR**

   a. Click **View** ..................... Alt + v

   b. Click **Sorting and Grouping** ........ S

3. Select desired field in **Field/Expression** column to group on.

4. Set sort order in **Sort Order** column.

5. Click in **Group Header** text box.

6. Click drop-down arrow and choose desired option:

**Yes** - to add a group header for this field to the report

**No** - remove group header for field from report

7. Click in **Group Footer** text box.

8. Click drop-down arrow and choose desired option.

9. Repeat steps 4-8 for each field to group on.

10. Double-click control menu box to close.

11. Add desired controls to new group header or group footer sections.

## GROUP REPORT DATA IN REPORT WIZARD

See Create Report with Report Wizard keystrokes in Exercise 23.

**At second screen of Report Wizard:**

1. Select field to be grouped.
   Click on > to move field.................. >

2. Select additional field, if necessary.

3. Set Priority, if necessary.

4. Click **Grouping Options** ......... Alt + O
   to select grouping intervals.

5. Click **Next** ................................... N

6. Click drop-down list to select sort fields.

7. Click button to determine sort order.

8. Complete Report Wizard steps.

## DEFINE AN EXPRESSION FOR A REPORT

   ✓ *An expression in a text box on a report is not stored in the database but calculated each time the report is displayed or printed.*

## ENTER EXPRESSION IN TEXT BOX

1. View in Report Design view.

2. Select text box to contain expression.

   **OR**

   a. Click **Text Box** tool in
      the toolbox................................ abl

   b. Click form at desired location of default-size text box.

   **OR**

   Click and drag pointer at desired location on report.

3. Click inside text box.

4. Press the **Equal Sign key (=)** ........... =

5. Type desired expression ....... *expression*

**Exercise**
# 27

## ■ Add New Fields to a Report

## NOTES

■ A saved report can be used to create a new report. Open the previously saved report design, make changes (such as adding new fields), and save the new design using a new report name.

■ To add a new field to a report, use the Field List option in the View menu in Report Design view to open a window that will list all fields in the

source table or query. To add a field, select a field and drag it to the desired detail position on the Design view screen. (The mouse pointer changes to a rectangular field name button as it is being dragged to the Detail position.) You can then add a label to the Page Header section and proceed as was discussed in previous lessons.

*You have been asked to create another report relating to your company's hardware inventory. You decide to use a previously created report as a basis for this new report since it contains only one additional field.*

## EXERCISE DIRECTIONS

1. Open the 🖾**COMPANY** database, or open 🖫**27COMPAN**.

2. Select the REPORTS tab section.

3. Open the COMPUTER EQUIPMENT report in Report Design view.

4. Select the Field List option on the View menu.

5. Add the ASSIGNED TO field to the end of the detail section items by selecting the label and dragging it to position. Delete the field label to the left of the field control.

6. Add a label item to the Page Header section; enter DEPT.

7. Adjust the size and position of DEPT. label and ASSIGNED TO detail item.

8. Extend existing lines to include the new entries.

9. Enter a subtitle **In Item Order** to the Report Header.

10. Change the subtitle font size to 12 point.

11. Extend Page Header boundaries to the new report width.

12. Center the new subtitle within the control box.

13. Create a Group Footer for ITEM using the View menu by setting the group footer to Yes.

14. Use the Properties box to remove duplicate entries from the ITEM and MFG. columns.

15. Set ITEM and MFG. detail items to print in Bold.

16. Add a Sum control footer for Cost in the ITEM footer and format to Currency using the Properties dialog box.

17. Change the label to read TOTAL COST = for the Sum footer label.

18. Print Preview; make any needed adjustments.

19. Change print orientation to Landscape, with all margins set for .5".

20. Print the report.

21. Save report as **HARDWARE INVENTORY WITH ASSIGNED DEPT**.

22. Close and save the database.

**Exercise**

**28**

■ **Create a Database with the Database Wizard**

## NOTES

■ All database objects can be created within the Database Wizard that is provided with Access. More than 20 database templates are provided. To access the Database Wizard, select New Database from the File menu and then select the Databases tab; or select Database Wizard from the opening screen.

■ The databases provided with the Database Wizard have all the database objects predefined. You are able to add fields but there are certain fields that are required or standard in these templates. If you have no data for these fields, you may delete the field once the database is created.

■ The Database Wizard creates a screen display or a Form view for you to enter your data. You may switch to Datasheet view if you wish to make entries on a table.

■ The Database Wizard presents you with a Switchboard, or a menu screen, so that you can maneuver within the database. You are given options such as entering data, previewing reports, changing switchboard items, or exiting the database.

■ Database objects created with a Wizard can be customized or changed using the toolbars, menus, design views, and other Wizards, as with a self-created database.

You will create an address book database using the Database Wizard. All the steps and mouse actions will be included in the exercise directions.

# EXERCISE DIRECTIONS

1. Open a new database using the Database Wizard by clicking Database Wizard on the opening screen or by Clicking File, New Database, Databases tab in the New dialog box.

2. Select the Address Book icon and click OK.

3. Name the database **ADDRBOOK**.

4. The Database Wizard screen appears and states what the database will accomplish.

5. Click Next.

6. The required fields in the database are checked in the field box. Additional fields are provided, shown in italics, and may be checked and added to the database. Do not check any additional fields.

7. Sample data for the database is offered. Check to include sample data.

8. Click Next.

9. Select the style for the screen display. Check each style and note the effect. Select the International style.

10. Click Next.

11. Select the Casual style for reports. Click Next.

12. Enter ADDRBOOK as the title of this database.

13. Click Next.

14. Answer Yes when asked if you want to start the database.

15. Click Finish.

16. At the Database Wizard main switchboard screen, select Enter/View Addresses.

17. View the form. Scroll through the records until you reach a blank form.

18. Enter the following data:

| First: | Michael |
|---|---|
| Last: | Westfield |
| Address: | 114 Zebra Road |
| City: | Seattle |
| State: | WA |
| Postal Code: | 98122 |
| Home Phone: | (504)555-6576 |
| Work Phone: | (504)555-7600 |
| Fax: | (504)555-7645 |
| Email: | mikew@anywhere.com |
| Birthday: | 12/18/62 |
| Send Card: | check |

✓ Note:  The form has two pages.

19. Switch to Datasheet View. Note that the extension field has not been used.

20. Switch to Form Design view. Select the Work Extension field and delete it.

21. Adjust the placement of the field names on the design screen by moving fields when mouse pointer changes to the hand shape.

22. Switch to Form view, and check that the field is no longer displayed.

23. Close the form, and return to the main switchboard screen.

24. Select the Preview Reports button, and view each report as listed.

25. Return to the Main Switchboard screen.

26. Close the **ADDRBOOK** database.

**Exercise**

**29**

■ **Summary**

*This summary exercise will review and apply all database concepts learned.*

*You have been hired by the Human Resources Department of Boynton College. One of your first jobs is to help organize information about the faculty. Once a database is created, you will be asked to update and modify the database, as well as create several reports requested by the President.*

## EXERCISE DIRECTIONS

### Creating and Saving a Database Table:

1. Create a new database file; name it **COLLEGE**.

2. Create a table using the field names and properties indicated at the right. Save the table; name it **TEACHERS**.

3. Save the table; name it **TEACHERS**. Set a primary key.

4. Change to Datasheet view of this table.

| Field Name | Type | Size | Description |
|---|---|---|---|
| NUMBER | AutoNumber | | |
| TITLE | Text | 3 | |
| LAST | Text | 10 | |
| FIRST | Text | 8 | |
| DEPT | Text | 4 | |
| BUDGET | Number | Integer | For Supplies |
| BLDG | Text | 1 | M=Main, A=Annex |
| NO OF CLASSES | Number | Integer | |
| START | Date/Time | Short Date | When Hired |
| TENURE | Yes/No | | |

### Entering Records:

5. Enter the records below into the table.

6. Adjust column widths to accommodate the longest entry in each field.

7. Print one copy.

8. Close the **COLLEGE** database.

| NUMBER | TITLE | LAST | FIRST | DEPT | BUDGET | BLDG | NO OF CLASSES | START | TENURE |
|---|---|---|---|---|---|---|---|---|---|
| 1 | Dr | Fernandez | Jose | Eng | 200 | M | 5 | 9/16/85 | Y |
| 2 | Ms. | Marcus | Diana | Eng | 250 | M | 4 | 9/16/85 | Y |
| 3 | Ms. | Hargrave | Sally | Eng | 250 | M | 5 | 9/16/84 | Y |
| 4 | Mr. | Bergman | Paul | Math | 150 | A | 3 | 9/16/83 | N |
| 5 | Mr. | Pax | Robert | Sci | 200 | A | 3 | 9/16/85 | N |
| 6 | Mr. | Chassin | Matthew | Math | 120 | A | 2 | 1/10/87 | N |
| 7 | Ms. | Blane | Jaime | PE | 120 | M | 3 | 9/16/87 | N |

| NUMBER | TITLE | LAST | FIRST | DEPT | BUDGET | BLDG | NO OF CLASSES | START | TENURE |
|--------|-------|------|-------|------|--------|------|---------------|-------|--------|
| 8 | Ms. | Chen | Julie | Sci | 160 | M | 4 | 9/16/85 | Y |
| 9 | Ms. | Brown | Donna | Hist | 200 | A | 5 | 2/1/88 | Y |
| 10 | Mr. | Anderson | Harvey | Hist | 200 | A | 5 | 1/10/86 | N |
| 11 | Dr. | Brown | Donald | Lang | 140 | M | 3 | 2/1/86 | Y |
| 12 | Mr. | Mastresi | William | Sci | 120 | A | 2 | 9/16/87 | N |
| 13 | Mr. | Zhan | Rafu | Sci | 200 | M | 5 | 9/9/83 | Y |
| 14 | Ms. | Browning | Paula | Eng | 150 | A | 4 | 9/9/82 | Y |
| 15 | Dr. | Ng | Tom | Lang | 180 | M | 3 | 9/9/87 | N |
| 16 | Mr. | Greene | Ralph | Math | 140 | A | 5 | 2/20/89 | N |
| 17 | Ms. | Linn | Sarah | Bus | 180 | A | 4 | 2/10/88 | N |
| 18 | Mr. | Fernandez | Ricardo | Bus | 180 | A | 3 | 1/20/88 | N |
| 19 | Dr. | Keltz | Mel | Bus | 200 | A | 5 | 2/10/90 | N |
| 20 | Mr. | Grosso | Lenny | PE | 140 | M | 2 | 9/16/85 | Y |

## Modifying the Datasheet/Adding Records:

1. Open the **COLLEGE** database table TEACHERS.

2. To keep track of faculty members' years of teaching experience, add one new number field (Field size - integer) to the table, EXP.

3. From the list below, enter the experience information into the table.

4. Adjust column widths to accommodate the longest entry.

| NUMBER | TITLE | LAST | FIRST | DEPT | BUDGET | BLDG | NO OF CLASSES | START | TENURE | EXP |
|--------|-------|------|-------|------|--------|------|---------------|-------|--------|-----|
| 1 | Dr. | Fernandez | Jose | Eng | 200 | M | 5 | 9/16/85 | Y | 15 |
| 2 | Ms. | Marcus | Diana | Eng | 250 | M | 4 | 9/16/85 | Y | 12 |
| 3 | Ms. | Hargrave | Sally | Eng | 250 | M | 5 | 9/16/84 | Y | 13 |
| 4 | Mr. | Bergman | Paul | Math | 150 | A | 3 | 9/16/83 | N | 14 |
| 5 | Mr. | Pax | Robert | Sci | 200 | A | 3 | 9/16/85 | N | 18 |
| 6 | Mr. | Chassin | Matthew | Math | 120 | A | 2 | 1/10/87 | N | 10 |
| 7 | Ms. | Blane | Jaime | PE | 120 | M | 3 | 9/16/87 | N | 9 |
| 8 | Ms. | Chen | Julie | Sci | 160 | M | 4 | 9/16/85 | Y | 13 |
| 9 | Ms. | Brown | Donna | Hist | 200 | A | 5 | 2/1/88 | Y | 8 |
| 10 | Mr. | Anderson | Harvey | Hist | 200 | A | 5 | 1/10/86 | N | 12 |
| 11 | Dr. | Brown | Donald | Lang | 140 | M | 3 | 2/1/86 | Y | 10 |
| 12 | Mr. | Mastresi | William | Sci | 120 | A | 2 | 9/16/87 | N | 16 |
| 13 | Mr. | Zhan | Rafu | Sci | 200 | M | 5 | 9/9/83 | Y | 15 |
| 14 | Ms. | Browning | Paula | Eng | 150 | A | 4 | 9/9/82 | Y | 15 |
| 15 | Dr. | Ng | Tom | Lang | 180 | M | 3 | 9/9/87 | N | 10 |
| 16 | Mr. | Greene | Ralph | Math | 140 | A | 5 | 2/20/89 | N | 8 |
| 17 | Ms. | Linn | Sarah | Bus | 180 | A | 4 | 2/10/88 | N | 9 |
| 18 | Ms. | Fernandez | Ricardo | Bus | 180 | A | 3 | 1/20/88 | N | 9 |
| 19 | Dr. | Keltz | Mel | Bus | 200 | A | 5 | 2/10/90 | N | 7 |
| 20 | Mr. | Grosso | Lenny | PE | 140 | M | 2 | 9/16/85 | Y | 11 |

5. Several teachers' records were omitted from the table. Add the following records.

| NUMBER | TITLE | LAST | FIRST | DEPT | BUDGET | BLDG | NO OF CLASSES | START | TENURE | EXP |
|--------|-------|------|-------|------|--------|------|---------------|-------|--------|-----|
| 21 | Dr. | Blanc | Pamela | Sci | 200 | M | 5 | 9/9/80 | Y | 17 |
| 22 | Mr. | Talley | Charles | Sci | 140 | A | 3 | 2/10/84 | N | 13 |
| 23 | Ms. | Goodcoff | Kayli | PE | 160 | A | 4 | 2/10/81 | Y | 16 |
| 24 | Mr. | Bergman | Thomas | Lang | 150 | A | 3 | 9/10/89 | N | 8 |
| 25 | Dr. | Knossos | Joyce | Math | 200 | A | 5 | 2/10/82 | Y | 16 |

## Doing a Quick Sort of the Datasheet:

6. Sort the datasheet in ascending order by LAST NAME.

## Searching the Database Table:

1. Using the Edit menu Find option, search the database for the answers to the following questions:

   a. Which teachers work in the English Department?
   b. In what building does Ralph Green work?

2. Using Edit Replace, search the database for all Hist. Dept. entries and change to S.S.

3. Using a Filter, find the answers to each of the following questions:

   a. Which teachers work in the main building and have more than 10 years experience?
   b. Which English teachers hold a doctoral degree (TITLE field)?
   c. Which Math teachers work in the Annex and have a supply budget of at least $140?

4. Create a Query of those teachers who work in the Main Building by Dept:

   Include the fields: DEPT (alphabetically), TITLE, LAST (alphabetically), FIRST, TENURE, and BLDG. Do not show the BLDG field.

5. Save the query; name it **MAIN BUILDING STAFF**.

6. Print the query.

## Preparing Reports:

**Report I:**

1. Create a new report with Report Wizard and respond as follows:

   - List fields in the following order: START, TITLE, FIRST, LAST, and EXP.
   - No grouping instructions.
   - Sort by START date.
   - Set Adjust the field width so all fields fit on a page to ON.
   - Set Portrait orientation, Tabular layout, Bold style.
   - Title report: BOYNTON COLLEGE.

2. Delete the Page Footer controls.

3. Add the subtitle **Faculty List**.

4. Center the Report Headers over the report.

5. Bold all headers without italics.

6. Change detail data:

   - START DATE to a descending sort
   - TITLE to alphabetical sort
   - START DATE with duplicate entries hidden

7. Change the Page Headers to read:

   | START DATE | TITLE | FIRST NAME | LAST NAME | EXPER-IENCE |
   |---|---|---|---|---|

8. Print Preview.

9. Make any adjustments necessary to make the report more attractive.

10. Add label:
    **Seniority Order as of**: to the current date function.

11. Adjust the date line to conform with the other two headers.

12. Print one copy.

13. Save and close the report.

## Report II:

1. Create a new tabular report. Respond to the Report Wizard as follows:
   a. List fields in given order: DEPT, BUDGET, and BLDG.
   b. Group by DEPT.
   c. Sort by BUDGET and set summary options for a SUM of BUDGET. Show Detail and Summary.
   d. Set Portrait orientation, Stepped layout, and Corporate style.
   e. Title report: DEPARTMENT BUDGETS.

2. Add a Report Header subtitle: **1996**.

3. Center all Report Headers and Building Detail.

4. Add, below the Sum function, a function to determine the Average of the budget figures for each department.
   Hint: Use =AVG([BUDGET]).

5. Shade the Sum and Average values in light gray.

6. Add appropriate labels to the Sum and Average amounts.

7. Change format of BUDGET to currency.

8. Print Preview.

9. Make adjustments as necessary.

10. Print Preview.

11. Print one copy.

12. Save and close the report.

## Report III:

1. Create and save a query to list those teaching in the Annex who have four or more classes.
   - List fields in given order: TITLE, FIRST, LAST, BLDG, NO OF CLASSES, and DEPT.
   - Set criteria to select Annex teachers who only teach four or more classes.
   - Save and close the query. Name it **Annex**.

2. Create a Tabular report using this query. Respond to the Report Wizard as follows:
   - List fields in given order: TITLE, FIRST, LAST, NO OF CLASSES, and DEPT.
   - No grouping settings.
   - Sort by NO OF CLASSES.
   - Set Adjust field <u>w</u>idth so all fields fit on a page to ON.
   - Set for Portrait orientation and Tabular layout
   - Set for Casual Style.
   - Title report: BOYNTON COLLEGE - ANNEX.

3. Add a subtitle: **Teachers with Four or More Classes**.

4. Change the column heading NO OF CLASSES to CLASSES.

5. Set main Report Header to italics.

6. Add a group footer at the bottom of the report.
   - Add a text box for the sum of the CLASSES field.
   - Label it: **Total # of Classes**.

7. Add another group footer directly under the first to determine how many teachers there are.
   - Add a text box for the count of the CLASSES field.
   - Label it: **Total # of Teachers**.

8. Change Page Footer items to Bold, without italics.

9. Print Preview.

10. Make adjustments, as necessary.

11. Print one copy.

12. Save and close the report and database.

# Microsoft
# PowerPoint 97

**Lesson 1:** Create, Save, and Print a Presentation

**Lesson 2:** Enhance Slides; Work with Text and Objects

**Lesson 3:** Work with Slide Shows

<table>
<tr><td rowspan="4">Exercise<br>1</td></tr>
</table>

| Exercise 1 | ■ About PowerPoint ■ Start PowerPoint<br>■ The Blank Presentation Option ■ Use the Template Option<br>■ Add Slides to a Presentation<br>■ Save a Presentation ■ Exit PowerPoint |

# NOTES

## About PowerPoint

■ PowerPoint is the presentation graphics component of Microsoft Office that lets you create and save presentations.

■ A presentation is a collection of slides relating to the same topic which may be shown while an oral report is given to help summarize data and emphasize report highlights. From the presentation slides, you can prepare handouts for the audience, speaker notes to use during the presentation, or outlines to provide an overview of the presentation. In addition, you can use slides as a table of contents and overhead transparencies. You can also create 35mm slides of your presentation.

■ PowerPoint slides may include text, drawings, charts, outlines, graphics, video, and/or audio clips.

■ Outlines created in Word or data created in Access or Excel can be imported into a PowerPoint slide. A PowerPoint slide may be imported into a Word document. (*See Integration Chapter, Exercise 9.*)

## Start PowerPoint

■ PowerPoint may be started using any one of the following procedures: (*See Office Basics, Lesson 1, page 3.*)

• Using the Windows 95 Taskbar: Click *Start*, highlight *Programs*, highlight and select *Microsoft PowerPoint*.

• Using the Windows 95 Taskbar: Click *Start*, highlight and select *New Office Document*. Click Blank Presentation, or click the *Presentation Designs* tab, select a presentation design and click OK.

• Using the Office Shortcut Bar: Click *Start a New Document* and click Blank Presentation, or click the *Presentation Designs* tab, select a presentation design and click OK.

■ If you launch PowerPoint using the first method, the following PowerPoint dialog box appears which presents options to Create a New Presentation or to Open an Existing Presentation. One of the options uses an AutoContent Wizard. As noted in the other applications, Wizards walk you through the presentation development process.

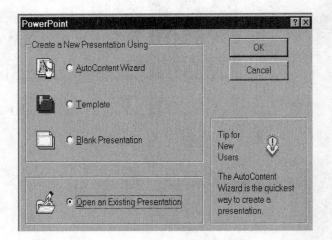

■ If you launch PowerPoint using methods two or three, you will have the option of creating a blank presentation or using a template design. Select the appropriate tab and option in the New Office Document dialog box.

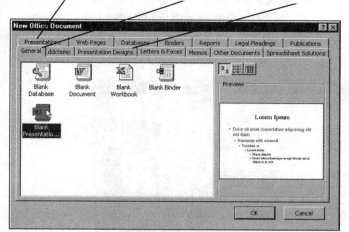

Click Presentations tab to display predesigned presentations

Click General tab to select Blank Presentation option

Click Presentation Designs tab to display templates

## The Blank Presentation Option

■ The Blank Presentation option lets you build your own unique presentation from blank slides that contain standard default formats and layouts.

■ After you select Blank Presentation and click OK, the New Slide dialog box appears.

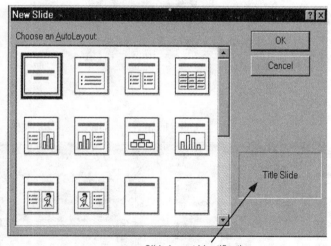

Slide layout identification

■ The New Slide dialog box includes a set of 24 different AutoLayout formats that arrange various types of objects on slides. Objects include such things as titles, charts, graphics, or bulleted lists—standard objects that you might want to place on the slide.

■ AutoLayout formats follow the natural progression of your presentation. They start with a Title Slide format and move to more complex layouts.

✓ Note: In later exercises, you will learn to rearrange objects and design your own layouts so that the slides become more suitable for your needs.

■ Each layout is identified in the box at the lower right corner of the New Slide layout window. Select a slide layout that is appropriate to the data you are presenting. The Title Slide is the default setting for the first slide in every presentation.

■ After you select the Title Slide layout and click OK, the PowerPoint screen appears.

## The PowerPoint Screen

■ PowerPoint places the generic title *Presentation* in the **Title bar** of each presentation you create. (*The PowerPoint screen is illustrated on the following page.*)

■ The **Standard toolbar** contains many buttons that appear in the other applications, but it also includes buttons unique to PowerPoint. Each button will be presented when it is relevant to an exercise.

■ The **Drawing toolbar**, located above the Status bar at the bottom of the screen, contains some of the most common tools used to add drawings to slides.

■ The **Common Tasks toolbar** is displayed when you open a new presentation. Several of the most common functions are available on this toolbar. You can close this bar if it gets in your way.

■ The **Office Assistant** appears when you first open a PowerPoint presentation. (*See page 12 for more on the Office Assistant.*)

■ **View buttons**, located at the bottom of the Presentation window, control the number of slides PowerPoint displays and the display layout. (*Views will be covered in Exercise 2.*)

■ The **Status bar**, located at the bottom of the PowerPoint window, contains information and buttons which make performing the most common tasks more efficient:

| | |
|---|---|
| **Slide number** | Identifies the slide currently displayed. |
| **Template Name** | Identifies the template design name. |
| **Spell Check** | Indicates if Automatic Spell Check is on or off. |

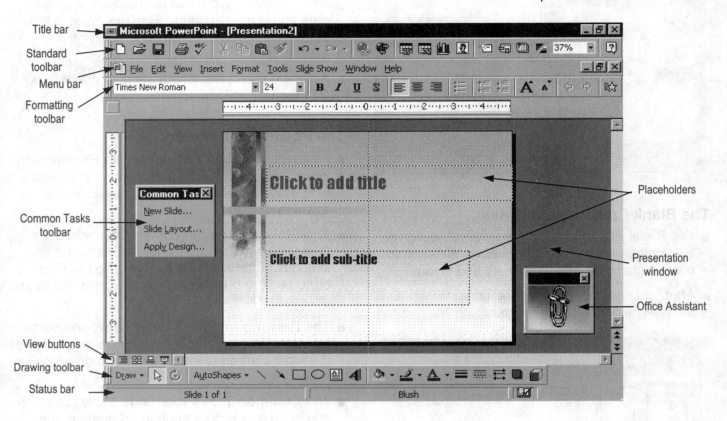

Title bar
Standard toolbar
Menu bar
Formatting toolbar
Common Tasks toolbar
View buttons
Drawing toolbar
Status bar

Placeholders
Presentation window
Office Assistant

## Create a Presentation Using the Template Option

■ The **Template** option lets you create slides with a predesigned format. PowerPoint provides over 100 professionally designed formats with colorful backgrounds and text from which you can choose.

■ After you select Template in the PowerPoint dialog box and click OK, a New Presentation dialog box appears. To select a template design, click the Presentation Designs tab. Each template is displayed by a large icon. (You can also display templates in List or Details view by clicking the appropriate icon.)

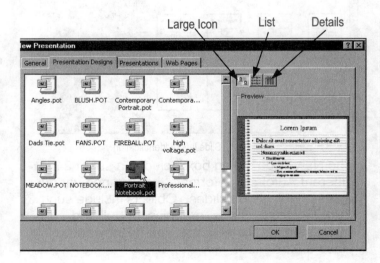

Large Icon   List   Details

■ PowerPoint also provides a set of slides that contain predesigned formats and suggestions for a specific type of presentation. For example, suppose you wanted to report the status of a project. PowerPoint contains a 10-slide presentation with suggestions for titles and bulleted information. To access specific slide presentations, click the Presentations tab in the New or New Presentations dialog box. Note below, 4 slides from a presentation about a food company.

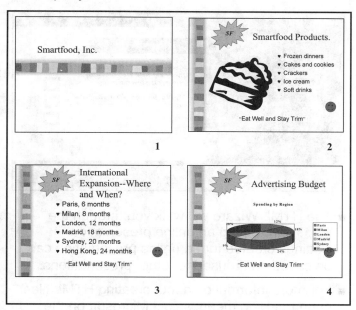

■ After you select the template design you desire and click OK, then select a layout from the AutoLayout screen and click OK, the PowerPoint screen appears.

■ Templates for designing online presentations are included in the Presentation design group. The designs of these presentations suggest the placement of buttons for links to other sites and other elements commonly used to create a presentation for the Word Wide Web. These designs can also be used for creating slide presentations.

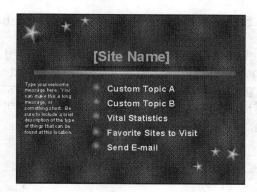

## Add Text to Placeholders

■ PowerPoint displays a slide containing **placeholders** (an empty box or boxes) which identify the placement and location of objects on the slide. Each placeholder contains directions to help you complete the slide.

■ Whether you select the Blank Presentation or Template option, **title placeholders** contain the format for title text while **body text placeholders** include format and design for subtitles or bulleted lists.

■ To type text into a placeholder, click inside the placeholder and note the handles that appear. Enter the text as prompted.

■ If you start typing without selecting the text placeholder, PowerPoint automatically places the text in the first text placeholder.

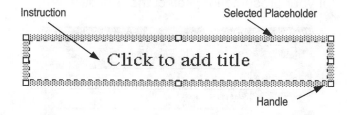

## Add Slides to a Presentation

■ To add a new slide to the presentation, click the Insert New Slide button on the Standard toolbar. When the AutoLayout dialog box appears, select a layout for the new slide.

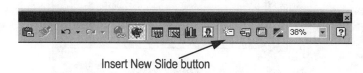

■ The Bulleted List format is automatically selected when you add a second slide to a presentation.

■ Five different bulleted sublevels are available. Pressing Tab indents text and produces sublevels of bulleted items. Different bullet shapes identify the tab levels, and the text size gets smaller with each sublevel. Pressing Shift+Tab returns you to the previous bullet level.

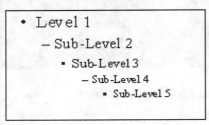

■ PowerPoint places the new slide immediately after the slide that is displayed or selected at the time you create the new slide.

## Save a Presentation

■ Presentations are saved using the same procedures used to save Word documents and Excel spreadsheets.

■ As in Word, selecting Properties from the File menu allows you to add summary information about your presentation. In the Presentation Properties dialog box under the Summary tab, you can add key words, a presentation title, comments, and other information you want to save with the file. To see a statistical summary of your presentation, select the Statistics tab.

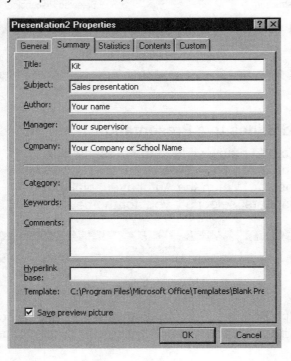

■ PowerPoint automatically adds a .PPT extension to presentations.

## Save File as HTML

■ Presentations created in PowerPoint can be saved in HTML format (Hypertext Markup Language) for publishing on the World Wide Web. When you select Save File as HTML on the File menu, the HTML Wizard, illustrated below, appears.

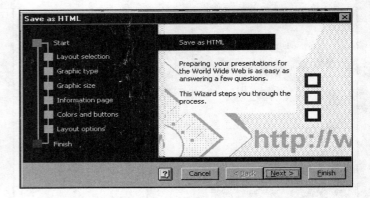

■ The HTML Wizard will walk you through the steps for creating an online presentation. Settings created for an online presentation can be saved and reused for other presentations.

■ For more information about creating HTML files, open the Help menu, select Microsoft on the Web and then click Product News.

## Close a Presentation/Exit PowerPoint

■ PowerPoint follows the same procedures for closing a presentation file and exiting as in the Word and Excel applications.

■ If the presentation you are working on has been modified or has not yet been saved, you will be prompted to save it.

*In Part I of this exercise, you will create a title slide and a bulleted list slide using the blank presentation option. In Part II of the exercise, you will create a title slide and a bulleted list slide using the Template option. You will save each as a presentation.*

# EXERCISE DIRECTIONS

## Part I

1. Start PowerPoint using the Windows Taskbar (highlight Programs) and create a new Blank Presentation.

2. Accept the default Title Slide layout for the first slide.

3. Type the title as shown in Illustration A.

4. Select New Slide and accept the default bulleted list slide for the second slide.

5. Type the bulleted list as shown in Illustration A.

6. Save the presentation; name it **KIT**. Fill in the summary information as follows:

   | | |
   |---|---|
   | Title: | (Accept the default) |
   | Subject: | Sales Presentation |
   | Author: | Your name |
   | Manager: | Your supervisor or teacher's name |
   | Company: | Your company or school name |
   | Category: | Sales |
   | Keywords: | Client, product |

7. Close the presentation window.

## Part II

1. Create a new Template presentation using the Zesty design.

2. Accept the default Title Slide layout for the first slide and the bulleted list slide for the second slide.

3. Type the title and bulleted list slides shown in Illustration B on page 378.

4. Save the presentation; name it **FLAGSHIP**. Fill in the summary information as follows:

   | | |
   |---|---|
   | Title: | (Accept the default) |
   | Subject: | Company Introduction |
   | Author: | Your name |
   | Manager: | Your supervisor or teacher's name |
   | Company: | Your company or school name |
   | Category: | Sales |
   | Keywords: | North Fork |

5. Close the presentation window.

## ILLUSTRATION A

### CREATIVE SALES

Sales Meeting
June 8, 1997

### SALES KITS

- Tool for making initial client contact
- A support system for sales rep
- Way to provide clients with material to make an informed decision about buying your product

**ILLUSTRATION B**

## FLAGSHIP REALTY

### Jawanza Hughes, President

## QUALIFIED LEADER IN DISTINCTIVE PROPERTIES

- Unparalleled knowledge of commitment to high-end properties on North Fork.
- Demonstrated track record.
- Unique ability to match client needs and inventory.
- Broad international client base.

# KEYSTROKES

## START POWERPOINT

**Using the Taskbar:**

1. Click **Start** ............................ `Ctrl` + `Esc`
2. Highlight **Programs** ....................... `P`
3. Select **Microsoft PowerPoint** ....... 🔲

   **OR**

1. Click **Start** ............................ `Ctrl` + `Esc`
2. Click **New Office Document** .......... 🔲
3. Double-click **Blank** ....................... 🔲
   **Presentation** to create a blank presentation.

   **OR**

a. Click **Presentation** ......... Presentation Designs
   **Designs** tab.
b. Select a Template design to create a designed presentation.
c. Click **OK** .............................. `Enter`

**OR**

1. Click **Presentations** .......... Presentation Designs
   tab.
2. Select Presentation.
3. Click **OK** .............................. `Enter`

**Using the Office Shortcut Bar:**

a. Click **Start a New Document** ...... 🔲
   button
b. Double-click **Blank Presentation**. 🔲
   to create a blank presentation.

   **OR**

a. Click **Presentation Designs** tab.
b. Select a **Template design** to create a designed presentation.
c. Click **OK** .............................. `Enter`

## SAVE A PRESENTATION

1. Click **Save** button ......................... 🔲

   **OR**

a. Click **File** ........................... `Alt` + `F`
b. Click **Save** ............................. `S`

2. Click **Save in** text box ............ `Alt` + `I`
   to select drive and/or folder.
3. Select desired .................... `↓`, `Enter`
   drive and/or folder.

**To select subfolder, if necessary:**

- Double-click folder ..... `Tab`, `↓`, `Enter`
4. Click **File name** .................... `Alt` + `N`
   text box.
5. Type presentation name .......... *filename*
6. Click **Save** ............................ `Enter`

   ✓ *Saved presentation files will be assigned the extension .PPT.*

## Exercise 2

- **Open a Presentation** ■ **Slide Views** ■ **Move from Slide to Slide**
- **Spell Checking** ■ **Print a Presentation**
- **Change a Slide's Layout or Template**

Open a          Print    Spell Check
Presentation

# NOTES

### Open a Presentation

■ Presentations may be opened by selecting Open an Existing Presentation from the PowerPoint dialog box or by using the procedures used to open documents in other Microsoft Office applications.

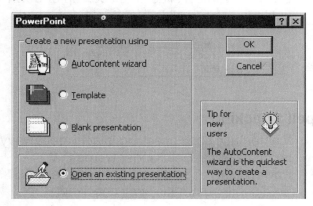

### Slide Views

■ PowerPoint lets you view your presentation in five different ways.

- **Slide view**, the default, allows you to see a single slide on screen. You can edit or modify a slide in this view.

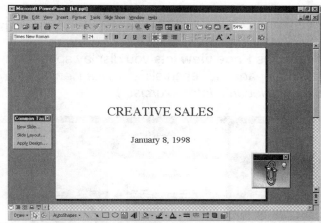

- **Outline view** displays slide text in a notebook page layout to give an overview of the content of a presentation. Use this view to organize a presentation. *(This view will be detailed in a later exercise.)*

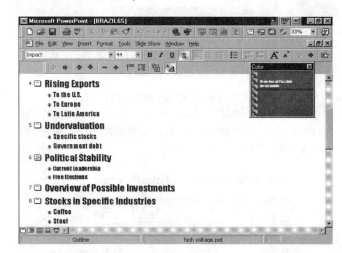

- **Slide Sorter view** lets you see miniature copies of your slides on screen so that you can see the flow of the presentation. Use this view to move, copy, and delete slides. *(Moving, copying, and deleting slides will be detailed in the exercise 8.)*

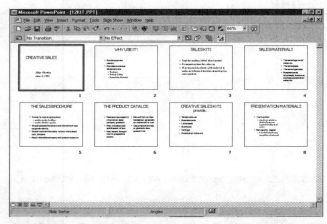

- **Notes Page view** lets you display speaker's note pages for each slide. *(This view will be detailed in a later exercise.)*

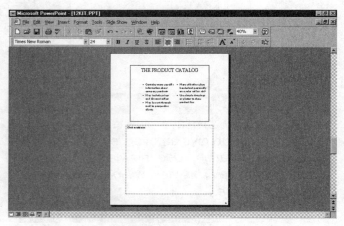

- **Slide Show view** lets you see your slides as an on-screen presentation. *(This view will be detailed in a later exercise.)*

■ Views may be changed by clicking the appropriate view button on the bottom left of the presentation window or by selecting the desired view from the View menu.

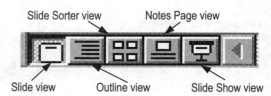

Slide Sorter view    Notes Page view

Slide view    Outline view    Slide Show view

## Move from Slide to Slide

■ When there are a number of slides included in a presentation, you will find it necessary to move from slide to slide to edit, enhance, or view the slide information. PowerPoint offers a variety of ways to select and display slides in Slide View:

- Press PgDn to display the next slide or PgUp to display the previous slide.

- Click the **Next Slide** or **Previous Slide** button on the vertical slide scroll bar.

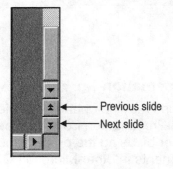

Previous slide
Next slide

- Drag the vertical slide scroll box up or down until the desired slide number is displayed.

## Spell Checking

- If automatic spell checking is activated, wavy red lines will appear under words that PowerPoint recognizes as possible errors. To disable automatic spell checking:

  - Click Options on the Tools menu.
  - Select the Spelling tab.
  - Deselect Spelling.
    **OR**
  - Click Hide spelling errors.

✓ *When you finish your presentation, you can deselect Hide spelling errors and check the words that have been identified as errors.*

■ The spelling feature may be used in PowerPoint as it was used in the other Office applications.

■ After creating your presentation, click the Spelling button ⌨ on the toolbar or select Spelling from the Tools menu.

## Print a Presentation

■ Slides in your presentation may be used as an on-screen show, transparencies, 35mm slides, notes pages, handouts, or as an outline. Therefore, you must specify certain setup information, depending on how you wish to use the slides or printouts. Select Page Setup from the File menu, and indicate your print specifications in the Page Setup dialog box that follows.

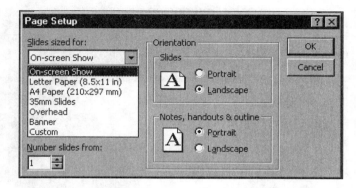

■ Printing PowerPoint slides is similar to printing pages in a Word document and worksheets in an Excel workbook. To print PowerPoint slides, select Print from the File menu, or press Ctrl+P. In the Print dialog box which follows, you may print the active slide, a selected slide range, or all slides in a presentation. When you print all slides of a presentation, each slide prints on a separate page.

The Print what feature lets you indicate whether you want your presentation printed as Slides, Notes pages, Handouts with 2, 3, or 6 slides per page, or as an Outline. *(Notes pages and handouts will be detailed in Exercise 17.)*

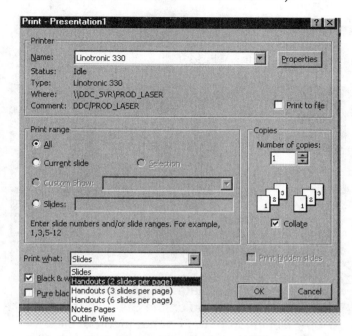

■ You can also click the Print button 🖨 on the Standard toolbar. When you use this technique, you bypass the Print window and send the print command directly to the printer. PowerPoint automatically prints information using the settings last selected in the Print window.

■ The default selection in the Print window prints All slides. Other options include:

| Option | Description |
|---|---|
| Properties | Changes elements specific to the printer, such as paper size, orientation, graphics, fonts, and so on. |
| Print to file | Prints the presentation to a disk file so that it may be sent to a service bureau for printing in an alternate format such as 35mm slides. |
| Print hidden slides | Prints slides that had been hidden. |
| Black & white | Turns all color fills to white and adds a thin black frame to all unbordered objects without text. Use this option if you plan to use your slides as overhead transparencies or if you have a printer that only prints black and white. |
| Collate | Prints multiple copies as collated sets. |
| Scale to fit paper | Scales presentation slides to fit a custom or different sized paper. |
| Frame slides | Adds a frame to the Slide when printed. |
| Pure black & white | Prints in black and white without gray scale. |

## Change a Slide's Template

■ Templates are organized by type and saved in the Presentation Designs subdirectory (folder) within the template subdirectory of the MSOffice directory.

■ As you select a template from the file list, an example of the template design appears in the right side of the window.

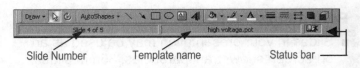

Slide Number          Template name          Status bar

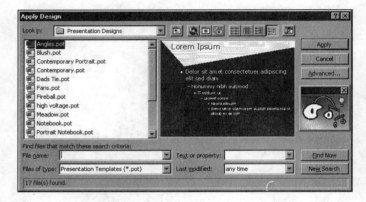

■ To change the template design, double-click the template name button on the Status bar or select Apply Design from the Format menu or click the Apply Design button on the Standard toolbar. The Apply Design dialog box appears, letting you make another template selection.

■ Sometimes it is distracting to see the color and design of the template while creating slide information. To display the slide in black and white, click the Black and White view button on the toolbar or select Black and White from the View menu. If Slide Miniature is selected in the View menu, a miniature slide appears on the screen with color and design displayed.

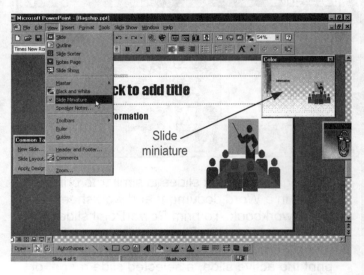

*In this exercise, you will add new slides to a previously created presentation. You will then use different slide views to see the flow of your presentation.*

# EXERCISE DIRECTIONS

## Part I

1. Start PowerPoint using the Windows Taskbar (click Programs) and select Open an Existing Presentation from the PowerPoint dialog box.

   ✓Note: *If PowerPoint is already running, select File, Open to open a presentation.*

2. Open ⊟FLAGSHIP, or open ⊟02FLAGSHIP.

3. Display slide two by clicking the Next Slide button.

4. Display slide one by dragging the scroll box.

5. Create a new bulleted list slide using the following information:

   ✓Note: *The slide will be inserted after slide one. You will move it into desired order in a later exercise.*

SERVICES INCLUDE
- Private financial evaluation
- Mortgage payment table constructed for each buyer
- Property tour videos
- Internet access for international sales and listings

6. Switch to Slide Sorter view.

7. Switch back to Slide view.

8. Correct all spelling errors.

9. View your presentation in Black and White.

10. In the Print dialog box, select Handouts with three slides per page as the Print what option. Print one copy in Black and white.

11. Close the file; save the changes.

## Part II

1. Open 📂**KIT**, or open 💾**02KIT**.
2. Display slide two using the PgDn key.
3. Display slide one using the PgUp key.
4. Create a new bulleted list slide using the following information:

   > CORPORATE IDENTITY
   > * Prepare a well-thought logo and corporate image
   > * Use logo on all company-related materials
   >   - correspondence
   >   - invoices
   >   - price sheets

5. Switch to Slide Sorter view.
6. Switch to Slide view.
7. Apply the Meadow template design.
8. Correct all spelling errors.
9. View your presentation in Black and White and display the slide miniature.
10. Use the default print slide setup.
11. In the Print dialog box, select Handouts with three slides per page as the Print what option. Print one copy in Black and white.
12. Close the file; save the changes.

# KEYSTROKES

## OPEN A PRESENTATION

*CTRL + O*

1. Click 📂 ........................ Alt + F , O
2. Click Look in box and select drive and/or folder containing file to open.
3. Type presentation name ............... *name* in **File name** text box, or select presentation in list.
4. Click **Open** ................................. Enter

## SPELL CHECK

*F7*

1. Click **Spelling** button ..................... ✓ on toolbar.

   **OR**

   a. Click **Tools**...................... Alt + T
   b. Click **Spelling** ............................. S

   ✓ *If Automatic Spell Check is activated, red wavy lines will appear under misspelled words. To correct the word(s), right-click on the word(s) and select the desired choice.*

## SWITCH VIEWS

Select desired view button:

* 🖥 **Slide** ................. Alt + V , S
* ▤ **Outline**................... Alt + V , O
* 🔡 **Slide Sorter**............ Alt + V , D
* 🖳 **Notes Page** ............. Alt + V , N
* 🛒 **Slide Show**.............. Alt + V , W

## ADD SUBLEVELS

Press **Tab**............................................ Tab
to indent text to next level.

   ✓ *Five different bulleted sublevels are available. Different bullet shapes identify the tab levels. Text size gets smaller with each sublevel.*

   **OR**

Press **Shift+Tab** ................... Shift + Tab
to return to previous level.

## DISPLAY SLIDES

Press **PgUp**............................................ Page Up
to display previous slide.

   **OR**

Press **PgDn**............................................ Page Down
to display next slide.

   **OR**

Click **Next Slide** ▼ or **Previous Slide** ▲ button on scroll bar.

   **OR**

Drag scroll box until desired slide is displayed.

## PRINT A PRESENTATION

*CTRL + P*

1. Click **File**............................... Alt + F
2. Click **Print** ...................................... P
3. Select desired options.
4. Click **OK** ...................................... Enter

   **OR**

   Click 🖨 to print presentation using settings last selected in Print dialog box.

**Exercise**

**3**

■ **Work with Object Slides** ■ **Use Undo**

*Standard Toolbar*

Insert Clip Art — Apply Design template

# NOTES

## Work with Object Slides

■ In Exercise 1, you learned that a placeholder is an empty box which identifies the placement of objects on a slide. You entered text into placeholders for a title and a bulleted slide. Some slides, however, contain special placeholders to hold a particular type of item, like clip art, a graph, or a chart. Some slides contain an object placeholder which holds any type of object—text, clip art, a chart, or a media clip.

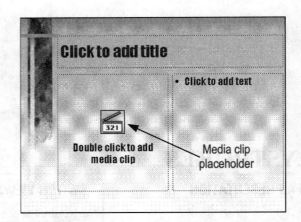

Click to add title

Click to add text

Double click to add media clip — Media clip placeholder

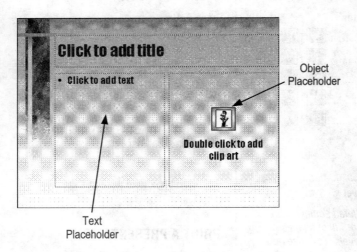

Click to add title

Click to add text

Object Placeholder

Double click to add clip art

Text Placeholder

■ When you select a slide layout containing a special placeholder, the placeholder prompts you to double-click within the placeholder to add the object. If you are adding clip art, for example, double-clicking the placeholder will open the Microsoft Clip Gallery so you can insert a clip art image in a clip art placeholder.

384

- You can also insert clip art by clicking on the Insert Clip Art button 🔲 on the Standard toolbar. In later exercises, you will learn how to insert a graph, a chart, or a media clip into placeholders as well as move and resize the objects inserted.

- The AutoClipArt feature suggests relevant clip art based on the text you type on your slides. To use AutoClipArt, select AutoClipArt from the Tools menu. The AutoClipArt dialog box which follows displays two list arrows. Clicking the first list arrow displays words in your presentation for which PowerPoint has found a relevant picture(s). The On Slide text box displays the slide number where the word has been entered. Select the word and slide number where you wish to add a suggested picture.

- To view the suggested picture(s), click the View Clip Art button. The Microsoft Clip Gallery opens and displays the picture(s) that best relates to the slide's wording.

### Use Undo

- As in the other Microsoft Office applications, the Undo feature reverses the most recent action. The keystrokes on page 387 review Undo procedures.

### Change a Slide's Layout

- The layout or template of a slide may be changed at any time. If you have objects on the slide when changing the layout, they will not be lost; they will be rearranged.

- Use Slide View when changing a slide's layout or template.

- To change the layout, click the Slide Layout button on the Common Tasks toolbar or select Slide Layout from the Format menu. The Slide Layout dialog box appears, letting you make another layout selection.

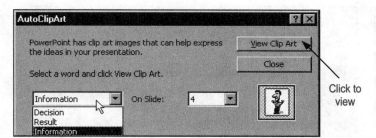

- You might find, however, that the picture(s) selected by PowerPoint is not one you desire. Remember, it is only a suggestion.

*In this exercise, you will add a slide to each of the presentations you created in previous exercises. You will also change the layout and template in each presentation.*

## EXERCISE DIRECTIONS

### Part I

1. Open 📖**FLAGSHIP**, or open 💾**03FLAGSHIP**.

2. Create a new slide using the Text & Clip Art layout.
   - ✓ *This slide will be inserted after slide one. You will move the slides into desired order in the next exercise.*

3. Enter the bulleted information shown in Illustration A of the exercise. Insert any relevant clip art.

4. Create another new slide using the Clip Art & Text Layout.

5. Enter the bulleted information shown in Illustration B of the exercise. Insert any relevant clip art.

6. Switch to Slide Sorter view.

7. Switch back to Slide view.

8. Use the default print slide setup.

9. Correct all spelling errors.

10. In the Print dialog box, select Handouts with six slides per page as the Print what option.

11. Print one copy in Black and white.

12. Close the file; save the changes.

**Part II**

1. Open ☷**KIT**, or open ▯**03KIT**.

2. Create a new slide using the Text & Clip Art layout.
   ✓ *This slide will be inserted after slide one. You will move the slides into desired order in the next exercise.*

3. Enter the bulleted information shown in Illustration C of the exercise. Insert any relevant clip art.

4. Create another new slide using the Clip Art and Text layout.

5. Enter the bulleted information shown in Illustration D on page 387; insert any relevant clip art.

6. Switch to Slide Sorter view.

7. Switch back to Slide view.

8. Change the template to the Angles design.

9. Change the slide view to Black and white. Display the slide miniature. Change the slide view back to color.

10. Use the default print slide setup.

11. In the Print dialog box, select Handouts with six slides per page as the Print what option.

12. Print one copy in Black and white.

13. Close the file; save the changes.

## ILLUSTRATION A

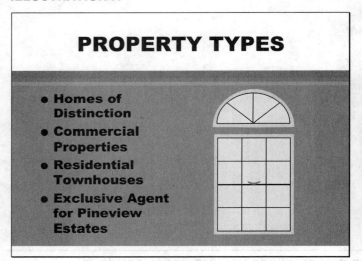

## ILLUSTRATION B

ILLUSTRATION C

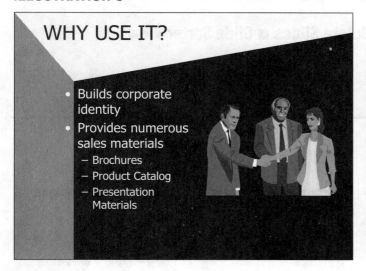

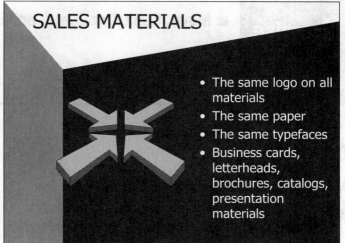

# KEYSTROKES

### DISPLAY SLIDE VIEW

Click **Slide View** button.......................🔲

**OR**

a. Click **View**......................... `Alt`+`V`

b. Click **Slide**............................. `S`

### CHANGE LAYOUT

**Display Slide view:**

1. Click **Slide Layout**........................ 🔲
   on Standard toolbar.

   **OR**

   a. Click **Format**...................... `Alt`+`O`

   b. Click **Slide Layout**....................... `L`

2. Select a desired layout.

3. Click **reapply**.......................... `Alt`+`A`

### CHANGE TEMPLATE

1. Click **Apply Design** button ............... 🔲
   on Standard toolbar.

   **OR**

   Double-click template name on Status
   bar (Angles, Blush, etc.).

   **OR**

   a. Click **Format**...................... `Alt`+`O`

   b. Click **Apply Design**...................... `Y`

2. Select a template design.

3. Click **Apply**........................... `Alt`+`P`

### UNDO

*CTRL + Z*

Click 🔙.............................. `Alt`+`E`, `U`

### USE SLIDE LAYOUT TO INSERT CLIP ART

1. Select a layout that has
   Clip Art option available.

2. Double-click Clip Art icon in template.

   **OR**

   a. Click **Insert**........................ `Alt`+`I`

   b. Click **Picture**............................. `P`

   c. Select **Clip Art**............................ `C`

3. Click desired Clip Art graphic.

4. Click **Insert**............................... `Enter`

### AUTOCLIPART

1. Click **Tools**........................... `Alt`+`T`

2. Click **AutoClipArt**........................... `U`

3. Click first list arrow to display words in
   presentation that have a relevant picture.

4. Select word.

5. Click **View Clip Art**................ `Alt`+`V`

6. Select relevant picture.

7. Click **Insert**............................... `Enter`

**Exercise**

**4**

■ **Move, Copy, Duplicate, and Delete Slides** ■ **Slide Sorter View**

# NOTES

## Move, Copy, Duplicate, and Delete Slides

■ Each slide in a presentation is part of the entire presentation. Slides may be moved, copied, duplicated, or deleted within the presentation. You can also move and copy slides from one presentation to another.

■ The **Duplicate** slide command lets you create a copy of a slide in Slide view. The Copy command is not available in Slide view. If you have created a custom slide that contains effects that you want to repeat on subsequent slides, you can duplicate the slide. You can also use the Duplicate slide command in Outline and Slide Sorter views. To duplicate a slide, select the slide and then select Duplicate Slide from the Insert menu. The duplicate slide will be inserted immediately following the original slide.

■ You should save a presentation before moving, copying, duplicating, or deleting slides to prevent loss of data. If you move, copy, or delete a slide and change your mind, use the Undo feature to reverse the action.

## Slide Sorter View

■ You can move, copy, or delete slides using menu commands or cut/copy and paste procedures. However, it is easiest and most efficient to perform these tasks in Slide Sorter view since all slides are displayed in miniature, and you can easily see the flow of the presentation in this view.

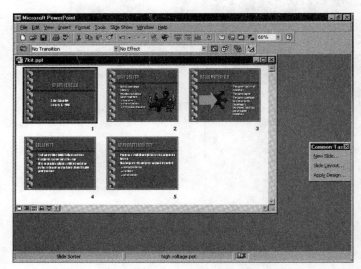

■ To move, copy, or delete a slide in Slide Sorter view, click the Slide Sorter view button 🔳 or select Slide Sorter from the View menu.

■ Select the slide to be moved, copied, or deleted. (Selected slides are outlined by a darker border.) You can select slides using a number of different techniques:

  • Click the desired slide.

  • Press the insertion point arrow keys until a dark border outlines the desired slide.

  • Press Shift and click each slide when you want to select multiple slides. Selecting multiple slides allows you to move, copy, duplicate, or delete them as a group.

■ The easiest way to move a slide in Slide Sorter view is to select it and drag it to a new location. When the slide is being moved, the mouse pointer becomes a slide icon and a vertical bar identifies the new position of the slide. When the bar appears in the position where you want to place the slide, release the mouse button.

- To copy a slide, press Ctrl and drag the slide you want to copy to a new location. The mouse pointer becomes a slide icon carrying a + sign.

- To delete a slide, select the slide and press the Delete Key.

### Return to Slide View

- Since you cannot edit slide contents in Slide Sorter view, you will need to return to Slide view to make changes and adjust text. You can return to Slide view using one of the following techniques:

  - Double-click a slide.

  - Select the slide and click the Slide view button 🔲 on the Status bar.

  - Select the desired slide and select Slide from the View menu.

---

*In this exercise, you will insert several slides into an existing presentation.*

---

## EXERCISE DIRECTIONS

1. Open 🖾KIT, or open 🖫04KIT.

2. Create a new slide using a Bulleted List layout.

3. Enter the information shown in Illustration A.

4. Create a new slide using a 2 Column Text layout.

5. Enter the information shown in Illustration B, on page 390.

6. Create a new slide using a Text & Clip Art layout.

7. Enter the information shown in Illustration C. Insert a relevant graphic.

8. Switch to Slide Sorter view.

9. Delete the slide entitled CORPORATE IDENTITY.

10. Move the slides into the order shown in Illustration D on page 391.

11. Switch to Slide view.

12. Correct all spelling errors.

13. View your Presentation in Black and white.

14. Print one copy of the presentation as Handouts with six slides per page in Black and white.

15. Close the file; save the changes.

## KEYSTROKES

### MOVE SLIDES

*–SLIDE SORTER VIEW–*

1. Select slide to move.

2. Drag slide to new location.

### COPY SLIDES

*–SLIDE SORTER VIEW–*

1. Select slide to copy.

2. Press Ctrl and drag slide to new location.

### DUPLICATE SLIDES

*–SLIDE SORTER VIEW–*

1. Select slide to duplicate.

2. Click **Insert** ..................... Alt + I

3. Click **Duplicate Slide** ...................... D

### DELETE SLIDES

*–SLIDE SORTER VIEW–*

1. Select slide to delete.

2. Press Delete ................................. Del

**ILLUSTRATION A**

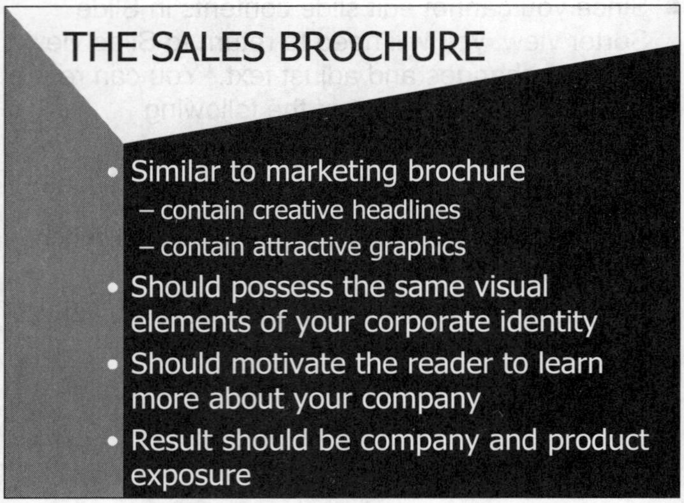

## THE SALES BROCHURE

- Similar to marketing brochure
  - contain creative headlines
  - contain attractive graphics
- Should possess the same visual elements of your corporate identity
- Should motivate the reader to learn more about your company
- Result should be company and product exposure

**ILLUSTRATION B**

## THE PRODUCT CATALOG

- Contains more specific information about company products
- May include prices and discount offers
- May be sent through mail to prospective clients

- More effective when handed out personally on a sales call or visit
- Use simple drawings or photos to show product line

**ILLUSTRATION C**

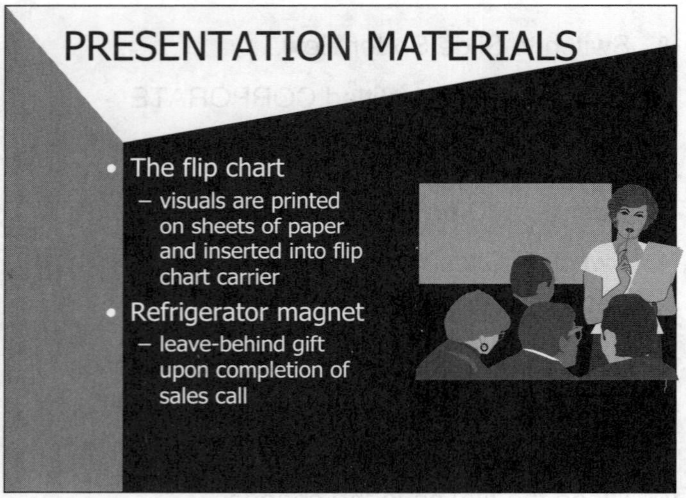

## PRESENTATION MATERIALS

- The flip chart
  - visuals are printed on sheets of paper and inserted into flip chart carrier
- Refrigerator magnet
  - leave-behind gift upon completion of sales call

## ILLUSTRATION D

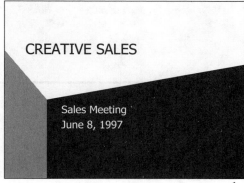

**CREATIVE SALES**

Sales Meeting
June 8, 1997

1

**WHY USE IT?**

- Builds corporate identity
- Provides numerous sales materials
  – Brochures
  – Product Catalog
  – Presentation Materials

2

**SALES KITS**

- Tool for making initial client contact
- A support system for sales rep
- Way to provide clients with material to make an informed decision about buying your product.

3

**SALES MATERIALS**

- The same logo on all materials
- The same paper
- The same typefaces
- Business cards, letterheads, brochures, catalogs, presentation materials

4

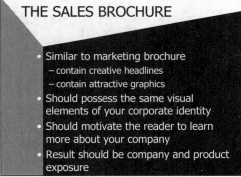

**THE SALES BROCHURE**

- Similar to marketing brochure
  – contain creative headlines
  – contain attractive graphics
- Should possess the same visual elements of your corporate identity
- Should motivate the reader to learn more about your company
- Result should be company and product exposure

5

**THE PRODUCT CATALOG**

- Contains more specific information about company products
- May include prices and discount offers
- May be sent through mail to prospective clients
- More effective when handed out personally on a sales call or visit
- Use simple drawings or photos to show product line

6

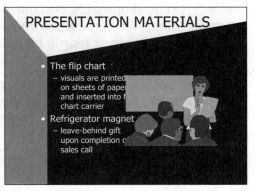

**PRESENTATION MATERIALS**

- The flip chart
  – visuals are printed on sheets of paper and inserted into flip chart carrier
- Refrigerator magnet
  – leave-behind gift upon completion of sales call

7

## Exercise 5

### ■ Outline View

## NOTES

### Outline View

- **Outline** view displays slide text as titles and subtitles in an outline format to give an overview of the content of a presentation. This view is used to organize a presentation.

- To display Outline view, click the Outline View button 📑 on the bottom left of the presentation window or select <u>O</u>utline from the <u>V</u>iew menu.

- Outline view can be used before creating text on slides to organize your thoughts in an outline format. Or, you may create your presentation in Slide view first, then switch to Outline view to see the flow of your presentation in an outline format. Outline View can also serve as a Table of Contents to distribute to your audience.

Note the illustration below of the KIT presentation displayed in Outline view. Slides are numbered down the left side of the screen, and slide icons identify the start of each new slide. A miniature of the selected slide appears in the window. If the miniature is not on screen, select Slide M<u>i</u>niature from the <u>V</u>iew menu.

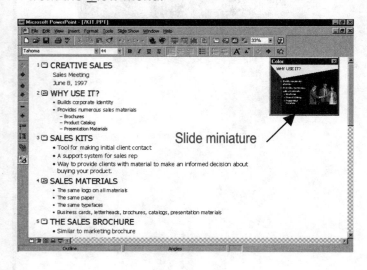

- If Slide Miniature is turned off, you will not see graphics and objects in Outline view. However, a slide that contains such items will be identified by shapes in the miniature slide icon 🖾 that appears to the right of the slide numbers.

- The Outlining toolbar replaces the Drawing toolbar in the presentation window. The Outlining toolbar contains tools for making some of the more common tasks associated with outlines more efficient. Many of these tasks are not available on the menus.

*Outlining Toolbar*

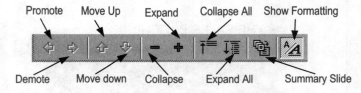

- **Promote/Demote** buttons ⬅ ➡ let you quickly reformat bulleted text to title text (promote) and title text to subitem text (demote).

- **Move up/Move down** buttons ⬆ ⬇ let you select text from one slide and move it to a new location. This procedure can be used effectively to move or rearrange individual text items or complete slides.

- **Expand Selection** button ➕ lets you display all title text as well as subitem text for selected slides and/or items containing multiple levels and subitems.

- **Collapse Selection** button ➖ lets you remove subitems from display for individual items or for groups of selected items.

- **Collapse All** button 🔲 lets you display only the title text for all slides in a presentation.

- **Expand All** button 🔲 lets you display all levels of text for every slide in a presentation.

- **Summary Slide** button 🔲 creates a new slide from the titles of slides you select in Slide Sorter or Outline views and creates a bulleted list of the titles.

- **Show Formatting** button 🔲 lets you display text formatted and enhanced, as it appears on the slide. When this feature is inactive, text for all slides appears as plain text in the default font.

### Add Slides in Outline View

■ The same four procedures can be used to add slides in Outline view that were used to add slides in Slide view:

- Click Insert New Slide button 🔲 on the Standard toolbar.

- Click New Slide on the Common Task toolbar.

- Press Ctrl+M.

- Select Insert, New Slide from the menu.

### Print an Outline

■ You can print an outline using the same basic procedures that were used to print copies of your slides. You must, however, select Outline View from the Print what drop-down list.

---

*In this exercise, you will create a presentation in Outline view. After creating the presentation, you will move slides, and print the presentation.*

---

# EXERCISE DIRECTIONS

1. Create a new Blank Presentation and select Title slide as the first slide layout.

2. Switch to Outline view.

3. Enter the following titles and subtitles to create your outline.

   1. Smartfood, Inc.
      "Eat Well and Stay Trim"

   2. Smartfood Products
      - Frozen dinners
      - Cakes and cookies
      - Crackers
      - Ice cream
      - Soft drinks

   3. Smartfood's Success…
      - People are eating healthier to reduce body fat.
      - People want low-fat, low-calorie foods that taste great!

   4. International Expansion--Where and When?
      - Paris, 6 months
      - Milan, 8 months
      - London, 12 months
      - Madrid, 18 months
      - Sydney, 20 months
      - Hong Kong, 24 months
      - ✓ *If the slide minature of slide 4 is not on screen, display it.*

4. Switch to Slide view.

5. Display slide 1.
   - ✓ *PowerPoint selected the slide layouts for you. You may, however, change them.*

6. Switch to Slide Sorter view.

7. Move slide 4 to become slide 3.

8. Switch to Slide view and display slide 2 (Smartfood Products).

9. Change the layout to Clip Art & Text. Insert a relevant graphic.

10. Apply the Dads Tie template design.

11. Insert a new bulleted list slide after slide 3 that reads:

> ### U.S. Markets
> - East-New York
> - North-Illinois
> - West-California
> - South-Florida

12. Change the layout to Clip Art & Text. Insert a relevant graphic.

13. Switch to Slide Sorter view, then to Outline view.

14. Correct all spelling errors.

15. In the Page Setup dialog box, change the orientation for Handouts to Landscape.

16. Print one copy as Handouts with six slides per page in Pure Black and White.

17. In the Page Setup dialog box, change the orientation for Handouts to Portrait.

18. Print one copy as Handouts with six slides per page in Pure Black and White.

19. Save the file; name it **FOOD**. Fill in the appropriate summary information.

20. Close the presentation window.

# KEYSTROKES

### SWITCH TO OUTLINE VIEW

Click  .......................... Alt + V , O

### ADD SLIDES IN OUTLINE VIEW

*CTRL + M*

Click **New Slide** button........................ 🖼
on Standard toolbar.

**OR**

1. Click **Insert**........................... Alt + I
2. Click **New Slide** .............................. N

### ADD TEXT IN OUTLINE VIEW

Click ⬅ ➡ to indent ................... Tab
or add subitems.

✓ *To add a bulleted item under the Title line, press Enter and then press Tab.*

**OR**

Click ⬅ ➡ ........................ Shift + Tab
to go back one text or
subitem level.

## Exercise 6

### ■ Summary

*In this exercise, you will create a presentation in Outline View. You will move the slides, change the layouts of selected slides, and print the presentation.*

# EXERCISE DIRECTIONS

1. Create a new Blank Presentation.

2. Switch to Outline view.

3. Create the outline shown on the following page. Display the Slide Miniature.

4. Print one copy of the outline (select Print what, Outline View from the Print menu).

5. Switch to Slide view.

6. Display slide 1 (Brazil).

7. Apply the High voltage template design.

8. Switch to Slide Sorter view.

9. Move slide 5 (Rising Exports) to become slide 4.

10. Delete slide 8 (Bonds).

11. Undo the last action.

12. Display slide 3 (Why is the Brazilian…) and change the layout to a Title slide.

13. Display slide 6 (Overview of Possible Investments) and change the layout to a Title slide.

14. Display slide 9 (Conclusion) and change the layout to Text & Clip Art. Insert a relevant graphic.

15. Display slide 8 (Bonds) and change the layout to Clip Art and Text. Insert a relevant graphic.

16. Insert a new slide after Undervaluation that reads:

    ✓ *Use a layout that includes clip art. Insert a relevant graphic.*

    | Political Stability |
    | --- |
    | • Current Leadership |
    | • Free Elections |

17. Correct spelling errors.

18. Switch to Slide Sorter view.

19. Print one copy as Handouts with six slides per page in Black and white.

20. Save the file; name it **BRAZIL**. Fill in the appropriate summary information.

21. Close the presentation window.

1 🗔 **BRAZIL**
- Investment Opportunities
- Simpson Investment Advisors, Inc.

2 🗔 **Brief History of the Brazilian Economy**
- Debt crisis in the 1980s
  - increased foreign borrowing
  - rising international interest rates
- Recent recovery of the economy
- Research Department's report on the history of the economy

3 🗔 **Why is the Brazilian Economy Ready for Foreign Investment?**

4 🗔 **Undervaluation**
- Specific stocks
- Government debt

5 🗔 **Rising Exports**
- To the U.S.
- To Europe
- To Latin America

6 🗔 **Overview of Possible Investments**

7 🗔 **Stocks in Specific Industries**
- Coffee
- Steel
- Chemical

8 🗔 **Bonds**
- Short term
- Long term

9 🗔 **Conclusion**
- Reasons to invest through Simpson Investment Advisors
  - rate of return on investments
  - global trading
  - highly trained professionals
- To Summarize...

**Exercise 7**

- **Select, Align, and Change the Appearance of Text**
- **Change a Slide's Color Scheme**
- **Change Case**

*Formatting Toolbar*

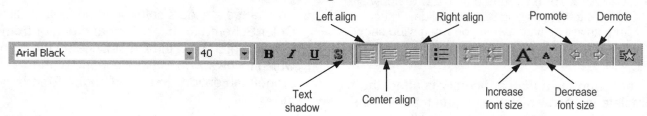

# NOTES

## Select Text

- When pointing to text with the mouse, the mouse pointer changes to an I-beam to signify that the text insertion mode is active, just as in Word. Click the text you want to edit, and use the same techniques for selecting blocks of text in PowerPoint that you used to select text in Word:

  - Double-click to select a word.

  - Triple-click to select a paragraph, complete title, or bulleted item, including all subitems.

- These techniques can be used to select and edit text in Slide or Outline views. Text may not be edited in Slide Sorter or Notes Pages views.

## Align Text

- PowerPoint lets you align text to the left, center, or right in a placeholder or textbox, as well as to justify text in the placeholder or textbox. Because the most frequently used alignments in PowerPoint are left, right, and center, buttons for these three alignment options are included on the Formatting toolbar. Justified alignment is available by selecting Alignment, Justify from the Format menu.

- To change the alignment of title text or text for one bulleted item, position the I-beam in the title or bulleted item and click the desired alignment button. To change the alignment for more than one bulleted item, select text for the bulleted

items you want to change before clicking the alignment button or selecting the alignment option from the menu.

- While you can set alignment in either Outline or Slide view, use Slide view to change text alignment because text formatting is displayed in this view.

- When you want to change the alignment of title text, all text in the title placeholder for that slide is realigned. To align text on one line of a title differently from text of other lines, remove the lines you want to align differently from the title placeholder and include them in the body placeholder. Each line in the body placeholder can then be aligned separately.

## Change the Appearance of Text

- PowerPoint controls font, size, alignment, emphasis (bold, italics, shadow, underline), and color on each slide layout. However, you can change these attributes using the same techniques described in Word and Excel.

- Use the Formatting toolbar to apply one formatting change to text quickly; use the Font dialog box to apply more than one formatting change to text.

- The Formatting toolbar in PowerPoint has several buttons not included on the Formatting toolbars in Word and Excel. These buttons perform tasks unique to PowerPoint:

- Use the **Increase/Decrease Font Size** buttons A A to incrementally increase or decrease the font size until it fits within the space you need.

- Use the **Text Shadow** button S to apply shadow effects to text.

- Use the **Promote (Indent less)** and **Demote (Indent more)** buttons ← → to adjust the levels of bulleted items.

- Use **Animation Effects** button to apply effects to objects and text on a slide. These effects will activate when you run a slide show. (*Animation effects will be covered in Exercise 15.*)

■ Format changes and enhancements affect the complete word in which the insertion point rests unless you have selected specific text.

■ You may replace one font face with another font face on all slides at once by selecting Replace Fonts from the Format menu. In the Replace Font dialog box which follows, select a font to replace in the Replace text box, select a font to replace it with in the With text box, then click Replace.

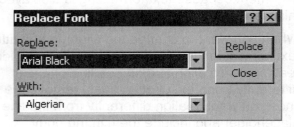

■ The Show Formatting button on the Outlining toolbar is defaulted to display font style, font size, bold, italics, and underline. When you turn off the Show Formatting feature, text appears in the default font with no enhancements. The Show Formatting button is available in Outline and Slide Sorter views.

## Change Case

■ As in word processing, the change case feature lets you change an existing block of text to sentence case, lowercase, uppercase, or toggle case. To change case, highlight the text and select Change Case from the Format menu. Choose the desired case in the Change case dialog box.

## Change a Slide's Color Scheme

■ Each template design has a predefined color scheme. Specific colors were chosen for the slide background, title text, fills, lines, shadows, and accents. PowerPoint lets you change the entire color scheme of your template or change individual parts (for example, line colors and slide background only) of the template. You may change the color scheme of one or all slides in your presentation.

■ To change a slide's color scheme, select Slide Color Scheme from the Format menu or from the shortcut menu. In the Color Scheme dialog box which follows, you may select one of the predefined options indicated on the Standard tab.

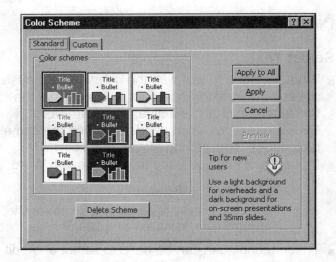

■ To make custom changes, click the Custom tab. You can then select the recommended color for each item (Background, Text and Lines, Title Text, etc.), or you can select other colors by clicking the Change Color button and selecting from a palette of colors. The preview window displays the results of your choices. Click Apply to All to change all slides or click Apply to change only the current slide.

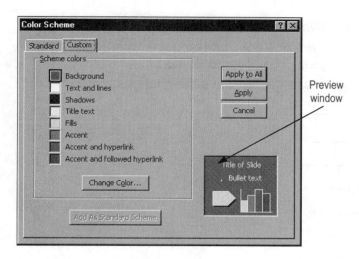

Preview window

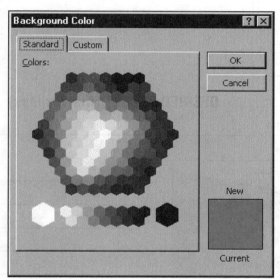

- You can also apply shaded, patterned, or textured background colors to slides by selecting Background from the Format menu and clicking the list arrow. A variety of color combinations appear. You can also click More Colors and Fill Effects for additional options. A preview window displays the results of your selection.

*In this exercise, you will manipulate placeholders and change the size and color of text on slides. Check your changes with the Desired Result shown on the next two pages.*

# EXERCISE DIRECTIONS

1. Open ⌨KIT, or open 💾07KIT.

2. Using Slide view, replace the font faces on all slides to Jester (or any other decorative font).

3. Center align the titles in slides 2-7.

4. Reduce the font size of the bulleted text on slide 5 (THE SALES BROCHURE) using the Decrease Font Size button on the toolbar.

5. Italicize subtitles on slide 1.

6. Switch to Outline view.

7. Use the Show Formatting button on the Outlining toolbar to turn the formatting off and on.

8. Insert a New bulleted Slide after slide 6 that reads:

> CREATIVE SALES KITS provide...
> - Sales Brochures
> - Business Cards
> - Letterheads
> - Brochures
> - Catalogs
> - Presentation Materials

9. Switch to Slide view.

10. Apply the same formatting changes to the new slide as you did to the other slides.

11. Change the color scheme on all slides as follows:

| Background | Dark Gray |
|------------|-----------|
| Accent | Yellow |
| Fills | Blue |

12. Switch to Slide Sorter view.

13. Print one copy as Handouts with 3 slides per page in Black and White.

14. Close the file; save the changes.

**CREATIVE SALES**

*Sales Meeting*
*June 8, 1997*

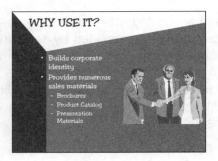

**WHY USE IT?**

- Builds corporate identity
- Provides numerous sales materials
  - Brochures
  - Product Catalog
  - Presentation Materials

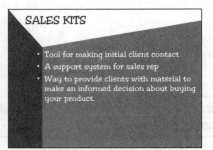

**SALES KITS**

- Tool for making initial client contact
- A support system for sales rep
- Way to provide clients with material to make an informed decision about buying your product.

**DESIRED RESULT (first 6 slides)**

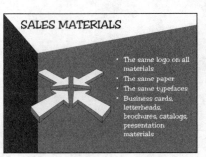

**SALES MATERIALS**

- The same logo on all materials
- The same paper
- The same typefaces
- Business cards, letterheads, brochures, catalogs, presentation materials

**THE SALES BROCHURE**

- Similar to marketing brochure
  - contain creative headlines
  - contain attractive graphics
- Should possess the same visual elements of your corporate identity
- Should motivate the reader to learn more about your company
- Result should be company and product exposure

**THE PRODUCT CATALOG**

- Contains more specific information about company products
- May include prices and discount offers
- May be sent through mail to prospective clients
- More effective when handed out personally on a sales call or visit
- Use simple drawings or photos to show product line

# KEYSTROKES

## CHANGE FONT

1. Position insertion point in word to format.
   **OR**
2. Select text to format.
3. Select......... `Times New Roman ▼` desired font from Formatting toolbar **Font** drop-down list.
   **OR**
1. Click **Format, Font** ......... `Alt`+`O`, `F`
2. Select desired font and options.
3. Click **OK** ..................................... `Enter`

## REPLACE FONT FACES

1. Click **Format** ......................... `Alt`+`O`
2. Click **Replace Fonts** ..................... `R`
3. Select font face to **Replace** .... `Alt`+`P`
4. Select font face ...................... `Alt`+`W` to **Replace With**.
5. Click **Replace** ......................... `Alt`+`R`

## CHANGE FONT SIZE

1. Position insertion point in word to format.
   **OR**
   Select text to change.
2. Select desired size ..................... `24 ▼` from Formatting toolbar **Font Size** drop-down list.
   **OR**
1. Click **Format, Font** ......... `Alt`+`O`, `F`
2. Select desired font size.
3. Click **OK** ..................................... `Enter`
   **OR**
   Click `A A` to increase/decrease font incrementally.

## CHANGE EMPHASIS (BOLD, ITALICS, SHADOW, UNDERLINE, COLOR)

1. Position insertion point in word to change.
   **OR**
2. Select text to change.
3. Click desired emphasis icon on Formatting toolbar.
   **OR**
   a. Click **Format, Font** ......`Alt`+`O`, `F`
   b. Click **Font Style** ................. `Alt`+`O`
   c. Select desired options.
   d. Click **OK** ................................ `Enter`

## ALIGN TEXT

1. Position insertion point in text to align.
2. Click Alignment option on Formatting toolbar:
   - Click **Left**............................ ▤
   - Click **Right** ............................ ▥
   - Click **Center** ......................... ▦
   **OR**
3. Click .............................. `Alt`+`O`, `A` **Format, Alignment**.
4. Select desired alignment:
   - **Left** ........................................... `L`
   - **Center**...................................... `C`
   - **Right**......................................... `R`
   - **Justify**....................................... `J`

## CHANGE CASE

1. Select text to change.
2. Click **Format**....................... `Alt`+`O`
3. Click **Change Case** ........................ `E`
4. Select desired case.
5. Click **OK** ................................... `Enter`

## CHANGE SLIDE'S COLOR SCHEME

1. Click **Format** ...................... `Alt`+`O`
2. Click **Slide Color Scheme** .............. `C`
   *–FROM STANDARD TAB–*
3. Click desired........................... `Alt`+`C` color schemes
   **OR**
   Click **Custom** tab.
   a. Click each item as desired (Background, Text and Lines, etc.)
   b. Click **Change Color** ........... `Alt`+`O`
   c. Select desired color.
   d. Click **OK**................................ `Enter`
4. Click **Apply to All** ................. `Alt`+`T`
   **OR**
   Click **Apply** ......................... `Alt`+`A` to apply changes to current slide.

## Exercise 8

- Copy Text Formatting ■ Move and Copy Text
- Increase/Decrease Paragraph Formatting
- Move and Size Placeholders

Format Painter

# NOTES

## Copy Text Formatting (Format Painter)

- As in Word, the Format Painter feature may be used in PowerPoint to copy formatting, such as font face, style, size, and color, from one part of text to another.

- To copy formatting from one location to another, select the text that contains the format you wish to copy. Then, click the Format Painter button on the Standard toolbar (the I-beam displays a paintbrush) and select the text to receive the format. To copy formatting from one location to several locations, select the text that contains the format you wish to copy, then double-click the Format Painter button. Select the text to receive the format, release the mouse button, and select additional text anywhere in the document. To turn off this feature and return the mouse pointer to an I-beam, click the Format Painter button or press Escape.

- When you use the Format Painter in Outline view, some formatting will not appear until you return to Slide view.

## Copy and Move Text on a Slide

- You can use the same methods to cut, copy, paste, and drag and drop text in PowerPoint that you used in Word and Excel. In addition, you may use the Move Up or Move Down buttons on the Outlining toolbar to reposition text up or down one line at a time.

- You can move text only in Slide or Outline views. However, it is more efficient to use Outline view to move or copy text on a slide.

- Use cut/copy and paste techniques to copy text to more than one new location or to copy text to a different presentation. Use the drag and drop technique in Outline view to move or copy text to a new location or to rearrange bulleted items. Use the drag and drop feature in Slide view to move text on one slide.

- To move or copy bulleted items in Outline or Slide views, position the mouse pointer on the bullet until it turns to a four-headed arrow and click once. The bulleted item, as well as the subitems, will be highlighted. Place the mouse pointer in the selection, and hold and drag it until you see a horizontal line positioned where you want to insert the text. Release the mouse button and your text will drop into place.

## Increase/Decrease Paragraph Spacing

- The space between paragraphs may be adjusted incrementally by selecting the paragraphs to be affected and clicking the Increase or Decrease Paragraph Spacing button on the Formatting toolbar. The spacing may also be adjusted by a specific amount by selecting Line Spacing from the Format menu.

## Move and Size Placeholders

- Text, clip art, and object placeholders can be moved, copied, sized, and deleted.

- To move, copy, size, or delete a placeholder, you must first display handles to put the placeholder into an edit mode. Click on the text to display the placeholder, then click on the placeholder border to display the handles. Click on the clip art or object to display the handles.

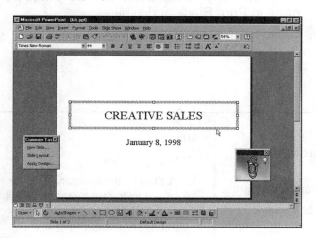

- When handles appear, you can **size** the placeholder as you did when working with pictures. Drag a top or bottom middle handle to change the vertical size (height); drag a left or right middle handle to change the horizontal size (width); drag a corner handle to size the placeholder proportionally. When you size a text placeholder, the text within it will adjust to the new borders.

- You can **move** the placeholder and its contents by displaying the handles, then placing the pointer on the border (not a handle), and clicking and holding the left mouse button while dragging the placeholder to a desired location.

---

*In this exercise, you will manipulate placeholders and change the size and color of text on slides. Check your changes with the Desired Result shown on the next page and page 405.*

---

# EXERCISE DIRECTIONS

1. Open 🖳**BRAZIL**, or open 🖫**08BRAZIL**.
2. Switch to Slide view.
3. Apply a new template design: Contemporary Portrait.
4. Change the font face on all slides to Times New Roman.
5. Using Format Painter, italicize all slide titles; then center them.
6. Display slide 1 (BRAZIL).
7. Move BRAZIL below the horizontal line.
8. Display slide 2 (Brief History) and change to Outline view. Display slide miniature.
9. Move the second bulleted item down to become the last bulleted item.
10. Switch to Slide view.
11. Change the color of the subitems to green.
12. Create a custom color scheme on all slides as follows:
    - Text and lines    Dark blue
    - Title text    Red
    - Fills    Red
    - Accent    Bright green
13. Display slide 3 (Why is ...?).
    - Change the layout to Clip Art and Text.
    - Delete the text placeholder.
    - Insert a relevant picture into the clip art placeholder. Move it into the center of the slide

and size it proportionally so it fills the center of the slide.
14. Display slide 7 (Overview of Possible Investments).
    - Change the layout to Clip Art and Text.
    - Delete the text placeholder.
    - Insert two relevant pictures into the clip art placeholder. Position them in the center of the slide and size them proportionally so they fill the center of the slide.
15. Display slide 8 (Stocks in Specific Industries).
    - Increase the bulleted text size to 48 point and increase the paragraph spacing so the text fits vertically into the placeholder. Highlight the text and click Format Painter.
16. Display slide 6 (Political Stability).
    - Use Format Painter to increase the bulleted text size to 48 point.
    - Delete the picture.
    - Use AutoClipArt to replace the picture with one that PowerPoint suggests.
17. Display slide 9 (Bonds).
    - Increase the bulleted text size to 48 point.
    - Reduce the size of the text placeholder.
    - Move the placeholder to the middle right of the slide.
18. Display slide 5 (Undervaluation).
    - Increase the bulleted text size to 48 point.
    - Reduce the size of the placeholder.
    - Move the placeholder to the center of the slide.

19. Display slide 4 (Rising Exports).
    - Increase the bulleted text size to 48 point.
    - Reduce the size of the placeholder.
    - Move the placeholder to the center of the slide.
20. Switch to Slide Sorter view.
21. View the Presentation in Black and white.
22. Print one copy as Handouts with six slides per page in Pure Black and White.
23. Close the file; save the changes.

# KEYSTROKES

## COPY TEXT FORMATTING

1. Position insertion point in text containing format to copy.
2. Click 🖌.
   ✓ *Double-click icon if format is to be applied to multiple selections of text.*
3. Select text with paintbrush ............ ☐ that you want to change or click to apply format to a word.
4. Press **Esc** to drop the .................... Esc paintbrush, if necessary.

## COPY

*CTRL + C*

1. Select the text to copy.
2. Click 📋 ...................... Alt + E , C
   **OR**
   Right-click and select **Copy** from the Shortcut menu.

## MOVE (CUT)

*CTRL + X*

1. Select the text to move (cut).
2. Click ✂ ...................... Alt + E , T
   **OR**
   Right-click and select **Cut** from the Shortcut menu.

## PASTE

*CTRL + V*

1. Position cursor where text is to be inserted.
2. Click 📋 ...................... Alt + E , P
   **OR**
   Right-click and select **Paste** from the Shortcut menu.

## DRAG AND DROP

1. Select text or bulleted section to copy or move.
2. Position mouse pointer on selected text.
   ✓ *Mouse pointer must be a white pointer arrow* ⬚.
3. Click and drag text until vertical bar (or horizontal bar, if in Outline view) appears in desired new text position.
   ✓ *To copy text using this process, hold down Ctrl* ⬚ *while dragging the text.*
4. Release mouse button.

## EDIT PLACEHOLDERS

**To display handles:**

1. Click inside the text placeholder.
2. Click on placeholder border.
   **OR**
   Click the clip art graphic or object.

**Move**

1. Display handles.
2. Position mouse pointer on border (not on a handle).
3. Hold down left mouse button and drag placeholder to new location.
4. Release mouse button.

**Copy**

1. Display handles.
2. Position mouse pointer on border (not on a handle).
3. Press **Ctrl** and hold down mouse button and drag text to new location.
4. Release mouse button.

## Size

1. Display handles.
2. Position mouse pointer on a top or bottom middle handle to change height, a left or right handle to change width, or a corner handle to change size proportionally.
3. Drag the handle until the placeholder is the desired size.

## Delete

1. Display handles.
2. Press **Delete** ............................. Del
   ✓ *If you delete a title or text placeholder, an empty text placeholder appears. Press Delete again to delete the entire placeholder.*

## INCREASE/DECREASE PARAGRAPH SPACING

1. Select paragraphs to be affected.
2. Click Increase 📏 or Decrease 📏 buttons on Formatting toolbar to adjust spacing incrementally.
   **OR**
   a. Click **Format** ................... Alt + O
   b. Click **Line Spacing** ................... S
   c. Enter desired amount in **Before paragraph** and/or **After paragraph** text boxes    Alt + B or Alt + A , *number*
   d. Click **OK** ............................. Enter

## ADD/EDIT TEXT WITHIN PLACEHOLDERS

1. Click inside placeholder until I beam appears.
2. Use I-Beam to edit text as usual.

**DESIRED RESULT**

---

BRAZIL

Investment Opportunities
Simpson Investment Advisors, Inc.

1

---

Brief History of the Brazilian
Economy

▮ Debt crisis in the 1980s
  ▮ increased foreign borrowing
  ▮ rising international interest rates
▮ Research Department's report on the history
  of the economy
▮ Recent recovery of the economy

2

---

Why is the Brazilian Economy Ready
for Foreign Investment?

3

---

Rising Exports

▮ To the U.S.
▮ To Europe
▮ To Latin America

4

---

Undervaluation

▮ Specific stocks
▮ Government debt

5

---

Political Stability

▮ Current
  Leadership
▮ Free
  Elections

6

---

Overview of Possible Investments

7

---

Stocks in Specific Industries

▮ Coffee

▮ Steel

▮ Chemical

8

---

Bonds

▮ Short term
▮ Long term

9

---

Conclusion

▮ Reasons to invest
  through Simpson
  Investment Advisors
  ▮ rate of return on
    investments
  ▮ global trading
  ▮ highly trained
    professionals
▮ To Summarize...

10

---

<table>
<tr><td>Exercise<br>9</td><td>■ Use Slide and Title Master ■ Insert Slide Numbers,<br>Date and Time, and Footer ■ Format Bullets</td></tr>
</table>

# NOTES

## Use Slide and Title Master

■ The **Slide Master** contains the default settings for the format of a slide. The **Title Master** contains the default settings for the format of the Title Slide. By changing the formatting (font style, font size, color, and/or position) of text or object placeholders on Slide Masters, all slides are automatically reformatted uniformly throughout the presentation. If, for example, you wanted to include clip art as your company's logo or a saying or quote on all slides in your presentation, you would include it on the Slide Master, and it would appear on all slides of your presentation.

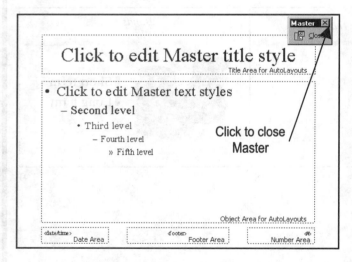

■ Text formatting on separate slides overrides changes made on the Slide Master.

■ Changes made on the Slide Master affect *all* slides in a presentation *except* Title Slide AutoLayout format. Changes to the Slide Master affect only the active presentation.

■ Slide Master may be accessed by selecting Master from the View menu, and then selecting Slide Master. Or, you can hold down the Shift Key as you click the Slide view button.

■ After making the desired changes on the Slide Master, click Slide view and display each slide in the presentation to see the effects. You may need to make adjustments to the Slide Master after seeing the results on individual slides.

## Insert Slide Numbers/Date and Time/Footers

■ Slide numbers, the date and/or time, and/or footer text may be included on individual or all slides. To do so, select Header and Footer from the View menu. In the Header and Footer dialog box which follows, click the appropriate check box to indicate whether you wish the Date and time, Slide number or a Footer to be on the current slide or on all slides (Apply to All).

■ If you wish to include the date and time or just the time and have it update automatically each time the presentation is accessed, click the Update automatically option. Click the list arrow to select a desired format for the date and/or time.

- If you do not wish to have page numbers, the date and time, or footers appear on the title slide, click the Don't show on title slide option.

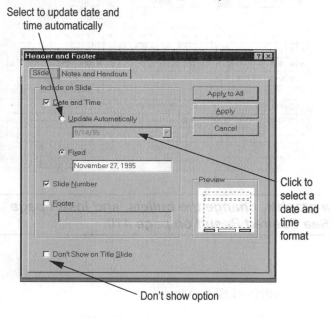

Select to update date and time automatically

Click to select a date and time format

Don't show option

- Since the Slide Master contains the default settings for the format of a slide, date and time, page number and footer placeholders have already been created and positioned by PowerPoint. *(See Slide Master illustration on previous page.)* The preview window in the Header and Footer dialog box lets you see how these items appear on the slide. The date and time appear on the bottom left of the slide, the footer appears in the middle of the slide and the slide number appears on the bottom right of the slide.

- If you wish to change the location of any of these items on the slide, you must make the changes on the Slide Master. To move the page number, for example, select the page number placeholder (so handles appear) and drag it to a new location on the Slide Master. If you wish to center the page number on the bottom of the slide, delete the footer placeholder and move the page number placeholder into the bottom center position.

- You may format the page number, date and time, and footer just like all other text within a text placeholder.

- The actual slide number will appear on your slides when you print and during a slide show. *(Presenting slide shows will be covered in Exercise 14.)*

## Format Bullets

- Many AutoLayout formats include bulleted body text. The bullet styles and shapes are set in the Slide Master. You can change the bullet style, size, and shape individually for each bulleted item on each slide, or you can save time and keep the format consistent by using the Slide Master. Bullets formatted individually will override formatting set in the Slide Master.

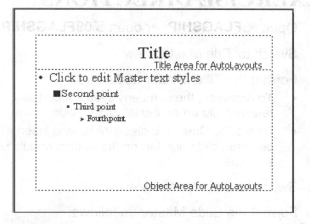

- If you wish to include text below bulleted items but would prefer no bullet on the explanatory text, you can remove the bullets. Click the Bullet On/Off button on the Formatting toolbar to turn bullets on and off on individual items or on selected text. You can also turn the bullet feature on or off by selecting or deselecting the Use a Bullet check box in the Bullet dialog box.

- To change the format and size of bullets, display the slide or Slide Master and position the insertion point on the bulleted item or bullet list level you want to change. Then select Bullet from the Format menu. If the insertion point is not positioned in bulleted text and no bulleted items are selected, the option will not be available. In the Bullet dialog box which appears, select a desired bullet, size, and color.

- You can select a bullet style from several character sets containing symbols and shapes (Wingdings, SymbolsA, etc).

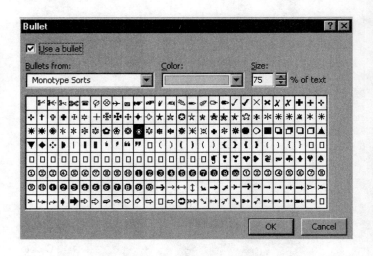

*In this exercise, you will use Slide Master to add a graphic, change the bullets, and insert page numbers, affecting all slides in the presentation. See Desired Result on page 410.*

# EXERCISE DIRECTIONS

1. Open 📷**FLAGSHIP**, or open 💾**09FLAGSHIP**.

2. Switch to Title Master view.

3. Format the Title Master as follows:
   - To represent the company's logo, insert any relevant clip art on the left of the slide.
   - Delete the Date/time placeholder and insert a centered slide number on the bottom middle of the slide.

4. Switch to Slide Master view.

5. Format the Slide Master as follows:
   - Decrease the width of the Master title style placeholder and move it slightly to the right.
   - Insert the same clip art used on the title slide on top of the square (see illustration on next page).
   - Insert a centered slide number on the bottom middle of the slide.

6. Change the format of the bullets as follows:
   - Main bullet to a blue flag (Wingdings character set).
   - First subitem bullet to a red arrow.
   - Fourth level bullet to bright yellow.

7. Switch to Slide view.

8. Display slide 2. (Property Types).
   - Move the graphic to the far right of the slide.
   - Widen the text placeholder.
   - Increase the paragraph spacing so the text fills the placeholder vertically.

9. Display slide 5 (Qualified Leader in…).
   - Click the decrease font size button on the Standard toolbar to reduce the title font size.

10. Display Slide 3 (Our Sales Force). Decrease font size of bulleted text until it fits within the slide.

11. View the Presentation in Black and white.

12. Print one copy as Handouts with six slides per page in Black and white.

13. Close the file; save the changes.

**TITLE MASTER**

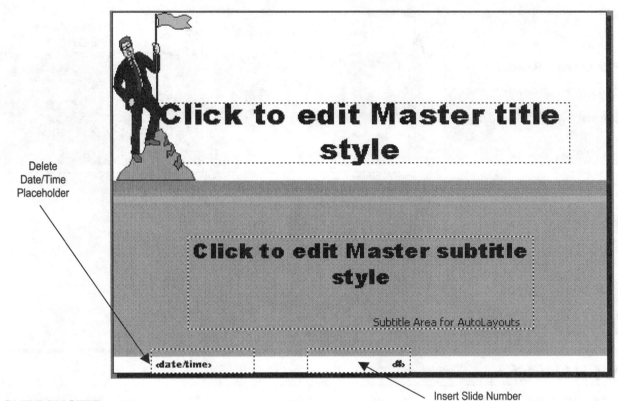

Delete
Date/Time
Placeholder

Insert Slide Number

**SLIDE MASTER**

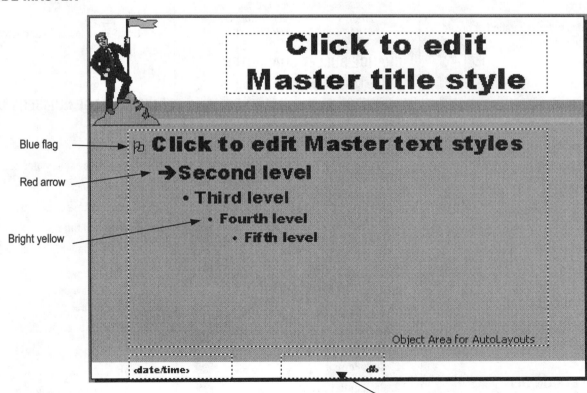

Blue flag

Red arrow

Bright yellow

Insert Slide Number

## DESIRED RESULT

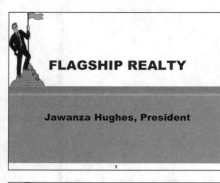

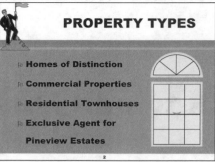

# KEYSTROKES

### FORMAT TEXT ON SLIDE OR TITLE MASTER

1. Open the desired presentation or create a new presentation.
2. Click **View** .............................. `Alt`+`V`
3. Click **Master** ............................ `M`
4. Click **Slide Master** .................... `S`

   **OR**

   Click **Title Master** ................... `T`
5. Select placeholder to change.

   **OR**

   Select text level to change.
6. Format text font, size, alignment, and enhancements as desired.
7. Click `▣` ........................ `Alt`+`V`, `S`

### DELETE PLACEHOLDER

1. Select placeholder to delete.
2. Press **Delete** ........................... `Del`

### TURN BULLETS ON/OFF

1. Select bulleted paragraph to turn off.
2. Click `☰` .. `Alt`+`O`, `B`, `U`, `Enter`

---

✓ An X in the box beside *Use a Bullet* indicates that the feature is active. An empty box means the feature is inactive and no bullet will appear.

### CHANGE BULLET CHARACTER

1. Position insertion point in desired bulleted item or select several bulleted items.
2. Click **Format** ........................ `Alt`+`O`
3. Click **Bullet** ............................. `B`
4. Select desired ............ `Alt`+`B`, `↓` character set from **Bullets from** list.
5. Select desired bullet character.
6. Click **Use a bullet** ............. `Alt`+`U` if necessary.
7. Click **OK** ............................... `Enter`

### CHANGE BULLET SIZE

1. Position insertion point in bulleted item to change or select several bulleted items.
2. Click **Format** ........................ `Alt`+`O`
3. Click **Bullet** ............................. `B`
4. Select **Size** box ..................... `Alt`+`S` in upper right corner.

---

5. Type desired percentage size ..... *number*

   **OR**

   Click `▲▼` to increase or decrease bullet size.
6. Click **OK** ............................... `Enter`

### INSERT PAGE NUMBERS/DATE AND TIME/FOOTER

1. Click **View** ............................. `Alt`+`V`
2. Click **Header and Footer** ........... `H`
3. Click **Slide** tab.
4. Click appropriate check box:
   - **Date and time** ............. `Alt`+`D`
   - **Slide number** ............... `Alt`+`N`
   - **Footer** ........................ `Alt`+`F`
   - **Don't show on** .............. `Alt`+`S`
     title **slide**.
5. Click **Apply to all** ................. `Alt`+`Y`

   **OR**

   Apply ............................... `Alt`+`A`

✓ Actual page numbers will display when printing or during a slide show.

## Exercise 10

- **Use Slide Rulers and Guides** ■ **Floating Toolbars**
- **Draw Graphic Objects** ■ **AutoShapes** ■ **Create Text Objects**
- **Group and Ungroup Objects** ■ **Layer Objects**

*Drawing Toolbar*

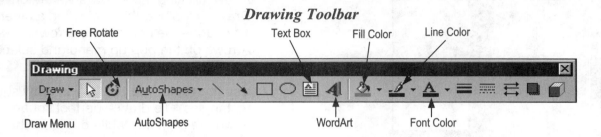

# NOTES

### Use Slide Rulers and Guides

■ In PowerPoint you can display horizontal and vertical rulers. Rulers allow objects and text to be placed on the slide more accurately. Rulers may be displayed by selecting <u>R</u>uler from the <u>V</u>iew menu.

■ Ruler measurements will display differently depending on what is selected on the slide. If an object is selected, the ruler displays in *drawing mode,* and the zero point is at the center of each ruler. If text is selected, the ruler is displayed in *text mode,* and the ruler highlights the measurement of the text placeholder.

■ A slide measures 10 inches wide by 7.5 inches tall. Note the screen illustration to the right in which the rulers are displayed in drawing and text modes.

■ As you move your mouse on the slide, a corresponding indicator displays on the Rulers showing you the horizontal and vertical position of your mouse pointer on the slide.

■ **Guides** may also be displayed by selecting <u>G</u>uides from the <u>V</u>iew menu. Guides assist you in aligning objects or text on a slide. Note the Text Mode illustration, which displays guides.

*Drawing Mode*

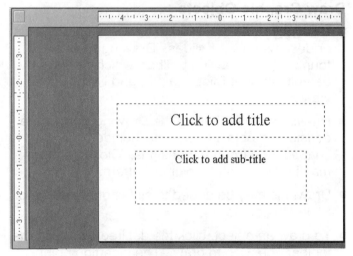

*Text Mode*

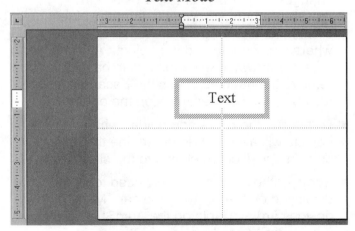

## Floating Toolbars

- If a submenu appears with a move handle, you can click and drag it away from the menu and leave it on screen. To close a floating toolbar, click the close box on the toolbar.

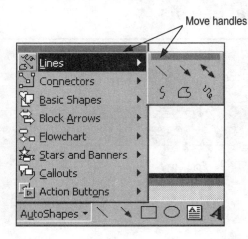

Move handles

## Draw Graphic Objects

- **Drawing tools** are used to create simple objects or designs on your slides. Drawing tools are found on the Drawing toolbar, which displays by default in Slide, Slide Master, and Notes Page views.

- Drawings created using the Drawing toolbar are considered objects. Objects include lines, shapes, and freehand designs. Closed shapes may be filled with a color or pattern.

- Drawings may be added to slides only in Slide or Slide Master views.

- To draw an object, click the desired object on the toolbar you wish to draw. The insertion point changes to a crosshair (+). Position the crosshair where you want to start the object; click, hold, and drag the crosshair to the point where you want to end the object. After the object is drawn, it will appear with handles. To remove the handles, press the Escape key. To redisplay the handles, click on the object.

- Displaying the rulers and guides when drawing objects will allow you to determine the object's size and position in relation to the slide's size.

- Some of the most commonly used tools are displayed on the Drawing toolbar. Many other designs are available on the AutoShapes menu (see AutoShapes).

- Use the **line tool** to draw a straight line. You can change the line style and color by selecting the line, then clicking the Line Style, Dash Style, Arrow Style, or Line Color button on the Drawing toolbar.

- Use the **arrow tool** to draw arrows. You can change the arrow style by selecting the arrow, clicking the Arrow style button on the Drawing toolbar, then selecting a different style. To change the color of the arrow, click More Arrows on the pop-up menu and select a new color.

- Use the **rectangle tool** to draw squares or rectangles. To draw a perfect square, hold down the Shift key while dragging the mouse.

- Use the **oval tool** to draw circles or ovals. To draw a perfect circle, hold down the Shift key while dragging the mouse.

## AutoShapes

- When you select **AutoShapes** on the Drawing toolbar, several menus containing a variety of shapes (lines, connectors, flowchart elements, callouts, etc.) display. Each menu can be dragged away from the pop-up menu so you can quickly access it. Below and on the following page is an illustration and explanation of each category available on the AutoShapes menu.

### Lines

Create curves, freeform, and scribble lines. The straight line and arrow tools are also available on this menu.

### Connectors

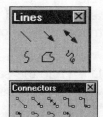

Connect objects using a straight, angled, or curved line. Connector lines stayed attached to the objects when they are rearranged.

### Action Buttons

Use to create a presentation for the Internet. Navigation buttons like Home, Help, Back, Next, etc. help you navigate a presentation.

**Basic Shapes**

**Block Arrows**

**Flowchart**

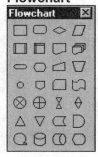

**Stars and Banners**

**Callouts**

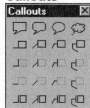

■ To draw an AutoShape, click the desired shape from a palette of shapes, then click and drag the mouse to expand the shape to the desired size. The color of the shape may be changed by selecting the shape with the selection tool, then clicking the Fill Color button on the Drawing toolbar.

## Create Text Objects

■ Text entered on slides thus far has been entered into placeholders. You can also add text using the Text Box Tool to create a separate object that can be moved, sized, deleted, etc., without affecting text in placeholders.

■ Use the Text Box Tool ⬛ on the Drawing toolbar to add text to pictures or other objects, including placeholders.

■ After selecting the Text Box Tool, outline the area of the slide that the text should occupy using the procedures you used to draw a rectangle. The textbox will expand as you enter text.

## Group and Ungroup Objects

■ When a drawing is comprised of several basic shapes, it is difficult to move, copy, or duplicate all the shapes as a whole object. **Grouping** allows you to select all the shapes in the group and treat them as a single object so that copying, duplicating, and moving the object becomes possible.

■ To group an object comprised of individual shapes, select each shape (hold the Shift key down while you click each shape). Select Group from the pop-up Draw menu on the Drawing toolbar. You can ungroup the grouped objects by selecting Ungroup from the Draw menu. You can also use the shortcut menu to execute these commands.

## Layer Objects

■ Shapes may be layered or stacked on top of each other to create interesting effects. You may adjust the layers by moving them back or bringing them forward in the stack. To adjust the layers of shapes or objects, click a shape or object and select Send to Back or Bring to Front from the Draw menu.

*In this exercise, you will create a logo using the AutoShapes and Text Box Tools on the Drawing Toolbar and place them on the Slide Master. You will then view each slide in your presentation to see their effects. See Desired Result on page Error! Bookmark not defined..*

# EXERCISE DIRECTIONS

1. Open 📷**FOOD**, or open 💾**10FOOD**.

2. Switch to Slide Master view.

3. Display Slide rulers and guides.

4. Format the Slide Master as shown in Illustration A. Illustration B shows results of changes made on Slide Master.
   - Shorten the Title placeholder so that it is 5" wide.
   - Insert a 2" Explosion2 AutoShape in the upper left corner of the slide and fill it yellow.
   - Using the text tool, create a text placeholder and insert the initials SF in serif 28 point bold italics. Center the initials in the text placeholder. Color the text blue and position it in the middle of the shape as shown.
   - Insert a .5" Smiling Face from the basic shapes palette and position it in the lower right corner of the Slide; color it blue.

   - Group the explosion shape and the text. Move the grouped objects to the bottom left of the slide, then back to the top left of the slide.
   - Using the text tool, create a text object with the words, "Eat Well and Stay Trim" in sans serif 28 point. Color the text blue and position it at the bottom center of the slide as shown.

5. Change the format of the main bullet to a green heart (Wingdings character set).

6. Switch to Slide view.

7. Display Slide 1 (Smartfood Products).
   - Delete the subtitle placeholder.

8. Print one copy as Handouts with six slides per page in Black & white.

9. Close the file; save the changes.

## ILLUSTRATION A

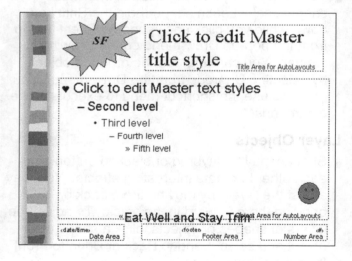

## ILLUSTRATION B

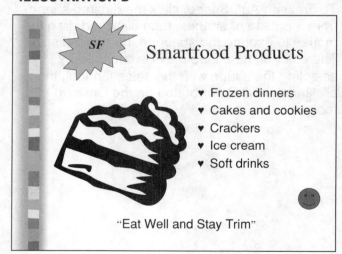

# KEYSTROKES

## DISPLAY RULER AND GUIDES

1. Click **View** ............................ `Alt` + `V`
2. Click **Ruler** ................................... `R`
   **AND/OR**
   Click **Guides** ................................. `G`

## DRAW AUTOSHAPES

1. Click **AutoShapes** ............... `Alt` + `U`
   on Drawing toolbar.
2. Click desired shape from pop-up menu:
   - **Lines** ...................................... `L`
   ✓ *See below for special instructions on drawing the curve, Freeform, and Scribble lines.*
   - **Connectors** .............................. `N`
   - **Basic Shapes** ........................... `B`
   - **Block Arrows** ............................ `A`
   - **Flowchart** ................................. `F`
   - **Stars and Banners** .................... `S`
   - **Callouts** .................................... `C`
   - **Action Buttons** ......................... `O`
3. Position crosshair (+) at point where shape will start.
4. Click and drag to desired end point.
   ✓ *Most drawing shapes require the same procedure. You click, hold, and drag the mouse point to the right and down. Some shapes require additional actions to get the desired result. The distance and drag direction determine the size and shape of the object.*

## DRAW A PERFECT CIRCLE/SQUARE

1. Click `▢` or `◯` on Drawing toolbar.
2. Position crosshair (+) at point where shape will start.
3. Press the **Shift** key while dragging mouse diagonally to ending point.
4. Release mouse button.

## DRAW ARROWS

1. Click arrow on Drawing toolbar.
2. Position crosshair (+) at start point.
3. Click and drag to end point.

## DRAW LINES AND FREEFORM SHAPES

1. Click **AutoShapes** .................. `Alt` + `U`
   on Drawing toolbar.
2. Click **Lines** ..................................... `L`
   from pop-up menu.
3. Select a line, arrow, scribble line, or freeform shape.
4. Move pointer to draw line or shape, clicking to change direction or angle, if necessary.
5. Double-click to stop drawing.

## CREATE TEXT OBJECTS

1. Click `▤` on Drawing toolbar.
2. Position I-beam at text box start point.
3. Click and drag to form confined text box.
   **OR**
   a. Click to type without outlining box.
   b. Type desired text.
   c. Press **Esc** when .......................... `Esc`
      text is complete.

## GROUP OBJECTS

1. Hold down **Shift** while clicking objects to group.
2. Click **Draw** ............................ `Alt` + `R`
3. Click **Group** .................................... `G`

## UNGROUP OBJECTS

1. Select desired grouped object.
2. Click **Draw** ............................ `Alt` + `R`
3. Click **Ungroup** ............................... `U`

## REGROUP OBJECTS

✓ *Regroups most recently ungrouped object. If slide containing ungrouped object becomes inactive, object cannot be regrouped using this procedure. It will have to be grouped.*

1. Click **Draw** ............................ `Alt` + `R`
2. Click **Regroup** ............................... `O`

## LAYER OBJECTS

1. Select desired object.
2. Click **Draw** ............................ `Alt` + `R`
3. Click **Order** ................................... `R`
4. Click **Send Backward** ..................... `B`
   to send object back one layer.
   **OR**
   Click **Bring Forward** ....................... `F`
   to send object forward one layer.
5. Repeat step 4 until object is properly placed.

**OR**

1. Select desired object.
2. Right-click selected object.
3. Click **Order** ................................... `R`
4. Select desired option:

| OPTION | MOVEMENT |
|---|---|
| **Bring to Front** | Places object on top of all other objects. |
| **Send to Back** | Places object beneath all other objects. |
| **Bring Forward** | Moves object one layer up on the stack. |
| **Send Backward** | Moves object one layer down on the stack. |

## CYCLE THROUGH OBJECTS

1. Press **Ctrl+A** to select ............. `Ctrl` + `A`
   all objects.
2. Press **Tab** until desired object ......... `A`
   is selected.

## Exercise 11

■ **Create a Chart, Table, or an Excel Worksheet on a Slide**

*Standard Toolbar*

Insert Chart

# NOTES

### Create a Chart

■ A chart may be added to a PowerPoint slide by importing one that was already created in Excel, or by using the Chart slide in PowerPoint to create one. *(See Integration Chapter to import an Excel chart and worksheet data.)*

■ To create a Chart on a slide, double-click a graph placeholder on an AutoLayout slide, or select Chart from the Insert menu or click the Insert Chart button on the Standard toolbar.

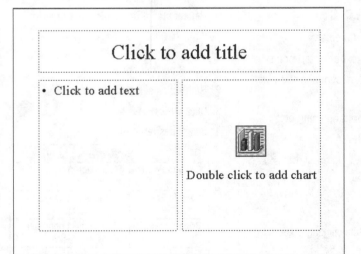

■ A datasheet window displays along with a Chart toolbar which replaces the Standard toolbar. Several charting features will appear on the Formatting toolbar. Enter the data you wish to chart (and delete the sample data) as you did in Excel. The chart will reflect the new data. Click on the slide (not the chart) to hide the datasheet. To see the datasheet again, double-click the chart.

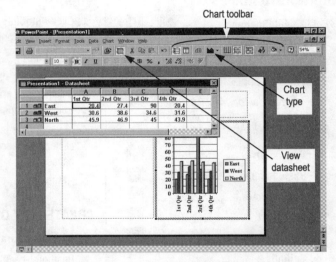

Chart toolbar

Chart type

View datasheet

■ The default chart type is 3-D Column. However, you may change the chart type before or after you enter data in the datasheet by clicking the chart on the slide and selecting Chart Type from the Chart menu or clicking the list arrow next to the Chart Type button ■ - on the Chart toolbar. Select one of the chart types from the choices displayed.

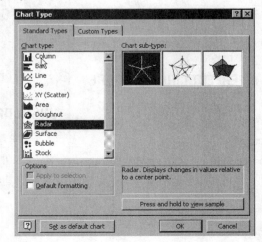

416

- You may enhance your chart with a title and data labels. Data labels allow you to indicate the exact value of each data point. Follow keystrokes to insert a chart title and data labels.

## Create a Table

- A Table may be added to a PowerPoint slide by importing one that was already created in Word, or by using a Table slide in PowerPoint to create one.

- Importing an existing Word table into a PowerPoint Slide will be covered in Chapter 6, Integration.

- To create a Table on a slide, double-click a table placeholder on an AutoLayout slide or select Microsoft Word Table from the Picture submenu on the Insert menu. PowerPoint offers one AutoLayout slide containing a table format.

- After clicking the table placeholder, the Insert Word Table dialog box displays for you to indicate how many columns and rows you need for your table.

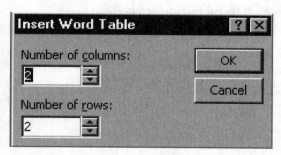

- You may also create a table by clicking the Insert Microsoft Word Table button ▦ on the Standard toolbar and dragging the mouse across the grid to indicate the number of rows and columns you desire. When you release your mouse, a table displays on your slide and PowerPoint's toolbars and menu bar are temporarily replaced by Word's toolbars and menu. This enables you to use Word's table editing features inside PowerPoint.

- Click in a cell and enter the desired text. Press the Tab key to move the insertion point from cell to cell.

- After you have entered all table text, click on the slide containing the table to return to PowerPoint or press Escape. You can return to the table

and make changes at any time by double-clicking inside the table.

- If you use a table slide to insert your table, the columns and rows will be evenly spaced within the table placeholder. You can adjust the column widths and row heights as you do in Word. If you create your table on a slide not containing a table placeholder and use the grid to create the columns and rows, you might need to reposition the table to a desired location on the slide. As you did with other objects, click within the table and drag it to the desired position; drag a handle to resize the table.

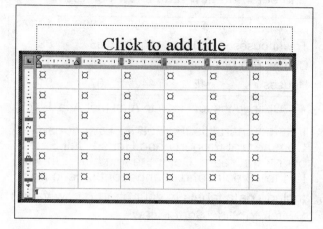

## Create an Excel Worksheet

- To create an Excel worksheet on a slide, click the Insert Microsoft Excel Worksheet button on the toolbar. A drop-down grid appears as it did with tables. Click and drag across and down the grid to indicate how many columns and rows you desire in your worksheet. When you release your mouse, a worksheet appears, ready for you to enter data. PowerPoint's Standard toolbar and menu are temporarily replaced by Excel's toolbar and menu. *(See Integration Chapter to import an Excel chart and worksheet data.)*

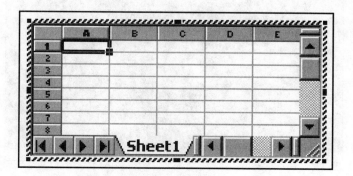

*In this exercise, you will insert a graph slide and a table slide into a previously created presentation.*

# EXERCISE DIRECTIONS

1. Open 🖳**FLAGSHIP**, or open 🖫**11FLAGSHIP**.

2. Insert a New Slide and select the Chart AutoLayout.

3. Display slide rulers and guides.

4. Enter the slide title shown in Illustration A and decrease the font size as needed. Double-click chart icon, delete the data from the datasheet and enter the new data shown below:

|             | 1994 | 1995 | 1996 | 1997 |
|-------------|------|------|------|------|
| Townhouses  | 20   | 40   | 85   | 88   |
| Comm. Prop. | 8    | 12   | 24   | 31   |
| Houses      | 45   | 44   | 87   | 91   |

   - Change the font face to Arial (not Arial Black).

5. Insert a chart title that reads, Townhouse, Commercial Property and House Unit Sales over Four Years. Color the text blue. Size the text to 18 point and change font face to Arial.

6. Include data labels in your chart (show value).

7. Switch to Slide Sorter view.

8. Move this new slide to become Slide 4.

9. Switch to Slide view.

10. Switch to Slide 3 (OUR SALES FORCE).

11. Create a callout AutoShape above the graphic and fill it pink. Using the text tool, insert the

words, "We care!" in serif 24 pt bold into the balloon shape as shown in Illustration B. Color the text and the line around the shape dark blue.

12. Insert a New Slide after slide 4, and select the Table Slide AutoLayout.

13. Enter the table data shown in Illustration C, on page 419.

   - Create 5 columns and 4 rows.
   - Set column heading text to Arial 24-point for columns 1-4; set column 5 heading to 18-point.
   - Set column text to sans serif 18-point.
   - Do not use Arial; use Arial Black if available.
   - Center column headings as well as column 2 and 3 text.
   - Adjust column widths and row heights so text appears as in the illustration.
   - Enter the slide title shown in the illustration.

14. Switch to Slide Sorter view.

15. View the Presentation in Black and white.

16. Print one copy as Handouts with 6 slides per page in Black and white.

17. Close the file; save the changes.

**ILLUSTRATION A**

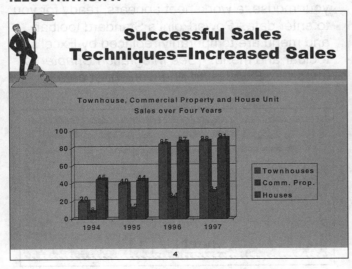

**ILLUSTRATION B**

ILLUSTRATION C

### SAMPLE INVENTORY

| TYPE | RMS | BATHS | PRICE | UNIQUE FEATURES |
|------|-----|-------|-------|-----------------|
| Country Estate | 7 | 4 | $1,300,000 | Swimming pool, spa & exercise rm |
| Townhouse | 8 | 3 | $500,000 | Formal dining room |
| Colonial Estate | 10 | 5 | $1,585,000 | Waterfront property w/400 ft. bulkhead |

5

# KEYSTROKES

## CREATE A CHART ON A SLIDE

1. Select a slide containing a Chart placeholder from Slide Layout.
2. Double-click the chart placeholder.
3. Enter the data you wish to chart in the datasheet.

   **To delete data in a Datasheet:**

   a. Press **Ctrl+A** ...................... `Ctrl` + `A`
      to select the data.

   b. Press **Delete** ............................. `Del`

4. Click the graph to hide the datasheet.

   **OR**

   Click **View Datasheet** button. .......

### Insert a Title:

1. Double-click the graph.
2. Click **Chart** ............................. `Alt` + `C`
3. Click **Chart Options** ........................ `O`
4. Click **Titles** tab.
5. Click **Chart title** ..................... `Alt` + `T`
6. Type title ......................................... *title*
7. Click **OK** .................................. `Enter`

## Color Chart Title:

1. Right-click Chart Title.
2. Click **Format Chart Title** ......... `Alt` + `O`
3. Click **Font** tab................................ `F`
4. Click **Color** ............................. `Alt` + `C`
5. Select desired color.
6. Click **OK** .................................. `Enter`

### Insert Data Labels:

1. Right-click chart.
2. Click **Chart Options** ............... `Alt` + `O`
3. Click **Data Labels** tab ..................... `D`
4. Select desired label type.
5. Click **OK** .................................. `Enter`

## CHANGE FONT

1. Right-click chart item to be changed.
2. Click **Format Legend** ..................... `O`
   or **Format Axis**
3. Click **Font** tab........................ `Ctrl` + `Tab`
4. Select desired font.
5. Click **OK** .................................. `Enter`

## CREATE A TABLE ON A SLIDE

1. Click Insert Microsoft Word Table button on the Standard toolbar.
2. Drag to highlight desired number of columns and rows.

   **OR**

1. Click **Insert** ........................... `Alt` + `I`
2. Click **Picture**................................ `P`
3. Click **Microsoft Word Table** ........... `T`

   **OR**

1. Select a slide from Slide Layout containing a Table placeholder.
2. Enter the title in the title placeholder.
3. Double-click the table placeholder.
4. Enter desired **Number of columns**.
5. Enter desired **Number of rows**.
6. Click **OK** .................................. `Enter`
7. Click the first cell and enter desired text.
8. Press **Tab** .................................. `Tab`
   to advance to the next cell.

   **OR**

   Press **Shift + Tab**............... `Shift` + `Tab`
   to move to the previous cell.

9. Click on slide to insert table and return to PowerPoint.

# Exercise 12

## ■ Insert Organization Chart Slide

## NOTES

■ An **Organization Chart** is used to illustrate a company's hierarchy or structure.

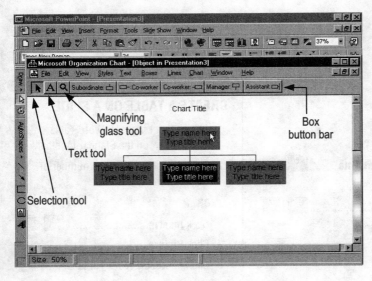

■ Organization charts may also be used to show the flow of a project or a family tree.

■ PowerPoint contains an Organization Chart AutoLayout. To create an organization chart, select the organization chart AutoLayout and double-click on the organization chart placeholder.

■ By default, four boxes display. However, you can attach additional boxes to existing boxes and rearrange boxes. In addition, you can format each box with different fonts, font sizes, fill colors and borders, as well as align text left, center, or right within the box.

■ There are four types of boxes: Manager, Subordinate, Co-Worker and Assistant; each box type attaches to the existing boxes differently. Note the box shapes available on the Box button bar.

■ You can enter up to four lines of text in each box. As you type, the box will adjust its size to fit the text.

■ After you have added the desired boxes and entered the desired text, select Close and Return to Presentation from the File menu.

*In this exercise, you will insert an organization chart and a graph slide to a previously created presentation.*

# EXERCISE DIRECTIONS

1. Open 🖮**KIT**, or open 🖫**12KIT**.

2. Switch to Slide view.

3. Insert a New Slide and select the Organization Chart AutoLayout.

4. Enter the organization information shown in Illustration A using a sans serif black font. Color the title yellow.

   ✓ Add an Assistant box to include box 5 information.

5. Insert a New Slide and select the Chart AutoLayout.

6. Enter the slide title shown in Illustration B. Delete the data from the datasheet and enter the new data shown below:

| Sales Before and After Using Creative Kits | | | |
|---|---|---|---|
| | Great Foods | Harly Hotel | Venus Graphics |
| Before | 100 | 485 | 195 |
| After | 200 | 555 | 305 |

   ✓ Since you will not need all the columns and rows in the datasheet, highlight the row and/or column you do not need and select Exclude Rows/Columns from the Data menu.

7. Switch to Slide Sorter view.

8. Move the chart slide to become slide 9 and the organization slide to become slide 10 (the last slide).

9. Switch to Slide Master view.

10. Shorten the title placeholder.

11. Using AutoShapes, create a curved ribbon banner and insert the initials CS in a red 48-point bold font in the center of the seal, as shown in Illustration C on the next page.

12. Insert a black slide number at the bottom right of the slide.

13. Switch to Title Master view.

14. Shorten the title placeholder and position it to the top right of the slide.

15. Using AutoShapes, create a curved ribbon banner and color it yellow. Insert the initials CS in a red 48-point bold font in the center of the seal.

16. Switch to Slide view and display Slide 1.

17. Display Slide 7 (CREATIVE SALES KITS provide...).

18. Change the Slide Layout to Text & Clip Art and insert a graphic using any desired art design AutoShapes.

19. Print one copy as Handouts with 6 slides per page in Black and white.

20. Close the file; save the changes.

# KEYSTROKES

**CREATE AN ORGANIZATION CHART ON AN AUTOLAYOUT SLIDE**

1. Select a slide from AutoLayout containing an Organization Chart Layout.

2. Enter the title in the title placeholder.

3. Double-click the Organization Chart placeholder.

4. Select box to enter text.

5. Type name and press **Enter**.

6. Type title and press **Enter**.

7. Type comment (if desired) and press **Enter**.

8. Click another box and repeat steps 5-7

   **OR**

   Click outside the box to close box.

9. Click **File** ............................... Alt + F

10. Click **Close and Return** ................. C
    **to Presentation**.

11. Click **Yes** to save your chart ....... Enter

**Insert a Box:**

12. Click the appropriate box tool you wish to attach.

13. Click existing box to which you wish to attach new one.

**Rearrange Boxes:**

14. Select the box to be moved.

15. Position mouse pointer on border of box to be moved.

16. Drag box to new location.

17. Release mouse button.

**ILLUSTRATION A**

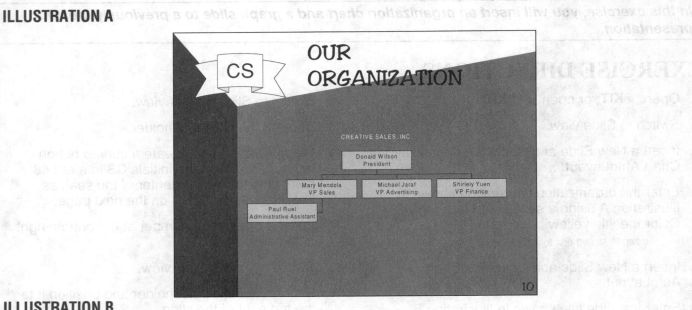

**ILLUSTRATION B**

**ILLUSTRATION C**

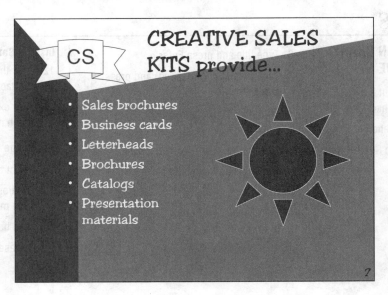

**Exercise 13**

■ **Summary**

*In this exercise, you will create a presentation for GreatGains Mutual Fund, a company that wants more investors to purchase their securities. This presentation will include a table, chart, and graph slides. You will use Slide and Title Masters to include information on all slides.*

# EXERCISE DIRECTIONS

1. Create a new Template Presentation; use the Fans template design.

2. Switch to Title Master view.

3. Display slide rulers and guides.

4. Create the logos shown on the top and bottom right corner (at the 4" mark) of the presentation in Slide 1 of Illustration A.

   *Hint: To create the double G logo on the top right, create two separate text boxes and enter the letter G in each. Size one of the letters to 54 point and the other to 28 point. Overlap the boxes, and draw a circle (using AutoShapes) around the boxes. Send the circle to back, and group the items. Then, adjust the size of the grouped items. You will need to use a similar procedure to create the text and AutoShapes balloon on the bottom right of the slide. Use a serif 14 point white font for the text and an aqua-blue fill for the balloon.*

   - Insert slide numbers where shown in 18 point using a pink font color.
   - Change the default first two bullet styles to another desired style.
   - Adjust the title placeholder so it does not interfere with the logo.

5. Copy the first logo.

6. Switch to Slide Master view.

7. Paste the logo in the same position as on Slide 1.

8. Copy the second logo.

9. Paste the logo in the same position as on Slide 1.

10. Switch to Slide view.

11. Create the presentation shown in Illustration B on pages 428 and 429, using the appropriate slide layouts.
    - Enter the data below to create the graph:

| Sales (in $ millions) | | | |
|---|---|---|---|
| | **1995** | **1996** | **1997** |
| GreatGains | 200 | 325 | 420 |
| FastMoney | 156 | 173 | 165 |

12. Use the names and titles below for the organization chart:
    - Rachael Black:  Head Fund Manager
    - John Chou:  Vice President
    - Pamela Haupt:  Vice President
    - Jaime Cohen:  Vice President
    - Harry Smith:  Associate
    - David Stuart:  Associate
    - Chandra Rao:  Associate

13. Display each slide.  Adjust the placeholders and/or the font size of the titles so they do not interfere with the logos.

14. Display slide 6.

15. Color the star bullet text (subtext) yellow.

16. Correct all spelling errors.

17. Save the file; name it **INVEST**.  Accept the default summary information.

18. Print one copy of each slide in Black and White. Compare each slide with those in Illustration B.

19. Print one copy in Outline view.

20. Close the presentation window.

**ILLUSTRATION A**
**TITLE MASTER**

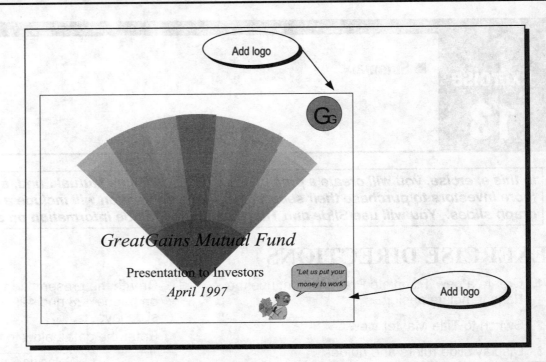

**ILLUSTRATION B**

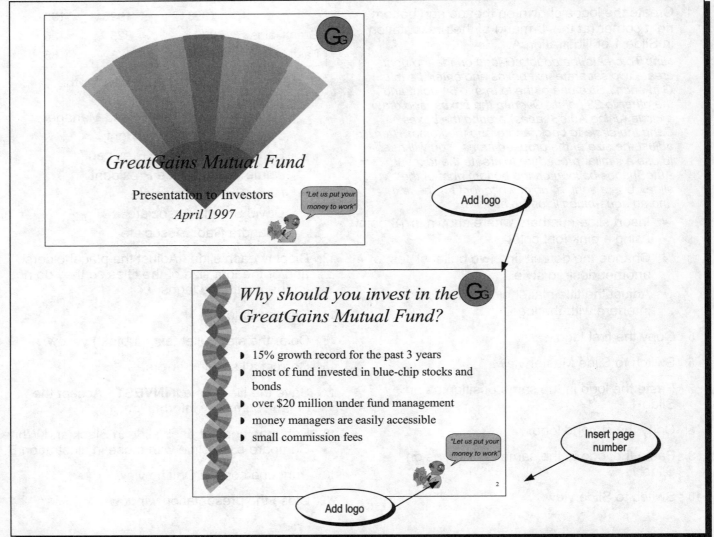

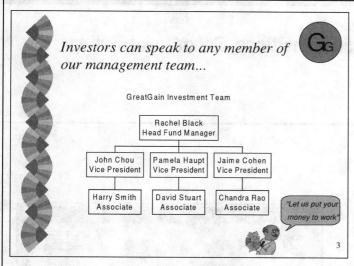

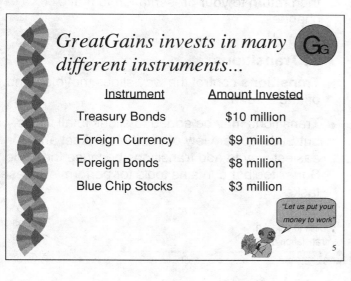

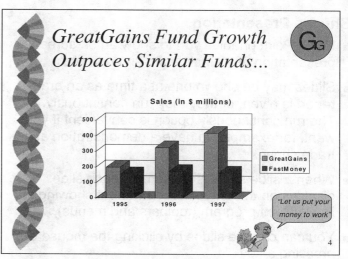

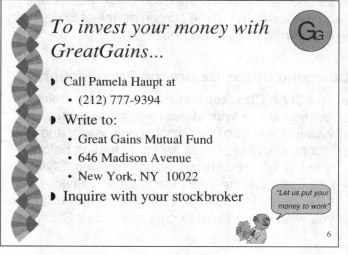

## Exercise 14

■ **Show a Presentation** ■ **Add Transitions, Sound, and Timing**

# NOTES

### Show a Presentation

■ PowerPoint enables you to show an on-screen presentation of your slides to an audience.

■ Slides may be shown one at a time as an oral report is given, or they may run continuously. The run continuously option is convenient if you want, for example, to have a demonstration at a trade show.

■ When a slide show is presented, each slide displays on the entire screen without showing the PowerPoint program (toolbars and menus).

■ You can change slides by clicking the mouse or pressing a key.

> ✓ *Note: If you plan to show your slide presentation to a large audience, you will need to project the computer image onto a large screen. This will require a projection device. See your local computer dealer for projection device information.*

■ To activate a slide show, display the first slide to be shown, then click the Slide Show button 🖳 on the lower left of the screen or select Slide Sho<u>w</u> from the <u>V</u>iew menu.

### Checking Slides Before the Presentation

■ The **Style Checker** feature within PowerPoint lets you check your slides for spelling errors, visual clarity (too many font styles used), and inconsistencies in case and punctuation before running the slide show. To do so, select St<u>y</u>le Checker from the <u>T</u>ools menu. In the Style Checker dialog box which follows, select what you wish PowerPoint to check and click Start.

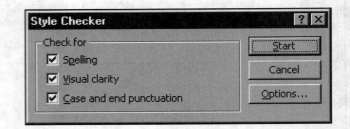

■ After checking the presentation, PowerPoint displays a summary of its findings. You may then return to your presentation to make changes.

### Add Transitions

■ **Transitions** control the way slides move on and off the screen.

■ Transitions may be added to slides in all views, but Slide Sorter view offers the quickest and easiest way to add transitions because the Slide Sorter toolbar contains tools for performing these tasks.

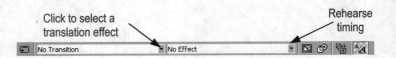

■ Click the list arrow next to the No Transition text box. A drop-down menu of transition choices appears. Select a transition effect.

- In Slide Sorter view, slides containing transitions are marked by a slide icon appearing below and to the left of the miniature slide image.

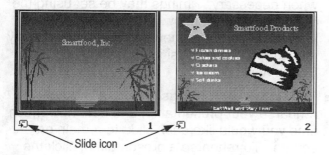

Slide icon

- To add transitions to slides in views other than Slide Sorter, select Slide Transition from the Slide Show menu. In the Slide Transition dialog box that follows, you can select a transition effect, the speed of the transition, and whether you want to change the slides manually (by a mouse click) or automatically (after a specified number of seconds).

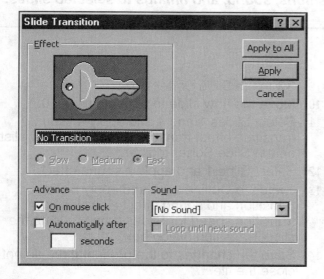

- Transitions include a number of special effects. Select a transition type and note its effect on the dog slide on the left of the dialog box. A description of transition types and their effect appears below.

| | |
|---|---|
| **Blinds** | Creates an effect of opening and closing venetian blinds and can be set for horizontal or vertical. |
| **Box** | Forms a box and opens from the center outward or the edges inward. |

| | |
|---|---|
| **Checkerboard** | Creates a checkerboard effect by placing small black squares randomly on the screen to reveal the new slide. |
| **Cover** | Replaces the slide with the next slide from the specified direction. |
| **Cut** | Replaces the slide with the next slide without directional motion. |
| **Dissolve** | Sprinkles the slide on and off the screen. |
| **Fade** | Gradually darkens the slide to black before revealing the next slide. |
| **Random Bars** | Reveals the new slide gradually by placing horizontal or vertical bars on the screen. |
| **Split** | Reveals and removes a slide from the center outward or inward, horizontally or vertically. |
| **Strips** | Reveals and removes a slide from one corner of the screen to the other using a variety of directions. |
| **Uncover** | Reveals a new slide as the active slide is removed. |
| **Wipe** | Removes one slide from the screen in the specified direction, revealing the new slide. |
| **Random** | Assigns a random transition effect as you move from slide to slide. Assigning Random to numerous slides generates a random assortment of transitions. |

## Add Sound

- In addition to adding a visual transition for moving slides on and off screen, you may add a sound effect when moving from slide to slide. If you want the sound to affect one slide, select the slide to receive the sound effect, then select the effect from the Sound drop-down list in the Slide Transition Dialog Box. If you wish the sound to remain until the next sound effect is encountered on a slide, click the Loop until next sound check box.

## Add Timings

- **Timings** control the speed with which slides replace other slides. Setting a time tells PowerPoint how long the slide will remain on the screen.

- Timings may be included as part of the transition. Timings are set in seconds with .05 representing 5 seconds.

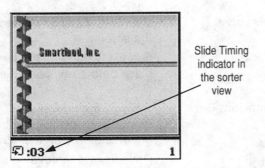

Slide Timing indicator in the sorter view

- Timings may be set individually for each slide or collectively for all slides. Slides containing timings may, however, be advanced manually when necessary. Timings may be set using the Slide Transition window in Slide view, Outline view, or Slide Sorter view. Slide timings display to the right of the transition slide icon in Slide Sorter view.

- The **Rehearse Timings** feature allows you to rehearse your presentation and note how much time you would like each slide to remain on screen. To rehearse a presentation, click the Rehearse Timings button 🖻 on the Transition toolbar. Each slide will appear on screen with a second counter clicking off time. Note how much time you wish each slide to remain on screen. Then, return to individual slides to reset their timing.

---

*In this exercise, you will edit a previously created presentation by adding items to the Slide and Title Masters, inserting new slides, and adding transitions, sound, and timings to selected slides. You will also view your slide presentation.*

---

# EXERCISE DIRECTIONS

1. Open 💾**BRAZIL**, or open 💾**14BRAZIL**.
2. Switch to Slide View.
3. Display Slide rulers and guides.
4. Switch to Slide Master view.
   - Delete Date Area and Footer Area Placeholders.
   - Insert the company name in the left corner of the slide (3" vertically) in a serif 20 point blue font. Using AutoShapes, create a red 4 point star following the company name as shown in Illustration A.
   - Insert a page number in the default position of the slide in the default font and size.
5. Switch to Title Master view
   - Insert the company name and star as described above.
6. Switch to Slide view.
7. Insert a New Slide and select the Organization Chart AutoLayout.
8. Enter the chart information as shown in Illustration B. (Do not include a chart title.) Format the title using the same font and style as other slides.
   - Set the text in each box to bold and set each box to a different color. Use bright colors for each industry name.

9. Switch to Slide Sorter view.
10. Move the new slide to become slide 10.
11. Select Slides 1 and 4 and apply a slide transition effect from the Effect drop-down list on the Slide Sorter toolbar.
12. Select Slide 1 and apply a sound effect.
13. Switch to Outline view and apply a slide transition and sound effect as well as a transition speed for Slides 2 and 3 using the slide Transition dialog box.
14. Save the changes to the presentation; do not close the file.
15. Using Style Checker, check your presentation. Make suggested changes, if appropriate. Do not remove the periods from U.S.
16. View the slide show.
17. Add slide timings to each slide as you desire.
18. Change the advance method to advance slides automatically.
19. View the slide show again.
20. Print one copy as Handouts with 6 slides per page in Black and White.
21. Close the file; save the changes.

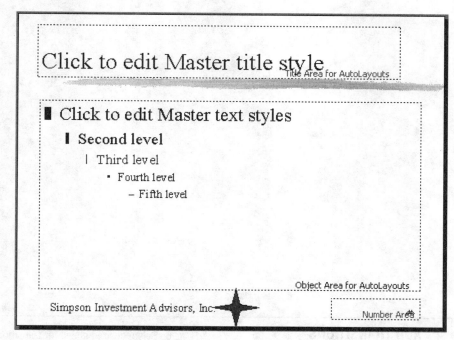

**ILLUSTRATION A**

**ILLUSTRATION B**

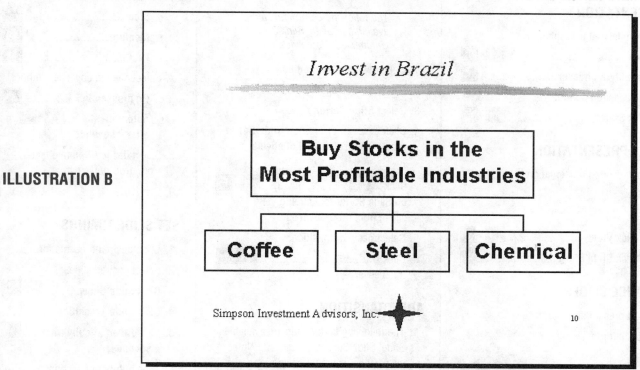

# KEYSTROKES

## CHECKING SLIDES BEFORE THE PRESENTATION

1. Open desired presentation.
2. Click **Tools** ............................ `Alt`+`T`
3. Click **Style Checker** ........................ `Y`
4. Click desired option.
5. Click **Start** ............................ `Alt`+`S`

## SHOW PRESENTATION

1. Open desired presentation.
2. Click `[icon]`.
   **OR**
   a. Click **View** ......................... `Alt`+`V`
   b. Click **Slide Show** ...................... `W`

## ADVANCE SLIDES

1. Start presentation.
2. Click left mouse button.
   **OR**
   Press **Enter** ............................ `Enter`

## ADD TRANSITIONS

✓ *The following commands are available in Slide, Slide Sorter, Outline, and Notes view.*

1. Open desired presentation.
2. Select desired slide.
3. Select **Slide Sorter** view.
4. Click `No Transition ▾` on **Slide Sorter** toolbar to display a list of effects.
   **OR**
   Click `[icon]` .............................. `Alt`+`E`
   on Slide Sorter toolbar and click **Effect** drop-down list.
5. Select desired transition.
6. Click **OK** .............................. `Enter`
   if necessary.

## ADD TRANSITION

1. The following commands are available in Slide, Slide Sorter, Outline, and Notes view. Open desired presentation.
2. Display desired slide.
3. Click **Slide Show** ................. `Alt`+`D`
4. Click **Slide Transition** .................... `T`

✓ *No transition options are available until a transition effect is selected.*

5. Select desired transition from **Effect** drop-down list.

6. Select desired speed for transition:
   • **Slow** ............................... `Alt`+`S`
   • **Medium** ......................... `Alt`+`M`
   • **Fast** ................................ `Alt`+`F`
7. Select desired advance method:
   • **On mouse click** ............... `Alt`+`O`
   • **Automatically** .... `Alt`+`C`, *number* after # seconds
8. Select desired **Sound** effect.... `Alt`+`U` from drop-down list.
9. Click **OK** ................................... `Enter`

## SET SLIDE TIMINGS

1. Open desired presentation.
2. Select desired slide.
3. Click **Slide Show** ................. `Alt`+`D`
4. Click **Slide Transition** .................... `T`
5. Click **Automatically after** ..... `Alt`+`C` **# seconds**.
6. Type number of seconds .......... *number*
7. Click **OK** ................................... `Enter`

## Exercise 15

- **Animate Text and Objects** ■ **Animation Effects Toolbar**
- **Preset Animation for Bulleted Lists** ■ **Custom Animation**
- **PowerPoint Central**

# NOTES

### Animate Text and Objects

- In addition to creating a variety of transitions from slide to slide, you can use PowerPoint's **animation** functions to control the way text and objects appear in a slide show. For example, on a slide with bulleted text, you can display the entire list all at once or one bulleted item at a time. During the slide show, the items in the list will appear when you click the mouse or at the time you designate. Displaying the contents of a bulleted list one at a time is frequently referred to as a *build*.

- You can also apply animation to objects, such as charts and clip art using the **Custom Animation** dialog box. Using this dialog box, you can assign an effect, arrange the order of the animation, determine the timing (when the effect will activate), and preview your settings.

  ✓Note: *PowerPoint has an additional number of animation/recording tools that let you create highly interactive multimedia presentations.*

### *Animation Effects Toolbar*

- The Animation Effects toolbar lets you apply effects to individual parts of slides. You can use this toolbar in Slide, Slide Sorter, and Notes Page views; however, many of the functions are available only in Slide view.

- Click the <u>V</u>iew menu and select <u>T</u>oolbars. Click Animation Effects to turn on the toolbar. You can also click on the Animation Effects button on the Formatting toolbar. The Animation Effects button is not available if you are in Slide Sorter view.

### Animation for Bulleted Lists

- To apply animation builds to bulleted lists, display the Animation Effects toolbar and switch to Slide view. Select the slide to which you want to apply animation and click in the bulleted list on the slide. Click the desired animation effect to build the bulleted list. Sound effects accompany many of the preset animation effects.

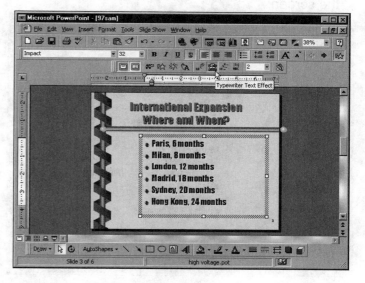

- You can also apply animation build effects to slides by selecting <u>P</u>reset Animation from the Sli<u>d</u>e Show menu. Select the desired build, or turn the current build <u>O</u>ff from this submenu.

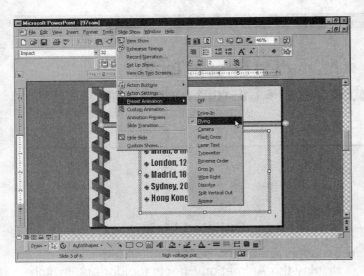

Selected slide element

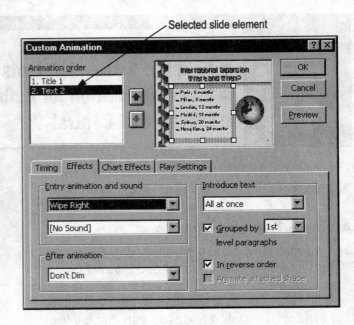

■ To preview how the build will appear in the Slide Show, click Slide Show menu and select Animation Preview. A miniature slide will display how the slide will appear during a slide show. Click the close box to remove the miniature from the screen.

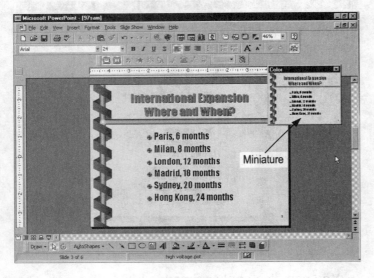

■ Below and on the following page are explanations of animation options. Options that are available depend on the object or text item that you are animating.

- **Animation order** Displays a list of objects that have been animated and the order in which they will appear. To change the order, select the item you want to move and click the arrows to the right of the Animation order box.

- **Timing tab** Displays objects that are not animated on the selected slide. Select an object, text, chart, or title to animate from the list. Click Animate to apply effects. The default timing is to have the effect start when you click the mouse. If you click Automatically, you can specify the number of seconds that you want the effect to wait after the previous event.

## Custom Animation

■ In the Custom Animation dialog box, you can control a variety of animation effects and apply them to different elements on a slide, including charts and clip art.

■ Switch to Slide view and select the slide to which you want to apply animation. Click the object you want to animate; then click Slide Show on the menu, and select Custom Animation. In the Custom Animation dialog box that follows, choose an animation option.

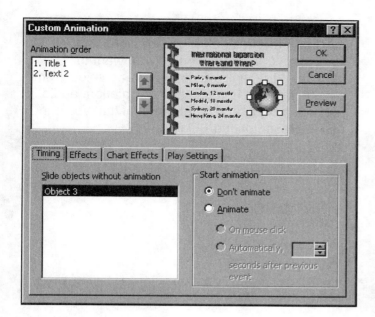

- **Chart Effects tab** Animate sections of a chart. The chart will appear all at once or by category. For example, a pie chart could appear piece by piece. You can also determine how the sections will appear and add sound effects.

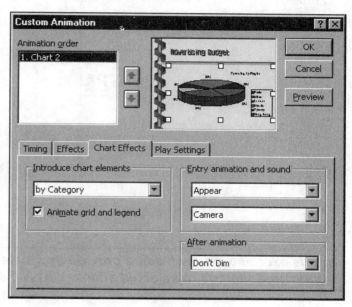

- **Effects tab** Lets you determine the way an element will display, apply a sound effect, adjust how the element appears after the animation, how much is displayed, or even reverse the order of, for example, a bulleted list. Some of these options are not available if you are working with an object.

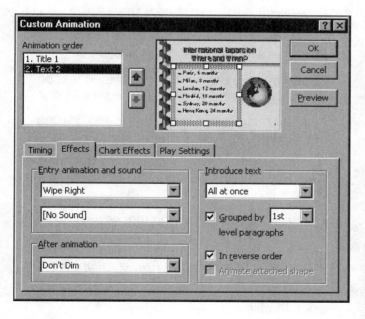

- **Play Settings tab** Adjust how audio and video clips will play during a slide show.

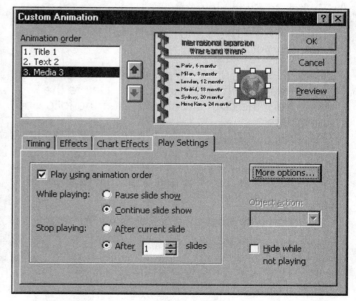

## PowerPoint Central

- If you have access to the World Wide Web, you can go online and access hyperlinks that will offer templates, the latest tips, and information about PowerPoint. To access PowerPoint Central, click Tools, PowerPoint Central.

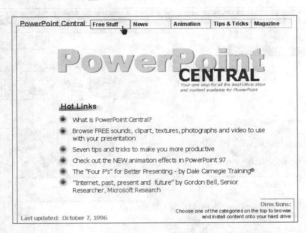

- If you installed Office 97 from a CD-ROM, you can open the Valupak to view options that are available. Click on the option you want to explore. You can also go online and select from several hyperlinks to access information, audio and video clips, and other material that you can use in presentations.

---

*In this exercise, you will edit a previously created presentation by adding a chart slide, builds, sound, and timings to selected slides. You will then view your slide show.*

---

# EXERCISE DIRECTIONS

1. Open 📀**FOOD**, or open 💾**15FOOD**.

2. Switch to Slide view.

3. Insert a New Slide and select the Chart AutoLayout.

4. Select Pie Chart as the chart type. Enter the slide title shown in Illustration A. Delete the data from the data sheet and enter the following new data:

| Paris | Milan | London | Madrid | Sydney | Hong Kong |
|-------|-------|--------|--------|--------|-----------|
| 400   | 600   | 800    | 300    | 300    | 900       |

- Create the chart title and position it as shown in the illustration.

- Insert data labels and select Show Percent.

5. Switch to Slide Sorter view.

6. Move the new slide to become Slide 4.

7. Create a transition effect for each slide.

8. Add a 5-second slide timing for Slide 4.

9. Create an animation build for bulleted text on Slides 2, 3, 5, and 6 using any desired option.

10. Animate the graphics on slides 2 and 5 using any desired effects.

11. Display the chart slide. Animate the pie chart by Category and add sound using any desired effects.

    *Optional: If you are online, access PowerPoint Central from the Tools menu, select a template from the www and apply it to all slides in the Presentation.*

12. Save the changes to the presentation; do not close the file.

13. View the slide show.

14. Print one copy of Slide 4 (the pie chart) in Black and White.

15. Close the presentation window.

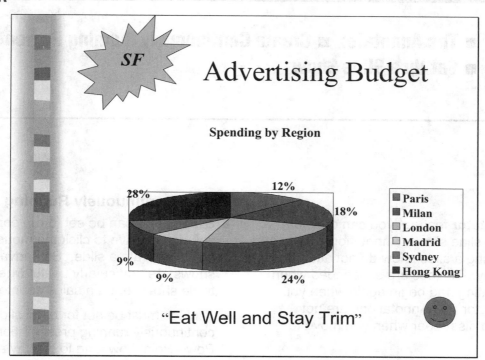

# KEYSTROKES

**APPLY PRESET ANIMATION TO LISTS, OBJECTS, OR CHARTS**

✓ *Many of the following steps can be performed in other views, but all the features are available in Slide view.*

*–FROM ANIMATION EFFECTS TOOLBAR–*

1. Select slide containing list, object, or chart that you want to animate.

2. Click anywhere inside list, object, or chart that you want to animate.

3. Click desired animation effect on the toolbar.

**To preview animation:**

  a. Click **Slide Show** .............. `Alt` + `D`

  b. Click **Animation Preview** ............ `E`

✓ *A miniature of the slide with the selected build appears on screen.*

*–FROM SLIDE VIEW–*

1. Select slide containing list, object, or chart that you want to animate.

  a. Click **Slide Show** .............. `Alt` + `D`

  b. Click **Preset Animation** ............... `P`

2. Select desired effect.
**OR**
Click **Off** ........................................ `O`
to turn off all effects.

**To preview animation:**

  a. Click **Slide Show** .............. `Alt` + `D`

  b. Click **Animation Preview** ............ `E`

*A miniature of the slide with the selected build appears onscreen.*

**APPLY CUSTOM ANIMATION TO LISTS**

*Many of the following steps can be performed in other views, but all the features are available in Slide view.*

1. Select slide containing list, object, or chart that you want to animate.

2. Click anywhere inside list, object, or chart that you want to animate.

3. Click Custom Animation ................... 
on Animation Effects toolbar.
**OR**

  a. Click **Slide Show** .............. `Alt` + `D`

  b. Click **Custom Animation** ............ `M`

4. Select options for list, object, or chart that you want to animate:

• **Animation order**
Select order for various elements to appear on slide.

• **Timing**
Select how, when and/or if elements will be animated on slide.

• **Effects**
Select animation and sound effects.

• **Chart Effects**
Select how chart elements will be introduced on slide that contains a chart.

• **Play Settings**
Determine settings for audio and video clips on slide.

✓ *Options that are dimmed are not applicable to the currently selected item that you want to animate.*

**To preview animation:**

  a. Click **Slide Show** .............. `Alt` + `D`

  b. Click **Animation Preview** ............ `E`

✓ *A miniature of the slide with the selected build appears onscreen.*

# Exercise 16

■ **The Annotator** ■ **Create Continuously Running Presentations**
■ **Set Up a Slide Show**

## NOTES

### The Annotator

■ With the **Annotator** feature, you can draw on slides during a slide show. Annotations made on the screen during a slide show do not alter the slide in any way. Timings are suspended when you are annotating and begin again when you turn the Annotator off. Annotations are not permanent and disappear when you move to another slide.

■ Annotator may be accessed by clicking on the Annotation icon ▨◸ , which appears in the lower-left corner of the screen during a slide show. Select Pen from the pop-up menu. Your mouse then becomes a pencil point so you can write on the slide. To turn Annotator off, click the icon and select Arrow from the pop-up menu.

■ To erase all annotations on the current slide, press the letter E on the keyboard.

> ✓ Note:  If the icon doesn't appear, move the mouse to display it. You can also right-click and select Pen from the shortcut menu.

### Create Continuously Running Presentations

■ Slide shows can be set to run continuously so you do not have to click the mouse or press a key to activate a slide. Self-advancing slide shows are particularly useful when displayed at trade shows or on a sales counter.

■ Timings must be set for each slide in a continuously running presentation to tell PowerPoint how long to display each slide. It is important to allow enough time for people to review the information presented on each slide when you set timings for a continuously running presentation.

■ To create a continuously running presentation, switch to Slide Sorter view; press Ctrl + A to select all slides. Select Set Up show ,Loop Continuously Until 'Esc' from the Slide Show menu.

■ A continuously-running slide show can be stopped by pressing Esc.

■ Select Slide Transition from the Slide Show menu. In the Slide Transition dialog box, select Automatically and indicate the number of seconds you wish each slide to stay on screen

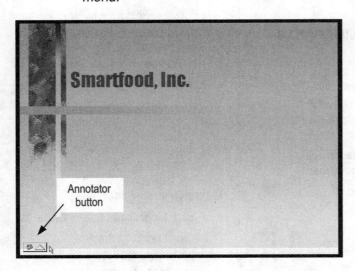

Smartfood, Inc.

Annotator button

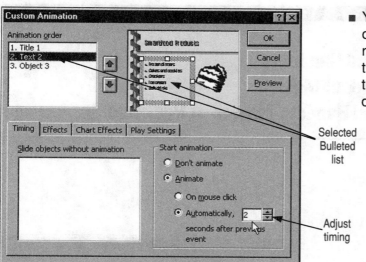

Selected
Bulleted
list

Adjust
timing

- You can control the timing of individual elements on bulleted lists, objects, and charts in addition to regulating the timing of the entire slide. Adjust the time of individual elements on slides using the timing options in the Custom Animation dialog box.

> *In this exercise, you will edit a previously created presentation by adding transitions, builds, sound, and timings to selected slides. You will also use the Annotator during your slide presentation.*

# EXERCISE DIRECTIONS

1. Open 🖫**FLAGSHIP**, or open 🖫**16FLAGSH**.

2. Switch to Slide view.

3. Apply a transition effect and a transition speed for each slide in the presentation in the Slide Transition dialog box.

4. Apply an animation build for bulleted text on slides 2, 3, 6 and 7 using any desired effect. Dim previous points in any color.

   - Animate and add sound to the clip art graphic on slide 3 and add a 5 second timing. Use any desired effect.

   - Animate callout graphic using any design desired effect.

   - Display Slide 4 (graph slide). Animate the chart by series and add any desired sound effect.

5. Save the changes to the presentation.

6. View the slide show. Use the Annotator to circle Pineview Estates on Slide 2 and the Country Estates row on Slide 5.

7. Add slide timings to each slide and change the advance method to advance automatically.

8. Set the slide show to run continuously and view the slide show again.

9. After viewing the entire presentation, stop the presentation.

10. Close the file; save the changes.

# KEYSTROKES

## ANNOTATE DURING SLIDE SHOWS

1. Open desired presentation and start slide show.

2. Click 🖱🔺 in lower right corner of screen to turn Annotator on.

3. Select **Pen** from pop-up menu.

4. Press left mouse button as you write on slide with the "pen."

**To turn Annotator off:**

1. Click Annotation button.

2. Select **Arrow** .................................. [A]

## RUN SLIDE SHOW CONTINUOUSLY

1. Open desired presentation.

2. Click **Slide Show** ................... [Alt]+[D]

3. Click **Slide Transition** ..................... [T]

4. Click **Automatically** ............... [Alt]+[C]
   after seconds

5. Enter number of seconds .......... *number*

6. Click **Apply to All** ................. [Alt]+[T]

7. Click **Slide Show** ................... [Alt]+[D]

8. Click **Set Up Show** ......................... [S]

9. Click **Loop Continuously** ....... [Alt]+[L]
   Until 'Esc'

**Stop Continuous Run of Slide Show:**

   Press **Esc**................................... [Esc]

**Exercise**

**17**

- ■ **Create Notes Pages and Handouts**
- ■ **Notes Master and Handout Master**
- ■ **Print Notes Master and Handout Master** ■ **Pack and Go**

# NOTES

## Create Notes Pages and Handouts

- ■ In the previous exercises, you printed your presentation either as individual slides or as Handouts with six slides per page. PowerPoint provides other options for printing your presentation.

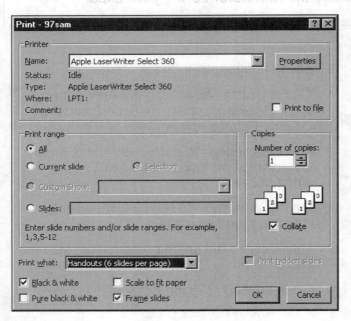

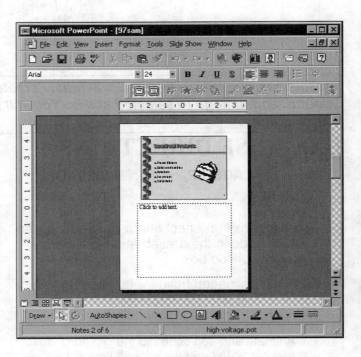

- ■ The **Notes Pages** option prints your presentation showing a small image at the top of the page and a blank box (notes placeholder) below the image. You can enter reminders and/or additional information about the slide in the notes placeholder, or you can leave the box blank so that your audience can use it for notetaking.

- ■ To add notes to your slides, click the Notes Pages view button on the bottom left of your screen or select Notes Page from the View main menu. Then, enter the desired text in the notes placeholder. Or you can add speaker notes while in Slide or Slide Sorter views by selecting the Slide to receive the Speaker notes and then selecting Speaker Notes from the View menu.

## Notes Master and Handout Master

- ■ In Exercise 9, you learned to use the Slide Master if you wanted to insert text or graphics on one slide and have it appear on all slides of your presentation.

438

- Using Notes Master and Handout Master also allows you to insert text and/or graphics on one page of your notes or handouts and have it appear on all pages. Often, the time, date, and speaker's name are added to audience handouts.

- Notes Master and Handout Master may be accessed by selecting Master, Notes Master or Handout Master from the View menu.

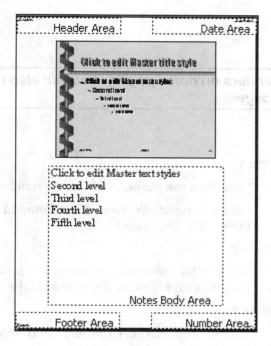

- The procedure to include the date, time, header and/or footer on the Notes and Handouts Master is the same as that used on the Slide and Title Master. See exercise 9 for explanation.

## Format Notes Pages

- You can format text on the Notes pages before or after you enter it. Use the commands on the Formatting toolbar, or all the commands (Font, Line Spacing, Bullets, etc.) on the Format menu.

## Print Notes Pages and Handouts

- Use the same procedures to print notes pages and handouts that you used to print slides.

## Prepare a Presentation for Viewing on Another Computer (Pack and Go)

- Using **Pack and Go**, you can save a presentation that can be "unpacked" and viewed on another computer. If the computer that will be used to view the presentation does not have PowerPoint installed on it, the PowerPoint Viewer will also be stored with the presentation. When the presentation is "unpacked" on the computer, the presentation can be viewed. If linked files are used in a presentation, those files will all be stored with the presentation.

- The **PowerPoint Viewer** is a program that lets you run slide shows created in PowerPoint on computers that do not have PowerPoint installed. It is available free and does not require a license. If you installed Office from a CD-ROM, you can find PowerPoint Viewer in the Office 97 ValuPack folder. The PowerPoint Viewer is also available from Microsoft on the World Wide Web.

- PowerPoint Viewer can be used with presentations prepared in PowerPoint 95 and PowerPoint 97.

- When you select Pack and Go on the File menu, the **Pack and Go Wizard** appears to walk you through preparing a presentation to view on another computer.

- Simply follow the steps to:
  - Pick the files to pack
  - Select where you want to save the presentation; for example, to the A drive.

- Include files that are linked to the presentation.

- Include PowerPoint Viewer, if the presentation will be used on a computer that does not have PowerPoint installed on it.

■ To view a presentation that has been packaged with Pack and Go:

- Use Windows Explorer to locate where the presentation is located, for example, on a disk in the A drive.

- Double-click on Pngsetup (Pack and Go Setup).

- Indicate where you want to copy the presentation.

- Double-click the PowerPoint Viewer (Ppview32).

- Click the Presentation that you want to run.

---

*In this exercise, you will create a table slide and add reminders on notes pages. You will also use Notes Pages master to insert text to appear on all notes pages.*

---

# EXERCISE DIRECTIONS

1. Open 💾**FOOD**, or open 🖫**17FOOD**.

2. Switch to Slide view.

3. Display Slide 4. Change the slide title to read International Advertising Budget.

4. Display Slide 5.

5. Insert a New Slide and select the Table AutoLayout.

   ✓ *The new slide should be Slide 6.*

   - Create 3 columns and 5 rows.

   - Enter the slide title and table data shown in Illustration A.

   - Set column heading text to sans serif 28-point italic bold. Use the default font size for column text.

   - Center column headings.

   - Adjust row heights so text fits attractively on the slide.

6. Switch to Notes Page view. Add the following notes to the slides indicated using a bulleted 16-point font size (see example shown in Illustration B):

**Slide 1:**

- **Introduce the purpose of the presentation.**

- **Give a general overview of the items to be covered in the presentation.**

**Slide 2:**

- **Review the different Smartfood Products available and identify the features of each.**

**Slide 3:**

- **Explain new market expansion and why these markets were selected.**

**Slide 4:**

- **Explain domestic markets and reasons for success in each.**

7. Switch to Notes Master.

8. Enter the footer information on the notes page shown in Illustration B in 12 point.

9. Switch to Handout Master.

10. Enter the same footer information using the same font size on the handouts master as you did on the Notes Page Master as shown in Illustration C on page 442.

11. Print one copy of notes pages 1-4.

12. Print one copy of the presentation as Handouts with three slides per page in black and white.

13. Close the file; save the changes.

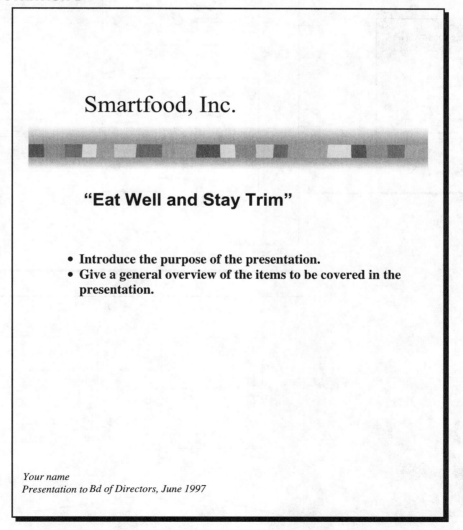

## ILLUSTRATION C

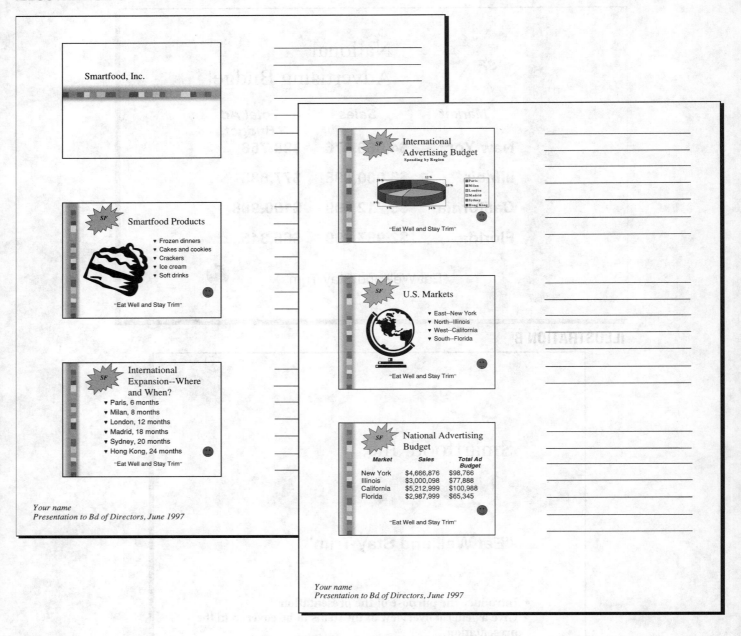

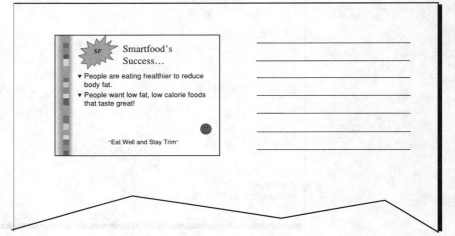

# KEYSTROKES

## CREATE NOTES PAGES

1. Open desired presentation.
2. Click 🖳 ........................ Alt + V , N
   to view Notes page.
3. Click on notes placeholder at bottom of page.
4. Type notes.

## PRINT NOTES PAGES AND HANDOUTS

1. Open desired presentation.
2. Prepare Notes Pages.
3. Click **File** ............................. Alt + F
4. Click **Print** ...................................... P
5. Click **Print what** ............. Alt + W , ↓
   list arrow.
6. Select **Notes Pages** or **Handouts**.
7. Select desired options, if necessary.
8. Click **OK** ................................... Enter

## INSERT PAGE NUMBERS/DATE AND TIME/HEADERS OR FOOTERS

See Keystrokes, Exercise 9.

## FORMAT TEXT ON NOTES PAGES

1. Enter text to format.
   **OR**
   Select text to format.
2. Click **Format** ......................... Alt + O
   to select desired formats.
   **OR**
   Use buttons on Formatting toolbar to apply desired format.

## FORMAT TEXT ON NOTES MASTER AND HANDOUT MASTER

1. Open a presentation or create a new presentation.
2. Click **View** ........................... Alt + V
3. Click **Master** ................................. M
4. Click **Notes Master** ......................... N
   **OR**
   **Handout Master** ........................... D
5. Select placeholder to change formatting.
   **OR**
   Using the text, drawing, and/or formatting tools, create desired master information.
6. Click 🖳 ........................ Alt + V , N
   ✓ To see effect of additions to Handout Master, print one copy of Handouts with any number of slides per page.

## Exercise 18

■ **Summary**

*In this exercise, you will get your presentation ready for a slide show. You will add transitions, builds and timings, prepare audience handouts and notes pages. You will use the Notes Page Master to add information to all notes pages.*

# EXERCISE DIRECTIONS

1. Open 📟**INVEST** or open 💾**18INVEST**.

2. Switch to Slide Sorter view.

3. Apply a transition effect, a transition speed, and a sound to each slide in the presentation.

4. Switch to Slide View.

5. Apply an animation build to text on slides 2 (Why should…) and 6 (To insert…) using any desired effect. Dim previous points in any color.

6. Display slide 3 (Investors…). Animate the organization chart in a series and add a sound effect using any desired effect.

7. Display slide 4 (Graph slide). Animate the chart by element in a series and add a sound effect.

8. Save the changes to the presentation; do not close the file.

9. View the slide show.

10. Use the Annotator to circle the highest bar on the graph.

11. Switch to Notes Master view.

12. Using the Text Box tool, create the company name and date as shown in Illustration A in sans serif 20 point. Use the line tool to create the horizontal line. Insert a page number on the top right corner of the page. Delete the footer and Number placeholders.

13. Add the following notes to the slides indicated:

    **Slide 1:**
    - **Introduce yourself and your position in the company.**
    - **Explain the purpose of today's presentation.**

    **Slide 2:**
    - **Review each reason to invest in GreatGains Mutual Fund.**
    - **Emphasize blue-chip stocks.**
    - **Give three examples.**

    **Slide 4:**
    - **Explain the reasons for significant growth in 1997.**

    **Slide 5:**
    - **Review each instrument.**

14. Using the copy feature, copy the bottom (company name and date) text to the clipboard.

15. Switch to Handout Master view.

16. Paste the company name and date text on the bottom of the page. Create a horizontal line below the name and date. Insert a page number on the top right of the page as shown in Illustration B. Delete the header, footer, and number placeholders.

*(continued)*

17. Print one copy of each notes page in black and white.

18. Print one copy of the presentation as handouts with three slides per page in black and white.

19. Add slide timings to each slide and change the advance method to advance automatically.

20. Set the slide show to run continuously and view the slide show again.

21. After viewing the entire presentation, stop the presentation.

22. Close the file; save the changes.

**ILLUSTRATON A**

GreatGains Mutual Fund

Presentation to Investors
*April 1997*

"Let us put your money to work"

•Introduce yourself and your position in the company.
•Explain the purpose of today's presentation.

**GreatGains, Inc.**                    April 1997

**ILLUSTRATION B**

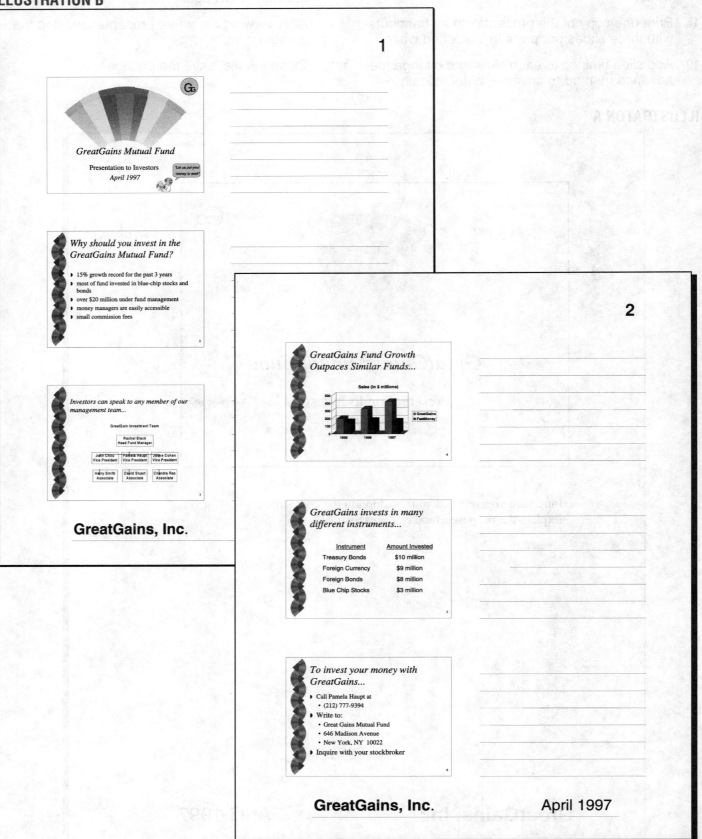

# Integration

## Exercise 1

- **Window Files in One Application**
- **Window Files From Different Applications**

# NOTES

### Window Files in One Application

- Microsoft Office allows you to work with several files simultaneously by displaying them in separate windows. The exact number of files that can be used at once depends on available memory. Windowing lets you view files as you work with them.

- When you begin a new application, Office provides a full-screen or maximized window for your work. The controls on the title bar let you size and arrange Office within the Windows screen. The controls to the left and right of the menu bar allow you to size and arrange the current application window and the application. *(See Chapter I - Office Basics, Exercise 2, and the illustration on the right.)*

- Minimizing a window, or reducing its size, allows you to view several files at once. To minimize a window, click the document minimize button near the right end of the menu bar. The file will be reduced to a small title bar which displays Restore, Maximize, and Close buttons and a menu when selected. The icon can be restored or maximized by selecting the desired feature. See the illustration to the right.

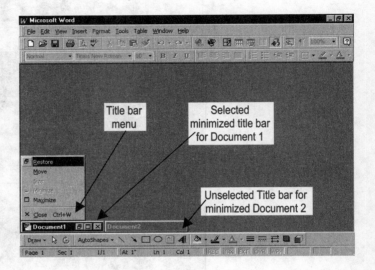

- You can move a minimized document by selecting it and dragging it to a new location. If you are viewing multiple files created in the same application, you may view the open documents on the screen at once using the Arrange All command on the Window menu. The files will be arranged so that all can be viewed and highlighted in a tiled fashion.

- When files are arranged or tiled, every file is visible without overlapping. The active window is indicated by the shaded title bar. Any window can be clicked to be made active, and the Maximize button ⬜ on the right end of the title bar can be clicked to enlarge or maximize the file. See the illustration below.

### *Arranged or Tiled Documents*

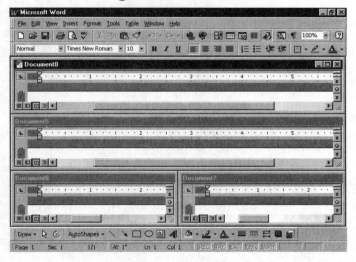

- In Excel, Access, and PowerPoint, a Cascade arrangement of files is available. Cascaded windows allow you to view the title bar of each open document. The windows overlap to display the title bar of each file. Note the illustration of three PowerPoint files cascaded with the active presentation on top. To make a presentation active, click any visible portion of the desired window.

### *Cascaded Documents*

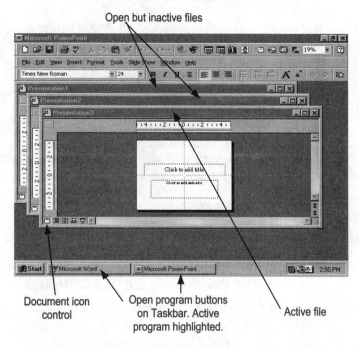

Open but inactive files

Document icon control

Open program buttons on Taskbar. Active program highlighted.

Active file

- You can also switch between file windows whether they are currently displayed or not by selecting Window from the menu and choosing the document from the open files listed.

- A window can be closed by clicking the Close button or by double-clicking the control menu icon, which is the icon at the left on the title bar.

## Window Files from Different Applications

- If you wish to move between an open Word document and Excel workbook file, or between any open Office programs, click on the appropriate button on the Windows 95 Taskbar at the bottom of the screen. As you open and switch out of a program, Windows 95 places a button on the Taskbar at the bottom of the screen. By clicking on the button you can access the opened file in the program you select. Note the taskbar in the previous illustration.

- If you wish to view files from several programs at the same time, right-click the Windows 95 Taskbar and select the view option you prefer. You may Cascade, Tile Horizontally, or Tile Vertically. Note the illustration of the menu that appears when the Taskbar is right-clicked.

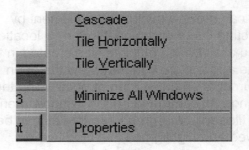

---

*In this exercise, you will work with four Excel workbooks and a Word document. You will arrange the workbooks so you can view each file and use the Taskbar buttons to view the worksheets and document.*

---

# EXERCISE DIRECTIONS

1. Create a new workbook in Excel.

2. Open ⌨**WAGON**, or open 💾**01WAGON.XLS.**

3. Open ⌨**PAYMENT**, or open 💾**01PAYMENT.XLS.**

4. Open ⌨**PRICE**, or open 💾**01PRICE.XLS.**

5. Open ⌨**INVENY**, or open 💾**01INVEN.XLS.**

6. Arrange all the worksheets.

7. Make WAGON (01WAGON) the active workbook.

8. Make PAYMENT (01PAYMENT) the active workbook.

9. Minimize INVEN (01INVEN) to a title bar icon.

10. Restore INVEN (01INVEN).

11. Select the Open Office Document item on the Start menu.

12. Look in the location where your files are stored.

13. Open ⌨**BLOCK**, or open 💾**01BLOCK.DOC.**

14. Switch back to the Excel screen by clicking the Excel button on the Taskbar.

15. Make WAGON (1WAGON) the active workbook.

16. Size the window so that it is larger.

17. Arrange the worksheets in Vertical, Horizontal, and Cascade layouts and view each.
    - ✓ *Note:* *The active file retains its status through the changes in arrangements.*

18. View the Excel and Word files by right-clicking the Taskbar and selecting the Tile Vertically option.

19. Use this method to view the Cascade and Horizontal views of all the files.

20. Close each window.

21. Exit Excel and exit Word.

# KEYSTROKES

## ARRANGE (ALL)

*Positions document windows next to each other as non-overlapping tiles. Keystrokes for Word and Excel.*

1. Click **Window** ........................ `Alt` + `W`
2. Click **Arrange All** ........................... `A`

   Excel, PowerPoint, and Access provide additional options:

   - **Tiled** ........................................ `T`
   - **Horizontal** ............................ `O`
   - **Vertical** ................................. `V`
   - **Cascade** ................................. `C`

## CLOSE WINDOW

Double-click Control menu icon of active document window.

**OR**

1. Click **Control menu** .............. `Alt` + `-`
2. Click **Close** ............................... `C`

**OR**

Press **Ctrl+W** (Word) ........... `Alt` + `W`

**OR**

Press **Ctrl+F4** ....................... `Ctrl` + `N`

(Excel or Access)

## MAXIMIZE WINDOW

*Fills the application window with the active file.*

Click Maximize box of .................... `□`
active file (not available if window is already maximized.)

**OR**

1. Click **Control menu** .............. `Alt` + `-`
2. Click **Ma_x_imize** ........................... `X`

**OR**

Press **Ctrl+F10** ..................... `Ctrl` + `F10`
(Word or Excel)

## MINIMIZE WINDOW

*Reduces active file window to an icon.*

Click Minimize box of .................... `_`
active file (only visible if window has been changed to resizable view with Restore command.)

**OR**

1. Click **Control menu** .............. `Ctrl` + `-`
2. Click **Mi_n_imize** ........................... `N`

**OR**

Press **Ctrl +F9** ..................... `Ctrl` + `F9`
(Excel)

## SWITCH AMONG OPEN DOCUMENTS

Click any visible portion of desired document.

**OR**

1. Click **Window** ..................... `Alt` + `W`
2. Click name of desired document.

## WINDOW FILES FROM DIFFERENT APPLICATIONS

1. Open first program.
2. Open desired file.
3. Open second program using the **Start**, **Programs** menu.
4. Open desired file.
5. Select taskbar button for first program.
6. Right-click a blank area of the taskbar.
7. Select desired option:

   - **Cascade** ............................... `C`
   - **Tile Horizontally** .................... `H`
   - **Tile Vertically** ........................ `V`
   - **Minimize all Windows** ........... `M`
   - **Undo Minimize All** ................. `U`

**Exercise 2**

- **Integrate an Excel Worksheet and a Word Document**
- **Internet Basics** ■ **Use Internet Features**

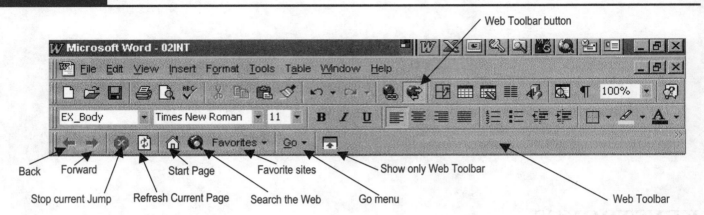

Web Toolbar button

Back
Forward
Stop current Jump
Refresh Current Page
Start Page
Search the Web
Favorite sites
Go menu
Show only Web Toolbar
Web Toolbar

## NOTES

### Integrate an Excel Worksheet and a Word Document

- Integration is the sharing or combining of data between Microsoft Office tools. The source file is used to send data; the destination file is used to receive data. For example, an Excel chart or worksheet (the source file) can add supporting or visual documentation of material to a Word document (the destination file).

- The Open a Document button on the Shortcut bar may be used to open files in different applications; while the Taskbar buttons may be used to switch programs to share information between applications. To integrate an Excel table into a Word document, for example, you can copy and paste the data or use the drag and drop procedure. Both of these methods place the table into the document, which may be edited. However, the integrated table has no connection to the original worksheet and the formulas are not accessible. These methods should only be used when updated or linked data is not necessary and when formulas do not need editing.

- Copying places the data onto the clipboard where it can then be pasted to the desired location. Open both the Word document and the Excel worksheet, make the Excel worksheet active, and copy the desired worksheet data. After you make the Word document active, paste the worksheet to the specific location in the document.

- The drag and drop technique may also be used to copy and paste the data if both the source and destination documents are made visible using the windowing options discussed in Exercise 1. When using drag and drop, you bypass the clipboard and directly copy the data. However, you must hold down the Ctrl key to copy (rather than move) the data.

  ✓ Note: If you have difficulty placing the worksheet, drag it to any spot on the document, then maximize the document, and adjust the placement.

## Internet Basics

- The **Internet** is a world-wide network of computers. These computers may be located in businesses, schools, research foundations, and/or individual's homes. Those who are connected to this network can share information with each other, communicate via e-mail, and search for information.

- The **World Wide Web (WWW)** is a service of the Internet in which pages, created by companies, individuals, schools, and government agencies around the world, are linked to each other.

- **Hypertext links** may appear in a different **color**, underlined, or **both**. Clicking your mouse on one of these links takes you to a new page with related information. When your cursor moves over a link, the arrow will turn into a hand.

- A Web **browser** is a program on your computer that displays the information you retrieve from the Internet in a readable format. The most popular Web browsers are Microsoft Internet Explorer and Netscape Navigator.

- A **Uniform Resource Locator**, or URL, is a World Wide Web address. The URL system is like an enormous card catalog that lets computers connected to the World Wide Web find the designated site.

- When you enter an address on the URL line, you will frequently start the address of the site with **http** or **ftp**. Http stands for **HyperText Transfer Protocol**, which refers to the communication protocol that allows web pages to connect to one another, regardless of what type of operating system is used to display or access the files. **File Transfer Protocol** (**ftp**) lets you transfer files from one computer to another over a network (or across the Internet).

- When you want to locate information on the Internet, you will access a **Search Engine Site**. Search Sites (Yahoo, AltaVista, InfoSeek, HotBoot, Magellan, etc.) are Web sites that contain catalogs of web resources that can be searched by headings, URLs and key words.

## Use Internet Features

- The Internet provides access to countless Web sites, many of which contain information and documentation that can be used for researching a particular subject or topic.

- Microsoft Office 97 provides easy access to the Internet through the menus and toolbar buttons. When you click the **Web toolbar** button 🌐 or click View, Toolbars, Web, the Web toolbar displays. Note the illustration on the previous page of the button and toolbar in Word.

- Below is an explanation of the buttons on the Web toolbar.

| | |
|---|---|
| ← → | Move **Back** and **Forward** among the pages that are stored in the history of your hyperlinks. |
| ⊗ | **Stop** a page from loading or refreshing. Use this when a page seems to take too long to load or you decide to take a different action. |
| 🗎 | **Refresh** the current page. This is convenient when a page doesn't seem to load completely or correctly. |
| 🏠 | Go the **Start Page**; also called a Home page. You can change the page that loads as the Start page. |
| 🔍 | When you click the **Search the Web** button, you will go to the main search page on the Microsoft World Wide Web site. |
| Favorites ▾ | Displays the current contents of your **Favorites** folder. Use the Favorites folder to store WWW addresses that you visit frequently. The favorites created in Internet Explorer will display when you open this folder. You can add folders and address using this option, even if you are off line. |

| | |
|---|---|
| 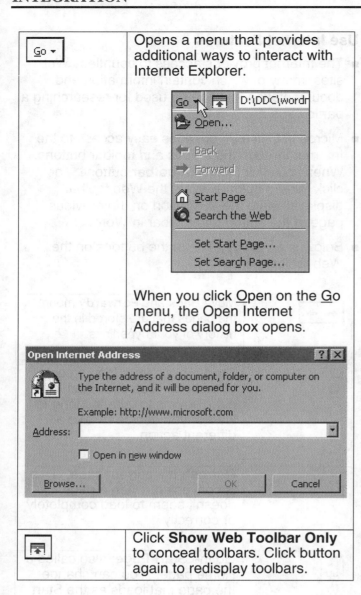 | Opens a menu that provides additional ways to interact with Internet Explorer.<br><br>When you click Open on the Go menu, the Open Internet Address dialog box opens. |
| (Show Web Toolbar Only button) | Click **Show Web Toolbar Only** to conceal toolbars. Click button again to redisplay toolbars. |

- You will gather information from the Internet for the rest of the exercises in this lesson.
  - If you are connected to the Internet, use the suggested sites or select other appropriate Web sites.
  - If you are not connected to the Internet, use the CD-ROM that accompanies this book. All the Internet actions described in the exercises are simulated on this CD. You can use the information on the CD-ROM to complete the exercises in this book.
- If you want to use the CD-ROM for these exercises, follow the installation directions on page viii.

**To launch the simulation from a hard drive:**

- On the Web toolbar, Click **Go**, then select **Open**.
- Type **C:\DDCPUB\OFF97INT.IMR** on the address line. If you installed the files to a drive other than C, use the letter of that drive. For example, if you installed the DDC files on the D drive, enter D instead of C.
- Click **OK** to open the simulation.

**To launch the simulation from the CD-ROM drive:**

- Install the files on a hard drive and be sure that the CD-ROM is in the drive.
- On the Web toolbar, click **Go**, then select **Open**.
- Type **E:\DDCPUB\OFF97INT.IMR** on the address line. Use the correct letter for your CD-ROM drive.
- Click **OK** to open the simulation.

In this exercise, you will edit a letter from Avi Lanch of Hemisphere Travel to include additional text and a worksheet showing prices for ski rentals. You must find the data for the worksheet by searching the Web for currency information and exchange rates. You will save the newly integrated document under a new name. If you plan to use the DDC simulation, be sure that it has been installed on your hard drive (see page viii) and that you have read the information on the previous page.

# EXERCISE DIRECTIONS

1. Click on the Open Office Document button on the Shortcut bar.

2. Keyboard the letter on page 456, or open 🖫**02SKI.DOC**, which opens in Word.

3. Add the additional text to the third paragraph as shown in Illustration A.

4. Click on the Open a Document button on the Shortcut bar.

5. Create the spreadsheet on page 457, or open 🖫**02CURRENCY.XLS**, which opens in Excel. See Illustration B.

6. Display your Web toolbar.

7. Use the Internet or the DDC CD-ROM simulation to complete the worksheet. Find the names of foreign currencies and the current value of the U.S. dollar in that currency. Do the following:

   a. Sign on to your Internet provider.

   **OR**

   • To access the DDC Internet simulation, click **Go**, **Open** on the Web toolbar.

   • Type **C:\DDCPUB\OFF97INT.IMR**. (Be sure that the simulation has been installed on your hard drive. If files are on a drive other than C, replace C with the correct letter.)

   • Click **OK** to launch the simulation.

   • Select **Exercise 2: Currency Convert**.

   b. Use the Yahoo search engine to search on the words "universal currency converter."

   ✓ *You may use other search methods.*

   c. View the sites that might provide currencies and conversion rates.

   d. Select a site and search for the currencies and conversion rates for Austria, France, Italy, and Switzerland.

   e. Write down the desired information.

   f. Exit from your browser and disconnect from your service provider, or exit the DDC Internet simulation.

8. Enter the COUNTRY CURRENCY and FOREIGN EXCHANGE data into the worksheet that you obtained as a result of your Internet search.

9. Use the FOREIGN EXCHANGE rate to determine the price of ski equipment in the foreign currency.

10. Copy the formula for all currencies.

11. Format money columns for two decimal places.

12. Copy the entire worksheet.

13. Switch to the Word document using the Word button on the taskbar.

14. Paste the worksheet in the memorandum as indicated.

15. Size the columns so headings fit on one line.

    ✓ *You can change data but cannot view or edit formulas. This is table mode.*

16. Select and delete the worksheet data in the document so that it can be integrated again using another method.

17. Display both the Excel file and the Word document on the screen using the Tile Vertically option.

    ✓ *Right-click the Taskbar in a blank area and select the Tile Vertically option.*

18. Use the Ctrl key and the drag and drop method to select and copy the worksheet to the Word document.

19. Make any size adjustments as necessary.

20. Include the following second-page header:
    • Upson Downs Ski Club
    • Page 2

21. Print one copy.

22. Save the file as **SKICUR**.

23. Close all files.

**ILLUSTRATION A**

**HEMISPHERE** *Travel*

555 World Class Way
Burlington, VT
Phone: (802) 333-3333
Fax: (802) 222-2222
E-mail: hemtrav@win.com

Date

Ms. Wendy Ascend, President
Upson Downs Ski Club
224 Mountaintop Lane
Burlington, VT

Dear Ms. Ascend:

Thank you for your inquiry about group rates for European ski vacations.

We will be glad to present a seminar to your group on the premier European ski resorts and the unique features of each.

*Insert text here*

Traveling to Europe can be very expensive. After hearing our presentation, you will be able to decide which vacation best suits your travel and economic needs.

As a sample of our services, note the table below analyzing ski rental charges with current foreign exchange rates.

Our Leisure Travel Department is available for consultation from 9 a.m. to 7 p.m., 7 days a week. We look forward to working closely with your group.

Sincerely,

*Insert worksheet here*

Avi Lanch, Vice President
Leisure Travel Department

av/yo

## ILLUSTRATION B

|     | A | B | C | D | E |
|-----|---|---|---|---|---|
| 1 | SKIS, POLES AND BOOTS RENTAL | | | | |
| 2 | | | | | RENTAL IN |
| 3 | | SKI RENTAL | COUNTRY | FOREIGN | FOREIGN |
| 4 | COUNTRY | US DOLLAR | CURRENCY | EXCHANGE | CURRENCY |
| 5 | Austria | 27 | | | |
| 6 | France | 28 | | | |
| 7 | Italy | 13 | | | |
| 8 | Switzerland | 37 | | | |
| 9 | | | | | |
| 10 | | | | | |
| 11 | | | | | |
| 12 | | | | | |
| 13 | | | | | |
| 14 | | | | | |
| 15 | | | | | |

Search the Internet for country currency and current exchange rate.

# KEYSTROKES

### COPY AND PASTE DATA BETWEEN APPLICATIONS

1. Open both applications and appropriate files.

2. In the source file, highlight the data to be copied.

3. Click **Edit** ............................. Alt + E

4. Click **Copy** ........................................ C

5. Switch to the destination file.

6. Place cursor at the point of insertion.

7. Click **Edit** ............................. Alt + E

8. Click **Paste Cells** ............................. P

   **OR**

   Click **Paste** ........................................ P

### COPY DATA BETWEEN APPLICATIONS WITH DRAG AND DROP EDITING

1. Open and display both applications and files.

2. In the source file, highlight the data to be copied.

3. Move pointer to right edge of selection until arrow appears.

4. Hold Ctrl while dragging the data to the location in the destination file.

### DISPLAY WEB TOOLBAR

**In all Microsoft applications:**

   Click Web toolbar button 🌐.

   **OR**

1. Click **View** ............................. Alt + V

2. Click **Toolbars** ............................. T

3. Select Web toolbar ............................. ↓

✓ *To hide Web toolbar, click the Web toolbar button or deselect the toolbar from the toolbar list.*

■ **Object Linking and Embedding** ■ **Link Files** ■ **Edit a Linked File**
■ **Embed a File** ■ **Office Links** ■ **Financial Data on the Internet**

# NOTES

## Object Linking and Embeding

■ **Object Linking and Embedding** or OLE is the system Microsoft uses to link or embed objects between applications.

## Link Files

■ As discussed in Excel, Exercise 25, linking files allows the data in the destination file to change if the source file is updated. Suppose you placed an Excel worksheet (source file) into a Word document (destination file), but you need to update your worksheet data on a weekly basis. By linking the worksheet and document files, the Word document automatically updates with the most current data. In addition, the linking procedure saves disk space since the file is stored in the source location and the link is a shortcut to that location.

■ Linking is accomplished by using Edit, Copy, and Edit, Paste Special commands with the Paste Link option selected. Before choosing Paste Link, you must identify the object or type of file since you are copying between applications, for example, "Microsoft Excel Worksheet Object."

## Edit a Linked File

■ When a linked file from one application is double-clicked within another application, the source application and file open for you to edit. For example, if you double-click on a linked Excel worksheet in a Word file, you are brought into Excel to do the edits. Changes made to the source file automatically appear on the linked file. Conversely, if you make changes directly into the source file and then open the destination file with the linked data, the updated worksheet will appear.

## Embed a File

■ Embedding files enables you to edit data within the source application but does not change or modify the source file. This is preferable if you wish to make changes within Excel that are not reflected in the source file or if the source file is not always available. Double-clicking on an embedded worksheet in a Word document allows you to make edits in Excel that will not change the source file. Unlike linking, embedding creates a larger destination file since the embedded file is included in the destination file.

■ To embed a file, use the Insert, Object, Create from File options or the Copy, Paste Special commands on the Edit menu without selecting the Paste Link option.

## Office Links

■ Office Links may be used to create a new embedded worksheet in a Word document by clicking the Insert Microsoft Excel Worksheet button 📊 on the Standard toolbar in Word. This worksheet may be sized using the handles on the worksheet and may be created by using the Excel menus that appear. To embed a new file using the menu, use the Insert, Object, Create New commands. The workbook you create within a document gives you all the capabilities of Excel within the document.

## Financial Data on the Internet

- The Internet provides a vast array of current financial information. All the major financial publications have web sites that provide market data, data on specific companies, and business news. The market prices are updated several times each hour and reflect the actual prices for that day.

- In most market quote web sites you must search for the stock using the ticker symbol. There is usually a search procedure for the ticker symbol as well. The DDC Simulation will provide stock prices, but the actual current prices must be obtained from the Internet.

> *In this exercise, Carol D. Jones is preparing a letter to a brokerage firm about transferring her portfolio to their firm. She will integrate a worksheet that contains her current investments using linked and embedded modes. The current prices for the stocks will be researched using the Internet.*

# EXERCISE DIRECTIONS

1. Click the Open a Document button on the Shortcut bar.

2. Keyboard the letter on page 461, or open 🖫**03INVEST.DOC**, which opens in Word.

3. Make the changes indicated on the document. as shown in Illustration A.

4. Click the Open Office Document icon on the Shortcut bar.

5. Create the spreadsheet on page 462, or open 🖫**03STOCK.XLS**.

6. Right-click the taskbar to arrange these files vertically.

7. Place the cursor in the Word document at the point where the worksheet is to be inserted.

8. Use the Insert, Object, Create from File options to embed the worksheet into the document.
   - ✓ *This is an embedded file that is part of the Word file. It may be edited without changing the source file.*

9. Double-click the embedded worksheet in the document and format the column headings to bold.
   - ✓ *The worksheet in Excel did not change.*

10. Select and delete the entire worksheet from the document.

11. Use the Internet or the DDC CD-ROM simulation to find the current market price of the investments, as follows:
    a. Sign on to your Internet provider.
       **OR**
       - To access the DDC Internet simulation, click **Go**, **Open** on the Web toolbar.
       - Type **C:\DDCPUB\OFF97INT.IMR**. (Be sure that the simulation has been installed on your hard drive. If files are on a drive other than C, replace C with the correct letter.)
       - Click **OK** to launch the simulation.
       - Select **Exercise 3: Stock Market**.
    b. Use the Excite search engine to search on the words "quick quotes."
       - ✓ *You may use other search methods.*
    c. View the sites that might provide stock quotes.
    d. Select Money Quick Quotes, if available.
    e. Find the ticker symbols for Apple Computers and Sun Microsystems.
    f. Find the current quotes for:
       ABR Information Services
       American Telephone and Telegraph
       Apple Computers
       General Electric
       Sun Microsystems
    g. Write down the last price for each stock.
    h. Exit from your browser and disconnect from your service provider, or exit the DDC Internet simulation.

12. Enter the current prices, using fraction format, into the STOCK in the MARKET PRICE column of the worksheet. Copy the worksheet.

   ✓ *The Market Value and gain or loss columns will change.*

13. Make the Word document active by clicking the title bar or by selecting Word on the taskbar.

14. Link the worksheet, using the Paste Special, Paste Link options to the location shown on the document.

   ✓ *This is a linked file that will reflect changes in the source file.*

15. Minimize the Excel worksheet.

16. Double-click on the worksheet in the Word file. (This brings you into Excel.)

17. Add a third worksheet title in B3: Market Prices as of March 1, 1997 (or insert current date).

18. Move the three-line title to Column A.

19. Click the Word button on the Taskbar to return to the document and note the updated worksheet.

20. Click the Excel button to return to the worksheet and insert one row below the heading.

21. Return to Word and note the updated worksheet.

22. Use Shrink to fit to keep text on one page.

23. Print one copy of the letter.

24. Close and save the file as **INVSTK**.

25. Close the Word file.

26. Save and close the Excel file; name it **STOCK**.

**Carol D. Jones**
470 WEST END AVENUE
NEW YORK, NY 10023
Phone: 212-999-9999
e-mail: CDJ@westlake.com

March 1, 1997

Ms. Winifred Thomas
Thomas & Young Securities
40 Wall Street
New York, NY 10001

Dear Ms. Thomas:

As we discussed, I am interested in transferring my entire portfolio to your firm. My investment objective has not been met with my present brokerage company, and after meeting with you, I have decided to transfer my account.

Your request for a summary of my portfolio is provided below. I have used today's market value.

*Insert*

*Insert worksheet*

I look forward to our scheduled meeting on Monday, March 15 to discuss investment strategies and to doing business with your company.

Sincerely,

Carole D. Jones

cdj

## ILLUSTRATION B

| | A | B | C | D | E | F | G | H |
|---|---|---|---|---|---|---|---|---|
| 1 | | CAROL D. JONES | | | | | | |
| 2 | | CURRENT INVESTMENT PORTFOLIO | | | | | | |
| 3 | | | | | | | | |
| 4 | DATE | | TICKER | COST | NO. OF | MARKET | MARKET | GAIN OR |
| 5 | BOUGHT | COMPANY | SYMBOL | PRICE | SHARES | PRICE | VALUE | LOSS |
| 6 | 3/18/96 | ABR Information Services | ABRX | 2955.45 | 100 | 25 1/2 | 2,550.00 | (405.45) |
| 7 | 4/15/96 | Am. Telephone and Telegraph | T | 8250.87 | 200 | 40 1/8 | 8,025.00 | (225.87) |
| 8 | 3/27/96 | Apple Computer | | 1943.95 | 100 | 17 3/8 | 1,737.50 | (206.45) |
| 9 | 3/12/96 | General Electric | GE | 10250.55 | 100 | 104 1/2 | 10,450.00 | 199.45 |
| 10 | 5/25/96 | Sun Microsystems | | 4568.75 | 200 | 25 5/8 | 5,125.00 | 556.25 |
| 11 | | | | | | | | |
| 12 | | TOTALS | | 27,969.57 | 700.00 | | 27,887.50 | (82.07) |
| 13 | | | | | | | | |
| 14 | | | | | | | | |
| 15 | | | | Locate the ticker symbol | | Replace these values | | |
| 16 | | | | from the Internet. | | with current market | | |
| 17 | | | | | | prices from the Internet. | | |

# KEYSTROKES

## LINK DATA BETWEEN APPLICATIONS

1. Open both applications and appropriate files.

2. In the source file, highlight the data to be copied.

3. Click **Edit** .............................. `Alt`+`E`

4. Click **Copy** ...................................... `C`

5. Switch to the destination file.

6. Place cursor at the point of insertion.

7. Click **Edit** .............................. `Alt`+`E`

8. Click **Paste Special** ........................ `S`

9. Select **Paste Link** ............................ `L`

10. Click in **As** box to select format ...... `↑↓`

11. Click ⎢ OK ⎥ ................................. `↵`

## EMBEDDED OBJECTS

**Create New:**

1. Click **Insert** ............................ `Alt`+`I`

2. Click **Object** ................................ `O`

✓ The Object dialog box will appear.

3. Click **Create New** tab ............. `Alt`+`C`

4. Click **Object type** list box ........ `Alt`+`T`

5. Select application .......................... `↑↓`
   from which to create object.

6. Click ⎢ OK ⎥ to create ................... `↵`

✓ The selected application will open.

7. Create desired information.

8. Click outside the object to return to original application.

**Create from File:**

1. Click **Insert** ........................... `Alt`+`I`

2. Click **Object** ......................... `Alt`+`O`

✓ The Object dialog box will appear.

3. Click **Create from File** tab ...... `Alt`+`F`

4. Click **Browse** ......................... `Alt`+`B`

5. Click **Look in** drop-down ........ `Alt`+`I`
   list box.

6. Type or select drive letter or .......... `↑↓`
   drive containing file you want to insert.

7. Double-click directory in Directories list box containing file you want to insert. ∗

8. Double-click file in ................. `Alt`+`N`
   **File name** list box.

9. Click ⎢ OK ⎥ ............................ `Enter`

∗ *This method may be used to Link the file by selecting Link to File check box at this point.*

## EMBED DATA USING PASTE SPECIAL

1. Open both applications and appropriate files.

2. In the source file, highlight the data to be copied.

3. Click **Edit** ............................... `Alt`+`E`

4. Click **Copy** ...................................... `C`

5. Switch to the destination file.

6. Place cursor at the point of insertion.

7. Click **Edit** ............................... `Alt`+`E`

8. Click **Paste Special** ........................ `S`

9. Click ⎢ OK ⎥ ............................ `Enter`

## Exercise 4

- **Integrate an Excel Chart and a Word Document (OLE)**
- **Embed a Chart** ■ **Link a Chart** ■ **Edit a Chart**
- **Favorites on the Web Toolbar**

## NOTES

### Integrate an Excel Chart and a Word Document (OLE)

■ You can insert an Excel chart into a Word document using Linking or Embedding commands. The OLE system and the consequences of using linking or embedding, as described in Exercise 3, apply to charts as well. If the chart is part of the worksheet, use the Copy, Paste Special procedure since the chart can be selected and isolated. If the chart is on a separate sheet, use the Insert, Object, Create from File procedure.

### Embed a Chart

■ If you wish to edit a chart in Word without changing the source material, you should embed the chart. When you double-click the chart, Excel menus and toolbars appear for editing purposes. You can return to the Word document by clicking outside the object or by clicking the Word button on the Taskbar.

### Link a Chart

■ If a chart refers to data that is updated periodically, or if you wish to minimize the size of the Word file, you should link the chart object. Edits you make on the linked chart object affect the source file; or, if you change the source file, the object in the destination file is automatically updated.

### Edit a Chart

■ A workbook may include multiple sheets and the chart may be on a separate sheet. The sheet that was active when the workbook was last saved will appear as the embedded object. By double-clicking on the object, you may adjust the sizing of the object, edit data, and switch to the proper sheet, if necessary.

### Favorites on the Web Toolbar

■ You can use the Web toolbar to move from one site to another or to move forward or backward through documents. If you find an interesting site that you wish to visit again, you should add it to the Favorites folder on the Web toolbar by clicking Favorites, Add to Favorites. When you want to visit the site again, click Favorites, Open Favorites, then click the Web page name. You may also click recently opened Web sites which appear on the menu, as illustrated below.

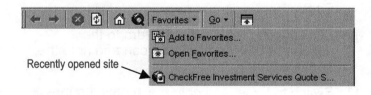

In this exercise, Avi Lanch of Hemisphere Travel, would like to chart the worksheet data included in her letter to the Upson Downs Ski Club. You will open a chart, link it to the Word document, and update the chart by adding Germany to the data.

# EXERCISE DIRECTIONS

1. Click the Open Office Document icon on the Shortcut Bar.

2. Open 🖭**SKICUR.DOC**, or open 🖫**04SKICUR.DOC** which brings you into Word.

3. Make the changes indicated on page 2 of the document as shown on page 466.

4. Click the Open Office Document icon on the Shortcut bar.

5. Open 🖭**CURRENCY.XLS**, or open 🖫**04CURRENCY.XLS**.

6. Switch to the Chart1 sheet.

7. Click Edit, Copy to select and copy the chart.

8. Switch to the Word document by clicking the Word Button on the Taskbar.

9. Link the MS Excel Chart Object, using the Edit, Paste Special, Paste Link options to the location shown on the document.

   ✓ Note: This is a linked file that will reflect changes in the source file.

   ✓ Note: Size the chart as necessary.

10. Double-click the chart in the Word file. (This brings you into Excel.)

11. Add a subtitle to the chart: Skis, Poles, and Boots.

12. Click outside the object to return to the document or click the Word icon and note the updated chart.

13. Switch to Excel and note the subtitle on the chart.

14. Switch to Sheet1 and insert a line for Germany below France on the worksheet as follows: Country: Germany   Ski Rental U.S. $: 32.00

15. Use the Internet or the DDC CD-ROM simulation to complete the worksheet. Find the name of the German currency and the current value of the U.S. dollar in that currency.

   a. Sign on to your Internet provider.

**OR**

   • To access the DDC Internet simulation, click **Go**, **Open** on the Web toolbar.

   • Type **C:\DDCPUB\OFF97INT.IMR**. (Be sure that the simulation has been installed on your hard drive. If files are on a drive other than C, replace C with the correct letter.)

   • Click **OK** to launch the simulation.

   • Select **Exercise 4: Currency Convert**.

   b. Use the Yahoo search engine to search on the words "currency convert."

      ✓ You may use other search methods.

   c. Find the German currency and conversion rate.

   d. Add the Currency Conversion site to your Favorites.

   e. Write down the desired information.

   f. Exit from your browser and disconnect from your service provider, or exit the DDC Internet simulation.

16. Add the new information to complete the worksheet.

17. Note the changes on the chart.

18. Switch to the Word document and note the linked updated chart object.

19. On page one of the letter, note the embedded worksheet that did not change with the update. Delete the original worksheet.

20. Insert the worksheet on page one as a linked object.

21. Switch to the Word document and size the chart so that it extends to the margins of the document.

22. Print one copy of SKICUR.

23. Close and save the Word file; name it **SKICUR**.

24. Close and save the Excel file; name it **CURRENCY**.

**HEMISPHERE** *Travel*

555 World Class Way
Burlington, VT
*Phone:* (802) 333-3333
*Fax:* (802) 222-2222
*E-mail:* hemtrav@wiz.com

Date


Ms. Wendy Ascend, President
Upson Downs Ski Club
224 Mountaintop Lane
Burlington, VT

Dear Ms. Ascend:

Thank you for your inquiry about group rates for European ski vacations.

We will be glad to present a seminar to your group on the premier European ski resorts
and the unique features of each.

Traveling to Europe can be very expensive.  After hearing our presentation, you will be
able to decide which vacation best suits your travel and economic needs.  As a sample of
our services, note the table below analyzing ski rental charges with current foreign
exchange rates.

SKIS, POLES AND BOOTS RENTAL

| COUNTRY | SKI RENTAL US DOLLAR | COUNTRY CURRENCY | FOREIGN EXCHANGE | RENTAL IN FOREIGN CURRENCY |
|---|---|---|---|---|
| Austria | 27.00 | Schilling | 11.87 | 320.49 |
| France | 28.00 | Franc | 5.70 | 159.60 |
| Italy | 13.00 | Lira | 1675.74 | 21784.62 |
| Switzerland | 37.00 | Franc | 1.47 | 54.39 |

Upson Downs Ski Club
Page 2

When the ski rental rates are charted, as shown below, you can see where your dollar buys more.

← Insert chart here

Our Leisure Travel Department is available for consultation from 9 a.m. to 7 p.m., 7 days a week.  We look forward to working closely with your group.

Sincerely,


Avi Lanch, Vice President
Leisure Travel Department

av/yo

# Exercise 5

- Office Links
- Export an Access Database to an Excel
- Copy Images from the Internet

## NOTES

### Office Links

- The Office Links button on the Access toolbar provides easy linking capabilities with an Access database and MS Word or MS Excel. Note the illustration of the Office Links button on the Access toolbar and drop down list of Office Links.

  *Access Database Toolbar (Office Links Button)*

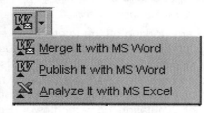

### Export an Access Database to Excel

- You may wish to use an Excel workbook to summarize and analyze information saved in an Access database. One method of accomplishing this is to export, or send, data from Access to Excel. Use Exporting if you wish to create a new workbook file with the database data or with part of a database table.

- To export an Access database to Excel, use the Office Links button and the Analyze It With MS Excel option. Analyze It With MS Excel will save and export the new file into Excel and open the new file.

- To export a table from Access, using the menu, select the Access table, then select the File, Save As/ Export commands. In the Save As dialog box, click To an External File or Database, and click OK. Select the Excel format, the drive or folder for the file, and select Save Formatted to preserve data formats. Then, switch to Excel to open the new file. As discussed, all these steps can be accomplished with the Office Links button.

- The Analyze It With MS Excel command may also be accessed by clicking the Tools, Office Links menus.

- Once the file is exported or output to Excel, you can work with the file as an Excel file. The column headings are the field names you used in the database and may be edited or changed in the Excel format.

### Copy Images from the Internet

- You may wish to insert a graphic image into a file that is not included in the Microsoft Clip Art Gallery. There are sites that provide public domain (free) images that you can use in your files. Image files can be cartoons, icons, art, photographs, or maps that can be copied and pasted to your document. Locate the object you wish to copy, select and copy the object, switch to your document and paste the object. Microsoft Office applications accept image files in .PCX or .BMP format. Files that are in .GIF format may be saved in one of those formats so that they can be pasted into Office documents.

In this exercise, Jane's Boutique would like to analyze the data in the Stock table in its inventory database. You will output the database to an Excel file and change the format of the data for presentation and analysis purposes. You will copy an image will be copied from the Internet to use to enhance the report.

# EXERCISE DIRECTIONS

1. Click the Open a Document button on the Shortcut Bar.

2. Open 🖴 **JANESHOP**, or open 💾 **05JANSHOP.MDB** which will bring you into Access.

3. Select the STOCK table, but do not open it.

   ✓ *If the Database toolbar is not displayed, select View, Toolbars and the Database toolbar.*

4. On the Access Database toolbar, click the Office Links drop-down arrow and select Analyze It With MS Excel.

   ✓ *The table will be output to Excel and will be opened as an Excel file.*

5. Make the following changes to the file in Excel:

   a. Insert five rows above the table to create room for a title and subtitle.

   b. Enter the following worksheet titles in cell A2:
   JANE'S BOUTIQUE
   INVENTORY - MARCH 31, 199-

   c. Format the titles for Metro font, 16 point, bold.

   d. Retype the column headings in uppercase letters.

   e. Size the columns to fit the longest entry.

   f. Insert a new column after the Color column.

   g. Cut and paste the Date Ordered column to the new column.

   h. Adjust the date format in Date Ordered column, if necessary.

   i. Insert a new column after J13 and enter the title TOTAL.

   j. Insert a new column after the PRICE column and title it VALUATION.

   k. Format the column headers to be consistent in shading (use the Format Painter).

   l. Find the total number of items in stock for each item in the TOTAL column.

   m. Find the Valuation of the inventory for each item by multiplying the Total number of items by the unit price.

   n. Format the Valuation data for currency.

   o. Skip one line below the table and enter the label TOTAL.

   p. Find the total Valuation of the inventory.

6. Use the Internet or the DDC CD-ROM simulation to locate, copy, and insert an image of a flower.

   a. Sign on to your Internet provider.
   **OR**

   • To access the DDC Internet simulation, click **Go**, **Open** on the Web toolbar.

   • Type **C:\DDCPUB\OFF97INT.IMR**. (Be sure that the simulation has been installed on your hard drive. If files are on a drive other than C, replace C with the correct letter.)

   • Click **OK** to launch the simulation.

   • Select **Exercise 5: Clipart Search**.

   b. Use the Yahoo search engine to search on the words "clipart collection."

   ✓ *You may use other search methods. The Clip Art Collection has Theme Specific Clipart.*

   c. If you are working off the Internet, save the image of a flower, a camelia or tulip, using a .BMP or .PCX file type. (These formats can be selected from Save as Type drop-down list in the Save dialog box.) Or, if you working off the Internet Simulation, copy the flower (Edit, Copy).

   d. Exit from your browser and disconnect from your service provider, or exit the DDC Internet simulation.

7. In the worksheet, place your cursor at K1.

8. If you saved the flower as a .BMP or .PCX, use Insert, Picture, From file to insert the image file into the worksheet. Or, if you copied the flower out of the simulation, paste the image into the spreadsheet (Edit, Paste).

9. Select the image and size it to fit in the K1:L6 range.

10. AutoFormat worksheet columns and data to the Classic 2 style.

11. Format the background color of rows 1:5 to gray to match the worksheet.

12. Save the file as **STOCKEX**.

13. Print one copy of the worksheet to fit on the page.

14. Close all files.

| | A | B | C | D | E | F | G | H | I | J | K | L |
|---|---|---|---|---|---|---|---|---|---|---|---|---|
| 1 | | | | | | | | | | | | |
| 2 | **JANE'S BOUTIQUE** | | | | | | | | | | | |
| 3 | **INVENTORY - MARCH 31, 199-** | | | | | | | | | | | |
| 4 | | | | | | | | | | | | |
| 5 | | | | | | | | | | | | |
| 6 | **STYLE** | **TYPE** | **COLOR** | **DATEORD** | J5 | J7 | J9 | J11 | J13 | **TOTAL** | **PRICE** | **VALUATION** |
| 7 | J7455 | JACKET | BLACK | 9/23/96 | 23 | 32 | 21 | 32 | 32 | 140 | $50.99 | $7,138.60 |
| 8 | J8510 | SKIRT | BLACK | 10/18/96 | 4 | 4 | 2 | 4 | 2 | 16 | $26.00 | $416.00 |
| 9 | P232 | SKIRT | BLACK | 2/10/97 | 5 | 5 | 5 | 5 | 7 | 27 | $29.50 | $796.50 |
| 10 | P987 | SKIRT | BLACK | 2/10/97 | 3 | 4 | 5 | 6 | 7 | 25 | $30.75 | $768.75 |
| 11 | J3254 | DRESS | BLUE | 7/16/96 | 4 | 15 | 16 | 3 | 14 | 52 | $61.99 | $3,223.48 |
| 12 | J3290 | DRESS | BLUE | 11/17/96 | 23 | 32 | 33 | 23 | 12 | 123 | $56.88 | $6,996.24 |
| 13 | J2121 | SWEATER | BROWN | 2/7/97 | 40 | 4 | 6 | 6 | 7 | 63 | $29.99 | $1,889.37 |
| 14 | J4230 | PANTS | GRAY | 12/12/96 | 24 | 4 | 6 | 12 | 13 | 59 | $49.99 | $2,949.41 |
| 15 | J5555 | BLOUSE | GREEN | 6/19/96 | 13 | 32 | 45 | 6 | 9 | 105 | $19.99 | $2,098.95 |
| 16 | J7654 | SUIT | GREEN | 9/18/96 | 12 | 17 | 34 | 12 | 12 | 87 | $85.50 | $7,438.50 |
| 17 | P287 | JACKET | NAVY | 2/10/97 | 7 | 9 | 11 | 14 | 14 | 55 | $75.50 | $4,152.50 |
| 18 | P998 | SKIRT | NAVY | 2/10/97 | 2 | 4 | 4 | 5 | 7 | 22 | $35.40 | $778.80 |
| 19 | J7699 | SUIT | NAVY | 2/7/97 | 12 | 10 | 10 | 8 | 7 | 47 | $110.10 | $5,174.70 |
| 20 | P999 | VEST | NAVY | 2/10/97 | 6 | 6 | 7 | 7 | 7 | 33 | $25.50 | $841.50 |
| 21 | J2123 | SWEATER | OLIVE | 2/7/97 | 5 | 5 | 6 | 7 | 9 | 32 | $35.75 | $1,144.00 |
| 22 | J5550 | BLOUSE | ORANGE | 8/21/96 | 12 | 24 | 43 | 7 | 4 | 90 | $23.99 | $2,159.10 |
| 23 | J5532 | SKIRT | PURPLE | 10/19/96 | 12 | 21 | 32 | 5 | 21 | 91 | $23.67 | $2,153.97 |
| 24 | P214 | BLOUSE | RED | 2/10/97 | 5 | 6 | 8 | 9 | 9 | 37 | $25.50 | $943.50 |
| 25 | J3290 | DRESS | RED | 10/8/96 | 17 | 21 | 35 | 32 | 18 | 123 | $48.25 | $5,934.75 |
| 26 | P765 | JACKET | RED | 2/10/97 | 7 | 9 | 11 | 11 | 11 | 49 | $60.99 | $2,988.51 |
| 27 | J9090 | VEST | RED | 2/7/97 | 23 | 22 | 22 | 25 | 25 | 117 | $20.00 | $2,340.00 |
| 28 | J4309 | PANTS | TAN | 11/17/96 | 2 | 12 | 12 | 4 | 4 | 34 | $44.50 | $1,513.00 |
| 29 | J5540 | BLOUSE | WHITE | 11/12/96 | 5 | 6 | 6 | 4 | 3 | 24 | $18.59 | $446.16 |
| 30 | J3317 | DRESS | WHITE | 1/7/96 | 3 | 6 | 7 | 3 | 4 | 23 | $62.65 | $1,440.95 |
| 31 | J7676 | SUIT | WHITE | 8/21/96 | 9 | 6 | 5 | 25 | 7 | 52 | $106.99 | $5,563.48 |
| 32 | | | | | | | | | | | | |
| 33 | | **TOTAL** | | | | | | | | | | $71,290.72 |
| 34 | | | | | | | | | | | | |
| 35 | | | | | | | | | | | | |

# KEYSTROKES

## EXPORT A TABLE FROM ACCESS

*Data will appear in default format of destination*

1. Open the database.
2. Select the table to be exported.
3. Click **File** .............................. Alt + F
4. Click **Save As/Export** ...................... A
5. Select the data destination:

   **To an External File or Database** ..... E

   **OR**

   **Within the Current Database as**...... C

   *(If you select this option, you may type the new title in the new name box.)*
6. Click [ OK ] ............................. Enter
7. In the **Save as** type dialog box, select desired format
8. In the **Save in** dialog box, select the drive or the folder to export to................. ↓
9. Enter the filename to export to
10. Click **Export**

## ANALYZE AN ACCESS TABLE WITH EXCEL

1. Open the database.
2. Select the table to be exported.
3. Click **Office Links** button ................ [icon]
   on the Database toolbar.
   **OR**
   a. Click **Tools**........................ Alt + T
   b. Click **Office Links** ........................ L
   c. Select **Analyze It with MS Excel** .. A
4. Choose **Analyze It with MS Excel**.

## IMPORT A PICTURE FROM A FILE

**In Excel:**

1. Place cursor in cell to receive image.
2. Click **Insert** ........................... Alt + I
3. Click **Picture** ................................... P
4. Click **From file**............................... F
5. Select directory and file
6. Click **Insert** ........................... Alt + R

# Exercise 6

- **Merge an Access Table with a Word Main Document**
- **Mail Merge** ■ **Use Internet Locator/Map Sites**

*Mail Merge Toolbar*

First record | Previous record | Mail merge | Check for errors | Merge to printer | Find record

Insert Merge Field ▾ | Insert Word Field ▾ | 《 》 | |◀ | ◀ | 1 | ▶ | ▶| | | | | | | |

View merged Data | Next record | Last record | Merge to new document | Mail merge | Edit record source

# NOTES

## Merge an Access Table with a Word Main Document

■ Database information from Access can be merged with a main document created in Word. This process is automated with the mail merge feature. This feature is covered in the advanced lesson Merge on the accompanying CD-ROM. Mail merge may also be accomplished using data from an Excel worksheet or a Word table.

## Mail Merge

■ The first step in the process is to set up the main document in Word to accept information from the Access database. Use the Tools menu in Word and select Mail Merge to access the Mail Merge Helper Dialog box as shown below:

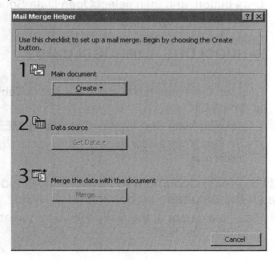

■ As you will note below, the three steps in the procedure are to create the main document, identify the source of the variable data, and merge the data and document files.

- First, create the main document in Word. An open document may be used by selecting the Active Window option in the form letter dialog box; otherwise, select the Create New option. After creating a mail merge document, the Mail Merge toolbar displays.

- Second, identify the source of the data as an Access table and select the specific table. The field names used in the Word main document must be the same as those used in the Access database. When the database is specified as the data source, the fields become available in a drop-down list as by clicking the Insert Merge Field bar on the Mail Merge toolbar. Insert the field names from the drop-down list into your main document. Use Edit the Main Document if the field names do not agree. If possible, the database should be planned using the commonly used titles to expedite the merge feature.

- Third, select Merge from the dialog box after all the fields are entered into the letter.

■ When you complete a merge, the information from the selected Access table merges into the form letter in the locations you specified for each field. A new document is created for each record in the database containing personal information in the field locations. Each letter should be separated by a section break, and the form letter is intact for future use.

■ You may start the merge operation from Access using the Merge It option in the Tools, Office Links command or by using the Merge it option from the Office Links button on the Database toolbar. When you click the Merge It button, the Microsoft Mail Merge Wizard appears which will guide you through the merge procedure, and transfer you to Word to complete the main document.

### Use Locator/Map Sites

■ The Internet provides sites that assist you in locating information from business and telephone directories, as well as National Yellow Pages. Once you enter a street address, many of these sites can provide door-to-door driving directions with maps for metropolitan areas.

---

*In this exercise, Nadine Ramaz, the President of the Users' Group, is sending a letter to the membership to inform them of a convention using a membership database. You will search the Internet for locator information to provide a map and locate tourist attractions. You will use this information to edit the form letter, which will then be merged with the database to create a letter for each member.*

*IMPORTANT: Before you do this exercise, it is recommended that you do the Word Merge lesson included on the accompanying DDC CD-ROM.*

---

# EXERCISE DIRECTIONS

1. Click the Open Office Document button on the Shortcut bar.

2. Keyboard the letter on page 474, or open ⊟**06NYMEET.DOC**, which opens in Word.

3. Enter today's date where indicated.

4. Add the paragraph as shown in the illustration.

5. Save the document as **NYMEET**. Do not close the file.

6. Create a main document from this file by selecting Tools, Mail Merge. Select Main document, Create and select the Active window option.

7. Select the data source by doing the following:

   a. In the Mail Merge Helper box, select the Get Data button, and then select Open Data Source.

   b. Select files of Type: MS Access Database.

   c. Select the correct directory to open 📠**HUGCLUB** or ⊟**06HUGCLU.MDB**.

   d. Click Open.

   e. Click on the Table tab and the Members Table, and click OK.

   f. Select Edit Main Document. Choose NYMEET.
      ✓ *The Main Merge toolbar appears, if it has not displayed before now.*

8. Edit the main document to insert merge fields to match the database by doing the following:

   a. Place the cursor at the first position for variable data (the Title field).

b. Select the first line of the address and click on the Insert Merge Field button.

c. Choose the field for Title (Titl), and enter a space.

d. Repeat until all the fields are inserted for the first and second lines of the address.

e. Since there is no State field in the database, enter the City field, a comma, CA (for California), and then the Zip field. Be sure to enter spaces and punctuation where necessary.

f. Insert fields into the proper locations in the salutation.

9. Use the Internet or the DDC CD-ROM simulation to locate a map of the vicinity of the meeting. Use the map to find and list tourist locations in the letter.

a. Sign on to your Internet provider.

   **OR**

   - To access the DDC Internet simulation, click **Go**, **Open** on the Web toolbar.
   - Type **C:\DDCPUB\OFF97INT.IMR**. (Be sure that the simulation has been installed on your hard drive. If files are on a drive other than C, replace C with the correct letter.)
   - Click **OK** to launch the simulation.
   - Select **Exercise 6: City Maps**.

b. Go to http://www.vicinity.com, which is a web site that provides locator/map services.

c. You may use other web sites that produce the same information.

d. Select MapBlast and Locate to display a detailed street map for the vicinity of 275 Madison Avenue, New York, NY,10016.

e. Copy the names of five tourist attractions in the vicinity.

f. Exit from your browser and disconnect from your service provider, or exit the DDC Internet simulation.

10. Use the information from the map to list five tourist attractions in New York in the vicinity of the meeting address.

11. Save changes to **NYMEET**.

12. Merge the files by doing the following:

a. Select Tools, Mail Merge.

b. In the Mail Merge Helper box, select the Merge button.

c. In the Merge dialog box, select the Merge button.

✓ *The default setting is to create a new document consisting of the merged letters.*

13. Save the new document as **NYHUG**.

14. Save and close all documents in Word

# KEYSTROKES

## ATTACH DATA SOURCE

1. Follow procedures under Set Up Main Document, Word, Lesson 9.

2. Click **Tools** ......................... Alt + T

3. Click **Mail Merge** ......................... R

   ✓ *Mail Merge Dialog Box appears.*

4. Click **Get Data** ...................... Alt + G

   ✓ *This option is unavailable if active Word document has not been set up as a mail merge main document.*

5. Select **Open Data Source** ............. O

6. Follow procedures to Open a File.

7. Select the Table tab and the table to be used.

8. Click ⌷ OK ⌷ ......................... Enter

**Nadine Ramaz**
**9012 Wilshire Boulevard**
**Beverly Hills, Ca  90210**
**(213)555-2211**

Today's date

«TITL» «FIRST» «LAST»
«ADDRESS»
«CITY», CA  «ZIP»

Dear «TITL» «LAST»:

As you know, this year the Users' Group Convention will be held on April 15-17 in New York City—the capital of the world!

Our meetings will be held at 275 Madison Avenue, in the heart of midtown New York.  As you can see from the enclosed map, there are numerous tourist attractions within walking distance of our meeting location.

On April 16 in the afternoon, we will have time to visit one or two sites. From the attractions listed below, select two that interest you most by checking them on the registration form which is on the back of this month's newsletter.

1.
2.
3.
4.
5.

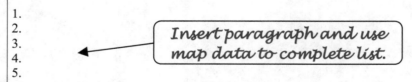

*Insert paragraph and use map data to complete list.*

Be sure to send in your registration form as early as possible.  We look forward to a very exciting convention and to your participation.

Sincerely,


Nadine Ramaz
President

Enclosure

# ■ Import/Export an Outline ■ Link an Excel Worksheet

## NOTES

### Import/Export an Outline

- An outline created in Word may be used as the text in a PowerPoint presentation. From PowerPoint, you may import the outline by converting the file format to a presentation file. You must close the Word outline before you can import it. You may also export, or send, an outline from Word by saving the file in RTF (Rich Text Format) so that you can open and use it in PowerPoint.

- In a Word outline, which can be viewed in Outline View, heading levels provide the structure for the data. When you import the outline into PowerPoint, each Heading 1 level becomes a separate slide. The other levels are shown as subtopics on the slide. The formatting or styles in the Word outline will be imported into PowerPoint. See the illustration below:

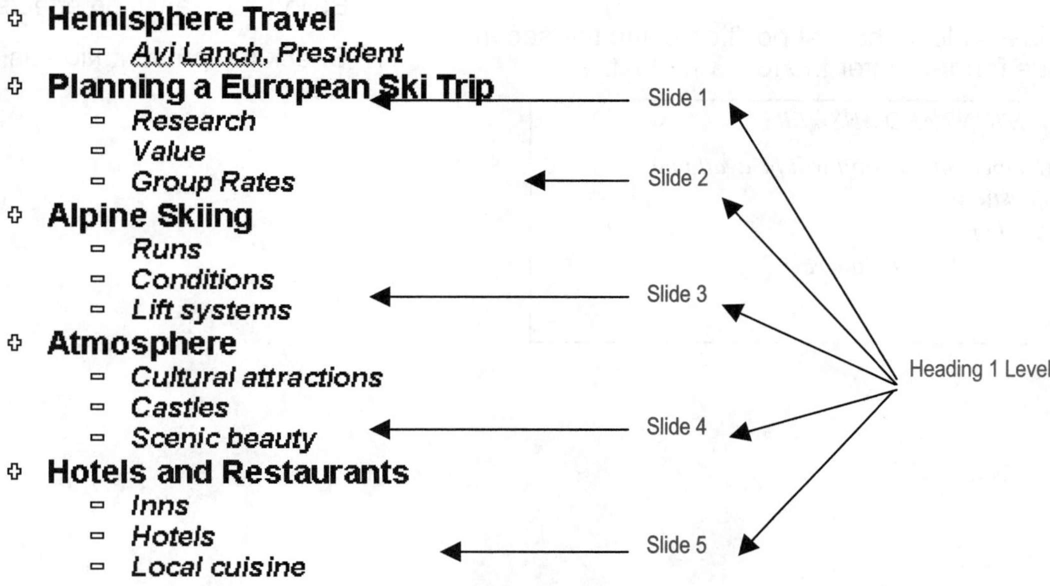

- You may edit and enhance the imported outline within PowerPoint. Apply a template to the outline to give it a professional appearance.

### Link an Excel Worksheet

- You can link data from Word or another application to PowerPoint so that the PowerPoint slide will update if the linked file is changed. You may link or embed charts into PowerPoint as well. As previously discussed, when linking Word and Excel files, the Copy, Paste Special, Paste Link options are selected to link application files in PowerPoint.

&#10010; **Hemisphere Travel**
&#9643; *Avi Lanch, President*
&#10010; **Planning a European Ski Trip** &rarr; Slide 1
&#9643; *Research*
&#9643; *Value*
&#9643; *Group Rates* &larr; Slide 2
&#10010; **Alpine Skiing**
&#9643; *Runs*
&#9643; *Conditions*
&#9643; *Lift systems* &larr; Slide 3
&#10010; **Atmosphere**
&#9643; *Cultural attractions*
&#9643; *Castles*
&#9643; *Scenic beauty* &larr; Slide 4
&#10010; **Hotels and Restaurants**
&#9643; *Inns*
&#9643; *Hotels*
&#9643; *Local cuisine* &larr; Slide 5

Heading 1 Levels

> In this exercise, You will import an outline created in Word for Hemisphere Travel into PowerPoint using two methods. You will enhance the slides, add a chart, and apply a template style to the presentation. You will research additional data for the presentation using the Internet.
>
> IMPORTANT: To do this exercise, you will need to use data files provided on the CD-ROM.

# EXERCISE DIRECTIONS

1. To import an outline:
   a. Open PowerPoint by using the Start, Programs, Microsoft PowerPoint selections.
   b. Click the Open an existing presentation option and click OK.
   c. Click All Outlines from the List Files of Types list in the Open dialog box.
      ✓ Files with a .DOC extension may be opened using the Outline type.
   d. Open 🖫07SKIOUT.DOC.
      ✓ The outline is converted to a presentation and imported into PowerPoint in outline view.
   e. Click Slide Sorter view to see the outline as slides.

2. To apply a template design to the slides:
   a. Click Format, Apply Design.
   b. Select High Voltage.
   c. Click Apply.

3. Edit the first slide; add the following text:

   ★ Presentation to:
   – Upson Downs Ski Club
   – Burlington, VT

4. Add a slide in the last position using the second slide format. Enter the following text:

   QUESTIONS AND ANSWERS

   ★ Members of our staff will be available for questions.
   ✍ Brochures
       ✍ Sample Itineraries
       ✍ Slides

5. Add a new slide after slide 9 with a Title only format.

6. Enter "Price Comparison Data" as the title.

7. Link an Excel chart to the slide:
   a. Click the Open Office Document icon on Shortcut bar.
   b. Open 🖫07CURREN.XLS, which opens in Excel.
   c. Go to the Chart1 sheet.
   d. Select and copy the chart showing comparison of ski rental prices.
   e. Switch to PowerPoint by clicking the button on the taskbar.
   f. In Slide view, Edit, Paste Special, Paste Link the chart on the new slide.
   g. Adjust the size of the chart to fit the slide.

8. Save the file as SKIOUTPP.

9. Do not close PowerPoint.

10. Switch to Slide Sorter view and add desired Build and Transition effects.

11. Check the presentation using the Slide Show view.

12. Use the Internet or the DDC CD-ROM simulation to research information about Bressanone/Brixen and Innsbruck to assist in your presentation. Enter the information on the speaker notes for the Bressanone/Brixen, Italy and Innsbruck, Austria slides.

   a. Sign on to your Internet provider.

      **OR**

- To access the DDC Internet simulation, click **Go**, **Open** on the Web toolbar.
- Type **C:\DDCPUB\OFF97INT.IMR**. (Be sure that the simulation has been installed on your hard drive. If files are on a drive other than C, replace C with the correct letter.)
- Click **OK** to launch the simulation.
- Select **Exercise 7: Skiing Europe**.

   b. Use the Yahoo search engine to search on the words "ski Europe" or use the address http://www.ski.europe.com.

      ✓ *You may use other search methods.*

   c. Use the Ski Europe site to research the information for each bullet (Elevation, Vertical Drop, Lifts, Trails).

   d. Write down the desired information.

   e. Exit from your browser and disconnect from your service provider, or exit the DDC Internet simulation.

13. Use the information to enter appropriate data on the speaker notes for slides 7 and 8.

14. Print speaker notes pages for slides 7 and 8.

15. Save and close all files.

## Exercise 8
- Hyperlinks
- Create Hyperlinks in Word
- Hyperlink to the Internet

# NOTES

### Hyperlinks

- A **hyperlink** is a "hot spot," or shortcut, that allows you to jump to another location. For example, by clicking on a hyperlink, you can jump to another file on your hard drive, your network, or to an Internet address. You do not have to be on the Internet to use hyperlinks.

- A hyperlink is a field that includes the path to the file, and may include switch codes for options during the link process. The format for the field code for a hyperlink is:

  {HYPERLINK"filename"[switches]}.

  You may either enter the field code to create a hyperlink, or use drag and drop to create a hyperlink between Microsoft files. Hyperlinks are represented by display text—which is usually blue and underlined. When you rest the pointer over a hyperlink the pointer changes to a hand.

  For example, suppose you wish to create a document that contains a hyperlink to an Excel worksheet. Samples of report text with the hyperlink code and report text with display text are illustrated below:

  Text with hyperlink field code: "The summary of production data shows an interesting trend. Click {HYPERLINK"C:\DATA\08TOYS.XLS"} for quarterly data."

  Text with display text: "The summary of production data shows an interesting trend. Click 1997 Production Report for quarterly data."

  Notice that in the second sample, the hyperlink field code was edited and replaced by display text that fits into your report. When you click the underlined blue display text, you will jump to the 08TOYS Excel file.

### Create Hyperlinks in Word

- You can create a hyperlink by clicking the Insert Hyperlink button or clicking Insert, Hyperlink. Enter the file or URL path and name in the dialog box, as illustrated below. You can use the Browse button to search for the file. You can also enter a named range or specific location in the file. The filename you select must be closed and saved. If you wish to link a chart, you should name the range the chart is in and enter it in the Named location in file box.

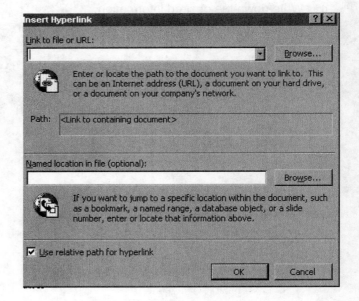

- You can create a hyperlink by dragging selected text, graphics, slides, ranges, or database objects from one Microsoft Office application to another. When dragging text or graphics to Word from another Office application, Word will create the hyperlink field entry.

- You can create a hyperlink by copying the destination data and using the Edit, Paste As Hyperlink commands or by dragging and dropping the destination data. To create a hyperlink in Word using the drag and drop method:

  - Display both files on the screen. Use Window, Arrange All if the files are both Word files.

  - ✓ Note: Use the taskbar shortcut menu to display files from different applications, as discussed in Exercise 1.

  - Select the text, graphic, range, or other item in the destination document.

  - Use the right mouse to drag the selection to the hyperlink location. Release the mouse.

  - Click Create Hyperlink Here on the shortcut menu.

- Editing a hyperlink presents a problem since clicking on the text jumps you to the location specified. To edit a hyperlink for display text, click just to the left of the text to edit, then drag the mouse across the text until it is selected, and then edit the text. You can also right-click on the hyperlink text, display the shortcut menu, and select Hyperlink, Select Hyperlink to select the hyperlink and enter the display text.

### Hyperlink to the Internet

- If you are connected to the Internet, you can click on hyperlinks to Internet addresses and automatically jump to your service provider and to that location when you are online. When you enter an Internet address in a Word document, it automatically formats as a hyperlink; the text is blue, underlined text. The mouse pointer becomes a hand and the Internet address displays in a box when you point to the hyperlink.

---

*In this exercise, the Tickle Toy Company is creating a report discussing its Production for the Eastern Division. They would like to include hyperlinks to a worksheet and charts in Excel and to the Internet.*

---

# EXERCISE DIRECTIONS

1. Click the Open Office Document button on the Shortcut bar.

2. Keyboard the report on page 481, or open 🖫08TICKLE.DOC, which will bring you into Word.

3. Note the bracketed areas in the illustration and in the document that indicate the location for hyperlinks.

4. Click the Open Office Document icon on the Shortcut Bar.

5. Open ⌨08TOYS.XLS, or open 🖫08TOYS.XLS, which will bring you into Excel.

6. Switch to the Pie Chart sheet and select the entire sheet. (Select the box in the left corner of the worksheet.)

7. Name the range: PIE.

8. Switch to the Line-Column Chart sheet and select the entire sheet.

9. Name the range: COMBIN

10. Switch back to the Datasheet.

11. Save and close the file; name it **TOYS**.

12. In the Word document, go to the first hyperlink location and delete the bracketed information.

13. Insert a hyperlink to the TOYS worksheet as follows:
    - Click Insert.
    - Click Hyperlink
    - Enter TOYS in the Link to File box or Browse to locate the file.
    - Click OK. A blue underlined hyperlink code field will appear.

14. Edit the hyperlink field code for display text as follows:
    - Right-click the hyperlink code.
    - Select Hyperlink, Select Hyperlink to highlight the hyperlink text.
    - Type Production Data.
    - Click on another location to stop display text entry.
    - ✓ *The blue underlined display text replaces the hyperlink code.*

15. Move to the second hyperlink location and insert a hyperlink for the Pie Chart in the TOYS worksheet. In the Named location in file box, enter PIE as the named range location.

16. Select the hyperlink field code and change the display text to "Pie Chart."

17. Move to the third hyperlink location and insert a hyperlink for the Line-Column chart in the TOYS worksheet. In the Named location in file box, enter COMBIN as the named range location.

18. Select the hyperlink field code and change the display text to "Comparison Chart."

19. In the last hyperlink location, enter the Internet address http://www.toy-tma.com to refer to a web site prepared by the Toy Manufacturers of America.

20. Select the hyperlink and select the text and change it to Our Web Site.

21. Check the hyperlinks.
    - Click the first hyperlink.
    - The Toys worksheet will display.
    - Close the Worksheet and select the Word file from the taskbar.
    - Repeat this for all hyperlinks except for the Internet connection.

22. If you have an Internet connection, select the Internet hyperlink. You will be connected to your service provider, where the site will be entered as the address.
    **OR**
    - To access the DDC Internet simulation, click **Go**, **Open** on the Web toolbar.
    - **Type C:\DDCPUB\OFF97INT.IMR.** (Be sure that the simulation has been installed on your hard drive. If files are on a drive other than C, replace C with the correct letter.)
    - Click **OK** to launch the simulation.
    - Select **Exercise 8: Toys.**

23. Exit from your browser and disconnect from your service provider, or exit the DDC Internet simulation.

24. Close and save the file; name it **TICKLE**.

# KEYSTROKES

### INSERT A HYPERLINK

1. Place your cursor on the link location.
2. Click **Insert** ............................. `Alt`+`I`
3. Click **Hyperlink** ............................... `I`
4. In the **Link to File or URL**: box, enter filename or URL .............. *filename*

**OR**

Click **Browse** to locate file ...... `Alt`+`B`

5. If desired, in **Named location in file**, ..................... `Alt`+`N` enter range name or bookmark.
6. Click **OK** ..................................... `Enter`

### EDIT AND SELECT HYPERLINK TEXT

1. Right-click hyperlink text.
2. Click **Hyperlink** ............................... `H`
3. Click **Select Hyperlink** .................... `S`
4. Type display text.

# TICKLE TOY COMPANY
## PRODUCTION ANALYSIS-EASTERN DIVISION
### First Quarter – 199-

We will be looking at our production capacities in the Eastern Division with an eye to improving efficiencies and increasing capacities.

Our Eastern Division consists of plants in Delaware, Georgia, and Virginia. The plant in Reston, Virginia is our largest in this division and its production data reflects that fact. Our Newark, Delaware plant is our next largest plant and the data is unsatisfactory in comparison to that from Marietta, Georgia, our smallest plant. Click on **<Enter hyperlink to TOYS.xls, display text "Production Data">** for more information.

The product lines manufactured at Eastern Division plants are Toys, Games and Stuffed Toys. This year our marketing department has succeeded in promoting our Toy line, especially the Tickle Tot Dolls. We have geared up our production capacity in our other divisions to meet the demand. The primary product of all Eastern Division plants has been Toys. Click on **<Enter hyperlink to TOYS.xls, PIE named range, display text "PIE">** to see the components of our Reston, Virginia production.

In order to improve the efficiency and output of the Newark, Delaware plant, we have had the plant under study by the Meister Efficiency Company. We have hired Mr. Tony Playsome to implement their recommendations as follows:

- Bring production equipment into good repair.

- Set manufacturing goals and develop production team involvement.

- Institute Quality Control circles within the production area.

- Upgrade employee facilities.

- Establish standards for the workplace and apply them evenly.

We are looking forward to improvement in the second quarter this year.

The overall production of the Eastern Division was satisfactory, and we expect that our Newark, Delaware plant will begin to show improvement. Click on **<Enter hyperlink to TOYS.xls, COMBIN named range, display text "Combination Chart">** to view the production volume for the Eastern Division. Our Eastern Division summary shows that our employees have continued to give us excellent products in varied markets.

You can view the Web site prepared by the Toy Manufacturers of America, of which we are members, by clicking on **<Enter hyperlink to http://www.toy-tma.com, display text "Our Web Site">**.

## Exercise 9

- ■ Export a PowerPoint Slide or File into a Word Document
- ■ Import a PowerPoint Presentation into a Word Document
- ■ Internet Research

# NOTES

■ You can send your PowerPoint notes and individual slide images to a Word document, or you can include a complete PowerPoint presentation in a Word document.

## Export a PowerPoint Slide or File into a Word Document

■ To insert a PowerPoint slide into a Word document, open PowerPoint, display Slide Sorter view and select the slide to be exported. Click Copy. Then, open the Word document and click Paste. The PowerPoint slide will insert into the Word document.

■ To link the slide so that any changes made in the Presentation file will automatically update the inserted slide in the Word document, click Paste Special (instead of Paste). In the Paste Special dialog box that follows, select Paste link and highlight Microsoft PowerPoint Slide Object.

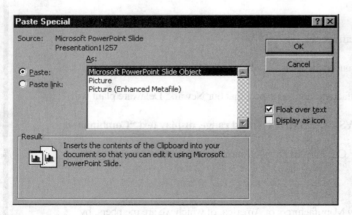

■ You can also send a PowerPoint file to a Word document by opening the PowerPoint file, then selecting File, Send To, Microsoft Word. In the Write-up dialog box that follows, select how you wish the PowerPoint slides to format once they

are imported into Word. You must also select the Paste or Paste link option.

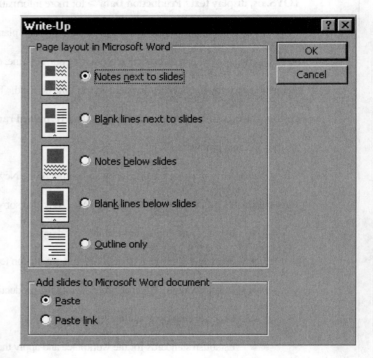

## Import a PowerPoint Presentation into a Word Document

■ You can import an entire PowerPoint presentation into a Word document by inserting it as an object. Word allows you to view the presentation, even if PowerPoint is not installed. To insert a Presentation while in Word, Place your cursor at the point of insertion. Select Insert, Object, and click the Create from File tab. In the Object dialog box, enter the Presentation file name, or click Browse and select the presentation.

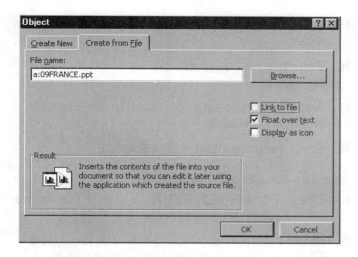

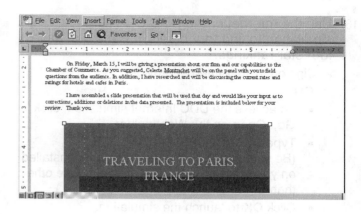

- Only the first slide of the presentation will appear in the document. You can size the slide can be sized to fit better in the document. To view the presentation, double-click the object. A full-screen view of the first slide will appear. Click to display the next and subsequent slides. When the last slide is clicked, you will be returned to the Word document. Note the illustration below of an embedded presentation.

## Internet Research

- If you access foreign Web Sites, you may find that resulting information is in the language of that country. However, many foreign Web Sites provide versions in several languages. Select the British flag icon to display the English version of the data.

---

*In this exercise, Claudine Vilmay of Allez-Vous Travel Consultants, is continuing to prepare for her presentation on French travel. Slide text will be used to create a Word document for prospective clients. In addition, she will use the Internet to research three or four-star hotels and interesting restaurants in Paris. The information will be added to the presentation and inserted into a letter about the travel seminar.*

*IMPORTANT: To do this exercise, you will need to use data files provided on the CD-ROM.*

---

# EXERCISE DIRECTIONS

**Export a Slide:**

1. Click the Open Office Document button on the Shortcut bar.

2. Open the Word file 🖫**09MEMO.DOC** or create the memorandum as shown in Illustration A.

3. Insert the additional text after the second paragraph.

4. Click the Open Document icon on the Shortcut bar.

5. Open the PowerPoint file 🖫**09FRANCE.PPT**.

6. In Slide Sorter view, select the last slide.

7. Copy the slide, switch to the memorandum in Word, and paste the slide to the location indicated.

8. Click on the slide to select it and size it appropriately for the memorandum.

9. Save the file as **MEMO**.

10. Close the file.

11. In Slide Sorter view of PowerPoint note that the Restaurants and Hotels slides need to be completed.

12. Edit the Restaurant slide and change the title to Cafes.

13. Use the Internet or the DDC CD-ROM simulation to find four hotels in Paris that have four star rankings.
    a. Sign on to your Internet provider.
       **OR**
       - To access the DDC Internet simulation, click **Go**, **Open** on the Web toolbar.
       - Type **C:\DDCPUB\OFF97INT.IMR**. (Be sure that the simulation has been installed on your hard drive. If files are on a drive other than C, replace C with the correct letter.)
       - Click **OK** to launch the simulation.
       - Select **Exercise 9: Paris Hotel Search**.
    b. Search on Paris and hotels, or France and hotels, or The Paris Pages.
       ✓ You may use other search methods.
    c. View the sites that might provide a list of four star hotels in Paris.
    d. Select four hotels from these sites and note their names. DO NOT DISCONNECT.
14. Next, you will find five Paris cafes that have good reviews. To research Paris cafes:
    a. Search on Paris cafes, or The Paris Pages.
       ✓ You may use other search methods. Your provider may supply travel pages for all countries that can provide this information.
    b. View the sites that might provide a list of Paris cafes.
    c. Select five cafes from these sites and note their names.
    d. Exit from your browser and disconnect from your service provider, or exit the DDC Internet simulation

15. Enter the names of the four hotels on the Hotels slide.
16. Enter the names of the five cafes on the Cafes slide.
17. Add any additional information to the Speaker Notes for the slide.
18. Save the presentation as **FRANCE**.

**Embed a PowerPoint Presentation:**

19. Open 🖫**09APPROVE.DOC** or create the memo as indicated in Illustration B.
20. At the insertion point specified, use the Insert, Object, Create from File tab procedures to insert the **FRANCE.PPT** file as an embedded object in the memorandum.
21. Find the edge of the presentation slide, click on it, and size the slide to fit appropriately into the memorandum.
    ✓ The first slide of the presentation will appear on the memorandum.
22. Double-click the slide to view it on a full screen. Click to change, and review each slide.
23. Save the memorandum as **APPROVE**.
24. Print one copy.
25. Close all files in all applications.

# KEYSTROKES

### COPY A POWERPOINT SLIDE INTO WORD

1. Open PowerPoint Presentation.
2. Select slide to be copied in Slide Sorter view.
3. Click **Edit** .............. `Alt`+`E`
4. Click **Copy** .............. `C`
5. Open destination document in Word.
6. Place cursor on insertion point.
7. Click **Edit** .............. `Alt`+`E`
8. Click **Paste** .............. `P`

### IMPORT A POWERPOINT PRESENTATION INTO A WORD DOCUMENT

1. Open the Word document to receive the presentation.
2. Click **Insert** .............. `Alt`+`I`
3. Click **Object** .............. `O`
4. Select **Create from File** .............. `Alt`+`F`
5. Select directory and .............. `↵``↑` PowerPoint file to be imported.
6. Click the edge of the file to size.
   ✓ The first slide of the presentation will appear on the memorandum.

### VIEW AN EMBEDDED PRESENTATION

✓ The PowerPoint Viewer, a separate application in PowerPoint, must be loaded into PowerPoint so that the presentation may be viewed in Word without having PowerPoint loaded.

1. Double-click on the first slide of the embedded presentation.
2. Click slide to change to the next slide.
3. After the last slide, you are returned to the document.

**M E M O R A N D U M**

TO:     Celeste Montrachet, Guide

FROM:  Claudine Vilmay, Vice President

RE:     March 15 Presentation

DATE:  February 15, 199-

On Friday, March 15, we will be giving a presentation about French travel, our firm and our services to the Chamber of Commerce.  In our presentation, we will be discussing French travel, tourist attractions, hotels and restaurants and will provide time for questions from the audience.

Since this will be a large meeting, I hope you will be able to attend.  The members of the Chamber may be using a trip to France for their annual fundraiser.

Thank you for your assistance with this important project.

*Insert last slide before third paragraph.*

*Insert text: Note the list of services we will be discussing.*

**M E M O R A N D U M**

TO:     John LeByron, President

FROM:  Claudine Vilmay, Vice President

RE:     March 15 Presentation

DATE:  February 15, 199-

On Friday, March 15, I will be giving a presentation about our firm and our capabilities to the Chamber of Commerce. As you suggested, Celeste Montrachet will be on the panel with you to field questions from the audience. In addition, I have researched and will be discussing the current rates and ratings for hotels and cafes in Paris.

I have assembled a slide presentation that will be used that day and would like your input as to additions or deletions in the data presented.  The presentation is included below for your review.

Thank you.

*Insert presentation here.*

# Exercise 10    ■ Summary

*In this exercise, Michael Miller, of the college Finance department, is making a presentation about investing in Brazil to his fellow college professors. He would like to obtain input from Ms Washington, his investment advisor affiliate, who will assist him at the meeting. You will incorporate her suggestions into the presentation and use the Mail Merge procedure to send a memo to the college professors who will be attending the meeting. You will incorporate a slide into the memorandum.*

*IMPORTANT: Before you do this exercise, it is recommended that you do the Word Merge lesson included on the accompanying DDC CD-ROM.*

*Since this is a comprehensive exercise and it may take more than one work session, we are indicating locations in the problem where you might stop and resume the scenario at a later time. The ✋ symbol before a step number indicates that this section should not be started unless you have time to complete the segment.*

## EXERCISE DIRECTIONS

1. Click the Open Office Document button on the Shortcut bar.

2. Open 🖫**10SHOW.DOC** in Word or create the letter as indicated in Illustration A.

3. Click the Open Office Document button on the Shortcut bar.

4. Open 🖫**10BRAZIL.PPT** into PowerPoint and switch to outline view.

5. Copy the outline from PowerPoint into the Word document in the location indicated in the letter.
   ✓ *Adjust font size to 12 pt, if necessary.*

6. Insert an appropriate header on the second page of the letter.

7. Save the file as **SHOW**. Print one copy.

✋ 8. Close the file.

9. Click the Open Office Document button on the Shortcut bar.

10. Open 🖫**10REPLY.DOC** or create the response as indicated in Illustration B.

11. Click the Open a Document icon on the Shortcut bar.

12. Open 🖫**10INFLAT.XLS** in Excel as shown in Illustration C.

13. Select the chart and use the Copy, Paste Special procedure to embed the chart into the Word letter where indicated in the text.

14. Save the file as **REPLY** and print one copy.

15. Switch to Excel and close the file.

16. Switch to PowerPoint. In Slide view, modify the presentation as follows:
    Insert a new chart slide as Slide 7 with the heading, "Low Inflation."

17. Switch to Word and select the Excel chart object by double-clicking on it. Copy and paste it below the Low Inflation heading on Slide 7 in the PowerPoint presentation.

18. Continue to modify the presentation as follows.
    - Edit Slide 1 title to read: Economic and Historical Prospective on Brazilian Investment
    - Edit Slide 1 subtitle to read: Presenter:    Michael Miller, Finance Department
    - Assistant:    Jennifer Washington, Simpson Investment Advisors

19. View the presentation.

20. Save the presentation; name it **BRAZIL**.

21. Switch to Word and close **REPLY**.

🖐 22. Open 🖫**10INVITE.DOC** or create the memorandum as indicated in Illustration D.

23. Switch to PowerPoint and select the first slide in Slide or Slide Sorter view. Copy it to the memorandum below the text.

24. Create a main document (form letter) using the memorandum.

25. Open 🖭**COLLEGE.MDB** or 🖫**10COLLEGE.MDB** as the data source.

26. Edit the main document to insert merge fields to match the database.

27. Merge the files into a new document.

28. Scroll through the newly merged document to check the merge.

29. Save the file as **INVITMER**.

🖐 30. Click the Open Office Document button on the Shortcut bar. Open a Word document.

31. Use the Internet, or the DDC CD-ROM Simulation to find current information about the Brazilian economy to add to your speaker notes.

   a. Sign on to your Internet provider.

   **OR**

   - To access the DDC Internet simulation, click **Go**, **Open** on the Web toolbar.
   - Type **C:\DDCPUB\OFF97INT.IMR**. (Be sure that the simulation has been installed on your hard drive. If files are on a drive other than C, replace C with the correct letter.)
   - Click **OK** to launch the simulation.
   - Select **Exercise 10: Brazil Economy**.

   b. You can use the Excite search engine to Search for Brazil Economy, and then select Trade Climate.

   c. Copy (Edit, Copy) the entire document.

   d. Exit from your browser and disconnect from your service provider, or exit the DDC Internet simulation.

   e. Paste the information into the Word document.

   f. Save the file; name it **BRAZIL1.DOC.**

   g. Print or copy data to add to slide 2.

32. Add information to the speaker notes section on slide 2.

33. Print slide 2 with speaker's notes.

34. Close and save all files.

## ILLUSTRATION A

Today's date


Ms. Jennifer Washington
Simpson Investment Advisors
777 Madison Avenue
New York, NY  10022

Dear Ms. Washington:

I am writing regarding the upcoming presentation we will be making to the staff at the college on the topic of investments in Brazil.  I will be using the historical and economic background of the country to interest the group in Brazilian investment.  It is my position that the Brazilian economy has substantially recovered since the Brazilian debt crisis in the 1980s and that this may be a good time to invest profitably in specific situations in Brazil.

Find below a preliminary outline, which I have drafted, for the presentation:

If you have any suggestions or anything to add to this outline, please contact me as soon as possible. Otherwise, I will be in touch with you the week prior to the meeting to confirm hotel arrangements.

Sincerely yours,

*Insert PowerPoint outline here*

Michael Miller
Finance Department

## ILLUSTRATION B

Today's date


Mr. Michael Miller
Boynton College
342 Palm Boulevard
Ocean City, VA  05555

Dear Mr. Miller:

Thank you for your letter regarding our presentation at the college on Brazilian investments.  I trust that you will be filling in the historical and economic background from your extensive knowledge of the country.

In addition to setting up an introductory heading in the outline, I would suggest that you include some data on the vast changes in the inflation rate.   I am including below a chart showing the trend of the inflation rate over the last 15 years.  This is a clear indication of the changes that have taken place and it should be included in the section where you discuss the current low inflation rate.

I look forward to seeing you in two weeks and will call to confirm my arrangements for the visit.  Thank you.

Sincerely yours,

*Insert chart here*

Jennifer Washington
Investment Advisor

## ILLUSTRATION C

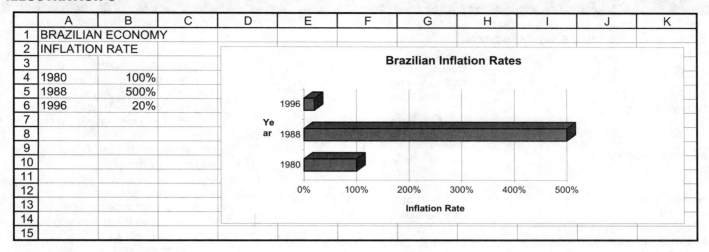

| | A | B | C | D | E | F | G | H | I | J | K |
|---|---|---|---|---|---|---|---|---|---|---|---|
| 1 | BRAZILIAN ECONOMY | | | | | | | | | | |
| 2 | INFLATION RATE | | | | | | | | | | |
| 3 | | | | | | | | | | | |
| 4 | 1980 | 100% | | | | | | | | | |
| 5 | 1988 | 500% | | | | | | | | | |
| 6 | 1996 | 20% | | | | | | | | | |
| 7 | | | | | | | | | | | |
| 8 | | | | | | | | | | | |
| 9 | | | | | | | | | | | |
| 10 | | | | | | | | | | | |
| 11 | | | | | | | | | | | |
| 12 | | | | | | | | | | | |
| 13 | | | | | | | | | | | |
| 14 | | | | | | | | | | | |
| 15 | | | | | | | | | | | |

## ILLUSTRATION D

# M E M O R A N D U M

TO:              Title FirstName LastName
DEPARTMENT:   Department
BUILDING:       Building

FROM:           Michael Miller
                Finance Department

RE:              Monthly Investment Seminar

DATE:            Today's date

　　　This month our meeting will focus on Brazil. Ms. Jennifer Washington Simpson Investment Advisors group will join us. The meeting will be held in Beaver Hall at 8:00 p.m. on the last Tuesday

　　　　As in the past, please note below the introductory slide of our presentation and post this notice in your department office.

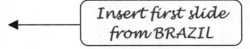

Insert first slide
from BRAZIL

# Index

Entries in all caps indicate keystroke procedures.

# NETWORK COMPATIBLE SITE LICENSE FOR DDC's LEARNING OFFICE 97 COMPANION CD-ROM

With the DDC Site License, all networked computers in your classroom or office
can access the Internet simulation, Office 97 multimedia tutorial, Multimedia Internet
Browser tutorial, and data files included on the CD-ROM that accompanies this book.
Install the CD once and access all files on all connected computers—
even the computers that don't have CD-ROM drives.

- - - - - - - - - - - - - - - - - - - - - - - - - - **ORDER FORM** - - - - - - - - - - - - - - - - - - - - - - - - - -

# Installation directions:

## To install the Internet Simulation, the Multimedia Internet Browser Tutorial, or the Demo of DDC's Office 97 Multimedia tutorial:

A separate installation is required for each program. At the designated prompt, indicate which program you wish to install. When installation of one program is complete, you may begin again from step one (below) to install another.

### System Requirements

| Software | Windows 95 or Windows NT 3.51 (or higher) |
|---|---|
| Hardware | 80486DX or higher, 16 MB RAM, 256 Color Monitor, and CD-ROM Drive- |
| Disk Space | 40 MB available hard disk space |

**To install the programs, place the CD in your CD-ROM drive and follow the listed steps below:**

1. **To install from Windows 95:**
   Click Start on the desktop and click Run.

   **OR**

   **To install from Windows NT:**
   Go to Program Manager in Main, click File,

2. In the Run window, begin a program installation by typing one of the following:

   - *CD-ROM drive letter:*\OFF97INT\SETUP to install the Internet Simulation.

   - *CD-ROM drive letter:*\OFFICE97\SETUP to install the Office 97 CBT.

   - *CD-ROM drive letter:*\NETSIM\SETUP to install the Browser tutorial.

3. Click NEXT at the Setup Wizard screen.

4. At the following screen, click NEXT to create a DDCPUB directory for storing program files. Then click YES to confirm the directory choice.

5. At the following screen, allow the default folder to be named **DDC Publishing**, and click NEXT.

6. At the next screen, choose one of the following options based on your individual system needs:

*NOTE: A **Typical** installation is standard for most individual installation.*

- **TYPICAL:** installs a minimum number of files to the hard drive with the majority of files remaining on the CD-ROM. ***NOTE: With this installation, the CD must remain in the CD-ROM drive when running the program.***

- **CUSTOM:** installs only those files that you choose to the hard drive. This is generally only recommended for advanced users of Innovus Multimedia software.

- **Server:** installs the programs on a network server (see directions below).

7. Click NEXT to begin copying the necessary files to your system.

8. Click OK at the Set Up status Window and then click YES to restart Windows.

To launch a program, click the Start button on the Windows 95 desktop, select Programs, DDC Publishing, and then select one of the following:

- **OFF97INT (to start the Internet Simulation)**

- **DEMO97 (to start the Office97CBT)**

- **NETCBT (to start the Browser tutorial)**

## To Copy the data files:

- Open Windows 95 Explorer (Right-click on **Start** button and click **Explore**).

- Be sure that your CD is in your CD-ROM drive. Select the CD-ROM drive letter from the All Folders pane of the Explorer window.

- Click to Select the **DDCdata** folder in the Contents of (CD-ROM Drive letter) pane of the Explorer window.

- Drag the folder onto the letter of your hard drive (usually **C:**) in the All Folders pane of the Explorer Window.

## Advanced Lessons

- For instructions on installing the advanced lessons, see page ix at the front of this book.